MW00573014

"The record of the Iron Brigade will not be dismissed by time. Not that they were better soldiers or patriots than others, but because the fortunes and misfortunes of war placed them where the fight was the thickest."

— O. B. Curtis, *History of the Twenty-fourth Michigan of the Iron Brigade*

"The young generation can hardly realize that their modest neighbors are soldiers who have fought on more fields of battle than the Old Guard of Napoleon, and have stood fire in far greater firmness."

— Rufus R. Dawes, Mauston, Wisconsin, 1885

"Wisconsin, Michigan and Indiana can say with truth that they have furnished the bravest soldiers of the war and they have had their shoulders to the wheel ever since the rebellion broke out. Their soldiers have never faltered . . . [and] they were confident that Right would be vindicated—and the result proved they were not wrong."

— *Milwaukee Sentinel*, July 1, 1865

"Almost every war brings some regiment or other military body to the front which distinguishes itself for special valor, consistence or endurance. Cromwell's Ironsides Regiment, Caesar's Tenth Legion, the Old Guard of Napoleon, the Light Brigade at Balaklava, are all illustrious of this fact. Among these bands of heroes should be enrolled the Iron Brigade."

— *Detroit Evening Journal*

THE IRON BRIGADE

in Civil War and Memory

Lance J. Herdegen

The Black Hats from Bull Run
to Appomattox and Thereafter

SB
Savas Beatie
California

Library of Congress Cataloging-in-Publication Data

Herdegen, Lance J.
The Iron Brigade in Civil War and Memory / Lance J. Herdegen. – 1st ed.
p. cm.
Includes bibliographical references and index.
ISBN 978-1-61121-106-1
1. United States. Army. Iron Brigade (1861-1865). 2. United States–
History–Civil War, 1861-1865–Regimental histories. I. Title.
E493.5.I72H46 2012
973.7–dc23
2012031744

First edition, first printing

SB

Published by
Savas Beatie LLC
989 Governor Drive, Suite 102
El Dorado Hills, California 95762

www.savasbeatie.com (web)
sales@savasbeatie.com (email)

Savas Beatie titles are available at special discounts for bulk purchases in the United States by corporations, institutions, and other organizations. For more details, please contact Special Sales, P.O. Box 4527, El Dorado Hills, CA 95762, or you may e-mail us at sales@savasbeatie.com, or visit our website at www.savasbeatie.com for additional information.

Printed in the United States of America.

For Shirley, whose grandmother was a daughter of
the Lac Courte Oreilles Ojibwa. Megwich

Iron Brigade Tiffany Flag

Contents

Contents (continued)

Contents (continued)

Contents (continued)

Bibliography

625

Index

639

List of Maps

Illustrations appear throughout the book for
the convenience of the reader

Introduction

Back to the Iron Brigade

The Iron Brigade may have been the best combat infantry brigade of the American Civil War. Composed originally of the 2nd, 6th, 7th Wisconsin, and the 19th Indiana, and supported by Battery B, 4th U.S. Artillery, its baptism of fire came on August 28, 1862, near Gainesville, Virginia, and continued on August 29-30 at Second Bull Run, September 14 at South Mountain, and September 17 at Antietam in Maryland. It was during those weeks the unit went from being just a "Black Hat Brigade" to an "Iron Brigade of the West." After the fighting at Sharpsburg, Maryland, the brigade was reinforced by the addition of the 24th Michigan. Of course, it was at Gettysburg on July 1, 1863, that the Iron Brigade won a place in American military history and was almost destroyed. The regiments—reinforced by volunteers as well as bounty and drafted men—fought on through 1864 and 1865 to Appomattox Court House. It was all chance that the forces of war, one veteran said, placed the Black Hats "where the fight was the thickest." At the end of the war, it was determined the Iron Brigade regiments suffered the highest percentage of loss of any brigade in the Union Armies.

What made the brigade unique was the simple fact all the regiments were from states on the nation's frontier. It was the only "Western" brigade in the Eastern armies. It was not until after Gettysburg in 1863 that the sectional makeup was lost with the addition of Pennsylvania soldiers. As individuals, the frontier boys were generally young men of energy and ambition. The five organizations were also well led and had a significant period of training—more than a year—before being called into action. As they learned to become soldiers, the volunteers were outfitted with the tall Model 1858 black felt hat of the U.S. Regulars and became a "Black Hat Brigade" recognized by friend and foe along the battle lines. The regiments became the fabled "Iron Brigade" during the hard fighting at Gainesville, Second Bull Run, South Mountain, and Antietam in 1862.

I was just finishing a journalism degree at Marquette University as Alan T. Nolan was completing his classic, *The Iron Brigade: A Military History*. Published in 1961 at the start of the Civil War Centennial, his book was an instant success and won wide acclaim. At the time, I was able to provide some minor research on the Wisconsin regiments and that led to a lifelong friendship. Over the years, Alan and I shared materials on our favorite brigade, argued minor points in the brigade's history, and walked the ground at Gainesville, Second Bull Run, Antietam, and Gettysburg where the Black Hats marched, fought, and died.

In the fifty years since Nolan did his careful scholarship, however, other important Black Hat sources have been found and published. It seemed every month since his book was released collections of letters, journals, photographs, and other accounts were discovered, many of them important and adding a flesh and blood dimension to the men of the Iron Brigade and their story. Some of these sources have been used in books and articles over the years while others remain hidden in old newspapers, family collections, and archival holdings. In 2011, for example, some 300 letters from Lt. Loyd Harris of the 6th Wisconsin were found with his relatives in Texas and presented to the Wisconsin Historical Society. They add to the many stories he submitted to the Old Soldier newspapers of the day regarding his service in the Western brigade. Other Iron Brigade materials surfaced in Michigan and Indiana, and even faraway places such as Idaho, South Dakota, Florida, Missouri, and Washington state.

Nolan, who passed away in 2008, ended his history after Gettysburg when the Iron Brigade lost its all-Western character. He wrote little of the hard campaigns of 1864, the final days to Appomattox Court House, and what became of the Black Hats. This book completes the story from Bull Run to Gettysburg to Appomattox and thereafter, relying on much previously unused material. The new sources found over the past half-century answer a lot of lingering questions: What were they thinking those dangerous days of civil war? How did they view their leaders as they sat around their campfires? What did they think of slavery and of those Confederates across the picket lines? What did they think and speak of during battle, or while lying wounded in a field? How did the war change them? It is fair to say that the plethora of new material turns names on rosters into three- dimensional characters in our mind's eye that live and breath and march and sweat and bleed and too often, die.

More importantly, I think, it reveals those young men of long ago—farmers, shopkeepers, mechanics, and piney camp boys—who wore the famous black hats were real people caught up in a war of unexpected magnitude and hardship. It is too easy when writing the history of military organizations to lose the simple truth that such storied units as the Iron Brigade were made up of individual flesh and blood sons, husbands, fathers, and brothers. Those who survived the war were changed in ways they never quite understood, and came home to an uncertain future. But one thing is certain: They never forgot they marched to the thump of history's drum.

So here then, often in their own unvarnished words, is their story of civil war and how they knew it to be.

Lance J. Herdegen
Town of Spring Prairie
Walworth County, Wisconsin

Acknowledgments

Writers spend a lot of time toiling alone as they work on a book, but the end result is never an individual achievement. Over the months and often many years of developing a manuscript, many people have an impact on the finished work. In fact, they are often woven into the very words themselves. It is customary to single out individuals for their assistance.

A special thanks to Daniel Netteshiem, Gary Van Kauwenberg, and Dan Joyce for their encouragement and suggestions, and to all those descendants of the Black Hats who came forward with letters, diaries, and photographs of their ancestors.

In no special order, others who deserve mention include Michel Keller, Paul Johnson, Dale Walker, Mary Rieder, Brett Wilson, Bill Christen, Scott Cross, Dale Niesen, Jennifer Eager Ehle, Gina Radant, Doug Dammann, Steve Victor, Kim J. Heltemes, Phil Spaugy, Andy Ackeret, Lance Myers, Brian Hogan, Alan Gaff, Sharon Murphy, Sharon Vipond, John Wedeward, William Washburn, William J. K. Beaudot, Scott D. Hann, Larry Lefler, Pat and Bob Sullivan, and, of course, the late Howard Michael Madaus and Alan Nolan. Many others helped with the effort, so many it is all but impossible to name them here. If you assisted any any way large or small, and your name is not here, forgive me and know that I appreciate all you have done to make this book possible.

And finally, to Hal Jespersen for drafting the outstanding maps and for insightful comments, and to the intrepid Theodore P. Savas and his great staff at Savas Beatie for publishing my work. Mr. Savas would have especially enjoyed a long conversation with "Mickey, of Company K," as they have much in common.

1861

Greenhorn Patriots

Unidentified members of the Iron Brigade

Author's Collection

An unidentified woman who sent her husband off to war.

Author's Collection

Part I: War! War! War!

The Rebellion Must be Put Down in Blood

The visitors came in family groups, with friends, and even alone. The old Wisconsin State Fairgrounds at Madison had been transformed into a sprawling soldier post. It was now "Camp Randall," enclosed by a high plank-board fence. Open ground in the center of the square was cleared and leveled for a drill field. Tents and temporary structures were strewn along one fence. The old frame livestock buildings were now barracks. The arrivals walked through the main gate past the new sentry posts to stand quietly near a wooden reviewing stand. They had come from cities and small towns and backwoods farms for a final goodbye to the soldiers of the 2nd Regiment, Wisconsin Active Militia. It was 10:00 a.m. on June 20, 1861, a bright and clear Thursday morning. And their boys were going to war.

Brought to Camp Randall by the call to activate the state militia, the 10 companies of the 2nd Wisconsin were to leave within the hour for Washington—the first of many departures of soldiers from Madison to faraway places. Mustered for 90 days, the state's first regiment left a month earlier from Milwaukee, and now the 2nd Wisconsin was about to be given a formal farewell. It was coming down to an emotional moment in which the flush of patriotic pride in seeing the new soldiers was overshadowed by the unspoken fear that it could be the last time they would be together with husbands, fathers, brothers, sons, and schoolmates. A pair of trains waited near the camp to carry "one thousand of the sturdiest and bravest of our Wisconsin boys" to war.

The great sectional crisis, so long threatened, came upon the nation with unexpected suddenness. The turning point arrived with the 1860 election of Republican Abraham Lincoln of Illinois as president. Just four days after the balloting of November 6, 1860, South Carolina issued the call for a secession convention and it was clear from the very start that the delegates would approve separation from the Union. The decision to sever the formal relationship with the

United States came amid hot words and cheers on Thursday, December 30, 1860, when the ordinance of secession was quickly approved 169-0. Mississippi left the Union on January 9, 1861, and was soon followed by Florida, Alabama, Georgia, Louisiana, and Texas. Delegates from the seceded states met in mid-February at Montgomery, Alabama, to work on a provisional constitution establishing a Confederate States of America. The announcement set off a wave of celebrations carried through the South on the shrill and wild yells that would soon echo on a hundred battlefields. In distant Wisconsin, Republican Gov. Alexander W. Randall raised a warning: "Secession is revolution; revolution is war, war against the government of the United States is treason. . . . Wisconsin is true, and her people steadfast. She will not destroy the Union, nor consent that it shall be done." His words were lost in the national clamor of the moment.[1]

More careful in his public statements was President-elect Lincoln, who was trying to organize his administration and pull together the many diverse elements of his new Republican Party. Around him, political insiders and others whispered that the new chief executive from the West was not up to dealing with the crisis. They pointed to his lack of administrative experience, his humble beginnings, and the fact that during his two years in the House of Representatives more than a decade earlier, one of his few accomplishments was his well-earned reputation for telling crude stories in Congressional hallways and cloakrooms. Lincoln's inauguration speech on a sunny but cold and windy day in early March did little to dispel this growing apprehension. Often vague and ambivalent, he called for conciliation between the states, repeating what he had been saying all along: He had no intention of acting against slavery in the states and territories where it existed. It was only when he addressed what he called the "formidably attempted" disruption of the Union that the flat prairie cadences of his high-pitched voice picked up a sharp tone that reached out to the edge of the large crowd gathered to hear him—almost as if he was now speaking across the miles to the very South itself. "In your hands, my dissatisfied fellow countrymen, and not in mine, is the momentous issue of civil war. . . . We are not enemies, but friends. We must not be enemies. Though passion may have strained, it must not break our bonds of affection."

The nation's reaction to the address—North, South, and West—was, as expected, mixed. It did little to improve Lincoln's political standing. Republicans hotly denounced secession as treason and talked of war; Northern and border state Democrats called for compromise and a peaceful reunion. All sides were critical of

1 Gov. Alexander W. Randall, Annual Message to the Wisconsin Legislature, January 10, 1861, *Messages and Proclamations of Wis. War Governors* (Madison, 1912), 43-44.

the new president. And then, in early April, attention turned to Charleston, South Carolina, where Maj. Robert Anderson held Fort Sumter in the harbor and refused Confederate demands that the Federal facility be surrendered. The situation was at a crisis point. The fort was low on supplies and in Washington the administration was sending mixed messages of what it would do in the face of strident Southern demands that Sumter be abandoned. A military attempt to rescue and hold the fort was not likely because the Federal government did not have on hand the 20,000 soldiers Lincoln's military advisors said were needed for such an effort. In an effort to buy additional time (some said later that it was a clever ruse to force the South's hand), Lincoln sent a message to alert South Carolina officials that he planned to send a ship to supply, but not to reinforce, the beleaguered garrison. Before the relief cutter could reach the harbor, however, at dawn on April 12, 1861, Confederate batteries opened fire on Fort Sumter. A civil war, so long threatened, was underway.

The news of war was announced from the pulpits of small town churches on a peaceful Sunday morning in Wisconsin. "The effect . . . can hardly be told upon those who had persistently insisted . . . that no American would ever open fire upon an American flag," said one witness. "[F]rom those of hotter temperament—those who had met the threat of secession with the counter-promise of hanging—there was instant willingness to make the promise good."[2] A hired hand working on a farm in Juneau County remembered the mood of the citizenry changed almost at once: "'We must lick 'em.' 'Southern rights be damned.' 'No Southerner or any other has a right to fire on our flag.' 'Charleston must be destroyed.'" These and other similar expressions echoed across the state. "War, war, war, was the theme of every fireside and gathering."[3] The excitement of morning gave way to what one man called "a palsied numbness" by afternoon. Sunday schools were "not well attended by the older boys that day," he explained. "They were out on the corners listening, thinking and talking. . . . There was very little loud expression, and no boasting or cheers. The saloons were not patronized. . . . There was a most ominous quietness among those who gathered on the streets from the different congregations. This semi-silence was more expressive than can be described."[4]

Within the week, Lincoln issued a proclamation declaring that an insurrection existed in the seceded states and calling for 75,000 members of the state militias to

2   Colonel C. K. Pier, "Wisconsin in the Civil War," *History of Wisconsin in Twelve Illustrated Magazines*, C.S. Matteson, ed., vol. I, no. 7 (Fond du Lac, WI., 1893).

3   James P. Sullivan, "Old Company K," *Milwaukee Sunday Telegraph*, May 16, 1886.

4   Pier, "Wisconsin in the Civil War," 47.

protect the national capital and public property. The call for troops to put down the rebellion sent North Carolina, Tennessee, Arkansas, and Virginia into the arms of the Confederacy. It was one thing for the president to proclaim an insurrection and call out the state militias; it was quite another to have the 75,000 soldiers in hand. Americans from the earliest days of the nation questioned the need and expense of a large standing army and displayed wariness of the man trained and educated solely to be a soldier. Part of this was caught up in the national memory of British red-coated regulars and their mercenaries on the streets of some American cities during the War for Independence. It also reflected an unshaken confidence that a small force of Regulars backed up in time of dire need by a militia army of citizen soldiers (like the "Minute Men" of old) was the most efficient as well as most thrifty course. In 1861, a statement generally accepted without challenge, in saloon and work place North or South or West, was that any ordinary citizen of good character and intelligence was capable of military leadership. It was, of course, simply not true.

Fort Sumter and the call for the active militia fanned a patriotic surge across the Upper Middle West. Union war meetings stirred by drum beats and screeching fifes spread in cities and backwoods towns amid calls to form military organizations to put down the rebellion. Patriotic and ambitious men held rallies seeking to gather the 100 enlistees needed to form a volunteer "company." Organizers of the would-be organizations scoured nearby communities in search of new recruits while bands played "Yankee Doodle" and "Hail, Columbia." Hundreds of young men stepped forward and those who did not make plans to go were left unsettled, as though, in some rite of passage to manhood they had been found wanting. "Parents tried to keep the youths back," one volunteer recalled, "but the enthusiasm in young America was too great, and they went forward with a determination paternal demonstration and threats could not prevent." In Madison, Governor Randall, busy organizing and equipping units of his militia for active service, expressed impatience with the Lincoln administration for not moving quickly enough. "This war began where Charleston is, and it should end where Charleston was," exhorted Randall. "These gathering armies are the instruments of His vengeance, to execute his judgments; they are His flails wherewith on God's great Southern threshing floor, He will pound rebellion for its sins."[5]

Wisconsin had achieved statehood just a dozen years before and few in the population were native born. But there were the sons of New England and Pennsylvania and Ohio and New York—and even Virginia and Tennessee and

---

5   Randall, May 15, 1861, *Messages and Proclamations*, 63.

Kentucky—to fill the ranks of the Wisconsin companies, as well as young tough fellows from Germany, Ireland, Norway, and other places across the ocean. In some of the backwoods companies being recruited could be found one or two free blacks and runaways and representatives of the Ojibwa, Oneida, Potawatomi, and Ho-Chunk—all to carry a musket with the rest. Whether born in America or "bred beyond her borders, or in foreign climes," they were proud of their new state and they rushed to fill the companies. "Not infrequently, every civilized nation on the face of the earth was represented in the rank and file of the same regiment. Every condition of social, religious and political faith, all the trades, occupations and professions were represented. The same tent covered the banker, lumberman, medical student, lawyer, merchant, and machinist. The millionaire's son touched elbows with the son of his father's hired man."[6]

A few of those who stepped forward were bored or wanted to be considered brave or sought advancement. Some saw the coming war as a fight against the evil of slavery; others felt they were called to protect the sacred Union created by their grandfathers and great-grandfathers. No one saw it clearer than Edwin A. Brown, a Fond du Lac attorney and young father who was among the first to go. "Thousands of patriotic lives may be laid a sacrifice on the Altar of our Country's good," Brown wrote, "but this Country will be purified of this blighting breath of treason and corruption, and history will record of the Republic, that in the year 1861, her patriotic children rallied around the emblem of the early fathers, and purged the land of the great curse of secession . . ."[7]

No sooner had Lincoln called for 75,000 volunteers than Governor Randall was active mustering, organizing, and drilling an 800-man regiment. The 1st Wisconsin, sworn in for three months of service, was outfitted at Milwaukee and sent by rail in early May 1861 to protect the nation's capital from an army of secessionists assembling outside the city gates. A second regiment was immediately called in to Madison and now, after just a few weeks, the day of departure was at hand. The new soldiers of the 2nd Wisconsin had been up since 3:00 a.m. packing knapsacks. The morning started chilly but turned pleasant as families and friends crowded around individual soldiers to exchange last minute and often tearful farewells while the new regimental band played quicksteps and waltzes. Finally, the

---

6   Pier, "Wisconsin in the Civil War," 49.

7   *Ibid.*, 49; Edwin A. Brown, letter to his wife, September 8, 1861, Institute for Civil War Studies, Civil War Museum, Kenosha, WI.; Edward Kellogg, "Letters from a Soldier," *Milwaukee Sunday Telegraph*, September 28, 1879; Earl M. Rogers, "A 6th Wisconsin Company," *Milwaukee Sunday Telegraph*, February 1, 1880; Michael H. Fitch, *Echoes of the Civil War as I Hear Them* (New York, 1905), 18-19.

order came to form companies before the reviewing stand. The crowd, proud as well as apprehensive, stirred and stepped back as the ranks formed, some individuals calling out to their soldier boys a last "Good Bye! Good Bye!" and "God Speed!" as young women raised a flutter of handkerchiefs.[8]

The 2nd Wisconsin was one of the first of the nation's Federal regiments sworn in for a term of three years of service or for the duration of the war. The longer term was required of new organizations in May after the Lincoln administration realized the conflict might well last longer than the ninety days of the first enlistments. Told only three-year regiments were being accepted, the men of the 2nd Wisconsin were given the choice of taking the longer term or disbanding. Only one company, mostly students from Beloit College, held back; it was quickly replaced by a unit from Milwaukee. Five would-be volunteers were turned aside for physical reasons, including one gallant patriot who confessed he was sixty and still wanted to go. Almost all of the remaining volunteers signed the three-year papers with light hearts and hardly a second thought—the war would surely be over once the rebels were given a sound licking. "I laugh now, when I review the impressions I then had of a soldier life," one of the Boscobel men recalled. "How enthusiastic the boys were! How idle they thought the ceremony of taking the oath! They would be soldiers for fifty years, if necessary, and then leave their muskets as a legacy for their children, enjoining them never to lay them down until the stars and stripes should wave in triumph from the St. Lawrence to the Rio Grande and the Atlantic to the Pacific."[9]

8   According to the *Milwaukee Sentinel*, July 2, 1861, the state provided each soldier with: "1 cap, 1 eagle and ring, 2 flannel shirts, 2 pair stockings, 1 woolen blanket, 1 tin or rubber canteen, 1 pompon, 1 coat, 2 pair flannel drawers, 1 leather stock, 1 haversack, 1 cap cover, 1 pair trowsers, 1 pair bootees or shoes, 1 great coat, 1 knapsack." The uniform prescribed by Wis. Adj. Gen. William L. Utley on April 27, 1861: "Coats—Grey cloth, plain—Single breast, standing collar—9 buttons on front and 2 behind—pockets in skirt—hook at neck—black lasting buttons—length, 2/3 from hip to knee. Trowsers—Grey cloth, plain—black welt 1/8 inch wide in outside seam. Caps.—Grey cloth—7th [New York State] Regiment Style—patent leather strap. N.B. Caps will be furnished by the state for the 2d regiment immediately. Note—whenever practicable, it is desirable that volunteer companies provide themselves with uniforms before departing from the homes for rendezvous, as the cloth can generally be procured. No uniform shade of grey is required, but a dark shade is objectionable. Whenever sufficient cloth of one shade cannot be procured at home for both coats and Trowsers, different shades may be used for the two, running uniformly through the company. It is not intended to confine the volunteers strictly to the above uniform, as circumstances may render it impossible for some companies to conform to it; but whenever practicable it is desirable." *Janesville Daily Gazette*, May 1, 1861.

9   "The exception was the Beloit City Rifles, many of whom were students in the college at Beloit, and had made no preparation for longer than a three months service. . . . The company

The tall and rangy Western boys and the new regiment outfitted in wool uniforms of militia grey made a good first impression and represented many sections of the state. There were the Light Guards from La Crosse on the Mississippi River, the Portage City Light Guards, the Belle City Rifles from Racine on Lake Michigan, as well as other companies from Fox Lake, Oshkosh, Madison, Milwaukee, Grant County, Janesville, and Mineral Point. The womenfolk—grandmothers, mothers, wives, sisters, and sweethearts—baked pies and organized packages of food and prepared socks and other items that might be needed by a soldier. The women of Watertown worked long hours to provide 500 flannel shirts for the new soldiers and the ladies of the Baptist Society in Janesville presented their hometown company with havelocks, a white cloth device to fit over caps and protect the neck from the hot sun. "The Ladies everywhere—God Bless them!" one volunteer wrote to his hometown newspaper.

The Best Fighting Rig Imaginable

Soldiers need uniforms, and finding the proper cloth was an ongoing concern for state officials as they struggled to outfit the 2nd Wisconsin. The uniforms of the 1st Wisconsin had been made by individual manufacturers and produced in small lots. Some of the uniforms were also commissioned by the individual militia companies through local tailors. An example of the complexity of the problem is found in the returns for the first regiment, which included thirty different uniform manufacturers including "20 or 30 men" employed at the Wisconsin State Prison at Waupun using what Commissioner Hans C. Heg described as a "good sewing machine."[10]

While the officers of the 2nd Wisconsin wore traditional dress coats "of blue cloth," the selection of grey for enlisted men harkened to militia tradition and the inability of the state to locate an immediate and dependable source of blue wool.

---

was afterwards disbanded, and many of the members entered other companies for three years." E. B. Quiner, *The Military History of Wisconsin: A Record of the Civil and Military Patriotism of the State in the War for the Union* (Chicago,1866), 59; Kellogg, *Telegraph*, September 28, 1879. One of those who paused at the three-year commitment was Capt. A. J. Langworthy, whose business partners objected, claiming their "large manufacturing establishment" was just formed and would "go down" if he went off for three years. "After a good deal of consideration, believing that my country needed my services," Langworthy explained later, he decided to go "if it strips me financially naked. Well it did, and I did not regret my course although at times I have found it inconvenient to say the least." A. J. Langworthy Papers, Wisconsin Historical Society.

10 *Papers of the 1st Wisconsin*, Series 1179-Box 1 and Wisconsin Quartermaster General Correspondence, Wisconsin Historical Society. Heg became colonel of the 15th Wisconsin and was killed in action at Chickamauga.

Private Frederick Lythson, Randall Guards, Co. G, 2nd Wisconsin

Lythson, posing in Madison in the Wisconsin militia gray frock coat and tall shako used by the 2nd Wisconsin early in the war. Frederick was wounded at Gettysburg and transferred to the Veteran Reserve Corps in 1864. *Author's Collection*

The supplies of two state woolen mills were soon exhausted, and even gray cloth of second quality proved difficult to find. The newly drafted regulations for state uniforms were based on the fatigue dress used by the famous Milwaukee Light Guard, a prominent and socially connected pre-war militia organization that went into the war as Company A of the 1st Wisconsin. Patterned after a design used by the English Volunteer Rifle Corps, the Milwaukee organization adopted a uniform consisting of "a single breasted grey frock coat and trowsers trimmed in red."[11] As a result, the order from the Adjutant General's office (which was unaware Southern states were adopting grey uniforms for their regiments) detailing the state's prescribed uniform followed the pattern of the Milwaukee Light Guard: "Coats—Grey cloth, plain-single breast, standing collar—9 buttons in front and 2 behind." The language was taken almost word for word from the 1st Wisconsin order book. The tall caps—in shako style—were ordered from J. H. Freeman of Milwaukee at $15.50 per dozen.[12] The color of the grey cloth gathered from state sources for the coats, however, was less than consistent in shade and the quality of the tailoring was often criticized. Caught up in the excitement of the moment, however, no one seemed overly concerned. "We have roundabout coats and loose pants," one enlistee wrote home. "It is the best fighting rig imaginable."[13]

The site of departure was about a mile and one-half from Madison on land under the operation of the Wisconsin Agricultural Society until accepted as a mustering post and renamed "Camp Randall" in honor of the governor. An army of workers—hampered by a wet and rainy spring—set out to clean the grounds, level a parade field, and clean, lay flooring, and install windows and wooden beds in the animal sheds along the southern and eastern walls of the enclosure. A large shed was remodeled to provide a mess hall and a nearby building turned into a kitchen where workmen and incoming soldiers were fed at a cost of 37-cents per day, per

11 Herbert C. Damon, *History of the Milwaukee Light Guard* (Milwaukee, 1875), 24-26.

12 The shako-style cap was ordered for the 2nd and 6th Wisconsin. Made roughly after the 1854 pattern U.S. dress cap, the headgear was held upright by a horsehair lining. Freeman was advertised as a "Practical Furrier" at 24 Wisconsin Street, Milwaukee, and also sold "Hats, Caps & Straw Goods." The firm also produced a "Haverlock [sic] Cape" which was "shaped differently from those previously made." These were ordered by the "Ladies of Milwaukee" and supplied to the 2nd Wisconsin. *Milwaukee Morning Sentinel,* June 1, 26, 1861.

13 See Howard Michael Madaus, Appendix III, in Lance J. Herdegen and William J. K. Beaudot, *In the Bloody Railroad Cut at Gettysburg* (Dayton, OH., 1990), 301-367. Also see J. Phillip Langellier, *Parade Ground Soldiers: Military Uniforms and Headdress, 1837-1910* in the Collections of the State Historical Society of Wisconsin (Madison, 1978); Regimental Order Book of the 1st Wisconsin Volunteers (3 months) in the collections of the Milwaukee Public Museum; Henry Matrau, *Letters Home: Henry Matrau of the Iron Brigade*, Marcia Reid-Green, ed. (Lincoln, NE.,1993), 7. A "roundabout" is a close-fitting jacket.

man. The first group of volunteers arrived in early May only to discover the buildings leaky and drafty. "Swimming out of the bunks, we care very little if it rains or not for we are used to it," wrote one new soldier. Several of the new inhabitants added to the misery of trying to sleep in old barns by cackling, mooing, honking, and quacking after dark to mimic the animals once housed there. Despite all its problems, Camp Randall would become the great mustering place for the majority of Wisconsin's regiments during 1861-1865.[14]

Madison itself was still much the frontier town in 1861, despite hosting the meetings of the Wisconsin legislature. Located on the isthmus between Lakes Mendota and Monona, the city was named for founding father James Madison and the first streets after each of the thirty-nine signers of the U.S. Constitution. The legislature first met there in 1837, and Madison became a city twenty years later with a population of 6,863. In 1861 the streets were still muddy during rainy seasons and crowded during legislative sessions when saloons and boarding houses were full. The intersection of Milwaukee, East Washington, Winnebago, and North streets became known as "Union Corners" when new military volunteers ran the guard to visit various drinking establishments located there.

Many of the formal farewell speeches to the departing 2nd Wisconsin had an Old Testament ring. "It remains to give you a parting word as you go forth on your great mission," Governor Randall informed his new soldiers. "By the shedding of blood atonement has always been made for great sins. This rebellion must be put down in blood, and treason punished by blood. You go forth not on any holiday errand, not on any Fourth of July excursion, but as men to perform great and urgent duties." It was just what the greenhorn patriots wanted to hear, confirmed one volunteer, and the governor was given three cheers accompanied by "tigers" and "big injuns." A national flag, completed by Mrs. R. C. Powers just an hour earlier, arrived too late to be formally presented but was handed off to one of the company commanders.[15]

---

14 Carolyn J. Mattern, *Soldiers When They Go: The Story of Camp Randall, 1861-1865* (Madison, WI., 1981), 3-4. The location today is the site of Camp Randall Stadium, home of the University of Wisconsin football team. Much of the detail in this chapter can be found in the ten scrapbook volumes assembled by Edwin B. Quiner entitled "Correspondence of Wisconsin Volunteers, 1861-1865," hereafter *Wisconsin Newspaper Volumes*. These are arranged by regiments and indexed and can be found in the archives of the Wisconsin Historical Society. The books include contemporaneous newspaper clippings, organized by regiment, and contain letters of Wisconsin soldiers printed in various newspapers. For more mustering of the 2nd Wisconsin and Bull Run is Alan D. Gaff, *If This Is War: A History of the Campaign of Bull's Run by the Wisconsin Regiment Thereafter Known as the Ragged Ass Second* (Dayton, OH., 1991).

15 *Wisconsin State Journal*, June 20, 1861.

While the departure of the regiment saddened many residents of Madison, others were delighted. Several "abuses and annoyances" had been visited upon the citizenry by drunken soldiers in recent weeks. One new recruit from neighboring Minnesota found the majority of the men in his Fox Lake Company "rough vulgar blackguards" and denounced Madison as "miserably dull" with "no life, no gayety & scarcely [any] amusement" and "scarcely a pretty woman here." The plank fence of Camp Randall had several loose boards that allowed the volunteers to evade the guards (who were only armed with a shout, one said) and walk the mile into town. The editor of the *Madison Argus and Democrat*, a newspaper critical of the Lincoln administration, thundered that the incidents showed undeniably "that the soldiers have not appeared to be under that restraint which a wholesome discipline would impose."[16]

The most notorious transgression came on the night before departure when a party of drunken soldiers attempted to get into Voigt's Brewery long after the closing hour. When the owner refused to open his saloon, someone broke a window and stole several bottles of liquor. A local newspaper reported what happened next: "Mr. Voigt, from a window above [in the second floor apartment where he and his family lived], fired a shot-gun over their heads with a view of driving them off, not intending to injure any one. Upon this they fired upon the house with revolvers and threw stones into the windows breaking glass, sash and blinds. Mr. Voigt fired several times over their heads with a revolver and finally discharged his shot gun aiming at their legs as nearly as he could upon which they decamped." It was subsequently reported that a soldier was found asleep near the brewery, dead drunk, and a member of the Racine company had a "wounded hand and leg." The *Madison Daily Patriot*, which favored the war, brushed off the reports, urging that "great care ought to be taken not to bring false and unjust charges against the volunteers. A great many exaggerated rumors prevail, which, if strictly investigated, would be found to be wholly without foundation in fact."[17]

All that was now behind the regiment and with the goodbyes and speeches at an end, the new companies marched to the nearby trains. The cars pulled out amid cheers, train whistle blasts, clanging bells, and not a few tears. The young soldiers waved caps from every window as the proud crowd made "the air ring with jubilant hurrahs." The rail trip had hardly begun before the trains ground to a halt less than an hour later at nearby Janesville where a "sumptuous dinner" awaited the new

16 Alured Larke, manuscript, Wisconsin Historical Society. Larke had enlisted in a Minnesota company, but came to Madison when the former unit was not called into service. He joined the company raised in Fox Lake.

17 *Madison Argus and Democrat*, June 14, 1861.

soldiers. Hundreds of citizens greeted them. Especially sought out were members of the Janesville Company under Capt. George B. Ely. There was only a little grumbling when soldiers late in reaching the tables found most of the food gone. As the train lurched ahead to begin the journey for Chicago, Henry N. Allyn stared through a window to catch a last glimpse of his home at Shopiere in Rock County. "I have one short view of the place where I have lived for the last 20 years & then it has passed from my sight," he scribbled in his new journal. "I may never again behold the old place, the home of my childhood . . . & if I do it will be one of the happiest moments of my life." Groups of citizens stood along the tracks watching as the soldier train crossed Turtle Creek, but Henry was unable to catch a glimpse of his mother among them.[18] A few hours later local militia units escorted the soldiers through Chicago's crowded streets of admiring crowds gathered on the sidewalks. Sandwiches, coffee, apples, and cigars passed freely through the cars. "The regiment is composed of the most soldierly looking fighting material of any we have ever seen," reported the *Chicago Times.*[19]

During the long ride to Washington in the swaying, bumpy cars, the Wisconsin boys whiled away the hours by looking at the passing scenery, talking, and playing cards. For many of the Wisconsin men it was their first ride on a train, and the noise, confusion, and smoke, together with the dazzling speed of more than thirty miles per hour, made a lasting impression. The states of the Upper Middle West—Minnesota, Wisconsin, Iowa, Michigan, Illinois, and Indiana—were crisscrossed with 7,000 miles of track by 1861, and the railroad was becoming a significant force linking the region both economically and socially. The rails also connected transportation canals back East to important waterways on the nation's western frontier. The arrival of the steam locomotives and their cars transformed communities. Chicago's growing network of rails, for example, allowed that city to make economic gains upon St. Louis' water routes. Agriculture and livestock were quickly becoming important industries.

At Toledo, Ohio, hundreds of citizens greeted the train to provide the boys with a fine breakfast. Pretty girls passed out doughnuts and pails of water. The trip across Ohio offered one ovation after another. Huge welcoming crowds awaiting the Wisconsin train of thirty-two cars at Cleveland offered yet more food and a dinner hosted by the ladies of the town. According to one officer, "hosts of little girls, dressed in white, with blue and red ribbons in their hair and ornamenting their dresses, came through the depot, and shook hands with the men, and over and over

18 Henry N. Allyn, journal, Henry Allyn Papers, Wisconsin Historical Society.

19 *Wisconsin Newspaper Volumes*, vol. 1.

again, wished them good bye, and a safe return." At almost every stop there was water, which was "greatly needed," recalled a 2nd Wisconsin man. "We missed our Wisconsin water very much and, in fact, have not any water that is as good as that we get in the old Badger state." Sometime after the Cleveland stop a sleeping officer awoke to find the train halted and his car deserted. Out a window he saw "about two hundred ladies on the platform, and about fifty of the regiment actively engaged in kissing them in such a business-like way, that at first I thought the regiment had got into active service in fact." A Janesville private wrote of the triumphant journey: "God bless the state of Ohio, her old men and young men, her women and fair damsels, who fed us, and cheered us on our way."[20]

Pittsburgh was reached the next morning—a "dingy, dirty, business-like town." The air was smoky and the cars traveled through a poor industrialized section of the city. The soldiers from the distant prairie used to open ground and clear air were not impressed. "The people seen by us generally looked poor, thin and haggard, but they cheered us most lustily," one officer wrote home. "Half-naked children climbed the fences and yelled and hurrahed at us." Pittsburgh, wrote one Wisconsin private, was "remarkable for its smoke. Even the little newsboys running around the street look as if they had [been] suspended over the funnel of some blacksmith's shop. You can smell smoke, feel smoke, & I will go so far as to say you can taste it."[21] At Mifflin, Pennsylvania, Pvt. Albert H. Stickney of Janesville climbed to the roof of his moving car to stand and return the salutes of the crowd at the station. The patriotic if oblivious private was waving his cap and hurrahing when he was struck and knocked off the train by the beam of a bridge. "He was shaken up considerably, but not fatally injured and is now doing fine," reported the *Daily Wisconsin*. In fact, the injuries were more serious than first believed and the private's days as a soldier were numbered.[22]

Finally, at Harrisburg, Pennsylvania, on June 22, the regiment was met by more crowds and city officials and ordered to pitch tents in an open field located "thirty rods west of the railroad round house." It was the 2nd Wisconsin's first camp since leaving Wisconsin, and it was at Harrisburg that the regiment was finally issued firearms: Harpers Ferry smoothbore muskets converted from flintlock to

---

20 "N.R." letter from "Camp Randall, Washington," June 28, 1861; John Hamilton, letter from Harrisburg, PA, June 23, 1861, *Wisconsin Newspaper Volumes*, vol. 1. "N.R." was probably Nathaniel Rollins.

21 *Janesville Daily Gazette*, June 21, 1861; Matrau, Letters Home, 9.

22 *Ibid.* Stickney, who enlisted at Janesville on April 20, 1861, was discharged that August 22 because of disability caused by his fall. *Roster of Wisconsin Volunteers, War of the Rebellion, 1861-1865*, 2 vols. (Madison, 1886), vol. 1, 358.

percussion, along with packets of deadly buck and ball cartridges carrying a .69-caliber round ball along with three smaller buckshot. "The Wisconsin boys were wild with delight," a correspondent reported. "One of the companies seized their guns and drilled for two hours before dropping them, though they were fatigued before receiving the guns."[23]

It was eighty miles from Harrisburg to Baltimore, where the 2nd Wisconsin would have to detrain and march through the city to reach another rail connection. When the train reached the Maryland state line, the boys in the cars raised cheers that continued for more than 30 minutes. "We were now in a secession state and all along the road there were squads of men stationed to prevent the burning of bridges and destroying other property," one new soldier wrote in his journal.[24] Delays added to the long trip, and just as the first of the two trains carrying the Wisconsin men neared Baltimore the grim order was given to fix bayonets on their new muskets. The city was regarded as full of "Plug Uglies" and other hooligans who favored the Southern cause. At the depot, the soldiers detrained and formed ranks on a nearby street. Weighing on the minds of the new soldiers was the secessionist mob that had attacked the 6th Massachusetts during its march through Baltimore streets on April 19. When shots were fired at the Bay State troops the soldiers returned fire. Four soldiers and a dozen civilians died. Adding to the tension was the fact that the second train carrying the rest of the companies was running late. "This taxed our patience severely, for expecting their arrival every minute, it was at least three hours before they arrived," complained one soldier. While some soldiers slept on the dusty road, others mingled with curious onlookers. The tired and hungry Badgers were not permitted to take food or water from the citizenry for fear of poison. Police guarded them the entire time.[25]

When the late second train finally arrived, the regiment formed for its journey through Baltimore. One private boasted with youthful vapor that he and his comrades "chafed like caged tigers" and were ready to teach the Plug Uglies a lesson that "they could have recited by heart for many a day." Many of the Wisconsin men, another private offered, "honestly wished for a muss with the sons of bitches; and our guns were loaded—one bullet and three buck-shot each—and we had a mighty nervous feeling about the forefinger." It was a mile and a half tramp to the next depot and officers kept the Badger column under strict discipline, the soldiers marching along with a police escort assigned to watch the crowd.

23 A quotation from the *Daily Wisconsin* cited in *Wisconsin Newspaper Volumes*, vol. 1.

24 Henry N. Allyn, journal.

25 E. K. McCord, from Washington, June 29, 1861, *Wisconsin Newspaper Volumes*, vol. 1.

Despite the approach of midnight, citizens gathered on the sidewalks to launch shouts and cheers for the Confederacy mixed with groans, jeers, and curses for Wisconsin. A few stones sailed through the darkness and a couple pistol shots fired without damage, but the regiment was held firm by the company officers and did not respond. When one onlooker called out that the Wisconsin men were quaking in fear, a cheeky Badger raised a fist and yelled back that he and his friends "were shaking like hell to get hold of Jeff Davis." Sprinkled here and there along the route were signs of loyalty and the display of the Stars and Stripes, which served to cheer the soldiers.

The second depot was reached and the regiment loaded onto a train for the short trip to Washington. Several miles from the destination two wheels of one of the cars derailed causing another three-hour delay. It was not until daybreak on June 25 that the dirty and exhausted Wisconsin soldiers reached Washington. The regiment was marched first to Woodward Block on Pennsylvania Avenue, and later in the day moved to Seventh Street Park, where it would remain for a week. A correspondent for the *New York Tribune* looked over the Wisconsin regiment and reported the soldiers were "mostly of hard fisted lumbermen from the pineries of the Badger State. They say they will fight if ordered and, if not ordered, will fight anyway." The 2nd Wisconsin men always believed they were the first three-year regiment to reach the Northern capital. Now, if only given the opportunity, the Wisconsin boys, with their frontier style and prairie manners, were ready to pitch into the rebels and give them a sound thrashing.[26]

"They are all young, stalwart, vigorous, splendid looking fellows," announced a writer for the *Chicago Journal* when describing the rank and file of the new regiment as it trooped through the streets of that city. The unit, he continued, included "200 lumbermen, hardy, cast-iron fellows from the north, who have not properly slept in a civilized bed in half a dozen years." It was the first time "iron" was used in describing a Wisconsin regiment.[27]

A Regiment of Badgers Led by a Coon

Washington was abuzz with excitement and the Western boys marveled at the clamorous war footing. Just outside the gates of the city were enemy picket lines and a rebel army. The capitol building boasted a bakery where 30,000 loaves of

26 Details were taken from the *Wisconsin State Register, Janesville Daily Gazette, Oshkosh Daily Northwestern, Grant County Herald,* and other newspapers in *Wisconsin Newspaper Volumes,* vol. 1.

27 *Janesville Daily Gazette,* June 1861, *Wisconsin Newspaper Volumes,* vol. 1.

bread were produced daily. A regiment was housed in the basement of the Treasury Building. Soldiers in new uniforms of various colors and design were everywhere— walking in filthy streets alongside wagons, buggies, and horses; sharing rough plank sidewalks with a swarm of citizens; camping in open areas that stretched as far as the eye could see; hanging out of the windows of buildings both public and private, and packed three deep in noisy saloons that never closed. "Everything in Washington looks lively," a Badger wrote home. The new arrivals in their long gray coats and tall caps were hardly noticed as they settled into camp life within a grove of trees in the Seventh Street Park. Someone named the place "Camp Randall" in honor of the Wisconsin governor. All around them, one soldier wrote, "can be seen the camping grounds of 40,000 men, all ready to fight for the good cause."[28]

When given the chance to explore the capital city with its large buildings of Federal stone, the first thing the curious new soldiers from the far West did was seek out the famous figures of the day. This was a time before photography was common and only crude woodcut likenesses of the notables could be found. Winfield Scott of Mexican War fame—"the greatest military man in the whole world"—was seen on a balcony before a flag-raising performed by soldiers from a New York regiment: "The old general is a very large man, looks very old and walks lame, but made a very graceful bow when three times three cheers went up for him," wrote one eyewitness. President Lincoln—"dressed in black with a white vest and turned down collar . . . tall and rather slim"—and Mrs. Lincoln appeared with Secretary of State William Seward, whom one soldier found "a great deal shorter than I expected." He concluded: "I must say Abe is rather homely, but he wears a very pleasant face, and I should say, an honest one, too."[29]

The Seventh Street Park camp was broken a few days later and the regiment marched to Fort Corcoran, one of a series of new military citadels guarding the approaches to Washington. When they arrived the Badgers were brigaded with three New York regiments, which they observed with backwoods wonderment. The 13th New York included city firemen in bright red shirts, another regiment was the famed Irish 69th New York, and the third was the 79th New York, whose flags were carried by bare-legged soldiers in kilts and whose trousers were a tartan plaid. The brigade commander was a nervous slender West Pointer named William Tecumseh Sherman. Young officers observed and noted that his brother, John, was the U.S. Senator from Ohio. Sherman had been out of the army at the start of the war, but in the rush to find qualified officers had been commissioned colonel of the

28 *Ibid.*

29 Letter to *Milwaukee Sentinel*, July 10, 1861.

13th U.S. Infantry. The regiment was still being formed when he was assigned to duty with Lieutenant General Scott, just then in command of all the nation's military forces. Scott assigned Sherman to the Third Brigade, First Division, of the new National Army under another former West Pointer named Daniel Tyler. It would not be too many months before Sherman was making a name, but in the Washington camps of 1861 he was just one of a handful of old Regular Army officers at the head of a brigade of green volunteers. Still, one of his Wisconsin soldiers wrote that he always believed Sherman was "as proud of his four superb regiments as an old hen could possibly be with four broods of chickens."

The burning question for the new soldiers, the citizenry, and the newspapers alike was when and where the great battle to end the secessionist rebellion would come. In the meantime, the days were marked by drills, alarms, inspections, guard duty, and long hours filled with talk. The boys were "very careless" with their new "shooting sticks," one wrote home when telling of a minor wound suffered by a Milwaukee soldier in the accidental discharge of a musket. The food, he went on, was plentiful and included "pork, fresh beef, rice, coffee, beans, hard and soft bread, and vinegar." He called the hard bread, or hardtack, a "great institution. You might soak a biscuit in a good cup of coffee six weeks, and then you would have to have a good set of teeth to eat it."[30]

The 1st Minnesota Infantry was camped nearby and was admired as exceptionally well drilled. Their military neighbors from the eastern states and the local civilians called the Wisconsin men "Badgers," a name given to early white settlers of the territory who burrowed into the ground to dig the valuable lead ore known as galena. The meeting of East and West was not always comfortable. Soldiers from such established and civilized states as New York, Pennsylvania, and New Jersey regarded the Westerners as backwoods rustics not far removed from being savages of the native tribes still living there. The farmer boys from the great prairie also found Virginia lacking. "Do you call that soil?" one Badger asked while toeing the ground. "The crops here are very poor," another soldier wrote his family. "I have not seen a field of grain that the farmers of Wisconsin would consider worth harvesting." Also laughed at around coffee fires was the encounter of two Racine soldiers with a curious local farmer. He questioned the two closely about the faraway frontier and their shooting ability. "Can you hit an Indian's eye at 40 rods?" he inquired. They nodded "of course" in solemn prairie fashion, adding that it would depend upon which eye. The men asked about an animal grazing in a nearby field. "Why, it is a cow!" replied the surprised farmer, at which the two Badgers

30 Charles Dow, letter, to friend James, July 10, 1861, *Wisconsin State Register,* July 13, 1861.

Non-commissioned officers, Oshkosh Volunteers, Co. E, 2nd Wisconsin

From left to right: W. S. Rouse, R. Ash, G. E. Smith, N. H. Whittemore, O. F. Crary, and Josh, a former slave working as a camp servant. *Wisconsin Historical Society 41937*

rolled their eyes in mock astonishment: There were no such animals in Wisconsin, they explained in pious and serious tones—only wild buffalo. Another much-laughed about episode was the report that a Connecticut boy "wished to know how many of us were half breeds," and another eastern soldier who "made the remark that he supposed that it did not come very hard, this camping out, to us, as we had probably been used to it the most part of our lives." The wildwood boys from the Wisconsin frontier were already an item of curiosity. "Our regiment is talked of a good deal," a Badger wrote the *Milwaukee Sentinel.* "All have an idea that we are all sharpshooters as we came from away out West and always lived out in the woods. . . . General Scott paid us a visit. He said we were all good, healthy looking fellows, and he must give Wisconsin the credit of clothing and equipping her men better than any other State had done."[31]

There was also news from the 1st Wisconsin regiment. These Badgers were serving as part of a force protecting the Baltimore & Ohio Railroad as well as the garrison established at Harpers Ferry, where the Federal arsenal had been destroyed earlier by the rebels and musket-making machinery and parts shipped to Richmond,

31 *Janesville Daily Gazette,* July 12, 1861.

Virginia. "We got reports from the 1st Regiment last night that they had a fight [the battle of Falling Waters] somewhere in the vicinity of Harpers Ferry and came out victorious, having captured quite a lot of baggage and a number of prisoners. Reports say that the officers had no control over the men—every one went in on his muscle, and their motto was 'Die dog or eat a hatchet.' I think this will be the case with the 2d Regiment if they ever come to a fight."[32]

There were more pressing matters, however, in the Washington camps of July 1861 where the 2nd Wisconsin and its green volunteers were learning to be soldiers. The regiment soon became mired in a leadership controversy. It was blamed on the Republican governor's well-meaning effort to include rival Democrats in the war effort by naming prominent and highly regarded Milwaukee lawyer Squire Park Coon, a former Wisconsin attorney general, as colonel. A native of New York, Coon was educated at Norwich University in Vermont, and he had no real military knowledge or experience. He assumed command of the regiment amid whispers about his respectable and notable thirst for strong drink. Recognizing a political favor with one of his own, Coon named the Madison mustering location "Camp Randall" after his governor-benefactor. The appointment of the new colonel was initially met with favor and his name led to a clever remark widely circulated: "Why is the Second regiment of Wisconsin Active Militia the greatest phenomenon of the age?—because it is composed of Badgers led by a Coon."[33]

The regiment was more fortunate in the selection of its second ranking officer. Henry W. Peck, a farmer in Jefferson Township, Monroe County, had been appointed from Ohio in 1851 to the U.S. Military Academy at West Point but did not graduate. With his two years as a cadet, however, and his new commission as lieutenant colonel, he soon took over drilling the regiment until the Western boys (using a manual authorized by General Scott) were able to move "by the left flank" or "left front into line" with a certain precision that even attracted the eye of soldiers in neighboring camps. Befitting a dashing and well regarded young officer, the citizens of Madison and Dane County presented Peck with a fancy black horse named "Wild Bill," a sleek animal known locally for its speed. Named major was Duncan McDonald of Milwaukee, an outgoing and friendly businessman called "Dunc." He was colonel of the Juneau Guards, a city militia company, and a

---

32 Charles Dow, letter, to Friend Butler, *Wisconsin State Register*, July 13, 1861. The letter referred to the battle of Falling Waters, June 2, 1861. The minor skirmish, also called the Battle of Hoke's Run, and the Battle of Hainesville, is often confused with the 1863 engagement. In the exchange of musket fire, George Drake of Milwaukee was shot and killed—the first Wisconsin man to die in the Civil War.

33 *Wisconsin Newspaper Volumes*, vol. 1.

railroad clerk and ticket agent as well as an officer of the Phoenix Insurance Company. The *Milwaukee Daily Wisconsin* described "Dunc" McDonald as "one of the most popular men in the city, and we are sure will make his mark when a chance is given."

It was soon clear to the whole regiment that Coon had no military ability and that during the long dull hours of the training camp had taken to "the inordinate use of stimulants." With what was expected to be the decisive battle ending the war just ahead, the concerned junior officers raised a petition asking Coon to resign. The letter was carried to the colonel by a delegation of the younger officers. Visibly shaken by the rent in his command structure, Coon stubbornly refused to leave his post. Undeterred, the officers selected a committee to go to the department commander, Brig. Gen. Joseph Mansfield, who informed the Wisconsin delegation that the proceeding was "decidedly against the regulations." In a move that was likely just as ill-advised and disruptive, Mansfield drafted a short note to be carried to brigade commander Sherman informing him of the situation and the desire by many in the regiment to see Coon replaced. Sherman, who described the incident in his memoir, admitted that political appointee Coon "knew no more of the military art than a child." To avoid any difficulties from strong political forces and a governor back in Wisconsin, and to improve the function of his new brigade, Sherman cleverly named Coon to his personal staff and promoted Peck to field command of the 2nd Wisconsin.[34]

At the very center of the excitement of the day and the calls to attack the Confederates outside Washington was Irvin McDowell, the commander of the new National army. The well-liked Regular Army officer had both a reputation for congeniality and an ability to consume and enjoy large amounts of food. During the War with Mexico he served with distinction on the staff of General Scott, demonstrating a marked ability in paperwork management. The new army commander, however, was also short-tempered and aloof. Not mentioned publicly, or at least little regarded at the time, was McDowell's lack of field or command experience. From the outset McDowell was whipped by violent political winds as he did his best to organize an army and prepare it for battle. Pressured by Lincoln to just do something, he told the president that he would need several weeks to get his new army in shape for an active campaign. "You are green, it is true, but they are

---

34 William T. Sherman, *Memoirs of General William T. Sherman by Himself*, 2 vols, (New York, 1875), vol. 1, 176-179, 182; Gaff, *If This Is War*, 143; Lucius Fairchild, manuscript, Wisconsin Historical Society; George Otis, *The Second Wisconsin Infantry, with Letters and Recollections by Other Members of the Regiment*, Alan D. Gaff, ed., (Dayton, OH, 1984), 107-108; *Milwaukee Sunday Telegraph*, March 14, 1886. Otis' history was originally printed in 11 parts in the *Milwaukee Sunday Telegraph* in 1880.

green also; you are all green alike," the president explained while pressing the need for immediate action because many of the enlistments of the 90-day regiments were expiring. Stung by shrill "On to Richmond!" newspaper editorials, unrelenting pressure from the Lincoln administration, and calls from across the country for action, McDowell gathered his inexperienced volunteers and a few Regulars and marched into northern Virginia.[35]

Bull's Run

The campaign that ended in the long-anticipated battle "on which a nation trembled" began July 15, 1861, when marching orders reached the 2nd Wisconsin of Sherman's brigade in Dan Tyler's division. The long days of waiting were at an end. The boys prepared for the campaign "right heartily," one recalled, because it was regarded that this time the marching orders "meant business" and the battle expected to end the rebellion and settle matters once and for all was really at hand. Three days' rations were prepared and surplus apparel discarded. Blankets were rolled lengthwise and carried across the shoulder. Baggage was left with camp equipage, tents standing. By 1:00 p.m. the regiment marched out to the Fairfax Road to take its place in the brigade formation. The column was on the move shortly, marching a dozen miles through Falls Church and then to Vienna, where it was halted for the night.

The march resumed the next morning at an early hour. The weather was hot and humid and the pace slow. Word coursed through the ranks that Rebels were lurking just ahead. Along the way the column discovered deserted farms and empty Confederate camps with "half cooked dinners left upon the fire." Soldiers trying to fill empty canteens surrounded water wells near empty farm houses while friends and comrades—despite strict orders against such deprivations—examined the empty structures for war souvenirs, milked abandoned cows, and gathered up chickens, pigs, sheep, and other foodstuffs. Felled trees blocked the roadway here and there, as did light breastworks. The regiment passed Fairfax Court House, marched through Germantown, and reached the Warrenton Pike. About three miles outside Centreville the column halted. It had covered about eight miles. "The march," admitted one of the new officers, "though tiresome, was gay," with the roadway ahead and behind crowded with men, horses, baggage wagons, and artillery. Alongside the column were discarded items the neophyte soldiers found too heavy or burdensome to carry. "Occasional shots were heard during the day," a

35 T. Harry Williams, *Lincoln and His Generals* (New York, 1952), 21.

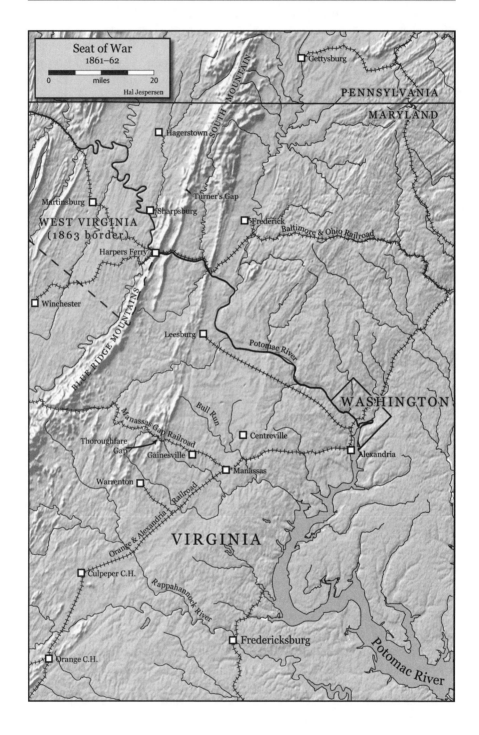

Seat of War
1861–62

0   miles   20

Hal Jespersen

Gettysburg

PENNSYLVANIA

MARYLAND

Hagerstown

SOUTH MOUNTAIN

Turner's Gap

Martinsburg

Sharpsburg

WEST VIRGINIA
(1863 border)

Frederick

Baltimore & Ohio Railroad

Harpers Ferry

Winchester

BLUE RIDGE MOUNTAINS

Leesburg

Potomac River

WASHINGTON

Manassas Gap Railroad

Bull Run

Thoroughfare
Gap

Centreville

Gainesville

Alexandria

Manassas

Warrenton

Orange & Alexandria Railroad

VIRGINIA

Culpeper C.H.

Rappahannock River

Fredericksburg

Potomac River

Orange C.H.

young and excited soldier wrote home, "and while the excitement is gradually 'growing on us,' the prospects are not so flattering for as early an engagement as anticipated."[36]

McDowell had an army of about 35,000 soldiers to face a Confederate army under Gen. P. G. T. Beauregard covering the key rail junction at Manassas in northern Virginia. The colorful Beauregard, with his French look and Napoleonic posing, had captured Fort Sumter and was at the moment the great hero of the new Confederacy—even though he was roundly denounced as a traitor and villain by Union loyalists. It was later determined that he had about 20,000 soldiers in his command. Farther north, another 12,000 Confederates under Gen. Joseph E. Johnston confronted a larger Union force (including the 90-day 1st Wisconsin) under Brig. Gen. Robert Patterson, a 69-year-old veteran of the War of 1812 who won the brief earlier skirmish at Falling Waters on July 2, 1861. The fighting withdrawal of the Confederates on that day, however, left Patterson convinced that he faced a much larger force. Aggression did not come naturally to the aging general.

The 2nd Wisconsin spent the night near the road and early on the morning of July 18 marched toward Centreville, where the brigade halted. The heavy cannonading thundering well to the front and beyond the town caused a stir in the ranks. About noon, the brigade was ordered to the support of troops engaged near a place known locally as Blackburn's Ford on a creek called Bull Run. The regiments moved forward at the double-quick through the midday heat for "better than three miles" claimed one soldier, with "a hot sun pouring down upon us and the roads so dusty that one can scarcely see his file leader." Blankets and other items are cast aside along the road. Many soldiers unable to keep the pace fell out along the way. As they approached the scene of the fighting, the regiment filed right into a patch of woods and formed a line of battle at right angles with the road. "We lay down to avoid the shot and shell which crash among the trees above our head," recalled a Badger. The artillery fire continued about three hours and demonstrated the Confederates were in large numbers across the creek. The young soldiers watched as their former colonel, Squire Coon, now on the brigade staff, rode up amid the shells with orders for Lieutenant Colonel Peck. "Men, don't stand up and expose yourselves needlessly," Coon advised in a quiet voice from his horse to the young men. "[L]ie down and take it cool and when we want you we will call you." The colonel, admitted a private, "showed more courage than we supposed him

36 Otis, *Second Wisconsin*, 33, 222. For a detailed and full discussion of First Bull Run, see William C. Davis, *Battle at Bull Run: A History of the First Major Campaign of the Civil War* (Garden City, NY, 1977).

capable of." It was the regiment's first experience with artillery, and the greenhorn soldiers were surprised to find how many escaped injury during the noisy shelling. Only four soldiers were struck and only one seriously. The unfortunate Myron Gardner, a 19-year-old farmer from Trempealeau in La Crosse County, died the next day—the regiment's first man killed in action.[37]

According to Capt. Thomas Allen of the Miners' Guard, being under fire for the first time without an opportunity to return it was "anything but agreeable." However, the shelling taught him and the others that while "the sound of the guns was more terrific, the real danger in battle was the whistling 'minnie' [bullet], which reached one without note or warning." Toward evening, the brigade was ordered back to the camp at Centreville, where Sherman bivouacked his brigade. It remained there for the next three days, the men expecting at any moment to move upon the Confederates. Orders arrived to prepare 10 days of rations.[38]

McDowell, meanwhile, devised a flanking movement to turn and crush the Confederate left. The ambitious movement began at an early hour on July 21, a bright clear Sunday morning. While Tyler's division, including Sherman's brigade, demonstrated near the Stone Bridge on the Warrenton Turnpike, two other Federal divisions moved toward the enemy flank. Tyler's movements were slow and carried little weight, however, and it did not take the Confederates long to realize that the bulk of the National Army was not sitting to their front but moving around their left. Despite hurried efforts to counter the move, the Union attack pushed the rebels off Matthews Hill, which in turn cleared the Stone Bridge when the Confederates retreated across the turnpike to a plateau-like area known locally as Henry House Hill. The enemy line stiffened there, but by any measure Beauregard's Confederate army was in trouble.

By this time Tyler's men had crossed Bull Run. Some slipped over the Stone Bridge, but Sherman's brigade, with the 2nd Wisconsin in the lead, splashed across a ford a quarter-mile upstream. Ahead of them on the hilltop, the Confederates made a stand with fresh reinforcements from Joe Johnston's Shenandoah army moving up to bolster their thin line. The cautious and elderly Patterson held his own Union forces in check, allowing Johnston to ship his rebels to Manassas just in time to meet McDowell's offensive. The Confederates covered the distance in crowded cars in one of the first usages of rail to transport troops directly onto a battlefield and into combat. The Union attempts to clear the hilltop, piecemeal and

---

37 Otis, *Second Wisconsin*, 33-34; Elisha R. Reed, "Both Sides of Life in Rebel Prisons," *Second Wisconsin*, 154.

38 Thomas S. Allen, "The 2nd Wisconsin at the First Battle of Bull Run," *Second Wisconsin*, 224.

delivered by worn and weary inexperienced soldiers in hot weather, stalled in front of a line anchored by a brigade of Virginians led by a Virginia Military Institute instructor named Thomas J. Jackson, a pious blue-eyed former West Pointer who held as firm as "a stonewall," and fought with the fanatical zeal of an Old Testament prophet.

Convinced victory was just one push away, McDowell mounted a series of frontal attacks in an attempt to clear Henry House Hill. It was during this effort that the 2nd Wisconsin and the balance of Sherman's brigade joined the fighting. The regiment crossed the Warrenton Pike upon the Sudley Springs Road, moving through what one Badger called "a terrific fire of shot and shell," only to halt at the base of the hill where a bluff along the roadway afforded some protection. Pvt. Philo Wright said it was while moving to the bluff that he saw and stepped over the first man he had ever seen dead on a battlefield. During the march forward he dodged a little to the right to "allow a cannon ball to have 'right of way' as it pursued its course in the opposite direction from which we were going. Casper Gardent to my left also stepped a little to the left to avoid meeting the ball and I shall never forget his look of horror and surprise as he, still advancing, turned to meet my look at him of equal wonder and fearfulness." Both men found a scene of horror. To their front, farther up the hill, the ground was littered with bodies and battle debris including dead artillery horses and wrecked cannon. Behind them, milling about in confusion and fear, gathered clusters of demoralized soldiers who had unsuccessfully charged up the hill. Dead and wounded alike were pressed along the shallow depression near the bank, "filling the ditch in some places three or four deep," wrote one Badger. "The smoke prevented us from seeing the length our line and the noise from hearing commands, even if any were given." Out of the smoke and confusion rode old Maj. James Wadsworth, a staff officer with General McDowell. Wadsworth directed Sherman to support a line closely engaged with the enemy. Holding two regiments in reserve, Sherman dispatched the 13th New York and the 2nd Wisconsin up disputed Henry House Hill into a swirl of bullets and artillery bursts. The regiments were caught up in what one called the "work of death and carnage."[39]

The 2nd Wisconsin surged over the embankment, climbed a wooden fence, and came upon a washed-out gully that split the unit into two parts. Twenty rods

39 William Lowry Morse, *Grandad and the Civil War* (privately printed, 1994). This book contains the written war memoirs of Philo Wright of the 2nd Wisconsin. Wright enlisted at Tafton, April 22, 1861. He was discharged May 25, 1864, as result of wounds. Gardent enlisted at Muscoda on April 22, 1861, and mustered out on June 28, 1864, term expired. *Wisconsin Roster*, vol. 1, 356.

more and most of the order lost. The line fitfully halted on its own just as enemy fire staggered it. "Soon there was a heavy fire opened up on us from the front which we returned with promptness and with such effect that it will cause them to remember until their dying day," one Wisconsin man boasted in his journal.[40] There was little to be gained, however, and the regiment was ordered back to the roadway to take shelter.

One of the Badgers in trouble from the heat and lack of water was Pvt. John Hinton. Remembered as orderly, intelligent, and responsible, Hinton joined friends in enlisting in the Belle City Rifles being raised in Racine. Now, with battle raging around him, Hinton was physically near the end of his rope as the untested and ill-trained soldiers of the 2nd Wisconsin fought along near the top of the hill. Hinton and several men of his company passed through the wreckage of a Federal battery halfway up the slope. When the advance stalled in the face of Confederate volleys, he and his company "kept up a brisk fire till our muskets became so hot we could scarcely hold them."[41]

When a fresh strong line of Rebels surged forward waving its battle flags, a soldier near Hinton fired and dropped one of the advancing Confederate color-bearers; Hinton shot the man to his right. He was one of three Confederates Hinton later claimed to have personally shot that hot afternoon. Nearby, another Belle City boy, Henry Benson— "his hat off, his cartridge box slung around in front of him, so that he could get at it handily"—was loading and firing. He was ramming home a charge when a ball struck his hand. Benson looked in surprise at the wound, held up his injured limb, and called out, "Boys, there's Wisconsin blood!" The soldier was urged to leave the line and get treatment, but refused to do so. He was shot dead a few minutes later. By this time the whole Union line was coming apart. Hinton stopped to give the rebels a parting shot. "Tearing my cartridge and inserting it into the muzzle of my gun, as I was upon my knees, I drew my ramrod to drive it down, when a ball struck me in the side," he wrote. "I staggered for a moment, but finding that I was not dangerously hurt, ran toward our column. Another ball went through my canteen as I was running. Discovering now for the

---

40 Henry Allyn, journal. To understand the movements of the 2nd Wisconsin and the tactical developments of the confusing early-war battle, see Bradley M. Gottfried, *The Maps of First Bull Run: An Atlas of the First Bull Run (Manassas) Campaign, including the Battle of Ball's Bluff, June - October 1861* (Savas Beatie, 2007).

41 Wright, in *Grandad*. The Hinton family had come to America from England when he was a child, living for a time in New York City and then Racine before moving to Waukesha. An 1859 graduate of Prairieville Academy, now Carroll University, he was working as a clerk when the war started.

first time that I had lost my ramrod, I stooped down and drew one from the gun of a man who was killed by my side."[42]

As the gray-clad Wisconsin soldiers fell back down the slope in a frantic effort to reach the road, they were mistakenly fired upon from the Union lines. "You are shooting your friends!" "Stop for God's sake!" cried the Badger men as they tumbled down the slope for the safety of the embankment. Private Elisha R. Reed halted to fire at the pursuing enemy. He discharged his musket and stooped to reload when a ball fired "from our own men on the hillside below me" struck him in the back, breaking his shoulder blade and lodging near the surface. Unable to keep shooting, he made for the rear just as Sherman ordered the 69th and 79th New York to relieve the 2nd Wisconsin. Reed was captured by Confederate cavalry the next day during his vain attempt to walk all the way back to Washington.[43]

As the New York regiments moved forward, some of the retreating Badgers turned around and slipped into the advance. Sherman's second effort was also shot to pieces and, as the general admitted, was "repulsed in confusion." The wounded Hinton huddled in the safety under the road embankment where other men of his company had halted. Within a few minutes he collapsed from sunstroke.[44] Nearby, another member of the Belle City Rifles—Willie Upham— struggled to breathe as blood from a gaping wound clogged his throat. He was forced to lay face down so the blood drained onto the ground. He would be left behind for dead.[45]

Long afterward, it would be noted that it was the second time Wisconsin men had faced Thomas Jackson's Confederates. The 1st Wisconsin had driven his rebels less than a month earlier in the skirmish at Falling Waters, but today's 2nd Wisconsin's engagement at Manassas ended badly. And the day was about to get much worse.

---

42 *Waukesha Freeman*, July 30, 1861; *Weekly Racine Advocate*, July 31, 1861; Benson, Burlington, WI., had enlisted less than a month earlier. *Wisconsin Roster*, vol. 1, 362.

43 Reed, "Both Sides of a Rebel Prison," 154. Reed returned to service when he was exchanged and was wounded again at Gettysburg. He transferred to the Veteran Reserve Corps until he was mustered out on June 11, 1864, at the end of his three-year term. *Wisconsin Roster*, vol. 1, 369.

44 Otis, *Second Wisconsin*, 35; Reed, "Both Sides of a Rebel Prison," 156; William Sherman's report, in *The War of the Rebellion, A compilation of the Official Records of the Union and Confederate Armies* (Washington, D.C., 1880-1901), Series 1, vol. 2, 369-370. Hereafter referred to as *OR*. All references are to Series 1 unless otherwise noted.

45 Upham was captured and sent to Libby Prison in Richmond, Virginia. He was paroled wounded, and subsequently appointed to West Point by President Lincoln. Two of the four young men appointed to the U.S.M.A. by Lincoln were from Wisconsin: Upham and Charles King, the son of Gen. Rufus King.

Repulsed in his vigorous if ineptly launched attempt to take Henry House Hill, McDowell realized the day was lost and ordered his regiments to withdraw across Bull Run and toward Centreville to reform. Sherman's brigade began the withdrawal more or less in order, and a friend took Hinton's musket because the young sun-stricken soldier could hardly walk. All around them the organization of the various regiments and companies was collapsing. Within an hour, the entire National army was on the run in panic and disgrace toward the nation's capital.

The Confederates would call the battle "Manassas" for the nearby town while the Federals called it "Bull Run" after the sluggish creek that meandered its way through the field. To 2nd Wisconsin men, it was always "Bull's Run" and, sometimes with a sour smile, "Big Run."

A Story of Bravery and Love Lost

As the survivors of the failed 2nd Wisconsin attack against Henry House Hill huddled in the powder smoke and wreckage behind the bank along the Sudley Springs Road, Confederates massed to their front and in the woods on their right. The crossfire that resulted proved untenable, and the Wisconsin men moved away from the road in groups of two or three, firing as they retreated. Private Wright suffered a minor wound, but did not discover it until the next day when he saw the sock on his left foot with "a fearful hole" torn by a bullet that had "gone close enough to the inside of my ankle to change the skin to a dark purple color." The initial hit felt "like a sharp blow with a stick," and it was only a day later that he realized "I had come near danger." Several Badgers, including Hinton, tried to form a rally point in a small hollow with some trees, but the holding action collapsed after four of them suffered wounds.

By this time the cartridge boxes of the 2nd Wisconsin men were all but empty (one corporal later discovered he had fired 32 rounds) and the muskets barrels so hot and fouled that some of the young soldiers drove ramrods against trees to get the cartridges down the muzzle. When enemy horsemen emerged from the woods, fleeing soldiers raised the cry, "It's the Black Horse Cavalry!"[46]

---

46 *Weekly Racine Advocate*, July 31 and August 7, 1861; Morse, *Grandad*, quoting the Wright memoir, 40; *Waukesha Freeman*, July 30, 1861. See Gaff, *If This Is War*, 203-216. The "Black Horse Cavalry" that evoked the fearful shouts at Bull Run referred to a famous pre-war militia company from Fauquier County, Virginia—which was not even on the field. The unit was originally formed in June 1859 and best remembered for escorting abolitionist John Brown to the gallows in December 1859. Now the storied name was lent to any and all Confederate cavalry at Bull Run.

The "Black Horse Cavalry" became the "great scarecrow" of the "skedaddle" at Bull Run, remembered one Wisconsin officer writing later with the grim amusement and experience of a veteran soldier. The feared horsemen of Bull Run never numbered more than a squad or two at any one place, he continued, and only made "a few faint dashes upon our forces." The Wisconsin men had earlier watched from a distance, however, when the 1st Virginia Cavalry under Col. James Ewell Brown (Jeb) Stuart charged and scattered the New York Fire Zouaves on Henry House Hill.[47]

The National army's retreat began reluctantly despite inexperienced officers and ill-trained soldiers. The men moved slowly with no real sense of panic, expecting they would rally and reorganize about where the first line of battle had formed that morning. In fact, some of the Federal soldiers began forming lines at that point. It was then, explained one Wisconsin officer, that more Confederate horsemen appeared near the Stone Bridge and charged "some stragglers, who came flying up the [Warrenton] pike shouting: 'the cavalry!' 'The cavalry are upon us!'" Reorganization became impossible, complained the officer, with "stampeding teamsters, ambulance drivers, musicians and a broken and demoralized army" filling and clogging the roadway. Farther on, he found Capt. Thomas Allen of his regiment using a stand of colors to rally a few hundred men in a half-circle as a protection against the enemy horsemen. No sooner "had the noble captain formed his impregnable wall of bayonets, than some mischievous cuss in the line called out: 'Here comes the cavalry!' and every man, as if by instinct, arose and dashed toward Centerville, leaving the plucky captain to take care of the colors as best he might." With his make-shift line dissolved, Allen turned his own face toward Centreville and safety with the rest of his men.[48]

Early in the withdrawal, Sherman tried to organize a hollow square to repulse cavalry. According to one Badger, however, it was incompletely filled and marked by "a great gap" through which cavalry might "pour without any trouble. I had heard of the French regiments forming hollow squares at Waterloo," he continued, "and I thought if there was anything that could save the country and turn back the tide of rebel victory, it was a hollow square." The advancing and jubilant rebels, however, were soon taking potshots at the island of National soldiers, flanking it, and then firing a crashing volley. Sherman admitted his little square "fell to pieces" and the disorderly retreat continued.[49]

47 Thomas Allen. "The 2nd Wisconsin at First Bull Run," 227-228.

48 Otis, *Second Wisconsin*, 36-37.

49 Gilbert Woodward, *Milwaukee Sunday Telegraph*, September 7, 1884; Sherman, *Memoirs*, 187.

There was one disconcerting moment just before the square was attacked that added to the despair of the moment: the sight of Lt. Col. Henry Peck of the 2nd Wisconsin riding past the formation on his pet horse "Wild Bill." His mount was a fast one and he was making for Washington and safety "at his best speed." Peck had fought with his regiment on Henry House Hill, but now he called out as he galloped past for his "boys to reach Washington as soon as possible and the best they could." More than one Wisconsin soldier watched the fleeing officer in dismay. "We have got to go too," concluded one, and elements of the "square dissolved and departed as quick as a covey of quails." The episode embarrassed Pvt. Henry Allen. "The retreat was one of the most ignominious that ever happened to American soldiers and I hope that it will never occur again," he told his journal. "The road for miles was strewn with artillery, muskets and the implements of war, also a great deal of ammunition, shovels, axes and baggage wagons loaded with provisions and clothing estimated about a quarter of a million all which fell into the rebels hands."[50]

Frightened civilians who had brought buggies and picnic baskets to watch the fighting passed the exhausted Wisconsin men in their haste to return to the safety of the nation's capital. Colonel Squire Park Coon and Rhode Island Gov. William Sprague, who had accompanied his state troops, did their best to rally the troops. Sprague was waving two revolvers and Coon was "mounted on a horse and waving a flag, with the tears rolling down his cheeks, as he implored the men to stand fast." It did no good and the disheartened soldiers moved past him. The old colonel, pushed aside by the young company officers and taken on Sherman's staff to avoid embarrassment, said one soldier, "won laurels for himself" for his conduct in the battle.[51]

One of the many moving in the stream of retreating soldiers was the wounded and sunstroke-ridden John Hinton, who was being helped along by a small party of Wisconsin men. He was barely able to keep up. About midnight, weary and drained of all energy, the group reached a point near Fairfax. In their frantic effort to get as far ahead of the Black Horse Cavalry as possible, Hinton's frightened comrades left him behind. About dawn, Hinton started on alone and made it to within three miles of Washington when, "perfectly exhausted," he sat down under a tree in a pouring rain. Luckily, some officers riding in a passing one-horse rig (how they acquired the buggy was not explained) took notice of the wounded soldier, loaded him aboard, and bumped along to Washington.

50 Woodward, *Telegraph*, September 7, 1884; Henry Allyn, journal.

51 Otis, *Second Wisconsin*, 110, 114; *Milwaukee Sentinel*, July 30, 1861.

The officers dropped Hinton off on a street corner. It was a hard fix for a Wisconsin soldier boy so far from home and friends. Sick, hungry, wounded, and suffering from heat exhaustion, Hinton was unsure what to do when a member of the Henderson Guards of the District of Columbia militia found him and took him into the armory, where the young soldier spent his second night after the battle. The next morning Hinton was served breakfast—his first real food since before the fighting. Refreshed and feeling better, Hinton wrote a long letter home to Waukesha describing the battle to his family before setting off in search of his regiment. Somehow his letter reached home before many details of the battle of Bull Run had even been reported in the newspapers. His account of Wisconsin's role in the great battle was shown to neighbors and friends, and the editor of the *Waukesha Freeman* and several other citizens urged the family to publish it. The account, highlighted by Hinton's lurid details of the fighting filled a long column and, despite the disaster of the defeat, lifted local pride in one of their own. A son of Wisconsin had stood up to rebel bullets, been wounded, and continued to do his duty in the face of all adversity imaginable. The Hinton family was besieged with a flurry of visits as neighbors and well-wishers congratulated them. Drinks and cheers were raised in local saloons, not only in Waukesha but the entire county—and even in neighboring Racine County.

A few days later, however, a man identified as "T. J. Johnson" sent his own letter to the *Freeman*. His account was fraught with bitter disillusionment and contained a charge of cowardice against Hinton who, wrote "Johnson," was no hero. The writer questioned the soldier's truthfulness about his role at Bull Run and alleged that Hinton "was sick in bed, unable to walk, at the time the battle was fought, and instead of being on the battlefield was no nearer than on a sick couch at Washington." The second letter created a sensation much as the first had, though a shameful one. The Hinton family closed its door to visitors. Saloons continued to do a good business, but no drinks were raised in Hinton's honor. The city, the counties, and yes, even the whole state of Wisconsin itself, it was said in quiet sorrowful whispers, was disgraced by Hinton's false story dreamed up to cover his cowardice.[52]

A long few days later another man appeared at the offices of the *Waukesha Freeman*. He claimed to be a friend of the Hinton family, and was there to respond to the accusations made by "T. J. Johnson." The stranger presented a letter offering a point-by-point refutation of the allegations before wondering aloud about Johnson's motives. Mr. Johnson, he alleged, had been courting John Hinton's sister

---

52 Details of the incident can be found in the Carroll University archives.

Adda, and "such meanness has been demonstrated heretofore, in cases where a young man has been rejected as a suitor." The letter was signed simply "Justice." When the details were published, John Hinton's reputation was again made whole. Less satisfying, however, was how the story played out over the coming months. The written record of those war days of long ago carried no information on the fate of the scoundrel known only as "T. J. Johnson," or what happened to the pretty Adda Hinton. John Hinton's own story had a sad ending. He was severely wounded in the fighting at South Mountain on September 14, 1862. His left leg was amputated but he died a month later at nearby Keedysville.[53] In March 1863, the *Freeman* reported that dozens of soldiers with Waukesha connections were involved in the war, and that several were among the "honored dead." One of those "honored dead" was John Hinton. His body was returned to Waukesha and buried in Prairie Home Cemetery.[54]

53 *Wisconsin Roster*, vol 1, 363; Gaff, *If This Is War*, 329.

54 Carroll University archives.

Part II: All Had to Learn the Business of War

Give Us Good Guns and Respectable Clothing

The defeat near Manassas Junction left the North stunned and the South jubilant. The embarrassment shook the very foundation of the new Lincoln administration and ended forever unrealistic and foolish notions there could be an early or easy end to the sectional crisis. Southern confidence soared in the mistaken belief that the chivalry of their soldiers would always triumph over any so-called "pluck" of Yankee "mudsills." Sober men on both sides realized it was going to be a real Civil War and a long one, and that no one could predict the outcome.

Some of the foot-sore and weary Bull Run survivors of the 2nd Wisconsin rallied near Centreville where they made coffee and spent the night under the command of Capts. David McKee and Thomas Allen. Lieutenant Colonel Henry Peck and Maj. Duncan McDonald were not among them. The survivors marched the next day to their old Camp Peck at Fort Corcoran near Washington. During the ensuing days other Badgers (like John Hinton) returned to the regiment in small groups or alone. In the bright light of the morning after the fighting, the survivors eyed one another in wonderment. What had become of the attractive gray uniforms and smart shakos of the regiment? Many of the caps were now missing and the coats sweaty, torn, and dirty to the point that they could be "stood in the corner of a tent at night where they stood at attention, acting as 'Randall sentinels.'"[1]

Officers calling the rolls found 785 men present or accounted for in the regiment two days after the battle. Sherman submitted the regiment's official loss as twenty-three killed, sixty-five wounded, and twenty-three missing and believed prisoners. The sad fact is that numbers and reports for every battle should be regarded as suspect. One historian of the 2nd Wisconsin used all available casualty

---

1 Otis, *Second Wisconsin*, 37.

lists, official and unofficial, and determined the loss at eighteen killed, seventy-six wounded, fifty wounded prisoners, and twenty-six unwounded prisoners—about twenty percent of the regimental strength. Overall in McDowell's army, 460 soldiers were killed, 1,124 wounded, and 1,312 missing or captured. Confederate casualties were 387 killed, 1,582 wounded, and thirteen missing. For a time many worried that the victorious secessionists would advance on Washington, but as the Confederates discovered, victory often left an army nearly as disorganized as defeat. To answer the crisis, President Lincoln the day after the event signed a bill providing for the enlistment of 500,000 men for up to three years of service.[2]

Governor Alexander Randall had been in New York at the time of the fighting and jumped the first available train back to Washington. He appeared in camp the day after the new call for troops, where he visited the sick and wounded, did his best to try and cheer up "the drooping hearts," and assured the new soldiers that they had not been forgotten in their home state. Dismayed by the tattered appearance of the boys, he immediately ordered—on his own initiative—the purchase of additional food, blankets, and other clothing. Randall was with his Badgers when President Lincoln and Secretary William Seward, accompanied by Sherman, arrived in the camps. As the Badgers crowded around the carriage, the president stood and made a short speech in a "mild, gentle way" promising better officers, improved arms, and new uniforms. It was all too much for former congressman and now Capt. Gabriel Bouck of Oshkosh. The officer pulled one of his private soldiers from ranks and turned him around in front of the president to display his torn trousers and expose the man's underwear. "Lincoln, look here!" the captain demanded. "Here is a specimen of the soldiers! Give us good guns and respectable clothing and there will be no trouble." He took a musket from another man to demonstrate that it was unacceptable. Another captain added a call for better officers and training, and the request was echoed by Captain McKee: "We are ready to fight but for God's sake give us officers who know something to command us." Lincoln took it all in stride and pointed toward William Sherman. "Here is your general and if your officers do not suit you, make your wants known to him." That bit of advice brought a hearty cheer and the boys crowded in to shake hands with the president. Lincoln was always much on the minds of his new soldiers those days. When the 19th Indiana marched past the White House sometime later, Pvt. A. D. Shaw spotted the president. "There in the door with head uncovered 'that man of the people' stood watching the passing regiment," the private recalled. "I could even at that distance recognize the sympathetic expression on his homely face. No

2   Gaff, *If This Is War*, 261.

doubt he felt in his great heart pity for the loved ones at home and pride in the men passing by."[3]

During the weeks that followed, as a growing federal army assembled and trained outside Washington, Lincoln traveled now and then from the White House to visit the Wisconsin regiment from a state neighboring his own Illinois. The president met for a time with the officers to talk politics and military matters before driving his carriage through the regimental camps to "receive the tumultuous greeting of 'the boys' [and] to wave his hat and smile at them, and sometimes, when they crowded around him, to stop and shake hands with the near most, and once or twice to tell some whimsical story that would set his hearer shouting with glee," recalled one who was there. "The President seemed to find himself thoroughly at home among those lads from the far West."[4]

There was much to discuss during the long hot summer days after the Bull Run disaster, and the young officers of the companies spent long hours talking over the situation. At first there was a call for a petition asking the governor to disband the regiment or take it back to Wisconsin for reorganization, but the idea was rejected. Also considered at length was the issue of .69-caliber Harpers Ferry smoothbore muskets. The guns, called "gas pipes" by the men in the ranks, "have proved to be of a very inferior quality and in no respect equal to those of the enemy." The muskets were awkward and clumsy and the barrels got so hot while firing "you can scarcely bear the hand upon them." The outdated weapons, difficult to keep clean and in good order, also had a vicious kick, "nearly taking a man's arm off at the shoulder every time they are fired."[5]

The regimental command situation was the most perplexing issue. The Badgers agreed that brigade commander Sherman had stood by them during the fighting, but there was little confidence in the regimental officers. Colonel Coon, who had shown bravery during the fighting and retreat, troubled many because of his lack of military experience and alleged drinking. Lieutenant Colonel Peck and Major McDonald performed well enough at Bull Run for inexperienced officers, but left the field and were "'up and gone' to Washington before the fight had fairly commenced." For the most part, it was the captains and lieutenants who had remained with their respective commands. Singled out as "capable" were Thomas

---

3   Otis, *Second Wisconsin*, 40; Quiner, *Military History*, 83; Gaff, *If This Is War*, 284; J. H. Stine, *History of the Army of the Potomac* (Philadelphia, 1892), 715. The quick decision by Randall to purchase the materials and bill them to the state without having authorization to do so was later sharply criticized by his political opponents in Wisconsin.

4   *Wisconsin Newspaper Volumes*, vol. 1.

5   *Milwaukee Sentinel*, July 9, 1861; Gaff, *If This Is War*, 145-146.

Allen of Mineral Point, Gabriel Bouck of Oshkosh, Wilson Colwell of La Crosse, David McKee of Lancaster, and George Stevens of Fox Lake. But none of these men desired promotion, and the only thing asked for by the captains was an experienced commander. A few days later the line officers asked Coon, Peck, and McDonald to resign. Peck did so on July 29, his decision announced to the full regiment the next day at evening parade. Coon resigned two days later. It was said that before he left, he was always "saluted by the boys with feelings of pleasure." McDonald, the regiment's last field officer, resigned on August 9 and returned home to Milwaukee.[6]

The hapless 2nd Wisconsin did not have to wait long for new officers. On August 2, Governor Randall again visited the regiment to deal with the mistakes that he had made in the original selection of officers. The truth of the matter, however, was the regiment would not have been in the field without Randall's unflagging efforts. At the start of the Civil War, Randall and other Northern governors turned to the flawed volunteer active militia system to fill the federal quotas for regiments.[7] Convinced the war would take longer than anyone expected,

6   Otis, *Second Wisconsin*, 36-37, 39; *Wisconsin Roster*, vol. 1, 345.

7   *Messages and Proclamations*, xiv; Frank A. Flower, *History of Milwaukee Wisconsin* (Chicago, 1881), 685-686. A native of Montgomery County, New York, Randall came to Wisconsin Territory in 1840 at age 18. He settled at Prairieville, later Waukesha, where he practiced law, served as a postmaster and was helpful in establishing Prairieville Academy, now Carroll University. Randall was associated with the Free Soil movement, but soon became a Democrat until the sectional crisis of the early 1850s sent him into the new Republican Party. He was elected to the Wisconsin Assembly in 1855 and that same year he was a candidate for the state attorney general on the Republican ticket, but was defeated. He was the Republican candidate for governor in 1857 and was elected in a close vote. Hampering the state militia was the fact the organizations were often ethnic-based and were used by the immigrants as a way to social acceptance or as an outlet for the energies of Germans and Irish who had military experience in the armies of Europe. As expected, the companies were marked by controversy, petty jealousies, and bitter feuds. Several organizations were formed and disbanded in the years before the war and most had ranks only half full. Whether the companies were effective in their role of being on hand in time of civil disturbance or natural disaster or Indian uprising was openly questioned. The militia movement was lifted for a time by a wave of enthusiasm for military training that swept England in the 1850s just after the Crimean War and soon reached the United States. In 1859, it was estimated that from one to one and a half million young American men—often regarded as the first generation possessed of leisure on a wide scale and attempting to find a national sport—were bearing arms and drilling. By 1860, however, military training and membership in militia units was yielding to cricket and baseball. It was also demonstrated during these first days that the administrative organization of the United States had weaknesses in time of war. The only officials of the national government in most other states were judges and postmasters and with the election of Lincoln those were in confusion with some postmasters expecting to be dismissed and others awaiting appointment in the patronage system of the day. The national subdivisions in the states were Congressional

Randall found much to be done. He sent representatives to Washington to confer with the new Lincoln administration and agents to New York to purchase uniforms and other military necessities. On April 23, Randall authorized creation of the "Second Regiment of Wisconsin Active Militia." Four days later he called on the ladies of the state for "blankets and quilts made for the use and benefit of the soldiers, until purchases can be made." A letter to Lincoln urged even more state men be put in the field and outlined Wisconsin's need for muskets: "The soldiers must go into camp and learn the use of weapons and the duties of soldiers." He also called in the arms held by militia companies not volunteering for active service.[8]

Now Randall was again in Washington in the aftermath of the defeat at Bull Run to face the very soldiers he had sent to war. He brought with him "a beautiful flag," a gift from the ladies of Madison, with the "eagle and stars . . . on one side, and the coat of arms" of Wisconsin on the other. The governor also admonished the soldiers to let whiskey alone—it was an "enemy more feared than the rebels," he chastised—before addressing his selections for the first officers of the 2nd Wisconsin. "I made a very great mistake," he admitted. "The men appointed were not such as the time and necessity demanded, and the mistake was one into which many of the Northwestern States fell. We had to make our officers out of the material we had, as we make our soldiers. All had to learn the business. The mistake has now been corrected, and I have to announce the appointment of a gentleman as colonel of this regiment—a thorough soldier and a brave man, in whom the fullest confidence may be placed, and under whose leadership you cannot fail of receiving the measure of credit which has been before allotted you."

His mea culpa now complete, Randall brought forward the man who accompanied him from Wisconsin to take his place as the 2nd's new colonel—Edgar O'Connor of Beloit.[9]

Our Higher Duty to the Constitution

The selection of a new colonel seemed promising despite the fact that the new appointee was well-known in Wisconsin as a Democrat. Edgar O'Connor was a Beloit lawyer of standing and reputation. Born in Cleveland in 1833, he moved to

---

districts, but they were without organization or staff. Randall and other war governors quickly came to realize that the raising of an army to defend the Union was going to be first a state effort, and then the state and national governments acting together.

8 Randall, *Messages and Proclamations*, 51.

9 *Milwaukee Sentinel*, August 8, 1861; Edward R. Chipman, *Madison Daily Patriot*, August 3, 1861.

Milwaukee with his family in 1842, six years before Wisconsin statehood. Most important was the fact that O'Connor was a graduate of the U.S. Military Academy at West Point. Upon earning his first straps in 1854, he was assigned to the 7th Infantry Regiment and served at Santa Fe, Pike's Peak, and three years at Fort Gibson in Indian Territory. In 1857, O'Connor married the daughter of a slave-owning Arkansas judge and two years later resigned his army commission to return to Wisconsin and Beloit to read law. He passed the bar in early 1861.

The appointment by Republican Governor Randall immediately generated a scattering of newspaper opposition because of O'Connor's political affiliation. More troubling was the fact that his wife came from the South and her father owned slaves. In reality, however, his father-in-law was a strong Union man and had moved his family to the North when the war started. The criticism was important enough to force O'Connor to publicly respond to concerns about his loyalty. He admitted that, until Fort Sumter he "was in favor of compromising the differences and difficulties [and] thereby avoid, if possible, the impending civil war." O'Connor had "relations, friends and property in the rebel States" and regretted the course the South had taken. "The separation has been painful, but when traitors take up arms, all personal relations, the ties of consanguinity and property, are to be merged in our higher duty to the Constitution."[10]

With his public response behind him, O'Connor set to work shaping his new regiment with a professional understanding of what was needed to be done. The stocky officer with sunken intelligent eyes set in a round face drafted early orders (perhaps in realization of the difficulty involving Squire Coon) that enlisted men caught drinking would be punished, and that intoxicated officers would be court-martialed. A drill schedule was re-established. Work details were assigned. The camp, which showed the lack of discipline and an absence of a firm hand, was cleaned and organized. The regimental drill manual was changed from the older Scott's to the new and improved Hardee's Tactics. Just as important in the history of the regiment were the appointments of the other field officers. Lucius Fairchild of Madison, then a new captain with the 16th U.S. Infantry and a man of reputation in the pre-war Wisconsin militia movement, was assigned lieutenant colonel. The final promotion for major lifted the well-regarded Bull Run veteran Thomas Allen from his Mineral Point company to be the number three in the regiment.

Of the new officers, Lucius Fairchild would become the most famous. Always friendly and outgoing, "Lush" (pronounced "Loosh") came into the war with a host of friends, both in the ranks and back home, and was the subject of much

Officers' Mess of the 2nd Wisconsin. Left to right: Surg. A. J. Ward, Maj. Thomas S. Allen, Lt. Col. Lucius Fairchild, and Col. Edgar O'Connor, as well as a butler, a cook, and other staff. *Wisconsin Historical Society 1908*

social gossip in his hometown because of his eye for pretty girls. The Fairchilds arrived in Wisconsin in 1846. Lucius' early education was marked by escapades and other matters. After an unimpressive semester he left Praireville Academy (now Carroll University, Waukesha, Wisconsin). It was whispered that his father failed to pay tuition costs. At age 17, he set off for the gold fields of California to seek his fortune. Unlike so many others, however, Fairchild returned home in 1855 with a full wallet. (He was always careful not to reveal the amount or how he made the money. Many believed it was not the gold he had found but his merchandising skills and ability to select good business partners that made his full poke.) Fairchild worked for a time for the Madison and Watertown Railroad, in which his father owned an interest, and engaged in an active social life that included several romances that made him the subject of town whispers. In 1859, he was elected clerk of Dane County at Madison and admitted to the bar the next year.

At the start of the war, Fairchild was an officer of the Governor's Guard, a prominent Madison militia company that had been trained for a time by drillmaster E. Elmer Ellsworth before Ellsworth's fame with the U.S. Zouave Cadets of Chicago. Fairchild used the company to create a stir shortly after the firing on Fort Sumter when he marched his Governor's Guard into a war meeting in Madison and quickly mounted the platform. As soon as the crowd quieted Fairchild lifted an arm and cried out, "I offer $50 and myself to go to war!" That set the crowd to cheering, and within a short time the young man took his militia company into the 90-day 1st Wisconsin. He saw action at Falling Waters in Maryland, a brief engagement now remembered only because Thomas Jackson (a few weeks away from winning his famous "Stonewall" nickname) and a young cavalry officer named Jeb Stuart were on the Confederate side. When the 1st Wisconsin returned home the three-month enlistment expired and Fairchild obtained a commission as lieutenant in the Regular Army, and then lieutenant colonel of the 2nd before joining the regiment at Washington.[11]

Allen, the new 36-year-old major, displayed bravery at Bull Run and was regarded as cool under fire. Tall and bewhiskered, he was one of the many "prints" in the 2nd Regiment, which had a proportionally large number of newspaper men in ranks. A native of New York, Allen was a student at Oberlin College in Ohio but

---

11 See Sam Ross, *The Empty Sleeve: A Biography of Lucius Fairchild* (Madison, 1964), 28-29. Ellsworth was born in New York State, but he lived in Wisconsin and Michigan before becoming a law clerk in Chicago. He joined the city's National Guard Cadets militia unit and introduced it to the colorful Zouave uniforms and drill of French colonial troops in Algeria. His Chicago unit won a national reputation. Ellsworth studied law with Abraham Lincoln before the Civil War and was killed in Alexandria, Virginia, on May 24, 1861, shot while cutting down a Confederate flag atop the Marshall House Inn.

left the classroom to take a job. He worked for a time on a Chicago newspaper and in 1847 he and family moved to Dodgeville in the Wisconsin Territory, where he worked as a mine surveyor, schoolteacher, and Clerk of the Dodge County Board. After moving to nearby Mineral Point in 1857, Allen was elected to the Wisconsin legislature and named Chief Clerk of the U.S. Land Office at Madison. In that city he became a member—along with Fairchild—of the Governor's Guard. Although he was serving as a lieutenant of the unit, Allen left Madison at the start of the war to take a captain's commission in the newly formed Miner's Guard Company at Mineral Point.[12]

These appointments generally satisfied the rank and file of the 2nd Wisconsin. A stir broke out when the rumor circulated that O'Connor, embroiled in the lingering controversy over his politics and a Southern wife, might be replaced by another officer from the recently returned 90-day 1st Wisconsin. "I believe I speak the sentiments of the regiment when I say that we have had no field officers as yet, except Major Allen, that we have had confidence in," one private admitted in a grumble over the promotion process. He added it was the hope of the ranks "that these we now have [O'Connor and Fairchild] may prove to be the men we need."[13]

The selection of officers for the early volunteer regiments proved a problem for the new army. In some instances the volunteers were allowed to elect their own officers, and candidates for the positions often used food, drink, and promises to campaign for their commissions. State governors could overrule such elections, but rarely did so and in fact used the system themselves to hand out appointments for a regiment's field officers as rewards to their political cronies or—as in the case of Governor Randall—to build support for the war effort. When the state regiments were turned over to Federal authorities, the practice of electing officers soon disappeared and boards of examiners and experienced Regular Army officers began weeding out those unsuited for leadership positions.

Many of the latest developments and promotions in the army and in the volunteer forces were reported in the weekly and daily newspapers. Newsboys hawked editions from Washington, Baltimore, and Philadelphia along with other papers. Weeklies also arrived by mail from back home. In the camps, soldier correspondents kept a steady flow of letters and columns moving to friends and folks. Letters and newspapers became an important part of camp life. In fact, the growth of newspapers changed American journalism and could be blamed in part for fanning the emotional flames of sectionalism in the 1850s. Literacy was

12 Quiner, *Military History*, 1,003-1,004.

13 *Madison Daily Patriot*, September 19, 1861.

widespread and technical advances—the telegraph, steam-driven presses, and expanding railroad links—made it possible for the first time to quickly reach mass audiences. Before the war, many a soldier-to-be followed the latest news swirling around the growing sectional crisis while sitting around his kitchen table under the big lamp while one of the family read the news aloud. The changes also made newspapers profitable, and editors used their growing power to push political agendas and inflame public opinion to expand readership. As a result, newspapers became important and influential and editors pushed coverage of the war. Some soldier readers found the growing power of the press troubling. "I find them teeming with false reports, false alarms, and what is worse, valuable information for the rebels at least," Pvt. Robert Beecham of the Randall Guards complained to his own newspaper back home in Madison. "I am surprised and vexed to think we have such fools and rascals among us, and would be glad to hear the order issued by the War department to take, and condemn as spies, every reporter found in our camp or at Washington. I would without hesitation help shoot every one of them." It was often true, Beecham continued, that newsmen or "specials" of the press often would "give a regiment, or an officer, a puff for $50 or $100, and then will puff the particular regiment, officer, or state that has been foolish enough to bribe them by slandering everyone and everything else." He went on to list the latest sensations about Bull Run produced in news columns—General McDowell was drunk; the battle was lost by the cowardice of men or officers, the soldiers were panic-stricken. "[L]et me use plain language—they lie."[14]

A more significant development in the history of the regiment transpired on August 27 when the 2nd Wisconsin was transferred to a new provisional brigade, joining the recently arrived 5th and 6th Wisconsin regiments as well as the 19th Indiana. The commander of the new brigade was Rufus King, a former newspaper man described by a friend as "favorably known to Milwaukeeans and to a large share of the people of Wisconsin, and so much beloved by them." Born in New York City, the new general was the son of Charles King, one-time president of Columbia College, and named for his grandfather Rufus, a Massachusetts delegate to the Continental Congress and Constitutional Convention. The younger King graduated from Columbia and enrolled in the U.S. Military Academy, finishing near the top of his class of 1833. His first assignment was as a lieutenant in the Engineer

14 "R. F. Beecham, Private Company Sec. Reg. Wis. Vol.," August 4, 1861, *Wisconsin Newspaper Volumes*, vol. 1. Beecham concluded: "When reporters become wise enough to keep out of camp, and newspaper publishers leave military matters to military men, then, and not till then, may we look for a speedy termination of this war. For the present, we have reason to fear the reporter's steel."

Corps at Fortress Monroe and his first commander was Virginian Robert E. Lee, now off in the service of the rebels. One of King's later duty posts was Lake Erie, where he was engaged in a topographical survey of Toledo Bay. King resigned from the army in 1836 to work as an associate editor for the New York newspapers *Albany Evening Journal* and *Albany Advertiser*. He even served a time as commander of the Albany Burgess Corps, described as "one of the most renowned volunteer militia organizations" of the day. King left New York in 1845 to become part proprietor and editor of the *Milwaukee Sentinel and Gazette* (later the *Milwaukee Daily Sentinel*)—a post he would hold until 1859—and also became active in education, serving as a regent for the University of Wisconsin and as superintendent of Milwaukee Public Schools. In his spare time, the indefatigable King served as captain of the Milwaukee Light Guard and—"in days when men of high degree 'ran with the machine'"—served as foreman of famous engine "No. 1" of the city's fire department. He also organized and took part in the first three baseball games ever played in Wisconsin.[15]

In March 1861, President Lincoln appointed King Minister to the Papal States. A prolonged goodbye with several ceremonies at Milwaukee and Madison was underway when news of Fort Sumter reached Wisconsin. A man of King's background and energy was not about to leave the country at a time like this, so he quit the appointment and offered his services to Governor Randall. King served in several capacities organizing state regiments before being commissioned as a brigadier general, first by Randall in Wisconsin (who had in his mind the formation of a Wisconsin brigade) and then by Lincoln, who named King to his post in the National Army training around Washington. A well-formed man with an attractive beard and neat manner, King found his new brigade camped at Camp Kalorama on Meriden Hill. Some of his new regiments marched to the Chain Bridge on September 3 to work on the earthworks of Fort Marcy and other defenses covering the approaches to the city. The hard work with pick, shovel, saw, and axe, marked an inauspicious beginning for the Western soldiers of what would become one of the most storied fighting brigades in American history.

We Regarded Them as Heroes and They Were

The 5th and 6th Wisconsin were still organizing at Camp Randall when the 2nd Wisconsin fought at Bull Run and the "disastrous news of the defeat of our army"

---

15 Damon, *Light Guard*, 20-22. The baseball games were played at the old State Fairgrounds in Milwaukee in 1859 which now includes the campus of Marquette University. Lincoln also spoke at the fairgrounds that same year.

Rufus King and Staff at Arlington House

The general and his staff pose on the step in front of the Arlington House opposite
Washington in 1861. The Lee Mansion was being used as a headquarters by several
officers at the time. *Milwaukee County Historical Society*

filtered back to the home state. The War Department ordered all state troops
immediately sent to Washington. The 3rd Wisconsin rendezvoused at Fond du Lac
and left the state July 12 for Harpers Ferry, and the 4th Wisconsin left July 15 to
report to Baltimore. Companies were selected for the 7th and 8th regiments, but
Randall declined calling them in before the end of the summer harvest unless
absolutely required to do so. The two regiments at Camp Randall (5th and 6th) were
told they would leave for Washington as soon as transportation could be arranged.
The former left Madison on July 24 and the latter four days later.[16]

The 5th Wisconsin arrived in Washington on August 8 and was assigned to
King's Provisional Brigade. Its colonel, Amasa Cobb of Mineral Point, a lawyer and

16 Quiner, *Military History*, 76-77.

man of good standing with experience as a private in the War with Mexico, was pointed to as an example of the quality of the regiment itself. His soldiers, who hailed from various towns across the state, were not the young hot bloods eager for adventure who had flocked to fill the early Wisconsin regiments, but solid men of their communities. These men needed extra time to make the necessary business and family arrangements before stepping forward to sign the rolls.[17] The association of Cobb's 5th Wisconsin with King's brigade would be short-lived, however. For reasons never fully explained the regiment was transferred to a neighboring brigade being organized under Winfield Scott Hancock, thus ending Randall's effort to create an all-Wisconsin brigade under King. Back home, the transfer was regarded as an underhanded effort by army officials to make sure the governor would not have much say over the operation of his regiments.

The 6th Wisconsin reached Washington on August 7 and was marched first to City Hall Park and then to Meridian Hill, where the Badgers laid out company streets along Rock Creek. The veteran 2nd Wisconsin arrived at the site a few days later, swinging up the hill with the confident stride of soldiers who had been in battle and were proud of what they had done—even if they had skedaddled with the rest of the National Army. The new volunteers of the 6th regiment gathered individually and in groups to watch the arriving column, taking in the tattered, dirty field-worn gray uniforms of the soldiers and their smooth and easy Western step. "They had been through the first battle of Bull Run," remarked one 6th Wisconsin man. "They had fought for their country. We looked up to them, regarded them as heroes, and they were." In the ranks of the 2nd Wisconsin were friends and relatives from back home who received a pleasant welcome. The Western men were often shy around strangers, but laughed and talked in an easy fashion amongst themselves.[18]

The "rattle of a large drum corps" a short time later marked the arrival of the 19th Indiana. "Looking up, our boys saw, astride a black horse, what seemed to us the tallest man we have ever seen," wrote one astonished Badger. The imposing figure was Col. Solomon Meredith, a 6-foot-7 citizen-soldier of unknown military

---

17 Amasa Cobb moved to Wisconsin from Illinois in 1842 to engage in lead mining. After serving in the Mexican War, Cobb returned to Wisconsin set up a law practice. While serving in the field in 1862, Cobb was elected as a Republican to represent the Third Wisconsin district in Congress. He resigned his commission and took his seat in March of 1863. During a Congressional recess, he raised the 43rd Wisconsin and was again commissioned colonel. Cobb left military service in 1865. Six years later he moved to farther west to Lincoln, Nebraska, where he set up another law practice. He also served on the Nebraska Supreme Court (1878-1892).

18 Jerome A. Watrous, *Appleton Crescent*, August 20, 1861.

abilities but rock solid political connections back home. A Quaker who as a young man walked from his native North Carolina to Indiana, Meredith had served as a sheriff, legislator, and U.S. Marshal and was Wayne County Clerk when Fort Sumter was fired upon. The colonel was a political crony of powerful Gov. Oliver P. Morton and as an Indiana delegate supported Lincoln for president during the Republican convention in Chicago in 1860. The giant of a man had the loud and forceful voice of a stump speaker and was not only singled out for his colorful use of the English language. (Lincoln, always clever with words, later liked to point him out as his "only Quaker general.") Described by one Badger as a "specimen of the genuine Hoosier," Meredith, he continued "put on no airs and frequently talks to the private soldiers and is therefore very popular with the men but is not much of a military man." Another veteran admitted a fondness for Meredith and noted the tall officer took double the risk in battle because he was twice as big as most men. After all, he concluded, "Stray scraps of iron running at large over the heads of a regiment are apt to pick out the tall ones."[19]

It was said around the coffee fires in the various Wisconsin companies that Meredith and his regiment were "the pets" of Indiana Governor Morton; the volunteer Badger officers—many sharply attuned to the direction of the political winds—made note of the fact. Also making the round was a story about a political rival back home in Indiana who quipped that "Long Sol" was so tall that he should be cut in half, and his lower and better half made lieutenant colonel of the 19th. That brought smiles, but the addition of the Indiana regiment was acceptable. After all, the Hoosiers were Westerners, and the men from Wisconsin looked them over and came away with satisfied nods.

The lieutenant colonel of the 19th Indiana was also a man of promise. New York native Robert A. Cameron was living at Valparaiso at the start of the war. A physician by training, his interest turned to politics in the 1850s and he became editor and publisher of Valparaiso's *Republic* newspaper. Alois O. Bachman served as the regiment's major. He was born at Madison into a family of Swiss settlers and was active in the Madison City Greys militia organization, which he took into the 90-day 6th Indiana. When that term expired he was commissioned as major of the three-year 19th Indiana. Bachman would be heard from during the coming months, as would William W. Dudley, Isaac May, Samuel J. Williams, and other Hoosiers in lesser positions. The ranks of the 19th Indiana were generally drawn from volunteers in the central portion of the Indiana, mostly near Indianapolis and

---

19 James P. Sullivan, "Charge of the Iron Brigade at Fitzhugh's Crossing," *Milwaukee Sunday Telegraph*, September 30, 1883; *Green Bay Advocate*, October 3, 1861.

Solomon Meredith, commander, 19th Indiana

With his 6-foot-7 height, Meredith cut a commanding figure when he brought his regiment to Washington and joined King's Brigade. One Wisconsin soldier called him a "true specimen of a genuine Hoosier." *Indianapolis State Library*

Muncie. The exception was the Elkhart Lake company, which came from the Indiana-Michigan state line near South Bend.[20]

The 19th Indiana left Camp Morton on two trains on August 5, but only after being issued weapons (some purchased from Canada), belts, and ammunition from state stores. Most of the volunteers received the smoothbore .69-caliber muskets converted from flint to percussion. The two flank companies—the Union Guards of Madison and the Richmond City Greys—received modern .577-caliber Enfield rifle-muskets along with the Winchester Greys, which was the color company and helped guard the regimental banners. Colonel Meredith rode in the smaller second train with two of his favorite horses. The regimental band stayed behind in Indiana waiting for their uniforms.

The train rolled through the states with women and children seemingly populating every front gate and doorstep waving handkerchiefs. Breakfast awaited at Bellefontaine and a crowd plied the men with cakes and lemonade at Crestline while the cars switched to the locomotives from another line. The best part of the trip was through Ohio where, recalled Pvt. John Hawk, the citizens greeted us with "baskets of well filled goodies and they stuff us Hoosiers until we were as stiff as gut sausage." The train stopped outside Baltimore and non-commissioned ordnance officers issued 10 rounds of ammunition to each soldier. There, the Indiana boys found squads of the 20th Indiana on guard and some general helloing and shouting was exchanged. The anticipated trouble in the city itself failed to materialize and the march through the city triggered only a few catcalls—the hooligans having apparently been cowed by the presence of Federal soldiers. Once out of Baltimore the bored soldiers trained their new muskets on "rebel" ducks and chickens along the railroad tracks. How much fowl was killed is unknown, but at least one horse was believed to be shot dead. Meredith, still much the farmer despite his new shoulder straps, was outraged that his men would shoot valuable livestock and stormed through the cars demanding to know who was pulling triggers. No one, of course, admitted to the deed.

When the train reached Washington at 6:00 p.m. on August 8, the weary Hoosiers marched to Soldiers Rest, a building used to sleep arriving regiments. They were told the next day they would be joining King's new brigade and marched to Kalorama Heights. Rain arrived before the regimental baggage did, so the wet Hoosiers set up camp in the mud.[21]

---

20 Alan T. Nolan, *The Iron Brigade: A Military History* (New York, 1961), 20-23.

21 Alan D. Gaff, *On Many a Bloody Field: Four Years in the Iron Brigade* (Bloomington, 1996), 29-36; John Hawk, letter to father, August 19, 1861.

The brigade association while at war seemed a natural fit for these two states. Wisconsin reached statehood in 1848 and has a rich heritage that sometimes escapes the history books. The first Europeans to reach the state were French fur traders from Canada in the late 1600s. They found dense woods, good soil and water, and the cold winters that produced prime pelts. Many of their trading posts, like the one established at the junction of the Wisconsin and Mississippi rivers and today known as Prairie du Chien, evolved into town and villages. When the blue-gray ore ("galena") was discovered nearby, claims were staked and a lead mining industry grew. Trade spread down the Mississippi and later to port towns on Lake Michigan, with links all the way east to New England and beyond. Despite the harsh winters, settlers joined the rough-living trappers and miners. By mid-century the population had spread across the southern third of the territory. Land was cheap and rich. Speculators acquired parcels and offered pieces to settlers from Indiana, Ohio, and Illinois, as well as a growing number of German, Irish, and Norwegian immigrants. By 1860 census takers counted 775,881 residents. More than one-third of the state's population was foreign-born. Two million acres were under plow and Wisconsin ranked second in the nation in wheat production. Mining was well established in the southwestern corner of the state and lumbermen were beginning to harvest the vast timber resources of the north. Several railroads crossed the state from east to west. Some in Milwaukee boasted that their city—and not rival Chicago—was the fairest port on Lake Michigan. Hard money was tight, "wildcat" banknotes freely circulated, debt was commonplace, and barter widely practiced. Men outnumbered women, swine outnumbered sheep, and sheep outnumbered cows.[22]

Having joined the Union in 1816 as the nineteenth state, Indiana was better established in 1861 than Wisconsin. A network of river, road, and rail transport supported fledgling river towns up and down the Ohio River Valley. In the coming month, Indiana would become a major source of food for the Union army with mills in communities along the Ohio River grounding wheat into flour while packing houses stuffed wooden barrels with salt pork and beef. Farmers harvested oats and hay to feed army horses and mules, lumberjacks felled trees for new wagons and artillery carriages, and a small boat-building industry would soon turn to constructing hospital and transport vessels. Indiana's coal production was about to triple and state industries were looking for a way to tap cheap and abundant sources of limestone and clay. Like Wisconsin, the state political scene was once dominated by Democrats but grew increasingly Republican in the 1850s during the

22 Frank L. Klement, *Wisconsin in the Civil War: The Home Front and the Battle Front, 1861-1865* (Madison, 1997), 3-4. A shorter version was first published in the *Wisconsin Blue Book* in 1962.

growing sectional crisis. Governor Oliver Morton, for example, was an active Democrat until 1854 before joining the new Republican Party. He would become one of the nation's most powerful state executives at a time when governors were important and significant in the United States. Facing a Democratic legislature and the need to raise and outfit his volunteers in 1861, Morton simply violated his state's constitution and spent the money without authorization. His actions were legalized by the next legislature, which had a Republican majority. In an effort to honor the five Indiana regiments that served during the Mexican War, Morton commenced the numbering of his new units at six. With 1,350,424 resident in 1860, his Indiana had about twice as many residents as did Wisconsin. Many of Morton's volunteers would one day pass through the new muster and recruiting station on the site of the state fairgrounds at 19th and Alabama Streets in Indianapolis. Befittingly, it was named Camp Morton.

It is a New Life for Us All

The final company called to complete the 6th Wisconsin was the Lemonweir Minute Men from Juneau County, and well down on that list of volunteers was a young man named James Patrick Sullivan. "I wanted to do something for my country," he explained. His family had come from Ireland via Canada when he was three. By the time the rebels fired on Fort Sumter, Sullivan was making his own way as a hired man on a farm near Wonewoc. Never clarified was his age on enlistment day or thereafter. Sullivan subtracted a few years from his age before a late-in-life second marriage to a younger woman, just as he had added a few years in early 1861. The only thing certain was he was younger than 18 when he stepped forward to sign the volunteer rolls. The young Irishman would soldier four years, suffer three battle wounds, and incur a pair of injuries—one when struck by a ramrod accidentally fired during a ceremonial volley of blanks. Slight in stature but with a quick intelligence and a certain Irish brashness, Sullivan called his comrades the "Greenhorn Patriots" and liked to say he was one of "Jumping Jesus Christers" on "bob-tail part of the line." To his family he was simply "J. P." or "Pat," but during his army days he was better known as "Mickey, of Company K."

The *Mauston Star* reported the "largest and most enthusiastic meeting ever held in Juneau County" assembled in late April at Mauston to discuss the raising of a company of volunteers. Those attending the war meeting resolved to "henceforth recognize but two parties—the Union and the Disunion party; that the Union party shall have our assistance, the Dis-Union party our most determined opposition." At a first call for volunteers, announced the paper, "FORTY-SEVEN brave fellows at once stepped forward." Sullivan was not among them. Another meeting was held Saturday, May 8, and on the following Wednesday Rescum "Reck" Davis, Jim

Barney, and Sullivan appeared at Bill Steward's adjoining farm, where John St. Clair was "acting in the dual capacity of the 'hired man' and 'beau' for 'Sal,' 'old Bill's' buxom daughter." St. Clair was a corporal of the provisional company and had the necessary enrollment sheets. The three young men added their names to the roll. A few days later the new company was authorized to rendezvous at Mauston to begin drills and await orders. Sullivan's group was the first to arrive, followed by men from New Lisbon and then the "Yellow River crowd" from the Necedah area.[23]

One of the leaders of these war meetings was Henry Dawes of Ohio. He was in Wisconsin operating a general store and buying land for speculation when war broke out. His son Rufus was with him from Marietta, Ohio, and the younger Dawes was active in the raising of the company. When it came time for the volunteers to select a captain, Rufus Dawes was elected and Juneau County prosecuting attorney John Kellogg became first lieutenant. That Dawes and Kellogg were named to the first two positions was met with favor. The new volunteers were impressed that the Dawes family had been part of the American story from the earliest days of the Republic. It seemed fitting that their captain, Rufus Dawes, was born on the 4th of July of 1838, and that his great-grandfather was William Dawes Jr., Paul Revere's companion on the night ride just before Lexington. Dawes' father and mother had obtained a legal separation the year after his birth and his father had moved to Wisconsin in 1855 and bought land in Juneau County. Rufus briefly attended the University of Wisconsin at Madison but graduated in 1860 from Marietta College in Ohio while living there with his mother. He joined his father thereafter and the two operated a general store and began to clear land outside Mauston. Kellogg's family arrived in Wisconsin from Pennsylvania in 1840. He was singled out during the company's organization and pointed to as one of the founders of the new Republican Party, being a member of the Madison convention of September 5, 1855.[24]

---

23 *Mauston Star*, January 8, 1885; "Mickey, of Company K," "Old Company K," *Milwaukee Sunday Telegraph* in two parts, May 9 and May 16, 1886. Sullivan wrote his reminiscences for several newspapers. They can be found in James P. Sullivan, *An Irishman in the Iron Brigade: The Civil War Memoirs of James P. Sullivan, Sergt., Company K, 6th Wisconsin Volunteers*, William J. K. Beaudot and Lance J. Herdegen, eds. (New York, 1983), 18-19.

24 Rufus R. Dawes, *A Memoir, Rufus R. Dawes* (privately printed, 1900), 11-13; Rev. William E. Roe, "Brigadier General Rufus R. Dawes," Dawes-Gates Ancestral Lines, Vol. 1 (privately printed, 1943), 3. John Azor Kellogg was born March 16, 1828, in Wayne County, Pennsylvania. His father was a tavern keeper, stage proprietor, and general contractor, and his grandfather served in the Revolutionary War. The Kelloggs moved west to the Wisconsin Territory about 1840, settling at Prairie du Chien. He began reading law at age 18 and was admitted to the bar at 29. He was elected district attorney of Juneau County in 1860, but resigned to enlist.

Captain Rufus Dawes, Lemonweir Minute Men, Co. K, 6th Wisconsin

Dawes still had an innocent, almost boyish appearance when he assumed command of
his new company from Juneau County in 1861. *Dawes Arboretum Collection*

Once officers and privates alike discovered they had much to learn they sought out men of experience such as John Holden of Wonewoc, a Mexican War veteran now serving as a corporal. The editor of the *Mauston Star* made much of Holden's patriotism, writing that even "though an old man" of 38, he had walked sixteen miles from his home to join the company. The veteran was greeted at the makeshift mustering place in the park near the Lemonweir River in Mauston with three cheers and a tiger. Holden's vaunted military experience, however, was of little assistance because the old soldier "had been an ordnance sergeant so long that he had forgotten all drill and tactics, except the 'salute.'" And so the young volunteers went endways and sideways in one row or two during those exciting days while under the direction of officers and sergeants who knew little more than they did. The marching, recalled Sullivan, was done on the public square near the river "to the great edification of school children, fathers, mothers, sisters, friends and the girls we had not yet left behind us, and if they judged by the loudness of the tones of command and our ability to charge the school house or church, they must have felt the rebellion would soon be a thing of the past." The *Mauston Star* reported company strength at ninety and that the volunteers included "the best men of our county; many of them leaving property and business interests that must suffer in consequence of their absence. The patriotism of such men cannot be doubted."[25]

It was soon determined with some late night discussion that what was now needed was a proper company name. The young men— "hardy lumbermen, rugged farmer boys and sturdy mechanics," said Sullivan—suggested "Rifles" and "Light Guards" and various versions of "Volunteers" before settling on "Minute Men" in honor of the patriots of older times and in respect to the heritage of their young captain. That suggestion was changed to the "Lemonweir Minute Men" to include the "peaceful and gently flowing river, in the beautiful valley of which most of the men resided." The name would remind the boys of home, wrote one of the recruits, and, said Dawes, "this argument carried the day."

It was during those early days that several members of the new company objected to Sullivan's enlistment because of his age and size. The diminutive young Irishman, they complained, "would disgrace the company by not being able to pitch rebels over his shoulder with a bayonet, or keep up on a march." As one asked rather pointedly, "What good would Mickey be in a charge 'bagnets?'" The young recruit was advised to "go home to mother" and wait until he was "feathered out." Dawes seemed about to reject Sullivan when Lt. John Crane marched the would-be private before a justice of the peace. The justice appointed himself Sullivan's

25 *Mauston Star*, May 14, 1861; *Wisconsin Roster*, vol. 1, 534; Sullivan, *Telegraph*, May 9, 1885. Holden would be discharged within six months for disability.

Private James P. Sullivan, Lemonweir Minute Men,
Co. K, 6th Wisconsin

Known for his bravery and lightning wit, "Mickey, of Company K" was wounded at
South Mountain in 1862, at Gettysburg in 1863, and again outside Petersburg in 1864.
Mr. and Mrs. Robert Sullivan

guardian, officially granted consent for him to enlist, and swore him into state
service "in one time and three motions." His enlistment would be dated June 21
instead of May 8, the day he actually signed the roll."[26]

26 Sullivan, *Telegraph*, May 9, 1886.

When the days passed without a call from Madison, concerned talk circulated that the company might not be needed after all. It was with much relief, then, when a telegraph informed Dawes that cars were on their way to transport the Minute Men to Madison. Last minute preparations were completed, goodbyes said, and personal items packed into carpet valises or tied up in handkerchiefs. When the day of departure arrived the company marched to the station—where to their great disappointment they were turned away because no cars had been sent to carry them away. Three times, said Sullivan, the new volunteers "bid farewell to every one in Mauston and twice we were escorted to the depot but each time no cars were provided, nor had the railroad any instruction to furnish transportation." Just before midnight on July 6, the depot agent yet again told Dawes that cars were attached to an incoming train. This time, Sullivan explained, there was no time for "good-byes or any escort, we hustled to the depot and took the train which carried many of the boys away never to see Mauston again."[27]

The Minute Men—called in to complete the 6th Wisconsin because of the failure of several other companies higher on the list to be filled—arrived at Camp Randall on July 7. En route, Dawes received a telegram from Col. Lysander Cutler asking about when the company would arrive. Dawes found out why when he herded his band of volunteers to the main gate. Arrayed inside the stockade walls to receive the new men with a formal welcome was the 5th Wisconsin and the nine companies of the 6th Wisconsin—almost 2,000 soldiers in long dressed lines. It was an "imposing spectacle," admitted Dawes, who did his best to keep the men in two ranks as they moved slowly across the parade ground kicking each other's heels and bumping into one another. The Minute Men did not make a good first impression. "A few wore broadcloth and silk hats, more the red shirts of raftsmen, several were in country homespun, one had on a calico coat and another was looking through a hole in the drooping brim of a straw hat. . . ," Dawes recalled. "The men carried every variety of valise, and ever species of bundle, down to one shirt tied up in a red handkerchief."

---

27 *Ibid.*, May 16, 1886. Dawes only made two documented visits to Mauston after leaving with his company in 1861. He came back in 1867 when his father died unexpectedly, and in 1869, when he closed the estate which was valued at between $50,000 and $60,000. His four sons, including Charles Dawes, who would serve as vice president under President Calvin Coolidge, returned to Mauston in 1926 when a pageant commemorating the Civil War was held. They took part in a ceremony placing a wreath on the grave of their grandfather in Evergreen Cemetery. Rufus Dawes' mother Sarah never visited Mauston or Wisconsin, and it was believed she did not do so because she regarded Wisconsin as little more than "Indian Country." Rufus' father, Henry Dawes, was described in the *Mauston Star* as "always a prominent and active man in the community in which he lived. He took a warm interest in politics and always for the right."

Even more intimidating than the long lines of waiting soldiers was the officer approaching them on "a spirited charger, and quite stunning in his bright uniform and soldierly bearing." Lieutenant Frank A. Haskell, adjutant of the 6th regiment, drew up his mount and asked Dawes to form his company by platoon. Hibbard's Zouaves of Milwaukee, part of the 5th Wisconsin, waited nearby as an escort. The unit with its bright and colorful uniforms was regarded as one of the best drilled in the state. "Good-afternoon, Sir," Dawes greeted Haskell in solemn fashion. "I should be glad to comply with the wishes of the Colonel, but it is simply impossible." And so the Minute Men moved across the large parade ground toward the welcoming stand "at their own gait" while the Zouaves with yells and shouts engaged in well-practiced maneuvers that "increased the distraction of my men, and they marched worse than before." The Minute Men were about to become Company K of the 6th Wisconsin, but "in recognition of our grand entrée, the camp had already christened us Company 'Q'."[28]

The welcome address from Colonel Cutler was brief and to the point. Julius P. Atwood, a Madison attorney and now the lieutenant colonel, gave the volunteers "quite a speech," recalled Sullivan, but it was former legislator Maj. Benjamin J. Sweet "who spread himself all over the American Eagle" and who was remembered with bitterness. "You call yourselves 'Lemonweir Minute Men,' but we had begun to think you were 'Lemonweir Hour Men,'" Sweet admonished the new arrivals. The sarcastic remark was taken to mean that the delay in reaching Madison was the company's fault. "I never liked the man afterwards," admitted Sullivan, "and frequently thought, after he left us that if Company K were hour men getting into camp they were also hour men in staying in the war."[29]

When the welcome ended the new company moved into the wooden barracks north of the main gate. That night at evening dress parade, the Minute Men formed behind the 6th regiment and Haskell assisted Dawes in handling his company.

28 Rufus Dawes, *Service with the 6th Wisconsin Volunteers* (Marietta, OH, 1890), 9-12. For more detail on the raising of the 6th Wisconsin, see Lance J. Herdegen and William J. K. Beaudot, *In the Bloody Railroad Cut at Gettysburg* (Dayton, OH, 1990).

29 Sweet was born in New York and came to Wisconsin at sixteen and his father moved to Stockbridge and homesteaded. He entered college three years later, but was forced to drop out. He studied law and was twenty-seven when he was elected to the Wisconsin Senate. He was commissioned major of the 6th Wisconsin, but resigned to take higher rank first in the 21st Wisconsin and then the 22nd Wisconsin. He was suffering from malaria at Perryville, but joined the fighting and was severely wounded. In May 1864, he took command of the prison at Camp Douglas in Chicago, where about 10,000 Rebels were confined. He won attention for his claim that he uncovered and thwarted a series of plans by anti-war Copperheads to liberate the prisoners and sack and burn Chicago. Frank L. Klement, *Dark Lanterns: Secret Political Societies, Conspiracies, and Treason Trials in the Civil War* (Baton Rouge, 1984), 187-218.

Dawes remembered the kindness, but admitted the adjutant was repaid in "the fun he enjoyed in watching us." A few days later he wrote his sister in Ohio: "My men are no more than half supplied with blankets, and, as we have cold drizzling weather, they have suffered. It is a new life to us all, but I hope we can get broken in without much sickness."[30]

The days passed with little change in routine with reveille, roll calls, company drills, breakfast, sick calls, fatigue calls, and more drills. "At one o'clock," one private grumbled, we "fall in and have three hours 'battalion drill,' supper, dress parade, tattoo and roll call at 9 o'clock, taps fifteen minutes later. Then the poor greenhorn patriot, tired as an ox after a day's hard logging, was at liberty to lay down on the soft side of a board and dream, if he slept at all of glory and the grave." The men ate at a long table in the mess hall, one company on each side. Dawes led them in grace, but the "rag-tag and bobtail of Company K" enjoyed crossing hands and assuming a pious look upward before uttering their own version:

> Oh, thou who blessed the loaves and fishes,
> Look down upon these old tin dishes;
> By thy great power those dishes smash,
> Bless each of us and damn this hash.

Sullivan remembered his messmates as "gay, brave, fun-loving boys" who would face "death just as cool and unconcerned as they then ridiculed Dawes' attempts at ready-made piety."[31]

The Juneau County boys took note of the other companies of their regiment. Two were from Milwaukee—one German and one Irish—and three from towns along the Mississippi River. The Anderson Guards included volunteers from their own Juneau County and nearby Dane counties. In addition to Milwaukee, cities represented included Baraboo, Prairie du Chien, Prescott, Fountain City, Appleton, Fond du Lac, and Beloit. One officer who attracted notice was the tall and formidable Capt. William H. Lindwurm of the German Citizen Corps. The Prussian with the stiff Teutonic manner and 300-pound girth reached Milwaukee in 1846 and was now a man of property and standing. Also admired was the Montgomery Guard, the Irish Company from Milwaukee first organized in 1857 as a militia organization. It was originally assigned to the 1st Wisconsin, but its ranks

---

30 Dawes, *Service*, 12-14; Sullivan, *Telegraph*, May 16, 1886. Atwood was a Madison attorney and one of his law partners was Frank Haskell. Haskell, Lucius Fairchild, and Atwood were also active in the Governor's Guard. Atwood would resign because of ill health.

31 Sullivan, *Telegraph*, May 16, 1886.

Captain William H. Lindwurm, Citizens Corps Milwaukee,
Co. F, 6th Wisconsin

Lindwurm's company of Milwaukee Germans raised a cry for bread in the
Washington camps. He resigned because of health issues. *Wisconsin Historical
Society 70131*

were insufficiently filled and another company was substituted. The first call to fill
the rolls was unsuccessful because the city's Catholic Irish were suspicious of the
war and unsure where it all was leading. Many were also still in mourning over the
Lake Michigan *Lady Elgin* excursion boat tragedy in September 1860 that claimed

more than 300 lives including many members of the Union Guards, the city's most prominent Irish Company.[32]

The state formed regiments in those days in response to a quota set by Federal officials. Companies of 100 volunteers were raised in local communities by individuals, who then offered the "company" to the state to be included in forming regiments. The state formally recognized the company and authorized the election of a captain and two lieutenants. When called up, the new companies gathered at a mustering place (such as Camp Randall in Madison or Camp Scott in Milwaukee) for organization into a regiment of 1,000 soldiers and given a numerical designation, such as the 6th Wisconsin Infantry. After being outfitted by the state with everything needed for war except arms and proper accouterments, Federal authorities inspected the new regiment and accepted it into Federal service.

For some, the Federal inspection process was intimidating. Pvt. Henry C. Matrau worried about being rejected because of his young age and slight stature. A native of Bainbridge in south Michigan, the underage Matrau tried to enlist in Chicago, but was turned away. The frustrated lad scolded the Chicago recruiting officer as a man who "didn't know his business," and then traveled to Beloit on the Illinois-Wisconsin line, where he joined the Star Rifles. According to the official returns Matrau was sixteen years old and stood 5-foot-6 ¾. A comrade, however, claimed Matrau was but fourteen years old and that he was not as tall as recorded. Officers suggested that the young teenager enlist as a drummer or fifer, but he refused, arguing that he wanted to carry a musket like the other men.

32 Richard Current, *History of Wisconsin*, 4 vols. (Madison, 1976), vol. 2, 277-281; Bayrd Still, *Milwaukee: The History of a City* (Madison, 1948), 153. The *Lady Elgin* disaster resulted when the Union Guards company was ordered to disband by state authorities. They were concerned the unit, with its Irish Democratic leadership, would not obey the orders of the governor in disputes involving the Federal Fugitive Slave Law, which demanded that states cooperate in the return of runaways. Randall opposed the measure and vowed to resist any effort to return slaves from Wisconsin to the South. Capt. Garrett Barry of the Union Guards, a prominent Democrat, West Point graduate, and treasurer of Milwaukee County, got into trouble for saying he would obey a call to arms by the Federal government, but not obey an "illegal order" from state officials. Barry was forced to surrender the company's weapons and belts, but managed to purchase eighty old muskets for $2.00 each from another source. To pay for the purchase, Barry scheduled an excursion to Chicago on the steamer *Lady Elgin*. Part of the proceeds from ticket sales would be used to pay for the muskets. The steamer was rammed by a schooner on the return leg to Milwaukee during a storm off Winnetka, Illinois. Among the dead were members of the German Black Jaeger and Green Jaeger militia companies, in addition to Capt. Barry and members of the Union Guards. The Irish Montgomery Guards militia company was called for the 1st Regiment, but was unable to muster enough men and was replaced by the Fond du Lac Badger Boys. As a result, the Irish Montgomery Guards were not able to fill their ranks until later, when the company did so, it was mustered into the 6th Regiment. *Ibid.*

The day of reckoning arrived when the Rifles, resplendent in their new gray coats and caps, were mustered by a U.S. recruiting officer.[33] The maneuver required each man, when his name was called, to step out and pass the mustering officer with a salute. Friends in his company helped Matrau prepare by providing him with a pair of large shoes with stuffed insoles and bigger heels to raise him up. Even the crown of his cap was stuffed to lift it. "I can see him as he looked when he started to walk past the muster officer," recalled a friend. "I can also see Captain McIntyre of the Regular Army, who mustered our regiment. The minute the boy started down the line his eyes were fixed upon him, and he watched him until he reached the left of the company. I can see the captain's smile of approval as the little fellow took his place. He had won the day. He was mustered into Uncle Sam's service for three years or during the war."

Matrau's youth and size were singled out again a few days later when the 6th Wisconsin paraded through Madison and a young lady on a sidewalk called out, "Look at that little fellow. He's only a baby." A fellow soldier would report over the coming months that "no soldier in the regiment carried a larger knapsack, kept up better in a long march, or loaded and fired more rapidly than [Matrau] . . . or behaved better under fire or in camp." By the end of the war in 1865 the "Baby of Company G" was known as the "Littlest Captain of the Iron Brigade.[34]

While Matrau settled into the ranks, the stern and fatherly Lysander Cutler assumed the regiment's top slot. The 53-year-old colonel was born in 1808 in Royalton, Massachusetts, and worked as a farmer, surveyor, and schoolmaster before moving to Dexter, Maine. He and a partner built what was then the largest woolen mill east of Massachusetts—employing 2,000 workers at one point—but the Panic of 1856 destroyed the business. Cutler moved to Wisconsin in an attempt to make a fresh start and worked for a time in the rough Lake Superior mining country. For two winters he organized a mining town thirty miles from the nearest supply post. One story circulating from those days claims Cutler obtained two of his packers at gunpoint from a saloon and forced them to deliver supplies to the snowbound community. The Indians and mixed blood Métis who worked for

33 Mickey Sullivan left a vivid description of the 6th Wisconsin uniform: "a short gray jacket reaching to the hips, faced with black at the ends of the collar, on the upper side of the cuffs, on the shoulders and straps on the sides to hold up the waist belt, gray pants with a black welt in the outside seam, a fatigue suit of pepper and salt gray cotton cloth (i.e., a sack coat and trowsers with red welt in outside steam,) two heavy dark blue woolen shirts, two pairs drawers, two pairs socks, a pair of cowhide shoes, a linen and glaze cloth cap cover, cap, etc., every article received from the state was of excellent quality." Sullivan, *Telegraph*, May 16, 1886.

34 Jerome A. Watrous, "The Littlest Captain in the Iron Brigade," unpublished manuscript, Jerome Watrous Papers, Wisconsin State Historical Society.

Colonel Lysander Cutler, 6th Wisconsin

Active in putting together the first Wisconsin organizations, Cutler was made colonel of the 6th Regiment. He proved an able leader and soon was promoted to brigadier general. *Howard Michael Madaus Collection*

Cutler called him "Gray Devil" because of the color of his long hair and trimmed whiskers.

Displaying what one admirer described as the "war-like enthusiasm of a young man of thirty," Cutler made for Madison when Fort Sumter was fired upon and assisted the governor in organizing regiments and purchasing components for the state's gray militia uniforms. When he was appointed colonel of the 6th Regiment, much was made of his experience leading a regiment of militiamen in the brief but bloodless 1839 border dispute between the U.S. and Canada known as the "Aroostook War." One of his privates said Cutler had a "stern, rugged, determined, yet kindly face, which, when a smile found place there, was rarely attractive; the gray, almost white and a full but clipped beard; the slim, tall, erect thoroughly soldier figure, and the grave, calm dignity of every motion." The colonel "imposed upon us severe duties—but only for our good as he told us, and we came to know this in time and thank him for it." According to Dawes, Cutler tolerated no nonsense and was "rugged as a wolf." The regiment, he continued, had great confidence in him.[35]

If the Western boys admired the solemn old Cutler, they came to despise regimental adjutant Lt. Frank Haskell. A graduate of Dartmouth (where a teacher described him as intelligent and able but "ambitious as Lucifer"), upon graduation Haskell followed a brother to Wisconsin and practiced law in Madison. He was active in the Governor's Guard militia along with Atwood, his law partner, as well as Fairchild and Thomas Allen now serving in the 2nd Wisconsin. Haskell was the grandson of a New Hampshire captain of the Revolution. At 33, his receding hair was trimmed close to his head and sideburns and a carefully trimmed mustache framed sharp intelligent hazel eyes. The Wisconsin boys did not like him, one veteran bluntly stated because he was rigid and drilled them like Regulars. "They were volunteers; they didn't want to be converted into Regulars," remembered Jerome A. Watrous. "They kicked and thrashed, but the harder they kicked and thrashed the more thorough was Haskell's discipline." In the end they recognized his worth and that he "was a martinet—a soldier from the foundation up—and had to be known before he could be liked." There was also a sharper explanation. "Haskell's soldierly bearing—I never saw a finer-appearing soldier—gave birth to ambition in the rank and file to become soldiers in the fullest sense of the word," continued Watrous. "Haskell's running fire of criticism and emphatic, plain instructions to individuals and companies as a whole . . . gave men . . . information without which no regiment can become thoroughly competent in either war or

---

35 Dawes, *Service*, 18, 25, 32-33; Flower, *History of Milwaukee*, 789-791.

Lieutenant Frank A. Haskell, Adjutant, 6th Wisconsin

Haskell served well as brigade adjutant, but is remembered today for his long letter describing Gettysburg, published after his death. *Wisconsin Historical Society 3343*

peace. Though others became adjutants of the Sixth, Frank A. Haskell never had a successor." Haskell, concluded Watrous, "was as perfect a soldier as I ever knew."[36]

Cutler from the first recognized the younger officer's worth and relied on Haskell in running the regiment more than he realized. In the end, "Haskell of Gettysburg" would become one of the most famous of all Wisconsin soldiers, the mounted officer who rallied the Union line and helped turn back the last great Confederate charge on the third day at Gettysburg. Haskell penned a description of the battle in a long letter a few days after the fighting and mailed it to a brother in Portage, Wisconsin. It would eventually be published, but not until long after his death at Cold Harbor in June of 1864. And it would be reprinted, over and over, for future generations to read and ponder. What Haskell saw and described would become so important that no historian of the epic battle dared overlook his words. Mostly forgotten would be his earlier role in shaping a tough Western regiment and the organization that would become famous as the Iron Brigade of the West.

The Only Casualty of Patterson Park

The journey of the 6th Wisconsin to Washington was marked by several incidents. The first came when the train was routed through Milwaukee and stopped on July 24 in what James Patrick Sullivan called the city of "beer and pale bricks." Colonel Lysander Cutler was a Milwaukeean with a pair of Milwaukee companies in the Irish Montgomery Guards and German Citizens Corps. Naturally, he wanted to show his regiment off. The stop opened with a tramp through the city streets before admiring crowds and was remembered for the kind treatment of "many beautiful ladies who seemed to think they could not do enough for us." After an "elegant dinner," one of the Sauk County boys recalled, there was the presentation of "the largest cake we ever saw and with it a handsome bouquet and this inscription: 'Flowers may fade, but the honors of the brave, never.'" Said one soldier of that long day: "That trip through Milwaukee sustained many a poor fellow afterward on a tiresome march, in the privation of soldier life, or in the fury of battle by reminding him that at home . . . he had many strong and warm friends, and nerving him with the thought that come what would they should have no cause to be ashamed of him."

---

36 Jerome A. Watrous, "Tribute to Adjutant Haskell," in Frank Aretas Haskell, *The Battle of Gettysburg* (Madison, 1910), xxi-xxviii; Jerome A. Watrous, "About the Boy Patriots," *Milwaukee Sunday Telegraph*, November 27, 1897. For more information about Haskell, see Frank L. Byrne and Andrew T. Weaver, eds., *Haskell of Gettysburg: His Life and Civil War Papers* (Madison, WI., 1970).

The men were returning to their train to depart when one cheeky bright-eyed private leaned out of his window, offered a bright smile for a comely young woman walking past, and asked, "Say, Miss, won't you kiss me for my mother?" To his surprise, she hugged him with both arms and kissed him for his mother before walking off with a smile of her own. The memory of the Milwaukee stop was enough to warm hearts for many a poor soldier boy.[37]

The journey to the front was "like a triumphal march," was how young Captain Dawes of the Lemonweir Minute Men remembered it. Cheering crowds at every stop greeted the regiment. Members of Maj. Robert Anderson's family were waiting at one halt in Pennsylvania. The old Regular Army officer was much hailed those days for his brave role in Charleston Harbor as commander of the Federal garrison manning Sumter. In fact, one of the companies in the new regiment was named after him. "You may be sure the Badger boys made the mountains ring with cheers for the daughters of the hero of Fort Sumter," confirmed Dawes, who wrote home that the oldest Anderson daughter was "a very handsome young lady." She presented him with a sprig of green that he said was probably given to the youngest captain of the regiment "wholly due to the superior lung power of Company 'K.'" He sent the sprig home to his sister with a note to keep it for him "until the war is over."[38]

When the 6th Wisconsin arrived at Harrisburg, the new volunteers were "dumped like a train load of stock" in a pasture. The next morning rations were brought in for the hungry solders—the first issue from Uncle Sam—that included "damaged hard tack of the consistency and nutritiousness of sole leather, green coffee, rusty bacon, sugar, vinegar, (if you had anything to get it in), and the everlasting bean," grumbled Sullivan. "Inasmuch as there was not a coffee mill, coffee pot, skillet or kettle in Company K, one many imagine how sumptuously we fared on the above menu." The hungry soldiers began to run the guard for Harrisburg where "bakers, pie dealers, hotel-keepers" experienced a boom in trade. The Sauk County boys remembered that Paul Will of Baraboo skipped camp and never returned—the company's only real deserter during four years of service.[39]

At Baltimore, the regiment halted for the night and camped in Patterson Park opposite Fort McHenry after marching through the streets without firearms but

37 Sullivan, *Telegraph*, May 16. 1886; Philip Cheek and Mair Pointon, *History of the Sauk County Riflemen, Known as Company "A" 6th Wisconsin Veteran Volunteer Infantry, 1861-1865* (Privately Printed, 1900), 16; *Milwaukee Sunday Telegraph*, April 8, 1883. The lucky soldier was not identified.

38 Dawes, *Service*, 15-17.

39 Cheek and Pointon, *Sauk County*, 17; *Wisconsin Roster*, vol. 1, 500.

escorted by 200 armed police. The Western boys expected trouble and had armed themselves with "brick bats." Hooligans who rushed the column were suppressed by the police. "The streets were jammed with people, as we marched, and the excitement was very great," wrote Dawes. The camp in the park was attacked after dark and shots were fired. The companies were turned out, but no one was injured and quiet was soon restored. When the disturbance erupted, Dawes formed his company in the company street and his men loaded up with brick bats. "We had no guns. Companies 'A' [Sauk County Riflemen] and 'B' [the Prescott Guards] only had been armed as yet and were on guard duty." During the dark and confusion, Lt. John Kellogg was sent to the colonel for instructions. After wandering around in the dark Kellogg finally found Colonel Cutler and returned to Dawes. "What instructions he received we never learned, as he fell into a dreadful hole [toilet] in his reckless rush to bring them to us, and his condition of body and mind was such that he did nothing but swear a blue streak about his own mishap." The lieutenant, it was remembered, was of "quick blood and it was not always safe to congratulate him as the only man wounded in the Battle of Patterson Park."

The 6th remained at Patterson Park until Aug. 7 when it was ordered to Washington. While waiting at Baltimore, the regiment received its first issue of weapons—Belgian muskets, "a heavy, clumsy gun of large caliber." The 6th Wisconsin was marched through the city streets with loaded muskets at half-cock and this time was met with silence. The soldiers were piled onto "filthy cattle cars" and reached Washington at daylight of the next day where they would be assigned to join King's Provision Brigade.

Remembered of those days was Pvt. Jerome Watrous' luck securing a pass to visit his brother Henry, who was camped nearby with the 4th Wisconsin. The two made the rounds of Washington. Both had campaigned as Republican Wide-Awakes in 1860 and they went to the White House to see if they could catch a glimpse of President Lincoln. They were on the sidewalk watching a Pennsylvania regiment when they found Lincoln standing behind them. "My boys, I see by your uniforms that you have come to help me save the Union, to be my partners in the enterprise." The president asked what state the two soldiers represented and when told said that Wisconsin was "sending many good men." He shook their hands and expressed the hope their lives would be spared, "and that we would never regret the partnership." Watrous said of the meeting: "To have looked into the Lincoln face, at close range, heard the Lincoln voice, had our hands enclosed in the ample Lincoln hand was glory enough for more than one August day."[40]

---

40 Jerome A. Watrous, "Old Days in Washington," *Milwaukee Telegraph*, January 14, 1890.

No one took to camp life in Washington with more of a flourish than did John H. Cook of Hartford, a private in the Irish company from Milwaukee who liked to call himself "the Tough One." On his first night in the nation's capital, Cook and several friends ran the guard for a spree. "When I returned to camp," he wrote in a brief memoir of his war days, "I got what I deserved and so did the rest; but we had a bully time. Three days on short rations and clothing. Of course you other fellows don't know anything about such things." He soon found a talent for producing passes carefully signed "Brig. Gen. King" and "Col. L. Cutler." His escapades landed him in the guard house four times in that camp alone. On yet another occasion, he was out looking for fun with friend Hamilcar McIntosh and cut the stripes off the uniform of Sgt. Andrew Gilmore while he was asleep and sent them to the captain in an envelope. "Of course, it got out. Cook and Mc. were in [the guard house] for three days."[41]

One camp incident was especially troubling for Cutler. After two days of little in the way of rations, the Germans in Company F—who were used to a full table of food back home—chanted "Brodt! Brodt! Brodt!" An orderly was sent to fetch the burly Capt. William Lindwurm, who arrived a short time later in full stride wearing his best regimentals. Two of the Sauk County Riflemen, knowing something was up, followed and watched. Cutler gave Lindwurm a stern look and lectured him about the lack of discipline: "I am very much surprised and chagrined that your company, Sir! should make such of a show of themselves and the regiment by crying: 'Bread! Bread! Bread! Bread!' It impairs the regiment's standing with the other troops . . . and shows a lack of attention on the part of the officers in permitting such a breach of good discipline to occur." Lindwurm's face flushed and he raised himself up to his full height—which was considerable—and the two watching privates noted he "was big in every way." When Cutler finally stopped, Lindwurm blurted: "See here, Col. Cutler, dem boys what is by my company in are de best boys in Milwaukee. Their father and mother come and say to me, 'Capt. Lindwurm, we let our boys go with you because we know you will be like a father by them,' and now my boys are all hungry; they have no bread for two days. I want to tell you something, Col. Cutler, were I the Colonel on this regiment I would have some one else but that fool brother-in-law of yours for Quartermaster. I tell you something now, Colonel, I am no lager beer Dutchman, I am a German gentleman what drink my Rhinish wine, when you, sir, was stinking fish inspector in Milwaukee. Mine boys want brodt!" After that, the two Sauk County men noted, bread was provided on a regular basis.

41 John H. Cook, "The Tough One Again," *Milwaukee Sunday Telegraph*, March 11, 1883.

Other than the "brodt" episode there was little excitement, and the long days were spent in the heavy work of constructing fortifications in Virginia beyond the Chain Bridge. On September 11, five companies of the 19th Indiana along with the 69th New York tramped five miles out into the countryside. Confederate cavalry attacked the reconnaissance and during the two hours of fitful shooting a Hoosier named W. H. H. Wood of Company D was killed. According to the 19th's Colonel Meredith, his companies "behaved with the utmost coolness and gallantry . . ."[42]

On October 7, the expected 7th Wisconsin arrived in Washington carrying orders attaching it to Rufus King's brigade. The order was a double-edged sword: Instead of losing the 19th Indiana to another brigade as many expected, the 5th Wisconsin was transferred to Gen. Winfield Scott Hancock, ending once and for all the idea of an all-Wisconsin brigade under King. The loss of the 5th was against King's wishes "and the wishes of a majority of the field and line officers and men of that gallant [5th] regiment." Word coursed through the ranks that Hancock, a West Pointer whose star was rising, took a "fancy" to the 5th Wisconsin and "begged or stole it away from Rufus King." King— "vexed at the loss of the Fifth," claimed one soldier— "insisted upon having another Wisconsin regiment in its place."[43] What was never determined was whether the transfer was the careless mistake of an army clerk or a way to prevent Governor Randall from having a say in the operation of his state's regiments. Despite the disappointment over the transfer of the 5th Wisconsin, King's command was still an all-Western organization—a fact that would have far reaching affects in the days ahead.

The 7th Wisconsin's arrival helped ease chapped feelings. "Our boys and those of the 2d made extravagant demonstrations of delight when they saw the gray uniforms and blue flags coming up the road from towards Washington," exclaimed a 6th Wisconsin man. Another remarked that it "seemed kind of natural to see someone fresh from Badgerdom." Long after the war, some would say the 7th Wisconsin proved to be the best regiment of the Western brigade, but that was not immediately apparent. The unit "makes a very good appearance in uniform," one soldier admitted, "but they don't carry bronze enough on their cheeks to give them a real good soldierly appearance." An officer left a more complete description of the new arrivals. The Wisconsin 7th, he said, was "said to be the finest body of

---

42 Cheek and Pointon, *Sauk County*, 19-20.

43 Quiner, *Military History*, 443; Jerome A. Watrous, *Milwaukee Telegraph*, September 26, 1896; Levi B. Raymond, diary, October 4, 1861, private collection; *Appleton Crescent*, October 19, 1861; *Green Bay Advocate*, October 10, 1861, Edwin A. Brown, letter, to his wife, October 2, 1861, Civil War Museum, Kenosha, WI.; Edward E. Bryant, "Our Troops!" *Milwaukee Sunday Telegraph*, October 26, 1879.

Private Phillip Bennett,
Lancaster Union Guards,
Co. F, 7th Wisconsin

Shown in the early Wisconsin
gray uniform, Bennett enlisted
from Potosi, Wisconsin. He was
wounded on July 1, 1863 at
Gettysburg and died three days
later. *Carroll Institute for Civil War Studies*

soldiers yet sent from our State. . . .
The men are not only of good size
and hardy looking, but they have an
intelligence and smart look, which
is assurance that they bring brain as
well as muscle to the work." The
6th Wisconsin's Lt. Edwin Brown,
however, was less than impressed:
"7th Wisconsin Reg. arrived here
yesterday and are encamped across
the road from us. They are not so
good looking Regt. as the Fifth and
Sixth are and never will be." Brown
reported with smug satisfaction
that the arriving soldiers set up their
small tents in a steady rain.[44]

That the soldiers of these four regiments were from the frontier West was
significant. The end of the Revolutionary War left the new United States with a
decision on what to do with open and unsettled land beyond the Appalachian
range. The Northwest Ordinance of 1787 set a framework for creation of new
territories and new states. Just as important, the ordinance barred slavery from the
territory and called for public support of education. The measure opened the lands
to settlement and led to the formation of the new states of Indiana, Illinois,
Michigan, and Wisconsin with a distinctive sectional interest and identification. The

44 Levi B. Raymond, diary, October 4, 1861; *Appleton Crescent*, October 19, 1861; *Green Bay
Advocate*, October 10, 1861; Brown, letter to his wife, October 2, 1861.

open land attracted folk of ambition and vigor, men and women interested in making a future. It mattered not if they came from Ireland, Germany, England, or other places across the sea or from New England, New York, or Pennsylvania—or even Virginia and North Carolina. Life in the harsh wilderness changed and shaped them. On the frontier, individuals were judged less by their family connection and money than for their skill with axe and plow and the strength needed to tame a wilderness. "They were young men and women in their very prime . . . their superiority was noticeable," confirmed one man. Poor boy Sol Meredith of the 19th Indiana, for example, walked out of North Carolina to prosper and grow strong in Hoosier political circles. Clayton and Earl Rogers in the ranks of the 6th Wisconsin came from Pennsylvania to the Wisconsin territory to open a sawmill "10 miles from the nearest white woman." Lucius Fairchild of the 2nd Wisconsin was a man just back from the gold fields of California. Even Abe Lincoln made his way from Kentucky to Illinois by way of Indiana, where he married well and became a lawyer of repute. The people on the new frontier, one explained, could drain a marsh, clear a wood for planting, and create a state. They were also quick to empty their purse for a poor widow or orphan, then sit down to play cards for more.

In many ways these settlers were a new kind of American. They had a certain kinship with those who pushed into the Ohio River Valley and Kentucky in earlier times, but they were better educated and rode the growing wave of industrial revolution. They were "Westerners" with a sharp sense of place fed by the growth of newspapers, railroads, highways, canals, and the telegraph. They counted among their friends others who were white, black, and red, immigrants, and native-born. They would become soldiers with a certain dash and sense of themselves never before seen in the United States. When the Western regiments appeared, one volunteer admitted, the "fine physique, the self-reliant carriage of its men at once challenged attention."[45] It was that "self-reliant carriage" and dash that even Rebels would in time come to see and cry out in recognition across the distance of rival battle lines.

45 Bryant, *Telegraph*, October 26, 1879.

Part III: As a Brigade We Get Along Finely Together

A Place They Called Secessiondom

The colonel of the 7th Wisconsin was an old Hungarian campaigner just then living in Milwaukee. His name was Joseph Vandor and he was recommended to the governor as "a brave man and thorough disciplinarian" with extensive European military experience—just the kind of officer needed given the recent troubles in the 2nd Wisconsin. A local newspaper touted the new colonel as educated at the "Imperial Military Academy of Vienna" and an "officer in the army of the celebrated Field Marshal Radetsky" with a distinguished role in the Hungarian Revolution of 1848-1849. "He is a thorough and experienced officer, and possesses all the requisites for the successful handling of a regiment in the camp or battlefield." One difficulty not mentioned in the newspaper columns, however, was that Vandor was barely able to speak English. Still, according to one of his new volunteers, the "old veteran seems to understand his business well and I think has the confidence of his men." Another volunteer made much of Vandor's European service, claiming the officer has seen service in 19 different battles and is "still suffering from the effects of a wound received in one of them. . . . He is a very intelligent man on all subjects and brings to the discharge of the duties of his position an ability and experience that will at once render him a very efficient and popular officer."[1]

One of Vandor's first orders prohibited the sale of intoxicating drinks. Anyone, citizen or soldier, found selling spirits would be put in the guard house. When someone tried to give him a barrel of beer as a present, the old campaigner refused it. As one observer put it, "This is adopting the right course and we are sure

---

1 *Kenosha Telegraph*, September 26, 1861. Johann Josef Wenzel Graf Radetzky von Radetz was a Bohemian nobleman and Austrian general.

Lieutenant Colonel William W. Robinson, 7th Wisconsin

The New Englander moved to Wisconsin in 1858. He came into the war as a lieutenant colonel of the regiment, but was soon promoted. *Howard Michael Madaus Collection*

that Col. Vandor has the firmness to carry out this excellent rule. We feel that this regiment is peculiarly fortunate in the selection of its Colonel."[2]

The 7th's second in command was William W. Robinson of Sparta, a 42-year-old Vermont native whose namesake was pastor of the Pilgrim Church that chartered the Mayflower. One of his kinsmen sailed on that ship and signed the Mayflower Compact. His father served as an officer in the War of 1812 and his grandfather was a veteran of the Revolutionary War. After attending schools in the East, Robinson moved to New Jersey and worked as a teacher before moving again to Cleveland, Ohio, where he and a partner ran a school. When President Polk called for men to fight in Mexico, he was commissioned an officer in the 3rd Ohio Infantry and served under Gen. Zachary Taylor. After the Mexican War, Robinson was sent by his father-in-law to scout land in the opening areas of the frontier and his family later moved to what is now Wisconsin. Robinson, however, set out for California, where he and partners built an 11-mile flume to supply water pressure for mines in the Minnesota and Smith Diggings. He returned to Wisconsin and moved his family to Minnesota and helped organize the town of Wilton, ran for state assembly, and served the state militia as colonel of the 9th Minnesota. Robinson moved back to Wisconsin in 1859 and trained with the militia company in which his brother-in-law, G. A. Fisk, was an officer. With the start of the Civil War, friends recommended him to the governor for the lieutenant colonelcy of the 7th Wisconsin. One observer described him as "a substantial looking man [who] seems perfectly at home in the discharge of his duties." Robinson's ability would soon lift him to higher rank.

Thirty-five-year-old Charles A. Hamilton of Milwaukee, a grandson of Alexander Hamilton, served as the regiment's major. His father was a New York attorney of wealth and reputation. After attending schools in England and Germany and reading law in New York, Hamilton arrived in Milwaukee in 1851 and developed an extensive practice. "He is in the prime of life and will, if we mistake not, prove a brave and competent officer," a newspaper reported, adding he was "a gentleman of sterling qualities and great courage." His brother, Col. Schuyler Hamilton, served on Gen. Winfield Scott's staff and would later introduce the officers not only to Scott but to Maj. Gen. George McClellan, a rising young star in the Army.

The companies for the 7th Wisconsin had been ordered into Camp Randall during the last week of August as the fall harvest was being completed. The soldiers were recruited at Lodi, Fall River, Platteville, Stoughton, Montello, Lancaster,

---

2 Sometimes spelled Van Dor. *Wisconsin Newspaper Volumes*, vol. 1; Julius Murray, letter, undated, Julius Murray Papers, Wisconsin Historical Society.

Grand Rapids (now Wisconsin Rapids), Fennimore, Beloit, and Dodge County. The men found Camp Randall "in excellent order." After the 5th and 6th Wisconsin left, grass sprouted on the parade ground and someone had cleaned the buildings. The Lodi Guards company was composed of 96 men, "all stalwart looking fellows capable of enduring the privations and fatigues of war." George Bill served as captain; his first lieutenant, Hollon Richardson of Chippewa Falls, would one day make a name for himself. The Beloit Badger Rifles was described as "a fine company of young men," and the three organizations from Grant County—the Platteville Guards, Lancaster Union Guards, and Badger State Guards—were said to be made up of "a remarkably intelligent and determined looking set of men."[3]

While the 7th Regiment was being readied for the war at Madison, the first companies of the 8th Wisconsin arrived. The one from Eau Claire in north central Wisconsin caught the attention of the Western boys because it included the "proud form" of a live large bald eagle perched on a painted shield and carried by a bearer. The eagle liked to spread its wings to retain his equilibrium while being carried. "It was the center of attraction during the day," admitted a 7th Wisconsin man. "The [Eau Claire] boys say they are going to take him with them and are not going to return until he shampoos his head in the Gulf of Mexico."[4]

Unlike the earlier regiments, the 7th Wisconsin mustered into Federal service by companies and left for the war front and active service on September 21 after a rousing send-off speech by Acting Gov. Louis P. Harvey. "Officers of the 7th," Harvey intoned to the formed companies, "we commit the care of these our fellow citizens principally to you. We feel that your responsibilities are fearfully great." Turning to the men in ranks, Harvey announced that there was no fear "your bravery will be daunted by any danger, or flinch before any foe." It was discipline and drill that was most important, he continued. "Undisciplined men upon the field of battle are but a helpless crowd, huddling for slaughters—all the weaker for greater numbers. Bound together by discipline, each secures the protection of his comrades, and all are interwoven in mutual dependence and strength as the strands in a cable of wire." Finally, Harvey reminded the regiment of the words of Gen. McClellan, now in command at Washington, who proclaimed in a recent order: "We have met our last defeat—we have beat our last retreat. You stand by me, and I will stand by you." Harvey paused for a moment before the hushed crowd and then

---

3 *Wisconsin Newspaper Volumes*, vol. 1.

4 The mascot would come to be known as "Old Abe," the famous Wisconsin war eagle carried by the regiment through camp life, skirmish, and battle. Indeed, the bird became the most famous "soldier" in the Civil War history of Wisconsin.

called out in a loud voice, "God bless the gallant Gen. McClellan! I have faith that he will make his words prophetic." The statement was met with cheers.[5]

Finally, the men boarded the waiting train cars and then, amid the booming of guns and the cheers and waving of handkerchiefs, started the long journey to the war front. It was about 11:00 a.m. The train, which was running late, halted for a welcome and dinner at Janesville shortly after leaving Madison. And it was there that one of the 2nd Wisconsin boys wounded at Bull Run boarded to travel back to his regiment, together with other recruits. The troop train reached Chicago at dusk and the regiment, led by the famous Ellsworth Zouaves, Scammon Light Infantry, and Anderson Rifles, began a long march through the city. Colonel Vandor and Lieutenant Colonel Robinson, both mounted, led the parade down streets lighted by gas and the rising moon. Along the line of march onlookers clapped and cheered. "I never thought that Chicago was such a big place," marveled one backwoods boy. Once at the depot Vandor thanked the escort and apologized for their later arrival. He singled out the band, saying "they played an air to which, as a Captain, [I] had marched [13] years ago in Hungary." A brief reception for officers followed at the Briggs House, where Vandor again enthralled the crowd with a story about how he landed in Chicago five or six years before after losing almost all of his property and with but $50.00 in his pocket. In the cars, meanwhile, the waiting soldiers—who were only served coffee—complained that it had taken twelve hours to move the regiment 135 miles.[6]

The train reached Fort Wayne, Indiana, the next morning, where the recruits filled their new canteens. A "sneaking rascal," caught by an officer behind the cars trying to provide whiskey for the soldiers, was administered a "severe kicking and forced to flee." The cars rolled into Pittsburgh the next morning, where breakfast was provided and 13 ladies "were detailed with cup and funnel to fill all the canteens with coffee." When they finally arrived in Harrisburg the Wisconsin boys detrained to camp in a clover field. "This 'living in clover' is not what it is 'cracked

---

5 *Kenosha Telegraph*, September 26, 1861. Harvey, a native of Connecticut, moved to Southport (now Kenosha), Wisconsin where he founded an academy and became associated with the Whig Party. He edited the *Whig Southport American* from 1843 to 1846. Moving to Rock County, he became a Republican State Senator, Secretary of State, and finally governor. He died in April 1862 when he fell into the Tennessee River and drowned while visiting Wisconsin soldiers wounded in the fighting at Shiloh, Tennessee. His body was found two weeks later. Lieutenant Governor Edward Salomon succeeded Harvey.

6 In Chicago the march went past the Galena depot across the Wells Street Bridge, down Randolph, past the Briggs House, down Clark, past the Sherman House and Tribune office, down Lake, past the Tremont, up Dearborn and then west past the Court House to the Wayne Railroad Depot.

up to be,'" grumbled a soldier in a letter home. "An oil cloth under us and a blanket over us is not a very good protection against the dew and cold of a September night." Baltimore predictably offered a mixed reception with both cheers and boos for Lincoln. "You could tell very easy the Secessionists when you met them on the street," recalled one Badger. "They would look awful sour, but they [dare not] say anything. The Secession streets in Baltimore were all dark, while the Union streets was well lit up." One soldier remembered a lady's friendly call: "Don't you dare come back here without Jeff Davis' head!" Before long it was on to Washington and what the boys called "Secessiondom." At one slowdown on a steep grade four black men jumped aboard, each carrying an instrument—tambourine, guitar, bones, and a triangle. The four sang Union and liberty songs, "collecting several dollars of loose change" while moving car to car.[7]

Once in Washington, the 7th Regiment Western boys reached King's brigade near the Chain Bridge and made camp under the watchful eyes and knowing smiles of the soldiers of the regiments already there. It was raining. "We have dared to set our foot upon the sacred soil of the old dominion," Capt. John Callis wrote home, "and . . . I must say it is enough to cast a gloom over the most impervious mind, to see the blighting influences of the present war, together with the relics of the accursed institution of slavery."[8]

On an unseasonably hot October 5, King marched the 2nd, 6th, and 7th Wisconsin and 19th Indiana across the Georgetown aqueduct to Fort Tillinghast on Arlington Heights in Virginia, where the brigade halted near the home of Robert E. Lee. There the brigade went into winter quarters, and there it would remain until March 10, 1862. The soldiers constructed cookhouses, stables, and officer quarters and fixed up small shebang houses of logs with tent roofs. Each had a mud chimney and in true Western fashion there was discussion about the proper design. "One squad, in building, contended that in order to draw successfully the chimney must be smaller at the top than the bottom. But the Lynxville boys of the Prairie du Chien Volunteers argued the reverse," recalled on observer. A test was proposed and the two squads each started a fire. A short time later the men of both squads were "smoked out into the street, where they stood in rain and cold, unhappy to the last degree." It was later decided that one of the designs was correct, but members of the other squad—fearing a failure— "had secretly stuffed an old pair of pants" in

7   Hugh Perkins, letter, September 29, 1861, in "Letters of a Civil War Soldier," Marilyn Gardner, ed., prepared for syndication, April 9, 1983, *Christian Science Monitor.* The letter was to Herbert Frisbie, great-grandfather of Gardner. *Beloit Journal and Courier,* October 1, 1861.

8   *Wisconsin Newspaper Volumes,* vol. 1.

the other's chimney. "It caused considerable swearing, but was voted the best joke that week."[9]

Of interest were Arlington's historic ties to George Washington and the earliest days of the nation. The columned home in Virginia just across the Potomac River from the nation's Capital was built by Washington's stepson John Parke Custis. It passed to Robert E. Lee through George Washington Curtis, his father-in-law. "We encountered a 69-year-old Negro who had lived in Arlington House for more than 50 years," one Badger wrote home. "He told us that George Washington had often visited there for days at a time. Several of the listening soldiers cried." "The property contains more than 1,000 acres," noted Julius Murray of the 6th Wisconsin, "and now for this act of treason he [Lee] loses it all, and his head with it if they do not succeed. It is the same way with thousands of others in the state." One of the Wisconsin soldiers exploring the house found a piano said to have belonged to Martha Washington and had "the historical, not exquisite pleasure, mind you, of performing on it. It was a small one, of a London make, and at that time in perfect order." He came back two months later to find it "half destroyed by vandals, curiosity hunters who had carried off first the keys, then the hammers and other portable parts."[10]

King's brigade was the only Western organization serving in the Eastern army and it set them apart. One of the captains in the 6th Wisconsin, Edward Bragg, announced that it was for the West that the brigade and the regiments would be fighting, for "the reputation of themselves and of their brothers, and the reputation of their state." Closer to home was the brewing rivalry to be the best regiment in the brigade, a desire that smoldered through guard mounts and other formations as they learned to be soldiers. The "veterans" of the 2nd Wisconsin provoked much of the heat with their boasting of their service at Bull Run. The 19th Indiana had also seen action, but only a simple inconsequential skirmish in the eyes of the Badgers. The 6th and 7th Wisconsin had not yet seen their baptism of fire. The four regiments would pull together as a brigade in battle, one observer predicted, but each "had, nevertheless, their individuality, their rivalry, their jealousies, if you will. The 2d had been through First Bull and swaggered a bit in consequence. They rather patronized the other regiments, put on veteran airs. They were superbly drilled, but decidedly given to sarcastic comment on the other commands. The 6th, 7th and 19th had not had the 2d's opportunities, but were cock sure that when the

9   Loyd Harris, *Milwaukee Sunday Telegraph*, March 11, 1883.

10 Longhenry Diary; Julius Murray, letter, undated. The piano player was Loyd Harris of the 6th Wisconsin.

time came they could fight every bit as well, stay as long in a hot place or charge just as daringly into a hotter."[11] It was not just loud talk that gave the men of the 2nd Wisconsin veteran airs. A 6th Wisconsin officer noted that the men of the 2nd "look as though they had been 'through the wars' ragged, and saucy, and without discipline." Another officer noted the soldiers of the 2nd "look dirty and more callus than ours. . . . The men are of good stuff, but . . . with little confidence in the officers & that they care little what they do." Another priggish officer sniffed that the men of the 2nd "did not have that exuberant, dashing, self-reliant manner that distinguishes the other Wisconsin men."[12]

Part of the hard appearance of the 2nd was the sad condition of their old uniforms in general, and their trousers in particular. Many were still wearing the state gray issued in Madison and worn for the many weeks of campaigning and in camp. There was nothing quite like the "view of their rear ranks when they attempted a dress parade," snickered a comrade, the "lively boys . . . were more like Highlanders minus kilts than model infantry." He added that even the gentlest of breezes were not hindered in cooling their "Adonis-like forms." In hard soldier fashion the 2nd Wisconsin was soon known as the "Ragged Assed Second," and none of the angry retorts served to comfort the maligned party. The 6th Wisconsin were known as "King's pet babies," because of suspected favoritism, the "Bragging 6th," and the "Calico 6th," the latter a reference to the homespun shirts worn by the farm boys in the back ranks. According to a 7th Wisconsin man, the 6th "was not well liked by the other regiments." The 7th Regiment fellows liked to call themselves the "Hungry 7th," but were more popularly known as the "Huckleberries" because they "liked to talk about pies and things to eat." The 19th Indiana men were described as "lean, lank" and a quiet set and became known as "Old Posey County" or "Swamp Hogs No. 19," and "every man of them did not care a goll darn how he was dressed, but was all hell for a fight."[13]

One frustrated officer in the 6th Wisconsin wrote home that some regiments "have the strange habit of christening their yet unborn reputation as for instance:

11 Edward Bragg, letter to Earl Rogers, April 3, 1900; Charles King, "Gainesville, 1862," *Military Order of the Loyal Legion of the United States, Commandery of the State of Wisconsin, War Papers*, 3 vols. (Milwaukee, 1903), vol. 3, 271.

12 Brown, letter to his father, August 28, 1861; Bragg, letter to his wife, undated; *Green Bay Advocate*, August 29, 1861.

13 Loyd Harris, "A Celebrated Case," *Milwaukee Sunday Telegraph*, August 5, 1883; Jerome A. Watrous, "The Old Brigade," *Milwaukee Sunday Telegraph*, September 27, 1885; William Ray, *Four Years with the Iron Brigade: The Civil War Journal of William Ray, Seventh Wisconsin*, Lance Herdegen and Sharon Murphy, eds. (New York, 2001), 16.

Officers of the 2nd Wisconsin

Left to right: Quartermaster J. D. Ruggles, Dr. A. J. Ward, Maj. J. S. Allen (standing), Lt. Col. Lucius Fairchild, Adjutant C. K. Dean (standing), and Col. Edgar O'Connor. The flag of the 2nd can also be seen, unfurled behind them. *Wisconsin Historical Society 5168*

'The Bloody This,' or 'Invincible That' or 'Ragged Other.' Please set us down as the plain 'Wisconsin Sixth' until we bring forth something for which history will have a name." It was with "great reluctance," one volunteer announced, "that we got up even a calling acquaintance with those other regiments, yet some of us had friends, cousins and even brothers in their ranks." Within the regiments there was some friction between American-born men and soldiers from other countries. "Americans are a materialistic people and are interested only in making money and raising hell," complained a German in the 7th Wisconsin. "Exceptions of course, are some well-bred and educated families and persons." One veteran admitted that the four regiments were "separate and distinct communities" until they were tested in battle. One 2nd Wisconsin soldier tried to explain their differences. The men in his regiment, he wrote, "are probably the hardest set of boys, but good natured and easy to get along with. They wear an air of fearless carelessness wherever found. The Sixth is more stately, and distant, and march to slower music than we do. The Seventh puts on the least style and crow the least . . . and is well drilled. It is the truest friend the 2d ever found. The 19th Indiana is an indifferent, don't care regiment. They pride themselves on their fighting pluck—which is undoubtedly good—more than their drill. As a brigade we get along finely together." Private Mickey Sullivan of the 6th Wisconsin said it plain: "If any one wanted to get into . . . difficulty, all that was necessary for him to do was go into the 19th and say a word against the 'Wisconsin boys' and the same held good in any of our regiments about them."[14]

Little Mac

The Western Brigade settled in for a long winter on the grounds around the Arlington House. More fresh regiments, meanwhile, arrived in Washington adding to the number of camps around the place while thousands of soldiers using axe, saw, and shovel expanded the capital's earthen defenses. The city's population exploded with not just soldiers but patriotic civilians, business men, speculators, office seekers, ladies of both proper and questionable backgrounds, individuals seeking patronage positions, and the various con artists and footpads war always attracts. New saloons were established daily and hotels and rooming houses slept visitors two or three or even five to a bed. Not forgotten, however, was the hard fact that just outside the city gates waited the victorious Confederate army of Bull Run.

The nation itself was mired in a conflict that suddenly extended from Virginia to Missouri. Gone were the earlier assumptions of a quick war and one quick battle, and then a negotiated peace. Now there was uncertainty and an awareness of an extended war that could last months and even years. The Confederates had won the opening engagement at Manassas July 21 and, just a few weeks later, in faraway Missouri, another Federal force was defeated at Wilson's Creek and its commander, Nathaniel Lyon, shot dead. The victory opened southern and western Missouri to Confederate invasion and a make-shift army under Confederate Sterling Price, an unlikely Old Testament figure who fought wearing his favorite straw hat and dingy white duster, quickly moved to Lexington, where the 3,500 man Union garrison surrendered on September 20. Half of Missouri was now under control of the secessionist forces. In western Virginia (now West Virginia), however, Union Gen. George B. McClellan, a West Pointer working as a railroad executive at the start of the war, was back in uniform and organized 20,000 troops in Ohio and sent troops across the Ohio River to occupy the important Baltimore and Ohio railroad

---

14 Harris, *Telegraph*, March 11, 1883; Jerome A. Watrous, "Heroes of Undying Game," *Milwaukee Sunday Telegraph*, September 26, 1896; *Janesville Daily Gazette*, July 10, 1862; Sullivan, *Telegraph*, March 16, 1883.

Major General George B. McClellan

His young soldiers called him "Little Mac," and he would capture their hearts and enthusiasm like no other army commander before or after. *National Archives*

connection at Grafton. He advanced his forces into western Virginia and won a minor victory at Cheat Mountain on July 1, then struck and damaged the retreating rebel rearguard two days later near Laurel Mountain. The successes left most of Virginia west of the Alleghenies under Union control and made the young

McClellan a newspaper hero. Confederate efforts in western Virginia never accomplished much beyond moving soldiers into the area. In late July, Robert E. Lee was released from a desk job in Richmond to take command. Rain, inexperience, and sickness, which sidelined a third of his soldiers, thwarted his plans to organize an attack. The newspapers in Richmond, still boasting of the victory at Manassas Junction, were quick to criticize the setback a failure and labeled the general "Granny Lee" in a move many believed doomed any chances he had for advancement.

The Confederate successes on the battlefield were balanced against a political situation that saw Lincoln and his operatives hold Missouri, Kentucky, Maryland, and Delaware for the Union. Federal control of northern Kentucky and eastern Missouri provided strategic access to the major river systems piercing deeply into the Western Theater. The gathering Federal host in Washington was anxious for another shot at the enemy. Army morale was high, especially in the mostly untested brigade of Western regiments. "If we only get a chance," one pleaded.

The failure at Bull Run convinced the Union high command that the North's military effort needed to be reorganized to meet the requirements of a long war against a resilient enemy. And so Lincoln turned to 35-year-old George McClellan to succeed the ill-fated Irvin McDowell, who was rushed into Bull Run before his army was ready. Always ambitious and sure of himself, McClellan moved quickly by consolidating two separate departments under McDowell and Joseph Mansfield into his new army, to which he added on July 26 the Department of the Shenandoah under Nathaniel P. Banks. To his new regiments, brigades, and divisions McClellan gave a mighty name that evoked the thump of history's drums: the Army of the Potomac.

Trailed by a flock of bright staff officers the young general seemed to be everywhere those days, dressed in his well-tailored uniform while riding his fancy black charger "Dan Webster." McClellan's steady hand brought order to the army camps in and around Washington. He oversaw the expansion and strengthening of the city's defenses, and was always on hand to personally supervise the layout of this new fort or that new line of earthworks. Company streets were policed. Sentry posts were established. Camps of instruction were scheduled. Provost guards swept the city to gather up off-duty soldiers and send them back to their camps. From his headquarters on Jackson Square, McClellan moved through army camps, political meetings, and social circles with ease and dash. He looked and acted the part of the great general. The newspapers hailed him as the "young Napoleon," but his soldiers simply called him "Little Mac."

It didn't take long for the new volunteers to come under the general's spell. "McClellan is very active," one Wisconsin man wrote his hometown newspaper, "and is in his saddle a large portion of the time. It is said he even visits the camps . . .

in citizen's dress—so determined is he to know that everything goes right and that his soldiers are properly cared for. Such conduct on his part is certainly well calculated to win the confidence of his men." Captain Dawes found the general "a splendid looking man, just in the prime of life. The boys are all carried away with enthusiasm for him. His youthful appearance causes very many to distrust his abilities," he cautioned. "He looks, however, as though he knew his business." Not mentioned in the newspapers or the letters was how the days slid into weeks and the weeks into months with nothing accomplished by the growing army until the active campaigning season was past.[15]

Put Him in the Band!

In addition to the troubling military situation in Washington, a pressing matter concerned the soldiers of at least one of King's four regiments. The command was serving as a provisional brigade and as a holding organization in which other regiments moved in and out on their way to various duty stations. As a result, a number of regiments passed through the organization and one of the few treats Wisconsin and Indiana soldiers enjoyed those long boring days was listening to the music played by the various bands at dress parade and between supper and tattoo "making the August air rich with martial music." Federal regulations allowed each volunteer regiment to have its own band of up to 24 musicians. In the event of a battle band members would help perform medical functions, such as setting up field hospitals and acting as stretcher-bearers to remove wounded from the field. The regulations included a pay scale for regimental musicians that had many making more per month than a regular enlisted man. The 5th Wisconsin band was generally regarded as one of the best in the Washington camps, but the band of the 2nd Wisconsin ran a close second. The 7th Wisconsin also brought a good band to Washington. "Each and every regiment believed and were ready to take an oath that their band was the best in the army," explained Loyd Harris, a young man who enjoyed the music and even brought his violin to camp. He added with some sadness that the men in his 6thWisconsin "were just as ready to wager anything from a box of cigars to a month's pay, rations included," that their regimental band was, without exception, the worst in the army. What did it matter if old Colonel Cutler drilled the 6th Wisconsin until the men marched like Regulars? What did it matter if Lt. Frank Haskell made the guard mount "a model for the whole army?" What did it matter if the men in the ranks were the pride of old Wisconsin? It always

15 *Mauston Star*, October 23, 1861; Dawes, *Service*, 21.

came down to the sorry performance of "that unfortunate brass band" that played just one tune—"The Village Quickstep"—at guard mount, dress parade, or on the march, over and over again, complained Harris. Even two decades later a veteran admitted that just the thought of that band "makes a cold chill creep over me." Another observer admitted that what he called that "peculiar" organization "had more dogged perseverance and fewer friends than anything of the kind in our neighborhood and the most emphatic bass drum I ever heard."[16]

The whole band matter reached a head during a brigade review. It was enough to "try the patience of a martyr," Dawes grumbled to his brother, citing "the performance of that contemptible band of ours. They played such slow time music that we passed the review officer at about forty-seven paces a minute. We had to hold one leg in the air and balance on the other while we waited for music." It was, some in the ranks complained, old Colonel Cutler's fault. They blamed him because he had no ear for music and used the band as a place to hide the awkward or useless soldier. It became so troublesome, one soldier admitted, that "if any man in the regiment is caught in a rascally trick, the whole regiment yells, 'Put him in the brass band.'" One private claimed the band's "discordant tootings" should have "brought a deserved shower of defunct eggs, but at that time we were willing to endure anything to whip secession."[17]

Cutler did not seem to mind that his band could not carry more than one tune, but Adjutant Haskell, who always did things in a neat and orderly way, was driven to despair. What made it more awkward was the fact that if the 6th Wisconsin had the worst band in the army, it may have had the best drum major. William Whaley was regarded "with pride and affection as the finest adornment of the regiment"—a leader of "stately" military bearing who "snuffs the air and spurns the ground like a war horse." One officer said that Whaley could "hold his head higher and whirl his baton faster than any other drum major" in the army. Soldiers came from miles around just to watch Whaley and his drummers and fifers parade the regiment. Pride always comes before the fall, however, and for Whaley and the regiment that moment arrived in the Grand Review ordered by McClellan that first November of the war.[18]

King's brigade was assigned the job of preparing the field, and his Westerners marched out each day to work on the parade ground. They carried with them

16 Harris, *Telegraph*, March 11, 1883; Dawes, *Service*, 30.

17 Loyd Grayson Harris, "Music in the Army, Chapter 2nd," *Milwaukee Sunday Telegraph*, November 26, 1882.

18 Dawes, *Service*, 30.

muskets and full cartridge boxes, and routinely complained about the need to carry the heavy ammunition. An agreement was reached to leave behind the cartridges. When the work was completed, Maj. Gen. Irvin McDowell ordered the brigade march on the ground to make sure it was ready. The brigade was halted and had stacked arms when Confederate artillery opened up on a picket post about one mile away. McDowell ordered King to rush his brigade to the danger point, utterly unaware that their cartridge boxes were empty. King turned to the colonels and repeated the order. After a long moment, Fairchild of the 2nd Wisconsin replied, "I am informed that the 2nd Wisconsin is without ammunition." The colonels of the other regiments reported the same. "General King appeared displeased, though I believe he knew it, but could not, of course, at the time confess it," explained one soldier. "General McDowell was in a great rage, and ordered the brigade to quarters with a sharp rebuke, and sent a staff officer post haste for Augur's brigade, which came forward at the double quick. We passed them not far from the crossroads. They were swearing mad at us, and did not hesitate to express themselves as they passed."[19]

The Grand Review was never forgotten. It was a sight that "no man this side of the Ocean has probably seen the like of," recalled an officer. A man in ranks agreed, adding that it was one of "the grandest sights I ever witnessed." One Westerner said the regiments marched that day "with eyes steady to the field without even a glance at either side. . . . [W]e were proud and thoroughly freemen, we were all volunteers, proud in that position, we were not forced into service, but had left our homes to fight for what we considered the best government on earth." The display included ninety regiments of infantry, twenty batteries of artillery and upwards of 5,000 cavalry moving at once all in sight with "all the pomp & circumstance of war." President Lincoln, members of his cabinet, and about 20,000 spectators watched. Captain Bragg of the 6th Wisconsin wrote that McClellan and his "splendidly mounted staff," with Lincoln alongside, rode at a fast gait "along the entire lines in front of each battalion—cheer after cheer filled the air as he passed, caps were flung high in the air."

One Badger took the opportunity to write home that "Abe looks first rate, and is not a homely man by any means. I think he will live to hang Jeff Davis yet." When the mounted party reached the Western regiments, however, the men offered the proper salutes—but remained deathly silent. "We have been taught and teach our men that perfect silence in the ranks is evidence of the true and well disciplined soldier," was how one officer explained the actions. "I was in command of this, and

19 Stine, *Army of the Potomac*, 103-104. Stine was a member of the 19th Indiana.

sat looking grimly to the front." McClellan and Lincoln took no note of the silence.[20]

It took five hours for the army to pass, but the day would come to a hard ending for the 6th Wisconsin. Embarrassed by the ill-tooting of their band, the young captains met in secret to talk, argue, and complain before coming up with a plan—a true Western plan to go forward with confidence. The scheme put Drum Major Whaley and his fifer and drummers at the head of the marching regiment so all eyes would lock upon their gyrations. The band would march silently just behind and could pass the reviewing stand unnoticed because they would not be playing.

Finally, the critical moment arrived. Whaley, puffed up with the honor of leading the regiment, was at his very best, pawing the air, spinning his baton, and leaning back almost to the point of falling. As he approached the stand, Little Mac caught notice of him and was "so overcome by the lofty pomposity" that the general took off his kepi and waved it as Whaley passed. The recognition came just as Whaley was indulging in a special "top loftical gyration of his baton" that he had been practicing as a surprise. Up . . . up . . . up went spinning baton to the long "ooh" of the crowd. It hung just an instant at the top of the arc before picking up speed as it plunged to the ground. At the last moment—his eyes transfixed on the device—Whatley's concentration broke and to the horror of the Wisconsin men— and accompanied by the gasps of the thousands of watchers—the twirling baton slipped through his hand. The drum major frantically dropped to his hands and knees in a mad scramble to pick up the bouncing shaft. "From the topmost height of glory he was plunged into the deepest gulf of despair," explained Dawes. The men of the silent regimental band, not knowing what to do in the face of such disaster, did the only thing they could and struck up the discordant "Village Quickstep." The lines of the 6th Wisconsin—some of the men losing time and stepping on the heels of the man in front—went past the reviewing stand as crooked as "a rail fence," wrote one of the marchers in despair.[21]

The tramp back to camp was a long and silent one, the brigade marching along a road lined with civilians and visitors. Among the four regiments several were noted as fine singers, none better than Sgt. John Ticknor of the Lemonweir Minute Men. And it was on that somber and troubling occasion that the young soldier, "as he was wont to do on such occasions," wrote Dawes, "led out with his strong and clear and beautiful tenor voice, 'Hang Jeff Davis on a southern apple tree.' The

20 Brown, letter to wife, November 23, 1861; Bragg, letter to wife, November 21, 1861; Henry Allyn, journal; Henry F. Young, letter, November 21, 1861.

21 Dawes, *Service*, 30; Harris, *Telegraph*, November 12, 1882.

whole regiment joined the grand chorus, 'Glory, glory hallelujah, as we go marching on.' We often sang this, the John Brown song, to our visitor appeared the 'Glory of the coming of the Lord,' and in our 'burnished rows of steel' and in the 'hundred circling camps' on Arlington [Heights] which were before her, Julia Ward Howe, our visitor, has said that the singing of the John Brown song by the soldiers on the march, and the scenes of that day and evening inspired her to the composing of the Battle Hymn of the Republic. We at least help to swell the chorus."[22]

With the excitement of the Grand Review behind them, the men passed the long hours of camp life by holding social gatherings, singing, listening to band concerts, organizing chess and checker tournaments, writing letters home, and waging the endless battle of ridding their clothing of lice and their bedding of what they called "graybacks." One pastime sure to cause excitement, recalled one of the Rock County men in the 2nd Wisconsin, Alvin Eager, a 19-year-old farmer from Union, was capturing a field mouse and slipping it into the trouser leg of a sleeping comrade. During the colder months, snowball fights offered some welcomed action, as did the chill fresh air. Before the weather prevented it, the Wisconsin men enjoyed walking down to willows along the edge of the Potomac River to watch the recently departed 5th Wisconsin drill. Brigade commander Winfield Scott Hancock, who was not yet well known, had "a voice like a trumpet." His orders and drills were sometimes complex, especially for citizen-soldier officers trying to learn such things as "Third battalion, deploy column, quick, march!" The flurry of orders often confused the 5th's Col. Amasa Cobb, which in turn triggered Hancock's "ringing, bell like tones, 'Colonel Cobb, where the damnation are you going with that battalion?'" Of course the Wisconsin boys watching from across the river would stand and chant in a fine imitation of General Hancock: "Colonel Cobb, where the damnation are you going with that battalion?" The boys liked to call the performance "Hancock whispering to his brigade."[23]

22 Dawes, *Service*, 29. Julie Ward Howe said later it was a Vermont regiment singing outside her window that inspired her to draft the new words. Bands were mustered with the first thirteen Wisconsin regiments, but when the war expanded following the defeat at Bull Run in July of 1861, the government questioned the value of regimental bands and began getting rid of them. As a result, Congress halted the enlistment of new regimental bands beginning in October of 1861, and permitted the discharge of musicians in January 1862. Most of the musicians in the Western regiments were gone by the fall of 1861, although some of them were mustered into the newly organized brigade band. Russ Horton, "Behind the Music: The Iron Brigade Band," *The Bugle: Newsletter of the Wisconsin Veterans Museum*, Volume 16:2, September 2010, 6-7.

23 Eager Family records compiled by Jennifer Eager Ehle; Dawes, *Service*, 24. Eager's mother had died in 1850 and his father in February 1861 of injuries received while unloading grain at Janesville.

Temperance-minded brigade officers battled camp drinking and the playing of cards and other games of chance. One private reported that in camp at Washington were "whole platoons of liquor stores, and then more liquor stores, and then, traveling on, you just begin to come to the liquor stores." Whiskey reached the camps in a "modest and demure way," wrote another soldier. "Cans, labeled 'Oysters,' and 'Pickles' and 'Preserved meats,' are very popular with the army." The nearby division under Louis Blenker, a German who served in several military positions in Europe before fleeing to America when the 1848 socialist revolutions failed, was a temptation. The two-brigade division was mostly manned by Germans. One of the customs in Teutonic military organizations of 1861, including regiments at Camp Randall during the early days of the war, was to make sure the regimental storekeeper kept a good supply of fresh lager beer. The brew had to be shipped daily and consumed with some haste to avoid spoilage. A Western boy, especially with a proper soldier attitude, made it to Blenker's camp on a regular basis along with many "who did not belong to the German division." All of them "filled up on lager beer and sang funny songs on the way back."[24]

Johnny "Tough One" Cook of the Irish Company found such excursions exactly to his liking: "German enthusiasm always ran high. They sell whiskey in quantities to suit; we do not, so our boys visit BLENKER frequently. Formerly, they would go over in small squads and some liberal German soldier would meet them with, 'Does you fight mit Blenker?' They reply would be 'Yah.' 'Dat is good. Come and take some lager beer.'" Cook joined the army "not for my country (being nothing but a boy did not know what that meant; did not know what my duty to country was), but for the sake of seeing the sunny south that I had heard so much about and to be considered brave." But he admitted that he "had cheek, which was very necessary to have in the army. When plenty of the boys were dry, I was wet. Some are awful slow in getting around."[25]

In the coming weeks the regiments camped about Arlington Heights assumed the look of real soldiers when their state militia gray coats and caps were replaced

24 John H. Cook, "Cook's Time in the Army," manuscript, August 9, 1865, John H. Cook Papers, Wisconsin Historical Society.

25 John H. Cook, "The Tough One Again," *Milwaukee Sunday Telegraph*, April 8, 1883; Charles Robinson, *Green Bay Advocate*, January 2, 1862. Robinson, who served as brigade quartermaster, was the editor of the *Advocate* before the war. Blenker, a leading member of the 1848 revolutionary government in German state of Bavaria, immigrated to the United States in 1849. A farmer and New York City businessman, he was commissioned colonel of the 8th New York and saw limited service at First Bull Run. Blenker was discharged in March of 1863 and died October 31 of the same year from injuries he had suffered in a fall from his horse earlier in the war.

Private Aaron Yates, Lemonweir Minute Men,
Co. K, 6th Wisconsin

Probably taken in the winter of 1861-62, Yates is shown here wearing the
newly issued frock dress coat. He had not yet received the Model 1858 felt
black hat that would make the brigade distinctive. *Carroll Institute for Civil War Studies*

with standard Federal blue. The changeover started first in the various companies
of the ragged and needy 2nd Wisconsin with the unusual issue of dark blue wool
trousers (the other regiments received sky blue trousers), a blue wool nine-button
frock coat, and the Model 1858 black felt hat, all of the kind worn by the Regular
Army. "The boys no longer look like beggars, with ventilated suits of clothing, but
present a very neat, tidy and soldier-like appearance," one of the Badgers reported

Private John Bissett, Columbia County Cadets,
Co. B, 7th Wisconsin

Bissett had this photo taken before the issue of the full Iron Brigade
uniform in 1861-1862. It is a good example of the transition from state gray
to Federal issue. *Brian Hogan*

in October. "Their new uniform consists of a handsome blue frock coat, pants of
the same, high felt hat, blue cord and black plume; now if we only had good rifles
instead of the sheet iron muskets, we should be fitted out." Another 2nd Wisconsin
volunteer picked up his pen to write to his hometown newspaper: "We now have
our entire new suit, all dark blue, with army hats with plume—the handsomest
uniform in the service." A 7th Wisconsin man noted in his diary that the new

The boys from Appleton, Bragg's Rifles, Co. E, 6th Wisconsin

Taken at Camp Randall, these seven were all from the Appleton area serving in Co. E, Bragg's Rifles, 6th Wisconsin. Front left to right: George W. White, John J. Dillon, Charles D. Elliott, James F. Parkhurst. Rear: Worthie H. Patton, William A. Dillon, Lyman L. White. *William J. K. Beaudot / Milwaukee Sunday Telegraph*

clothing made the men in his regiment "look very well . . . especially when they put on their tall hats."[26]

In all the regiments, the replacement of blue for gray continued here and there by company and by regiment. "In a few days the men will receive new uniforms of blue, the new U.S. regulation pattern," a 6th Wisconsin soldier reported home, "the grey is to be thrown away; it being exclusively worn by the rebels. Some of our regiments in grey were fired upon by our own men at the battle of Bull's Run, supposing them to be the enemy. Such mistakes will hereafter being prevented." It would not be until late October 1861, however, before the changeover for the 6th Regiment was complete and the remaining grey uniforms, except for pants and

26 *Wisconsin Newspaper Volumes*, vol. 1; Papers of John Webb, La Crosse Historical Society; Charles Walker, diary, May 6, 1862.

overcoats, ordered, packed, and boxed for return to Wisconsin. Once they returned the gray issue, however, volunteers worried they were being charged double for the new uniforms—the blue issue being deducted from their monthly pay of $13. The change was especially slow for the 7th Wisconsin, which arrived in gray. Private James M. Perry scribbled in his diary on October 23, 1861, that he had received one cap at sixty-three cents, the price for Federal forage caps. It was not until Nov. 27 that he received "1 dress coat" at the price of $6.71. The allotment was part of 838 "Infantry Frock Coats" received by the 7th Wisconsin.[27]

Many of the boys in the three Wisconsin regiments were sorry to see the old state gray caps replaced. The Wisconsin uniforms were of excellent quality, one volunteer argued, "except the dress caps and that was something wonderfully and fearfully made." Using what he said were carpenter terms he described the shako-like headgear as "made of hair cloth, the frame and studding of wire and whalebone, and the siding of gray cloth; the inside finish of black alpaca, and the cornice based boarded, and outside trimming of patent leather, the front vizor or porch square with front elevation and projecting on a level; a rear vizor or piazza extending downwards at one-third pitch, and the whole heavily and strong put together according to specification." The use of both a front and back visor was troubling, but as the boys stood around, hands in pockets, discussing the cap, one Irish private "solved the vexed problem" in an undisputable manner: "That we were fi'tin, the inimy couldn't tell win we ware advancin' or retreatin.'" The explanation was accepted with solemn nods "as the only correct and reasonable hypothesis." The caps also provided many hours of entertainment. When placed on the ground and stepped on, the caps "sprang up refreshed after every disaster, the hair cloth acting as an indestructible spring to restore them to the original shape after the pressure was withdrawn, and it was not till they were remodeled by taking out the hair cloth and cutting off the rear vizor that the boys took to them kindly and generally."[28]

The Model 1858 Hardee dress hat made the best impression. It was a showy black felt affair, looped up on the side with a brass eagle and trimmed with an infantry-blue cord, black plume, brass infantry bugle, company letter and regimental numeral. "We have a full blue suit, a fine black hat nicely trimmed with bugle and plate and ostrich feathers," boasted a proud 7th Wisconsin man to the

27 *Wisconsin Newspaper Volumes*, vol. 1; Regimental Order Book, 6th Wisconsin Infantry (Record Group No. 94), National Archives Washington, D.C., General Regimental Orders No. 27 (1861); Papers of Lt. H. P. Clinton, quartermaster, 7th Wisconsin Infantry, Milwaukee Public Museum, "Civil War Papers," vol. 3, 80 and 82.

28 Sullivan, *Telegraph*, May 23, 1886.

Private Charles Keeler, Prescott Guards, Co. B, 6th Wisconsin

Keeler is wearing the full Iron Brigade uniform of black hat, frock coat, and linen leggings. This picture was probably taken in early 1862. He was shot through the legs at Gettysburg.

Alan Nolan Collection

folks back home, "and you can only distinguish our boys from the regulars, by [our] good looks." The black hats made the tall Westerners look even taller and would give them a distinctive look on both the drill field and the battlefield.[29]

One bit of excitement lifted the boredom of the training camps when Capt. William Strong of the 2nd Wisconsin returned wounded from a trip to a sentry post. A group of Confederates, he explained, had captured him but failed to take his pair of pistols. Near "a thicket of undergrowth," he pulled the pistols, one in each hand, and shot the two infantrymen and ran. "The confusion of my captors was apparently so great that I had nearly reached cover before shots were fired at me," explained the injured captain. "One ball passed through my left cheek—passing out of my mouth. Another one, a musket ball, went through my canteen." According to Strong, he exchanged several shots with two mounted cavalrymen and knocked one off his horse. Another shot at the second horseman failed when the gun misfired. A blast from the enemy's carbine, fired so close that it "burned the cloth out the size of one's hand," passed through his coat and shirt. Some of the Badgers were unsure Strong's story was completely true, but a double-page spread in *Harpers Weekly*

29 *Mineral Point Tribune*, October 22, 1861. For a description of the evolution of the Iron Brigade uniform, see Howard Michael Madaus, "The Uniform of the Iron Brigade at Gettysburg, July 1, 1863," in Herdegen and Beaudot, *Railroad Cut*, Appendix 3, 301-367.

"showing the position of the captain and the rebels" along with an article applauding the captain's gallantry and bravery ended most doubts.[30]

More troubling that fall was the appointment of army boards to examine the qualifications of the officers of the volunteer regiments to see if they lacked military experience and/or were unfit for command. Most of the regimental officers were appointed by the governors and the appointments were not always made on merit but political expediency. The effort by army authorities to weed out incompetent officers caused a considerable stir and quickly reshaped leadership in the regiments of King's brigade. It is difficult to determine which officers left on their own accord and which resigned under pressure, citing illness, family responsibilities, or other causes.

At first glance the purge seems to have singled out many of the German and Irish in command positions while passing over those who were "American-born" of certain social classes. The legislation providing for establishment of boards of examination was passed July 22, 1861, and the panels were soon active in the Army of the Potomac. General James Wadsworth was president of the board that examined officers in King's brigade. Six officers in the 19th Indiana resigned before the end of the year, most citing "domestic matters at home" as the reason for leaving. Colonel Sol Meredith escaped the examinations though several of his company officers thought he lacked military experience and was unfit for command. The 6th Wisconsin saw several officers resign "under the thin disguise of failure to pass examinations before a certain commission of officers." Irish Company D of Milwaukee (the Montgomery Guard) was stripped of Capt. John O'Rourke and both lieutenants, John Nichols and Patrick H. McCauley. In the Beloit Star Rifles, the examinations claimed Capt. M. A. Northrup (one of the organizers of a Lincoln appearance at Beloit before the war) and his lieutenants, George C. Montague and William Allen. Other forced resignations included Lts. Daniel K. Noyes of the Sauk County Riflemen, Amos S. Johnson of the Anderson Guards, and John Crane of the Lemonweir Minute Men, who had come to Mickey Sullivan's assistance in those early days at Mauston. Captain Leonard Johnson of the Anderson Guards resigned on December 13, and the physically imposing Capt. William Lindwurm of the German Citizen Corps of Milwaukee went home ill on December 11. The resignation of Lt. Col. Julius Atwood of the 6th Wisconsin moved Benjamin Sweet into the second spot and elevated Edward Bragg of Company E to major.

30 Otis, *Second Wisconsin*, 43-44. Strong's full report can be found *ibid.*, 115-117. *Wisconsin State Register*, October 5, 1861.

Corporal Cornelius Wheeler, Miners' Guard,
Co. I, 2nd Wisconsin

Wheeler is wearing the leggings and early issue dark blue Regular Army
trousers given only to the 2nd Wisconsin. Light blue trousers were the issue
to the other regiments. *Wisconsin Historical Society 25110*

Rufus Dawes found Crane's resignation troubling, for he believed the young lieutenant was "making a fine young officer" and was "one of the best instructors in the manual of arms in the regiment." He blamed Crane's "too close a sympathy" with the Irish officers of Montgomery Guard for bringing the "attack upon him." Lieutenant Edwin Brown of Fond du Lac County escaped the examinations and wrote home blaming the purge on Cutler and Bragg. "They have caused several Capts and Lieutenants to be reported for a vigorous examination while myself and others have been allowed to go scot free although we probably knew no more than those who were examined. Some who passed the ordeal, that they desired to get rid of, have been annoyed in other ways." According to Brown, the "consequence is quite a bad state of feeling in some of the companies which I fear will impair our efficiency when called upon to fight." He concluded: "Most of those officers [who resigned] opposed Bragg's promotion. This much of my letter," he warned his wife, "must not be made public at all, as my head would come off if it were known that I had let 'the cat out of the bag.'"[31]

Sickness also swept the companies those winter months. The hardest hit, naturally, enough, were the backwoods boys, for they had not developed a natural immunity as children. Men from cities were more likely to have been exposed to disease. The first illness to strike was usually measles, followed by small pox. Regimental doctors who knew little more than their patients used whiskey and rest to treat most of the ailments. Just as troubling was a form of chronic diarrhea called the "Virginia Quickstep" or "the bloody flux" by the men. This disease left soldiers weak, dehydrated, and drained of energy. In some cases the disease ran its course quickly and the patient survived. When the disease lingered, however, death was a frequent result. Contaminated water and food spread typhoid, various fevers, diarrhea, and severe headaches. Because these symptoms were very similar to dysentery, the treatments were much the same—a variety of mostly ineffective drugs.

At one point that long winter, 263 of the 3,669 men in the brigade were reported on the sick list. Sixty soldiers in the Indiana regiment died of disease during those late months of 1861; no regiments escaped unscathed. Illness peeled away eighty-five enlisted men from the 6th Wisconsin, all of whom were sent home for good. In the Lemonweir Minute Men, twenty-five caught the measles and another ten fell sick from measles and other ailments. Rufus Dawes, however, was able to report to his sister on August 24: "My men are getting through with the

---

31 Dawes, *Service*, 26-27; Brown, letter to his wife, October 22, 1861; Gaff, *Bloody Field*, 87-88. Six officers from the 19th Indiana resigned before the end of the year.

measles, and I hope to soon have out full ranks. We are drilling every day and improving rapidly."[32]

Mud was sometimes a problem, recalled Dawes. On one occasion, he and his company were marching out to a sentry post when "the mud rolled down upon the men in a kind of avalanche. They wade up the hill through a moving stream of red clay mortar." A few days later he reported: "Mud-mud-mud precludes drill, everything."[33] The Western boys took the hardship in stride. Confined to their tents on rainy days, they "beguiled the weary hours" by "croaking like frogs, quacking like ducks and barking like dogs." On the march one would call out, "When our army marched down to Bull Run, what did the big bull frog say?" Hundreds would respond in "deep base, bull frog croaks, 'Big Thing, Big Thing.'" The leader would then call out, "When our army came back from Bull Run, what did the little frogs say?" "Run Yank. Run Yank" they screeched in reply, offering "an excellent imitation of a swamp full of frogs." In the 6th Wisconsin, one leader asked, "What does the bully Sixth say?" The soldiers, in "bull frog bass voices," answered, "Hit 'em again! Hit 'em again!" Said Dawes: "Brave boys, how they contended against adverse circumstances with their cheerful and courageous spirit."[34]

The job of learning to soldier proved a challenge for privates and officers. One remembered incident was a regimental drill involving the 7th Wisconsin and Colonel Vandor, the old Hungarian still working on his English. The regiment was firing blanks by front and rear ranks. Vandor was mounted and in his proper place behind the regiment in battle line when he ordered, "Rear rank, about face! Ready, aim . . ." The rear rank sharply came around and, according to the manual, leveled muskets. The "sudden innovation," one soldier remembered, "brought the long line of file closers and officers to their knees, while the gallant Lt. Col. and major was seen charging toward some friendly trees." The adjutant called out to Vandor, "Colonel, that is not correct; you will shoot the file closers." The stubborn Vandor replied, "I don't care a tam. If your colonel ish te mark, fire anyway." And so it was, continued the soldier, that "a thousand muskets emptied their blank cartridges at the noble colonel."

The colonel's harsh European manner (one of his orders required the hair of soldiers cut to one inch in length and beards trimmed once a month) upset his young frisky volunteers, especially when he called the officers "a worthless Set of

32 Dawes, *Service*, 26-27.

33 *Indianapolis Daily Journal*, November 27, 1861; *Wisconsin Newspaper Volumes*, vol. 3. Nolan, *Iron Brigade*, 307, note 16; Dawes, *Service*, 19-20.

34 *Ibid.*, 23.

Men." It was an insult hard to ignore, and a letter was drafted by Capt. Samuel Nasmith and signed by others asking Vandor to resign. To make matters worse, the letter was circulated to all brigade and division officers and the governor. By this time the situation was simply unmanageable and the old campaigner resigned on January 30, 1862, to take an appointment as the United States representative to Tahiti. Vandor had escaped the army examiners and critics, but his European manner and sharp temperament proved beyond his control. "Our Dutch Col. is at last removed," one soldier wrote. "The regiment came to the conclusion that he was too much a tyrant & sputter to command this glorious 7th." Some months after the resignation and in light of further developments, an anonymous letter to a Wisconsin newspaper put the matter in better context: "The officers feelings were hurt by his strictures on their military knowledge. They, as well as the men, were raw then and some of them have since regretted their opposition to him. . . . Had you [Vandor] adopted a less candid policy in your intercourse with men you would have been with us yet. It is but justice to say, however, that the military examining Boards could find no flaw in your ability, and that you voluntarily resigned."[35]

35 Special Order No. 5, October 9, 1861, Order Books of the 7th Wisconsin, Record Group 94, National Archives; Samuel Nasmith, letter, September 30, 1861, Nasmith Papers, Wisconsin Historical Society; *Wisconsin Newspaper Volumes*, vol. 3.

Henry Fonda,
Co. E, 7th Wisconsin

David Lyons

Capt. Geo Burchell,
24th Michigan

Kim Heltemes

1862

Iron Brigade of

the West

Mary Beman Gates

Author's Collection

An unidentified member of
the 7th Wisconsin

Author's Collection

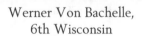

Werner Von Bachelle,
6th Wisconsin

Author's Collection

Part I: Black Hat Brigade

A Dashing Young Officer and a Maiden Fair

The weather turned harsh just before the New Year of 1862 and King's Western Brigade hunkered down at Arlington Heights to wait out the winter. Reveille was at 4:00 a.m. and the day ended with tattoo at 9:30 p.m. The weeks were first marked by a heavy schedule of drills and instruction. "The Colonel took us up hill and down double quick and by the right flank, right face, double quick march, close column on the tenth company, left flank, left face, double quick march," a Wisconsin farm boy wrote home. "After the drill was over we went back to camp, held dress parade, eat our supper; went to bed and slept til morning. Then we got up, washed up, combed our hair, ready for another day's labor at drill." Private Henry Allyn of the 2nd Wisconsin took stock of the year just ended: "It has indeed been a year fraught with the events of the most stirring kind. It has passed away amid scenes of bloodshed and war and the New Year has been ushered in much the same way. What may be the result at the close of 1862 no one can tell."

The sharply colder weather during the first weeks of 1862 sent the woodcutters deeper into the countryside because trees in the immediate area had all but disappeared. Except for picket patrols, active campaigning stopped and the days were spent gathering wood and hauling food, water, and other necessities. "I will never forget that awful winter," confessed one private. "The Potomac [River] froze and during the January thaw we were compelled to split puncheons and plank our street in order to be able to go from one end to the other, while the blood-thirsty editors at home were asking 'why don't the army move?'"[1]

---

1 Stephen Vesper, letter, to his sister, Clarissa, November 15, 1861, as quoted in Rena M. Knight, "The Civil War Letters of Stephen Vesper," *North-South Trader*, May-June 1989, 31-32; Henry Allyn, journal; Sullivan, *Milwaukee Sunday Telegraph*, May 16, 1886. Vesper was in the 6th Wisconsin.

One topic of interest around the cook fires, especially in the 7th Wisconsin, was the developing difficulty between Lt. Hollon Richardson of Chippewa Falls and Col. William Robinson. The Western Brigade's camp near the Arlington House across the river from Washington was a pleasant location, and Robinson was one of several officers who had wives and families, including his pretty daughter Leonora, visit him. The young lady was soon a favorite of the unattached officers. "Lieutenant Richardson was particularly well pleased with her," recalled Jerome Watrous. "Indeed, he soon learned to love her, and loved her very ardently, and her heart warmed toward him as thoroughly as his did toward her." Her father liked the handsome 25-year-old Richardson well enough as an officer and man, but he refused to allow his daughter to marry "a man who might be felled with windows made by rebel bullets the day after he became his son-in-law. He was emphatic in the matter and was not at all backward in making known his opposition to the proposed union."[2]

The objection was puzzling. A native of Poland, Ohio, and the son of a construction contractor, Richardson passed the bar in 1857 and moved to Wisconsin to practice law. He was elected prosecuting attorney of Chippewa County and was the first man from the county to enlist for the coming war. Gathering together a makeshift squad of volunteers, Richardson needed to get his recruits to Lodi where a company was being formed. Should they walk to Reed's Landing on the Mississippi River he was asked? "We'll use the river," he replied. Soon the detail was chopping and sawing and shaping a huge flat raft to carry them down the Chippewa River to the rally point. The sight of the arriving raft full of would-be soldiers was met there with laughter and cheers, and the volunteers from Chippewa County were labeled the "Wet Feet Division." Richardson developed into a capable officer. Despite the efforts of the young couple to win his approval, the colonel stubbornly continued to oppose the match.[3]

Of course, love would win out and the pair were married a few months later outside the colonel's influence and knowledge. There are two family stories about the ceremony. In the first, the lieutenant and Miss Robinson "met in Washington by accident—such as an accident, as they had carefully planned to bring about—and were married." In the second, told by a Richardson descendant, the pair were traveling together by carriage to Washington on May 9, 1862, to stand up at the wedding of another young couple. Sometime during the ride, the lieutenant (a relative called him a "a good talker") convinced Leonora to join him in a double

2 Jerome A. Watrous, "A Badger Traveler," *Milwaukee Sunday Telegraph*, December 22, 1878.

3 *Soldiers and Citizens Album of Biographical Record*, 2 vols. (Chicago, IL, 1888), vol. 2, 578-582.

wedding. It was "some months" before the old colonel discovered he had a new son-in-law, and the length of the deception made it all the worse. When Robinson found out "the true state of affairs he was unwise enough to let his angry passions come to the surface." In one report, the colonel went looking for Richardson with a revolver unaware that his wife had emptied it of bullets. In any case, the two officers were no longer on speaking terms and many months would pass—well into 1864— "before the sun shone, the ice broke and melted away and they became warm friends." In the meantime, however, the colonel and the lieutenant suffered through a stiff relationship watched with dismay by many in the brigade because Richardson was a great favorite and his new father-in-law was well respected as well.[4]

One casualty of the family difficulties was the 7th Wisconsin's Chaplain Samuel I. Brown of Beaver Dam, who resigned after the marriage was discovered. The rank and file believed the clergyman married the young couple without the colonel's permission and then denied it when confronted. "Being as he was not liked by any of the regiment," one soldier wrote home, "he was requested to resign or stand a court martial which ever he pleased." No one would miss Brown: "He has never done the Regiment the first particle of good. He preached but a very few sermons and then did not amount to but very little. What little he did was for the benefit of his pocket, not for the Regiment."[5]

The highlight of the Western Brigade's social events that winter was an impromptu banquet organized by the "prints"—editors, newspapermen, and printers of the 2nd Wisconsin—on the evening of January 17 to honor the memory of Benjamin Franklin. Captain David McKee of the 2nd Wisconsin was chosen as President of the Day. The toastmaster for the "grand supper" was Gilbert Woodward of La Crosse, then an enlisted man. He was remembered for his "short, witty and fine" poem written for the occasion. The invitations to the banquet were printed at the *Washington Chronicle* office, which published a full and complete report of the proceedings. There were letters from various generals, including George McClellan and Irvin McDowell, as well as a series of toasts and responses including one to the "Printer Volunteers," proclaiming their "shooting sticks will batter every type of treason, and knock the whole form into pi." Brigade commander Rufus King, late of the *Milwaukee Sentinel,* was unable to attend but was cited as "an editor, who, in fifteen years at the head of a political newspaper, never said an

---

4   Hollon Richardson family records.

5   George Eustice, letter to Mother, April 20, 1862, Civil War Museum, Kenosha, WI.

ungentlemanly word, nor did an unmanly thing." The music was provided by the 2nd Wisconsin band.[6]

One other matter of far reaching consequence that winter of 1861-62 was the addition of Battery B of the 4th U.S. Artillery to King's brigade. The outfit was one of the most famous organizations in the Old Army and one of thirty-six artillery companies (the "companies" officially became "batteries" in 1861) created in the artillery reorganization of 1821. Battery men fought as dragoons in the Seminole War and served with distinction as artillery at Monterrey and Buena Vista during the War with Mexico in the 1840s. Battery B was stationed at Camp Floyd, Utah, for the Mormon Uprising and served as cavalry escorts to guard the Pony Express route. In fact, it was a Pony Express rider who brought word of the firing on Fort Sumter. The battery was ordered overland to Fort Leavenworth in Kansas and then traveled by rail to Washington. Its commander was West Pointer Capt. John Gibbon.

Battery B was equipped with six Model 1857 muzzle-loaded 12-pound bronze smoothbores, often called "Napoleons" (a mobile field gun of the type favored by France's Napoleon III) or "Light Twelves" to distinguish them from an earlier model. They were officially categorized as "gun-howitzers" and got their name in part by the weight of the ammunition—a 4.62-inch caliber, 12-pound solid shot. Napoleons would prove the workhorses of the Army of the Potomac. In addition to solid shot, the guns fired bursting shells using a timed fuse as well as canister, a thin iron can of lead or iron balls packed in sawdust. The canister was used on infantry at close ranges, much like a blast of a giant shotgun.[7]

The December 1861 roll showed Battery B with three lieutenants and 47 enlisted men—well below a full complement. It was during this time that Gibbon, already a familiar figure to the volunteers of the 2nd, 6th, 7th Wisconsin and 19th Indiana, sought volunteers to fill his ranks. Standing before the assembled 6th Wisconsin, he had trouble convincing soldiers to join his battery, partly due to their distrust of West Pointers. Only one man stepped forward following his opening appeal. Colonel Cutler then intervened to explain again what was needed and then a "large number stepped forward." Cutler cautioned, "There, there, that will do—you needn't all come out—they don't want the whole regiment for the battery." Gibbon and two battery officers carefully picked the men from the various regiments. They would become some of the best artillerymen in the Army

---

6   Otis, *Second Wisconsin*, 45; Cornelius Wheeler Diary, Cornelius Wheeler Papers, Wisconsin Historical Society; *Milwaukee Sentinel*, letter, January 19, 1862.

7   The common shell, with bursting change and fuse, weighed 9.5 pounds.

Brigadier General John Gibbon—"Johnny, the War Horse"

Gibbon was the second commander of the Western Brigade, an Old Army no-nonsense Regular who is justifiably credited with turning his four Western regiments into an Iron Brigade. He would go on to a long and distinguished career, both during the Civil War and after. *Charles Foster*

of the Potomac. One volunteer called Battery B one of the best in service and explained why he made the transfer: "I pity the poor infantry when they move, for they have got to carry five days' rations in their knapsacks and three days in their

**Cpl. Jasper Daniels,
Fox Lake Citizen Guard,
Co. A, 2nd Wisconsin**

Daniels enlisted from Port Washington in 1861 and was soon promoted to corporal and then to sergeant. He veteranized in 1864 and served as quartermaster sergeant of the 2nd Wisconsin Independent Battalion. *Dan and Gretchen Farwell*

haversacks, besides their clothing and blanket, while we have only got a canteen of water to carry. When we get tired of walking we can ride. I never have been better suited than I am at present."[8]

The occasion of Washington's birthday in 1862 was marked in the camp with a formal formation and the booming of artillery salutes. King's regiments drew up in a "semicircle in close column" before the Arlington house. The general's Farewell Address was read and King offered a few remarks before closing with a call for cheers for the United States and the recent victories at Forts Henry and Donelson in Tennessee. "They were hearty cheers I tell you," recalled one soldier. The columns were then deployed in lines of battle and battalion volleys of blanks fired in honor of General Washington. At the first crash of muskets, Pvt. Mickey Sullivan of Company K received his first wound of the war—a whack on the back from a spinning steel musket ramrod fired by a careless private in the 7th Wisconsin standing behind the men of the 6th. The heavy bruising landed the Irishman in a hospital for two days.

Several other ramrods were also launched in that volley of "blanks" when soldiers forgot to withdraw the shafts. According to Pvt. William Ray in the 7th Wisconsin, one of the flying ramrods broke into three sections and dropped near him, "one piece going through the right leg of the man that stood behind me and

8 Watrous, *Milwaukee Sunday Telegraph*, September 7, 1884; Augustus Buell, *The Cannoneer: Recollections of Service in the Army of the Potomac* (Washington, D.C., 1897), 26. The battery train also included a battery wagon, mobile forge, and extra caissons. Adolphus Shepherd to Mother, Sisters and Brothers, February 15 and April 21, 1863.

another piece went through his bootleg. The other piece run into the ground with three inches of the mans foot that stood beside him. The but [butt] of the ramrod struck in his leg until he pulled it out. The but piece run through his leg to the boot on the other side and there stoped. The middle piece . . . went through bootleg in another place. The other piece not touching anybody." The firing of blanks continued for a number of seconds and Pvt. William Atkinson near Ray was struck and stepped out of line "stooped over." Ray saw Atkinson's musket on the ground and thought it had burst. A second look revealed the injured soldier "throw down the but of the ramrod [which had struck him] and it was bloody and I turned and shot and looked again and he was gone." Officers quickly picked up the pieces of the ramrod. As Ray attested, the incident "caused a great excitement." When the regiment got back to camp, he admitted, "there was two ramrods missing out of the Co." Atkinson's wound was minor, wrote Ray, the news welcomed in the Union Guards of Lancaster because he was a soldier "well liked by all [and] always at his post."[9]

The volley fire demonstration on George Washington's birthday did little to improve the relationship between the regiments.

Ready to Smell Powder

The winter of 1861-62 witnessed Union success in the Western Theater and the rise of Ulysses S. Grant with his capture of Fort Henry on the Tennessee River and Fort Donelson on the Cumberland. The war in the Eastern Theater, however, stalled when Army of the Potomac commander George B. McClellan found one reason after another for delay. His army needed to be outfitted. His army needed more training. His army needed to know the dispositions of the enemy outside Washington. His relationship with President Lincoln went from barely cordial (in part due to McClellan's inbred disdainful view of the lower class origins of his commander-in-chief) to downright hostile. There was no important military movement in the three months following Bull Run, during which time the National Army at Washington swelled to 120,000 men while facing some 50,000 Confederates south of the Potomac. McClellan always believed himself outnumbered, and never found the will for immediate action. He saw every possibility for defeat but rarely the possibility for victory—a man of intelligence, training, and personal courage paralyzed by the fear of failure.

9 Sullivan, *Irishman*, 38; Gaff, *Bloody Fields*, 108; Ray, *Iron Brigade*, 54-55. Atkinson enlisted at Ellenboro on August 19, 1861, and mustered out July 3, 1865. *Wisconsin Roster*, vol. 1, 558.

In addition to organizing and training his large army, the young general also spent much of his time in an ongoing effort to remove and replace his immediate superior Winfield Scott, commander-in-chief of all the Union armies. The elderly general was barely able to walk because of age and girth, and McClellan believed the old hero of the War with Mexico was slipping into his dotage. It was a classic example of an ambitious and talented younger man trying to replace an older man that he felt was in the way. When he was finally offered the higher post on Scott's resignation, McClellan was asked if being commander-in-chief of the entire war effort and leading the Army of the Potomac was too much responsibility for one man. "I can do it all," he replied.[10]

His relationship with the president was one of the most curious in American history. The young general, a life-long Democrat, misjudged Lincoln's intelligence and from the first made no secret of his dislike of the loud and active new Republicans and their abolitionist allies. His letters to his wife included snide references about Lincoln and boasts of how he kept the administration in the dark about his military plans to the point that he was making an effort to "dodge all enemies in the shape of 'browsing Presidents, etc.'" One night in November 1861, Lincoln and Secretary of State William Seward went to visit McClellan. Told the general would soon be home, the two waited. When McClellan returned and learned of his visitors, he walked upstairs without seeing them. Thirty minutes later a servant informed Lincoln and Seward that the general had gone to bed.

The two had different views about the war effort. The general had many old friends and former classmates in the Southern army and he wanted to fight a war designed for political settlement rather than military conquest. He opposed what he viewed as crude and misguided Republican attempts to curtail or control slavery and believed a harsh solution to end the conflict would alienate Southerners and force a long bloody war. McClellan seemed blind to the idea that such policy decisions were not his to make. His views, expressed freely in camp and to influential friends, spread to his volunteers, raising the notion that the Army of the Potomac must be protected against the very ill-informed government officials who created it. In the end, McClellan became too protective of the great army he forged. The very soldiers he sought to shield would pay the price.[11]

10 See Russel H. Beatie, *Army of the Potomac: McClellan Takes Command, September 1861-February 1862*, vol. 2 (New York, 2004), 266.

11 Lance J. Herdegen, *The Men Stood Like Iron: How the Iron Brigade Won its Name* (Bloomington, IN, 1997), 214-215; William Harries, "In the Ranks at Antietam," Otis, *Second Wisconsin*, 270 (a typed manuscript is also in the Jerome A. Watrous Papers, WHS); Fitch, *Echoes*, 304. McClellan and his officers believed their service and patriotism earned them a special voice in the conduct

If McClellan's influence drove much of the nation's history of those early days of the war it also was a significant force in the development of a Western Brigade in his Army of the Potomac. Most of the young volunteer officers came under Little Mac's spell and endorsed his view of the administration. However, one new lieutenant in the 6th Wisconsin, Edwin Brown of Fond du Lac, saw the danger in recent developments. "Everything that patriotism could devise, everything that the almost unlimited resources of the North could provide, has been lavishly poured at the feet of McClellan," Brown wrote. "President, Cabinet & people respond to his every wish, almost before it is expressed, and wo[e] to him if the vast power that he exercises is not wielded for the general good. Wo[e] to him, and the administration that appointed him, if the hour of trial he provides incompetent, or insufficient for the emergency—an enraged soldiery and an outraged people would be difficult to control."

Brown's friend and immediate commander, Capt. Edward Bragg, who would use his war days as a stepping stone to a three-decade career in Congress, reached a slightly different conclusion. McClellan—for all his failings—also did much that was good, Bragg believed. A life-long Democrat and in his soldier days always critical of Lincoln, Bragg told a meeting of veterans at Chicago long after the war that the Army of the Potomac was "organized, equipped and drilled by one who, whatever else may be said of him, had no superior in that branch of the service, and in defense. He was a master of grand strategy, but he did not meet the requirements of popular demand by more rapid progress. . . . He blended the untutored enthusiasm of a nation unused to war, and taught it by bitter experience to yield itself to the cunning hand of discipline. . . . It was this drill and discipline that made the army."[12]

Finally, in early 1862, McClellan came forward with a bold plan to flank the Confederate forces in Virginia by moving his large army to Richmond via water. Desperate for any action at all President Lincoln agreed—but with the provision that sufficient troops be left to protect Washington and seize the important railroad connections at Manassas Junction upon the expected Confederate withdrawal south to counter McClellan's move toward Richmond. Long frustrated by

---

of the Civil War. Unfortunately, Little Mac's shadowy game of politics and service would forever follow and forever hamper the Army of the Potomac. His words and attitude created a lingering mistrust within his army that "the meddling politician and the bullheaded Senator"— as one Wisconsin soldier boldly put it—would use the army's fortunes for their own political ends.

12 Brown, letter to wife, October 13, 1861; Edward Bragg, speech to an Army of the Potomac reunion at Chicago, undated; Edward Bragg Papers, WHS.

One of the Huckleberries

This unidentified member of Co. A, Lodi Guards, 7th Wisconsin, posed for a studio portrait with his black hat set nearby showing a distinctive hat cord. *Dale Niesen Collection*

McClellan's inactivity and under political pressure to do something, on March 8 the president directed the establishment of the corps organization of the Army of the Potomac.

The Union army would be made up of four infantry corps. McDowell's division, which included the Western Brigade, became the First Corps along with divisions under Gens.

Adj. Charles Dean, 2nd Wisconsin

A veteran of First Bull Run, Dean enlisted at Boscobel in Co. K. He was captured in September 1862 and rejoined his regiment on December 22, 1862. Dean resigned on May 18, 1863. *Wisconsin Veterans Museum*

Officers of Co. I, 7th Wisconsin

Left to right: Lt. Joseph N. P. Bird, Capt. George H. Walther, and Lt. Christopher Lefler. Alonzo Gambel, their black servant, is standing in the shadow of the tent. *Wisconsin Historical Society 25588*

George A. McCall and William B. Franklin. The command of the corps was given to McDowell, who had been demoted after his failure at Bull Run in July. Rufus King of Wisconsin was promoted to division commander. His brigade was temporarily taken over by its senior colonel, Lysander Cutler of the 6th Wisconsin. No sooner had the army's reorganization been announced than word reached Washington of a Confederate withdrawal south from northern Virginia to an area closer to the Rappahannock River. McClellan ordered an immediate advance into the Virginia countryside and Cutler's brigade joined the movement on March 10.

When the orders for active service were read to the assembled ranks of the 7th Wisconsin, the men were told to be "held in readiness to march at a minute's warning with knapsacks packed, and three days rations cooked, ready at all times." Overcome by the excitement of the moment, an officer stepped forward, pulled the hat off his head, and waved it high while yelling, "Boys, if them orders exactly suit you, you may cheer!" The orders suited them fine, and the ranks roared out a yell.

"You better believe that we roused him up three times good," recalled one soldier in a letter home. "The boys seemed to be in the best of spirits, and anxious to smell powder."[13]

The careful and deliberate advance of the army to Centreville, however, found only abandoned camps with empty parapets and wooden logs for cannons. The countryside was in ruins. "You can hardly form any idea of the terrible havoc and desolation this war has occasioned in old Virginia," a Western farmer-turned-soldier wrote home. "Splendid houses deserted, some knocked partly to pieces, some burnt up and one large mill past still burning, fences all burnt up, excellent orchards entirely destroyed. It is a sorrowful sight, but they have brought it on themselves." The road back to the Union camps was "strewn with gloves, socks, shoes, blankets and all kinds of clothing thrown away by our troops who were too tired to carry them." It began to rain and the roads became muddy and slow going. Private Julius Murray of the 6th Wisconsin stopped to throw away a blanket, a pair of new shoes, two shirts, one pair of boots and one pair of drawers. His son also emptied his knapsack of some clothing and a $4.00 pair of boots. Major Edward Bragg, who was "wet through," came up and asked what they were doing. "I told him I was lighting up, well said he—hurry up for we all have a hard time of it." The great advance was a bust. "The men were greatly disappointed. They had made their wills, and written their farewell letters, and wanted to fight a battle," confessed a Badger officer.[14]

McClellan's limited activity and delay in beginning his flanking movement led Lincoln to a hard decision: if McClellan would not move the army he would do so himself. He issued a presidential order directing McClellan's advance on Richmond via the Chesapeake Bay to begin no later than March 13—provided the capital at Washington was left "entirely secure" in the judgment of McClellan and his four corps commanders. Of course, the developments and the details of the presidential order and the recent reorganization of the army were carried in the columns of the Washington newspapers and made their way south. In the Western regiments, the news was received with enthusiasm. Finally, after all these months of drilling and waiting, they might see action. While the rest of the army was to travel by boat, McDowell's corps would operate in northern Virginia and move overland toward Richmond to threaten the Confederate flank as Little Mac and the balance of the Army of the Potomac embarked for the move on Richmond. The order also assigned the First Corps to the Department of the Rappahannock. As a result,

13 Hugh Perkins, letter, March 17, 1862.

14 Dawes, *Service*, 39-40; Murray, letter, March 17, 1862.

McDowell's 23,000 men, another army under Maj. Gen. John C. Fremont at Wheeling in western Virginia, and a third Federal force under Maj. Gen. Nathaniel P. Banks, head of the Department of the Shenandoah, were left to protect Washington.

On April 4, McDowell's brigades tramped out of Washington for Fredericksburg, Virginia, the proposed headquarters for the Department of the Rappahannock about midway between the warring capitals. The blue columns reached Fairfax Court House and moved on Bristoe Station south of the Manassas Junction on the Orange and Alexandria Railroad. Heavy rain and wet snow swept the area, turning roads to mud and stalling the advance until April 13 at a place the soldiers called "Camp Snowy." The brigades halted again for a week at Catlett's Station to make repairs to damaged tracks on the Orange and Alexandria Railroad. The army finally reached Falmouth on April 23. Enemy pickets could be seen roaming the hills around historic Fredericksburg on the far side of the river. The stop at the "thriving little village" was remembered as a happy one, especially for some of the boys in the 2nd Wisconsin who used captured Confederate currency to clear the shelves in three stores.

The long march to Falmouth had been a hard one in wicked weather. A "heavy whiskey" ration was issued one night while the brigade was camped in a muddy field, its members "wet, wood scarce and mud deep, air chilly and everything in a forlorn condition. There were many who would not drink their liquor at all, and others, as a result obtained a double or triple portion," one officer complained to his journal that evening. "A thousand drunken men in the brigade, made a pandemonium of the camp all night." In his own letter to his hometown *Appleton Crescent*, Jerome Watrous of the 6th Wisconsin never mentioned the drinking or the hard weather. He concluded his upbeat report with a line to ease the concern of the folks back home: "With two or three exceptions, the Appleton boys are well, and as tough as so many bears."[15]

Cutler's brigade settled into a routine of work details, patrols, and drills. Railroad bridges were repaired on Potomac Creek. Another bridge was rebuilt at Brook's Station. Finally, the brigade moved down to the river and camped on the bank of the Rappahannock in front of Fredericksburg. Two 2nd Wisconsin companies were detached with the construction corps to help repair and build bridges, including one across the Rappahannock 600 feet in length and 65 feet in height. "It will be seen that the enemy made us heaps of work; they engaged us in good, honest labor," joked one Black Hat. But the days passed without orders to

15 Dawes, *Service*, 39-40; Otis, *Second Wisconsin*, 47.

enter Fredericksburg, and were spent instead in hard manual labor and an occasional foray to watch for enemy movement. "We are playing a big game of 'hide-and-go-seek'," one soldier said, "making short and rapid marches, back and forth over a strip of country for the sole purpose of keeping the enemy from slipping into Washington. At the same time, the enemy scarcely keeps up an appearance; if anything he is playing with us, toying us about here and there, as a kind of ruse which has more or less of the Confederate smartness in its makeup. As we are not in on the secret or the part we are expected to play, we take to the work right kindly."

Two incidents from these days of construction and marching stand out. The first involved a halt at Warrenton, where "haughty and arrogant" Southern women delighted in taunting the "Lincoln chaps" guarding their property. "Very likely many of the brigade will remember the free bath conferred on the guard by the ladies . . . and will recall to mind the naughty words spoken in the heat of excitement." The second more troubling incident involved a pet gray squirrel named "Bunnie" that Crawford County boys in the 6th Wisconsin had taken in as their own. The "little fellow was tamed in a day or so and was a great pet with the Badger boys," recalled one of them. During a march, the squirrel ran free between the small trees and "never failed to join them when called especially if tempted by a lump of sugar." One day the men were sitting around a large fire watching the squirrel run up trees only to jump "to the broad shoulders of some kind friend." During one jump he leapt from a tree directly into the flames. "It was a clear case of cremation. Bunnie did not know what a fire was." The story is an example of how soldiers used the recollection of a small tragedy as a means of keeping away the hard memories.[16]

An announcement arrived on May 8 that Capt. John Gibbon of Battery B, 4th U.S. Artillery, was being promoted to brigadier general and given command of the Western Brigade. Cutler returned to his 6th Wisconsin. The announcement caused only a minor stir because the long-awaited move to occupy Fredericksburg was of more immediate interest. The Western boys found the city "surrounded by high land, and being built with strict regularity." It contained "many handsome private residences and public buildings" and was supplied with water power by the Rappahannock Falls. The soldiers also discovered a marble monument in an old graveyard marking the final resting place of George Washington's mother.

---

16 Loyd G. Harris, *Milwaukee Sunday Telegraph*, February 13, 1881; Otis, *Second Wisconsin*, 49-51; Dawes, *Service*, 38-39; Cheek and Pointon, *Sauk County*, 24-25. The "bath" occurred while guarding the home of former Virginia Governor "Extra Billy" Smith.

According to one Black Hat, "It was shamefully mutilated and disfigured by reckless soldiers."[17]

There was also news from the West. A Confederate surprise attack against U.S. Grant's army at Shiloh in Tennessee had been turned back after two days of the bloodiest fighting the war had yet witnessed. Federal forces had also captured New Orleans and were seeking to move up the Mississippi River. A desperate worry began coursing through the ranks that McDowell's corps might never join McClellan's army, which was moving slowly up the Virginia peninsula toward Richmond. If the Southern capital fell quickly, as most expected, the war might end. How could the Western boys go home without even getting a chance to strike a blow? One Wisconsin officer wrote in his journal, "General McClellan presses steadily on to Richmond. We are left out in the wet."[18]

Other more important developments occurred closer to home as Gibbon gathered the reins of his new brigade. His tightening of discipline was not greeted with enthusiasm. The new general was a Regular, after all, and the volunteers were distrustful of Regulars and their old Army manner. Especially upset was Col. Sol Meredith of the 19th Indiana, who had made known his own ambition to win the promotion. Volunteers should be commanded by volunteer officers, he told anyone who would listen, and he began a letter writing campaign to his powerful friends in Indiana and Washington to see what might be done. Gibbon discovered, much as his friend George McClellan had during the Mexican War, that volunteer troops were frisky and rather undisciplined. The Wisconsin and Indiana men had been in service almost a year, but the relationship between enlisted man and volunteer officer was still casual and discipline inconsistent.[19]

Gibbon was an unusual case himself. Born in Pennsylvania in 1827 into the family of a physician, he grew up in North Carolina and it was from that state he entered West Point, graduating in the Class of 1847. He was assigned to the artillery, served in Mexico and against the Seminoles in Florida before returning to the academy as an artillery instructor from 1854 to 1859. He won some attention in 1859 for his publication of a highly regarded Artillerist's Manual. Gibbon left West Point when he was promoted captain and joined Battery B at its duty post at Camp Floyd in the Utah Territory. With the start of the Civil War, despite his North Carolina roots and even though three brothers went into Confederate service,

---

17 Otis, *Second Wisconsin*, 51-52.

18 Dawes, *Service*, 44. See also Frank A. Haskell, letter to his brothers and sisters, September 22, 1862, Frank Haskell Papers, WHS.

19 Levi B. Raymond, diary, March 20, 1862 (privately held).

Gibbon stayed with the Union. When his battery joined the army outside Washington, he served as McDowell's chief of artillery before taking the infantry promotion. The general's star did not come to Gibbon as early as it should have (given his past service); some said his promotion to brigadier was delayed in Congress because of his Southern background and the fact that he had no patron. When Gibbon sought out James Wadsworth, the politically connected New York general saw that the promotion was advanced, winning Gibbon's gratitude.[20]

In his order taking command, Gibbon referenced the Western roots of his brigade, adding that he hoped his men "will emulate the gallant deeds of their brave Statesmen in the West, and prove to them that the heroism displayed at Fort Donelson and Pittsburg Landing, can be rivaled by their brothers, who have come East, to fight the cause of the 'Union.'" Gibbon was familiar with the Westerners because of their ongoing association with his Regulars in Battery B. "The first marked feature I noted with these men was their quick intelligence," he wrote in his memoir. "It was only necessary to explain a thing but once or twice to enable them to catch the idea and then with a little practice they became perfect." Part of the difficulty, he went on, was that in "such mass of raw material it not infrequently happened, that brothers, fathers and sons were serving in the same company, the son, perhaps, being senior to his father!" The "fearless, independent" Westerners, wrote one of the artillerists who helped train the volunteers after they joined Battery B, were "splendid raw material [but] 'quick on the trigger' and would not take any nonsense from anybody, with or without shoulder-straps. . . . They were ready to fight anything on earth at any time or in any shape!"[21]

Readying his infantry brigade would be a difficult task, but Gibbon was a competent, steady, and respected professional who had the intelligence to recognize that his volunteers could not be handled in the same fashion as the Regulars. His dark side was a fierce ambition that embroiled him in lingering

20 Herdegen, *The Men Stood Like Iron*, 67.

21 Gibbon's General Order No. 52 is cited in Gaff, *Bloody Field*, 124; John Gibbon, *Personal Recollections of the Civil War* (New York, NY, 1928), 12-14, 27-28; Buell, *Cannoneer*, 24-25. The accuracy of Buell's memoir is in question. Milton W. Hamilton, "Augustus C. Buell, Fraudulent Historian," *Pennsylvania Magazine of History and Biography* (1956), 80-156, 478-492. Hamilton proved Buell did not enlist until August 21, 1863—six weeks *after* Gettysburg, and then joined the 20th New York Cavalry. Author Silas Felton, however, pointed out that Buell's account of Battery B included solid information supported by the battery's veterans. Felton concluded that Buell's account is likely based on extensive interviews with at least three Battery B veterans. Felton also noted that Buell's story was first published in the *National Tribune*, the major veteran newspaper of the day, and reprinted in book form—a publication path to avoid if the story was bogus. Obscure Wisconsin sources also confirm minor details of Buell's account. Silas Felton, "Pursing the Elusive Cannoneer," *Gettysburg Magazine*, No. 9 (July 1993), 33-39.

Captain Samuel Stevens, Grand Rapids Union Guards,
Co. G, 7th Wisconsin

Stevens enlisted from Grand Rapids, Wisconsin, on August 17, 1861, and
resigned on May 24, 1862. *Wisconsin Veterans Museum*

Capt. Homer Drake, Grand Rapids Union Guards, Co. G, 7th Wisconsin

Enlisted from Simmonds and promoted to 1st lieutenant on May 24, 1862, Drake resigned on February 11, 1862. *Author's Collection*

disputes with other officers over slights imagined and real. His war memoir includes long passages justifying his military actions and decisions others had criticized. That fact he was raised in North Carolina and had brothers in Confederate service was also noted by his volunteers. Behind the general's back they called him "The Southern Renegade" and the "Gigadier Beneral" and made jokes about his "comical appearance . . . when mounted because . . . his legs were abnormally long and he rode a small horse." One of his first orders required each soldier take a bath once a week. Another instituted a "daily review at what seemed to us an unwarrantably early hour in the morning—5 o'clock, I think—to be followed immediately at its close by the drinking of a cup of hot coffee by each member of the brigade whether he liked it or not." Regimental officers who had not been attending the early morning roll call were now required to do so. After inspecting the 19th Indiana's camp, Gibbon forced the Hoosiers to completely realign the tents on their company streets according to regulations. "The impression in relation to our new Brigadier, on first sight, is rather unfavorable," concluded an Indiana man obviously upset with Regular Army manners and style.[22]

22 Albert Young, "His Pilgrimage," *Milwaukee Sunday Telegraph*, July 1, 1888; William Murray diary as cited in Gaff, *Bloody Field*, 125.

Iron Brigade Soldiers

Six Wisconsin soldiers tentatively identified as members of Company C (Grant County Grays) of the 2nd Wisconsin. The individual seated in the center is thought to be Cpl. Spencer Train. This photo was probably taken between May and August 1862 opposite Fredericksburg, Virginia. Train died in 1863 from wounds received at Gettysburg.
Wisconsin Historical Society 41960

Gibbon was also upset with the uneven appearance of his regiments. Uniforms varied from company to company with some soldiers in caps and others in the tall black felt dress hats of the Regulars. Trousers varied from dark blue to sky blue. The transition actually began before he took command when acting Brigade Commander Cutler decided to make the Model 1858 dress hat a consistent item for all the soldiers. The 6th Wisconsin was issued hats a few days later and the 19th Indiana about the same time. The new headgear made a striking impression on the already rangy Westerners, who now looked even taller under the impressive hats. Gibbon took the uniform matter a step further by requiring that all soldiers be issued the felt hats and the nine-button dark blue frock coat of the Regulars along with white linen leggings and cotton white gloves. In the ranks it seemed a bit fancy for the boys from the piney camp, but one 7th Wisconsin man wrote home, "We have a full blue suit, a fine black hat nicely trimmed with bugle and plate and ostrich feathers, and you can only distinguish our boys from the regulars by their [our] good looks." An officer in the 6th reported his regiment was in "fine feather" during its next dress parade.[23]

If the additions were generally greeted with "the greatest merriment," there was loud grumbling when it was discovered that each soldier would pay for the gloves and leggings out of his clothing allowance. The required items included extra underwear, stockings, and shoes. Lieutenant Colonel Lucius Fairchild outfitted a soldier according to Gibbon's new rules and found the entire outfit weighed 85 pounds. "It is impossible for men on the march, in active service, to transport on their persons anything more than they actually need. And the Yankee soldier won't," stated one veteran, who noted the extra clothing was thrown away on the first march. In making his requisition for the supplies for his regiment, sly Sol Meredith asked for four extra mule teams to transport the extra luggage. The colonel's request was denied.

The displeasure over the issue of linen leggings would linger. In addition to the additional cost, they were cumbersome to put on and uncomfortable to wear in warm weather. The angry mood was well expressed one morning when Gibbon emerged from his tent to find his "pet horse" equipped with four leggings. The breach of discipline upset the by-the-book Regular, who never discovered the culprits responsible for the prank. The incident led to another that became part of the lore of the Black Hat Brigade, and that was how the general got even. It came long after the war during a soldier reunion in Wisconsin. At the time Gibbon was in civilian clothing and was passing through Boscobel headed for his duty station at Fort Snelling in Minnesota. He was waiting at the depot for a train when told of a veteran's reunion then underway nearby. Gibbon made his way to the hall and at the door inquired if there were any members of the old Iron Brigade present. One veteran was gathered up and brought to him. When Gibbon asked if he had been a member of the old Western Brigade the man, with some pride, answered in the affirmative. The general smiled and said in a quiet voice, "Well, I am looking for a man."

"What man?" asked the old soldier.

Gibbon, smiling more broadly now, said sharply, "Why the man who put the leggings on my horse when we were opposite Fredericksburg in 1862."

---

23 For a description of the distinctive apparel, see Appendix II, Howard Michael Madaus, "The Uniform of the Iron Brigade at Gettysburg, July 1, 1863," in Herdegen and Beaudot, *Railroad Cut*, 301-371.

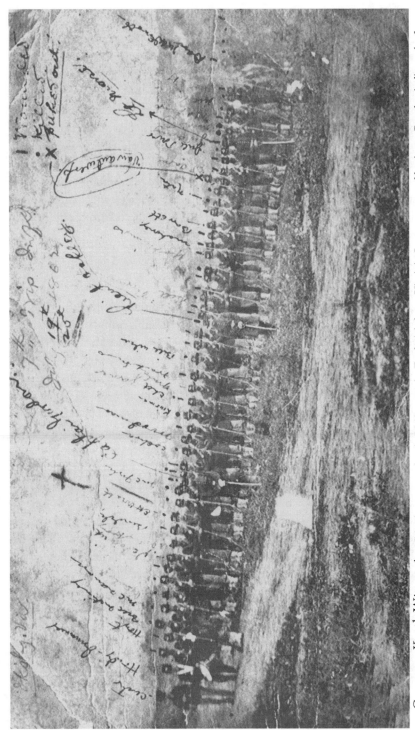

Company K, 7th Wisconsin. This photo was taken in 1862 opposite Fredericksburg, Virginia. It was annotated by Amos Rood to indicate the fate of individual soldiers. *Alexander Gordon Jr. Family*

The old soldier blinked and looked closer at the figure standing in the dark doorway. "Geewilikins," he said (or words to that affect), motioning to other soldiers nearby. "Come over here, boys, quick, here's Johnny, the War Horse."[24]

Gibbon would command the Western men for only six months, but his influence carried them to the end of the conflict. "He soon manifested superior qualities as a brigade commander," Rufus Dawes, a veteran of several major battles, wrote long after the war. "Thoroughly educated in the military profession, he had also high personal qualifications to exercise command. He was anxious that his brigade should excel in every way, and while he was an exacting disciplinarian he had the good sense to recognize merit where it existed. His administration of the command left a lasting impression for good upon the character and military tone of the brigade, and his splendid personal bravery upon the field of battle was an inspiration."[25]

Tied to Granny Lincoln's Apron String

At Fredericksburg during those weeks of early summer of 1862 the Western Brigade drilled and then drilled some more as McClellan's main command slowly moved on the rebel defenses at Richmond. "We expect 'Little Mac' will celebrate the 'Fourth' in, or near that place," one Westerner wrote his sister. "We will not participate, but will move to there soon after it is taken." As the dismayed Wisconsin and Indiana men watched the Federal offensive from afar, they spent the days training and on work details. One such effort involved rebuilding a railroad track destroyed by the Confederates. A party of Wisconsin men was marched out to one site along the line and issued shovels. The Badger officer in charge looked over to a nearby wood and saw troops from New York City "hacking around trees until they could push them over and then trying to make railroad ties from the trees." The Western officer was a man used to working in the woods and, "his face the picture of disgust," turned to the colonel in charge and announced, "If you will give those shovels to those counter jumpers and give us the axes we will cut all the ties and bridge timber you will need on the road in a week but if you give us the shovels we could not dig a hole big enough to bury a cat in a month." The axes were soon in Wisconsin hands and in short order the wood needed for the roads and bridges was available. One of the Western men recalled an "old darky slave" who had watched

---

24 Dawes, *Service*, 44; Brown letter to parents, September 1, 1961; Cheek and Pointon, *Sauk County*, 27; Fitch, Echoes, 39.

25 Dawes, *Service*, 43.

Pvt. Levi Raymond, Beloit Star Rifles, Co. G, 6th Wisconsin

Raymond was promoted to corporal, but was discharged on November 15, 1862, for disability. He was a native of Chicago, Illinois. *Institute for Civil War Studies*

the effort in wonder. "It took we uns four years to build dat dar bridge and de Yankee soldiers done gone and build dat dar bridge in three days." The statement brought a round of laughter.

The Western boys soon had the run of Fredericksburg, taking over wagon shops, blacksmith and other workshops, and even the local newspaper. Joseph I. Weirich (who had been volunteered from the *Baraboo Republic* newspaper by proprietor A. N. Kellogg along with a Sharps Rifle) and other printers soon began issuing a much sought-after soldier newspaper on brown store wrapping paper called the *Christian Banner*. The local shopkeepers had run up their prices for the intruders. Common note envelopes were $1.00 per package and tea $7.00 a pound. At first the store owners refused to accept U.S. greenbacks and wanted only Confederate money. Enterprising individuals among the printers soon started to make facsimile Confederate "notes" available to the soldiers at 10-cents per $1,000 dollars. "We accommodated them and bought out the town in the line of supplies they had that we thought we wanted and did not kick on the price charged, as we got our money cheap," announced one Badger. "The boys felt that all was fair in war."[26]

The weather was pleasant, the countryside lush and beautiful, and the lonesome Western boys were soon thinking of tender matters. The Southern ladies of the town, however, were quick to show their scorn and turn away. The "women and girls are worst of all," complained a soldier in the 7th Wisconsin. "Whenever

26 Loyd G. Harris, letter to his sister, July 2, 1862, Loyd Harris Papers, WHS; Cheek and Pointon, *Sauk County*, 8, 24-26, 29-30.

they would pass a Yankee soldier they would twist their pretty faces all out of shape." A 6th Wisconsin soldier described the city inhabitants as "mostly colored, a few old hoary headed white men, rosy cheeked damsels (all in their sweet sixteenth). They all think we are 'right smart looking fellows and wear right good clothes' but can't become reconciled to that name Yankee." Some of the more zealous of the fairer sex, said another soldier, showed their patriotism for the Confederate cause by "making mouths at the Union soldiers as they pass through the streets, in some cases even spitting at them and threw water upon them from the windows." The boys got their own form of revenge. A Union flag hung over a sidewalk on Caroline Street in the city where the Federals had an office. A group of ladies were nearly under the flag before seeing it, then walked out into a muddy street to escape going beneath the banner. "The boys looked on and enjoyed the scene," recorded an observer. Soon seven flags were strung across the whole street and the ladies "did not walk on that street at all."[27]

No soldier of the time had a more bittersweet memory of those long ago war days at Fredericksburg than young Lt. Loyd Harris of Prairie du Chien. Harris boasted an outgoing and sunny attitude, a love for music (he took his violin with him to war), and an eye for a pretty girl. His first

Unidentified Sergeant of the 6th Wisconsin

This unidentified sergeant is wearing the dress coat of the Iron Brigade along with a non-commissioned officer's belt and buckle. It came out of an estate sale in Wisconsin.
Author's Collection

27 George Eustice, letter, undated: Watrous, *Appleton Crescent*, May 31, 1862; Edward P. Kellogg, "Another Regiment," *Milwaukee Sunday Telegraph*, September 28, 1879; Cheek and Pointon, *Sauk County*, 29-30.

brush with "the rudeness" of the local inhabitants came when "two young ladies" approached along a street. "As we neared each other, I gave away toward the outside of the walk, when the ladies crowded me into the gutter and swept by. I had just time to raise my hat and say Thank you, my pretty 'secesh.'" This so troubled Harris that he recounted the incident in a letter to his sister.

A more important task those days was learning discipline and military life under their new general. "My, my, how the boys disliked John Gibbon in those days of hard work—work which they thought was not necessary," admitted one Badger. "They had enlisted to fight for their country, not to wear themselves out in drilling and marching around. Gibbon was a soldier. They were not when he took them. He knew what was before them; he knew how much they needed the discipline he was giving them, and they learned to most keenly appreciate it before they were a year older." Another veteran said that the general proved "a most thorough disciplinarian. . . . There were early morning drills, before breakfast, forenoon drills, evening and night drills, besides guard mounting and dress parade. Probably no brigade commander was ever more cordially hated by his men. He was all soldier, both in looks and deeds. When Gibbon's Brigade marched there was no straggling."

Gibbon soon recognized the competence and ability of Frank A. Haskell of the 6th Wisconsin, who had been acting as brigade adjutant under Cutler, and made the adjutant post permanent. Both Gibbon and Haskell were cordially hated by the men in ranks, but proved a formidable pair. The officers made the rounds each morning and supervised the drinking of coffee by each soldier at the regimental mess tents. They also provided instruction in drill and other important matters. "One especial and untiring effort of Adjutant Haskell was to exact cleanliness and neatness of appearance, an essential condition of the soldierly bearing," one volunteer recalled. "The cotton gloves, which he required the men to wear, were kept snow white; nor did he allow them to cover dirty hands. It was a dreaded ordeal for a man to step four paces in front and face the adjutant before the assembled guard and in fear of this he went there clean at however great and unusual a sacrifice of customary habit."

The sergeants were held responsible for the cleanliness of their squads and if one soldier was dirty, they all suffered. "Now this is wrong to have the whole Co. condemned on account of one man being dirty and it is not right to expect us to do as regulars when we are on the field and been marching and lying about the mud like so many boys," complained one of the boys. "Oh damn this way of putting regular officers over volunteers. It don't suit me at all." It was Haskell who enforced the discipline, one veteran grumbled, and "so elevated his office, that some men then thought the Adjutant must be at least next to the Colonel in authority and rank."

Haskell, a 7th Wisconsin man wrote in his journal, is "just as bad now as the Gen. The boys used to think considerable of him but they hate him just as bad now."

In the end, Gibbon found just the right way to handle his frisky Western boys when he discovered them to be intelligent and willing and more responsive to reward over punishment. "I was already impressed with the conviction that all they needed was some discipline and drill to make them first-class soldiers, and my anticipations were more than realized," wrote Gibbon. The 2nd and 6th Wisconsin "had decidedly the advantage" over the other two regiments and "each strove to become the 'crack' regiment of the brigade." One difficulty in all the regiments was that some company officers knew nothing of drill. Schools of instruction were established. "As it was, discipline and drill gradually advanced, slowly but surely."

In addition to drills and instruction were matters of discipline. The young soldiers often knocked down fences for firewood, so Gibbon ordered the regiment camped the closest to rebuild it. Soldierly appearance was encouraged with an order giving the properly turned out soldier a 24-hour pass to go "blackberrying." He also found a way to make his volunteers man a picket post. "Men who had been working hard all their lives for a purpose could see no use in pacing up and down doing nothing," Gibbon explains. "Hence logs of wood, a convenient rock or campstool, were frequently resorted to as resting places, and often I would ride by a sentinel without any attention being paid to me whatever, the men on the post being entirely too much occupied enjoying his ease, perhaps even smoking a cigar, to notice my approach." One day, the general— "perhaps being in a less amiable frame of mind than usual"—had a lax sentry relieved from his post, stripped of equipment, and placed "on the head of a barrel in front of the guard tent." Other soldiers came by to laugh and point at the hapless private. "I never had any more trouble after that about my sentinels, either saluting me or walking their posts, and that is the only instance in which I ever resorted to arbitrary punishment in that command," wrote Gibbon.[28]

If the general was enforcing a sharper brand of discipline than wanted by his soldiers, he also saw to the general welfare by visiting the brigade hospital to make inquiries about the care of the men of his regiments. On one occasion he found some of his sick volunteers lying on the ground with their blankets instead of on cots. "Well he quizzed them pretty close and told a pretty hard story, but a true one and he seemed very much dissatisfied," William Ray of the 7th Wisconsin wrote in his journal on June 30, 1862. "He then sent one of the waiters to have the Doctors come in and one of our boys that was just able to [move] about told us that the

28 Gibbons, *Recollections*, 27-28, 37.

General gave him hell (in his way of speaking). Told them they ought to be ashamed to treat them so. . . . I suppose from what I have heard from other sources that he gave him to understand that kind of work wouldn't do. I guess he is the only General or officer higher than our Col that ever was to the hospital."

If the general was making his volunteers into real soldiers he was also instructing the young Western officers about commanding troops. Gibbon was glad for the professional training of West Pointer Colonel O'Connor of the 2nd Wisconsin, but dismayed at the political posturing of the 19th Indiana's Colonel Meredith. He also recognized the merit of Colonels Robinson of the 7th Wisconsin and Cutler of the 6th Wisconsin. Gibbon's careful handling of a dispute between Cutler and Benjamin Sweet, the regiment's lieutenant colonel, showed his ability to head off a serious problem. Sweet publicly complained that one of the old colonel's orders contained a falsehood and refused to back down. Gibbon investigated and wrote a careful letter upholding Cutler, but declined to press charges against Sweet. The letter could be read to the regiment, Gibbon said, which placated Cutler. Sweet recognized his dilemma and change of standing in the regiment and did some maneuvering of his own. A month later he resigned to become colonel of the 21st Wisconsin, taking some of the regiment's better officers with him by use of promotions in the new outfit. One of those who left to take a higher post later explained Gibbon's impact on the inexperienced younger officers: "The regiment became finely drilled before I left it. But of course that did not foreshadow its fighting qualities. Its real efficiency depended upon the way it was handled under fire by its officers. Its death list of officers tells the real tale of how the men were held under fire in many battles. It was one of the nineteen volunteer regiments in service that lost sixteen or more officers killed or mortally wounded. It is the only Wisconsin regiment which lost as many as sixteen."[29]

On May 23, President Lincoln and Secretary of War Edwin Staunton arrived at Fredericksburg to review the troops. Shield's division also arrived, the soldiers dirty and much used up, their commander with his arm in a sling from a wound he had received in the Shenandoah Valley. The Western Brigade was in full uniform of Hardee Hats and dress coats and made a striking appearance during the review, which brought hoots and catcalls from some of Shield's men about "bandbox soldiers." A Wisconsin officer replied to his journal with proper literary sniff, "Shield's division are the dirtiest ragamuffins we have yet seen in the service." About that time Maj. Gen. Irvin McDowell paid a high compliment to the Western Brigade: "Many times I have shown them to foreign officers of distinction, as

29 Fitch, *Echoes*, 330; Ray, *Iron Brigade*, 97, 99.

specimens of American Volunteer soldiers, and asked them if they had ever anywhere seen even among the picked soldiers of royal and imperial guards, a more splendid body of men, and I have never had an affirmative answer."[30]

After the review, the president received the general officers at the Lacy House directly across the river from Fredericksburg where McDowell made his headquarters. When Gibbon was introduced, Lincoln shook his hand and made a sly joke, asking if the general had written *The Decline and Fall of the Roman Empire*. A puzzled Gibbon blurted back that the only thing he had written was an artillery manual, to which Lincoln smiled, placed a hand on the general's shoulder, and replied, "Never mind, General, if you will write the decline and fall of this rebellion, I will let you off." The president made a few more remarks that "put everyone on an easy footing which I suspected afterwards was Mr. Lincoln's object," recalled Gibbon. The president also approved McDowell's planned march on Richmond and agreed that King's division should lead the advance.

In the Western ranks, the arrival of the president was viewed as "the forerunner of something to happen. Speculations of all sorts are in order, and the boys come to believe that it was for fear of something dreadful as likely to happen that they were kept from participating in McClellan's on to Richmond via the Peninsula." The brigade received marching orders the next day and as the joyful soldiers readied to leave ("As soon as old Abe saw our brigade, he knew it could take Richmond, and he has sent us to do it," boasted one), there was additional excitement when powder and other munitions housed in a small brick building used as a magazine exploded, killing one of the guards. "He was blown on top of a building some 4 or 5 rods distant," confirmed a Wisconsin man. "One leg blown of [off] close his body & and the other just below his knee." It was a sight never forgotten: "The hair was burned of his head. He had scratches all over his body and besmeared with blood, blood and dirty. There was not a thread of clothing left on him. I saw him & it was the most horrible sight I have ever seen. It is beyond description. His brother was the first to get hold of him, he being on another post not far distant. I have not heard as there was any body else got even a scratch."[31]

To the disappointment of many, the brigade marched but eight miles south before the advance was halted because of the political fears that Washington would be left unprotected. (In fact the nation's capital, with its ring of impressive fortifications, could hardly be threatened except by more men than the

---

30 Dawes, journal, May 24, 1862; Dawes, *Service*, 45.

31 Gibbon, *Recollections*, 34-35; Otis, *Second Wisconsin*, 48; Ray, *Iron Brigade*, May 26, 1862, 88-89; George Eustice, letter, undated.

Confederates could ever put into active service.) Before long news arrived that Nathaniel Banks had been beaten in the Shenandoah Valley and was retreating, and Confederate forces under Thomas "Stonewall" Jackson were making a swift advance north—with the more fearful reports claiming that Jackson was making a dash for Washington. McDowell was ordered to mount a pursuit, but what followed was two weeks of hard marching in what one officer called "a wild goose chase." In the immediate panic, troops were shifted hither and yon by what Gibbon called "wild orders. One brigade was at once shipped by water whilst the balance of the command, our troops, apparently under the command of nobody, was in a few days strung from Fredericksburg to Front Royal, some marching and some on the cars rushing, helter-skelter, as was supposed to 'cut off' Jackson," Gibbon complained. "What was done by the other portions of the command, we only learned from time to time by rumors."[32]

The marching was especially hard on the men, the hot and sultry weather and issue of extra clothing adding to their burden. One tramp of twenty miles saw 150 men in the 6th Wisconsin fall out exhausted. "Our young boys were broken down by the needless overtaxing of their strength," observed one officer. "I can not say who was responsible for such management. I know, however, that General McDowell, whether justly or unjustly, was thoroughly cursed for it." Some of the stronger soldiers in the regiment, such as Abe Fletcher of Lemonweir, would carry two or three knapsacks to help "the little fellows" of the regiment, "young, slight, round cheek boys, who endured their hardship with a cheerful patience that won us all." Also in good form during the hard marching was Mickey Sullivan, whose sharp Irish wit eased the long road hours. Even Rufus Dawes shouldered a knapsack to help out. William Ray of the 7th Wisconsin was ill, but kept up. "The catarrh in my head troubles me very much of late when I get my blood heated. I was completely given out and should have had to [have] stopped for the night if they had went much further," he noted in his journal. The next day he reported that two men in the 6th Wisconsin died from the heat along with one soldier in the 2nd Wisconsin killed by sunstroke and another left helpless. Two of the men in his own Lancaster Union Guards were put on the backs of the officer's horses to keep them with the column.[33]

Soldiers began throwing away the newly issued extra clothing and overcoats as well as discarding the overburdened knapsacks they derisively called "Saratoga trunks." The "sides of the road were literally blue for miles," one man confided to

32 Dawes, *Service*, 47-48; Gibbon, *Recollections* 34-35.

33 Dawes, *Service*, 46-47; Ray, *Iron Brigade*, 91.

his diary. The Western boys joked that they were "issuing overcoats to the rebel cavalry." One said the first to go was the extra coat, "then the pants, then the socks, and last of all the shoes, accompanied by the shoe brush and the box of blacking." The vast shedding of clothing dismayed Gibbon, who recalled the "quantities of perfectly new clothing" being left along the roadway. Confederate deserters from Stonewall Jackson's army were also flushed by the soldiers and brought in as prisoners. One came to the side of the road to watch the marching columns. He was ragged and dirty and looked over the Black Hats with professional interest, taking in their knapsacks, coats, and many accoutrements. "We uns durst leave our mammy," he said with a sly grin. "You uns is tied to granny Lincoln's apron string."[34]

They Fight Like Devils

Despite the hard marching and the panic over the threat of Stonewall Jackson's army, Gibbon's brigade found itself back in camp opposite Fredericksburg without having "seen an enemy nor heard a gun fired during the time." Although McCall's division of McDowell's corps was being transferred to McClellan's growing army opposite Richmond on the Virginia peninsula, the Westerners were once again left behind as part of the force to protect Washington. The hard work of the past two weeks, however, had one beneficial result. "The experience and marching," explained Gibbon, "were valuable to our new troops." Still, the general—with the ingrained penny-pinching tradition of the Old Army—was deeply troubled by the careless disposal of so much valuable clothing and equipment. Much worse was yet to come.

Gibbon reviewed his brigade on June 12 and praised the "military bearing and appearance of the regiments on review," but singled out the "marked contrast" between the Wisconsin units and the 19th Indiana. "Three weeks ago, when reviewed by the President, every one remarked [upon] the neat and cleanly appearance of this Regiment, and the General noticed with regret, the contrast presented in review yesterday." Gibbon made a sour reference to the clothing discarded on the recent marches before adding, "Such foolish waste of Stores provided by the Government can not be tolerated, and would never occur in a properly disciplined body of men. . . . At the approaching muster, every man of this regiment, who has not now in his possession, the clothing issued to him during the

---

34 Dawes, *Service*, 47-48; Gibbon, *Recollections*, 35; *Milwaukee Sunday Telegraph*, July 1, 1888; George Fairfield diary, George Fairfield Papers, WHS.

past month will be charged on the muster rolls the cost of such clothing, and have the amount deducted from his pay."[35]

The order set off a fire storm, particularly in the 19th Indiana, where the white linen leggings were especially hated. Upset with the insult to his command, Meredith secured a leave to meet with his Indiana political friends in Washington to see about replacing Gibbon or having his regiment transferred to another brigade. In the Hoosier ranks were hot words and threats against "one of the meanest Brigadier genarls that ever lived. Gibens is his name. He is a regular and if we ever get in a fight he will Be the first to fall. every Body hates his very name." Opposition to the clothing orders was also felt in the three Wisconsin regiments. "The officers are coming right down on us as if we were so many slaves now," complained Private Ray of the 7th to his journal on June 18. He continued:

And they are forcing leggings and blous [blouse or frock] coats on us and forcing us to wear them. It's a dime for this and a quarter for that and so it goes. And whatever the General says we must have, we must take it or be arrested. It is said that the Col of the Indiana Regiment has gone to Washington to see if he cannot get his Regt out of his Brigade and our Colonel [Robinson] has gone some place and been gone two or three days and the talk is that he has gone for the same purpose as the Ind. Col and if this be true, I hope he will succeed and we will be from under the old tyrant Gen. Gibbons. It is him that causes the truble. he comes down on the regimental officers and they come down on the Co officers and as a matter of course, they must come down on us and that is the way it goes. I don't blame any of them for reminding us of keeping clean but I hate this putting on so much style. The boys call it . . . French airs.

Most of the Indiana men and those in the 6th Wisconsin had thrown away their extra clothing and would have to draw more. "The Gen is bound to make us carry the extra clothing, thereby causing a great many to give out on the march," added Ray, "and then they will have to haul them & their knappsacks too. And if they oblige me to carry so much, I will sit down when tired and they have got to haul me."[36]

Despite the efforts of Meredith and his political friends, the Indiana regiment was not transferred nor Gibbon removed. Secretary of War Stanton replied that the matter was in the hands of McDowell who, despite pressure from Hoosier

35 Gibbon, *Recollections*, 33-35; General Orders No. 58, cited in Gaff, *Bloody Field*, 132.

36 The threat against Gibbon is found in the manuscript of Sgt. Jeff Crull and cited in Gaff, *Bloody Field*, 133; Ray, *Iron Brigade*, 99-100. The rumor Robinson was seeking to have his regiment transferred to another brigade was not true.

politicos, refused to move the 19th Indiana from Gibbon's brigade. Meredith returned to his regiment, where his unspoken manner made clear that he supported his Hoosiers in resisting a re-issue of the infamous white leggings. "This fretted the General," remembered one Indiana man, "who, with numerous dress-parades and orders and lecturers to the officers on parade sought to carry his point. The officers exhorted, pleaded, threatened, swore, but the boys would not take the leggings." An exasperated Gibbon drew a line in the sand and told the Hoosiers that if they did not appear in their leggings the next morning, he would order his battery to open fire on their camp.

The Hoosiers defied the order by gathering on their company streets the next morning without leggings. Just as they were forming, a burst of cannon fire sent the startled soldiers to their knees or face down in the dirt. "Lay down boys, lay down!" some shouted while others called out "We'll take the leggings! We'll take the leggings!" After a few seconds, no injuries, and laughing and pointing Wisconsin men, the Hoosiers discovered a nearby battery drilling with blank rounds. The story stayed with them throughout the war and remained around even the old soldier campfires decades later. In a wry twist of soldier humor, whenever the brigade endured artillery fire or an especially loud blast, some Wisconsin regiment would cry out, "Will you take the leggings now?" The Hoosiers would call back, "No! No!" If a second loud blast followed, the cry would be taken up by all the regiments, "Yes, yes. I'll take the leggings!" In the end, the leggings were not reissued and those worn out were not replaced. Indiana men viewed it a victory, and convinced one another that Gibbon was not forcing the issue and "acknowledged that his brigade made a volunteer of him."[37]

And so the rough Western volunteers began to act and look like real soldiers. Their transformation was further enhanced when the regiments were armed with rifled weapons. This was important because these men believed they "were all crack shots with the rifle" because they "came from away out West and always lived in the woods." The new rifles helped morale even though they created a minor ordnance supply problem for the brigade. The 2nd Wisconsin carried the Model 1854 Austrian Lorenz rifles in their original .54-caliber, while the shoulder arms of the other regiments were in the more standard .58-caliber. The volunteers in the 2nd, like the boys in all the regiments, were used to handling firearms and generally liked their Lorenz rifles ("a splendid gun to shoot," one said). "Is there any wonder, then that we should weep for joy rather than sorrow," a Wisconsin man wrote home when the old muskets were exchanged for "true and trusty rifles that will bite as well

---

37 For a much more detailed account of the leggings mutiny, see Gaff, *Bloody Field*, 130-138.

as bark and kick. We now have the best guns in the Brigade, and I think they are in the hands of men who know how to use them." After a firing drill a week later, he reported the new weapons proved satisfactory. "They are a splendid piece, rough as they look; and in the hands of the Second will do good execution when the opportunity for their use occurs."

The men in the 6th Wisconsin and the 19th Indiana were issued the Model 1861 .58-caliber Springfield pattern rifle-muskets (a rifle-musket has the length of a musket, but a rifled bore) and believed they were superior to the Lorenz. There was some prejudice in the 19th Indiana against the English Enfield rifle-musket because of a lot of 240 initially issued to the flank companies in August 1861. Many were out of order and the regimental armor declared "a portion of them were not worth repairing." In addition, some of the Enfields had irregular calibers and many of the ramrods were too short. "A large share of the men composing my Regiment have from childhood been accustom to the Rifle and are accomplished Marksmen," Colonel Meredith wrote to McClellan. "If armed with the Springfield Gun, I would desire whenever you think us competent, an advanced position—and will cheerily perform the outpost and Picket duty." The 19th Indiana got the Springfield rifle-muskets.[38]

Private Mickey Sullivan of the 6th mounted his rifle-musket with "some silver ornaments and fixed the screw in a stock against the dog [sear] so it [the trigger pull] worked almost as easy as a squirrel gun, and I felt very proud of it." The fix involved a wood screw by the trigger guard that extended into the lock. It was the kind of trick used back home on the frontier and demonstrated Sullivan's skill with a firearm. During an inspection one day, an officer asked about the screw in the gunstock. "I told him so that I could hit a canteen at one hundred yards and he asked me no more questions."[39]

The 7th Wisconsin was also issued Austrian Lorenz rifles, but unlike the smaller caliber guns of the 2nd Wisconsin, they were re-rifled or reamed to .58-caliber—the standard being adopted by the army. The new rifles had been exchanged for the old muskets in February. The regiment was formed and "they were given out as the roll was called and the guns being numbered, we took guns accordingly," recalled one private. The new rifles were "colored black except for the lock guard and rammer, which are bright." The rifles were four inches shorter than the old musket and a half-pound heavier, but "they carry very nice and much

38 Oliver Morton Papers and Correspondence, Indiana State Library, Indianapolis, as cited Gaff, *Bloody Field*, 41.

39 Mickey, of Company K, [James P. Sullivan], "The Charge of the Iron Brigade at Gettysburg," *Mauston Star*, undated clipping.

Lt. J. N. P. Bird and his soldiers, Miner's Guards, Co. I, 7th Wisconsin

Lt. Bird (holding the newspaper) and Lt. Christopher Lefler, with men of the 7th regiment in front of Capt. George H. Walther's tent at Fredericksburg, Va. in 1862. *Wisconsin Historical Society 33555*

easier than the musket. So we are ready for the secesh now." By late June of 1862, the weather had bleached nearly yellow the beech wood stocks of the Lorenz rifles and an order came down that they be stained and "varnished" at a cost of ten cents per soldier. The initial "strong opposition" faded with the improved look of the stained weapons.[40]

One week slipped into another week without action. One frustrated soldier remarked that "a year's fight was bottled up in them and it was spoiling to come out." A Western boy wrote home of his desire to be in battle: "I hope we will give

40 *Milwaukee Sentinel,* June 10, 1861, August 17, 1861, January 20 and 27, 1862; *Madison Journal,* May 3, 1861; James P. "Mickey" Sullivan of Company K, "The Charge of the Iron Brigade at Gettysburg," February 13, 1883, *Mauston Star;* Ray, *Iron Brigade,* February 16, 1862 and June 19, 1862. Ray wrote: "We got everything pertaining to the new guns, which are as follows. First a brass Stopple, a very pretty one, a good wormer and a good screwdriver and wrench. They are in one piece." The Lorenz was the second most common imported shoulder arm used by both sides in the Civil War. It was regarded as a sound weapon to use while production of U.S. arms caught up with demand. The Union reported purchases of 226,924 and the Confederacy as many as 100,000. *Ibid.*

them hail Columbia and then the thing will be played out. As it is it is on the last legs and I wish I could get a chance to hit them one blow." Adding to their growing sense of dismay was an order combining several independent commands (including McDowell's First Corps) into the new Army of Virginia to protect Washington. Gibbon's Black Hats were yet another step removed from their beloved General McClellan; any hope of joining his army outside Richmond seemed more remote than ever.

Throughout these many weeks all eyes remained focused on McClellan's operations against the Southern capital. The homesick Capt. Edwin Brown of the 6th Wisconsin took the situation especially hard and his morale dipped as the days passed without conclusion. Attorney Brown had left his practice to fight the rebellion, and had left behind his wife Ruth and their children in Fond du Lac to do so. The conflicting news and growing realization that McDowell's corps had missed the fighting, and there would be no march south against the Rebel capital, left him angry and bitter. In a biting letter home to his father, the young officer mistakenly blamed McDowell (rather than the War Department) for his stationary circumstance:

> [B]y preventing any men of whatever [officer] grade from visiting Washington on any pretence and by his continued presence there, he [McDowell] bids fair to thwart the wishes of his entire command. Thus the Country if they do not suffer from his treachery or the betrayal of that command to the enemy, will at least have to pay the expenses of 30 or 50,000 troops in the field who will not be permitted to strike one blow at treason or rebellion. . . . If McDowell had given McClellan his hearty cooperation Richmond would be ours today. As it is if McClellan should be defeated in the approaching great battle which will doubtless determine the fate of the Southern Confederacy, the loyal American people have no one to blame, no one to curse but McDowell and the Blindness of the War Department.

Captain Brown also targeted division commander Rufus King for some of the blame:

> The general is a sluggard, a man of no force of character, or he would not be here with his division," Brown continued. "But King will play up the 'gentleman General' have luxurious headquarters, dispense hospitality to notable individuals get up parades shows for their edification, have fine band playing evenings around 'these Head Quarters' pass the wine cup around to his satellites and friends, ride splendid horses when he goes out to see be seen attended by his parasites and staff. Ah! it is a great thing for men Bankrupt politically & financially to old high place in the Army . . . without rending if any aid in its death struggle with rebellion. Too many men who are

entirely satisfied with the place they hold have been appointed as Generals. Why? When the war is ended they will go back to the obscurity from which they came."[41]

Frustration mounted when John Pope, the new commander of the Army of Virginia, got off to a troubling start. A native of Kentucky, Pope graduated from the U.S. Military Academy at West Point in 1842 and served in the Mexican War. He was a captain in the Regular Army when the Civil War broke out and, upon Abraham Lincoln's election, used his political connections (his father was a judge in Illinois) to travel on part of the president-elect's journey east to Washington. Rebuffed in his attempt to be named the president's military secretary, Pope accepted a commission as brigadier general of volunteers and was placed in command the Army of the Mississippi. He earned wide newspaper attention, much of it through his own efforts, for the capture of New Madrid and Island 10 on the Mississippi River. Although modest successes, the victories caught Lincoln's eye (and probably his political attention in a time of Federal failure and inactivity) and Pope was brought East. His new assignment and army was to protect Washington, threaten Confederate rail lines in central Virginia, and open a second front to threaten Richmond.

"I come to you of the West, where we have always seen the backs of our enemies," the general proclaimed to his new army in a boastful order. "I am sorry to find so much in vogue amongst you . . . certain phrases [such as] 'lines of retreat,' and 'bases of supplies.' . . . Let us study the probably lines of retreat of our opponents and leave our own to take care of themselves. Let us look before us and not behind. Success and glory are in the advance, disaster and shame luck in the rear." Pope's clumsy swipe at McClellan did not go down at all well with soldiers recently associated with the Army of the Potomac. "General Pope's bombastic proclamation has not tended to increase confidence, indeed the effect is exactly the contrary," grumbled a Wisconsin officer in a letter home. Mickey Sullivan took a dimmer view when looking back at those troubling days long after the war: "General Pope who had captured the rebels that the gunboats had dislodged from island No. 10 and New Madrid, and in consequence fancied himself the greatest general of the age . . . issued his first order dated 'Headquarters in the Saddle,' and the soldiers, with their usual aptitude to ridicule all attempts at self-glorification on the part of generals, said that he must have his brains where most persons have their hindquarters . . . and after events fully justified their judgment." To be fair, Pope strenuously denied ever having written an order using the phrase "Headquarters in

---

41 Edwin A. Brown, letter to his father, June 15, 1862.

the Saddle," but once the story began making the rounds, he was never able to escape it.[42]

Despite the interminable wait, one of the 2nd Wisconsin men reached the conclusion that the volunteers of 1861 were more sure of their loyalty than when they enlisted. "I believe the boys are as patriotic now as then, only an inexperienced person might not think so, if he should happen along about the time something goes wrong, and hear them cursing the war, and the generals, and the country, sometimes even the cause that brought them here," he wrote home. "They are not so ardent and fiery, experience has tamed them. They are cooler, and I believe fight better and endure more. . . . The mass of the army is true and tried."[43]

News seeping in from McClellan's front was at first encouraging. The Army of the Potomac was attacked on May 31 at Seven Pines, where Confederate Joseph E. Johnston, one of the heroes of Bull Run, tried to crush an isolated portion of the Federal army south of the Chickahominy River. It all went sour quickly for the Rebels, who did not have enough experience to pull off the complex offensive plan. About dusk, Johnston was struck in the right shoulder by a ball and in his chest by a spent piece of shell. He was succeeded by G. W. Smith, who was replaced the next day by Gen. Robert E. Lee.

As he was wont to do after any serious fighting, McClellan paused his offensive operations to extend his lines and bring up the necessary armament and supplies. It was not until June 25 that Little Mac began a serious movement, winning a minor victory at Oak Grove. Troubling telegraph reports reached the Western boys that told of heavy fighting and setbacks at Beaver Dam Creek, Gaines' Mill, and Savage's Station, where the rearguard of the Union army was sharply attacked. Befuddled by Lee's relentless attacks and alarmed that he was heavily outnumbered,

---

42 Dawes, *Service*, 51; James P. "Mickey" Sullivan of Company K, "Ready, Aim, Aim Low," *Milwaukee Sunday Telegraph*, November 4, 1883. "A good deal of cheap wit has been expended upon a fanciful story that I published an order or wrote a letter or made a remark that my 'headquarters would be in the saddle,'" wrote Pope. "It is an expression harmless and innocent enough, but it is even stated that it furnished General Lee with the basis for the only joke of his life. I think it is due to army tradition, and to be the comfort of those who have so often repeated the ancient joke in the days long before the civil war, that those later wits should not allowed with impunity to poach on this well-tilled manor. This venerable joke I first heard when a cadet at West Point . . . and I presume it could be easily traced back to the Crusades and beyond. Certainly I never used this expression or wrote or dictated it, not does any such expression occur in any order of mine; and as it has perhaps served its time and effected its purpose, it ought to be retired." John Pope, "The Second Battle of Bull Run," *Battles and Leaders of the Civil War*, Robert U. Johnson and Clarence C. Buell, eds., 4 vols. (New York, NY, 1956), vol. 2, 493-494.

43 Kellogg, *Milwaukee Sunday Telegraph*, September 28, 1879. Kellogg served with Co. C, 2nd Wisconsin. The quotation was from a letter he wrote May 24, 1862, reprinted in the *Telegraph*.

McClellan was retreating toward the safety of Harrison's Landing and the Union gunboats on the James River. The Lee criticized as "Granny Lee" because of his caution during the early days of the war was gone forever. Now reinforced by Thomas "Stonewall" Jackson command from the Shenandoah Valley, he maneuvered to intercept McClellan at Glendale on June 30. The attacks fell apart and the Federals escaped to a strong defensive position on Malvern Hill. Lee hit them again there on July 1, but the Federals threw back the effort and inflicted heavy casualties.

McClellan's grand advance undertaken with such hope and promise had failed. Much of the Confederate success was properly attached to Lee's assumption of command and his unexpected boldness. The slashing attacks shook Little Mac to the core, and he withdrew to Harrison's Landing to dig in. He bombarded Washington with requests for troops and supplies and told anyone who would listen that the setback was Washington's fault for failing to release McDowell's corps and other troops he had requested. McClellan protested that he was overwhelmed by superior forces (in fact, he outnumbered the Rebels). The bravery of his own soldiers had kept the defeats from turning into something much worse.[44] "There has been terrible slaughter, but we are well satisfied that McClellan is safe," a soldier in Gibbon's brigade wrote home. "We did not have half force enough. When we get there we will make them skedaddle, where ever we meet them we drive them back, but it must be admitted they fight like devils."

It is Admitted We are Not Bad on a March

Despite the distressing news from outside Richmond, the Western Brigade celebrated the Fourth of July in proper fashion. Private Ray noted in his journal that it was a fine day for the 86th birthday "of this great and once happy Republic." Still, it was "awful to think of that a portion of its inhabitants have tried to & and Disgraced it to their utmost." The morning opened in the Federal camps at Fredericksburg with the usual reveille and roll call, but there was laughter and catcalls in ranks as the companies formed. In the 7th Wisconsin, new officers from the boys in the back ranks were "elected" on the spot and took command. Colonel John Callis was called out and ordered to carry breakfast to the guards. "This rather plagued him but go he must," wrote Ray.

---

44 The fighting during the Seven Days' Battles (June 25-July 1, 1862) was the heaviest of the war up to that point, its 30,000 killed and wounded equal to the number of casualties in all the battles in the Western Theater fought during the first half of 1862. James McPherson, *The Battle Cry of Freedom: The Civil War Era* (New York, NY, 1988), 471.

Other officers were named to the cooking and water carrying details. Non-commissioned officers were assigned to the police details cleaning up the campgrounds under the watchful eyes of privates. The guards came out dressed in their dirtiest and "most comical" uniforms. "Our corporal had an old haversack for a hat, got an old knapsack which had been thrown away, and put it on with the canteen tied to the knapsack behind dangling about his legs and instead of a gun he had a verry large crooked stick, with paper stripes cut in a fantastic form on his arms," one soldier reported. As the unusual detail formed, a large Newfoundland dog owned by Capt. Alexander Gordon Jr. of Beloit was let free just as the guards passed. "This scattered the boys all over and the officer of guard with sword drawn tried to defend the guard and gets run over by three or four the guard which caused greater confusing in the ranks of the guard." It was all accepted in good humor by officers and men alike.

The merriment went on most of the day and included mule and horse races around a circular track. "The mules without number was run, then the horses, then foot races were run," Ray reported. "I guess every officer in the division was there and the whole of Gibbons Brigade and a few privates from other Brigades, but it was made for this Brigade only." Officers gathered prize money and Pvt. George Williams of the 2nd Wisconsin collected the purse for the best mule rider, with the track behind him littered with unseated soldiers. The fastest horse was a gray mare named "Bet" belonging to Adj. John Russey of the 19th Indiana (and Colonel Meredith, who had a good eye for horseflesh, won $140.00 in the wagering). A 6th Wisconsin soldier named John C. Ismael of Cassville won first prize and $10.00 as the fastest runner. Ismael was immediately challenged to a final race by Capt. Hollon Richardson of the 7th Wisconsin. The officer beat Ismael but refused any money, claiming he just wanted to see if he "had lost speed any since coming to the army." Other informal races continued until evening.

A rather unusual dress parade took place late that afternoon where, to Gibbon's surprise, the men who still had them strapped white linen leggings to coats, hats, belts, accouterments, and other pieces of equipment. The clever tweaking of his original order made even the stiff general smile. The new "officers" of the 7th Wisconsin issued a series of humorous orders before thanking the real commanders for their forbearance. Colonel Robinson was singled out "for the levity he has allowed us &c and expressing the greatest confidence in him as a man to lead us to the battle." Private Ray closed his long account of the Independence Day celebrations by admitting the brigade had made "quite a demonstration" that could have been done at home. "But when we do get home," he concluded, "we will try to raise a Co for the next fourth after." How such an unusual day could occur in a military organization during those innocent days was explained by a 2nd Wisconsin man. The Western boys, he observed, were "more lively by far than the other troops that are with us. We have more music, more dancing, more athletic sports and more real fun and good humor than the Eastern boys, and it is generally admitted that we are not bad on a march." There was truth in his assessment.[45]

During those weeks opposite Fredericksburg in mid-1862, Gibbon served as both stern teacher and brigade commander, with the 4,000 men and boys under his care his often unruly students. Gibbon's heavy schedule of drills and inspections turned the volunteer regiments into effective organizations. The men quickly recognized that the well turned out soldier was given a day of "blackberrying" and so sought to emulate him. The soldier who failed to properly maintain a picket post became the object of ridicule standing on a pickle barrel. Inexperienced officers pondered and studied their drill manuals to help them master unfamiliar formations. Even Gibbon worked to better himself on the drill field. After overhearing a comment from an officer that he did not drill his regiments as a brigade because he was only an artillery officer, the general pulled out his pocket edition of Coppee's *Evolutions of the Line*. "It was slow work at first and both officers and men looked wearied and bored at the long and tedious explanations but this improved as we progressed, and I gained confidence in myself when I discovered how much more I know than my pupils and how that knowledge was increased by experience, with now and then a sly peep at my copy of Coppee which I carried in my pocket," confessed Gibbon. "In a few days practice the regiments got so they would move at this as one man, and the open ground about the Lacy House re-echoed with the solid tramp of the four regiments."

What happened on that drill field during the early summer of 1862 would have a lasting positive impact on a brigade of Western men in tall black hats. Some of it came from the confidence of knowing they could move easily and well as regiments from one formation to another. The unexpected blending of Gibbon's Old Army professionalism with the enthusiasm and desire of intelligent and willing young volunteers to become real soldiers helped glue the units together. It was not merely efficiency in drill that was gained during these weeks of instruction, explained Gibbon, but the "habit of obedience" and the "subjection to the will of another, so difficult to instill into the minds of free and independent men" that became marked characteristics of the command. "A great deal of the prejudice against me as a regular officer was removed when the men came to compare their own soldierly appearance and way of doing duty with other commands, and although there were still malcontents who chafed under the restraints of a wholesome discipline and

45 Ray, *Iron Brigade*, 110-115; Gaff, *Bloody Field*, 139-141; Stine, *Army of the Potomac*, 114.

would have chafed under any, these were gradually reduced in number and influence."[46]

The men in the ranks had also taken Gibbon's measure as well as the measure of their own officers. "The men who carried the knapsacks never failed to place an officer just where he belonged, as to his intelligence and bravery," one veteran explained. "Even if they said nothing, yet their instinctive and unconscious action in battle placed upon the officers the unavoidable brand of approval or disapproval. For no regiment acted well its part under fire and great danger, without the officers had the confidence of the rank and file."[47] The three Wisconsin and one Indiana regiments were moving away from being just an unlikely brigade of Western volunteers in an army of Easterners to becoming Gibbon's "Black Hat" Brigade—a significant development at a time when "wholesome discipline" and "efficiency in drill" and confidence in officers would be sorely needed. [48]

Gibbon was later credited with shaping the Western regiments into an effective "Iron Brigade," but it is easy to overlook Adj. Frank Haskell's role in this development. Gibbon found a willing associate in Haskell, and the former adjutant of the 6th Wisconsin found a mentor as well as a friend. Haskell's interest in military matters stretched back to his days in Madison where he helped organize the Governor's Guard, a militia company with a pre-war reputation for social dinners, parades, and picnics. ("I go in for a reasonable amount of fun, and [the] military has some little fun together with some nonsense in it," fellow Guardsman Lucius Fairchild wrote a friend.)

Help turning the Governor's Guard into an elite unit also arrived from an unexpected source in the form of New York's E. Elmer Ellsworth, who was in Wisconsin and developing his skill as a drillmaster. One of the unit founders, E. W. Keyes, said young Ellsworth was the "inspiration of the military spirit which afterward made the guard so famous in the matter of furnishing competent and experienced officers" to the Badger regiments. Ellsworth appeared in Madison shortly after the company formed and spent time, without compensation, drilling the amateurs. He was months away from national fame as a drillmaster of a Chicago company of Zouaves and his untimely death as a Union martyr at the beginning of the Civil War. "His heart and soul were in the work. His enthusiasm was boundless,

---

46 Gibbon, *Recollections*, 37.

47 Fitch, *Echoes*, 330.

48 Gibbon, *Recollections*, 37-38. See Capt. Henry Coppee, *The Field Manual of Evolutions of the Line* (Philadelphia, PA, 1862).

although at the time of his work here no one dreamed that the rebellion was possible," said Keyes.[49]

No one of the young Madison organization was more captivated with Ellsworth's instruction than Haskell, although his climb in rank in the militia company came rather slowly. He was elected first corporal on August 24, 1858, first sergeant on April 13 the next year, and a successful contender for first lieutenant in 1860. Haskell was remembered as a rather severe drillmaster. On one occasion, Keyes recalled how he and a friend walked out of one of Haskell's long sessions, stacked muskets, and "hunted for a cool restful place." They were both fined for their lack of discipline. Keyes said the incident revealed Haskell's "peculiar disposition; that he had little sympathy for a raw soldier no matter how much he was suffering from the heat dust and thirst when on duty or on the march." Several other Guardsmen in addition to Haskell and now soldiers in what would become the Iron Brigade fell under Ellsworth's instruction and influence, including Lucius Fairchild, Julius Atwood, Thomas S. Allen, John F. Randolph, and Nathaniel Rollins.[50]

Still, the coming of the Civil War and Ellsworth's tragic death in April 1861 while pulling down a secessionist flag in Alexandria, Virginia (his friend and mentor President Lincoln was rendered speechless by the news) caused many of the Guardsmen to hold back when the company was activated for service in the 90-day 1st Wisconsin Militia. It was not until June 20, 1861, that Haskell finally accepted a commission as a volunteer and that was as first lieutenant and adjutant of the 6th Wisconsin. The staff position, however, blocked quick promotion. Haskell's ambition displayed itself in 1862 in a sharp lesson in the type of politics that swirled through the volunteer regiments of the day. His friends at Madison were already petitioning new Republican Governor Louis P. Harvey to advance Haskell to a field-grade position when Haskell's former law partner, Julius Atwood, resigned as lieutenant colonel of the 6th Wisconsin and was replaced by Benjamin Sweet. The vacancy at major was filled by Edward Bragg. When Sweet resigned to accept a higher commission, Bragg moved to lieutenant colonel, which created a field-grade opportunity for Haskell, who was quick to seek the position. He had the backing of Gibbon and Cutler, but the latter tired to placate his line officers and allowed his

---

49 E. W. Keyes wrote in 1910: "His association with the Governor's Guard at that period of our history is an historical reminiscence to be well remembered." Judge E. W. Keyes, "Madison's First Governor's Guard," *Madison Democrat*, April 24, 1910. Julius Atwood, Haskell's law partner, was elected president at the February 5, 1858 organizational meeting in Madison and would become lieutenant colonel of the 6th Wisconsin.

50 Keyes, *Madison Democrat*, April 24, 1910; Haskell, *Haskell of Gettysburg*, 12-16.

four captains of equal seniority to draw lots. When young Rufus Dawes won the contest, Cutler convened a caucus in an attempt to induce the captains to select Haskell. The caucus voted to recommend Dawes. Haskell refused to accept the close vote, and he and Dawes both agreed to continue to seek the post, shook hands, and sent off letters to friends in Madison. Dawes was unsure about his chances. "Colonel Cutler, General Gibbon, General King, and, I suppose, all Madison, Wisconsin, recommended Haskell," Dawes wrote home. "Lieutenant Colonel Sweet, Major Bragg, seven captains, fourteen Lieutenants and three regimental staff officers recommended my appointment."[51]

An unforeseen development had a direct effect on the selection process. Governor Harvey, who favored Haskell's promotion, drowned on April 19, 1862, while on a relief mission to aid Wisconsin troops after the battle of Shiloh. Harvey was succeeded by Lt. Gov. Edward Salomon, a German-American lawyer and Democrat from Milwaukee who was on the Republican ticket to garner war support and the German vote. Salomon's position on the appointment of a new major was unknown and Haskell's friends besieged him so aggressively that the new governor began to resent the pressure. Benjamin Sweet, the former lieutenant colonel of the regiment who had squabbled with Cutler, added to the chaos by visiting Salmon to oppose Haskell as a means of getting back at Cutler. The matter concluded when Salomon gave the major straps to Dawes. The new major viewed his promotion favorably at the time, but Dawes could never shake its affect on Haskell because "it put entirely out of the line of promotion one of the finest officers Wisconsin sent to the war." Gibbon, who was intimately associated with Haskell, later wrote that his adjutant "was better qualified to command an army corps than many who enjoyed the honor." Haskell continued serving on Gibbon's staff until 1864, when he finally won appointment as colonel of the 36th Wisconsin. Haskell was killed that June at Cold Harbor when he stood up under fire in an attempt to encourage his green regiment to attack the enemy's works.[52]

While Gibbon's regiments drilled, squabbled, and played politics, events well beyond their control shaped the future of the Western volunteers. With the Army of the Potomac inactive at Harrison's Landing, Lee's Army of Northern Virginia was situated between McClellan and John Pope's new Army of Virginia farther to the north. For an aggressive commander like Lee it was a position of opportunity, and there was concern in Washington that he would concentrate near Gordonsville

51 Dawes, *Service*, 50-51.

52 Haskell, *Haskell*, 18-20, 42; In September 22, 1862, Haskell wrote he had pretty much given up any attempt for promotion. Governor Salomon "will not appoint me. I have got done asking for promotion—I should like it—I think I deserve it—but I shall not get it."

against Pope. Rufus King's division was ordered to make a series of marches and patrols to determine if the Confederates were on the move. Gibbon's brigade, with Battery B of the 4th U.S. Artillery and a few squads of the 3rd Indiana Cavalry, ran into enemy skirmishers near the Orange Court House on July 24. Unwilling to risk an engagement, Gibbon withdrew in the face of increasing opposition. It was only later that he learned he was trading shots with some of Stonewall Jackson's regiments. On August 5, Gibbon led another reconnaissance with the 2nd and 7th Wisconsin, 19th Indiana, and Battery B to intercept rebel communications along the Virginia Central Railroad. At the same time, another detachment under Col. Cutler with the 6th Wisconsin and some soldiers from the Harris Light Cavalry and a section of the 1st New Hampshire Battery moved toward Frederick Hall Station near the North Anna River. Gibbon retreated when a screen of Confederate cavalry moved into his rear and threatened his wagons. Cutler reached Frederick's Hall Station, burned Confederate supplies, and destroyed two miles of railroad track. Three days later Gibbon's brigade was once again assembled near Fredericksburg. Cutler's troops had marched ninety miles in hot weather in nearly four days. Gibbon's losses were fifty-nine, most of them exhausted soldiers left behind and captured by enemy cavalry.[53]

With Pope moving to threaten rail junctions northwest of Richmond, General Lee, emboldened by his success against McClellan, seized the initiative and dispatched Jackson and three divisions to Gordonsville. Thereafter Lee began moving other brigades by rail to catch up with Jackson, who was moving against two Union divisions under Nathanial Banks at Cedar Mountain. Expecting to be reinforced, Banks attacked Jackson's larger command and nearly defeated him before events went against the Federals and they were driven from the field. Lee began shifting additional brigades to swell Jackson's ranks with the hope he could strike Pope before the Union general could be reinforced.

New York and Pennsylvania Monopolize All the Glory

The official reports of those days of marching to find Tom Jackson and his Confederate divisions appear detailed and precise. The columns moved here and then there, the papers explained, with little indication of confusion or how the hot sultry weather thinned the columns. In the end, little real intelligence was gained. The Confederate cavalry screen commanded by Jeb Stuart blinded the Federals to

---

53 Nolan, *Iron Brigade*, 66-69; Otis, *Second Wisconsin*, 50-54.

the movements of the enemy and the old Bull Run fear of the "Black Horse Cavalry" played on the minds of the soldiers.

In truth, the marches were not as well organized or performed as hindsight suggested. Private William Ray, whose fever and poison ivy left him in camp, recorded a very different view. The regiment was not gone long, he wrote in his journal, when weary stragglers began stumbling into camp, done in by the heat and fast pace. One of them was a distraught Louis Kuntz, who brought news of a near-escape from Rebel horsemen and the capture of several Black Hats. According to Kuntz, he and another played-out soldier from the 19th Indiana spent the night at a farm house and were eating breakfast when a squad of enemy troopers surrounded a wagon of exhausted boys from the 2nd Wisconsin, which was just then passing by the farm. Kuntz and the Hoosier made a run for it, but the latter stopped when ordered and was captured. Kuntz made his way into a stand of woods with bullets flying around him and hid there. "He said all those along the road was taken prisoner & and that not being a few," wrote Ray. "They took all of our provisions train but three wagons before coming up to this house. They just cleaned up everything that was behind the main body of troops." Many of the supply wagons were recaptured later that night.[54]

The regiment finally returned to camp on August 8 much the worse for wear. Ray tried to describe the scene in his journal: "A couple of the boys have come in bringing the news of the Regt coming in soon. Here some two or three more boys come. There some more. Well, they coming in separately, every man for himself. Here Cap comes with two or three more and they kept coming in for an hour." Ray gathered up buckets of cold water for the soldiers. "They complain of being tired & and sore all over, some lame and some one thing and some another complaint. They have had plenty to eat but hard marching and not much rest and very little sleep." The soldiers threw themselves on the ground and slept for two or three hours only to wake extremely stiff. "It being warm dry weather all the time and the dust intolerable and scarcity of water and the excitement at times & doublequicking some, and altogether it was a wonder that some of our Co didn't die."[55]

After a day of resting and some preparation, during which some of the sick were sent to Washington, the Black Hat brigade was given orders to "strike tents and fall in." In the 7th Wisconsin, a delay ensued to fix a mix-up getting the knapsacks of the men loaded into wagons. The column of some 1,900 officers and

54 Ray, *Iron Brigade*, 125-126. Kuntz enlisted in Co. F on August 19, 1861, and was killed at Antietam on September 17, 1862. *Wisconsin Roster*, vol. 1, 560.

55 Ray, *Iron Brigade*, 127-128; Otis, *Second Wisconsin*, 53-55.

men was soon on the road and, despite the hard week just experienced, moved with a quiet professionalism that demonstrated the Westerners with their big hats were no longer awkward volunteers. There seemed to be a great urgency to the march and the thick column moved quickly over dusty roads under a "scorching" August sun and heat "like a great hot sponge, which sucked the moisture out of every pore of the soldier's body." The ambulances traveling with the regiments were soon filled with "sick or given out men." Water disappeared. "When a streamlet or spring was reached," one Black Hat said, "it was lined with eager soldiers scraping the muddy bottom with cups in order to provide for their exhausted canteens." The hours passed slowly along a road with no end. Swept by a sudden rain, the roads "were soon over shoe top deep with soft mud." The column halted to wait out the weather. Private Chester Wyman of the 6th Wisconsin found a small rise and fell asleep. When he awoke, he discovered he was in a graveyard and had been sleeping on a grave.[56]

The column reached the Rappahannock River at Kelly's Ford at dusk. The bridge was out. Under a rising bright moon, the soldiers took off trousers, tucked up shirts and, holding their muskets and cartridge boxes high, pushed waist deep into the river. Some of the soldiers without under drawers were naked from the waist down and the moonlight made their bare legs seem almost white. One cheeky half-naked Hoosier approached Colonel Meredith, who was sitting on his horse watching the men wade across. The soldier told the tall officer that he wanted to show off the perfect fit and durability of the "uniform" he had been wearing the past 22 years. Long Sol guffawed out loud. The night was cool but pleasant and the crossing marked with friendly catcalls. "Now and then, when a poor devil slipped from the stone and went, ca-souse, into the water, a great cry went up." Once on the far side, the soldiers marched a short distance before halting to spread oil cloths to sleep. They had marched 20 miles.[57] The night was an unhappy one. During the day, word reached the marching column about the Cedar Mountain fight "and that our folks was whipped and all kinds of rumors," one Badger wrote in his journal. When the column drew near the scene of the fighting, the battleground and flags of truce could be seen some distance to the south on higher ground. More important to

56 Chester A. Wyman, letter, May 28, 1918 (privately held).

57 Otis, *Second Wisconsin*, 54; Ray, *Iron Brigade*, 128; Cheek and Pointon, *Sauk County*, 30; Edward Bragg, letter to Earl Rogers, April 3, 1900, Jerome A. Watrous Papers, WHS; Gaff, *Bloody Field*, 149. The number of 1,937 for Gibbon's brigade can be found in Alan Gaff, *Brave Men's Tears: The Iron Brigade at Brawner Farm* (Dayton, OH, 1983), 157. Gaff credited the 2nd Wisconsin with 430, the 6th Wisconsin with 504, the 7th Wisconsin with 580, and the 19th Indiana with 433.

some of the men in the ranks of the 7th Wisconsin was the dozen beehives found along the way. Private Ray was still sick. "Well now we knew what the forced march was for and didn't regret it any although the complaints were loud about soreness and sleepiness." Wines and whiskey meant for medicinal purposes proved a problem on the march. The officers drank up the spirits, complained a private, and the "doctors are so drunk they can hardly sit on their horses and they don't notice the poor fellows that are lying by the roadside panting and feeling as if they don't care whether they live or die for such is their feelings." Even the second lieutenant of his company was so tight that "he couldn't walk and that was all and was perfectly foolish which I hated to see."[58]

After tramping forty-five miles the tired Wisconsin and Indiana men went into bivouac near the battlefield. They had finished some hard days, wrote two of the Sauk County men: "Weather muggy, hot, no rest except to make coffee, wading streams, marching in mud very little rations (hardtack tasted good those days)." Other brigades in King's division were thinned by worn-out soldiers who fell behind. "Straggling became almost a mania, some regiments not being able to account for half their men," said one Badger. "It was here Gibbon's brigade showed its wonderful discipline and high morale. Our regiments had comparatively no stragglers, not through the immediate influence of the officer alone, but a feeling of personal responsibility, each man for the man whose elbow he touched in ranks, and the responsive thought, 'I must not fail myself in the duty I demand of my comrade.'"[59]

Gibbon rode ahead to take a look at the battlefield and "discovered evidence of a severe struggle, but from what I could learn it was not a very decisive one," he wrote later. Captain Brown in the 6th Wisconsin told his father in a letter two days later that General Pope "was so badly scared that on the night we arrived he caused all the stores everything belonging to the army to be shipped on the R.R. He expected to be attacked as Jackson was large reinforced." The 3rd Wisconsin, which had fought in the battle, was found camped alongside the roadway. Someone by a fire called out, "What regiment, boys?" When told the 7th Wisconsin, laughter and a few cheers broke out before questions about this or that man who belonged

58 Ray, *Iron Brigade*, 129.

59 Therron W. Haight, "King's Division: Fredericksburg to Manassas," *War Papers*, vol. 2 (Milwaukee, WI, 1896), 348; J. O. Johnson, "Army Reminiscences," *Milwaukee Sunday Telegraph*, November 30, 1884; Gibbon, *Recollections*, 43; Cheek and Pointon, *Sauk County*, 30. Johnson served in the 6th Wisconsin. Haight, who was living in Wisconsin in 1861, returned to his native New York and joined the 24th New York. He returned to Wisconsin after the war and became publisher of the *Waukesha* (Wisconsin) *Freeman* newspaper.

to each regiment. "They were very glad to see us and we to see them. They said we were the only Wisconsin boys they had seen in the service. A great many found friends." Brown penned in his letter home that the 3rd Wisconsin "suffered greatly in the fight but no mention is made of it. N.Y. & Penn Reporters monopolize all the glory for their own State troops, although they never do as well as the New England & Western troops—The marches made by our Regt. were the longest & most severe made this century. We cut off Jackson's Communications with Richmond & then marched here to help whip him, and the Sixth Wis. never even got a Newspaper puff for it. Two New York Regts. who acted as our support 30 miles in our rear got all the newspaper Credit for what we did," he added.

Brown put the situation in perspective:

> Our division arrived at this point [Cedar Mountain] just after the battle. We made a forced march to get here at that. Before that we had been out on an expedition to Frederick Hall Station on the Va. Central Rail Road. The Sixth Wis., did all that was done. The balance of the expedition failed. We tore up the track for miles and blowed up two Culverts, burned the Depot, and destroyed the commissary stores & and other confederate property including 1,400 sacks of flour. . . . [W]e made a forced march of 39 miles crossing the branch of the Pamunkey, which was not fordable, going 10 miles beyond the Bridge over it. And only left a guard of 100 men who were tired out to guard it. On our retreat we burned the Bridge which was a wooden structure 150 long & 70 feet above the water. We think we did a big thing. We marched 102 miles in 3 ½ days, accomplishing a good deal. As above stated, had no support within 30 miles hardly slept or eat during the time, rested one night & half a day, were ordered peremptorily to march here.[60]

The Black Hat regiments set up picket lines and established camps. That night, one of the non-commissioned officers named John Johnson of the 6th Wisconsin was making the rounds when he came upon a badly shaken Dennis Kelly of Fountain City. "Sergeant," he told Johnson, "I have seen ghosts of spirits." Kelly was a steady young fellow and known to the sergeant. "I knew the man to be truthful, and told him to be still and I would examine the cause, being afraid that some of the men would raise a false alarm. I started in the direction of the field, and marched directly to the nearest point," continued Johnson. "There I found a dead body, interred very shallow, and a phosphorescent light oscillating from the head to the foot of the corpse. And so it proved in every instance." Johnson puzzled over

60 Gibbon, *Recollections*, 43; George Eustice, letter, undated; Ray, *Iron Brigade*, 129; Brown, letter to his father, August 13, 1862.

the cause. "It being a very warm, sultry night and dark, must have been the reason of it, or some gas from the decaying bodies. Some of the corpses were covered so slightly, that the head and feet protruded under the sod."

It was the 6th regiment's first contact with "one of the real horrors of war." According to Mair Pointon and Phil Cheek in the Sauk County company, the fallen soldiers were buried so shallow "that the tops of the trenches were moving like gentle waves with living corruption. This is the only place we could distinguish between the scent of dead animals and human beings in the state of decomposition. The human is very much more offensive than the animal." Private Hugh Perkins of the 7th Wisconsin wrote to a friend that "it looks hard to see men buried like a lot of hogs, 12 to 15 together. But I suppose they feel as well as though they [had] ever so nice a grave and coffin. We had nothing to brag about in this fight." Lieutenant John Shafer of the 19th Indiana wrote home, "the piles of dead horses upon both sides, the remnants of arms, accouterments and clothing, the fresh soil covering the remains of the fallen, were silent but melancholy evidence of the deadly conflict." [61]

The Black Hats spent a week near the battlefield, much of the time building cremation fires for the dead horses sprawled everywhere. The word making the rounds was that Jackson had fallen back behind the Rappahannock River and that Pope had reported to Washington that the enemy was "in full retreat towards Richmond, complete demoralized." Mickey Sullivan complained bitterly that Pope compelled the army "to remain encamped more than a week during the hottest part of the year, on the battlefield, subject to the overpowering stench of decaying horses and half buried bodies, when fifteen minutes march would have placed them in adjoining grove of timber where they would have shelter from the sun and have plenty of good water, and be removed from the filth and unwholesomeness of the battlefield."[62]

Despite the stench and sickening work, however, appetites remained good. "Today the boys took everything they wanted if they could find it such as horses, mules, chickens, ducks & geese & honey which there was a plenty," Private Ray wrote in his journal while another Badger reported that "the officers, though against this, acted as if they didn't see anything. Only when it got too bad they raised hell with the soldiers." The Sauk County men said simply that "it was here not a

61 Johnson, *Milwaukee Sunday Telegraph*, November 30, 1884; Cheek and Pointon, *Sauk County*, 31; Dawes *Service*, 56; Perkins, letter, August 17, 1863; Gaff, *Bloody Field*, 150. Kelly was wounded during the Spotsylvania Campaign at Laurel Hill and died on June 23, 1864. He is buried at Arlington National Cemetery. *Wisconsin Roster*, vol. 1, 526.

62 Sullivan, *Milwaukee Sunday Telegraph*, November 4, 1883.

question of what you should eat, but what you could get."[63] The incident showed the Wisconsin and Indiana boys were much changed from the awkward greenhorn patriots who tramped away from home in 1861. Just weeks before Cedar Mountain, in writing a friend, a Wisconsin officer reported that the "cowards have been sifted out of the ranks, and the huge talking men, the braggarts, and boasters have gone home. The men who are left are real warriors, and not the holiday party that you saw us when we went away." His 2nd Wisconsin was thinned by hard service, he said, but "I think what there are left of us are made of the 'real ould stuff.' I don't think it would be safe for any disease as the cholera, smallpox, or typhoid fever to attack us single-handed. Perhaps take the three combined they might make us sick—nothing more; for nothing short of a Minie [ball] can kill us, or we should have been dead ere this." Another Black Hat said that "we have some hard boys, I admit that; but when they get where there are any secesh they are not afraid."

Just ahead of them, not too far down the road, was a farm rented by John Brawner near the old battlefield of Bull Run.[64]

Matt Bernard and Kindred Stories

It was on one of the marches returning to Fredericksburg that the young officers of Co. C of the 6th Wisconsin—the Prairie du Chien Jayhawkers—discovered their black cook Joe Allen had walked off without any notice. He was one of the hundreds of runaway slaves who flocked to the army seeking safety in the circle of "Massa Linkum's men." The fugitives were young and old, men and women, family groups and alone, and they "came in clouds," one Badger officer said. "The first party I ever saw was a family of some sixteen—an old couple with some children, a young married couple with one child, and some men and boys." In the camps, they approached the fires "as composedly as if it had been built for them." One of the "little darkies" kept the camp alive "for an hour with plantation jigs," he continued. "For the information of those who are interested in the great moral question as to the effect of freedom upon this opposed race, I will state that this particular offshoot . . . is as graceless a vagabond as ever assisted in upheaving a nation and producing civil war."[65]

---

63 Ray, *Iron Brigade*, 129; Cheek and Pointon, *Sauk County*, 31.

64 Kellogg, *Milwaukee Sunday Telegraph*, September 26, 1879; Charles Dow, "Wartime Letters of Charles C. Dow, Co. G, 2d Wisconsin," in Otis, *Second Wisconsin*, 146 (originally in *Wisconsin State Register*, July 5, 1862); Edwin R. Hancock, *Columbus Weekly Journal*, January 22, 1862.

65 *Green Bay Advocate*, July 10, 1862.

Prairie du Chien Volunteers, Co. C, 6th Wisconsin

Several of the Jayhawkers of Company C post near their shelter in an image believed taken opposite Fredericksburg in the summer of 1862. *Institute for Civil War Studies*

Senior army officials had no idea what to do with the fugitives. There were no regulations for dealing with runaways and no plan to feed or care for them. Looking into the hard face of slavery the enlisted men at first backed away, only to come to accept them as part of army life. They called them "contrabands," after a statement made by Union Maj. Gen. Ben Butler that fugitives reaching his lines were "contraband of war." Butler refused to return them to their previous owners. If the army did not know what to do with them, that was not a problem in the lower ranks, where many were hired to cook and wash, tend horses and mules, polish boots and saddles, and do all sorts of tasks for coins and food.

The "contrabands" can be found over and over again in the dim photographic histories of the war—black cooks, teamsters, and strikers—in twos and threes, usually looking at the camera from the background of a posed shot. By the time the Black Hat brigade reached the area around Fredericksburg, every company had at least one servant attached to the mess details of the various officers. The runaways would soon be wearing blue uniforms themselves. Often forgotten is the simple fact that these men were part of the Union Army—and a very important part at that—from very early in the war.

It was for that reason of convenience that the officers of the Prairie du Chien Volunteers were "completely upset" over the disappearance of Cook Allen, a runaway late of Culpepper remembered for his ability to predict the weather and a fondness for big words. Allen approached the officers' cook fire for the first time with what one remembered as a "half-afraid" manner. When greeted with a welcoming hello, Allen exclaimed, "Bressed de Lawd, dat I found freedom and kind frien's at de same time." Now Allen was gone, apparently for good, and three company officers—Captain Plummer, his brother 1st Lt. Tom Plummer (recent immigrants from England), and 2nd Lt. Loyd Harris—wore long faces that night. Harris insisted he would do the cooking, and "after several mishaps, such as upsetting the coffee pot and allowing the fire to communicate with the pork in the frying-pan," a hardscrabble supper was eaten with grim faces and little talking.[66]

Not far away, company privates observed the young lieutenant's inept efforts with amusement. After a brief discussion Orrin D. Chapman ("with a mischievous smile playing around the corners of his mouth," remembered Harris) approached the officers struggling to eat Harris' fare. The boys heard about the missing cook, Chapman said, and sent him "to say that we have got an old colored man who has been with us for some time doing our washing." The runaway claimed to be able to do common cooking. "Now if you want him you are welcome to hire him and we'll get another one somewhere." The kind offer was quickly accepted and Chapman introduced the young officers to "the best old darkey that ever followed the 6th."[67]

The man's name was Matthew Bernard, wrote Harris, who "must have been fifty years old the day he made his first blow, and in a quiet voice said, "Gemmn, I hopes I'll always suit you." The introduction went well. "Bless his kind, old heart, he always suited us, never failed us, and even in the hour of danger . . . brave old Matt waited for his orders to seek safety." Bernard told his story to Harris, who later put it on paper. "Over the river, just below Fredericksburg on Mass Arthur Bernard place, was born," began "old Matt." "It was dar I grew up as a slave, and with the consent of Massa Bernard I married one who was raised on de same place. We was very happy, sah; had a little baby girl who is now almost grown. Just before the war, I heered that my wife was to be sold. I sent to Massa Bernard wid tears in my eyes, and begged him not to sell her. He would do it; and he sold her to go far south. When she was gone I went to him and said Mass Bernard, I's always been your

66 Loyd G. Harris, "The Cooks of Our Mess," *Official Bulletin, Grand Army of the Republic, National Encampment*, April 16, 1889.

67 "Grayson," Loyd G. Harris, "Old Matt Bernard (Colored)," *Milwaukee Sunday Telegraph*, April 8, 1883. Chapman, originally from Westfield, New York, enlisted as a private in Prairie du Chien. He was promoted several times to 2nd Lt. and killed at Gettysburg on July 1, 1863.

faithful slave, but you have dun sold my wife and the first chance I get I will leave you, and de old place. Soon after dat," added Matt, "de federal solders come along and I sent to see him and said Mass Bernard, good bye, and den I jined de old Sixth." This was an example of the unusual relationship developing between soldier and runaway during those days—a changing relationship that sometimes was harsh and cruel and took on a golden glow only long afterward.

Another runaway was William Jackson, who was hired by Rufus Dawes. Known for his abolitionist leanings, the captain assembled the company and announced that he had found a man to be both company cook and his servant. He would raise half the pay, he said, if the company would raise the balance for the day-to-day cooking. Mickey Sullivan, in harsh soldier fashion, later described the combined duties of Jackson as the captain's "dog robber" and the fellow in charge of the company kitchen, "which consisted of all outdoors and a hole in the ground for the fire." The arrangement proved satisfactory, however. Jackson was always on hand "and the meals ready in proper season, and the coffee had not lost its blackness nor when the beans or rice burnt or scorched any oftener than before." The captain's boots and sword, Sullivan added, "shone like new chromo, and at night William would relate to an attentive audience stories of his former slave life in de cotton and de cane and terbqacker fiel's of de souf." [68]

The initial reaction of the frontier men to contraband blacks ranged from friendly curiosity to outright hostility. "Had a regular negro dance," one soldier wrote home. "[Negroes] monarchs of all they survey—tell some curious tales. Negros more intelligent than their masters." Another volunteer told his sister that the "more I see of them the more I hate them. I wish that the Nigger lovers in Boston were down here and had to take charge of them. I did once have more sympathy for them. Now I do not think are better than cattle and I will use them as such." Lieutenant Brown blamed "the almighty Negro" for the fix the country found itself in. "Why more lives will be lost in the next big battle, more treasure expended than the necks of the whole Negro race are worth." Another Badger officer wrote he was upset with "this great national nigger question," saying he had not come as soldier "from the grand west . . . to wrangle over Virginia niggers and South Carolina niggers and other niggers."[69] At one point a "colored boy" walked into camp "bare-footed and ragged" and was taken in by the volunteers intending

68 James Patrick "Mickey" Sullivan of Co. "K," "How we lost our Cook: An incident of Rappahannock Station," *Milwaukee Sunday Telegraph*, October 21, 1883; Sullivan, *Irishman*, 40.

69 James M. Perry, diary, April 22, 1862, WHS; Horace Emerson, letter to his sister, May 21, 1862; Brown, letter to his parents, undated; *Green Bay Advocate*, December 19, 1861; *Milwaukee Sentinel*, May 12, 1862; Harris, *Milwaukee Sunday Telegraph*, April 8, 1883.

to cloth and feed him. Two officers appeared and sharply "ordered him out of the company at once, and threatened with severe punishment the man who should attempt to shelter him." It was an "atrocious act," one private exclaimed, "turning out a child of ten years from a place where, if caught by his unnatural master, nothing could save from a brutal and barbarous flogging—such as a Western farmer would be ashamed of." One of the two officers who ordered the boy out of the camp was Lieutenant Harris, the same Harris who, scarred by memories of war and infused with the wisdom that only time provides, would come to write with affection two decades later of his friendship with Matt Bernard.

During those days of soldiering, the frontier mechanics, farmers, and piney camp workers now in uniform confronted slavery and found it unsettling. The war began as an adventure in defense of the Old Flag and Union, but was now becoming something deeper and more complex. There were so few blacks back in Wisconsin and Indiana, but here there were so many. In Wisconsin, where a man was pretty much judged for his ability and strength, blacks could freely travel, own property, serve on juries, and send their children to public schools. Two enlistees in the 6th Wisconsin from the town of Forest in Bad Ax (later Vernon) County were from a "settlement of colored people" and were listed as "colored" on the 1860 census rolls. The two "were faithful soldiers, each of them receiving wounds in battle," Earl Rogers, a former officer in the company, wrote in a history of his home county. The two enlisted together sometime after Fort Sumter. One was killed in 1864, and the other made it home with the regiment and was remembered for his "faithful service." Sullivan of Company K always liked to say the black barber who accompanied the regiment from Fond du Lac was as "well known" as the brigade commander.[70]

"I really wish you could see as much of negro life as I have the past month," one of the "prints" of the 2nd Wisconsin, Boscobel newspaperman Edward Kellogg, wrote a friend. "I never dreamed they were as a race so unique, so foreign to the soil in language and custom, so clearly distinguished from the ruling race in every habit and feeling." In another letter to the same friend, he wrote: "How intense your interest is, in the cause of the Negro is stronger than mine, I confess, but I can have no controversy with you, or with any other sympathizer with the down-trodden. For, however good men may differ with regard to the policy which should be pursued in dealing with our great national evil, all who ever felt a single heart-beat for the good of humanity, are anxious that the great wrong should be

---

70 Earl M. Rogers, ed., *Memoirs of Vernon County* (Madison, WI, 1907), 21; Sullivan, *Milwaukee Sunday Telegraph*, October 21, 1883.

righted. . . . It would have done your slavery hating heart good to have seen the contrabands pouring into our lines during the past few weeks," he added. "Thousands upon thousands have found refuge among us." The 6th Wisconsin's Albert Young was one of the soldiers who entered the army to defend the Union and found his view changing. "I never thought I had entered the army in the interest of the slave," he wrote after the war. "But here I came to feel that I wished the war might result in the freeing of the colored people of the South. I was glad I was in the army if it might that our battling would result in the doing away with what I then for the first time fully recognized as being a most gigantic wrong." All that would have to be sorted out later, long after the uncomfortable week the Western Brigade spent camped near Cedar Mountain.[71]

And it was during their sojourn on the August 9 battlefield that it became apparent that something was seriously amiss. The Confederates under Jackson, as well as others from Lee's army, were on the march, but Federal commanders did not seem to know where or why. The divisions ordered north from McClellan's army outside Richmond to reinforce Pope's army were slow in coming. When Pope finally realized his army was the target, he pulled back and concentrated his command. As one private in the Western Brigade wrote, it was not "all quiet on the Potomac," adding, "It may be quiet now, but it was the damnest lively Potomac that I ever saw."

John Gibbon's brigade crossed the Rappahannock near the Orange and Alexandria Railroad on August 20. "We had been hunting the rebels, and now we were trying to keep them away from us," one private wrote the home folks. To Gibbon's dismay, the army-sized move triggered only confusion: "Wagon-trains, Divisions, Brigades, and Regiments were all mixed up, apparently in the most inextricable confusion, nobody seeming to know where to do and where anyone else was, and there was such a total absence of all order and authority as to produce a most painful impression of the mind." The officers were slow to regain control and the soldiers could see troubling clouds of dust on roads opposite the river in such a way "we could trace the advance of the rebel army." The next day a Confederate artillery battery swung into action and fired across the river. It was the first artillery some of the Western men had seen in battle. Union guns responded and silenced the opposing pieces, "showing a better practice and more accurate shooting." According to Mickey Sullivan, "Our fellows, who had never heard a rebel cannon before, but had been kept well posted about the 'black flags' and 'railroad' iron of the rebels by the warlike editors at home, and thinking that nothing

71 Kellogg, *Milwaukee Sunday Telegraph*, in a wartime letter printed September 28, 1879; Albert Young, "His Pilgrimage," *Milwaukee Sunday Telegraph*, July 1, 1888.

else could make such unearthly screams, they said the 'greybacks' were slinging railroad iron."

The 6th Wisconsin was ordered to march behind the Federal guns in range of Rebel artillery. The move distressed Private Ray of the 7th Wisconsin because he was cooking "some very fat pork" using his plate and a split stick. It was the first salt meat he had had for a week. When the column moved into the open, the Confederates turned their fire upon the regiment. "This was our initiation," said Dawes. "The shells whizzed and burst over us and around us. The men marched steadily, keeping their places and holding their heads high. They soon learned that a discreet and respectful obeisance to a cannon ball is no indication of cowardice."[72] A skirmish line of 6th Wisconsin men was thrown out and shots exchanged. Several rebels were wounded and a lieutenant and two privates captured. "These officers and their men won the first glory for the 6th Wisconsin on the field of actual battle," said Dawes.

Toward evening the regiment was again ordered to the river. When a Rebel battery opened fire, Colonel Cutler halted and carefully, according to all regulations, established guides and alignments before allowing his soldiers to lie down. "You must get used to it," he said. The cannonade did little damage, recalled Mickey Sullivan, except for one bounding cannon ball which hit the colonel's mess chest. It was then "the old greybeard, who had been an indifferent spectator hitherto, ordered the regiment to 'fall in' and he marched it about a length to one side, out of the line of fire." The entire experience, wrote the Sauk County boys, "was valuable in showing the men that artillery fire was not so dangerous as they (or the officers) had anticipated." Sadder news came from the 19th Indiana: a shell killed two horses, including one owned by Lt. Col. Alois Bachman and the other named "Bet," the fast mare that won all the races on the Fourth of July at Fredericksburg.[73]

The Black Hats received "several good shellings" over the next two days. On the 25th, King's division moved to Warrenton and then on to Sulphur Springs, where enemy artillery batteries and skirmishers shielded the enemy movements. The next day, King's division was ordered to "march with the utmost haste" to Centreville. During the move the Black Hats observed clouds of dust beyond the river: Jackson's brigades had somehow gotten between Pope's Army of Virginia and Washington. Word also reached the marching column that four days earlier, Rebel cavalry attacked Pope's wagon park at Catlett's Station and captured

72 Cheek and Pointon, *Sauk County*, 36; Cook, *Milwaukee Sunday Telegraph*, April 8, 1883; Dawes, *Service*, 46, 47-56; Sullivan, *Milwaukee Sunday Telegraph*, October 21, 1882.

73 Dawes, *Service*, 57; Brown to his father, September 5, 1862; Sullivan, *Milwaukee Sunday Telegraph*, October 21, 1882; Cheek and Pointon, *Sauk County*, 35; Ray, *Iron Brigade*, 134.

prisoners, dispatches, and baggage—including one of Pope's uniforms. The 21 wagons of Gibbon's brigade, however, had been successfully defended by the wagon guard and the sick and lame soldiers left behind. The Sauk County men serving with the guard had erected a small tent and were getting ready to sleep when the first shots were fired. "Blow out the lights!" someone shouted. When they got out of their tents, several bullets passed over their heads: "Rebels! Rebels!" The attack arrived about midnight during a thunderstorm and the 400 horsemen had to "climb over" a railroad track. The volleys fired by the sixty guards, together with a shower of stones thrown by the wounded and sick, turned back four attempts to rush the wagons. One trooper got close enough to slash the hand of a Badger with his saber. "Our boys felt pretty good over saving our brigade train, the only one saved, from injury or destruction in the entire army train," boasted one of the Sauk County men.[74]

One incident was long remembered. Cavalry general Fitzhugh Lee, the nephew of Gen. Robert E. Lee, reached the wagons amid the darkness and confusion. "Don't shoot boys, those horsemen are our men!" he yelled. The ruse did not confuse Pvt. Herman Kellner, who had already discharged his own musket. The private screamed back above the din, "Shoot the son of a rooster (or 'words to that effect') he's a damned rebel!" Fitz Lee left "as fast as a scared horse could carry him." Jerome Watrous said Lee recalled the close call in a conversation the two had long after the war. Watrous said in telling the story in his Milwaukee newspaper columns that if "Kellner had a charge in his gun the moment he discovered that the man on the white steed was a rebel, he would have brought down big game, sure." One of the brigade officers labeled the defense of the wagons "a very gallant deed, and of especial value to us as all of our paper and much property were with the wagons."[75]

Mickey Sullivan left a telling view from ranks of what was transpiring on the operational stage:

> Pope was startled by the news that instead of being in a demoralized retreat towards Richmond, 'Stonewall' was crossing the Rappahannock on his right flank and rear.

74 Dawes, *Service*, 57-58. Frank A. Haskell, to his brothers and sisters, September 22, 1862, *Wisconsin State Register*, Portage, October 4, 1862; Cheek and Pointon, *Sauk County*, 32; *Soldiers and Citizens' Album of Biographical Record*, 2 vols. (Chicago, IL, 1892), vol. 2, 722; Ray, *Iron Brigade*, 134.

75 Watrous, "Fitzhugh Lee's Close Call," *Milwaukee Sunday Telegraph*, December 3, 1882. Kellner would be wounded at South Mountain and taken prisoner at Gettysburg. He was mustered out February 18, 1865, at the end of his enlistment. *Wisconsin Roster*, vol. 1, 518.

Our whole force immediately started in pursuit and all the talk was (which we understood originated at headquarters) that Stonewall Jackson had got into a bag and General Pope was to tie the string and keep him there. But the next news was that 'Stonewall' had taken the army train and Pope's headquarters train at Catlett Station and the next news that 'Stonewall' had captured . . . [Manassas Junction] and had telegraphed to Washington for and received supplies and entire new outfit for his army. Our men lost all confidence in Pope's abilities and it was openly remarked in ranks that McDowell was a traitor.[76]

Gibbon's chance meeting with two Old Army friends—John Reynolds and George Meade—only added to the uncertainty. The two were up from the Army of the Potomac as part of the reinforcements sent to aid Pope. Meade asked Pope what he was doing at Manassas Junction. "This is no place for the army," he told Gibbon. "It should fall back so as to meet the rest of the Army of the Potomac coming up and by superior forces overwhelm Lee." According to Meade, Pope replied that he had orders from Washington to hold the Rappahannock line for two days, and by that time McClellan's men would be on hand. Pope "querulously added that the forty-eight hours had passed and the "reinforcements had not arrived."[77]

The Western men had now been in the service for a year and some weeks. The long uncertain road of civil war that began in Wisconsin and Indiana had taken several unexpected turns over ground low and high and camps dry and wet. Home seemed far off and distant—a fading memory caught in a clutch of treasured letters and pictures of those left behind. The soldiers were loyal to their men around their cook fires and in the ranks of their company and even their regiment and the brigade. They still grumbled about Gibbon and his old Army ways and worried that Lincoln would undo what had been accomplished with unnecessary political posturing and maneuvering. These volunteers were fiercely loyal to the Union, troubled about the whole matter of slavery and what to do about it, homesick, and worried the war might end without getting a chance to strike a blow.

---

76 Sullivan, *Milwaukee Sunday Telegraph*, November 4, 1883.

77 Gibbon, *Recollections*, 47-48. Gibbon said the exchange between Meade and Pope demonstrated that Pope was "lacking in that sort of independence of character which not only prompts but enables an army commander to do on the spot that which he knows the exigencies require, independent of orders received from superiors at a distance and ignorant of the situation." *Ibid.*

Part II: Baptism of Fire

A Hard Day for Mother

The day that changed everything opened much the same as the day before and the day before that—with the expectation of more marching. The Black Hats were roused at 4:00 a.m. in the dim light of false dawn for an early start. It was a Thursday, August 28, 1862, and when the sun set later that evening Gibbon's brigade would be changed in ways even the soldiers and officers were never quite able to explain.

The last several days had been hot and dusty with rations short. Gibbon had sent riders ahead the previous day (August 27) as the column approached Warrenton to have food placed along the town's sidewalks so the men could pick it up as they marched through. When he reached the main intersection, however, Gibbon found it "packed with troops, and trains slowly making their way forward, but everything else seemed to be hurried and confused." Major General Franz Sigel had his wagons with his column despite orders to leave them behind. The hungry soldiers could see "wagon-loads of hard tack and pork" being burned, but when the Wisconsin and Indiana men halted in the street to stuff their haversacks, Maj. Gen. Irvin McDowell ordered the Westerners to "push forward at once."

A frustrated Gibbon rode to the porch where General McDowell was standing and tried his best to explain the situation to the corps leader, but was turned away with a sharp order to keep his column moving. The weary and hungry soldiers, Gibbon recalled, "were obliged to turn our backs on and abandon the much-needed food. This was all the more to be regretted since scarcely had we cleared the town than the road was found so blocked up in front that our progress was very slow and after marching till long after dark we bivouacked for the night only five miles beyond Warrenton." Gibbon managed to load a few boxes of hardtack and bacon on the caissons and limbers of Battery B, but there was not nearly enough to go around. "The officers know how to take care of themselves.

Nobody worries about us. They care very little," grumbled a hungry Wisconsin soldier to his pocket diary.[1]

As the Black Hats slept alongside the roadway, General Pope reached the conclusion that Jackson's Confederate brigades might be exposed at Manassas Junction. If he moved quickly, reasoned Pope, he could trap Stonewall and his isolated command there before Lee could reinforce him. Dispatch riders galloped to the various commands with orders to concentrate at Gainesville and Haymarket or—in the case of McDowell's division—at Centreville. But Pope was wrong. Jackson was already on the move.

Stonewall Jackson's wing, about 25,000 men, had left the rest of Lee's Army of Northern Virginia along the Rappahannock River on August 25 and marched quickly around the exposed flank of Pope's Army of Virginia. Stonewall's "foot cavalry" seized the huge Federal supply depot at Manassas the next day. The always hungry Confederates ("wiry, fleet-footed, half-soled, full-souled men," was how one Badger described them) ate as much of the food as they could, filled their wagons with food, ammunition, and other supplies, and burned the rest. Jackson decided to await the arrival of the rest of the Confederate army hastening to join him. Well aware of how vulnerable he was, Jackson selected a strong defensive wooded position north of the Warrenton Turnpike just west of the old Bull Run battlefield where the year before he had won fame. But his legendry reticence to disclose his plans to anyone, including his top lieutenants, created confusion, and by daylight on the 28th only one Confederate division was on the ridge. His second division was near Centreville, and a third at Blackburn's Ford. As his men filed in along the embankments of a stony railroad grade prepared for the still-unfinished Manassas Gap Railroad, Jackson turned to the possibility of adding to the confusion of the marching Federal army. The confidence exhibited by Jackson and his veterans was not felt in Union ranks. "This Country is all woods & hills & they lay in ambush for us everywhere," one Wisconsin officer wrote home of those days. "I am afraid Pope is not equal to the task before him."[2]

Brigadier General John Hatch's brigade of Rufus King's division was the first to move on the morning of August 28, followed by Gibbon's four regiments and Battery B. King's two other brigades and their attached artillery followed. As the division's senior brigade commander, Hatch was in charge of the march because King was ill. The column was soon strung out along the Warrenton Turnpike with

---

1   Gibbon, *Recollections*, 47-48; Dawes, *Service*, 58-59, Longhenry, diary, August 28, 1862.

2   Douglas S. Freeman, *Lee's Lieutenants: A Study in Command*, 3 vols. (New York, NY, 1943), vol. 2, 102-107, Gaff, *Brave Men's Tears*, 43-54; Nolan, *Iron Brigade*, 72-79; Brown, letter to his father, August 19, 1862.

about a mile between each brigade. The movement was tiring and slow, and it went that way most of the day: march and halt, march and halt. The frustrating effort, combined with the heat and dust, threw the soldiers out of sorts. Many men spotted the disheveled King standing by a log fire, and whispers coursed through the ranks that he was drunk. In fact, King was suffering from the affects of an epileptic seizure. The Federals passed through Gainesville, "a cluster of two or three houses where the Manassas Gap railroad crosses the turnpike," before turning right down a farm lane. They marched another mile and stopped. "Orders were given for us to form a line of battle and then countermanded," reported Gibbon. "We remained halted in this position for many hours, and everybody was busy speculating as to what was going on and what was to be done." The men stacked arms and boiled coffee, paying little heed to the low rumbling thunder of distant artillery fire.

When a large body of Confederate prisoners passed, some of the Wisconsin and Indiana men stepped out for a look. The Johnnies were dirty and pretty much used up. They were Jackson's men, they said, and had not been able to keep up. One weary rebel studied the Wisconsin boys, with their knapsacks and profusion of belts and accouterments, and exclaimed, "You uns is pack mules, we uns is race horses. All old Jackson gave us, was a musket, a hundred rounds and a gum blanket, and he 'druv us so like hell,' that I could not stand it on parched corn." Dawes, who overheard the exchange, admitted later, "With us, ponderosity was a military science."[3]

Mounted on his small horse, Gibbon rode ahead during the halt and found McDowell with several officers with field glasses glued to their eyes. "In that direction heavy clouds of dust [were] seen rising about the tree tops, indicating the movement of columns of troops," he wrote. When nothing further developed, Gibbon returned to his brigade and ordered beef cattle killed and eaten. Marching orders arrived before the bloody meat could be distributed. According to a Hoosier in the 19th Indiana, hunger forced "many of us [to] cut off chunks and [eat] them warm and raw."[4]

A dispatch rider arrived at 4:00 p.m. with orders to return to the Warrenton Turnpike and on to Centreville, where Jackson might be lurking. King's division was to "move rapidly" along the roadway and be ready to bag Stonewall the next morning. Word quickly spread down to the ranks and the tired soldiers (who had lived on "corn for several days, roasted and raw," wrote one) "sprang to guns" and marched back up the lane. While McDowell and King conferred at the turnpike

3   Dawes, journal, undated; Dawes, *Service*, 45-47, 59.

4   Gibbon, *Recollections*, 56; Gaff, *Bloody Field*, 155.

Hatch deployed skirmishers and moved his brigade forward behind the thin line of blue sweeping over the fields near a house, barn, orchard, and woods north of the turnpike. One of the regiments was the 14th Brooklyn, still wearing the bright red trousers of its New York state militia uniform. When no enemy was found, Gibbon's brigade filed onto the road in column to follow Hatch. The 6th Wisconsin was in the lead, followed by the 2nd and 7th Wisconsin, with the 19th Indiana and Battery B bringing up the rear.

The men would remember later that there was little apprehension in the ranks. Gibbon recalled "the sun was shining, the birds were singing." The soldiers chatted and joked in the usual manner as they moved along the roadway in a "leisurely" fashion. "There was no thought of battle," one private recalled. Another remembered moving along "the turnpike on that quiet summer evening as unsuspecting as if changing camp." To the north was a farm house and cluster of outbuildings leased by John C. Brawner from a widow in nearby Gainesville. He had worked the 300 acres since 1858. Just past the buildings the turnpike passed through "an ugly piece of woods," where the road had been excavated leaving a three-foot embankment. Once past the timber the soldiers could "look ahead for some distance over the flat country, part fields and part woods." The horizontal rays of the setting sun cast long shadows ahead of the moving soldiers, flashing now and then on the bright musket barrels. A distant brass band played "the jolly notes of a popular soldier song, and here and there in the sprawling ranks bearded men or laughing boys" took up the chorus: "Johnny stole a ha-a-am, And didn't care a da-a-a-m."[5]

When the band fell silent the singing gave way to the usual murmur of voices and the thump and clanking of the moving column. Gibbon was riding with the leading 6th Wisconsin. His four regiments and six-gun battery were well closed along one-half mile of roadway. The general moved ahead as the regiment cleared a wooded area in order to ride to a gentle rise north of the Warrenton Turnpike for a better view of the open ground. A movement to the left caught his eye: horses coming out of the woods a mile away. "I looked closely, and one thing struck me as peculiar—there were a good many light colored Horses. . . . The next thing I noticed was the size of the horses and I knew guns were coming 'into battery.'" One marching private also saw the horses. He thought they were pulling army wagons

5   Alan T. Nolan, "John Brawner's Damage Claim," *Giants in Tall Black Hats*, Sharon Vipond and Alan Nolan, eds. (Bloomington, IN, 1998), 1; Edward Bragg, letter to Earl Rogers, April 3, 1900. Edward Bragg Papers, WHS; George Fairfield, diary, August 28, 1862; Cheek and Pointon, *Sauk County*, 37. Confederate reports refer to the engagement as Groveton, while the Federals called it Gainesville. Author Nolan correctly located the fighting at Brawner's Farm. Nolan, *Iron Brigade*, 315-316.

and wondered what they were doing in the woods. "That don't look like any of our batteries," a Sauk County soldier remarked to his friend Gus Klein. Klein shook his head and replied, "See here! We have been in the service over a year and except a few skirmishes, we have never been in a fight. I tell you, this damned war will be over and we will never get into a battle!"

Gibbon recognized the immediate danger and called to an orderly, "Ride back and bring up Battery B on a gallop." The Southern artillery opened fire just moments later, with the first shell hissing over the heads of the marching 6th Wisconsin. "We never saw so polite a bow made by a regiment as we made, men and officers, as it passed over," wrote one soldier. The shell exploded harmlessly in the woods south of the turnpike. The enemy battery fired more shots in quick succession. "It is not necessary to tell the outside world how awfully scared we were," Gibbon admitted. "I know it, for there was no worse scared man in the brigade than I was." For a long instant the Wisconsin men seemed ready to bolt, but then Colonel Cutler's voice rang out firm and steady: "Battalion, halt! Front! Load at will! Load!" The soldiers responded instinctively to the commanding voice heard so often on so many drill fields the past months, their ramrods clanging as they pushed cartridges down the muzzles of their rifle-muskets. Two more artillery rounds cut through the air, knocking one horse over against a fence and just missing two officers of the 2nd Wisconsin. "Lie down!" Cutler ordered, and the Badgers hugged the ground as more "shells came quick," sweeping the area and exploding in a clap of thunder and smoke. "When this shelling commenced," said Gibbon, "I realized that the enemy in search of whom we had been marching for days and days, were right there and somebody ought to have known it."[6]

Down the roadway at a gallop rolled "Gibbon's old pets"—the six bronze guns of Battery B under the command of Capt. Joseph Campbell. The wheels kicked up clods of dirt and stones as the wide-eyed straining artillery horses hauled the heavy smoothbores to the front. The guns were handled with the smooth efficiency of Regulars and passed along the right of the Wisconsin men crouching against the side of the road. Several infantrymen jumped forward to kick down a section of rail fence. Leaping up to assist was contraband cook Matt Bernard, who was still carrying his pack of pots and pans. The guns rolled through the gap to a knoll. Gibbon swung his arm to show where he wanted them placed and yelled, "Into

6 Dawes, *Service*, 60; A. R. Bushnell, "How the Iron Brigade Won Its Name," *Grant County Herald*, undated clipping. Watrous Papers, WHS; Brown, letter, to his father, September 5, 1862; Cheek and Pointon, *Sauk County*, 37-38; Young, *Milwaukee Sunday Telegraph*, May 6, 1888; Harries, "In the Ranks at Antietam," 250; Sullivan, *Milwaukee Sunday Telegraph*, November 4, 1884; Gibbon, *Recollections*, 51-52; Watrous, *Milwaukee Sunday Telegraph*, September 7, 1884.

battery, here!" The guns swung around, the trails dropped, and the gunners moved into position. The battery opened with a terrible roar, the blasts flattening the grass in front of the flaming muzzles.

Gibbon rode into the nearby woods where he and his aide, Frank Haskell, watched the effects of the fire. He was convinced the enemy battery was only horse artillery sent to disrupt the marching Federal column. Farther back down the column, more Confederate cannons opened fire on the division's two rear brigades. When Battery B's accurate shooting slowed the rate of fire of the first Rebel battery, Gibbon believed he had a chance to capture the guns. Haskell moved to bring up his most veteran regiment—the 2nd Wisconsin. "I don't suppose that more than half a minute had elapsed before I got impatient (I sometimes do)," reported Gibbon, "and rode back to meet the regiment coming through the wood."[7]

Back on the roadway, the Wisconsin and Indiana men huddled along the embankment waiting for orders. One 7th Wisconsin man gaped in astonishment when Haskell jumped "his horse over the fence and rode up toward the battery to reconnoiter the enemy's position, and then turn and walked his horse back as calmly as though there was not a rebel within a thousand miles." Within a few minutes Gibbon's order to come up reached the 2nd Wisconsin and the men stood up. "What luck!" called out a disappointed Sauk County man in the 6th Wisconsin. "There is the Second in again before us." The 2nd moved by the left flank and disappeared into the woods as the 6th Wisconsin boys, regardless of the long rivalry between the regiments, raised a ragged cheer for them. The men of the 2nd Wisconsin, who had been bloodied at Bull Ran and bragged so long about it, were marching directly into the waiting guns of Jackson and half of the Confederate Army of Northern Virginia.

Gibbon met the advancing Wisconsin officers in the shade of the woods. Ahead was probably a Confederate cavalry battery, he told them, and "if we can get you up quietly we can capture the guns." The regiment formed its line in a clearing north of the woods. Two companies were pushed forward as skirmishers with the remaining eight behind, closely aligned on the flags and marching abreast. "As soon as it reached the brow of the hill," Gibbon wrote, the "line of skirmishers was quickly thrown forward, the enemy's skirmishers driven in and the regiment advanced to the plateau beyond." When the skirmish fire opened the Confederate artillery fell silent. The 2nd Wisconsin had not moved more than a few steps more when "a very heavy musketry fire was opened upon it."

---

7   John Gibbon in an 1884 speech to the Iron Brigade Association at Lancaster, Wisconsin; Earl Rogers Papers, Wisconsin Veterans' Museum, Madison; King, *War Papers*, vol. 2, 212.

The infantry fighting that erupted was wholly unexpected. The Badgers were marching in line of battle by the left oblique near the farm buildings when rips of musketry tore into their exposed flank. One astonished skirmisher saw a thick line of Confederate infantry coming on "three lines deep." What he did not yet know was that the gray infantry was from the famous Stonewall Brigade—the same five veteran Virginia regiments that had turned back the 2nd Wisconsin at Bull Run the previous year. Although reduced to about 800 men, the brigade (now under Col. William S. H. Baylor) outnumbered the Black Hat regiment almost two to one. The sudden appearance of the heavy enemy line shocked Gibbon, who witnessed what he called "the worst infantry fire begun I ever heard. I was more afraid than ever, and afraid that the regiment was scared, but it was not." According to one Wisconsin officer, the "bullets came thicker than rain and it seemed as if our whole regiment must soon be annihilated." To a soldier in Hatch's brigade a mile or so ahead, the sheets of musketry made a sound "like that of hailstones upon an empty barn."[8]

The Woods are Full of 'Em!

Colonel Edgar O'Connor, selected to command the 2nd Wisconsin during the troubled reorganization after the Bull Run defeat, moved forward believing he had something to prove. He was still under a political cloud because of lingering questions of his loyalty to the Union centered around allegations that his marriage to a Southerner and West Point education made him friends with many who were now serving in the ranks of the Confederate army. O'Connor also made an unwise (if true) statement to a newspaper in his hometown of Beloit that the new Union volunteers might need more training before being ready for a battlefield. It was a remark that was still being recalled in print now and then by Republican editors back home as an example of what might reflect O'Connor's lack of courage. A lingering bronchial illness that required him to give commands in a whisper to an

8 Bushnell, *Herald*, undated; Cheek and Pointon, *Sauk County*, 38; Sullivan, *Milwaukee Sunday Telegraph*, November 4, 1883; Cornelius Wheeler, journal, August 28, 1862, Cornelius Wheeler Papers, WHS; King, *War Papers*, 217; Dawes, *Service*, 60; Watrous, *Milwaukee Sunday Telegraph*, September 4, 1884; Gibbon, *Recollections*, 53-54; Harries, "In the Ranks at Antietam," 251; Thomas Allen, letter, September 4, 1862, *Civil War Times, Illustrated*, November 1962, 32-33; Theron W. Haight, "Gainesville, Groveton and Bull Run," *War Papers*, vol. 2, 361. "The regiment met a heavy body of the enemy's infantry; here for nearly twenty minutes, until succored by the other regiments of the brigade, the Second Regiment alone sustained and checked the whole of 'Stonewall' Jackson's division, under one of the intensely concentrated fires of musketry probably ever experienced by any troops in this or any other war." Wheeler, journal, August 28, 1862.

aide, who then repeated them in a loud voice, only added to the colonel's difficulties.[9]

O'Connor had fewer than 450 men in his line, many of whom were veterans of Bull Run. He halted the regiment and held it steady before the advancing Confederate brigade. The small Wisconsin regiment, standing alone in an open field, appeared doomed as the thick enemy ranks swept down upon it as if to engulf everything in its front. Then, to "the amaze" of the Confederate officers, reported one Badger, the front rank of "the Black Hats knelt in their tracks as though bidding them to come on." The 2nd Wisconsin men "bethought themselves of all they had told the Sixth and Seventh of what it meant to stand fire, and if fifty brigades, instead of five, had burst upon them, there were men in those stubborn ranks that would never have yielded an inch." Holding "their pieces with a tighter grasp and expressing their impatience with low mutterings in such honest, if not classic phrases, as 'Come on, God damn you,'" they waited for the command to fire.[10] Finally, with the Rebels nearly upon his regiment, O'Connor whispered the order to an aide and the blue line exploded with a crash of smoke and noise. The brigade of Wisconsin and Indiana boys had finally found the battle for which they had so long yearned.

When he realized the depth of the Confederate lines, Gibbon ordered the 7th Wisconsin and 19th Indiana forward. Sol Meredith pushed his Hoosiers in line of battle at the double-quick. "Boys," he called at one point, "don't forget that you are Hoosiers, and above all, remember the glorious flag of our country!" The 19th Indiana took its place on the left of the embattled 2nd Wisconsin. A Rebel regiment hidden by a fence and scattered haystacks let loose with a volley into the 19th Indiana at a range of just seventy-five yards. It was then that the fight began in earnest.

The 7th had come up on the right side of the 2nd Wisconsin, but its flank companies advanced too far and were bowed forward. They halted, about faced, and marched back to correct the alignment. It was during this maneuver that Private Ray was hit. "We halted to dress & and the flanks of the Regt being ahead so they had to about face, march back on line but before this there was three wounded in our Co. I saw two go down," Ray said. "Well just as I had to face about, there was a ball struck me in the back of the head & as it appeared to me, I spun around on my heels like a boys top and fell with my heels in the air and spun around again for a few

---

9   A 19th Indiana soldier who saw O'Connor during the Gainesville battle on August 28, 1862, observed, "I thought I never saw a handsomer man." Stine, *Army of the Potomac*, 132.

10 King, *War Papers*, 273.

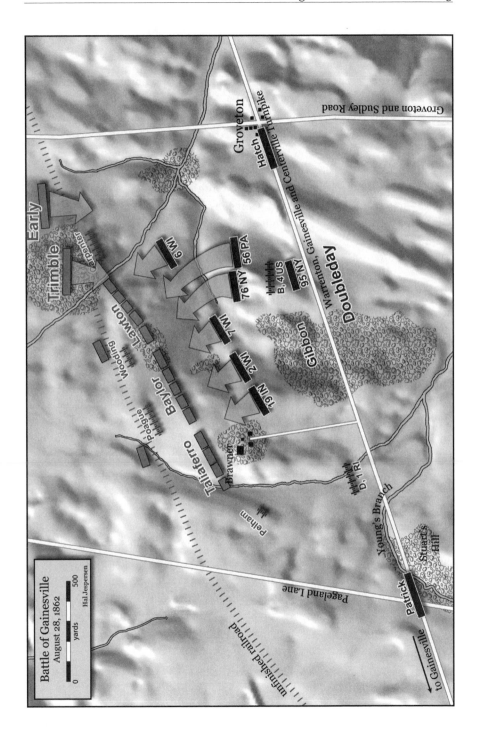

Battle of Gainesville
August 28, 1862

0   yards   500

Hal Jespersen

seconds." When he came to his senses, Ray rolled to his knees and crawled a few rods before walking out of the fight.[11]

Lieutenant Colonel Lucius Fairchild of the 2nd Wisconsin, sleeves rolled up and sword in hand, ran through the smoke and confusion to the 7th Wisconsin. "For God's sake colonel, deliver your fire up to the left. We are all cut to pieces, and the enemy are advancing on us." The 7th's Col. William Robinson was a stiff-mouthed Vermonter who had served in the Mexican War before going off to the gold fields of California. After calmly looking over the situation he ordered, "Battalion! Change front forward on tenth company! By company, left wheel—March! Forward—March!" "Company after company came into alignment along the foot of that slope, and poured in their fire, our right striking right into the enemy's lines along the edge of the woods, and they broke and fell back," wrote a relived 7th Wisconsin man before adding, "Who does not remember the cheer we gave?"

All three regiments were soon battling the Rebel lines expanding to the left and right. Galloping staffers were sent by Gibbon to the two brigades behind him for immediate help. Another aide, James Wood of the 2nd, was sent to the 6th Wisconsin waiting in the turnpike. The young officer was a bit excited after an artillery bolt knocked his horse out from under him during the first minutes of the firing and left him standing on the pike. Somewhere Wood found a remount. Pale and shaken, he called out to Cutler, "Colonel, with the compliments of Gen. Gibbon, you will form your regiment by battalion front, advance and join on the right of the Seventh, and engage the enemy." Wood looked about in wild fashion and blurted, "Colonel, for God's sake, go over and help the Second. They are being cut to pieces." Cutler was sitting on the rail fence by the roadside watching the fight with his field glasses. "Yes," he replied, "the woods are full of 'em. Get ready boys, for the fun is coming."[12]

Cutler would prove steady under fire. "We can not let our comrades be slaughtered in that manner," he announced. The Badgers pulled down portions of the fence along the north side of the roadway and formed on the brow of the ditch. The regiment was dressing its line when three soldiers ran up with their rifle-muskets and belts in hand—Pvts. Harry Dunn of Menekaunee, John Burus of Oakfield, and William Campbell of Mauston. Footsore and exhausted by hard marching, the three had been riding in the ambulances but ran to join their

---

11 Gaff, *Bloody Field*, 156; Ray, *Iron Brigade*, August 28, 1862. "Come too, rolled over on to my knees, crawled off to the rear a few rods, got up, walked till come to little gutter in small hollow, laid down to rest but the balls fell around like hail striking very close so that wouldn't do."

12 Watrous, *Milwaukee Sunday Telegraph*, September 4, 1884.

companies at the first fire.[13] They found their places in their companies and the 6th Wisconsin moved into the open field "in line of battle with full regimental front and step, and 'guide left,' as regular as if on parade." Major Dawes remembered marching to his first battle "with something of the feeling that one would hurry to save a friend from peril." His mare was caught up in "the fierce excitement" and "ran up the bank and leaped a fence like a squirrel." He could now see the 2nd Wisconsin "under the concentrated fire of at least six times their own number of the enemy. Our regiment, five hundred and four men in ranks, pushed forward rapidly in perfect line of battle, field officers and Adjutant E. P. Brooks mounted and in their places and colors advanced and flying in the breeze. Colonel Cutler was on a large dark bay, well known to all the men as 'Old Prince.' Colonel Bragg rode a pure white horse, of high mettle, which was skittish and unmanageable." The young Dawes recalled that he "never felt before in my life that feeling of intense horror that came over me when on mounting that bank I saw the Second gallantly struggling and staggering under the fire of not less than six regiments of the enemy." To his right, Bragg—unable to control his horse—dismounted and went forward on foot.[14]

Private Albert Young looked ahead to "a meadow sloping down in front of us for some distance" before rising to a wooded ridge. "Slightly to the left of our immediate front, and extending a long distance to the left from this ridge came a line of fire—it was then early dusk—and much nearer to us and the road," Young wrote, "but still on our left was another similar line of fire. We did not need to be informed that these lines of flame were reb and Union lines of infantry, and that the fight was an exceedingly hot one. As soon as our line was formed we were ordered forward. We knew we were in for it."[15]

About forty rods into the field and half way to the wood line, Mickey Sullivan looked back to see Cutler "sitting on his big horse as straight as a rod. We had never been engaged at close quarters before, and the experience was new to all of us. I don't know how the others felt, but I am free to confess that I felt a queer choking sensation about the throat, but someone in the rear rank awkwardly stepped on my heel and I instantly forgot all about the choking feeling and turned to him angrily to

13 Burus died May 7, 1864, of wounds suffered in the Wilderness fighting; Dunn mustered out at the end of his three-year enlistment; Campbell resigned his commission as 1st Lt. on October 11, 1864. *Wisconsin Roster*, vol. 1, 513-514, 533.

14 Gaff, *Brave Men's Tears*, 73; Cheek and Pointon, *Sauk County*, 38; Marsh, *Milwaukee Sunday Telegraph*, January 16, 1886; Fairfield, diary, August 28, 1862; OR 12, pt. 2, 382; Dawes, *Service*, 61; Dawes journal, undated. He later noted in pencil that it was written in 1862 and 1863.

15 Young, *Milwaukee Sunday Telegraph*, May 6, 1888.

demand if there was not room for him to march without skinning my heel; and we were jawing and fussing until the colonel shouted halt, and there," continued the Irishman, "about six or eight rods in front of us was a heavy column, marching by the flank, which I supposed was part of our division . . ." In fact, the tramping command was Isaac Trimble's Confederate brigade, about 1,200 men from Georgia, Alabama, and North Carolina. Trimble was trying to envelop Gibbon's line, but the growing darkness and billowing smoke made the approaching Wisconsin regiment all but invisible.

"Sixth regiment, Ready! Aim—Aim Low, Fire!" shouted Cutler. The regiment, which had practiced the maneuver on many drill fields, delivered a sharp and crashing volley that Sullivan never forgot: "Every gun cracked at once, and the line in front, which had faced us at the command 'ready' melted away, and instead of the heavy line of battle that was there before our volley, they presented the appearance of a skirmish line that had rallied by fours, there being only groups left, here and there, but another line moved up and took their place, and we stood there, firing at each other, at short range, until our men fired away twenty rounds of cartridges and the rebs fell back and another line took their place, and we engaged them."[16]

The 6th Wisconsin had "advanced without firing a shot," making a slow half wheel "as accurately as if on the drill grounds." Inside the ranks could be heard the sound of "rip-rip," but the marching soldiers did not realize this was caused by bullets until the boys began to fall. The 6th was well to the right of the line of the three other regiments. "Through the battle smoke into which we were advancing, I could see a blood red sun, sinking behind the hills." reported Dawes. "I can not account for our immunity from the fire of the enemy while on this advance." The 6th Wisconsin joined the shooting and the united fire of the four Black Hat regiments seemed to do "great execution," continued the major, throwing the "rebels into complete confusion" as they fell back into the woods. "We now gave a loud and jubilant cheer throughout the whole line of our brigade." Because the 6th Wisconsin was on lower ground and darkness was falling, the Confederates fired too high. "The three other regiments," Dawes explained, "were on higher ground than the enemy. There was space enough vacant between our regiment and the others for a thousand men."[17]

Private Young was struggling with a range of emotions during the harrowing exchanges of lead. His initial thought "was that the prospects for getting killed were growing bright, and the question I first put to myself was, 'Are you a coward?' to

16 Sullivan, *Milwaukee Sunday Telegraph*, November 4, 1884.

17 Dawes, journal, undated.

this I without an instant's hesitation answered, 'Yes.' Should I run? I must have been very pale. It seemed as if my blood had stopped circulating," he admitted. "Waves of intense heat flashed in quick succession through my entire being. I trembled so I could with difficulty keep from dropping my musket, but I hung on to it because I realized I should soon have need of it if I were not knocked out very early by a rebel bullet." But Young kept moving. He continued:

> My legs quaked so they would scarcely support my weight, slight though it was. Should I run? Although I could hardly move one foot before the other toward the enemy, I felt that were I to head the other way I could beat the record. My mouth had in an instant, as it seemed, become dry and parched. I was suffering a terrible thirst. With trembling fingers I managed to get my canteen to my lips and took a long draught. It did not quench the thirst by which I was consumed. Again the question presented itself to me, 'Shall I run?' I answered it in the negative, because I was too much of a coward to run. I was too cowardly to endure being called a coward by my comrades if I survived. . . . A black mass was moving out from the timber in front, directly towards us. I will not be certain, but I shall always think my hair began rising at this time. At least something lifted my hat from my head, and I had to grab quickly for it or I should have lost it. But I caught it and pulled it down tight so it would not be liable to come off again. Just at this instant, our colonel's voice was heard giving the commands. There was not the suspicion of a tremor in his voice, while I could not, I felt sure, utter an audible sound.[18]

The 6th Wisconsin was "in the middle of an open field," one Badger recalled, "the confederates behind a fence, on the edge of the field in the timber." He stood and fired the ammunition he carried, "and I do not know how many rounds I received from the killed and wounded in rear of our lines." Ahead in "an opening in the timber," the rebels "placed some artillery on rising ground, but they never fired a shot. We killed the cannoneers, as fast as they came up to load. On the right of the line was a thicket of timber brush, "which, we could see the enemy file into at a run to rake us in flank," he continued. "Command, fire right oblique, 6th Wisconsin, and I did not see one man go back out of that copse of woods. . . . They tried again and again to form, brought reinforcements time after time, and each time 'steady, boys,' would run along the line, and before they came to the fence they were a disordered mass, and our swift and sure fire kept them so during the fight. The rattle of our musketry sounded all along the line, like a piece of canvass tearing in a storm."

18 Johnson, *Milwaukee Sunday Telegraph*, November 30, 1884.

The 6th's crashing first volley—fired at a point blank range of fifty yards—brought a cheer from the other three embattled regiments that was answered by a "Whoop, Whoop, Whoop" yell from the Rebels, a sound once heard and never forgotten. "There is nothing like it this side of the infernal region and the peculiar corkscrew sensation that it sends down your backbone under these circumstances can never be told," a Wisconsin man admitted. "You have to feel it, and if you say you did not feel it and heard the yell you have never been there." The men of the 6th stood and fired, with Cutler mounted and just behind the two flags in the center of the regiment. Dawes watched from the left side. "It was quite dark when the enemy's yelling columns again came forward, and they came with a rush," wrote the major. "Our men on the left loaded and fired with the energy of madmen, and the sixth worked with an equal desperation. This stopped the rush of the enemy, and they halted and fired upon us their deadly musketry. During a few awful moments, I could see by the lurid light of the power flashes, the whole of both lines. . . . It was evident that we were being overpowered [on the left] and that our men were giving ground. The two crowds, they could hardly be called lines, were within, it seemed to me, fifty yards of each other, and they were pouring musketry into each other as rapidly as men could load and shoot."[19]

According to Pvt. Chester Wyman, the men of his company fired at the flash of the enemy muskets "as fast as we could load and fire. I did not know what second I might get hit but I would give them the best I had in me as long as I could." The man next to him was knocked out of line, "apparently dead," right before Wyman was hit in the right thigh. He took a step but his leg gave way and he fell heavily. Around him the firing again flared up.[20]

Fighting on the other end of the line was Capt. John Marsh. "The sun was sinking behind the horizon when from my position near the right I saw a confederate officer to the left form his command as for a final effort to break our line," reported the officer. "They were on rising ground, every man standing, boldly out from a sky radiant with the golden state of a summer sunset. Recklessly placing himself in front of the line, he gave the command to charge. Down they came at double quick over that green slope, their gallant leader waving them on. Men drop from the ranks by scores, but the column sweeps bravely forward until half their number lie bleeding on the ground. The living hesitate," Marsh continued, "and the bold leader rides fiercely along the line to urge them on, but the leaden hail is too

19 Johnson, *Milwaukee Sunday Telegraph*, November 30, 1884.

20 Dawes, journal, undated; Cheek and Pointon, *Sauk County*, 39; Dawes, *Service*, 61-62, Chester Wyman, letter, May 28, 1918.

potent, and they fall back, but with the steady pace of veterans." It was not over. "Twice more they charge down that bloody slope only to be repulsed with fearful slaughter. Strange to say neither rider nor horse that led this gallant charge had fallen, when darkness shut off my view, and only the flashing guns marked the contending lines of friend and foe." A shell burst in the darkness and nearly blinded the Union captain, who felt as though he was "wounded near the knee, but I can walk and don't mind it. Every man in my company seems a hero, and, when a corporal, whom I had disliked, quietly says, during the hottest of the battle: 'Captain, my gun's so foul I can't get the cartridge down, can you find me another?' I felt like embracing him. He was soon supplied, for we had a surplus of guns just then, many a brave fellow having turned his in for the final settlement."[21]

It was "a roaring hell of fire," was how one Badger described the long minutes of the early evening fight. "Retiring never an inch, with no confusion, now standing up, now flat upon the earth, now swaying backwards or forwards to get advantage of ground, the devoted 1800 blazed with fire. Line after line of the rebels confronted them and was swept away, or broke in confusion. Fresh regiments would again appear . . . and with a cheer would rush for a charge upon the 'Black Hats,' but their rebel cheer was drowned in one three times louder by the Badger boys, and their lines met the fate of its predecessors. No battle was ever so fierce before—no men ever did better than did the men of Gibbon's Brigade."[22] At one point the Rebels "rallied and in a line lapping ours both ways there burst from that dark wood volley after volley by battalion that roared and crashed in a manner not surpassed in any action I have seen." The men "loaded and fired with the energy of madmen, and a recklessness of death truly wonderful, but human nature could not long stand such a terribly wasting fire. It literally mowed out great gaps in the line, but the isolated squads would rally together and rush up right into the face of Death."

The 19th Indiana and 2nd and 7th Wisconsin were pressed together, left to right, with the 6th Wisconsin well to the right with a large gap between its left and the other three regiments. Together, Gibbon's brigade faced an overwhelming force, but Jackson was having trouble coordinating his attacks and his regiments were thrown in piecemeal. Part of this was due to the stiff and unexpected fighting done by the Black Hats, coupled with the loss of several of Jackson's regimental officers and two division commanders. One of the latter was William B. Taliaferro, who was on the right when hit in the foot, neck, and arm and knocked out of action.

21 John Marsh, "Army Life Incidents," *Milwaukee Sunday Telegraph*, January 16, 1886.

22 Haskell, letter, September 22, 1862.

The other, Richard S. Ewell, was commanding on the left when he knelt to see under the musket smoke and a minie ball shattered his left kneecap and smashed his tibia into several pieces. The terrible wound required the amputation of his leg.

On the left of Gibbon's line, the men of Indiana's 19th "suffered terribly" because the "lines of battle were close enough to do effective work." In the approaching dusk Meredith's horse, "Old Roan," was hit by a ball and fell, pinning the colonel. Two officers pulled the stunned Meredith free. Lieutenant Colonel Alois Bachman assumed command. Meredith's son, Samuel, serving as a lieutenant in one company, was shot in the neck about the same time. At one point in the fighting two Rebel guns were posted on the 19th's flank and two companies were ordered forward. Confederates surged forward to take advantage of the resulting gap. "The regiment great felt the loss of those two companies, and swung back a little," one soldier wrote. Out of the smoke and confusion appeared a horseless Gibbon, who helped reform the battered line. The general had left his small "sorrel horse" tied to a peach tree, but the animal broke loose and ran away, leaving the general on foot and "in a dangerous and exposed position."[23] Gibbon, who would see heavy fighting during the coming months, later claimed that Gainesville was "the most terrific musketry fire I have ever listened to rolled along those two lines of battle. It was a regular stand up fight during which neither side yielded a foot. My command exhibited in the highest degree the effects of discipline and drill, officers and men standing up to their work like old soldiers."[24] One of those "old soldiers" noted it was "one of the most stubborn, tenacious infantry fights . . . that history has any record of," while a 7th Wisconsin man called it "a stand-up-and-shoot fight in line of battle." Captain Edwin Brown of the 6th Wisconsin described the combat as a "baptism of blood & carnage." Bragg said it was a fight at "close range, from late in the afternoon until after dark, with old Battery B ringing its case shot and canister up and down the line, and the roar of musketry filling the air, deadening the cries and groans of the wounded as they fell and passed away."

The men remembered the fighting through a blur of confusing sights and incidents. Private Philo Wright of the 2nd Wisconsin was shot about an hour into the battle. "I must have been kneeling on my right knee with my left knee bent up with its left side toward the Rebels," he said, "for a 'minnie' entered the left side of my calf...tearing out the ligaments and making a bad wound. How it missed all

---

23 *Beaver Dam Home League*, October 18, 1862; Dawes, journal, undated; Rufus R. Dawes, "Skirmishes of the Rappahannock and Battle of Gainesville," T. C. H. Smith Papers, Ohio Historical Society, Columbus; Bushnell, *Herald*, undated; Stine, *Army of the Potomac*, 131-132; Gaff, *Bloody Field*, 158.

24 Gibbon, *Recollections*, 54.

bones and arteries it would be hard to say." It would be four months to "straighten the knee and get it in working order." Private Alvin Eager of the Janesville company of the same regiment was shot through the mouth. (After the war he grew a beard to hide the disfigurement). Nearby, his younger brother, Amos Eager, who was in the Stoughton Light Guard of the 7th Wisconsin, was also wounded, once in the hand, carrying away his thumb and a finger, and again in the right leg above the ankle.[25] In the 6th Wisconsin, Pvt. Richard Warham of DeSoto was shot through the arm. Unable to load his rifle-musket, he "busied himself giving the remaining cartridges of his box to the comrades." Dawes watched a mounted Confederate officer ride within twenty paces of his line. "He was, of course, killed."[26] The two lines were so close together, wrote Sauk County men, "that by the flash of the muskets we could see the enemy distinctly, as they could see us. We did not remember to have heard another order than the first given, except an occasional one from the officers, 'Give them hell! boys, give them hell!' For after the first volley we fired as fast as we could load." One of the Crawford County men, George Fairfield, said Battery B "was throwing shell over our heads which made it seem as if the heaven was a furnace." One of the Juneau County boys in the 6th Wisconsin, John St. Clair of Summit, recalled firing "45 times at the Devils" and a member of his company wrote that "Many of our men fired forty rounds of ammunition without stirring out of their tracks. Our brigade could not advance and the rebels could not drive us one foot, and it was a straight stand up and take it between the two rebel divisions, and our brigade, in which the advantage of numbers, more than three to one, was on the side of Jackson and also that he had the cover of the timber while our men were in the open field."

The Western cheers "were promptly answered by the rebel yell," claimed a 7th Wisconsin man. He continued:

> They rallied, brought up reinforcements, and charged on our lines—and didn't they make it hot for us? Bullets from front, at right flank—the air full of them, whistling by our ears—scratching our clothes—burning our faces—bullets seemingly everywhere.

25 Eager family records compiled by Jennifer Eager Ehle. Amos Eager enlisted August 10, 1861, about three months after his brother. Alvin Eager was subsequently captured by the Confederates, but exchanged. He would be wounded again at Gettysburg and mustered out with his regiment in 1864, term expired. *Wisconsin Roster*, vol. 1, 357.

26 Johnson, *Milwaukee Sunday Telegraph*, November 30, 1884; Bushnell, *Herald*, undated; Brown letter to his father, September 5, 1862; Edward Bragg letter to Earl Rogers, April 3, 1900; Earl Rogers, *Milwaukee Sunday Telegraph*, August 29, 1884; Dawes journal, undated. Warham's arm was amputated and he was discharged for disability on December 31, 1862. *Wisconsin Roster*, vol. 1, 532.

The sixth came in on our right—the 19th Indiana on the left of the second; and as battery B got into position on a little hill to our rear, firing over our heads, gave them canister, and the charge was repulsed. Twice more they brought up more men and charged down upon us. Line behind line they came, their flags flying, and we plainly heard the voice of their commander, 'Forward! Guide, center!' On they grandly came; and as they got near enough, and we poured in our fire, through the dim and smokey light, we saw their ranks swept down grow thinner and beautifully less until the last man of them seemed to drop into the ground. And yet, again they came; and again their dim ranks outlined against the sky above the hill went out into nothingness."[27]

Help in the Nick of Time!

With both lines bathed in the light of heavy musket fire, the gap between the 6th Wisconsin and the rest of the brigade was clearly visible in the darkness. From the turnpike behind them approached two regiments from Abner Doubleday's brigade double-quicked into the fight. Major Dawes always remembered how the 531 men of the 56th Pennsylvania and the 450 of the 76th New York slid into the gap and fired a crashing volley. "Hurrah! They have come at the very nick of time," he wrote a quarter century later, still feeling the excitement of the moment. The Confederates made three attacks against the 76th New York, which the Wisconsin officer labeled "the only genuine attempts at bayonet charges I have seen in this war."[28] The outcome of the fighting was still in question. The Federal line stretched nearly a mile and included almost 2,800 soldiers. Jackson had three brigades in the fighting, about 3,000 men of the 20,000 he had available. It seemed as though the weight of the Confederate numbers would finally roll back the Black Hats despite the arrival of Doubleday's men. Col. Cutler asked the worried Dawes, "Our men are giving ground on the left, Major?" No sooner had Dawes replied "Yes, Sir" when he "heard that tchug so ominous in battle." Cutler "gave a convulsive start, and clapped his hand on his leg," but "not a muscle of the old man's face quivered as he quietly asked, 'Where is Col. Bragg? I am shot.'" At the same instant, the

27 John St. Clair, letter to his parents, September 6, 1862; John St. Clair Papers, WHS; Cheek and Pointon, *Sauk County*, 39; Fairfield, diary, August 28, 1862; Sullivan, *Milwaukee Sunday Telegraph*, November 4, 1884; Jerome A. Watrous, *Milwaukee Sunday Telegraph*, September 4, 1884; Bushnell, *Herald*, undated. A native of Hartford, Ohio, Bushnell moved to Wisconsin in 1854 and settled in Platteville where he studied law and set up a practice in 1857. In 1860, he was elected Grant County District Attorney but resigned to join the 7th Wisconsin. Bushnell was a captain in 1863 when he resigned and returned to Wisconsin, where he was elected the first mayor of Lancaster. He also served one year in Congress.

28 Dawes, journal, undated.

colonel's horse "Old Prince" was also struck, but "he carried his master safely from the field." Dawes left to find Lt. Col. Edward Bragg, who was still on foot. When distant cheering broke out on the left, the two officers concluded the Federal line "was again standing firmly." General Doubleday's pair of regiments, wrote Dawes of the moment, "by their opportune arrival and gallant work, aided much in turning the battle in our favor." Bragg was "always eager to push forward in a fight" and advanced the 6th Wisconsin several rods. "Soon the enemy came on again just as before, and our men on the left could be seen on the hill in the infernal light of the powder flashes, struggling as furiously as ever." Dawes "could distinctly see Lieut. Col. Fairchild, of the 2nd Wisconsin and Lieut. Colonel Hamilton of the 7th Wisconsin, and other officers whom I recognized, working among and cheering up their men. Men who had been shot were streaming back from along the whole line. Our regiment was suffering more severely than it had been; but, favored by the low ground, we kept up a steady, rapid, and well aimed fire. How long our men withstood this last attack, I cannot estimate," added Dawes, "but, in the history of war, it is doubtful whether there was ever more stubborn courage than was displayed by the 2nd and 7th Wisconsin and 19th Indiana regiments on this field of battle." On Gibbon's left, continued Dawes, the 19th Indiana "gradually fell back. It did not break but slowly gave ground, firing as savagely as ever. The rebels did not advance. Colonel Bragg," continued Dawes, "directed our regiment to move by a backward step, keeping up our fire and keeping on a line with our brigade. But one of the companies of the right wing ('C') became broken by the men marching backward into a ditch. Colonel Bragg halted the regiment to enable them to reform their line, and upon this ground we stood until the enemy ceased firing."[29]

Unable to see and thoroughly exhausted and bloodied, the fighting sputtered to a halt on both sides of the line. The first battle fought by Gibbon's brigade, opened with the boom of an artillery piece on a quiet August late afternoon before erupting into a standup musketry fight at close range, was finally at an end. It was 9:00 p.m. The infantry fighting had lasted less than ninty minutes. It was not like anything they had expected. There were no gallant charges, just a frantic scramble to load and shoot, load and shoot, again and again at the flashes illuminating the enemy line. It had been all noise and confusion, the opposing lines surging crowds of soldiery. Overheated muskets became so foul that the men hammered ramrods with rocks or against the ground to push down the lead bullet. Officers on foot pulled shaken soldiers to fill gaps and straighten the line. Dawes was surprised to discover that he "alone of all field officers in the battle remained mounted and

29 Dawes, *Service*, 63.

unhurt." Across the dismal field could be heard "the groans of the wounded, their cries for help and calls for water. It was more difficult to endure than going into the battle," admitted one Wisconsin soldier. Another described the calls as "the most pitiful sounds I ever heard." Details were organized to carry the wounded to the rear. "Now was the hardest part of the battle," confessed one soldier, "to learn who of our friends were killed or wounded. In the copse of trees in front of the regiment, remembered John Johnson of the 6th Wisconsin, came "such lamentations . . . as 'O, God,' 'O mother,' that would make the stoutest heart quail and shudder, even if they were enemies to our country. I would not like to hear it again."[30]

After an "interval of quiet," Colonel Bragg called for "three cheers." The defiant "Hurrahs!" echoed into the blackness. The enemy offered no response of any kind. Satisfied the fighting had truly ended and his line was secure, Gibbon rode to the Warrenton Turnpike in "a very bad temper" because he was convinced his brigade had been left unsupported. He found General King and his staff sitting in a fence corner alongside the road with two other brigade commanders, John Hatch and Abner Doubleday. Hot words were exchanged, after which Gibbon calmed down when he learned Doubleday had sent two regiments to assist his brigade. Hatch had reversed his march but arrived too late to help. A short time later Brig. Gen. Marsena Patrick arrived and the generals discussed their next move. King's orders were to march to Centreville.

"From whom were those orders received?" someone asked.

"From General McDowell," replied King.

"Where was General McDowell?" another asked. No one knew.

Jackson's entire wing of the Southern army might be camped in the woods just a few hundred yards away. "I was the junior general present," Gibbon recalled, "but none of the other officers expressed an opinion except General King, and he seemed disposed to attempt to obey the orders he had received to march to Centreville. I opposed this because I did not think it practicable to do it in the darkness, and as a better plan, proposed we should take the road to Manassas Junction with the hope that we might meet troops coming from there to support us." When no one else "expressed any opinion, either for or against the proposition," continued Gibbon, "I took a piece of paper and by the light of a candle wrote what I proposed and showed it to the other generals, finally handing it to General King. They all agreed that it was the best thing to do under the circumstances and General King, after adding something in his own handwriting,

30 *Ibid.*, 62-63; Dawes, journal, undated; Young, *Milwaukee Sunday Telegraph*, May 6, 1888; Fairfield, diary, August 28, 1862; Johnson, *Milwaukee Sunday Telegraph*, November 30, 1884.

signed it as a dispatch to General McDowell." The officers returned to their commands to make ready for the march to Manassas Junction.[31]

The Western men never forgot the especially grim darkness of August 28, 1862, or the troubling cries of the wounded. The night air was damp and thick and greasy with the smoke of the fighting. Private Alvin Eager of the 2nd Wisconsin, shot through the mouth and in pain, searched and located his wounded younger brother, Amos, who was with the 7th Wisconsin. Amos had been shot in the hand and leg and was unable to walk. He was to be left behind with the wounded. Alvin assisted his brother to a tree for shelter, said a hurried good-bye, and then joined his regiment as it prepared to march off. After a time, Amos, desperate not to be left behind, dragging and limping along on his wounded leg, caught the rear of a passing ambulance. He pulled himself in, falling on the wounded already in the wagon. It would be nearly all night before the ambulance reached a hospital camp.[32]

Chester Wyman of Hillsboro, wounded in the right leg, was in a field hospital in the small woods by the turnpike. Many of the wounded were piled around at different points in the trees and there were few men to help them. The walking wounded did what they could to find water and food for the others, but there was little to go around. The small field station would be surrounded by the fluid fighting of Second Bull Run during the next three days, and eventually about 500 wounded would crowd the place. "With no . . . help it was every man for himself," Wyman stated. "Many died there. One man that was near me died and he had a blanket. I did not. After he died I took his blanket and spread over myself and was more comfortable than I had been for it kept me warm." It would be ten and painfully long sunrises before Wyman would see a real hospital.[33]

---

31 Haskell, letter to his brothers and sisters, September 22, 1862; Dawes, *Service*, 63, 70; Stine, *Army of the Potomac*, 132; Gibbon, *Recollections*, 55-57. According to Marsena Patrick, he refused to put his brigade in on Gibbon's left flank because he disagreed with Gibbon's decision to make the attack without more consideration and knowledge of the strength of the enemy in his front.

32 Eager family records compiled by Jennifer Eager Ehle. The ball that hit Amos Eager entered about six inches above the ankle. It broke no bones, but injured the cords of the leg so he was not be able to bring his heel to the ground while standing. Standing on the leg caused pain. He was transferred to the Veteran Reserve Corps on November 15, 1863. *Wisconsin Roster*, vol. 1, 552.

33 Wyman, letter, May 28, 1918. He added: "Our men came with a flag of Truce and carried us to Washington some 50 miles from there. The city of Washington contributed carriages to bring in the wounded, but the suffering we endured that night over the rough roads can be imagined but not told. When we arrived there, a number of dead were removed from the carriages and at least one third of the wounded died within 2 weeks after we were in the hospital." Wyman was soon discharged and sent home.

Flickering torches and lanterns flitted about the field as soldiers from both sides searched for fallen friends and messmates. "We found all our dead and wounded along a line, a rod or two in width," wrote a Wisconsin man. "It was then very dark and once we got outside of our line and ran into the enemy's pickets, who fired on us but missed." Lieutenant Colonel Fairchild formed the 2nd Wisconsin on the roadway only to be shaken to find so few. "Where is the regiment—have they scattered?" he asked. Out of the darkness someone replied, "Colonel, this is all that is left of the Second, the rest lay on the field." Through tears Fairchild managed, "Thank God, they are worthy of their name." Several lost Confederates stumbled out of the darkness into the Wisconsin line and were disarmed. They were from Richard Ewell's division, they said, before asking with friendly curiosity about the soldiers in the "big hats" they had been fighting.[34] When told they were Wisconsin and Indiana men, one Johnny private nodded and said that one of his officers had remarked, "It was no use to fight them damn fools; they did not know enough to know when they were whipped." Captain Brown reported proudly in a letter to his wife that an 18th Georgia soldier told him it was the first time his brigade "ever turned their backs to the foe." The rebel then asked "if we were not western troops, saying they knew we were not Yankees."[35] Toward midnight, the line moved back to the edge of the timber where the weary soldiers bivouacked for an hour or two. "While here," said Capt. John Marsh, "the Seventy-sixth New York, marching by the flank, usual route step, passed in front. The colonel was near the center of his regiment and opposite me when he gave the command: 'Seventy-sixth New York, halt.' The head of the column, however, kept on and the rear closing up. 'Seventy-sixth New York, won't you halt?' shouted the colonel, but it didn't, and the colonel pleaded: 'Seventy-sixth New York, you have behaved so well tonight, won't you halt?' But on they went with steady tread."[36]

The sort of combat just experienced was the kind of thing to stampede any regiment, especially one staggered and battered in its first fight, but the Wisconsin and Indiana men, drilled so hard the past year, stood steady in the darkness. It was about half past midnight when the regiments were marched through the woods to the turnpike. "Painful to relate, to this woods many of our wounded had gone when shot in the battle," wrote one officer. "They were now scattered about under its

---

34 The 6th Wisconsin engaged the 12th Georgia and 21st North Carolina of Isaac Trimble's brigade. Otis, *Second Wisconsin*, 253; *Beaver Dam Home League*, October 18, 1862; Dawes, *Service*, 63-64; Bragg, letter to his wife, September 13, 1862.

35 Sullivan, *Milwaukee Sunday Telegraph*, October 21, 1883; Brown, letter to his father, September 5, 1862.

36 Marsh, *Milwaukee Sunday Telegraph*, January 16, 1881.

dark shadows, suffering and groaning and some were dying. In the pitchy darkness we stumbled upon them. This was the battle for which we had so long been yearning. On the turnpike we found hasty preparations for retreat and at about one o'clock a.m. we silently filed away into the darkness, muffling the rattling tin cups, and turning our course toward Manassas Junction." Captain Brown wrote his father: "We were obliged to leave our dead unburied, and those of our wounded that we were unable to move to the tender mercies of the Rebels. Doctors & nurses were left to wait on them. Lieut. [Jerome B.] Johnson was left with many others. I regretted it much but could not help myself." Johnson, who suffered a severe wound to the groin, and a dozen of the company had been wounded.[37] Private Ludolph Longhenry of the 7th Wisconsin was "among the last" to leave the battleground. "I was all alone. The Seventh Regiment had marched ahead. As I was leaving I came across one of our wounded . . . shot through the lungs. I gave him the last drink of water from my Canteen. But I could do no more." Longhenry pushed after his regiment. "Just before sunrise I left the dangerous rebel area. Every now and then a sharp-pointed bullet whizzed past me."[38]

Frank Haskell recalled that the men and officers were somber as the column trudged away from the wounded and took as "many as the ambulances would hold we silently took up the line of march for Manassas Junction." One private said the men were "bleeding, angry, hungry, tired, sleepy, foot-sore and cut to pieces." The march from the bloody fields on Brawner's farm was the hardest of the war. Drained of all energy by the hot emotions and numbing fear, the bone-weary young men were just able to put one foot ahead of the other. The column moved with little talking over the scuffling feet, the dull clink of accouterments, and the creak of the wagons. "I never saw men more in need of sleep," said one soldier. "We would halt for a few minutes and half would go to sleep, each man sitting or laying down upon the spot where he halted." Now and then the quiet night was broken by a soft sigh or the jarring cry of a wounded man. The thought of being left behind was worse than enduring the agonizing weariness, so on they walked through a night that seemed endless.[39] Captain Marsh was just about played out. When the division resumed its march toward Manassas, he admitted, "I found my wounded knee too painful to walk, but Maj. Dawes . . . kindly dismounted and helped me on his horse,

37 Dawes, *Service*, 64; Brown, letter to his father, September 5, 1862. Johnson, of Fond du Lac, rose from ranks and received his commission in September 1861. He resigned December 27, 1862. *Wisconsin Roster*, vol. 1, 513.

38 Cheek and Pointon, *Sauk County*, 40-41; Longhenry diary, August 27-29, 1862.

39 Haskell, letter to brothers and sisters, September 22, 1862; Sullivan, *Milwaukee Sunday Telegraph*, October 21, 1883; Fairfield, diary, August 28, 1862.

saving me a journey to Richmond as a prisoner of war." Dawes remembered the same event:

> As major I rode at the rear of our regiment. Presently there sifted out from the marching column numbers of wounded men, who had been struggling to keep with their comrades and to avoid falling into the hands of the enemy. I saw Captain John F. Marsh, who had been shot in the knee, drop to the rear, and dismounting from my horse, I lifted him to the saddle, marching through on foot myself. My steady old mare did the service of a good Samaritan. Each stirrup strap and even her tail were an aid to help along the weak and weary. The cry at such times is for water, water. There was none left in the canteens. But we deemed ourselves very fortunate.[40]

The next few hours were hard. "I would travel a few rods, then finding myself going to sleep as I walked, my gun dropping out of my hand," said one Badger. "I would start up with a sudden jerk, and then for a short distance, with supreme effort, would march along, trying to keep awake. Many times since then have I been tired, footsore and weary, but I cannot recall one instance where the feeling of fatigue was so great as one this night's march from Gainesville. When we halted at Manassas Junction in the morning, I dropped down in my tracks and was immediately lost in slumber, from which I did not awake, until the sun was several hours high, and shining in my face."[41] Gibbon called it a "sad, tedious march" and "contrary to expectations we met nobody on the road and reached the vicinity of the [Manassas] Junction just as day was breaking. Here a halt was made, our poor, tired men lying down alongside the road for a much-needed rest, whilst steps were at once taken to supply them with food and ammunition . . . . The Junction was a scene of desolation and ruin," continued Gibbon, "long trains of cars which had been filled with supplies for our army, were now a smoldering mass of ashes, the rebel troops, first supplying themselves, having set the balance on fire two nights before."[42]

Among the wounded left behind was Private Wright of the 2nd Wisconsin, who sat beside a hollow tree in the woods. He shoved his musket into the hollow and waited through the long night "with many uttering death groans around me." Daylight found the Confederates in possession of the woods and the Federal wounded prisoners. "I am sorry to write it, but it is true, that some who wore the

---

40 Marsh, *Milwaukee Sunday Telegraph*, January 16, 1881; Dawes, *Service*, 64.

41 Harries, "In the Ranks at Antietam," 255.

42 Gibbon, *Recollections*, 58.

blue uniforms cried like babies and whined to the Rebel captors that they were not to blame for being there, that they had been obliged to enlist and were drafted!" Wright said. "Not many were they who played the game, but there were a pitiful few." The battle sounds resumed and Wright realized his only hope was to crawl for safety. He said he crawled about twenty rods when some Pennsylvania men gathered him up, telling him "You will make better time with us." He was taken to a small field hospital. The hospital was soon in danger from the fighting and Wright and other wounded were hauled to ambulances. "I was the last man put in the rear ambulance. Two soldiers, each shot in the leg, lay at full length on the bottom." Wright was made to sit beside the driver, but when the ambulance crossed a ditch 80 rods away, a wheel broke and he was thrown to the ground. A surgeon riding a horse near the ambulance told the two soldiers in the ambulance to crawl to the woods and wait. He loaded Wright on his horse and took him to a field hospital. Wright was ultimately taken to Alexandria, Virginia, and did not return to his regiment until December.[43]

Not far away dawn brought with it a sober realization for the rest of the brigade. "I hardly knew our brigade," said Mickey Sullivan. "It was so reduced in size and the men looked so dirty and powder-stained that I could scarcely tell my own tentmates, and it seemed as if their dispositions changed with their appearance. The intensest feelings of anger were manifested against the commander [King] who allowed one brigade alone and unaided to fight the best divisions in the rebel army." Sullivan was not finished. "The remainder of the division had the excuse that they had no orders, and did not know that we were so hard pressed, but we thought they were pleased to see 'them Western galoots' get fits. Our men halted and made coffee, and 'Little Johnny Gibbon' won the affect of the brigade for all time by his manly sympathy for his men. It may seem strange that our brigade was allowed to be cut to pieces without getting help," he concluded, "but that seemed to be the way with Pope's army, every one for himself and the devil take the hindmost."[44]

43 Morse, *Grandad*, 43, quoting from the Wright Memoir.

44 Sullivan, *Milwaukee Sunday Telegraph*, October 21, 1883. Sullivan's belief that his brigade fought the battle without assistance was contested in a dispatch printed November 11, 1883, in the *Milwaukee Sunday Telegraph*. It was signed "Orderly," but was penned by Charles King, the son of Brig. Gen. Rufus King: "Mickey says that except Gibbon's brigade and Battery B, he has 'no knowledge of a shot being fired by any of King's division.' More than that he says 'although the rest of the division lay there in sight and hearing, not a shot was fired nor a man sent forward to our assistance.' Here Mickey is in error. When the fight began, Hatch's brigade was sent out of sight a mile ahead. Patrick's brigade was over a mile behind. Doubleday's was the only one close at hand, and that Doubleday's brigade was speedily ordered in to support Gibbon, and that the 56th Pennsylvania and the seventh-sixth New York pushed right forward

Haskell felt the same way, writing home that "none of us could look upon our thinned ranks, so full the night before, now so shattered, without tears. And the faces of these brave boys, as the morning sun disclosed them, no pen can describe. The men were cheerful, quiet and orderly. The dust and blackness of battle were upon their clothes, and in their hair, and on their skin, but you saw none of these— you saw only their eyes, and the shadows of the 'light of battle,' and the furrows plowed upon cheeks that were smooth a day before, and now not half filled up. I could not look upon them without tears, and could have hugged the necks of them all."[45]

Regimental officers made their reports. When the general determined the "frightful loss," one soldier wrote, "Gibbon dropped his head and wept most bitterly. His sorrow was as sincere as that of the father who had been bereft of his children." Even four weeks later, "whenever the losses were referred to, his eyes would fill with tears and he would ask that the subject be dropped." It was remembered the fighting removed all dislike for "the strict disciplinarian, and how great became the admiration and love for him, only those who have witnessed similar changes can appreciate."

The 6th Wisconsin lost eight killed, 61 wounded (including Colonel Cutler), and three missing. Losses in the other three regiments were much worse. The 7th Wisconsin lost 164 of 580; the 19th Indiana, 210 of 423; the 2nd Wisconsin 276 out of 430. According to initial reports, more than one-third of the brigade, or 725 men, fell that day. Eight of the brigade's 12 field officers were wounded with Edgar

---

on the same line with the 6th Wisconsin wherein Mickey was blazing away for all he was worth, is attested by the reports of General Doubleday and Colonels J. William Hoffman and Charles B. Wainwright, and by the fact that right there on that line the 56th lost their colonel, four captains, two lieutenants and 55 enlisted men, shot down and the 76th 10 killed, 72 wounded (including five officers) and 18 missing. The 95th was sent to the right in support of old Battery B and did not get into the heavy fire. Mickey is hardly to blame for his lack of information on this point, as it was quite the custom to speak of it as Gibbon's fight as though no other brigade was engaged. In saying, too, that not until midnight was General King aware that his division was attacked, and that that officer allowed our brigade to fight alone and unaided, Mickey does grave injustice to a man who yielded to none in his love and admiration for the Iron Brigade. It was General King who sent orders to Patrick to push in to Gibbon's support, to Hatch to hasten back, and to Doubleday to hurry forward, and though it was barely dark by the time Hatch and his men did return and though Patrick's orders failed to reach him in time, it was no fault of General King. More than this, at nine o'clock at night King wrote to General William Ricketts, telling him to come to his support as Jackson was there in full force, and that hour, 9 o'clock, Hatch, Gibbon and Doubleday were there with King talking over the situation and 'Little John Gibbon,' as Mickey affectionately calls him, was vehemently urging General King to fall back and push for Manassas—the very move that resulted in their wounded being left on the field."

45 Haskell, letter to brothers and sisters, September 22, 1862.

O'Connor of the 2nd Wisconsin killed—"shot four times" Dawes wrote in his journal. Colonel Meredith of the 19th Indiana was hurt when his horse was shot in the neck and fell on his leg. All three field officers of the 7th Wisconsin were wounded with Colonel Robinson carried bleeding from the field. Lieutenant Colonel Charles Hamilton was shot through the thighs but maintained his seat in the saddle as his boots filled with blood. Major George Bill suffered a slight head wound. In the 2nd Wisconsin, Maj. Thomas Allen was shot in the neck and left arm, but did not leave the field. "Our Col. fought bravely until killed and the Lt. Col. [Fairchild] was under the hottest fire but escaped unhurt," Allen wrote home. With no field officers available in the 7th, Gibbon consolidated the 2nd and 7th Wisconsin under Fairchild, the senior field officer still on his feet.[46]

Confederate Brig. Gen. William B. Taliaferro, who was severely wounded in the fight, tried to catch in words what the combat at Gainesville involved:

> [I]t was a stand-up combat, dogged and unflinching. There were no wounds from spent balls, the confronting lines looked into each other's faces at deadly ranges, less than one hundred yards apart, and they stood as immovable as the painted heroes in a battle-piece. There was cover of woods not very far in the rear of the lines on both sides, and brave men—with the instinct of self-preservation which is exhibited in the veteran soldier, who seizes every advantage of ground or obstacle—might have been justified in slowly seeking this shelter from the iron hail that smote them, but out in the sunlight, in the dying daylight, and under the stars, they stood, and although they could not advance, they would not retire. There was some discipline in this, but there was much more of true valor.

The 2nd Wisconsin had been "almost mortally wounded," reported Rufus Dawes. "Never afterward could be filled the places of such soldiers as went down at Gainesville. For free and easy movement, combined with exact precision and perfect time, that battalion had a little surpassed us all on the brigade drill ground. The élan of the old second Wisconsin could not be excelled." He added a grim afterthought: "Our one night's experience at Gainesville had eradicated our yearning for a fight. In our future history we will also be found ready but never again anxious."[47]

---

46 Gaff, *Brave Men's Tears*, 156-158; Stine, *Army of the Potomac*, 132; Dawes, journal, undated; Allen, letter, September 4, 1862; Wheeler, journal, August 30, 1862; Watrous, *Milwaukee Sunday Telegraph*, December 7, 1879.

47 W. B. Taliaferro, "Jackson's Raid Around Pope," *Battles and Leaders of the Civil War*, vol. 2, 510; Dawes, *Service*, 64-65, 69-70.

Wisconsin and Indiana Blood Spilled for Naught

Major General John Pope later admitted that the decision to march King's division from Jackson's front to Manassas Junction was a tragic error. He also said that he had directed orders to King to "hold his ground at all costs"—a claim refuted in print by King's son. In fact, by August 28 Pope's Army of Virginia was scattered and no one in high command circles knew much about the movement of the Confederate columns. One Federal division had been ordered to Thoroughfare Gap to contest the arrival of the rest of the Rebel army, but the Federal commander realized he was outnumbered and retreated when the head of James Longstreet's wing arrived. Hearing King was taking his division to Manassas Junction, another Union general, James Ricketts, marched his men to Bristoe. Pope insisted later that it was the worst move King or Ricketts could have made—if they had maintained their positions, the two might have kept Longstreet's soldiers from reinforcing Jackson.

News of the bitter late day fighting convinced Pope that Jackson was in full retreat to Thoroughfare Gap. His solution was to shove troops after the withdrawing Rebels while King and Ricketts moved to blocked Jackson's retreat. In reality, the situation was much different. Jackson was not retreating; he was digging in along a strong defensive position. His lines of communication to Longstreet

were open and the head of Longstreet's column was already through the gap and bivouacked within supporting distance. Pope, however, was not expecting Longstreet to arrive before Saturday night or even Sunday, and issued orders for an attack on Jackson. Even

Pvt. Joseph Helms, Wisconsin Rifles, Co. K, 2nd Wisconsin

Helms fell wounded and a was taken prisoner at Gainesville, Virginia on August 28, 1862. He was discharged on October 31, 1865, for wounds.
Wisconsin Veterans Museum

Sgt. John Banderob, Oshkosh Volunteers, Co. E, 2nd Wisconsin

Baderbob was shot in the right arm at First Bull Run and wounded again at Gainesville and Gettysburg. He mustered out in 1864, term expired. After the war he became the mayor of Oshkosh. *Brett Wilson Collection*

as his aides rode off to the various division commanders, Federal skirmishers were exchanging fire with Jackson's men along the turnpike east of Groveton. Other Union forces would soon join in.

As time passed, Gibbon's decision to advance a regiment on the Rebel battery shelling his column was questioned because it stirred up Jackson and could have led to the defeat of a portion of the Union army. Massena Patrick admitted that he declined to put his brigade in on Gibbon's left because he disapproved of Gibbon's attack without more consideration and knowledge of the strength of the enemy he was assaulting.[48] The decision to leave the battlefield to the enemy was also scrutinized, with much of blame for doing so placed on Rufus King. "It would not do for Gen. McDowell's troops to have had a battle when he was not there, Or to have found any Confederate force of the enemy where according to his theory of the situation there was only a reconnoiter party," a Wisconsin officer, unaware that General King was ill and not drunk, wrote in his journal. "It might look as though he didn't know where the enemies were. Neither would it do for a division General (King) to have his troops fight a battle at the beginning of which he was almost dead drunk, and which he did not show his precious head. Nor is he anxious to any thing particularly said about the matter of his withdrawing his division without orders, ill-natured folks would say hurriedly, to Manassas." The same sentiments were

48 Stine, *Army of the Potomac*, 132.

echoed in the ranks by a 2nd Wisconsin soldier: "Then our division commander, Brigadier General Rufus King, orders a retreat, the first and only command he is known to have given since the opening of the battle, and we march by the Bethlehem road to Manassas Junction."[49]

Long after the war, however, in a written defense of his father, Charles King explained that "no order or message of any kind, sort, or description reached General King that night from General Pope or another superior officer; no staff-officer of General King saw or heard from General Pope that night." He also quoted from a letter of May 7, 1863, from Gibbon to King. "I deem it not out of place to say that the retreat was suggested and urged by myself as a necessary military measure," was how Gibbon put it. "I do not hesitate to day, and it is susceptible of proof, that of the two courses which I considered open to you, of obeying your orders to march to Centreville or tread on Manassas on your own responsibility, the one you adopted was the proper one." In the end, of course, the decision to march King's division away from Jackson's front was indeed a mistake and it played a large role in the defeat of Pope's Army of Virginia on August 29 and 30.[50]

All that was yet to come. In their make-shift camp along the railroad at Manassas Junction the morning of the 29th, the Wisconsin and Indiana men cooked the remains of their beef ration and boiled coffee. The brigade's ammunition wagons arrived and each man drew sixty rounds. About mid-morning they began to hear the "heavy sound of cannon and an occasional ripple of musketry" from the scene of the previous night's fight.

Major Dawes, sleeping alongside the roadway, awoke to the "heavy tramp of hurrying feet" and found a thick blue column moving back along the very road the 6th Wisconsin had covered the previous night. The soldiers belonged to Fitz-John Porter's corps, just up from McClellan's Army of the Potomac (a "happy sight to see," added one Badger). The new arrivals were marching to the sound of the fighting. Porter's men, who had withstood the battles outside Richmond several weeks earlier, were fresh and in good spirits—and filled with the contempt of veterans for Pope's soldiers, especially those dirty specimens in fancy plumed hats standing alongside the road to cheer and gawk as they passed. "We are going up to show you 'straw feet' how to fight," one infantryman yelled, which triggered "a

---

49 Rufus Dawes, journal, undated; Wheeler, journal, August 28, 1862. For a full discussion, see John J. Hennessy, *Return to Bull Run: The Campaign and Battle of Second Manassas* (New York, NY, 1993), 193.

50 General King, "In Vindication of General Rufus King," *Battles and Leaders*, vol. 2, 495. See also Gaff, *Brave Men's Tears*, 164-169.

running fire of disparagement" by both sides. One of Porter's regiments was the 5th New York, a colorful Zouave organization still outfitted in baggy red trousers. As it passed, a frustrated Badger stood by the road, narrowed his eyes, and raised his fist. "Wait till you get where we have been," he yelled. "You'll get the slack taken out of your pantaloons and the swell out of your heads."[51]

Once the regiments passed, Gibbon's brigade and the rest of the division fell in behind Porter's men to march back along the road traveled the night before. The Westerners could hear fighting and see dust clouds stretching toward Thoroughfare Gap. To the rank and file, these signs meant Jackson was on the run for safety. "The cannonading is getting stronger and closer," a Wisconsin soldier wrote in his diary. "It sounds like the continuous thunder of a storm: boom-boom-boom-boom. We now have hope seeing a quick ending of this unhappy war."[52] When he reached the junction of the Manassas-Gainesville and Manassas-Sudley roads, Porter continued on toward Gainesville. He had orders to attack Jackson's right—an order Porter never followed or was unable to follow. The road upon which he marched would carry him into one of the most the bitter controversies of the war and destroy his career.

When they reached the crossroads, staff officers waved King's men up the Manassas-Sudley road. They soon reached the Warrenton Turnpike and found Irvin McDowell on his horse. "We have been driving the enemy all day," the general announced. "Give him a good poke boys. He is getting sick." Some suspected that McDowell was a Southern sympathizer. He was wearing what one Badger called "the oddest looking hat I ever saw," and it was believed in the ranks that the general wore the distinctive headgear "so the rebels could distinguish him, and not direct their fire in his direction." The division finally halted and formed in two lines of battle, but Gibbon's regiments were detached and marched to the right, climbing the hill north of the Warrenton Turnpike to support Federal artillery. Men in the 2nd Wisconsin recognized the ground as the same they had fought upon during the first battle of Bull Run. It was near sunset. Off to the left the fighting was dull and indistinct. "Listening to this musketry, we deemed ourselves exceedingly fortunate to have escaped a fight," wrote Dawes. "A few artillery shots from the enemy whistled over us, but we soon fell into a profound and much needed slumber."

51 Sullivan, *Milwaukee Sunday Telegraph*, May 16, 1884; Longhenry, diary, August 29-30, 1862; Dawes, *Service*, 68-69. "Fitz-John Porter's corps from the army of the Potomac passed as we lay along the road. We felt good thinking we would be reinforced by the Army of the Potomac." Cheek and Pointon in Sauk County, 42.

52 Longhenry, diary, August 29-30, 1862.

A long time afterward, after examining the records, Dawes sat down to write a history of his regiment, including his bitter summary of Gainesville. "On the afternoon of this day, August 28th, 1862, was lost the only opportunity that occurred in that campaign to attack Jackson with superior forces while separated from Lee. The verdict of history is likely to be, that the opportunity was 'lost in the woods.' The best blood of Wisconsin and Indiana was poured out like water, and it was spilled for naught," believed Dawes. "Against a dark background of blunders, imbecilities, jealousies and disasters in the Pope campaign, stands in brief relief the gallant conduct of our heroic leader, John Gibbon. Whatever history may do for others, his fame is as safe as that of the faithful and gallant heroes of the brigade he commanded."[53]

The Wisconsin and Indiana soldiers slept in line of battle wearing belts and accouterments, with rifle-muskets at hand. "We understood that Lee had been beaten and tomorrow would finish the job, and that the much dreaded 'Stonewall' was bagged with his army," recalled Mickey Sullivan, "but the next day brought a very different story."[54]

Left to Fight the Whole Rebel Army by Himself

The sun rose into a clear sky on Saturday, August 30, 1862. It was as "quiet as a Sabbath morning at home," observed one of Gibbon's men. Far away skirmish fire sounded "like a dozen carpenters shingling a roof." The men were on a low hilltop and enjoyed a "fine view" of the Union army with "divisions, brigades and regiments" arrayed before them. The dark columns were moving toward various positions. Farther on, out of sight behind thick timber waited Jackson's Confederates. The minutes became hours, however, and little developed. "We dared not make coffee there as the smoke would show where the infantry was and the rebels would commence to shell us," one Badger said. Some of the soldiers moved behind the hill to boil their brew. Later, they would remember (with smiles) that their campfire talk included serious discussions of whether Stonewall and his men would get away without being "bagged."

Gibbon eventually rode off to find army headquarters. He located John Pope and several officers occupying a command post, not one in the style of George McClellan—there were no tents, no guards, and no flags—but a scattering of wood boxes for seats. An excited Pope complained to Gibbon of what was called "the

53 Dawes, *Service*, 68.

54 *Ibid.*, 69-70; Sullivan, *Milwaukee Sunday Telegraph*, May 16, 1884; Gibbon, *Recollections*, 61.

inaction" of Fitz-John Porter. He had done nothing, asserted Pope. "That is not the way for an officer to act, Gibbon." The comments surprised the brigade leader. "I knew Porter's reputation as a soldier well and felt confident that he was not a man to stand by and do nothing when he ought to fight," Gibbon recalled later. "But I knew little or nothing of the military situation and said nothing."[55] Pope was convinced the enemy was beginning to retreat and issued orders for a pursuit.[56]

Because of King's lingering illness, John Hatch was in command of his division. Under Pope's new orders, Hatch marched the command to the Warrenton Turnpike, then west one-half mile before moving north of the road. The four Black Hat regiments formed there in two lines with another brigade in front. To their front was a patch of woods and beyond that, though not in sight, a railroad embankment full Rebels who had no intention of retreating. The Union line stepped off, and when it reached the woods Gibbon ordered his regiments into a single line. The 6th Wisconsin held the right. The brigade in front disappeared into the timber. Gibbon's regiments moved perhaps thirty yards more when musketry erupted to their front. "We pushed on without delay or halt," Gibbon wrote, even though the "underbrush was thick and impassable for horses." Mounted officers moved forward on foot. "It was with difficulty that any alignment could be preserved. Bullets came thick from the front and very soon shells were bursting among us, coming from the left." The line moved into heavy underbrush, where the regiments became tangled as the heavy foliage forced them one way and then another. Showers of leaves and branches fell when "scraps of railroad iron" tore through the trees. "We pushed on," one officer said, "advancing as the lines in front of us advanced and lying down on the ground when they stopped." Suddenly, the Rebels "raised a tremendous shout and poured in a heavy fire of musketry" and the Federal line on front of the brigade gave way in disorder. A New York regiment behind the 6th Wisconsin "took the contagion and ran away not having fired a gun." A flurry of artillery fire also swept the end of the Federal line, adding "to the panic and confusion."

Behind the 6th Wisconsin, Lt. Col. Edward Bragg (in command of the regiment since the wounding of Colonel Cutler) came up on foot. With squinted eyes and his hat pulled down tight to one side, he shouted to the right and left through the smoke and noise: "Sixth Wisconsin down! Captains, keep your men down! Let nobody tramp on them!" Gibbon, revolver in his hand, was also there.

55 Sullivan, *Milwaukee Sunday Telegraph*, May 16, 1884; Dawes journal, undated; Fairfield diary, August 30, 1862; Gibbon, Recollections, 62.

56 Gibbon, *Recollections*, 62-63.

"Stop those stragglers—Make them fall in!—Shoot them if they don't!" yelled the general. "Stop them or shoot them like dogs." The Black Hats knelt and set their bayonets forward to receive the running fugitives. The line trembled and bucked as soldiers and officers clubbed, cuffed, and cursed the fleeing men in a frantic effort to halt the panic. Some halted to join Gibbon's line, but most others didn't stop until well to the rear.

Once the woods in front of Gibbon's brigade were empty the firing stopped. Was the enemy rushing toward them in pursuit? When Gibbon called on Bragg to throw forward a company of skirmishers, he selected the second platoon of Company K from Juneau County. "It was a fearful duty to go into the face of an advancing army," Major Dawes wrote, but the skirmish line deployed and Capt. David Quaw moved it smartly into the woods. A flurry of bullets clattered through the trees. Private Levi Gardner of Fountain City was shot "dead in his tracks," and Hoel Trumbull of Lemonweir was upended. Trumbull had folded his rubber blanket into a three or four-inch strip tied around his waist to keep it out of the way. "He was running forward when a bullet hit him on the waist belt and rubber blanket and he turned the completest somersault I ever saw, and some of us laughed heartier at it than at the antics of circus clown," wrote Mickey Sullivan. Trumbull was on his feet as quickly as he was knocked down, gasping for air while trying to understand what had happened.[57]

The skirmish line of Juneau County boys pushed deeper into the woods, snapping off shots as they dodged from tree to tree. When they spotted a line of Confederates the firing increased dramatically and the Black Hats took what cover they could find. The earlier "panic and retreat" of the first line of Federals amid the "exultant shouts of thousands of rebel soldiers did not daunt these men," boasted one officer. In the first wave of shooting, Captain Quaw shouted, "Tree!" and jumped behind a small sapling where he admitted "I must have shrunk to the dimensions of a wafer." A dozen bullets jerked the thin tree back and forth. Quaw recalled his skirmishers; he had located the Confederate line and it was heavy. Crouching down behind a small tree, Sullivan did not hear the order to retreat. "I began to peg away at the Rebs until I exhausted the rounds that was in the top compartment of my cartridge box. When I stopped to refill it I saw I was alone and I dug out of there in a hurry." He found the men of his regiment lying down to

---

57 Quaw, of Friendship in Bad Ax (Vernon) County, enlisted as a private May 10, 1861. He rose from the noncommissioned ranks to become 1st Lt. of Company I. He gained the captaincy on June 24, 1862, but resigned in October. *Wisconsin Roster*, vol. 1, 533. Gardner was the first man of Co. K killed in battle. Rufus R. Dawes, letter to J. T. Hanson, November 23, 1884, printed in *Mauston Star*, January 2, 1885.

escape artillery shells slicing through tree branches and leaves just above them. "I was very angry at [Lt. John] Ticknor, thinking he had carelessly left me there alone and not yet having arrived at the dignity of using . . . 'a good mouth filling oath,' I still clung to the 'cuss' words of my boyhood, I ask him in a indignant 'doggone' why he had left me there to fight the whole rebel army alone." Bragg, standing nearby watching the exchange, quietly told Sullivan to lay down. Ticknor added, "Lay down, Mickey, you damfool, before you get killed." Sullivan went to ground and transferred his cartridges to the upper part of his cartridge box.[58]

Before long all Federal troops in the woods withdrew except for the 6th Wisconsin, which was under fire from sharpshooters. Quite a number of the Badgers had been killed or wounded. Nothing transpired, one soldier said, until "the state of affairs were reported to the General and orders received as to what should be done." The long minutes under fire in the smoky woods strained Western nerves. "A bullet would strike a man who would writhe, groan and die or spring up, throw away his impediments, and start for the rear," one officer wrote. "Our men peered through the leaves, shooting at the puffs of powder smoke from the muskets of the rebels." Dawes was walking behind the line when a soldier called out, "Major, don't go near that tree." Dawes jumped to one side. "Spat went a bullet against the tree, cutting a corner from my haversack." The soldiers had noticed that the tree had been several times struck by the bullets of a sharp shooter.[59] Another soldier remembered "hugging the earth to escape the thick-flying musket balls from in our front," and when he looked back was astonished to find Bragg standing behind him. "Our colonel stood erect and motionless, alertly watching every development, ready for any emergency. And when the enemy brought artillery into position on our left and began throwing shells which came down the line and through the thick timber with a hair-raising clatter, he never moved nor even appeared conscious of the appalling danger." It was that moment under fire in the smoky woods at Second Bull Run that Bragg became in heart as well as title the "little colonel" of the 6th Wisconsin.

Edward Stuyvesant Bragg had been with the regiment from the first and was showing the kind of ability to lead men that would earn him a general's star later in the war. He moved from New York State as a young man to Fond du Lac in the

---

58 Dawes, journal, undated; Sullivan, *Milwaukee Sunday Telegraph*, May 16, 1884; Dawes, *Service*, 71-72. John Johnson of the 6th Wisconsin claimed the skirmishers received "such a withering fire that they came running back inside of three minutes, with half their numbers lost." Johnson, *Milwaukee Sunday Telegraph*, November 30, 1884.

59 Sullivan, *Milwaukee Sunday Telegraph*, May 16, 1884; Fairfield, diary, August 30, 1862; Dawes, *Service*, 72.

Capt. Henry B. Converse,
Co. A, 2nd Wisconsin

Enlisted in 1861 from Randolph, Converse was promoted through ranks. He was wounded at Second Bull Run and discharged on July 1, 1863, for reasons of disability.
Wisconsin Veterans Museum

Wisconsin Territory, where he practiced law and began to make a name for himself. When the war began the 37-year-old abandoned his law practice. "I'm in favor of suppressing the rebellion" he told a war meeting in his home town. "I want these young men and my neighbors to enlist. I will set the example." He walked to the front of the hall, signed the enlistment roster, returned to his law office, and announced he was shutting down until the insurrection was put down. Bragg began to raise a company of volunteers and decided to call it "Bragg's Rifles," which said something about the man. His restless energy created a good impression. As one volunteer put it, "he takes on the duties of a soldier as naturally as a tree takes on the burden of her fruit. He observes shrewdly, combines and infers rapidly, and intuitively separates important things from unimportant. He hates sham pretension and gives and demands perfectly straightforward and frank intercourse."[60]

There was much more to Bragg than the volunteer's simple description. He was one of those complex individuals tossed up in the volunteer organizations—a combination of ambition and patriotism, part politician, part soldier, and an

60 Watrous, *Milwaukee Sunday Telegraph*, December 10, 1898; *Milwaukee Sentinel*, October 4, 1861; Dawes, *Service*, 19; Murray, letter, June 22, 1861; Watrous, "An Appleton Contribution," manuscript.

individual one fellow soldier called "the brightest man" of Wisconsin volunteer officers. This man of ability and intelligence could also be petty. His letters to his wife are filled with bitter complaints against the older Cutler who Bragg believed blocked his advancement. One of his lieutenants noted that Bragg "seems to be engaged in fishing for some higher place and not in promoting the health or good feeling" of what would become his company.[61] The descriptions of him from his war days are enlightening. Bragg employed what one volunteer called an "awful vocabulary" while handling the regiment under fire. "He is rather under medium height, does not talk much and when he does speak it is in a low tone. But . . . he was like a fiend when fighting, raving and storming at his men and urging them on to the more daredevil acts, himself leading the way." Another soldier described the captain as "small and wiry; eyes and hair black as coal voice penetrating." Bragg, he continued, once comforted a wounded soldier with a pat on the back before adding, "You're all right chicken."[62]

There are dozens of Bragg stories, and one of the best involved a Massachusetts clergyman down to see the Army of the Potomac. The visitor confided to the regimental chaplain of the 6th Wisconsin that he was "much pleased with the general appearance of the men." He found the Badgers a "clean and orderly set, who drank and gambled much less than the soldiers in other regiments." The clergyman mused the reason was probably "the example of your colonel. . . . They feel the force of his beautiful Christian spirit, and they are afraid of shocking him by the use of profane language." To what denomination is Colonel Bragg, the clergyman asked? The regimental chaplain was an honest man and he mentally recalled "some of the highly picturesque expletives which the colonel was apt to use while in action, and the sultry anathemas which the men of the Sixth directed at the enemy along with the bullets." The chaplain coughed "violently to smother a laugh before replying, "Well, really, Brother Clark, I don't know to what church Colonel Bragg belongs. I never asked him, and I have never heard him say anything that would give me a hint."[63]

On August 30, the salty Bragg found himself holding his regiment under fire in a woods during one of the darkest days for Union arms. One of the fleeing New York soldiers collared by Gibbon was now dying near Bragg behind the line. The

---

61 Brown, letter to his wife, August 13, 1861.

62 Jerome A. Watrous, "Famous Iron Brigade," *Milwaukee Telegraph*, March 27, 1896; Watrous, "The Old Captain," pamphlet, undated; Watrous, *Milwaukee Sunday Telegraph*, December 10, 1898; James P. Sullivan, *Milwaukee Sunday Telegraph*, May 16, 1884.

63 Watrous, *Milwaukee Sunday Telegraph*, March 27, 1896.

soldier was halted and forced into the Wisconsin line and almost immediately mortally wounded. After Capt. Edwin Brown's hat was clipped by a bullet, he claimed in a letter home that the Rebels were using "globe sighted target rifles." In front of the Badger line, a wounded New York soldier begged for water. Unable to take the horrible cries any longer, Pvt. Charles Lampe of Milwaukee ran forward canteen in hand and was shot dead. Henry Petit of Lynxville was then shot through the body. He cried out "loud enough to be heard a mile" and fell into the arms of Sgt. August Miller. "What's the matter you great calf?" Miller said in rough soldier fashion. "I'm killed! On my God! I'm killed!" "Well," replied the sergeant, himself under a bit of a strain, "what the hell is the use of making a fuss about it?" Petit was carried to the rear, out of the war and on his way home. An unexpected legacy from Europe and an easier life awaited.

Especially troubling to Maj. Rufus Dawes was the wounding of Pvt. William Bickelhaupt of Milwaukee. Shot through the lungs, the unlucky soldier was crazed with pain and fear, and "the poor little boy, for such he was, in plaintive broken English telling his comrades what to write his 'Mutter.'" The wounded soldier wandered between home and the fighting. "Oh, I am dying," he cried out at one point. "I am killed. Tell my mother I was a good soldier." His body lurched and he fell silent for a minute or two before rising up and shouting, "Give them hell! Give them hell!" only to fall back again, his bloody chest heaving with every strained breath. Bickelhaupt lifted up again and uttered, "Tell her that I did my duty in battle—Poke it at 'em boys! Poke it at 'em!—Tell her that I . . . " Bickelhaupt would lay wounded three days before being taken to a hospital. At first he seemed to be recovering, but infection set in and he was dead within the month.[64]

The deadly sojourn in that stand of timber seemed endless. Gibbon arrived and told Bragg and Dawes that he had no orders to retire and that he would stay until he got them. No orders arrived. After a few minutes Gibbon became convinced that no staff officers could reach them. He directed Bragg to form skirmishers to cover the retreat. The squads deployed and Bragg ordered the 6th Wisconsin to face about. "But the moment we turned our backs we received a galling musketry fire and heard the exultant shouts of the enemy in our rear," writes a Black Hat. "Our commanding officers and Adjutant Haskell saw that we would be destroyed in no time, if we did not face them. To do this was a difficult maneuver under the

---

64 Dawes, journal, undated; Dawes, *Service*, 72; Brown, letter to his father, September 5, 1862. Petit would be discharged on February 25, 1863. Miller of Cassville was wounded at Gettysburg and was sick and absent when the regiment mustered out in 1865. Bickelhaupt died in Washington on October 22, 1862. *Wisconsin Roster*, vol. 1, 507, 519, 517. Brown said his men killed two rebel sharpshooters carrying target rifles.

circumstances, and I never saw it executed during the war but that once but we accomplished it, and retreating backwards, towards our lines, facing the confederates."[65]

A Slow Backward Step Under Fire

The 6th Wisconsin was in a tough place. The enemy had gotten around both flanks and was still in force to their front. When the regiment began moving out of the woods with "a slow backward step," Gibbon discovered that all other Federal troops had withdrawn. Private Francis Deleglise of Appleton was concentrating on the Rebels to his front and did not hear the orders to fall back. A friend rushed back, caught hold of his coat and gave a yank, telling to get back quick. "Without the least excitement but with a little longer stride than usual," said his friend, "he went back to the command, about faced and resumed his deliberate firing.[66]

Bragg faced the regiment by the rear rank and took a steady double quick toward the Union lines. When he reached the edge of the woods, he ordered the color bearers forward to wave the national flag to keep his own forces from firing on them as the line cleared the woods. The lieutenant colonel, one soldier said, began "taking long quick strides himself, his regiment imitated him." When the 6th Wisconsin "emerged from the trouble [in] splendid order . . . great old cheers went up from the spectators." The line moved steadily across the field for ten or fifteen rods before Bragg halted it. "About face!" he ordered. "Shoulder arms! Ready, aim fire! Recover arms! About face! Forward march!" Again they moved forward in quick time twenty or thirty rods more. There was another halt, another volley, another "About face!" and another march to the rear. "That was the way that Western regiment fell back."[67]

It was about three-quarters of a mile across a generally open field to reach the main Union line. The 6th Wisconsin "alone upon the plain, in full sight of both

---

65 Johnson, *Milwaukee Sunday Telegraph*, November 30, 1884.

66 Jerome Watrous on Deleglise: "No one had a brighter, better kept uniform. His rifle was as clean as a rifle could be made. His spare clothes and blankets were always folded just so, and he was sure to get everything in the way of rations that belonged to him and he knew just how to cook them." But Deleglise had one mannerism troubling to a soldier: lying down while shooting. Two days previously at Gainesville, Capt. Edwin Brown found the private flat on the ground working his rifle-musket with cool deliberation. "Private Deleglise, why are you lying down?" asked the astonished officer. "Because I can get better aim, Captain," Deleglise replied. Brown nodded and walked down the line. Watrous, manuscript, undated, Jerome A. Watrous Papers, WHS.

67 Watrous, manuscript, WHS; Brown, letter to his father, September 5, 1862.

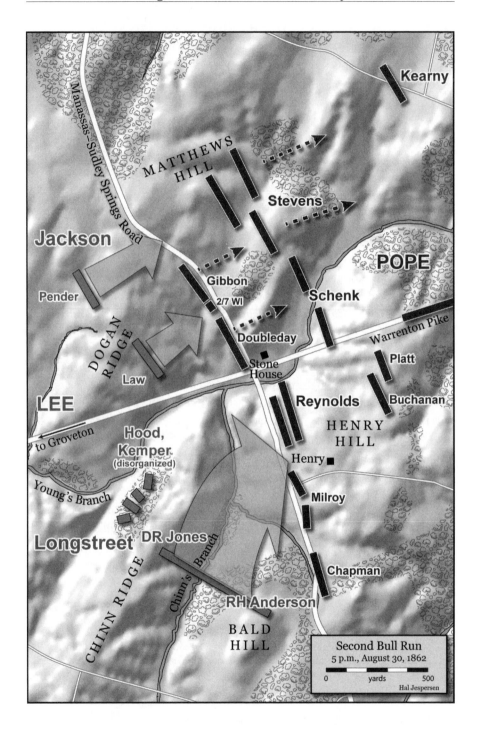

Kearny

MATTHEWS
HILL

Stevens

Jackson

POPE

Pender

Gibbon

Schenk

2/7 WI

DOGAN
RIDGE

Doubleday

Warrenton Pike

Law

Stone
House

Platt

LEE

Reynolds

Buchanan

to Groveton

Hood,
Kemper
(disorganized)

HENRY
HILL

Young's Branch

Henry

Milroy

Longstreet

DR Jones

CHINN RIDGE

Chinn's Branch

RH Anderson

Chapman

BALD
HILL

Second Bull Run
5 p.m., August 30, 1862

0   yards   500
Hal Jespersen

armies, marched this distance," reported Dawes. There was a disruption as the line passed through a small orchard and the regiment's flag became caught in the branches. Adjutant Frank Haskell rode to the front of the line and that "prince of good soldiers"—as Mickey Sullivan called him—lifted his sword and began pumping up and down, calling "Left, left, right, left" as he had done on all the drill fields from Washington to Fredericksburg. The regiment straightened and "marched as well as it ever did on review," one soldier said. In his official report, Rufus King noted the regiment was "the very last to retire, marched slowly and steadily to the rear, with the column formed and colors flying, faced the front as they reached the main Federal line and saluted the approaching enemy with cheers and a rattling volley." The general was in error as to the final volley, corrected Dawes. "We should have killed our following skirmish line by such fire."[68]

Gibbon's four regiments were ordered to support Battery B on a rise overlooking the Warrenton Turnpike. Two dozen Federal guns were arrayed on the hill, some facing west and others south. It was late in the afternoon. Heavy columns of Rebel infantry were spotted moving toward their left flank. Several hundred yards ahead a Confederate line moved to the edge of the woods. "By rising on our hands and knees we could see the magnificent corps of Longstreet coming toward us in close column by division, the closest formation at that time of infantry," a Sauk County boy recalled. "Their artillery was opening a close and destructive fire on the guns in front of us," wrote another Black Hat, "and canister and case shot were flying in all directions." One of the chunks of metal ripped Pvt. Ed Simmon's haversack as it lay on his thigh and "scattered his stock of hardtack and coffee in all directions, and he mourned more over the loss of his 'grub,' as he called it, than if it had been his arm." Also never forgotten was the soldier whose leg was shot off and made "such good time for the rear with the aid of his musket," or the rabbit "so much scared by the tremendous noise" that it took shelter under one soldier."[69]

Another artillery bolt careened through the six guns of Battery B, cut off the tail of one of the bay battery horses, and left "a deep cut across the rump." The wounded horse was named "Tartar," and his adventures tangled themselves into the lore of the Black Hat brigade. After the war, one veteran said, his small children asked him over and over at bedtime for the "horse story," and he admitted he might

68 Sullivan, *Milwaukee Sunday Telegraph*, May 16, 1884; Dawes, *Service*, 73.

69 Johnson, *Milwaukee Sunday Telegraph*, November 30, 1884; Cheek and Pointon, *Sauk County*, 43; Sullivan, *Milwaukee Sunday Telegraph*, May 16, 1884. Edward Simmon of Marion enlisted May 10, 1861. He was wounded at South Mountain in 1862 and at Petersburg in 1865. He veteranized in 1864, but was absent (wounded) when the 6th was mustered from service in July 1865. *Wisconsin Roster*, vol. 1, 353.

have romanced it a fact or two. The truth was just as interesting. Four-year-old Tartar entered service at Fort Leavenworth, Kansas, in July 1857 just before the battery left on the Utah expedition. Sick with distemper, the horse was abandoned at Green River in Utah a short time later. The following spring, two Indians returned him back to the battery. The shell at Second Bull Run carried away Tartar's tail and cut him on both flanks. When the army retreated the next day, Tartar was left behind in a small fenced pasture. Sometime that night he jumped the fence and was discovered the next morning with the rest of the battery horses. Tartar was also wounded at Fredericksburg in 1862 and once again left behind, only to show up on a Federal cavalry picket line a month later. Late in the war during a review attended by President Lincoln, Lt. James Stewart's battery was passing the reviewing stand when Lincoln spotted the horse, smiled, and remarked to the generals around him, "This reminds me of a tale." Lincoln's son Tad, who had accompanied his father, was much taken with Tartar. Tad was mounted on a pony and followed the battery pestering Lieutenant Stewart to trade horses. "I told him I could not do that, but he persisted in telling me that his papa was the President, and would give me any horse I wanted in trade for Tartar," remembered the officer. "I had a hard time to get away from the little fellow." When Stewart was promoted and transferred to the 18th U.S. Infantry in 1866, Tartar was still in harness with Battery B—the tenth year of "his honorable and distinguished service." What became of the famous battery horse is unknown.[70]

Watching the steady advance of Longstreet's infantry was an awesome sight. "We could see regiment after regiment of the enemy moving in column by division, and forming into lines of battle as they advanced upon our men. Our batteries were all actively firing upon the advancing columns of the enemy. Their artillery was also in action," recalled an officer. "The solid shot and shell," he continued, "struck around us and whizzed over us. Occasionally a horse would be killed by them, and one man's head was carried away entirely. Such sights very severely test one's nerves. A solid shot will plow into the ground, spitefully scattering the dirt and bound a hundred feet into the air, looking as it flies swiftly away like an Indian rubber playing ball." One ball almost hit Pvt. John Johnson. "The shot must have struck the ground in front of us, then I could see it as plain as if we were playing ball," he wrote. "The instinct of boyhood was predominant in me and my left hand stretched out to catch it. It just touched the top of my left shoulder."[71] The Black Hats could see other Federals engaging the Rebels. "Regiments would sweep

---

70 James Stewart, letter, December 8, 1889, quoted in Buell, *Cannoneer*, 30-31.

71 Johnson, *Milwaukee Sunday Telegraph*, November 30, 1884.

splendidly forward into the front line, fire a crashing volley . . . then work with great energy," observed an officer. "But they quickly withered away and then would appear to be a mere company crowding around the colors. The open fields were covered with wounded and stragglers, going to the rear."

In front of the line, a Massachusetts regiment supporting an Ohio battery panicked and broke, wrote one Black Hat, the fleeing soldiers taking "shelter in a ditch that had been used as a rear [toilet] by all hands while we had been on the field, much to our indignation and disgust." A disgusted Pvt. Tom Flynn exclaimed to the men around him, "There is not divils enough in the confederacy to make me put my head in that ditch." The Buckeye battery was left exposed and its commander rode up to Lt. Col. Bragg "crying worse than a whipped schoolboy." Shouting and swinging his hands, the officer cried over and over, "Mine pattery was gone, mine pattery was gone!" Bragg, in his "cool, indifferent way, with one eye shut and the other not open," replied simply, "We'll take care of your battery." The German had no sooner left than Gibbon rode out with an order to the artillery to hold fire. The German quickly returned. "Got in Himmil! General, why you no say shoot by my battery! By Jesus Christus, who you no say shoot!" Gibbon shot the officer an icy stare and snapped, "Go to your battery, Captain, and obey orders when given."[72]

"Masses of the enemy" were clearly visible approaching "a bald hill in front of the Henry House," but would disappear in the rolling clouds of gun smoke. A Confederate line also stepped out of the woods to advance on the Ohio battery. The combined 2nd and 7th Wisconsin under Lucius Fairchild were aligned on the brow of the ridge, one wing on each side of the German guns. The Confederates came on with a steady step in good discipline. "When we . . . found the Johnnies flanking us on both sides and saw those double-shot Napoleon guns, we knew there was to be music," wrote one of the Black Hats. Gibbon waited until his infantry could "see every detail of their outfit" before yelling "Batteries, ready! Aim! Fire!" The heavy bronze guns belched smoke and flame, bucked back on their wheels by the firing. The blasts "tore great bloody gaps in the Rebel lines and piled the dead and mangled in rows like hay raked in windrows in a hayfield," observed a farmer-turned-soldier. "It was an awful slaughter." The Confederates were "pretty close when the front line arose and fired, cutting them badly and turning them about after they fired one volley without much effect. . . . The bullets came over our heads like a show or hailstone." The 2nd and 7th Wisconsin boys poured in another volley that halted the Rebels "right then and the order to fix bayonets and charge cause them to conclude that they did not want that battery, and they scampered

72 Edward S. Bragg, letter to Rufus Dawes, December 21, 1890, Dawes Papers, WHS; Cheek and Pointon, *Sauk County*, 43.

back for the woods as fast as they could go, under a withering fire of all the guns could bear on them." An Irish private, watching the Rebels retreat, called out, "Set them up on the other alley boys, they're all down on that." The remark brought laughter that spread along the line of Black Hats.[73]

Despite the easy repulse of the enemy thrust, the day was turning decisively against Pope's army. Off to their left, the Westerners watched Union brigades being driven back in confusion. Longstreet's broad heavy attack would soon outflank the Federal army, crush and sweep it off the field, and destroy John Pope's reputation. One of Maj. Gen. Joseph Hooker's staff officers arrived and advised Gibbon to retreat. "General Hooker was almost a stranger to me and belonged to a different corps," Gibbon wrote. "I called the attention to the officer, bringing the order, to the importance of the position we held, especially in view of the fact that our troops appeared to have retaken possession of the hill near the Henry house and that if we fell back the whole line would have to do so and requested him to so state to General Hooker." The officer left but returned a short time later, this time with different news: General Pope had ordered a general retreat.

By now Gibbon could see Hooker riding along the batteries ordering the guns and supporting infantry to retire. "Regiments moved steadily by the right of companies to the rear, the batteries moved also in retreat," confirmed a Black Hat officer. About the same time a heavy line of Confederate infantry rose in front of the position and began a slow advance after the retreating Federals. When the Union line halted, the Confederates stopped as well and went to ground, hugging but not pressing the retreat. "Get, you sons of bitches, get!" some of the Johnnies called out. "We got, not talking back," admitted a Wisconsin man. Another Black Hat added, "How I skedaddled with my short legs. . . . In fact, I wished I hadn't been born. We stood when commanded to stand, and when ordered to go—we got!" Long after the war Mickey Sullivan was still bitter about the retreat. "I fail to see why we did not win, as I am very sure we held the key [position] and were not driven an inch by the rebels, nor did our pieces have to 'limber to the rear' until we were finally marched off the field."[74]

73 *Ibid.* Gibbon's men faced two brigades, one under William D. Pender (Jackson's wing), and the second under Evander M. Law (Longstreet's wing).

74 Johnson, *Milwaukee Sunday Telegraph*, November 30, 1884; Cheek and Pointon, *Sauk County*, 44; O. B. Curtis, *History of the Twenty-fourth Michigan of the Iron Brigade* (Detroit, MI, 1891), 466. The quotation is from Phil Cheek of the 6th Wisconsin to a postwar meeting of veterans in Michigan; Sullivan, *Milwaukee Sunday Telegraph*, May 16, 1884. For an interesting account of the general, see John Pope, *The Military Memoirs of General John Pope*, Peter Cozzens and Robert I. Girardi, eds. (Chapel Hill, NC, 1998).

The brigade moved across a valley and up a hill, passing a pike of knapsacks and other equipment left in a woods. Just before pulling out, Gibbon saw Hooker watching the Confederate advance. He rode over to explain his hesitancy to retreat. "That is all right," Hooker replied, adding "some complimentary remark" about the way the brigade had behaved. According to Gibbon, the exchange "at once excited my pride and attracted me to him." Soon after leaving Hooker, Gibbon came upon Irvin McDowell, who smiled and said he had heard Gibbon was dead. Gibbon assured him that was not the case, pointed out his passing brigade, and spoke with enthusiasm about his Wisconsin and Indiana soldiers. "If you have such troops as that," McDowell said, "you shall act as a rearguard and be the last, except myself, to pass Bull Run!" The order astonished Gibbon. "I must admit that up to this time I had not got it through my head, that there was such a thing as a retreat or that we were to be a rearguard."[75]

Gibbon's brigade deployed with Battery B's six guns on a ridge alongside the Warrenton Turnpike near the Robinson House. "The sun was now just disappearing and the atmosphere so thick with smoke that the eye could not reach to any great distance," the general later recalled. "We could not see any of the enemy's movements but the sound of cannon was still heard both to our right and left."[76]

An erect officer rode out of the growing darkness, an empty sleeve of his military tunic pinned to the shoulder. Major General Phil Kearny, who had lost his arm in the War with Mexico, was one of the most famous general officers in the entire Union army.

"Whose command is this?" yelled Kearny. Gibbon stepped forward to reply that he was acting as the rearguard.

"You must wait for my command, sir," Kearny ordered. When Gibbon asked the location of the general's command, the one-armed general snapped back, "Off to the right, don't you hear my guns? You must wait for Reno, too," he added, referring to Jesse Reno's division. Gibbon inquired as to Reno's position, and Kearny shot back, "On the left—you hear his guns? He is keeping up the fight and I am doing all I can to help."

Kearny leaned forward to look Gibbon in the face. "I suppose you appreciate the conditions of affairs here, sir?" When Gibbon did not reply, he continued, "I suppose you appreciate the condition of affairs? It's another Bull Run!"

Gibbon was taken aback: "Oh! I hope not quite as bad as that, General."

75 Dawes, *Service*, 74; Gibbon, *Recollections*, 64-65.

76 Gibbon, *Recollections*, 64-65.

"Perhaps not," Kearny replied. "Reno is keeping up the fight. He is not stampeded. I am not stampeded, you are not stampeded. That is about all, sir, my God that's about all."

Kearny set his spurs and rode off to meet his fate two days later at Chantilly, where he would be killed. He left behind a letter that included a sentence describing Second Bull Run: "The army ran like sheep, all but a General Reno and a General Gibbon."[77]

The Country was Shocked and Discouraged

Second Bull Run ended about 9:00 p.m. with the onset of darkness. Gibbon's men were so close to the enemy lines they could hear the commands of the Rebel officers. When nothing developed, Gibbon rode to the left and found a brigade of Reno's command and a battery. Their officers gathered to ask that he give the command to retreat. Gibbon hesitated, unsure of the command situation, but finally told Reno's men to retire to the Warrenton Turnpike. During his ride back Gibbon learned that Kearny's troops had also left the field. Reno confronted him a few moments later and asked, "What the devil are you ordering my troops off the field for Gibbon?" After hearing Gibbon's explanation replied, "All right, all right. All my troops have gone back, and now you can leave as soon as you please."[78]

It was close to midnight when the Black Hats—after building fires to confuse the enemy— "leisurely fell back all night," crossing Cub Run the next morning. The brigade halted once more to form and face the enemy. When no Confederates showed themselves the Westerners marched to Centreville, where they met a Union force just up from the Army of the Potomac to reinforce Pope. "[A]fter marching, starving and fighting a week, without a night's rest, we lay down in the mud and rain and slept as only the tired soldier can when he has a chance," reminisced Mickey Sullivan. By this time Gibbon was well aware that Kearny's conclusion that "It's another Bull Run!" was accurate. The Warrenton Turnpike was "blocked up with a mingled mass of stragglers, wagons, artillery, ambulances

---

77 *Ibid.*

78 Dawes, *Service*, 75; Gibbon, *Recollections*, 69. Reno was killed at South Mountain on September 14, 1862. Several units claimed to have acted as the Union army's rearguard at Second Bull Run. See Joseph Mills Hanson, *Bull Run Remembers* (Manassas, VA, 1953), 131-132. Frank Haskell, who was serving on Gibbon's staff, wrote home: "On the night of the Thirtieth after the battle the army fell back to Centreville and Gibbon's Brigade with Campbell's (formerly Gibbon's) Battery, Co. "B" Fourth Artillery, was the rearguard of the whole army. This is no small honor, and you may set it down as a fact, the lying newspapers to the contrary notwithstanding. Haskell, letter to brother and sisters, September 22, 1862.

and wounded, some of whom were in hand litters as they left the field." The scene at Centreville "baffled description," wrote a Black Hat. Officers of all grades, from all branches of service, were milling about "looking for their commands and mobs of men looking for their organizations. Infantry, artillery, cavalry, ambulances, wagons and all the impediments used in an army all mixed up with dire confusion."[79] Still, there was a key difference between the situation now and that of First Bull Run, observed one Badger:

> It was a different class of men. They had seen service; they had been in a number of hard battles; they had learned how to fight. It was not their fault that a great victory was not won at the second battle of Bull Run. They had lacked competent leadership. It was fortunate for that defeated army and Washington that Lee's army had been so severely punished that it did not follow up its advantage. At no time, in all of the four years of war was Washington so disturbed or in such great danger. . . . The country was shocked and discouraged.[80]

An example just how confused matters were was made plain when the brigade bivouacked at Centreville. Picket lines were established around the entire command. "Nobody knew when the next blow would come," explained one officer. "Ignorance of the situation, and disorder and lack of discipline among the troops was the rule." There was one tragic mix-up. Worn out by three days of battle, a confused Wisconsin soldier on picket duty faced the wrong direction. When a detail arrived to relieve him, the soldier mistook the men for the enemy and fired. His round killed Pvt. Rudolph Fine, one of the Hillsboro boys of Co. I of the 6th Wisconsin. Gibbon summed up the last few days in a single terse sentence: "Again had faulty strategy defeated us, and again the folly of attempting to command armies in the field from a distance had been demonstrated."[81]

The next day, the first of September, the Western Brigade "in regular form with no demoralization" led the retreating army toward Fairfax Court House. Having been without food for a couple of days, the hungry soldiers spied an opportunity to fill their stomachs when they came upon a wagon train carrying fresh bread. "As the wagons passed we got on each side and with our bayonets speared out the whole contents of the wagon. Real fresh bread don't go far with a

79 Sullivan, *Milwaukee Sunday Telegraph*, May 16, 1884; Dawes, *Service*, 74-75; Gibbon, *Recollections*, 69, Cheek and Pointon, *Sauk County*, 44.

80 Watrous, manuscript, undated, Jerome A. Watrous Papers, WHS.

81 Edward Bragg, letter to Earl Rogers, April 3, 1900; Dawes, *Service*, 75. Fine enlisted at Hillsboro on May 10, 1861. *Wisconsin Roster*, vol. 1, 531; Gibbon, *Recollections*, 69.

half starved soldier," wrote one of the bread thieves. Despite the food, it was heavy going for the "exhausted, tired, footsore soldiers," and those unable to keep up the pace dropped to the side of the road to rest. Gibbon, mounted and accompanied by a one-horse spring wagon carrying his provisions showed his dark side when he ordered the drum corps to play the "Rogue's March" to shame stragglers back into the ranks. It was, complained a Badger, "the only instance on record . . . outside of his own cruelty, barbarity and indecent humidity, where the outrage was imposed on volunteer soldiers unless sentenced by a court martial."

Later that day a heavy storm swept the area, and Gibbon formed his regiments in a line of battle when distant artillery and rippling musketry intermingled with the thunder. "The darkness incident to a sky overcast with heavy, rolling clouds, lighted up alternately by flashes of lightning and the flames of artillery, made a scene long remembered," wrote Rufus Dawes. Although none of them knew it, the fighting involved a Union effort to block an attempt by Stonewall Jackson to get around the Federal right and block their retreat.[82] The Western men escaped the combat, but not the confused tangle of wagons and marching soldiers fitfully tramping along the Warrenton Turnpike. The next day an ambulance rolled past the marching brigade carrying the body of Phil Kearny. He had been killed at Chantilly and his corpse returned from enemy lines under a flag of truce. As the head of the column approached Upton's Hill six miles from Washington, regimental commanders told their color bearers to wave their flags to prevent "being fired upon by the Union guns in the front upon the height, so demoralized were they were the crushing defeat the Union army had received."[83]

Despite the hard marching, harder fighting, and crushing defeat, good news was at hand: McClellan had been given command of the capital's defense and much of the Army of the Potomac had arrived from the peninsula. Loud yells and cheers greeted the news. General Hatch, a McClellan partisan, swung his sword over his head and led the huzzahs and cheers that were given with "uproarious good will and repeated." One Black Hat summed up the matter thusly: "There was a loud call for a new leader to gather up the reins, reorganize the army and enter upon the next campaign. Where was the leader? There was no time to lose. McDowell had twice been defeated at Bull Run. He wouldn't do. Pope . . . had met disaster. He wouldn't do. President Lincoln did what he believed was the best thing to do. He named

---

82 The battle at Chantilly on September 1, 1862, considered the last combat of the Second Bull Run Campaign took the lives of two Federal division commanders, Isaac I. Stevens and Philip Kearny.

83 Cheek and Pointon, *Sauk County*, 45; Earl Rogers Papers, Wisconsin Veterans Museum, Madison; Dawes, *Service*, 75-76.

Gen. McClellan." Frank Haskell agreed, writing home that "Poor, lying Pope was played out. The man alone who is fit for the place, McClellan, took the army." Edward Bragg of the 6th Wisconsin described Pope as "a braggart & villainous perverter of facts & McDowell too fussy & and confused to have any combinations successful." McClellan's return to command, wrote Gibbon, sent the "weary fagged men into camp, cheerful and happy to talk over their rough experience and speculate to what was ahead."[84]

The past three weeks had thoroughly changed Gibbon's brigade. The hard bloody combat at Gainesville had been well beyond the imagination of innocent volunteers, and so many friends and camp mates were gone. But there was also deep satisfaction because the Western Brigade had been tried under the harshest conditions and demonstrated courage and ability at every turn. The men discussed their experiences around campfires eating salt pork and hard tack provided by a German commissary sergeant of an Ohio regiment (given without requisition or receipt to keep "the men alive during the night"). "Great as our loss has been it is better than defeat," concluded one Badger, "and everybody feels proud of belonging to 'Gibbon's Brigade,' commanded by John Gibbon, or 'Fighting John' as our boys call him." Haskell told his family, "I have no touch of bullet or shell upon me. I cannot give you particulars or write home, as the terrible weariness of a long fight is upon me." In the Lemonweir Minute Men, Pvt. Hugh Talty told his messmates, "Arrah, if the big generals wus wurth a cint, we'd show thim rebels what dilgant hands we were a fightin.'" His nephew, Mickey Sullivan, agreed. "The feeling was universal that the miserable result of all our hard fighting was due to lack of skill in our commander and the meddling interference of the war department in keeping several different armies to protect Washington, neither of which was strong enough for any purpose but that of defeat. Pope, McDowell and several more of that ilk were relieved from command," continued Mickey, "and 'Fighting Joe' Hooker took command of our corps. Our brigade camped at Upton's Hill and once more received enough to eat."[85]

"I know that our part of the army had no idea that we were defeated," Mickey wrote many years later after a chance to consider the larger picture and examine the written record. "I think, had he [Pope] been an energetic commander, with two fresh corps coming up to his support, and his centre and right wing intact, there was no occasion for Pope to retreat from Bull Run, leaving his dead and wounded

84 Frank Haskell, letter to brothers and sister, September 22, 1862; Edward Bragg, letter to his wife, September 13, 1862; Watrous, manuscript, undated; Gibbon, *Recollections*, 70.

85 Edward Bragg, letter to Earl Rogers, April 3, 1900; Thomas Allen, letter, September 4, 1862; Frank Haskell, letter to his brothers and sister, August 31, 1862.

uncared for, many of the latter of whom died for want of care before the ambulance corps and citizens of Washington went out and brought most of them in." During the roughly two months Pope commanded the Army of Virginia, he continued, it was "one uninterrupted series of disasters, and although they fought well and lost heavily, there was no talent to direct the men." Pope blamed his defeat on the actions or lack of actions of Fitz-John Porter,[86] "but the enlisted men of the army thought that he should blame his own ignorance and self conceit," Mickey argued, "for, if he had handled his army half as well as Porter's men fought at Bull Run, the result would have been different." Pope had come from the West to show the Army of the Potomac how to fight, and now he blamed Porter "to have some excuse for his ignominious failure. I don't wish to be understood as being unfair and prejudiced against Pope any more than against any of the other military failures of the war," he concluded, "but when Pope took command he made such a braying of trumpets in his own praise as to render him particularly conspicuous."[87]

As was often the case, the postwar assessment offered by Rufus Dawes was more measured. "General Pope made a grave blunder" in sarcastically attacking the army's "ingrained hero worship of General McClellan, which feeling can be little understood now, because conditions akin to those affected us have passed away," he explained. "Such a feeling, as that for General McClellan, was never aroused for another leader in the war." Because of that "feeling" in the ranks, it was all but certain that McClellan would return to at least partial command of the army. In fact, the Army of the Potomac, created and inspired by "Little Mac," one soldier wrote,

---

86 Porter was relieved of his command on November 1862 to face courts-martial charges leveled by Pope for disobedience, disloyalty, and misconduct in the face of the enemy. He was found guilty. In 1878, a special commission exonerated Porter, and President Chester Arthur commuted his sentence and restored his commission as a colonel of infantry in 1886 (backdated to May 1861, though without back pay). The vindicated Porter retired from the Army two days later. *Dictionary of American Biography*, 20 vols. (New York, NY, 1928-1937), vol. 15, 91.

87 James P. Sullivan, "A Private's Story," *Milwaukee Sunday Telegraph*, May 13, 1888; Sullivan, *Milwaukee Sunday Telegraph*, May 16, 1884. Sullivan prefaced his biting criticism with an unsubstantiated report passing through the ranks: "A recent writer narrating how his company, after a fatiguing march (in dust so thick that one was unable to see the length of the company), was turned out and worked all night constructing a bridge only to get orders as the last plank was laid at daylight, to destroy it, described the campaign as a 'blunder,' and that is the only word that does justice to Pope's Bull Run campaign. It was said, but I did not see it, that Pope, McDowell and Sigel quarreled on the battle-field, and that Sigel drew his pistol to shoot Pope, calling him a cowardly ignoramus, who was not qualified to hold the rank of corporal." Sullivan concluded: "It is a mystery to the men who served in the late war why McDowell, who never won a battle, and Pope, who was continually defeated from the time the enemy appeared in his front until he took shelter in the defences of Washington, should hold high commands at this day." *Ibid.*

was "smarting under criticism and its own frustration that it had disappointed its own hopes and those of the people." Richmond remained in Southern hands, Pope proved a failure, and the Confederate army was once again outside the gates of Washington. As one Wisconsin officer put it, "there were those even in high position, who seemed to glory in the fact." Against the advice of others, Lincoln pursued the only course left to him by restoring McClellan to the soldiers who loved him. The return cheered officers and men alike and lightened the step of the very volunteers who had failed a second time at Bull Run. Dawes recalled of that time that common and severe throughout the army was "animadversions against the President himself, for what was called 'interference' with the plans of his Generals."

"What is reserved for us in the future I don't know," Capt. Edwin Brown wrote home. "We have been out generalled. Jackson, Lee & Longstreet are too much for 'the Pope' and McDowell, who have commanded the army since we left Culpepper." The troops have no confidence in either of them, added the captain. "They curse them continually as the cause of our disasters. When the army heard that McClellan was restored to original command, 150,000 voices broke forth in a multitude of grand old cheers—The soldiers have faith in him whether politicians do or not—Gen. Pope is the greatest imposition that has been palmed off on a credulous army of people. McDowell even, is a giant in comparison to him."

With some sectional bias, Brown also wrote that most of the New York and Pennsylvania troops behaved badly in the battle, saying they "did not stand fire well, broke & run in confusion when the thing became hot. New England troops did well and so did Western. So far as I could judge, this was universal, yet those that make the best time get the most Newspaper puffs. They buy correspondents to fight their battles on paper." Then he added his assessment of the enemy: "I must say this the Rebels fight furiously desperately, madly and have great system in their madness. We always have to fight them in strong positions generally in the woods, and their sharpshooters play the very devil with our officers and artillerists."[88]

What one officer called the brigade's "terrible ordeal" lasted from August 23rd to the 30th. The Black Hats were in a battle or skirmish nearly every day during that time at the cost of some 800 men. "The country knows how nobly our men have borne themselves," Dawes wrote home. "I have been at my post in every battle."[89]

One of the troubling discussions that made the rounds of the campfires and continued long after the war was that the "disgraceful defeat" at Second Bull Run

88 Edwin Brown, letter to his father, September 5, 1862.

89 Dawes, *Service*, 78.

may have been caused by McClellan's desire to see Pope fail. "The bulk of the Army of the Potomac under McClellan was within reach of that field and could have had a part in the battles of the three days," one Badger explained. "It would be difficult to convince unprejudiced people who recall the condition of things during that frightful campaign of destruction, disorder and slaughter, that General Pope was not purposely left to fight the battle with his inferior force and suffer just such a defeat as came to him and his splendid army." As proof, the 6th's Jerome Watrous related a story told to him by a 5th Wisconsin veteran whose friend worked as an orderly at McClellan's headquarters. The orderly was visiting his old company just up from the peninsula. "Boys," he told his friends, "you will get orders to move tomorrow morning, early. You will prepare five day's rations. You will start for the battle, but you will not reach there." Why is that? he was asked. What do you mean? "I have heard talk at headquarters which would chill the blood," the orderly continued. "It is definitely settled that Pope must be defeated. A victory . . . would mean John Pope at the head of the United States Army; that would never do." And Watrous (and others) claimed that is exactly what happened. "If the truth and all of the truth ever comes out pertaining to the second battles of Bull Run, every patriotic man and woman in the country will be shocked at the perfidy, the infamy, which prevented a great Union victory, instead of a disgraceful defeat, a rout."[90]

At Upton Hill, the dismay of defeat gave way to grim acceptance. "You see we are back near our first starting point," a Wisconsin officer wrote home. "It is a sorrowful conclusion of a mismanaged campaign Pope has played out with the army." Otherwise, there was little change and routine again became normal. Peddlers appeared, but pockets were empty. "Sutlers are asking outrageous prices," one Black Hat complained. "Molasses 50 cents a bottle. . . . As a result the soldiers are obliged to steal."[91]

The campaign just ended left Capt. Edwin Brown of the 6th Wisconsin near the end of his rope, physically and emotionally. He hadn't seen his wife and young children back in Fond du Lac for more than a year, and the close brush with a sharpshooter's bullet that clipped his hat unnerved him. "I have seen enough of the horrors of war, imagination cannot picture it, it is too horrible to write about," he

---

90 Watrous, "New Facts Touching a Long Ago Time," manuscript, Jerome A. Watrous Papers, WHS. Watrous identified the soldier as Oscar H. Pierce, a Milwaukeean who served with Company B of the 5th Wisconsin. The orderly was George H. Cooper of Beloit, who after being wounded in the Seven Days' fight, was transferred to various headquarters posts. *Wisconsin Roster*, vol. 1, 442-443.

91 Cheek and Pointon, *Sauk County*, 46; Thomas Allen, letter, September 4, 1862; Longhenry, diary, September 3, 1862.

penned in a revealing letter to his father. He also admitted his health was suffering. "I am weary, worn out. I don't weigh over 115 pounds, and would like to seek repose with my family & friends. I have been on every march. In every place of danger, that my Co. & Regt. have. I have been broken so much of any rest, have had such hard fare that I am weak, tired and thin. I tried to get leave of absence for one week to rest in Washington but was refused. What the end will be I can't tell. Probably a fit of sickness." Just before he sent the letter, he scrawled a disturbing line across the top of the page: "I don't know as I shall ever get a chance to come home—I think the south will maintain their independence."[92]

92 Edwin Brown, letter to his father, September 5, 1862.

Part III: The National Road at South Mountain

I Have Seen Enough of the Horrors of War

Captains of infantry, privates, and even the president of the United States were unsure all the sacrifice and suffering would be enough to preserve the Union. Robert E. Lee and his soldiers had beaten McClellan and lifted the siege at Richmond, turned and defeated the Union armies at Cedar Mountain and Second Bull Run, and were now on the march in search of new opportunities. On September 4, elements of the Army of Northern Virginia began crossing the Potomac River into Maryland, posing a threat not only to Washington but to Baltimore and beyond. Lee wanted to shift the fighting north to allow Virginia farmers time to harvest their crops, feed his army with Maryland food, and raise men to swell his ranks. Lee also knew that his series of victories had left Lincoln's Eastern armies in disarray, and that another significant victory on the order of Second Bull Run might prompt European recognition of the new Confederacy and convince the Northern populace that the war was simply too expensive in blood and treasure to continue. The Southern army, however, was exhausted, hungry, ill-clothed, and low on just about everything from ammunition and food to horse flesh and shoes. Despite their own travails morale remained high, with unbounded trust and enthusiasm for the generals leading them from one success to another. Moving north of the Potomac, however, dramatically increased Lee's rate of desertion; thousands of soldiers simply refused to cross because they had enlisted to defend the Confederacy and not invade the North.

McClellan's task in the face of Lee's thrust north was a heavy one. His command structure was in a chaotic state and the men in the ranks shaken by the defeats of recent days. Little Mac had to not only take the wreckage that was Pope's Army of Virginia (which was stricken from the Army rolls) and blend it back into his own Army of the Potomac, but reclaim order, discipline, and morale. Everything had to be done in a hurry and there was so little time. Animals had to be gathered and made ready for an active campaign. Wagons had to be repaired, and food and ammunition found to fill them. Soldiers needed refitting with uniforms, shoes, munitions and rations. Orders had to be drafted for a possible movement into Maryland after Lee. The man who had built the Army of the Potomac into a force so strong that it was able to withstand almost any blow or any defeat proved equal to the task. It was McClellan at his very best—working long into each night to sign this order or that, inspect new wagons, ensure his regiments were equipped and his artillery ready. In the final result, his was a feat of military skill and organization that no other Union general (or Confederate for that matter) could have pulled off. Advance elements of his army were on the road and giving chase just one day after Lee's army crossed into Maryland. Cursed with unfortunate luck and limited ability, Irvin McDowell left active service, while the able and active Joseph Hooker was given command of First Corps.

High command changes that would directly affect Gibbon's brigade began with the ill Rufus King, who left his division for a diplomatic post. Brigade leader John Hatch was given King's command. Once the threads of change came together, Gibbon's 2nd, 6th, 7th Wisconsin and 19th Indiana became the Fourth Brigade, First Division, First Army Corps, Army of the Potomac.

Marching orders arrived at 10:30 p.m. on September 6. Gibbon's men assembled in darkness, tramped to Washington, and stopped in front of the Executive Mansion. Private John Johnson of Stevens Point curled up for a "good nap, on the pavement up against the fence enclosing the grounds of the White House."[1] The night was "terribly hot and sultry" and the president's lawn thickly strewn with played-out soldiers. When a bobbing lantern approached, the soldiers lifted themselves on an elbow to watch "the tall form of the President ('Old Abe,' as they called him) in shirt sleeves, water pail and dipper in hand, stepping over and among the boys lying around all over the grounds giving them water to drink."[2]

The march resumed at dawn north into Maryland. The columns pushed along again the next day and stopped briefly near Brightwood so the soldiers could boil coffee. "We have to carry our knap-sacks again," one soldier grumbled in his diary. "Corn, potatoes, apples . . . are being taken from the countryside because we had only crackers and coffee with us. We went into camp about eight miles north of Washington on the way to Frederick."[3] The army was moving at "a tremendous pace" and the weather was "very warm, and the clouds of dust nearly suffocating." The column pushed toward Rockville "with only the shortest possible halts and no

1   John O. Johnson, "Recollections of Soldier life, read on the Meeting of the GAR Post 186 by J. O. J.", undated, Bragg Papers, WHS. Johnson was promoted to second lieutenant of Company H, 45th Wisconsin, September 17, 1864. *Wisconsin Roster*, vol. 1, 526.

2   Cheek and Pointon, *Sauk County*, 46.

3   Longhenry, diary, September 7, 1862.

stoppage for coffee." The 7th Wisconsin's Pvt. Ludolph Longhenry tracked the progress in his diary:

> September 8, Monday: All kinds of rumors are floating around but no one knows definitely where we are going.

> September 9, Tuesday: We resumed our march toward Frederick. Five crackers for rations. Now and then we see the Stars and stripes floating over farm houses. Some farms are abandoned. This is a great orchard country. In the forest can be found enormous sweet grapes in abundance. This is beautiful country, with great farms and beautiful girls.

> September 10, Wednesday: After an all day march northward, we camped about sundown near Slideltown.

> September 11, Thursday: We marched today to a small community called Lisbon.

> September 12, Friday: We marched today through Poplar Springs, Ridgeville, and toward Newmarket, where we bivouaced. Yesterday the rebels had abandoned Newmarket.[4]

Two stories made the rounds. The first involved Edward Bragg, who a few days earlier received several letters urging him to stand as a "War Candidate" for Congress back home. His return letter did him honor: "[T]he Government must be sustained, but my services can not be taken from the field. I command the regiment and can not leave in times like these." The other story involved old Lysander Cutler, who was in the capital healing from his Gainesville leg wound and desirous of meeting Secretary of War Edward M. Stanton. He acquired a new uniform and went to the War Department, waited a long while, and was finally admitted. Cutler awkwardly used his canes to thump his way to Stanton's desk. The secretary looked up, took in the bright buttons and new coat, and asked sharply, "What in hell and God Damnation are you doing in Washington?" Cutler, a man of steady manners, paused before replying: "If I had not been shot and a fool, I would never have come here. Good day, Mr. Secretary." With that, the colonel limped off without a backward glance—or at least that was the tale told around the campfires.[5]

---

4 *Ibid.*, September 8-12, 1862.

5 Dawes, *Service*, 78-80.

The brigade was outside Frederick on the night of September 13 when John Gibbon rode into town to visit McClellan's headquarters. McClellan spoke freely about the pursuit of Lee's Army and at one point held up a folded piece of paper. "Here is a paper with which if I cannot whip 'Bobbie Lee,' I will be willing to go home," he exclaimed. The general would not show the officers the contents of the document, but he folded it to display the signature "R. H. Chilton, Adjutant Gen." Chilton was Lee's chief of staff. McClellan told the assembled officers the information provided the movements of every division of the Confederate army. "Tomorrow we will pitch into his center and if you people will only do two good, hard days' marching I will put Lee in a position he will find hard to get out of." Little Mac's confidence added to Gibbon's own growing sense that the army had "a General who knew his business and was bound to succeed." Gibbon replied to McClellan, "Well, we will do the marching and I have a command that will do its part." He added some praise for his Wisconsin and Indiana regiments, but admitted his brigade was much reduced and another unit should be assigned to it—a Western command. McClellan smiled. "You shall have the first western regiment I get."[6]

The document signed by Chilton was the famous "Lost Order" (Special Orders No. 191) that outlined Lee's widely separated army. As he had done at the beginning of the Manassas Campaign, Lee again boldly divided his army to better enable him to capture Harpers Ferry. Somehow, a copy of the marching order was lost—an event never satisfactorily explained—and a detail of Union soldiers discovered it in a field. They, in turn, sent the paper up the chain of command to McClellan, who now had a good idea about the location of Lee's army and how best to attack and defeat it. The Federal army was soon in motion, and before long a puzzled Lee learned of the enemy's activity. After the thrashing they had taken at Second Manassas, Lee did not believe anyone could reorganize the Federal divisions and move them out against him so quickly or aggressively. Lee dispatched small portion of his army to South Mountain to watch the passes through which the Union columns would have to pass.

Reveille came at 4:00 a.m. for Gibbon's brigade on the 14th day of September. It was "as beautiful a morning as one could wish to see," remembered one soldier.[7] The panorama of swarming camps stretched out in every direction, and every soldier "felt his courage rise at the sight." Morale was high that morning. "The deep

---

6   Gibbon, *Recollections*, 71-73.

7   Longhenry, diary, September 14, 1862; Zebulon Russell, *Columbus* (WI) *Republican*, August 24, 1895.

feeling of almost affectionate admiration among the soldiers for the commander of our army, General McClellan, was often thus expressed: 'We have got a General now, and we will show the country what we can do.'" Not far away were the spires of Frederick, where church bells rang in one officer called "a rejoicing at the advent of the host of her deliverance, the Army of the Potomac." However, there was also the dull mutter of cannon fire off to the southwest, later found to be Jackson's attack on Harpers Ferry.

Gibbon's brigade reached Frederick about 8:00 a.m. "Our entry into the city was triumphal. The stars and stripes floated from every building and hung from every window," gloated one officer. "The joyful people ran through the streets to greet and cheer the veterans of the Army of the Potomac. Little children stood at near every door, freely offering cool water, cakes, pies and dainties." The reception was strikingly different from those received by the Federal army in Virginia. The "generous and enthusiastic welcome by the ladies of Frederick City," claimed one Black Hat, "helped us all through the balance of the day."[8]

Gibbon watched McClellan and his entourage enter the city. "When Gen. McClellan came through he was overwhelmed by the ladies, they kissed his clothes, threw their arms around his horse's neck and committed all sorts of extravagances. Those who saw it say there never could have been such a scene witnessed in this country since Washington's time." An inspired Gibbon told his Black Hats that McClellan himself had told him two days of hard marching would see to the destruction of Lee's army, to which the ranks let out loud cheers. Gibbon went on to say he knew they would "march well and without straggling." More cheers. And, he said, he wanted them to hoot and jeer "every man they saw on the road straggling from his command." More loud cheers. Finally, Gibbon concluded, McClellan had promised the first Western regiment received by the army would be assigned to the brigade. That news set off the loudest yells of all. "I suppose he made the promise because he knew of no better place where a new regiment could learn to fight," wrote one who knew firsthand. The march resumed "with everybody in high spirits."[9]

The column pushed on over the dusty roads through a beautiful valley. It was a moment never forgotten, the "bright guns glistening in the sun," the long trains of wagons, the generals "with their fine bodyguards," and the bright flags made it one

---

8   Dawes, *Service*, 79; Longhenry, diary, September 14, 1862, Russell, *Columbus Republican*, August 24, 1895.

9   Gibbon, *Recollections*, 74-75. To follow the movements of the armies, see Bradley M. Gottfried, *The Maps of Antietam: An Atlas of the Antietam (Sharpsburg) Campaign, Including the Battle of South Mountain, September 2-20, 1862* (Savas Beatie, El Dorado Hills, CA, 2012).

of the "grandest sights we have ever looked upon." Citizens stood along the side of the road to watch the passing soldiers; others rode beside the column on saddle horses. When stragglers appeared, Gibbon moved forward a detail and the brigade drum corps. Guards gathered in the footsore soldiers and pushed them along while the drum corps rattled the "Rogue's March" to force the tired soldiers forward amidst laughing and jeering from the Black Hats. "Look at that fellow, hasn't he a regular hospital gait," one Westerner joked. "Wonder if he has been to the sick call, this morning," a friend added. The stragglers soon disappeared, hiding in the woods and shrubs as the Western Brigade swept along. "What was of more importance to my command," Gibbon later wrote, "[was] a strong spirit of opposition to straggling was created and it became an honorable ambition to remain the ranks, instead of constantly inventing pretexts to fall out."[10]

During this march Pvt. Bill Palmer made a place for himself in the company lore of the Sauk County boys. A camp favorite, Palmer sported a "great good nature and natural dry wit." The company was near the end of the column when McClellan passed with his staff in a great show of bright buttons and fancy horses. Stepping out of ranks and waving a $5.00 banknote, Palmer walked up to one staff officer.

"Here, old man take that," Palmer said pushing the money toward the officer.

"My man, what do you mean?" asked the staffer.

"Nawe, you just take it," said Palmer, drawling it out "in his Yankee Vermont twang" so everyone could hear him. "When I left Wisconsin I said that the first galoot I met with a longer nose than mine had to have a fiver—so here 'tis."

The staffer scowled, waved the private away, and rode off without a backward look or the banknote with the laugher of the Sauk County boys trailing him. The cheeky private was soon known throughout the brigade as "Nosey" Palmer.[11]

The column reached Catoctin Mountain late that morning. Fences and trees bore witness to some fighting. From the summit the soldiers looked down Middletown Valley at the heavy smoke rising miles away. The low telltale rumble of

---

10 Gibbon, *Recollections*, 74-75.

11 *Milwaukee Sunday Telegraph*, July 9, 1882; Cheek and Pointon, *Sauk County*, 212-213. Cheek and Pointon also included this story: "While in camp at Arlington in the winter of 1862, Adjutant [Frank] Haskell was trying to get the company details for guard into line so as to hold 'Guard Mount,' but one fellow down the line persisted in remaining so his breast was back of the line Haskell was trying to establish. Several times he told the men to dress on the line, but it was no use, there was a sag in the line—finally becoming out of patience, he stepped a pace to the front where he could see every man in line and said 'No. 6, move up into line.' No. 6 was totally ignorant that he was the sixth man from the head of the line, and did not move. Haskell could stand it no longer and he yells out: 'I mean that man with a plow coulter for a nose.' Bill Palmer of Company A immediately stepped up in line. Palmer became a First lieutenant, a promotion dated August 28, 1862, for his behavior in the battle of Gainesville."

distant firing reached their ears. Citizens stepped out to look at the passing soldiers march through Middleton. Here and there a "bloodstained soldier" made his way in the opposite direction. When a report raced through the ranks that an Ohio officer had been wounded, Rufus Dawes inquired as to his identity in case he knew him. The officer was Rutherford B. Hayes of the 23rd Ohio, a name Dawes did not recognize.

A short distance beyond Middleton, the men turned into a field and stacked arms near a creek along the base of South Mountain. "Here we laid down along side the turnpike which crossed over the Mountain in front of us, and saw a systematic movement of the troops begin, which we could plainly see from our elevated position," recalled a Black Hat. "The army was disconnected. The right wing moved up the mountain about two miles from us on our right. The left wing started up about one and one-half miles to our left. We could follow the course of our troops as well as the Confederates, by the smoke of their musketry rising about the timber." The Rebels were being pressed back by the weight of the Union lines with the fighting "stubborn and heavy going." The Johnnies held the pike and about one-half mile on each side of the roadway. "We felt very good, that we would have seen a splendid view of the battle, and enjoyed it out of harm's way, seeing where our boys would push them back, or when our shells would do some good execution in the rebel rank, until we grew quite hilarious, when the drum call to fall in was heard."[12]

The march to South Mountain had been both joyous and hard going, and the welcome by the citizens in the towns lifted soldier hearts. The reality of a pending battle, however, had a sobering effect. Captain Edwin Brown took a few moments during one halt to write his loved ones:

> I have just time to write you a line—nothing more. You are doubtless informed of the defeats of our Army which explains our being here. Three times has my life been in jeopardy, where the danger was in every inch of space. You can say to your friends that your husband was no coward, where so many showed 'the white feather.' The troops had no confidence in Pope or McDowell, therefore many behaved badly. The only troops that really maintained for themselves a good name every where was Hooker's & Kearney's divisions and Gibbon's Brigade of King's Division. The Army is discouraged, having no great confidence in anyone. They have more confidence in McClellan than any one else. None too much in him however. Rebels are in force in Maryland, we are 'massing' to meet them.

---

12 Dawes, *Service*, 78-80. Rutherford B. Hayes was elected president of the United States in 1876.

I am weary & sick if the enemy was off from our soil I should go to Hospital. Honor requires that every one who has any patriotism left should meet the insolent foe. Should I live to see them driven out of this State & away from Washington, I will have rest at some rate.

Kiss the babies for their war worn father,

Good Bye Wife, E. A. Brown

It was Brown's last letter home.[13]

They Must be Made of Iron

First Corps commander Maj. Gen. Joseph Hooker was under orders to carry the crest of South Mountain and Turner's Gap before dark. Turner's was the right-most passage, with Fox's Gap farther left, and farther left still toward the Potomac River. If McClellan could force the gaps, Lee's army would be in grave peril, divided into widely separated pieces with the Army of the Potomac in the middle of them. Gibbon's brigade was marched onto the National Road and then west into a field where the lines formed. Hooker deployed George Meade's division well to the right, where it was advancing to capture the Frosttown Plateau and turn the defenders out of Turner's Gap. Hatch's division would advance more directly, using the National Road, which sliced through the pass, as a guide. With the pike just to their left, the 7th Wisconsin and 19th Indiana made up the first line with the 2nd and 6th Wisconsin in the second—the rear line about forty yards behind the front. An Ohio battery was also in the field firing shell toward the heights.[14]

In front was a slight dip and beyond the steep and rocky slope. Long lines and heavy columns of dark blue infantry were visible pressing up the green mountainside to the right, "their bayonets flashing like silver in the rays of the setting sun, and their banners waving in beautiful relief against the background of green."[15]

13 Edwin Brown, letter, September 13, 1862.

14 Johnson, "Recollections."

15 Dawes, *Service*, 78-80. For a full description of South Mountain and the various battles there, see Brian Matthew Jordan, *Unholy Sabbath: The Battle of South Mountain in History and Memory, September 14, 1862* (Savas Beatie: New York, 2012), and Ezra A. Carman, *The Maryland Campaign of September 1862, Vol. I, South Mountain*, Thomas G. Clemens, ed. (Savas Beatie: New York, NY, 2010).

Turner's Gap was not that wide, and the terrain ideal for defensive operations. Confederate Alfred Colquitt's brigade straddled the National Road well up the hillside, with two skeleton-thin brigades of Virginians haphazardly aligned under James Kemper and Richard Garnett beyond Colquitt's left. Other Rebels were on their way, marching up the backside of South Mountain. Unfortunately for Maj. Gen. Daniel H. Hill, the Confederate commander on that long and trying day, there was simply too much mountain and not enough infantry to man the three passes and the various approaches to and through them. Little Mac was moving with uncharacteristic speed, motivated by the belief the Lee's lost orders was one of those unusual historical turning points that would give him a victory. As a result, Lee had no choice but to hold the passes as long as possible to allow Jackson time to capture Harpers Ferry and reassemble the army to recapture the initiative or withdraw across the Potomac.

Gibbon's brigade would advance once other Union forces were well committed. Hatch's other brigades, battling the Virginians, were having "a hot time in dislodging the rebels from their strongly fortified position," recalled one eyewitness. When an orderly galloped up to Gibbon, saluted, and exchanged words, the boys began "to brace up," one said. Orders coursed up and down the line: "Attention, Battalion!" "Load at will!" "Shoulder arms!" "Forward by file right, MARCH!" The regiments stepped off with "a hearty cheer" and displayed what Gibbon called the "drill and efficiency acquired by the brigade." Ahead, the sun was sinking behind the mountain, "casting long shadows over the stone walls, fields, woods, ravines, and farm buildings alongside the road."[16] It was between 5:30 and 6:00 p.m.[17]

The Western regiments moved with an easy step, at first. But with each yard the slope increased and the lines entered wooded areas strewn with large rocks. The 19th Indiana and 7th Wisconsin moved in line of battle on either side of the turnpike with the right two-gun section of Battery B poised to move up the roadway in support. The 2nd Wisconsin was behind the 19th left of the road and the 6th Wisconsin behind the 7th on the right. Both support regiments were held in double columns. Each Black Hat carried 100 rounds of ammunition. "The turnpike

---

16 Cheek and Pointon, *Sauk County*, 48; Gibbon, *Recollections*, 75.

17 Russell, *Columbus Republican*, August 24, 1895; Sullivan, *Milwaukee Sunday Telegraph*, May 13, 1888; George B. McClellan, *McClellan's Own Story* (Philadelphia, PA, 1887), 579-580. In one of those strange turns during the Civil War, the fighting at South Mountain pitted two Old Army friends against each other. John Gibbon's brother Lardner was serving in the Confederate army and both brothers had been groomsmen at the prewar wedding of Maj. Gen. Daniel H. Hill, the commander of the South Mountain defenders.

Battle of South Mountain
September 14, 1862

0   yards   500
Hal Jespersen

Zittlestown

Rodes

Evans

Meade

Turner's Gap

Jenkins

Garnett

Hatch

27 GA 13 AL 6 GA

Colquitt

23 GA 28 GA

Colquitt's
skirmishers

7 WI

6 WI

19 IN

2 WI

B-4 US

Gibbon

National Road

Fox's Gap

is steep and winds up among the hills," Adj. Frank Haskell wrote later. "The ground descends from both sides to the turnpike—is wooded save for a belt from one hundred and fifty to three hundred yards wide upon each side, and is crossed here and there with strong stone fences and abounds in good natural covers for troops, altogether an ugly looking place to attack, the enemy's center, and held by artillery and we knew not how much infantry."[18]

The answer was five Alabama and Georgia regiments, about 1,350 men comprising Alfred Colquitt's brigade. The 28th Georgia held his left flank with the 23rd Georgia next in line stretching toward the National Road. Both were in timber with a stone wall covering much of their front. Colquitt's remaining three regiments were positioned on the right side of the National Road extending the line southwest toward Fox's Gap, the 13th Alabama on the far right and the 27th Georgia and 6th Georgia completing the line. Clouds of Southern skirmishers were active well in front of the main line, and a battery of artillery directly supported Colquitt.

Where the slope began to climb, Confederate pickets were flushed and scattered shooting broke out. The thin line of men in tall hats astride the turnpike kept moving. Shielding the right side were skirmishers from two companies of the 6th Wisconsin—the Prescott Guard from the Mississippi River under Capt. Rollin Converse and the Lemonweir Minute Men of Juneau County under Capt. John Ticknor. They quickly moved forward pushing the Confederate skirmishers up the slope. "Nothing could be finer than the conduct of these two companies, or more gallant than the bearing of their young leaders," said one Wisconsin officer. The thin line of skirmishers pushed on for half a mile in a "deadly game of 'Bo-peep,' hiding behind longs, fences rocks and bushes."

On the left front, the skirmish line command fell to Capt. Wilson Colwell of the 2nd Wisconsin and his La Crosse Light Guard. Colwell's order was always "Forward! Forward!" His soldiers and friends watched the recklessly brave officer with concern and apprehension. He pushed his men forward with but little caution for himself. The captain had recently been passed over for promotion to another regiment because of a false allegation contained in a letter from the Army to the state of Wisconsin that he had not "behaved well" at First Bull Run. It was not true, but Colwell "was naturally very sensitive, and this affected him so much that he went into battle determined to die," claimed one officer. Colwell told his friends he "had no desire to survive the fight" and he "boldly stood up, fighting with the bravery and desperation, which has characterized him in every battle."

---

18 Johnson, "Recollections"; Haskell, manuscript, September 22, 1862; Haskell, *Gettysburg*, 32, 35.

Captain Wilson Colwell, La Crosse Light Guard, Co. B, 2nd Wisconsin

Colwell had this picture taken in his fighting rig immediately after First Bull Run. He was killed while directing the skirmish line at South Mountain on September 14, 1862. *Wisconsin Veterans Museum*

The captain was in many ways typical of the citizen-soldier officers from the frontier. Of medium height with a thick black beard and handsome face, Colwell arrived in Wisconsin from Pennsylvania and opened a bank in La Crosse in 1858. He was active in the social life of the Mississippi River town and a leader of the Wide Awake movement backing Lincoln for president. Colwell was elected mayor in 1861, but stepped aside to become captain of the Light Guards. He took one of his cashiers, Frank Hatch, with him as first lieutenant. "His kindness and generosity, with a pleasant humor, often veiled under an affected gruffness, caused the men to regard him with a positive feeling of affection, and this in his company, to a great extent, supplied the place of discipline," said a private in the company. "He was incapable by nature of enduring or enforcing a martinet discipline; but the men knew him so well, and were so strongly attached to him that he easily maintained a perfect discipline when necessity called for it." He would, it was said with some truth, just as soon dine with one of his privates than with Gen. Winfield Scott.[19] And so it was that under this unwarranted cloud of suspicion Captain Colwell moved methodically up the rocky slope, sometimes ahead of his skirmishers. Then a bullet pierced his body and his comrades carried him to the rear. He was dead within the hour. "His place cannot be filled," lamented Lucius Fairchild in his official report.[20]

The advance offered a textbook example of how to employ skirmishers, with one line advancing and the other giving way. The Juneau County boys reached a "cultivated field with a heavy wood on the right," with their line extending from the woods down to the road. The field was full of large boulders. "Part of the men would fire and then rush forward while the others covered them and fired at the rebels, and then the rear line would pass through to the front," explained Mickey

---

19 *Milwaukee Sentinel*, August 12, 1861; *Milwaukee Sunday Telegraph*, September 23, 1883. The private was Gilbert Woodward.

20 *Milwaukee Sentinel*, October 31, 1862. The correspondent added: "I give the story as it is told here by Wisconsin men. If it is true, the cowardly assassin who wrote such a letter to the Governor, derogatory of the bravery of such a man as Captain Colwell, may have the gratification of feeling that his malice, or envy perhaps, has succeeded in destroying one of the bravest and noblest men that Wisconsin has sent to the field. For the sake of humanity, I trust that what everybody believes may not prove true, and that there is no craven-hearted coward among the troops from the Badger State, who has been thus guilty." Haskell described Colwell as a "brave and accomplished officer." Haskell, manuscript, September 22, 1862, Wisconsin Historical Society. See also OR 19, pt. 1, 254. On September 22, 1862, the *Milwaukee Sentinel* carried a dispatch from the *Chicago Times* of the previous day: "Among the killed was Capt. Wilson Colwell of Company B, 2nd Wisconsin. . . . His body was enclosed in a metallic coffin and brought here [Chicago], but was so much decomposed on its arrival that the process of embalming was found to be impossible."

Sullivan. Here and there from behind a boulder, three or four men would gather to hold it until the enemy retreated. "The utmost enthusiasm prevailed and our fellows were as cool and collected as if at target practice, and, in fact, on more than one occasion . . . one would ask the other to watch his shot and see where he hit."

Sullivan was suffering from a case of the mumps and his cheeks had reached "a respectable rotundity." Lieutenant Lyman Upham loaned the Irishman "a big silk handkerchief" which the private tied around his face. The handkerchief, however, obstructed his shooting so he stuffed it in his pocket. Sullivan's immediate "comrades in battle" included George Chamberlain of Mauston, Ephraim Cornish of Lindina, and Franklin Wilcox of Lemonweir. Dusk was rapidly approaching. The four were behind a boulder, said Sullivan, with two firing from each side. Sullivan was working with Chamberlain, the boyish private who doubled as his best friend in the army ("inseparable companions and fast friends"). Chamberlain left a circus to enlist, joining the infantry to find relief from a hard life. Both were regarded as the "stray waifs" of Company K, forced "to suffer all the misdeeds or mistakes, no matter by whom committed." It was commonly uttered, Sullivan explained, that if Captain Dawes "stub[bed] his toe he'd put Mickey and Chamberlain on Knapsack drill."[21]

Confederate artillery posted high up the mountainside overshot the advancing Federal line. Whenever the skirmishers halted, two guns from Battery B would "wheel into action and fire shell at the houses, barns or thickets where the rebels found a cover." Gibbon rode back and forth watching over his advancing brigade, issuing orders in a "voice loud and clear as a bell and distinctly heard throughout the brigade"—"Forward! Forward!" The line reached a fence and just ahead was "a large pasture full of logs, stumps, big bounders . . . behind which" the skirmishers were "having a picnic with the 'Rebs' in front, trying to dislodge them from the position and to make them get for the woods." One Rebel shell exploded in the 2nd Wisconsin line, killing four men and injuring five others. Battery B responded and the Confederate artillery fell silent.[22]

The climb seemed endless. Canteens were almost empty and bullets zipped through the lines from a variety of directions. McClellan and other officers, who had gathered to watch the advance, enjoyed an unobstructed view from their observation point in the rear.

21 Sullivan, *Milwaukee Sunday Telegraph*, May 13, 1888.

22 Dawes, *Service*, Russell, *Columbus Republican*, August 24, 1895; Haskell, manuscript, September 12, 1862.

Pvt. Asahel Gage,
Janesville Volunteers,
Co. D, 2nd Wisconsin

Gage was killed in action at South
Mountain on September 14, 1862.
Wisconsin Veterans Museum

Who the Thunder is Your Father?

Up the rocky slope of South Mountain climbed the Indiana and Wisconsin soldiers, higher and higher into a steady Confederate fire. Behind them rode John Gibbon shouting "Forward! Forward!" The Black Hats took a few steps, stopped to shoot, loaded, and then climbed onward. The intensity of the fighting increased with every passing yard as darkness closed around the combatants like a heavy cloak. For a time, Col. Solomon Meredith's 19th Indiana stalled in front of a farmhouse and outbuildings filled with Johnnies. The old colonel sent his son to Battery B to request that a pair of guns roll forward to clear the strong point. The battery commander, Lt. James Stewart, looked up at the new arrival whom he described as "the youngest and tallest, as well as the thinnest man I ever saw."

The younger Meredith saluted and announced, "Father wants you to put a shot into that house; it is full of rebel sharpshooters."

The blunt speaking Stewart asked, "Who in thunder is your father?"

"Colonel Sol Meredith of the 19th Indiana."

The old Regular looked the young man up and down. "You go back with my compliments to your father, Colonel Sol Meredith, of the 19th Indiana, and tell him I will require him to give me a written order to shell that house."

Young Meredith rode off as directed, and the colonel himself arrived a few minutes later. "I want you to shell that house," he told the artilleryman. When Stewart asked for the order in writing, Sol replied, "By Jinks, I will give you a written order!" And that is just what he did.

Satisfied, Stewart guided the guns forward and threw what Meredith called "several splendid shoots . . . causing a general stampede." The 19th Indiana pressed up the hill.

"It was a most magnificent sight to see the boys of the Nineteenth going forward, crowding the enemy, cheering all the time," reported the colonel. One of the battery boys watching the advance was John "The Tough One" Cook, late of the 6th Wisconsin and now serving as a volunteer gunner. He had been in the battery just two days. "I did not know a hand spike from the fifth wheel," he admitted, "but I was there just the same, and when they wanted ammunition, it all depended on me whether I had it or not. You see I was a sort of promiscuous supernumerary fellow. That is, I just as leave be in Milwaukee as at South Mountain. The boys voted me thanks and said it was the greatest maneuver of the campaign."[23]

The Rebel position was "one of great advantage," recalled one soldier, "and it was only by stubborn fighting that they were driven back." The 19th Indiana and 7th Wisconsin rolled over one fence "pell-mell, yet in good order" and passed through a pasture toward woods in which Rebel skirmishers were seeking cover.[24] "[George] Chamberlain, who was brave as a lion, kept continually rushing forward leading the squad [and the skirmish line] and of course we had to follow up and support him," said Mickey Sullivan. "It was now sundown and being in the shadow of the mountain, it was getting dark very fast, and our fellows pushed the rebel skirmishers up to their line of battle, and our squad took shelter behind a big bounder." The main 7th Wisconsin line opened fire as the Union skirmish line continued moving toward the woods, still heavily engaged with their opposites.[25]

The heaviest fire was coming from a stone wall running along a ravine left of the 7th Wisconsin and Lt. Col. John Callis moved the right of his regiment to face the wall, only to expose his line to rebels hiding in the trees. "[W]ith a yell accompanied with a withering volley," the Confederates fired into the backs of the Wisconsin men. It was a test of training and mettle, but the 7th Wisconsin stood its ground and slowly wheeled back into line "being at least ten minutes under this heavy fire without returning a shot." One Black Hat called it "a most terrific fire," and that it "seemed no one could survive." It was later discovered that the shooting wounded many but killed few. "We were soon back into line," wrote a 7th Wisconsin man. "'About face!' and orders are given to 'fire and load and fire at will!' We commence to fire. By this time it was quite dark," he continued, and "the rebel

23 OR 19, pt. 1, 25; Cook, *Milwaukee Sunday Telegraph*, March 11, 1883; Gaff, *Bloody Field*, 177.

24 Harris, *Milwaukee Sunday Telegraph*, September 9, 1883; Russell, *Columbus Republican*, August 24, 1895; ibid., clipping, undated "Written by a soldier from Company B, 7th Wisconsin"; Dawes, *Service*, 81.

25 Sullivan, *Milwaukee Sunday Telegraph*, May 13, 1888.

line was at the edge of the woods behind a fence, and all we could see of the enemy was a streak of fire as their guns were discharged."[26]

Mickey Sullivan was fighting well in advance of the main battle line behind a cluster of large boulders, against which splattered lead rounds. "When the crash came, either a bullet split in pieces against the stone or a fragment of the boulder hit me on the sore jaw, causing exquisite pain, and I was undetermined whether to run away or swear," he recalled. Somewhere in the shadow of the rock Eph Cornish cried out, "Mickey, Chamberlain is killed and I'm wounded!" Another "crashing volley" of musketry followed, wrote Sullivan, and "a stinging, burning sensation in my right foot followed by the most excruciating pain." Frank Wilcox, fighting next to Mickey, "toppled over wounded." All around him the skirmish line was falling back and Sullivan, using his musket for a crutch, hopped downhill "a good deal faster than I had come up." The game of "hide and coop" by the skirmishers was ending as the heavy battle lines stepped up in reasonably good order.

Almost as soon as he left the skirmish line, Mickey passed through the 7th Wisconsin and into his own 6th Wisconsin moving up in support. The Irishman was hobbling through the Jayhawkers of Company C when Sgt. Edward A. Whaley appeared out of the gathering darkness to inquiry as to his wound and advise him to continue to the rear.[27] Sullivan made his "best time" despite the pain in his foot, helped along by the angry zip of bullets buzzing past him. Mickey passed the two guns of Battery B, which "made almost continual roar and they were being pushed forward by hand at every discharge." The mountain seemed "aflame and the noise and uproar and cheers and yells were terrific."[28]

Pressing toward Turner's Gap, the Black Hat line stalled in front of a stone wall. Bullets flew from several directions through almost total darkness. The 7th Wisconsin's Zeb Russell was loading and firing when he was struck in the right leg. "I went down, of course. The first thought was 'the limb is shot off!' . . . I got back of the Company the best I could, perhaps a couple rods, more or less." Russell was growing faint when "Someone came along and I asked for a drink of water. He gave me a drink and asked where I was wounded. I said my leg was shot off." Russell ran

---

26 *Columbus Republican*, clipping, undated, "Written by a soldier"; Cheek and Pointon, *Sauk County*, 48; Dawes, *Service*, 82; Longhenry, diary, September 14, 1862; Russell, *Columbus Republican*, August 24, 1894.

27 Whaley enlisted as private in 1861 and was wounded three times during the war. He would be in command of the 6th Wisconsin and lose a leg at Five Forks, Virginia, on April 1, 1865. Whaley later served as postmaster at Prairie du Chien. *Wisconsin Roster*, vol. 1, 505.

28 Sullivan, *Milwaukee Sunday Telegraph*, May 13, 1888; George Fairfield diary, September 14, 1862.

his hand down his leg, only to discover it was still there. "About this time, another bullet came and hit me on the other foot. It lodged under the heel of my shoe; no harm done, but my heel was sore a great many days after, but I was thankful that I did not receive a bullet in some other tender spot, as they were coming thick and fast."[29]

With the 7th Wisconsin line twisted under a heavy fire, Hollon Richardson ran back to the 6th Wisconsin waving his arms and shouting. "Come forward Sixth!" he called while motioning toward the beleaguered sister regiment. Lieutenant Colonel Edward Bragg took in the situation with a glance and displayed the coolness for which he would become known. "Deploy column!" he ordered. "By the right and left flanks, double quick, march!" The regiment jumped forward to deploy as it had done on a dozen drill fields. "We came up on a run and just then the right wing of the Seventh Regiment were tumbling in every direction from a withering, raking fire into their flank," wrote one Badger. The 6th Wisconsin's left was behind the 7th Wisconsin and the right flank facing an open field. Bragg saw an opportunity. "Boys, you must save the Seventh," he called. Dawes was nearby and Bragg shouted over the musketry, "Major take command of the right wing and fire on the woods!" "Attention, right wing, read, right oblique, aim, fire, loaded at will, load!" Dawes ordered. The leveled rifle-muskets of the right wing crashed as one and the sound rolled up the hillside. In the smoke and confusion, Bragg called, "Have our men lie down on the ground, I am going over you!" Dawes nodded his understanding and called out in a sharp voice, "Right wing, lie down! Look out, the left wing is going over you!" As soon as the soldiers of the right wing hit the ground, Bragg and the left wing moved through and over them. The left wing volleyed into the woods and the soldiers dropped to the ground. Dawes ordered the right wing to their feet and passed it through the prone Badgers and fired a third crashing volley. Four volleys by wing were fired on command. One Badger called it the "nicest, quickest movement under fire that I saw during the war, and it must have been very destructive to the Johnnies. They receive the volleys so rapidly that it could not have been otherwise, being in plain sight of them." In his long combat experience, wrote Dawes "this was the one single instance I saw of other than a fire by file in battle. The characteristic of Colonel Bragg in battle was a remarkably quick conception and instant action."[30] The crashing volleys, he always believed, saved the day, and Capt. Patrick Hart of the 19th Indiana, shot through the hips and helpless on the ground, later told Dawes "that he 'cried like a child' when he heard

29 Russell, *Columbus Republican*, August 24, 1895.

30 Johnson, "Recollections"; Dawes, journal, September 14, 1862; Dawes, *Service*, 82.

An Iron Brigade man

This unidentified sergeant wears a noncommissioned officer's sword and belts (a late 1862 Iron Brigade uniform). He may have posed for this picture near Fredericksburg during the summer of 1862. *Kim Heltemes Collection*

those volleys so steady and fired at the word of command for, said he, 'I knew they (the rebels) couldn't stand that and I should not fall into their hands.'"[31]

One Wisconsin soldier recalled "a stone fence in front, 80 or 90 paces distant" with Colquitt's Confederates fighting behind it. "After the third volley, we could see them no more for the bank of smoke laying in front of our line." The infantry fire "was incessant and forcible and the artillery roared to beat anything I had yet heard," Pvt. George Fairfield told his diary. "It was while the battle was its full strength and while the column was advancing I was wounded." The soldiers would "kneel down and look under the smoke to see the flash of the Rebel muskets not to waste our ammunition," said one man. The gun barrels grew so hot they could not be held with a bare hand. "I shifted my haversack on my left side and in firing would stick my hand inside of it to rest the musket and load the cartridges."[32]

The lines were close enough now that the fighting became personal. "Oh you damned black hats we gave you hell at Bull Run!" yelled a Rebel. "Never mind Johnny, it is no McDowell after you now!" came the quick reply. One Badger "elbowing his way along, loading and firing" under the cloud of smoke would yell

31 Dawes, journal, September 15, 1862.

32 Johnson, "Recollections."

after every shot, "Roll your tails, God Damn you! Gibbon and McClellan are after you now!" Portions of the Union line would jump up and move, only to take cover when another flare of musketry illuminated the enemy line. "Hurrah for Georgia!" someone yelled; a crash of Federal musketry answered the boast.

After several long minutes of close-quarter fighting, the rate of fire coming from the Confederates hunkered down behind the stone wall slowed. The long day was taking its toll on both sides. Union canteens were empty. One Badger wrote that he was "parched, his lips and tongue swollen and cracked by the powder taken into the mouth while biting off the end of the cartridges in loading." Nearby two of the 6th Wisconsin men—John Weidman of Freedom and Jack Langhart of Prairie du Sac—were shot dead and two others were mortally wounded, while a third, Pvt. James Whitty, was laying on a rock when a bullet tumbled him backward. "For the love of God!" he announced with some astonishment, "a 'Wild Irishman is hit." He was carried to the rear.[33]

The advance had moved smartly on both sides of the National Road, but was now stalled before the wooded and mostly walled Confederate line. When a gap appeared between the 19th Indiana on the left and 7th Wisconsin on the right, the 2nd Wisconsin pushed into the space to pour in additional fire. By this time all four of Gibbon's regiments were in one line, with the 6th and 7th fighting on the right of the road, and the 2nd and 19th on the left. "At that point they were annoying us very much," admitted the 19th Indiana's Colonel Meredith, who saw an opportunity to break the stalemate on his front. The colonel rode to the commander of Company G with orders to "wheel his company . . . until he could command the line of battle lying directly behind the stone fence." The move was promptly executed and, caught in the rear and front, the pair of companies from the 27th Georgia began to fall back or surrender where they stood. Meredith reported that his men "opened a flank fire upon the enemy, causing them to retreat precipitately."

"It was dark and our only aim was by the flashes of the enemy's guns," wrote one Wisconsin officer. "Many of our men were falling, and we could not long endure it." When Bragg moved the left wing of the 6th Wisconsin into a patch of woods, it was so black the soldiers kept from being separated by holding on to each

33 Dawes, journal, September 15, 1862; Dawes, *Service*, 82-83; D. H. Hill, "The Battle of South Mountain or Boonsboro," in *Battles and Leaders*, vol. 2, 275-276; Cheek and Pointon, *Sauk County*, 47-49. Of the vocal exchanges, Dawes wrote: "Not very refined or moral but reflective of an anxious enmity loosened in battle." The ball that entered Whitty was never removed, wrote Cheek and Pointon, "and the after effects of this wound finally killed him in 1906." Whitty was wounded in three engagements, the last in the Wilderness in 1864, where he would lose a leg. "Poor Jim, he was a great soldier." He was first wounded on August 28 at Gainesville.

other. When he finally got to a position where the regiment could fire into the Confederate flank, Bragg sent a runner back to Dawes to bring up the right wing. The Badgers stumbled and clawed their way through the brush and darkness up "the stony side of the mountain" while the left wing poured a quick hot fire into the Rebel flank. Closing the gap between the wings was finally completed. During the movement Pvt. William Lawrence of DeSoto, singled out for bravery at Second Bull Run, fell wounded. William Clawater of Bad Ax helped drag him to the cover of a tree and found two blankets, one for Lawrence's head and the other to cover him.[34]

With the cartridge boxes nearly empty and the rifle-muskets so "dirty with bad powder" and so hot "it was not safe to load them," the fighting fell away into a fitful patter on both sides. "It was about as trying a place to be in as you can imagine," said one soldier, "with the enemy peppering you and you cannot shoot back." The living had been pilfering cartridges of the dead and the wounded for some time, but it was not enough. "Ammunition commenced to give out," Bragg reported, "no man having left more than four rounds, and many without any. It was dark, and a desperate enemy in front." The colonel told his men to cease firing and lay still. In the pitch darkness the shooting, finally, gave away to quiet. A shaken Wisconsin soldier called out, "Captain, I am out of cartridges!" Rebels just ahead heard him and opened another wave of sharp firing. When that fell off, the fighting finally came to an end.[35]

Before too much longer Bragg heard the enemy withdrawing. "Three cheers boys, the battle is won! Three cheers for the Badger state!" he ordered. The "Hurrahs!" seemed louder in the dark and echoed into the night. The Johnnies answered with a yell of their own, but it came from well up the hillside and perhaps beyond, and so told its own story: the Black Hats had carried the day. A few skirmishers were sent forward, but it was too dark to do much and pursuit was not possible.

The rush of adrenaline slowed and a great weariness settled on the men. Try as they might, the officers were unable to keep the soldiers awake. The Black Hats "fell fast asleep from exhaustion without a cartridge in the boxes, and with their commanding officer and a captain as their pickets. One private wrote that he was

---

34 "I take great pleasure in calling especial attention to the conduct of Pvt. William Lawrence of Co. I of the Sixth Wisconsin Volunteers, whose coolness and bravery under fire fell under my personal observance of the thirtieth," wrote John Gibbon in his official report, *OR* 12, pt. 2, 379.

35 Bragg's report, *OR* 19, pt. 1, 254; Cheek and Pointon, *Sauk County*, 48; Dawes, *Service*, 83; Lewis A. Kent, "Capt. Kent's memory," *Milwaukee Sunday Telegraph*, September 25, 1884.

"so wet from perspiration that running my hand down my wool sleeve the water would run down in front of it."[36]

In the 6th Wisconsin line, one of the wounded officers, John Marston of Appleton, heard Col. Bragg tell Edward Brooks, "Adjutant, go and find General Gibbon. Tell him the Sixth Wisconsin is on the top of the mountain, that we are out of ammunition, but we will hold our position as long as we have an inch of iron left." When Brooks returned he was panting with exertion: Gibbon told him it was impossible to furnish ammunition, but he hoped the 6th would be soon relieved. The last part of the message was a grim one—hold the position gained as long as there was "an inch of bayonets left."

The gloomy night was chilly, which only added to their weariness and misery. The wounded, scattered up and down the mountainside, suffered "untold agonies." Out of the blackness came their cries for water, but Western canteens were empty. Captain John Kellogg and Dawes tried to ease the suffering of William Lawrence, who had been shot in the stomach and was dying in terrible agony. The two officers looked for water or liquor, but there was none to be had. The mortally wounded Lawrence recognized them and, though unable to speak, nodded his appreciation. "They dreaded reality of war was before us in this frightful death, upon the cold, hard stones," wrote Dawes many years later. "The mortal suffering, the fruitless struggle, to send a parting message to the far-off home, and the final release by death, all enacted in the darkness, were felt even more deeply than if the scene had been relieved by the light of day."[37]

The Iron Brigade of the West

The long climb up South Mountain astride the National Road was a transforming moment for the soldiers of John Gibbon's four Western regiments. Not long afterward, other soldiers in other regiments were not talking about a Western Brigade, or even a Black Hat Brigade, but an "Iron Brigade of the West"—a powerful name that rings down through the decades to this very day. General McClellan claimed to have a role in the new name, and perhaps he did. The story he told Col. John Callis of the 7th Wisconsin during a reception at the Continental Hotel in Philadelphia after the war included this exchange he claimed took place between himself and Joe Hooker:

---

36 Dawes, journal, September 15, 1862; Dawes, *Service*, 82-83; D. H. Hill, "The Battle of South Mountain or Boonsboro," *Battles and Leaders*, vol. 2, 559-565; Cheek and Pointon, *Sauk County*, 47-49.

37 Dawes, *Service*, 83.

McClellan: "What troops are those fighting on the pike?"

Hooker: "General Gibbon's Brigade of Western men."

McClellan: "They must be made of iron."

Hooker: "By the Eternal, they are iron! If you had seen them at Bull Run as I did, you would know them to be iron."

McClellan: "Why, General Hooker, they fight equal to the best troops in the world."

According to Little Mac, it was sometime after the fighting on South Mountain that Hooker rode up to headquarters and called out, "General McClellan, what do you think now of my Iron Brigade?" It was a plausible exchange that may well have taken place, although questions remain whether McClellan and Hooker were even together that day. Gibbon stated in his memoir, "How or where the name of the 'Iron Brigade' was first given I do not know, but soon after the battle of Antietam the name was started and ever after was applied to the brigade." As will be seen, his use of Antietam as a starting point for the name Iron Brigade has some merit, although the fighting there occurred just three days after South Mountain. Dawes' history of the 6th Wisconsin never identified the origin of the immortal name.[38]

Other evidence suggests a more acceptable explanation. The slope of South Mountain is more heavily wooded now than in 1862. Back then it was much more open and less cluttered, with clumps of woods, some large clusters of boulders, and lines of stone fences marking open fields. Little Mac had a clear view of the advance from the viewing platform built by his engineers on a rise of ground near his headquarters well back from South Mountain. In his account of the battle, McClellan wrote a glowing description of the combat: "The [Gibbon's] brigade advanced steadily, driving the enemy from positions in the woods and behind stone walls, until they reached a point well up towards the top of the pass, when the enemy, having been reinforced by three regiments, opened heavy fire on the front and on both flanks. . . . Gen. Gibbon, in this delicate movement, handled his brigade with as much precision and coolness as if upon parade, and the bravery of his troops could not be excelled."[39]

The display of military discipline and bravery was recognized and remembered because it took place in full view. At Gainesville, the four regiments fought almost alone in the gathering darkness against the Stonewall Brigade (another fighting

38 Gibbon, *Recollections*, 93.

39 McClellan, *Own Story*, 582.

organization with a storied name and reputation) and other infantry. But the Western men were still untested men fighting in the as yet unacclaimed "Black Hat Brigade." The Westerners covered the retreat from Second Bull Run but won little fame for the effort. At South Mountain, however, the general commanding the Army of the Potomac and many others of all ranks watched Gibbon's brigade fight its way up to Turner's Gap. And perhaps—just perhaps—Little Mac did indeed ask what brigade was moving up the hill, and when told replied with a clever remark about "iron men."

A newspaper reporter standing near McClellan and his entourage overheard something along these lines from McClellan and his officers and noted it in his notebook long before McClellan's memory of the movement was romanced a bit. The correspondent worked for the *Cincinnati Daily Commercial*. His report appeared on September 22, 1862, just eight days after South Mountain and five days after Antietam. In it, he described Gibbon's four regiments thusly: "The last terrible battle has reduced this brigade to a mere skeleton; there being scarcely enough members to form half a regiment. The 2nd Wisconsin, which but a few weeks since, numbered over nine hundred men, can now muster but fifty nine. This brigade has done some of the hardest and best fighting in the service. It has been justly termed the Iron Brigade of the West."[40]

In the years after the war, New York men claimed the famous name was stolen from their regiments. The original "Iron Brigade," they argued, was actually the 22nd, 24th, and 30th New York regiments, and the 14th Brooklyn (officially the 84th New York). When the two-year New York regiments mustered out (the 14th Brooklyn, a three-year regiment, remained), the name was "taken" by the Wisconsin and Indiana regiments. "I do not know that I can blame those western kids for taking up our name after we mustered out; but they should have added jr. making it the 'Iron Brigade, jr.,'" huffed a New Yorker after the war. An officer in the 24th New York claimed the name was first attached to his brigade after a march that covered fifty miles in two days. "Sixteen miles a day is considered good march," he wrote, "so you can see why we are sometimes called the 'Cast Iron Brigade.'" General Marsena Patrick was also cited as the originator of the name for telling a New York officer, "Your men must be made of iron to make such marches."[41]

---

40 Cincinnati, Ohio, *Daily Commercial*, September 22, 1862.

41 Tom Clemens, "'Black Hats' off to the original 'Iron Brigade,'" *Columbiad*, vol. 1, No. 1, Spring 1997, 46-58; William R. Fox, *Regimental Losses in the American Civil War* (Albany, New York, NY, 1889), 177.

Wisconsin and Indiana men never believed there was any confusion attached to the name and that it was McClellan, the hero of the Army of the Potomac, who singled them out—not as a two-year "Cast Iron Brigade," but as the "Iron Brigade of the West." From the first they were careful to include the reference to their Western roots, and boasted the name was won not by long marches but by hard fighting. Jerome Watrous of the 6th Wisconsin, one of the "prints" himself, first told the correct version of how the name was publicly attached to the brigade by a correspondent for a Cincinnati newspaper who was at McClellan's headquarters during South Mountain. Watrous was asked about the famous name in an interview with the *Chicago Chronicle* before the 1898 Iron Brigade Association reunion at Baraboo, Wisconsin. When published by the Chicago newspaper, Watrous ran the story in the columns of his own *Milwaukee Telegraph* on September 12 that same year.

The war of words over the origin of the name was a regular feature in the old soldier newspaper, with this soldier and that soldier claiming the correct version. S. E. Chandler of the 24th New York, for example, in a letter written to a Washington newspaper, claimed his brigade was "the old original Iron Brigade." He added: "The cat is out of the bag. The game is ended. Wisconsin, Indiana and Michigan have been wearing a mask. It is indeed a sad, sad exposure." In copying the letter, editor Watrous of the *Milwaukee Sunday Telegraph* admitted with a written smirk on July 5, 1885, that there "was a brigade in the Potomac army whose name sounded a little like 'Iron Brigade,' but the spelling was markedly different. It was known as the 'I-run-brigade.'"

Protestations to the contrary, available evidence firmly demonstrates that the Wisconsin and Indiana men linked the name to McClellan and the time of South Mountain and Antietam. As an example, Capt. Aleck Gordon Jr. of the 7th Wisconsin wrote the folks back home just four days after Antietam on September 21, "Gen. McClellan has given us the name of the Iron Brigade." Private Hugh Perkins of the same regiment penned a letter to a friend five days later announcing that "Gen. McClellan calls us the Iron Brigade." As early as September 18, the day after the bloodiest day in American history, Rufus Dawes used the word "iron" to describe the fortitude displayed by the men of his regiment: "I have come safely through two more terrible engagements with the enemy, that at South Mountain and the great battle of yesterday [Antietam]," he wrote his mother. "The men have stood like iron."[42]

---

42 *Wisconsin Newspaper Volumes*, vol. 4; Hugh Perkins, "Letters of a Civil War Soldier," *Christian Science Monitor*.

We Who Got Through Were Happy

The wounded and ill Mickey Sullivan made it safely down the mountainside using his musket as a crutch. Once at the bottom, he picked his way along a road and ran into a line of cavalrymen stretched across the pike. "What regiment?" he asked. "McClellan's body guard," came the reply. A little farther on he came across a small fire in a clump of bushes and found Emory Mitchell of his own Company K helping several wounded men. Mitchell had been left behind because of a bad hernia that prevented him from keeping up. Once he situated Mickey on the ground and filled his canteen with water from a nearby stream, Mitchell soaked the sleeve of his extra shirt and the silk handkerchief, rolled them up, and tied the makeshift bandage around Sullivan's foot. The sound of battle was growing fainter. "Our fellows are giving 'em Wisconsin hell," said Mitchell with some satisfaction, adding "we had some generals now." Mitchell scrounged up a cup of hot coffee, fixed his gum blanket, and gave Mickey a knapsack for a pillow. It was a long night, and Mitchell "kept him awake all night twitching [his] injured foot." The next morning the pair found a "hospital established in a barnyard, which was filled with wounded laying on blocks of hay and straw." Dr. Abraham D. Andrews dressed Sullivan's wound, but was not able to extract the ball wedged between the bones. An operation in a proper hospital was needed. "We got some tea and crackers and some of the severely wounded had wine or brandy served them," recalled Mickey. "An attendant offered me some of the latter, but I told him I'd rather take another wound sooner." The attendant shot Sullivan an incredulous look before downing the brandy himself.[43]

The house of horrors that was the barnyard hospital was filled with hundreds of wounded soldiers from both sides. "One who lay next to me was hit by a cannon ball," wrote Sullivan, "which carried away his arm and part of his side, exposing the heart and vital organs and at ever respiration their action as visible." Nearby lay a Rebel "shot through the forehead, diagonally from the temple on one side to the hair to the other, and his eyes were closed and I heard a doctor remark, 'That fellow must have no brain or he would be killed.'" A day or so later, Sullivan was surprised to see the same follow in a church hospital in Middletown, where "he was recovering." Sullivan and other wounded who could travel were hauled to Frederick, "where there was a regular hospital with those white winged angels of mercy, the Sisters of Charity, for nurses." From there, Sullivan was sent on to

43 Mitchell, a sawmill hand at Yellow River before the war, enlisted in 1861 and served his three years, mustering out July 15, 1864. Andrews was assistant regimental surgeon of the 6th Wisconsin from October 1861 to November 1863. *Wisconsin Roster*, vol. 1, 535, 494.

Washington and placed in the House of Representatives, which had been temporarily converted into a hospital. There, finally, he was put "under the influence of ether" and his foot operated upon. He would remain in the nation's capital until December 22, away from the regiment for many long and trying months.[44]

While Sullivan was making his way to safety, the survivors of Gibbon's brigade were still clinging to South Mountain awaiting relief. Stretcher bearers finally reached the line to carry away the wounded, and a runner found Lieutenant Colonel Bragg to let him know his regiment would soon be relieved. "How glad we were to hear [that]," said one Wisconsin officer. Only those who have experienced hard combat can fully understand "the feeling of prostration produced by such scenes and surroundings, after the excitement of bloody battle." When a brigade from John Sedgwick's First Corps division came up to relieve Gibbon, the Western regiments withdrew in succession as the fresh troops arrived. The 2nd and 7th Wisconsin and the 19th Indiana left the front just before midnight. The 6th Wisconsin, however, far in advance in the rocks and timber and in close contact with the enemy, was the last to be withdrawn. As the minutes passed and no soldiers appeared, Adj. Edward Brooks was sent back to find Brig. Gen. Willis Gorman, who was slated to provide the relief. "I can't send men into that woods to-night," the general admonished Brooks with a shake of his head. "All men are cowards in the dark." The news angered Rufus Dawes, who accused Gorman of forgetting "that the men who he condemned to shivering and misery for the rest of the night had fought and won a bloody battle in the dark. We were not relieved until eight o'clock in the morning of September 15 when the Second New York of Gorman's Brigade came up." Dawes wasn't finished. "Some men may be cowards in the daytime."[45]

The ground over which they advanced and were now occupying was "so rough and rocky that more than one of the boys had to use his dead comrade for a pillow," observed a Sauk County Black Hat. "It was fortunate that we were old enough in the service to sleep at any time." Recalling the long climb under fire, he added, "We who got through were happy."[46]

When dawn arrived, the Wisconsin men slowly advanced on the stone wall to take a look at what lay beyond. In one of those strange turns during the Civil War,

---

44 The Sisters of Charity was an order of Catholic nuns that established hospitals. The second toe and a portion of Sullivan's right foot were amputated.

45 Dawes, *Service*, 84; Dawes, journal, September 15, 1862; Gibbon, *Recollections*, 77-78.

46 Cheek and Pointon, *Sauk County*, 49.

the fighting at South Mountain pitted two Old Army friends against each other. John Gibbon's brother Lardner was serving in the Confederate army, and both brothers had been groomsmen at the prewar wedding of Daniel H. Hill, the Confederate general in command of the South Mountain defenders. Behind and on the wall were many dead and wounded Confederates, nearly all from Colquitt's brigade (the 6th, 23rd, 27th, and 28th Georgia, and 13th Alabama). One wounded Georgian, his face "a gore of blood," jumped up in fear and attempted to fire at the approaching Badgers. "We could hardly persuade him that it was not our purpose to kill," wrote Dawes.[47]

It was not until nearly 8:00 a.m. before a column of relieving infantry came swinging up the road. It was the 2nd New York, which, Bragg wrote with unfeigned sarcasm, "had been lying in the field . . . a safe distance in the rear, refreshing themselves with a good night's sleep, after a long and fatiguing march of some 10 miles." The exhausted 6th Wisconsin survivors tramped down the mountain and halted at the bottom to light coffee fires. "We cleaned our muskets and ourselves, and needed it," said one Badger. The boys were black from the musket smoke, and "did not look anything like the trim Sixth Wisconsin soldiers, 'band box' and "Calico Sixth' the rest of the boys used to call us." In true army fashion, orders arrived before the coffee was ready for the regiment to march back up the slope. "It was hard, but the men fell in promptly and marched along munching on dry hardtack," grumbled one of the Badgers. "It was now 24 hours since [we] had had [our] coffee." Word coursed through the ranks that Gibbon's brigade would lead the army's advance up and over South Mountain to seek out the rest of Lee's Army of Northern Virginia.[48]

The fighting at Turner's Gap was indeed costly. The Wisconsin and Indiana regiments lost 318 officers and men—about twenty-five percent of their effective number. This was twice as severe as had any other brigade in the First Corps. "I can only call your attention to their list of casualties," General Hooker said of the Western Brigade in his official report. Its loss "speaks for itself. The 7th Wisconsin,

47 Dawes, *Service*, 85; Dawes, journal, undated. Major General D. H. Hill, in writing about the battle years later, described Gibbon's regiments as a "choice brigade, strong in numbers and strong in the pluck of his men, all from the North-west where habitually good fighters are reared. . . . The Western men met in the . . . Georgia regiments men as brave as themselves and far more advantageously posed. . . . General Gibbon reports officially 318 men killed and wounded—a loss sustained almost entirely, I think at the stone-wall. The colonel of the Seventh Wisconsin reports a loss of 147 men in killed and wounded out of 375 muskets carried into action. This shows that he had brave men and that he encountered brave men." Hill, "The Battle of South Mountain," 275-276.

48 OR 19, pt. 1, 254; Johnson, "Recollections."

caught at the stone wall, suffered the worst with 147 men shot out of 375 carried into the fighting."[49]

McClellan, meanwhile, was sending a flurry of telegraphs to Washington announcing his great victory and claiming he had delivered Maryland and Pennsylvania from the Rebels. He based his (mistaken) assumption on Lee's decision not to continue the fighting for South Mountain on September 15. There were never enough Confederates in the area to hold the gaps for long against a determined effort to take them, but Little Mac assumed the open passes indicated that Lee was in headlong flight out of the state. True to form, however, it was not until late the next morning before McClellan began his pursuit in earnest. When it set off it was methodical and slow. Later that day, reports filtered in that Lee's army had halted along Antietam Creek near the town of Sharpsburg.

The advance of the Army of the Potomac off South Mountain was a grand sight that included several large groups of Confederate prisoners moving along with the marching Federal infantry brigades. The day was very hot and movement was slow. The marching soldiers and artillery cleared the road and the army ambulances pulled onto the turnpike only to become entangled with baggage and supply wagons. It was several hours before officers were able to unscramble the trains.[50]

One of the details following in the column included Pvt. George Fink of Milwaukee. A new recruit in the 6th Wisconsin, Fink had previous service in the 90-day 1st Wisconsin and was bringing with him eighty recruits from Wisconsin to the war front. In his possession was a stack of descriptive lists and instructions to turn the new soldiers and their papers over to the commander of the 6th Wisconsin. The small detail spent most of September 15 marching, and the men were taken back by what they found at South Mountain. "What we saw there was too terrible to tell," Fink wrote. "The dead, many of them had been left without burial. The bodies were decomposed. Dead Horses, gun wheels, exploded shells and arms and accoutrements were on every hand. The ruin and desolation made us read the meaning of war more plainly than we had ever before." Fink and his squad of recruits finally caught up with the army's wagons where he found Otto Schorse of Milwaukee serving as brigade quartermaster. The wagons stopped in a secluded wood where the teamsters and recruits set up camp. "Here we slept that night," Fink said.[51]

49 OR 19, pt. 1, 215.

50 Longhenry, diary, September 15, 1861.

51 *Milwaukee Free Press*, September 22, 1912.

Gibbon's brigade was not far ahead, and an incident that day ever after carried a bright memory for the Westerners. Gibbon was in the long column on the main pike and had to pass forward to reach his brigade. The Black Hats—"footsore, sleepy, weary, battle-stained and hungry," wrote one—were being marched back up the mountain and through Turner's Gap to pursue the Confederates. The Westerners were near Mountain house at the summit when they came upon Maj. Gen. Edwin Sumner's men halted just over the crest. "Bull" Sumner, a tough old dragoon and Indian fighter, had watched Gibbon's men fighting up the mountain the previous day. The general issued orders for his regiments to cheer the passing Wisconsin and Indiana men. Accompanied by his staff, Sumner moved to the roadside to salute with swords and raised hats. The gray-haired general remained uncovered until the head of the column passed. Gibbon was behind his regiments and missed the display, but halted to speak with Sumner and his officers. Sumner's adjutant told Gibbon that the old general had ordered his corps to cheer the brigade "as a testimonial of the gallantry it had exhibited the night before in the fight which he had seen from the hill behind us." Gibbon said the action on the part of Sumner was "all the more gratifying from the fact that it was well known in the army that he was very much opposed to such demonstrations as not being proper for disciplined troops."[52]

The 6th Wisconsin was at the head of Gibbon's column when it reached the crest, and it was Bragg who heard the "Present Arms!" and saw Sumner and his staff motionless by the roadside. The old general himself lifted his hat to the passing Black Hats he had "witnessed climb a high mountain the face of a lead and iron storm." The event was never forgotten "while memory remains unclouded," boasted Jerome Watrous. Bragg later confirmed it was "a very proud moment for me, although I had been on my feet nearly forty-eight hours without sleep." Another Wisconsin officer, Loyd Harris, said he did not understand the significance of the honor until much later—that "a distinguished corps commander could not pay a brigade a higher honor." When the importance finally sunk in, he added, "I always felt like lifting my hat whenever General Sumner's name was mentioned."[53]

52 Watrous manuscript, Jerome A. Watrous Papers, WHS; Gibbon, *Recollections*, 85-86. Gibbon was unaware of the salute by Sumner and his staff and wrote in his memoir that he was "very much disappointed at the time that his orders to his troops had not reached them until after they passed by."

53 Edward Bragg, letter to Rufus Dawes, December 21, 1890; Watrous, manuscript, undated. Bragg explained to Dawes that the salute was given "in recognition of our sturdy fight of the night before."

I Can Whip Lee Without Any Trouble at All

A story circulated in the Western Brigade the day after the long afternoon and night of fighting on the slope of South Mountain. Apparently, some Confederates were captured and a squad of Black Hats with a corporal in charge was sent to the rear with orders to turn them over to McClellan's headquarters. The headquarters was a sizeable two-story private stone home taken over by the general and his large staff. The corporal found the house and was wandering through the halls looking for someone to turn over his prisoners when he came upon an open door and entered. An officer, seated at a desk and writing, was annoyed at the interruption and asked in a sharp voice, "What do you want?" The corporal was face-to-face with George Brinton McClellan.

Taken aback, the soldier but straightened up just a bit and spoke. "I have some prisoners, General, I am ordered to turn over to you."

"Who are you and where do you come from?" When the corporal mentioned his regiment, McClellan exhibited interest. "Ah, you belong to Gibbon's brigade. You had some heavy fighting up their tonight."

"Yes sir," he replied, "but I think we gave them as good as they sent."

"Indeed you did," confirmed the general, "you made a splendid fight."

The corporal was green on some military matters, such as how to have a conversation with the general commanding the Army of the Potomac, but he was a Western boy with sand and a certain amount of cheek. "Well, General, that's the way we boys calculated to fight under a general like you." Little Mac got up out of his chair and did just the kind of thing that made him beloved by the men in ranks. He took the corporal by the hand and said with some emotion, "My man, if I can get that kind of feeling amongst the men of this army, I can whip Lee without any trouble at all."

Back among his comrades, the proud soldier told the story to the hoots, laughs, and leg slaps of his friends about how McClellan had taken an enlisted man by the hand and complimented him on the way his brigade had behaved in the fight. "By such bearing as this," concluded Gibbon, "is the confidence of the soldiers won."[54]

Little Mac was going to need all the help he could find if he was to beat Lee and the Army of Northern Virginia—even with a copy of Lee's marching orders in hand. There was much at stake during that second autumn of the war. The string of Union victories in the West was now threatened by Confederate thrusts across the country. Confederate columns were driving north into Kentucky, and the Rebel

54 Gibbon, *Recollections*, 78-79.

victory at Richmond, Kentucky, on August 30 (the last day of Lee's stunning victory at Second Bull Run) allowed the enemy to threaten not only Louisville but Cincinnati, Ohio. Lee's quick march into Maryland following his success at Manassas sent chilling ripples throughout the North just when Congressional elections were approaching and some Democratic candidates were talking about a peace settlement that would result in a divided country. Lee's defeat was thus of paramount concern. The march from South Mountain was pressed with the idea of catching the various elements of the Southern army before they could reassemble. Instead of retreating quickly across the Potomac, however, Lee had gathered with a portion of his army on the west bank of Antietam Creek near the small Maryland town of Sharpsburg.

Pulled together with the elements of Pope's disbanded Army of Virginia, the Army of the Potomac feeling its way toward Antietam Creek now numbered seven infantry corps. The new commander of the First Corps was Joseph Hooker, who had a new commander in John P. Hatch at the head of his First Division. In Gibbon's brigade, three officers were promoted to replace those killed at Gainesville. George H. Stevens of Fox Lake moved to lieutenant colonel of the 2nd Wisconsin to replace mortally wounded Col. Edgar O'Connor, who was in turn succeeded by Lucius Fairchild. John Callis, a native of North Carolina and like Fairchild a '49er in the California gold fields, took the reins of the 7th Wisconsin in place of the wounded John Hamilton. In the 19th Indiana, William W. Dudley, a 19-year-old New Englander who in 1861 was operating a grain milling business at Richmond, Indiana, was appointed acting major to replace Isaac May. Stevens, Callis, and Dudley were men who would be heard from in the coming days.

One of the lasting memories of this march was how Capt. Werner von Bachelle's Newfoundland trotted along with him. When the dog wandered into camp a couple months earlier, the landsmen of his company presented the animal to the courtly Milwaukee officer of the 6th Wisconsin. The captain had a fondness for animals and taught the dog "to perform military salutes, and other remarkable things." The dog was von Bachelle's constant companion, so much so that one officer concluded that the pet was probably the captain's "most devoted friend on earth." Von Bachelle had extensive military service in Europe (one account had him serving "with distinction in the French Army in Algiers") and was widely regarded as a capable officer. His limited English and Old World aloofness, however, left him with few friends among the regimental officers and prevented any familiar associations with his countrymen in lower ranks. The reserved captain also possessed a certain fatalism. One Wisconsin officer told the story about a conversation with von Bachelle "under a holly bush" after the fighting on South Mountain as the two "stood picket" for their sleeping soldiers. The native of Hanover, who arrived in the United States in 1851, talked at length about his life before coming to America and believed he would not die "until his time came in regular order."[55]

When the column drew near Boonsboro, west of South Mountain, the Western men came upon a party of "old gray haired men, citizens of Maryland" gathered by the roadside. They cheered "almost frantic with joy," swinging their hats as they "laughed and cried without regard for appearances." The town at first seemed deserted, but when the head of the column reached the main street, doors and windows flew open and the people poured out to greet the Union soldiers. The column turned south at the intersection and pushed on five or six miles over good roads before reaching the small town of Keedysville, where the rearguard of the Confederate army was located west of town. When several enemy batteries closer to Sharpsburg opened with case shot, the shells burst over and around the Federal column but did little damage. Gibbon turned his brigade into a ravine for protection. Union guns arrived on the gallop almost immediately, wheeled into battery, and opened fire. The veterans paid little heed to the gunnery, heading instead for the wood fences to start coffee fires "with little regard for the fragments of shell flying around." It was almost midday.[56]

A curious Wisconsin officer climbed the ridge overlooking Antietam Creek and could clearly see the Rebel line on the hills surrounding Sharpsburg. Joe Hooker, who was also there, told the officers around him that at least 40,000 enemy waited just across the creek. Soon, McClellan and his staff arrived to study the Confederate position. Nothing of immediate consequence came out of the long distance reconnaissance. About 3:00 p.m. orders arrived for the brigade to move out of the range of the Rebel guns. Once we did so, "Our greatly exhausted men were soon sound asleep," remembered Maj. Rufus Dawes.[57]

The four regiments rested out of danger but enjoyed a good view of the artillery exchanging fire. McClellan spent the day concentrating his army for what was shaping to be a major battle. He had about 75,000 soldiers at hand, but was convinced the Confederates had at least 50,000 men along the front. Lee only had

---

55 Dawes, *Service*, 93; Edward Bragg, letter to Dawes, December 21, 1890; Dawes Papers, WHSW. Von Bachelle was born in Hanover and immigrated to the United States in 1851. He arrived in New York and filed an initial declaration for citizenship. At the start of the war, he was living in Granville (now Milwaukee) with William H. Lindwurm. Lindwurm, von Bachelle, and another immigrant, Frederick Schumacher, organized the Citizen Corps' Milwaukee, which became Company F of the 6th Wisconsin. William J. K. Beaudot, "A Milwaukee Immigrant in the Civil War," *Milwaukee History: The Magazine of the Milwaukee County Historical Society*, vol. 7, No. 11 (Spring, 1984), 11-25.

56 Longhenry, diary, September 16, 1862; Dawes, *Service*, 86.

57 Gibbon, *Recollections*, 80.

perhaps 15,000 men readily available, but Little Mac was convinced the six Southern divisions that had taken part in the siege of Harpers Ferry had reached the field, increasing the Confederate army to close to 100,000. In fact, the six divisions would not reach Sharpsburg until late the next afternoon—September 17—and even then, Lee would have fewer than 40,000 men.

At 4:00 p.m. September 16, Hooker's First Corps moved across Antietam Creek beyond the army's right flank and marched to the Hagerstown Pike a couple miles north of Sharpsburg. The supply wagons were well behind and there was little food. The Westerners filled pockets and haversacks with apples from nearby orchards by cutting off the branches. When McClellan was spotted riding along the column he "was received with great enthusiasm by the troops." The light was fading when artillery and small arms fire broke out to the south. The fitful fighting continued for perhaps an hour, slowed, and stopped altogether about 9:00 p.m. No one was sure what the gunfire signified. The four Western regiments formed in close column, muskets loaded and the lines parallel to the turnpike. John Gibbon remembered a certain uneasiness with the army's "very confused and huddled up condition." A drizzling rain, coupled with what seemed to be certain battle in the morning made for a difficult night. "Nothing can be more solemn than a period of silent waiting for the summons to battle," confessed one officer.[58] Just after dusk, Gibbon rode to a barn near the turnpike that doubled as Hooker's First Corps headquarters. Artillery opened in the distant darkness. The fire is puzzling, commented Hooker, because it seemed as though the enemy was shooting into his own troops.[59]

Gibbon's brigade was much reduced. The four regiments arrived in Washington in 1861 with 1,000 men in each. On the eve of Antietam, the entire brigade numbered fewer than 1,000. Sickness, disability, promotions, transfers, and other things had taken many, but the heavy fighting of the past weeks had winnowed the units and changed them in ways even the soldiers themselves did not yet understand. The large brigade marched in late August with some 2,100 bayonets and fought three major battles in less than three weeks: Brawner's Farm or Gainesville, Second Bull Run, and South Mountain. The latter fighting at Turner's Gap claimed 37 killed and 251 wounded, or about 25 percent of the brigade's strength. Gone were some of the major figures of the brigade, including Rufus King, whose illness hampered him on the battlefield and ruined his reputation. In the 2nd Wisconsin, Col. Edgar O'Connor of Beloit was shot dead at Gainesville in

---

58 Dawes, *Service*, 87; Gibbon, *Recollections*, 80-81.

59 *Ibid.*, 81.

the flurry of bullets that wounded Maj. Thomas Allen, who remained in the fight. In the 6th Wisconsin, Col. Lysander Cutler was in Washington recovering from his leg wound, and farmer boy Mickey Sullivan was on his way home after being shot in the foot at South Mountain. Reuben Huntley of Yellow River was shot dead on the skirmish line at South Mountain where circus boy George Chamberlain was also killed outright. "I never saw better work than old Huntley did," remarked his captain. Private William Lawrence of DeSoto died a slow death in the dark near Turner's Gap. The 7th Wisconsin's Pvt. Willie Ray of Cassville lay in an army hospital with a Gainesville head wound, the same battle where Col. Charles Hamilton was shot through both legs. Lieutenant Colonel William Robinson was shot in the leg, and Maj. George Bill shot in the forehead. Respected and admired Capt. George H. Brayton was also killed there. Col. Solomon Meredith of the 19th Indiana was injured when his horse fell on him at Gainesville and Maj. Isaac M. May suffered a mortal head wound in the Brawner farmyard. He died September 6.

If some of the surviving officers had proved themselves brave and competent, others were found wanting. "I call the Capt. a coward," one Badger wrote home. "He will not run but he is so terrified that he can't give at command. At Bull Run . . . you would have thought he was trying to sneak up to a wild turkey. I did not see a single man in ranks but what stood right up like men. I was really ashamed of him."[60] At the other end of the spectrum, everyone recognized that the tireless efforts of John Gibbon and Frank Haskell had molded the brigade into an effective fighting force. "We will go in not eagerly, as ferocious stayers-at-home say, but willingly and to win," explained one officer who proved himself in combat. "A battle to veterans is an awful experience. There is not with our men the headlong recklessness of new men, who start it, acting as though they would rather be shot or not, and then lose their organization and scatter like sheep, but there is a conviction from much experience in fighting, that safety is best had be steadiness, persistence in firing, and most of all by holding together."[61]

The Army of the Potomac created and shaped by McClellan was also much changed, and some of the shift involved Little Mac's ongoing fight with the Lincoln administration. Cooled now was the hot flush of patriotism that had driven the "Boys of '61" to flock to the Old Flag following Fort Sumter. Inept generals, ambitious officers, and influence peddlers who used the fortunes of the army for their own ends had pulled the men closer to the small circle of their cook fires,

60 George Fairfield, letter to his sister, October 2, 1862. Fairfield Papers, WHS. Fairchild, who served in Company C, referred to Alexander S. Hooe of Prairie du Chien as a capable officer frozen by the danger of battle. He resigned his commission on February 7, 1862.

61 Rufus Dawes, letter, to Mary Gates, August 6, 1863; Dawes, *Service*, 197.

where they voiced simmering anger at the manipulators, the stay-at-homes, the peace-at-any-price proponents, and the bombastic newspaper editorials calling on the army to move. Even the homefolk seemed unwilling to accept the reality of war. Bright flags and heroics and victory in broad swaths was still appealing. The hardship through which their men suffered and the senseless killing was better left unspoken.

We Have Held Our Lives Cheap

On the eve of the fighting at Sharpsburg, Maryland, the soldiers of the Army of the Potomac were keenly aware that they still had to prove themselves—despite all the months of fighting and hardships. A 2nd Wisconsin officer wrote "in a weak and trembling hand" from the bed, where he was dying of a festering wound suffered at Gainesville, of his own stiffening resolve to see the war through. "We have held our lives cheap and counted our blood of no value," explained Lt. Edward P. Kellogg of Boscobel, who continued:

> We have dared and done all that was the most exacting could require, but the stupidity of our leaders has squandered all this wealth of bravery and patriotism, and enthusiasm and energy, and has made all of no avail. We are not disheartened. We are willing to go on, even if it be in our own homes that we have to fall. We have been disgracefully beaten, but we are not conquered, and I humbly trust that neither Stonewall Jackson nor Robert E. Lee, nor things present, nor things to come, will be able to accomplish the feat. It seems to me that in spite of our undeniable reverses, the rebellion never before was in so fair a way to be speedily wiped out. I think the North may well feel jubilant at the prospect.[62]

For many Western men down in the rolling countryside north of Sharpsburg that night, however, their primary concern was simply trying to keep dry.

The first streaks of dawn arrived "misty and foggy." Brigadier General Abner Doubleday was in command of the division after Hatch fell wounded on South Mountain. "Move the troops out of there at once," Doubleday ordered Gibbon. "You're in open range of rebel batteries." The drummers beat the "long roll," but

---

62 A former newspaperman, Kellogg enlisted May 18, 1861, at Boscobel and was promoted to 2nd Lt. of Company C on March 28, 1862. He was wounded at Gainesville and taken prisoner. He returned to the army and regained enough strength to return to Wisconsin, but died on October 9, 1862. *Wisconsin Roster*, vol. 1, 363. His letters were given to editor Jerome Watrous after the war, who published some of them in the *Milwaukee Sunday Telegraph*, September 28, 1879.

the men were in "heavy slumber" because of the hard matching of the past days and it took "shaking and kicking and hurrying" to get them up. Well to the south, a sharp picket fire erupted, followed by the low thump of artillery. It died out rather quickly. Frightened by the noise, a rabbit sought a hiding place in the coat of one of the officers, but "that poor, trembling thing was left behind as the regiments started to form." The fighting picked up again. This time it didn't fade away. The bloodiest day in American history was upon them.[63]

Corps commander Joe Hooker arrived in a clatter with staff officers, mounted on a "large white horse" and donned in his "full regimentals of a Major General." "General Gibbon," he called. "Get your brigade close column by divisions in to line and follow me." "We were hungry, ragged and dirty," recalled a Badger. "Before starting we pulled up our belts a notch or two. As we had very little to eat the day before and no breakfast at all, this was an easy thing to do." As soon as they stepped off, the six guns of Battery B of the 4th U.S. Artillery opened with a crash, firing rounds over their heads in the direction of an as-yet unseen enemy.[64]

The brigade that set off that morning numbered about 800 men. Its regiments marched in a column of divisions with each regiment two companies wide and five companies deep. The 2nd and 6th Wisconsin took the lead with the 6th on the right facing south. Behind them tramped the 19th Indiana and 7th Wisconsin. With Col. Lucius Fairchild of the 2nd Wisconsin suffering from severe and chronic diarrhea and Solomon Meredith of the 19th hampered by an earlier wound, the 2nd went into action under Thomas Allen and the 19th under Alois Bachman.

The formation had not moved fifty yards in the dim light of dawn before Confederate batteries opened on them. The first shots whizzed overhead, but a case shell exploded with a lurid red flash in the center of the 6th Wisconsin. The blast killed two outright and injured eleven others, including one Sauk County soldier who had his arms ripped off. A piece of shell lacerated Capt. David Noyes' right foot. The "dreadful scene" left Pvt. Francis Deleglise staggering half-blind with his ears ringing. After a few moments he discovered he was the only soldier standing left of the gap. The explosion swept away the men on his right and behind him. The voice of Lt. Col. Edward Bragg "rang out loud and clear" in the half-light: "Steady, Sixth," he called. "Close up!" Bragg "stepp[ed] over the quivering bodies of dead and wounded comrades [and] the regiment moved to the front." The "shock was momentary," Bragg later wrote, and his column moved on "leaving the

---

63 Edward S. Bragg, letter to Col. Ezra A. Carman of the Antietam Battlefield Commission, December 26, 1894. Bragg Papers, WHS; Wheeler, journal, September 17, 1862; Dawes, journal, undated; Dawes, *Service*, 87; Pointon and Cheek, *Sauk County*, 51, 215.

64 Harries "In the Ranks at Antietam," 261; Dawes, *Service*, 132.

mangled bodies of their comrades on the ground." The sudden carnage was the "severest test of discipline," wrote Gibbon, who worried the "shock would scatter the regiment like a flock of frightened sheep." As it turned out, he worried for naught: "I had not yet learned the powers of discipline in that brigade, nor what extent of tests it could take and successfully pass through." A few minutes later the soldiers reached the shelter of a barn on the Joseph Poffenberger farm. Just ahead was a stand of timber. The brigade halted to deploy for battle. "The artillery fire had now increased to the roar of a hundred cannon," reported a Wisconsin officer. "Solid shot and shell whistled through the trees above us, cutting off limbs which fell about us."[65]

The brigade was moving steadily along a slight ridge marked by outcroppings of rock. The ridge carried the Hagerstown Pike south into Sharpsburg. Just ahead about one-half mile and left of the road was a farm owned by David Miller and beyond that, his large cornfield. South of the corn was a meadow and, farther on, a small white church belonging to the German Baptist Brethren sect called "Dunkers" because of their practice of baptism by total immersion. The church sat in the fringe of a large stand of trees on the western side of the Hagerstown Pike later known as the "West Woods." On the other side of the pike across from the Miller cornfield was another stand of timber later called the "East Woods." Gibbon advanced his regiments from the Poffenberger farm with skirmishers well forward. Rebel pickets made themselves known around the Miller farm. Despite "a vigorous fire," the Black Hats on the advance line dashed ahead at a run, the regiments following with the air above their heads alive with "screaming missiles of the contending batteries." Adjutant Haskell pulled up to and ordered Bragg of the 6th to "advance as far as it was safe." The slight lieutenant colonel gave the staff officer a hard look. "Give General Gibbon my compliments, and tell him it has been

---

65 Frank Haskell, letter to brothers and sisters, September 22, 1862; Soldiers' and Citizens' Album, vol. 1, 722; Gibbon, *Recollections*, 81; John Gibbon, "Antietam Eighteen Years After," *Milwaukee Sunday Telegraph*, December 5, 1880; Edward Bragg, letter to his wife, September 21, 1862; Dawes, *Service*, 87-88. Bragg's Report, OR 19, pt. 1, 255; Rufus R. Dawes, "On the Right at Antietam," *Sketches of War History, Ohio Military Order of the Loyal Legion of the United States*, vol. 3, 252-263, reprinted in Dawes, *Service*, 333-334; Eugene Anderson, letter to his mother and father, September 22, 1862, private collection. Haskell added that Noyes "has had his right foot amputated, saving the heel and ankle joint, is doing well, and undoubtedly will recover." On September 27, 1862, The *Milwaukee Sentinel* carried a story taken from the Washington correspondent of the *Chicago Times*: "I have just been shown a piece of shell, weighing a quarter of a pound, which was cut out of the thigh of E. Fletcher, Company E, Wisconsin Sixth. For twenty-four hours this murderous piece of iron was buried in the thigh of the wounded soldier. The surgeon reports that his patient is getting along finely. The shell to which this piece belonged exploded in the ranks of the Sixth Wisconsin at the battle of the 17th." *Wisconsin Newspaper Volumes*.

dammed unsafe here for the last thirty minutes." Bragg gave his hat a final tug and ordered, "Forward, 6th Wisconsin!"

The 6th Wisconsin lost several casualties trying to work through the trees and shrubs on the Miller farm. Corporal Eugene Anderson of Mauston was struck climbing a fence. The ball hit him in the upper part of the leg below the right knee, glancing off the bone and lodging just behind the skin. The right wing of the regiment swept ahead, but a stout fence around a small garden impeded the left wing. Dawes urged his men to pull down the boards, but frantic tugging and shoving failed to conquer the fence. He finally called on the left wing to pass through a gate and with "utmost haste" reform in the garden. "[W]orn out and so lame that he could scarcely walk," Capt. Edwin Brown pushed forward to get his men through the fence. He lifted his sword and in a "loud and nervous voice" ordered, "Company E, on the right by file into line!" Just then a piece of shell struck him in the face and carried away part of his jaw. Sergeant Andrew Deacon heard the captain's "shriek" of pain and saw Pvt. Lute Murray of Shawano kneel beside the fallen officer. Deacon moved on, remembering how Brown told him he would see the Rebels out of Maryland and then apply for a furlough, and if he could not get that he would resign.[66] The captain—described by Bragg as a "good officer and genial gentleman" and known to enjoy the singing of the regimental officers—returned to his wife and children in Fond du Lac in a metallic casket.

Just pass the Miller garden was a small orchard. The line pushed to a rail fence skirting the front edge of a woodlot. "Before us was a strip of open field, beyond which on the left-hand side of the turnpike, was rising grown covered by a large corn-field, the stalks standing thick and tall," remembered one officer. "The rebel skirmishers ran into the corn as we appeared at the fence. Owing to our headlong advance, we were far ahead of the general lines of battle." Running south to Sharpsburg, the Hagerstown Pike dips to a flat area around the Miller farm

---

66 John P. Hart of Fond du Lac, letter, to Sgt. Andrew Deacon dated October 2, 1862, from Keedysville. Deacon enlisted in Fond du Lac and was also among the Antietam wounded. His arm was amputated and he was discharged December 10, 1862. Deacon said Murray stayed with Brown until he died, and the officer gave Murray "his revolver and he thinks his watch wishing them to be sent home to his wife." Deacon was mistaken. Brown's loaded revolver was found in a belt on his body when his casket broke apart and the body fell out as it was being moved after the war from one Fond du Lac cemetery to another. "Company E will long remember him," the letter concluded. "He was ever kind and noble and human man. It is a loss to the Company, deeply regretted by all. He had not a single enemy in the whole Regiment, and may he rest in peace is the wish of the whole company." In a letter dated September 28, 1862, Edward Bragg wrote his wife: "Mrs. Capt. Brown must feel the loss of her husband severely. I wrote her a letter of condolence, a day or two since, it was difficult for me to do, but I thought it would be something to her feelings and gratifying to the family. But, such duties, I do not like to perform they are not to my taste."

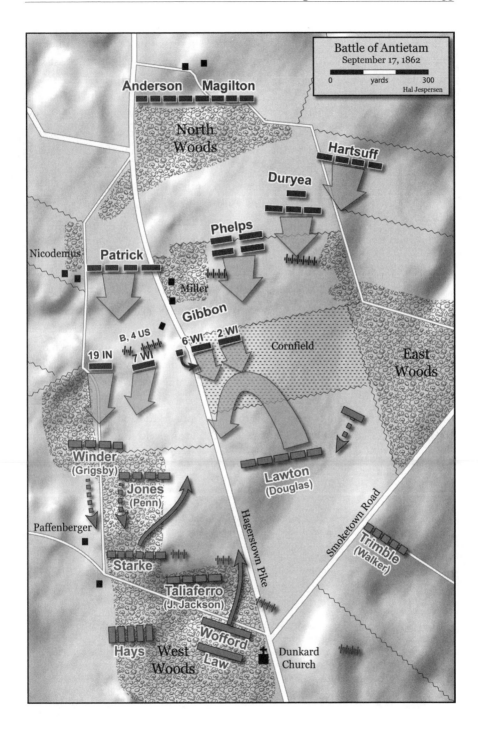

buildings before gradually climbing the low ridge several hundred yards farther on. The roadway was flanked by wooden fences about five feet tall. On the east side was a mature and dense cornfield, with the East Woods beyond. To the west and south was an open field with two stacks of straw and a rocky area with trees—the West Woods. The 6th Wisconsin held the left center of Gibbon's brigade front, moving through the corn with one company out on the road and two other companies in the open field on the right. The German company from Milwaukee was on the roadway with the Beloit Company G and the Juneau County men of Company K in the open field. On the left of the 6th Wisconsin holding the far left of the brigade was the 2nd Wisconsin. West of the road the landscape dropped sharply away, and it was there the 7th Wisconsin and the 19th Indiana had moved from behind the front line, formed, and advanced into battle.

The line of Black Hats spilled over the fence and through the open field into the heavy corn. It was heavy going, the stalks planted in clumps and as high as the soldiers' tall hats. As Bragg put it, his soldiers had "a sniff of blood in their nose that morning, sweeping along like a storm cloud, over skirmishers, everything opposing." Behind them, near the Miller farm, Battery B "opened fire upon a foe, as yet, scarcely seen by the gunners." The advancing skirmish line in the open field right of the corn, wrote Bragg later with bitterness, drifted away as the commanding captain "dodged behind a tree and grew there, letting his line go helter skelter without direction." Bragg ordered the skirmishers to move forward, but they hung back in the patchy morning mist and were left behind. Farther left, musketry rattled the morning air when other Federal units advanced along the east edge of the cornfield. Within minutes a "terrific fire flared in the cornfield immediately to the left as well as in the woods to the right."[67]

---

67 Dawes, journal, undated; Dawes, *Service*, 88-89; Edward Bragg, letter to Ezra Carman, December 26, 1894, Ezra A. Carman, Manuscript Division, Library of Congress; Gibbon, *Recollections*, 82. In his official report, Bragg wrote Carman "the right of my line of skirmishers having failed to advance, either from a failure to hear or heed commands." *OR* 19, pt. 1, 250. To Carman, however, he wrote that his skirmishers failed to go forward because Capt. Alexander Hooe of Company C "showed the white feather." Hooe organized the Prairie du Chien Volunteers in 1861 and his son was elected captain. The elder Hooe (some records spell the name Hove) was a Virginian who moved west to Prairie du Chien on the Mississippi River in the 1830s after graduating from West Point. He was cited for bravery during the War with Mexico and fought at Palo Alto in and Resaca-de-la-Palma the same year, losing his arm in the latter combat. The editor of the Prairie du Chien newspaper in 1861 described the younger Hooe as a "patriotic and efficient officer who has a thorough knowledge of the duties of a soldier.... He is the most capable man in this part of the country to lead a company." Hooe was discharged from the 6th Wisconsin on February 7, 1863. *Prairie du Chien Courier*, May 2, 1861; *History of Crawford and Richland Counties, Wisconsin* (Springfield, IL, 1884), 497-499; *Wisconsin Roster*, vol. 1, 505.

The Men with Their Tall Hats Looked Ten Feet Tall

The advance of the line revealed more of the terrain that awaited them, as well as the enemy. Bragg watched as horses pulled enemy artillery across the rise just ahead. He called to Capt. Werner von Bachelle to take his company up the road and shoot the battery horses.[68] The Germans ran up the road, but when the pike sloped upward a heavy line of Confederate infantry rose out of a cover field near the West Woods delivered a blast of musketry into them.[69] The volley knocked down several men, ripped furrows on the roadway, and splintered rails lining the turnpike fences. Von Bachelle was struck several times and fell heavily on the roadway. Aware that his wounds were fatal and trying to achieve some dignity even as life slipped away, the captain crossed his feet, drew down the visor of his cap, folded his arms, and died while his company fell back in confusion. Despite the urging of several privates, von Bachelle's pet dog refused to leave his master's body and was left behind.[70]

The companies in the field were ordered to the Hagerstown Pike, where the soldiers dropped and poked the barrels of their rifle-muskets between the rails on the five-foot fence. Dawes halted the left wing and ordered his men to lie down. "The bullets began to clip through the corn, and spin through the soft furrows—thick, almost as hail," he wrote. "Shells burst around us, the fragments tearing up the ground, and canister whistled through the corn above us." Artillery fire from "our own batteries," complained Dawes, swept portions of the roadway as the Union gunners tried to get the range. One of the rounds killed Lt. William Bode of Milwaukee on the Hagerstown Pike and wounded another. "This has happened often in the war," admitted Dawes. "The rebel artillery shot way over our heads." Bode was struck by a piece of exploding case shot. In the field west of the road, Capt. John Ticknor of Company K received a painful but not life-threatening

68 The guns were probably from Cutt's battalion of the Confederate Artillery Reserve under William N. Pendleton. Carman, manuscript, 23. Carman was the colonel of the 13th New Jersey at Antietam. He also served on the Antietam Battlefield Board after the war. His manuscript of the campaign is based upon an exchange of thousands of letters and conversations with men who fought on both sides. It has been fully edited and annotated by Thomas G. Clemens, and published in two volumes entitled *The Maryland Campaign of 1862* (vol. 1: *South Mountain*; vol. 2: *Antietam*).

69 The force was comprised of J. R. Jones' and Charles Winder's Virginia brigades of Stonewall Jackson's division. Carman, manuscript, 24.

70 Bragg's report, *OR* 19, pt. 1, 255; Edward S. Bragg, letter to Rufus Dawes, December 21, 1890; Dawes, journal, undated; Edward Bragg, speech to Chicago reunion, undated; Gibbon, *Milwaukee Sunday Telegraph*, December 5, 1880; Carman, manuscript, 23.

Pvt. Anthony Olson
Prescott Guards
Co. B, 6th Wisconsin

Olson was wounded at South Mountain and Antietam and transferred to the Veteran Reserve Corps on September 17, 1862. *Wisconsin Veterans Museum*

wound when a shell fragment knocked the breath out of him and left him spitting blood. He had been hit in the leg by a spent ball at Gainesville.

Amid the smoke, falling stalks, and clatter of bullets appeared Sgt. Maj. Howard Huntington looking for Dawes. "Major," he shouted over the noise. "Colonel Bragg wants to see you, quick, at the turnpike." Once there, Dawes found Bragg leaning against the rails. His face was pale and he was obviously shaken. "Major, I am shot," Bragg said before collapsing to the ground. "I saw a tear in the side of his overcoat which he had on and I feared that he was shot through the body," Dawes recalled. Bragg had been hit just as the 2nd Wisconsin came up on the left of the 6th Wisconsin. "I thought my elbow fractured," Bragg later wrote, "as I had not then discovered the ball hole in the breast of my coat." A soldier trying to help the lieutenant colonel found the hole in a side pocket and seeing "the red linings were sure I was shot through the body. To make sure I was not dead, I gave an order to withdraw the line on the right under cover of a fence and there I must confess things began to look pretty dark."[71] Convinced Bragg was severely wounded, Dawes called on two nearby soldiers for help: "Take a tent and carry him to the rear at once." The men bundled Bragg in a

---

71 Dawes, *Service*, 89; Dawes, journal, undated. In his war memoir, Dawes deleted reference to the fact that it was Federal artillery that struck Bode and Ticknor. Bode enlisted May 10, 1861. He served as corporal and 1st sergeant before being commissioned July 16, 1862. *Wisconsin Roster*, vol. 1, 517, 533; Eugene Anderson, letter to his parents, September 22, 1862.

Pvt. Abel H. Johnson,
Anderson Guards,
Co. I, 6th Wisconsin

Private Johnson was severely
wounded in the right foot while
fighting at Antietam on the
morning of September 17,
1862. He later transferred to
the Veteran Reserve Corps on
November 8, 1863. *Scott D. Hann
Collection*

shelter half and carried him
through the corn and out of
danger. "Colonel Bragg was
shot in the first fire from the
woods and his nerve, in
standing up under the shock
until he had effected the
maneuver so necessary for the safety of his men, was wonderful," said Dawes. "I
felt a great sense of responsibility, when thrown thus suddenly in command of a
regiment in the face of a terrible battle."[72]

The men carrying Bragg set the wounded officer down near the north end of
the Miller cornfield, where it was found that his left arm was numb and paralyzed,
but he could still walk. Bragg ordered the two soldiers to return to the regiment and
began moving slowly for the rear. After a handful of yards a mounted Gibbon
appeared. "Old man, are you hurt? You are very white," asked the general with
obvious concern. Bragg replied that he was indeed wounded, and warned Gibbon
that the enemy was "flanking the brigade." The general dismounted and withdrew a
pocket flask, from which Bragg took a long pull. Somewhat revived, Bragg
continued to the rear. (A few hours later in the kind of pious letter a soldier might
write to his wife, Bragg claimed that the whiskey was "the first I have tasted since I
have been in the service.")[73]

72 Edward S. Bragg, letter to his wife, September 21, 1862.

73 *Ibid.*; Watrous, "Old Man, are you Hurt?" *Milwaukee Sunday Telegraph*, December 10, 1898.

Private William P. Harrison, Lemonweir Minute Men,
Co. K, 6th Wisconsin

Harrison was mortally wounded with a bullet through the spine at Antietam on
September 17, 1862. He lingered for three long days at Boonsboro, Maryland, before
finally expiring. *Scott D. Hann Collection*

Sergeant, 7th Wisconsin

This unidentified image arrived with many others in a collection of 7th Wisconsin pictures. *Author's Collection*

Back at the front, meanwhile, Major Dawes oversaw the 6th Wisconsin along the rail fence lining the Hagerstown Pike. In an effort to slow the enemy fire, Gibbon ordered the right two-gun section of Battery B to move forward in front of the two straw stacks southwest of the Miller buildings. Division commander Abner Doubleday ordered Marsena Patrick's New York brigade forward in support.

On the ridge line near the West Woods, Dawes spotted "a group of officers, whom I took to be a general and staff." Taking muskets from the men around him one at a time, Dawes rested the barrel on the fence and squeezed off a half a dozen shots. He reported with some satisfaction that the group of officers "suddenly scattered." On his left, he spotted a thick line of Federal infantry sweeping through the cornfield. Thomas Allan of the 2nd Wisconsin appeared and asked Dawes to join the general advance. When "Forward-guide left-march!" cut through the air, the soldiers of the 6th Wisconsin jumped to their feet and moved south through the green stalks. Dawes caught Huntington by the arm with an order for Capt. John Kellogg: "If it is practicable, move forward the right companies, aligning with the left wing." Huntington ran off, ducking through the stalks as he disappeared. He returned a short time later with a response: "Please give Major Dawes my compliments, and say it is impracticable; the fire is murderous." Dawes nodded his understanding and told Huntington to tell Kellogg to take cover in the corn and rejoin the regiment if possible. Although struck by a bullet on the way, Huntington carried the message to

Kellogg, who ordered his men up only to have so many shot that he ordered them back down again.[74]

"The union line, which I afterward discovered to be my own brigade was marching toward . . . the rebel line, and the men looked as if they were ten feet tall on account of the tall hats they wore, quite in contrast with the low, tight fitting caps of the volunteers and the rebels," wrote a 6th Wisconsin soldier watching the unfolding battle from the brigade's wagons near the North Woods. "The rebels were in a cornfield and in the woods and at their rear about 250 feet was a fence. As the union men advanced up the slope, man after man would make a convulsive grab at some spot on his body, or perhaps merely drop his musket, then fall himself." It was "a frightful thing to witness," he continued, "for I was not near enough to tell whether or not those who fell were my best friends. Finally as the union men advanced, the rebels lay down and then a volley tore into the union men and was returned with more vehemence than that with which it was sent. The rebels jumped and began running back. Some tried to get over the fence and could not and hung there until take prisoners. The union men were firing at will and standing their ground."[75]

The 2nd and 6th Wisconsin line moving through the corn was now on the right side of a long line of Federal infantry. A second line of Union soldiers was not far behind. The 2nd Wisconsin men had yet to receive or fire a shot. At the southern edge of the cornfield was a "low Virginia rail fence" and beyond an open field. "As we appeared at the edge of the corn, a long line of men in butternut and gray rose up from the ground," wrote Dawes. "Simultaneously, the hostile battle lines opened a tremendous fire upon each other. Men, I can not say fell; they were knocked out of the ranks by dozens. But we jumped over the fence and pushed on, loading, firing, and shouting as we advanced. There was, on the part the men, great hysterical excitement, eagerness to go forward, and a reckless disregard of life, of every thing but victory."[76]

The flurry of Rebel bullets took an immediate and terrible toll. Private Nick Gaffney of the 6th Wisconsin was shot and his tent mate, Francis Deleglise, stopped to assist him. Still shaken by his own narrow escape from the shell that ripped through his company just before daybreak, Deleglise was convinced

74 Dawes, *Service*, 89-90.

75 *Milwaukee Free Press*, September 22, 1912.

76 Carman, manuscript, 27; Dawes, *Service*, 99-111. The two Wisconsin regiments faced the 26th, 38th, and 61st Georgia regiments of Alexander Lawton's brigade (under Col. Marcellus Douglass). The distance between the two lines was about 200 yards.

Sgt. Waldo A. Stearns,
Co. H, 2nd Wisconsin

Stearns enlisted as a corporal and was promoted to sergeant. He was severely wounded in Maryland while fighting at Antietam on September 17, 1862, and discharged for disability on January 21, 1863.
Brett Wilson Collection

Gaffney was as good as dead. He pulled off Gaffney's knapsack to make a pillow then ran ahead to find only four of his company still in line. As he bit the tail off a paper cartridge and rammed the ball home, a bullet struck the man next to him in the left eye and exited the right ear, splattering Deleglise with blood and brains. Deleglise put down his musket, pulled the dead soldier's knapsack under the blood-soaked and ruined head, picked up the man's weapon, and fired. At the same instant, a Confederate bullet grazed his right cheek, breaking a tooth. When the stunning numbness gave way to pain, he turned back to the corn to seek assistance only to be hit in the left thigh, the bullet spinning him around and knocking him down.[77]

One survivor called the slaughter on both sides "enormous." Walker Barcus of Harmony fell wounded, discovered he could not run, and yelled, "Here is where you get your stiff legs!" Pvt. Reuben Sherman shot at a Rebel flag and saw it fall. He was boasting how he had "fetched it" when a bullet struck and paralyzed his arm. By this time Deleglise was again on his feet. He hobbled toward the fence, dropped behind it, and loaded the musket. He aimed at a color bearer in "a solid line of rebels 60 feet away," but another ball caught him on the upper right side of his forehead before he could fire. "Not feeling equal, under the circumstances, to the emergency of a struggle with a solid line of advancing foes," he wrote with poetic understatement, Deleglise dropped the musket, pulled off his cartridge box and belts, and limped back through the bloody corn.[78]

The air was filled with a "hail-storm of bullets," wrote a survivor. The fighting at "Gainesville, Bull Run, South Mountain were respectably battles, but the

---

77 *Soldiers' and Citizens' Album*, vol. 1, 722. Gaffney was discharged due to disability. After the war he was a farmer in Osceola in Fond du Lac County, where he served several terms as town clerk. Watrous, "Bragg's Rifle," *Milwaukee Sunday Telegraph*, January 4, 1880.

78 Frank A. Haskell, letter to his brothers and sisters, September 22, 1862; Dawes, *Service*, 93-94; *Soldiers' and Citizens' Album*, vol. 1, 722.

intensity and energy of the fight and the roar of firearms, they were but skirmishes in comparison to this of Sharpsburg."[79] By this time the front of the attacking Union line resembled something akin to a surging crowd, the soldiers biting cartridges, ramming and firing, and repeating the process. Dawes perhaps summed this part of the fighting best: "Whoever stood in front of the corn field at Antietam needs no praise."

Steady Infantry Work

The Federal line was fighting along the cornfield's southern fence with the Confederates slowly giving way in what had evolved into a furious musket fight punctuated with fitful bursts of artillery. Another thick line of the enemy with red flags emerged from the woods to the southwest. These men belonged to William Starke's Louisiana brigade and a Virginia-Alabama brigade led by E. T. H. Warren. This new threat, about 1,100 men, opened "murderous" volleys that staggered Dawes' line. Lieutenant Colonel Allen of the 2nd Wisconsin ordered a change of front to the right. He halted his men at the roadway fence, where they began piling fence rails for a make-shift barricade. The 6th Wisconsin moved in on Allen's right; other Federals extended the line westward. Other Confederates fired into the exposed flank as a supporting second line of Federals came up with a loud shout, moving into the Union lines to close "the awful gaps."[80]

One of the arriving regiments was the famous 14th Brooklyn in their colorful red trowsers. "Now is the pinch," explained Dawes. "Men and officers of New York and Wisconsin are fused into a common mass, in the frantic struggle to shoot fast. Every body tears cartridge, loads, passes guns, or shoots. Men are falling in their places or running back into the corn." It was a defining moment in this part of the fighting. Dawes continued: "The soldier who is shooting is furious in his energy. The soldier who is shot looks around for help with an imploring agony of death on his face. After a few rods of advance, the line stopped by common

---

79 Frank A. Haskell, letter to brothers and sisters, September 22, 1862; Dawes, *Service*, 93-94.

80 Carman, manuscript, 28; Dawes, journal, undated. The attacking line consisted of William Starke's Louisiana brigade and William B. Taliferro's brigade of Alabama and Virginia regiments. Starke had about 650 men and Taliaferro about 500. Starke aimed his attack against the southwest corner of the cornfield, where the Wisconsin men made their appearance in pursuit of the three beaten Georgia regiments. The Federals extending the Union line were from the 2nd U.S. Sharpshooters. Report of Marsena Patrick, OR 19, pt. 1, 235. Patrick said his brigade was "35 paces" behind the Wisconsin line when he ordered his men to line down in the corn before moving up in support.

impulse, fell back to the edge of the corn and lay down on the ground behind the low rail fence."[81]

One of the last soldiers to leave the advance line to run back to the fence was Pvt. Bob Tomlinson of the 6th Wisconsin. The private was from the tough Mississippi River country and a good soldier. "God, you ain't going back, are you?" he asked his fellow retreating soldiers with "disappointment in every feature of his face." An officer tugged at his sleeve, but Tomlinson shook his head. "Not yet," he replied. "I have a few more cartridges left." Standing almost alone and well forward in an open field, Tomlinson fired his last rounds with cool deliberation, "a target for hundreds to turn their guns on," recalled an officer. When he finished, Tomlinson walked slowly back to the cornfield.[82]

One soldier described this part of the fighting as "steady infantry work," with the yelling Confederates pushing closer to exchange near point blank shots with the Wisconsin men crowded in the southwest corner of the cornfield and along the fence. Lieutenant Colonel Allen of the 2nd fell wounded. One of his soldiers, Horace Emerson of Portage, flinched in horror when the man in front of him was struck in the face and "blood and brains run out his shoes." Another 2nd Wisconsin man, William Harries, was shot in the left shoulder and left the field just as Alexander Hill of Portage was struck by a heavy lead bullet that drove into his groin a ring of keys carried in his pocket.[83] The Black Hats poured a sharp fire on Johnnies trying to climb the high fence across the road in fighting that was "fast, furious and deadly." More New Yorkers from Walter Phelps' supporting brigade moved into the embattled Union line, and the added musketry halted the Confederates, who clung grimly to the opposite fence. When "three cheers and a rattling fusillade" erupted off to the right and out of sight behind the Confederates,

81 Dawes, *Service*, 90.

82 Dawes, journal, undated; Dawes, *Service*, 214-215; Tomlinson, who enlisted from Diamond Bluff in the Prescott Guards, Company B, was later wounded at Gettysburg and captured at Haymarket, Virginia, a few months later. He died June 28, 1864, in the Confederate prison at Andersonville, Georgia. *Wisconsin Roster*, vol. 1, 405.

83 Dawes, *Service*, 214-215; Horace Emerson, letter to mother and sister, September 28, 1862. Emerson identified the soldier struck in the face as Gustave Elterman, and added: "He did not know what hit him. He was a good man and had never been hit before and had been in all the fights that the Regt had been in." Elterman, a native of Germany, was just eighteen when he enlisted at Portage April 19, 1861. Of Hill's wound, Emerson wrote: "It made a very bad wound and a very painful one." Otis, *Second Wisconsin*, 18. Charles Dow of the 2nd Wisconsin wrote on September 24, 1862: "I got a letter from Lieut. Hill the other day. He was wounded in the groin on the 17th. It is a bad wound, but not considered dangerous; he is doing well and going home (to his wife I suppose) as soon as he is able to ride." Dow, letter, September 24, 1862. Hill resigned June 1, 1863. *Wisconsin Roster*, vol. 1, 364.

a Wisconsin soldier fighting in the corn yelled, "Bully! Bully! Up and at them again. Our men are giving them hell on the flank." The ceaseless musket fighting had been going on for about 30 minutes.[84]

The new musketry eruption emanated from the 7th Wisconsin and 19th Indiana. When he spotted Confederates moving to the Hagerstown Pike, Col. John Callis of the 7th Wisconsin swung his Black Hats to the left to a waist-high rocky ledge where they could fire into the rear of Starke's advancing Louisiana brigade. The Confederate advance rolled up to the rail fence on the pike and opened fire in places as close as thirty yards. Bullets splintered fence rails and knocked down men on both sides, but the tactical excellence of the 7th Wisconsin and other troops was the undoing of the Confederate thrust. When Gibbon ordered a section of Battery B to move up another fifty yards to sweep the roadway and its fences, Lt. James Stewart protested that his guns and limbers would be exposed to small arms fire. When Adj. Frank Haskell dismissed Stewart's objection, a two-gun section rolled up, deployed, and added its deep-throated bass tones to the higher pitched musketry action. "We were brought up in rear of a brigade of Rebels and laid in the woods and fired 20 rounds before we was discovered," was what one Badger wrote home. "After they discovered our position they threw down their arms and broke for the woods (what was left of them). Then we had fun picking them off. Killed every one of them," he boasted, "even a wounded man could not be seen creeping off without being plugged by a minie. They refused to surrender to us, but had to our minie balls."[85]

With the Confederates on the run, the Wisconsin and New York troops jumped the fences on the southern edge of the cornfield and pushed into the open field beyond. "The men are loading and firing with demonical fury and shouting and laughing hysterically and the whole field before us is covered with rebels fleeing for life, into the woods," said Dawes afterward. "Great numbers of them are shot while climbing over the high post and rail fences along the turnpike. We push on over the open fields. . . . The powder is bad, and the guns have become very dirty. It takes hard pounding to get the bullets down, and our firing is becoming slow."[86] The disordered Federal line crested the ridge and continued south down a long slow slope. Several hundred yards ahead was a small white church on the eastern fringe of the West Woods. It was about 7:00 a.m.

---

84 Dawes, journal, undated.

85 Hugh Perkins, letter to a friend, September 26, 1862. The letter was to Herbert Frisbie, great-grandfather of Gardner.

86 Dawes, journal, undated.

Dawes watched a "long and steady line of rebel gray" emerge from the woods around the church. This, he would later learn, was the division of John Bell Hood and included his famous Texas Brigade. The Johnnies had been called from their cook fires in a last-ditch attempt to stem the Federal advance. Hood's 2,300 soldiers crossed a pasture south of the cornfield in a charge that would become fabled in the annals of the Confederate Army of Northern Virginia. The Confederates gave a loud yell and halted to allow fleeing survivors to pass through their line. Once their field of fire was clear, Hood's men lifted muskets and squeezed off a ripping volley of bullets "like a scythe running through our line," said Dawes. "The auspicious moment has passed. The great victory has passed away from our grasp. Five minutes sooner and our reinforcements would have broken the enemy in the rear." The Badgers and New Yorkers turned and made for the corn as fast as they could. "The Sixth and its support were too weak in numbers to withstand this force and were pushed back, fighting as they went," Lt. Col. Bragg wrote in a report for his 6th regiment at Antietam. "It is not to be presumed they had a dress parade alignment after the blows they had given and received that morning, but acted as if he thought he was the Sixth Wis., and had its honor in his every man of the Sixth keeping."[87]

With the contest suddenly going against them, it was a "race for life" with Black Hats and other Federals tumbling backward in chaotic retreat, companies and regiments disorganized and intertwined. By this time most cartridge boxes were empty and muskets fouled and hard to load. A bullet stung the calf of Dawes' leg but did not slow him down. Back to the corn and back through the corn, the line retreated. The Johnnies, firing from behind and from along the fences lining the turnpike, caught the retreating soldiers in a vicious crossfire. Knots of bluecoats tried to stem the tide to no avail. Now and then a squad would make a stand here or there only to suffer through a flurry of shooting that hastened their retreat. The veritable storm of lead and iron splintered rails and slapped through the corn stalks. Battery B's guns slammed heavy blasts of canister into the corn and against the Confederates crossing the field between the woods and the pike. Dawes grabbed the blue Wisconsin state flag from a color bearer near the northern end of the cornfield and waved it over his head to rally his men. Within minutes several dozen Black Hats gathered around him. Broke and disorganized soldiers stumbled out of the corn stalks in twos and threes; every man able to hold and fire a musket would be needed. Behind them could be heard the screams of pursuing Confederates

---

87 Dawes, *Service*, 90-91; Dawes, journal, undated; Edward Bragg, letter to Carman, December 26, 1894.

surging toward Battery B's flaming guns. For a time it seemed the six bronze Napoleons might be lost.[88]

The artillerymen—Regular and volunteer alike—had been doing good work from the first light. No sooner had the 2nd and 6th Wisconsin reached the southern edge of the cornfield than did Gibbon begin moving the guns forward. The right two-gun section under Stewart was the first to reach the advanced position west of the Hagerstown Pike in an open field forward of two stacks of straw. The two guns came up on the run, swung around and dropped their tails with practiced smoothness, and opened fire. The loud crashing musketry was clearly heard rolling back toward them after the Union line broke and retreated. Stewart called for spherical case shot with the fuses crimped to burst just one and one-half seconds after leaving the muzzles—near point blank range.[89]

Stewart's battery's included 15-year-old bugler Johnny Cook of Cincinnati. "No sooner had we unlimbered when a column of Confederate infantry, emerging from the so-called west woods, poured a volley into us, which brought fourteen or seventeen of my brave comrades to the ground," wrote the bugler. "It was a sickening sight to see those poor, maimed, and crippled fellows crowding on top of one another [behind the straw], while several stepping a few feet away, were hit again and killed." Stewart's horse fell in the hail of bullets, spilling him to the ground, but he jumped up unhurt and ran to the limbers to gather a makeshift force of horse holders and drivers to take the places of the downed gunners. The other four Napoleons of Battery B arrived and were rolled into position on the left of Stewart's two guns. Three were at the top of a gentle slope, two slightly advanced, the far left gun in the turnpike behind the others. The ammunition limbers with horses and drivers crowded into a narrow space bounded by the guns, the Hagerstown Pike fence on the left, and a barnyard fence behind them.[90]

88 Gibbon, *Telegraph*, December 5, 1880.

89 Ibid.; Stewart's report, *OR* 19, pt. 1, 231. Stewart cited Meeds' "cheerful and very effective service." Meeds, of Perry, Wisconsin, was a member of Company B. He would be wounded at Chancellorsville in 1863, discharged on January 31, 1864, but would later enlist in the Regular Army. *Wisconsin Roster*, vol. 1, 503. A 12-pound Napoleon could be fired two or three times a minute.

90 "John Cook, the Boy Gunner," in W. F. Beyer and O. F. Keydel, eds., *Deeds of Valor*, 2 vols. (Detroit, MI, 1903), vol. 2, 75-76; Gibbon, *Milwaukee Sunday Telegraph*, December 5, 1880. Cook was born August 10, 1847, and was 14 when he enlisted. Gibbon reported three cannoneers were killed and 11 wounded in the space of a few minutes. Bugler Cook was not related to John "Tough One" Cook of the 6th Wisconsin. Both served with the battery at the same time.

Part IV: Butchery Along the Hagerstown Turnpike

Into the Cornfield

While the six guns of Battery B of the 4th U.S. artillery fired to stem the Confederate advance, a "terrific fire" of musketry erupted in the cornfield. The confusion and smoke made it difficult for General Gibbon to determine the progress of his brigade or what was happening. Wounded men poured out of the corn, including Edward Bragg, who warned Gibbon the Black Hats were being flanked. The cornfield was a hellish swirl of smoke and shouting soldiers, the air full of bullets and exploding shells.[1] It was about thirty minutes into the advance, and the fighting seemed to be rolling back through the corn toward Gibbon's prized bronze guns. Out of the shambles of the bullet-ripped field, "torn and broken and with thinned ranks," reported Gibbon, tumbled the black-hatted survivors of the 6th and 2nd Wisconsin and those of Phelp's brigade. Artillerymen and horses were falling at alarming rate, and his brigade looked to be broken and in disorder.[2] Just ahead, advancing Rebels were firing at point-blank range into the gun crews and horses. "It seems almost incredible that any man could have escaped in a battery working in an open field with veteran infantry under dense cover sharpshooting at it with 28 or 30 paces," related one gunner. The gunners were using canister and then double canister. Captain Joseph Campbell was down. "He had dismounted when he was hit twice, and his horse fell dead with several bullets in the body," wrote teen bugler Cook. "I started with the captain to the rear and turned him over to one of the drivers. He ordered me to report to Lieutenant Stewart and tell him to take command of the battery." The steady firing of Battery B's guns began to falter.

1 Buell, *Cannoneer*, 34; Carman, manuscript, 59-60.

2 Gibbon, *Milwaukee Sunday Telegraph*, December 5, 1880; Edward Bragg, letter to Ezra Carman, December 26, 1894; Gibbon, Recollections, 83-84.

Capt. Joseph B. Campbell, Battery B, 4th U.S. Artillery

Campbell was in command of the battery opposite the cornfield when he was seriously wounded in the neck, shoulder, and side. *Scott D. Hann Collection*

Turning back toward the guns, Cook came upon a dead artilleryman, struck down while carrying ammunition to the guns. "I unstrapped the pouch, started for the battery, and worked as a cannoneer," said the 15-year-old, who would one day be awarded a Congressional Medal of Honor for his service.[3] Moving along the firing guns, Stewart organized his crews to maintain a steady rate of fire. When he spotted an infantry volunteer trying to jam two complete canister rounds with powder bags attached into the gun he was serving, Stewart stopped to show the soldier how to knock off the powder container of the second round against the hub of the wheel. The volunteer did as instructed, only to painfully slam his finger on the metal rim. After that, explained Stewart, every second round went into the muzzle powder and all just as it came from the arsenal.[4] The heavy blasts from the double-charged 12-pounders deafened and stunned the men working the guns, who pushed the pieced back into place after each recoil. The Regulars trained the new men and infantry volunteers to stand on their toes to absorb the concussion, explained volunteer Henry B. Foster of the

---

3 "John Cook," 75-76.

4 A canister round was made up of a powder charge and a metallic container filled with cast-iron or lead balls or long slugs set in dry sawdust. The canister ruptured on firing, scattering the slugs much like a round fired from a modern-day shotgun. It was mainly used against infantry and had an effective range of between 100 and 400 yards. Occasionally, a gun would fire double or even triple canister. In those cases, the drill called for the powder container to be broken off the second round before loading.

2nd Wisconsin. Foster was holding a lead team, but left the horses to another man to carry ammunition to one of the pieces. Some of the men tied handkerchiefs around their heads to ease the pounding, but "I have seen some of our men bleed at the nose and be deaf for a number of days after a hard battle, and . . . you know that them twelve pound brass guns is the worst kind to be close to when firing."[5]

When Henry Klinefelter, a 7th Wisconsin man serving as an artillery gunner, noticed the two guns to his right had stopped firing he discovered "all the men were shot down."[6] Two or three of the injured gunners "crawled on their hands and knees several times from the limber to the pieces and loaded and fired those guns in that way until they had recoiled so far that they could not use them any more. Not until then were they entirely silenced." Another 7th Wisconsin volunteer serving in the battery less than a week was Horace Ripley of Bristol. Left with the limbers, Ripley helped a wounded sergeant to the rear. He was given a pair of horses to hold when he returned to the battery. One animal was hit in the flank, its thrashing body and hooves threatening Ripley as he danced out of danger. "In a moment," he said, the second horse "had his bits complexly shot out of his mouth, carrying away his whole under jaw." One of the Regular artillerymen stepped out of the smoke with a belt revolver, walked over to the crazed animal, and "blew his brains out to put him out of his misery." The young Badger was sent forward to carry ammunition to one of the embattled Napoleons, but within minutes enemy bullets knocked out everyone serving the piece except Ripley and one other man.[7]

Despite the killing blasts of double canister and musketry, the yelling Confederates seemed about to carry all before them. John Johnson of Janesville, one of the 2nd Wisconsin men, was working a handspike with Sgt. Joseph Herzog to shift a gun back into firing position. The piece had fired 10 to 15 rounds of canister in what Johnson later called "as fierce and murderous a combat as ever surged about a six-gun battery." Herzog was shot through the lower bowels and slumped against the trail of the piece in great agony. Johnson watched in horror as

---

5   Foster enlisted at Racine on April 23, 1861. He was detached to Battery B from November 27, 1861, until June 18, 1864. He was mustered out June 28, 1861, term expired. *Wisconsin Roster*, vol. 1, 363.

6   Klinefelter enlisted in Co. D, 7th Wisconsin in 1861 and served with that regiment until he transferred to battery B of the 4th U.S. Artillery on March 7, 1862. He served with the battery until January 1864. He was wounded at the Wilderness in May 1864 and mustered out on March 6, 1865. He accepted a commission with the 51st Wisconsin Infantry, but the war ended before the regiment was readied for the war. *Wisconsin Roster*, vol. 1, 552.

7   Buell, *Cannoneer*, 38-39. Ripley was transferred to Battery B on September 12, 1862, and served with the guns until August 1864. He mustered out on September 1, 1864, at the end of his enlistment. *Wisconsin Roster*, vol. 1, 547.

the tough Regular pulled a belt revolver and shot himself in the right temple. Not far away, Gibbon watched the gunners and horses "falling thick and fast in the combined space." The crew working a Napoleon on the pike was down to just four men. The piece was on an incline, so every time the gun fired it rolled backward, tipping the muzzle higher into the air. "In the hurry and excitement of the battle," said Gibbon, the elevating screw was permitted to run down (as it will do in firing) until . . . the muzzle was sticking up in the air in such a way as to throw the projectiles entirely over the heads of the closely approaching enemy." Gibbon spurred his mount toward the skeleton crew shouting, "Run, run up the elevating screw," but could not be heard above the noise and confusion.[8] Gibbon swung off his horse and, to the astonishment of the watching artillerymen, ran up the gun and shouldered aside Henry Klinefelter. The general straddled the trail of the gun to spin the elevating screw so the canister blast would bounce off the ground into the advancing Confederates. Gibbon jumped away and yelled, "Give them hell boys!" nodding to the man on the lanyard. The heavy gun bucked, the rear of the tube lifting in recoil as Gibbon ducked under the smoke to see the discharge. The blast "carried away most of the fence in front of it" and produced "great destruction in the enemy ranks." Hood's Confederates, wrote Gibbon, "got so close to the battery in this desperate attempt to capture it that that pieces were double-shotted with canister before which whole ranks went down, and after we got possession of the field, dead men were found on top of each other." The men rolled the gun forward to fire again. During one of the hurried firings, Sgt. John Mitchell was badly hurt when the gun recoiled over him.[9]

A 6th Wisconsin soldier stumbled out of the ruins of the cornfield carrying his regiment's blue state flag and a Confederate banner he found on the ground.

---

8 "John Cook," 114-115; Gibbon, *Recollections*, 83; Gibbon, *Milwaukee Sunday Telegraph*, December 5, 1880; Buell, *Cannoneer*, 34-35.

9 Often discussed around Black Hat campfires was how the Confederates missed killing Gibbon that morning as he stood amongst the guns. "His escape was miraculous," marveled one soldier, "as he wore the full uniform of a Brigadier-General, and the enemy was so close they could not help discerning his rank, unless the smoke obscured him." Bugler Cook agreed, adding that Gibbon "was very conspicuous, and it is indeed surprising, that he came away alive." Buell, *Cannoneer*, 39; Gibbon, *Recollections*, 83-84. After the war, William Harries shared the story of Gibbon and his old battery at Antietam with former Confederate Harry Heth, who had been a classmate of Gibbon's at West Point. "John, did you leave your brigade during a fight and act as gunner of your old battery?" Heth asked his old friend during a conversation at the Army and Navy Club at Washington. "Why, you should have been court-martialed for it." Gibbon replied, "Yes, I did do that. I knew the men of my old brigade would fight without me and just at that particular moment that gun needed looking after to make its fire effective." Harries, "In the Ranks at Antietam," 262.

Unsure what to do, the man approached Gibbon near the guns, but the general had no time for trophies. "Throw down the flag and take your place in ranks!" snapped the general. Not one to disobey an order—especially from an excited general—he did as he was told. A few seconds later, Gibbon "grimed and black with powder," found Major Dawes at the edge of the cornfield rallying his broken regiment. "Hurray for the Sixth! Three cheers men, for the Sixth!" Gibbon shouted. "Major, bring your men over and save that gun," he added, pointing to the long Napoleon on the roadway. With the state flag in hand, Dawes waved it above his head and ran to the artillery piece. "Let every man from Wisconsin follow me!" he called. Looking back, Dawes would write, "it did not seem possible then to carry that flag into the deadly storm and live." Soon, gathered around him was "every 'black hat' within sight of the blue emblem of the Badger state." Also coming up were men from the 20th New York State Militia, sent to support Battery B. The moment of decision had arrived. The Wisconsin survivors and New Yorkers pushed ahead to shoot at the Confederates in the corn. The enemy, recalled Bugler Cook, made "three desperate attempts to capture us, the last time coming with ten or fifteen feet."[10]

A 2nd Wisconsin man working the guns "as if artillery was his forte" remembered the "terrible ordeal" lasted fewer than ten minutes, during which Gibbon and his gunners "literally filled the air with fence rails, haversacks, guns and limbs of rebel soldiers." Dawes was "fairly stunned [by] a report as of a thunderclap" from a Napoleon near him firing a double blast of canister that threw "the rails of a fence" high into the air. When all seemed lost, a line of blue infantry came sweeping from the right across the field in front of the battery and into Hood's Rebels holding the southwestern quarter of the Miller cornfield.[11] It was "our gallant Nineteenth Indiana," exclaimed Dawes. On its left was the 7th Wisconsin, with three other New York regiments from Patrick's brigade joining the counterattack. The Federals fired into the flank of the Confederate attack, halted under a hot exchange of musketry, and rolled forward again with a loud yell.

The genesis of this counter assault began with the skirmishers of the 19th Indiana, who spotted Hood's men closing on Battery B from their position in the fringes of the West Woods. Lieutenant Colonel Alois Bachman, who could not see

---

10 Buell, *Cannoneer*, 34; "John Cook," 75-76.

11 Dawes, journal, undated; Dawes, "Sketches of War History," 252-263; Gibbon, *Recollections*, 82-84; John Gibbon, letter to James Stewart, August 4, 1893, National Archives, Antietam Studies; "John Cook," 76; Edward Bragg letter to Carman, December 26, 1894; "Choice Reminiscences," *Milwaukee Sunday Telegraph*, March 4, 1883; It was Gibbon's recollection the 20th New York did not advance beyond the caissons of Battery B.

the Rebels because of a rocky ledge, called in his skirmishers and sent runners to the 7th Wisconsin and the New York regiments: he was changing front for an attack. With the 7th Wisconsin coming up on its left, the 19th Indiana moved to the rocky ledge and opened fire on the Confederates. Some of the Rebels fled, but most stood ground. When the Hoosiers began shouting "Charge! Charge!" Bachman pushed through his line and looked right and left. He had been with these men since the first days of the war. "Boys, the command is no longer forward, but now it is follow me!" he called. Hat in hand and sword drawn, Bachman led his yelling Hoosiers into the open. The 7th Wisconsin joined the attack, followed by the 21st and 35th New York (with the 23rd New York in support). The Confederates stood for a short time before turning to run. One regiment, the 4th Texas, was in danger of being cut off. The Texans tried to move by the left flank, halted, and fired into the Black Hats. The crashing musket fire knocked back the Badgers and the Texans slipped away.

The Hoosiers of the 19th drove forward, crossing the Hagerstown Pike into the cornfield before wheeling right to follow fleeing Confederates to the brow of the ridge. There, not far from the small white church, another line of enemy infantry was seen moving northward through abandoned artillery pieces. A murderous volley swept through the Indiana ranks. A bullet struck Bachman on his right elbow and spun him around. A second shot pierced his body, killing him instantly. "We got into a hornet's nest" and were "nearly cut to pieces," remembered one of the Indiana Black Hats. With Bachman down, command fell to a young man of nineteen named William Dudley, the youngest captain in the line. Just months before he had been quietly milling grain in Richmond, Indiana. Now, the boyish captain was doing his best to keep his men together and alive.

Rebels seemed to cover the front, and everyone was shooting. A group of men carried Bachman's body to the rear. Dudley ordered the Indiana regiment to fall back to the road, where it rallied with the 7th Wisconsin on its left and Patrick's men gathered farther north. The line held there for a time. Without warning, Confederates fired from the West Woods and advanced north. The exhausted Federals gave way again, rallied, changed front, and continued firing. Muskets were so hot and dirty that the Indiana boys had to throw their ramrods into the barrels to thump down the ball. Finally, when the Rebel attack fell apart and withdrew into the timber, Dudley pulled back his command to a rocky ledge where some of Patrick's soldiers and the 7th Wisconsin were stitching together yet another make-shift line. With cartridge boxes empty or nearly so, the Indiana and Wisconsin regiments fell back north, leaving the New Yorkers behind. The battle continued just a couple hundred yards to the east as a fresh Southern attack drove toward the cornfield and the East Woods. Patrick's men also withdrew soon thereafter to a meadow near the Miller barn in search of fresh ammunition and new orders.[12]

One soldier described the charge of the 19th Indiana and its fellow regiments as "gallant, but ill-advised," but an officer of the Iron Brigade credited the furious rush with saving Battery B. The quick and timely advance, he argued, was made "regardless of consequences to themselves, but to protect Battery B, and save their Brigade brothers so hard pressed in the cornfield. It was bold, and it was bravely met, as the line of dead along that pike on that front testified more forcibly than word may do."[13]

With the Confederate attack turned back, fighting west of the pike dribbled to a close. When Gibbon ordered Battery B to the rear, the damaged teams and enervated gunners worked like fiends to haul their guns out. "The attack was beaten off, the bullets gradually ceased to come, and during the lull the battery was rapidly limbered to the rear and quickly withdrawn from its dangerous position," wrote Gibbon, "leaving the corner of the field thick strewn with its dead men and horses, while the thinner ranks of the brigade followed after it."[14] The 2nd Wisconsin man serving with the battery hopped a caisson with one of the Regulars. The caisson had only rolled "a few rods when the thing turned over and came near breaking their necks," wrote a witness. "They got the thing righted and made another start when the caisson blew up; the full force of the charge went out of the end on which sat the regular, and blew him into shreds," while the Badger was "stood on his ear" into apple tree tops that had been cut off and piled in heaps. Somewhat worse for wear, the Black Hat calmly brushed himself off. "For the first day in a battery I've been used rather rough," he commented to a man standing nearby. He had been serving the battery only 20 minutes, he added, and was fully convinced "that battery was inclined to take too many risks."[15]

---

12 Carman, manuscript, 60-62; Jeffry D. Wert, *A Brotherhood of Valor: The Common Soldiers of the Stonewall Brigade, C.S.A., and the Iron Brigade, U.S.A.* (New York, NY, 1999), 183.

13 Dawes, *Service*, 91; Dawes, journal, undated; Edward Bragg, letter to Carman, December 26, 1894; William Dudley's report, OR 19, pt. 1, 252; Stine, *Army of the Potomac*, 193. The Confederate line on the brow of the hill south of the Miller cornfield was made up of survivors of Roswell Ripley's brigade. Carman, manuscript, 59-60.

14 Gibbon, *Milwaukee Sunday Telegraph*, December 5, 1880.

15 *Milwaukee Sunday Telegraph*, March 4, 1883. Another incident often related at veteran meetings involved the fighting at Antietam. One of the brigade chaplains, a pious man who was "always at hand when the boys were double shooting, sleeves rolled up, working their guns to the best." As he watched, one gunner stepped back before firing, telling comrades, "Now boys, give 'em hell!" The clergyman stepped in to reprimand the gunner. "How do you expect to have the support of Divine Providence when you use such language!" The gunner gave the chaplain

A Wisconsin officer boasted his regiment rallied to save the battery as "readily and cheerfully as for a companion in arms." The heavy bronze guns "had voices," he continued, "and the voice of B had always been to them the forerunner of victory, and they loved the guns as if they were part of themselves." Gibbon, too, admitted that the escape of his pet Napoleons was very close indeed. "Had we succeeded even in getting the pieces out through the double gate-ways of the barn yard, there beyond was that long straight stretch of turnpike, perfectly under command of the enemy the moment his riflemen reached the top of this little ridge up where the guns stood. A single horse killed or badly wounded in that narrow 'gorge' and Battery B would be numbered among the trophies of Lee's Army." One of the gunners, a veteran of several fights, remembered the service of September 17, 1862, as the hardest of the war for Battery B. "The recruits of 1863, even with Gettysburg on their records, always took off their caps to the old Antietam boys whenever there was a campfire debate about prowess, and cordially yielded the palm to the Iron veterans who had braved the butchery of that fatal Cornfield on the Sharpsburg Pike."[16]

What Grim-Looking Fellows They Were

With the guns leaving the front, Major Dawes set about gathering the survivors of his 6th Wisconsin on the pike. When he spotted Brig. Gen. Abner Doubleday nearby, Dawes informed the division commander of his availability. Doubleday told him to remain in position. A few minutes later, Gibbon arrived and ordered the young major to withdraw his men to the North Woods, replenish ammunition, and await orders. "Bullets, shot and shell, fired by the enemy in the corn-field, were still flying thickly around us, striking the trees in the woods and cutting off the limbs," observed Dawes as he marched his regiment back to the trees and halted it in their shade. Next came the grim task of calling the roll to determine the regiment's "dreadful losses." The Wisconsin regiment carried 315 officers and men into the battle. Company C drew skirmish line duty that morning and escaped the heaviest fighting with only two casualties of the thirty-five engaged. Of the 280 men who

---

a hard look. "To hell with the Divine Providence, the Iron Brigade supports us," he shot back—or at least that is how the story was told long after the war. Cheek and Pointon, *Sauk County*, 214.

16 Gibbon, *Milwaukee Sunday Telegraph*, December 5, 1880; Edward Bragg, letter to Earl Rogers, April 5, 1900; Aubrey, *Echoes*, 51; Buell, *Cannoneer*, 35. For additional detail, see generally, Ezra A. Carman, *The Maryland Campaign of September 1862, Vol. II, Antietam*, Thomas G. Clemens, ed. (Savas Beatie: El Dorado Hills, CA, 2012).

fought in and around the cornfield and on the turnpike, 150 were killed, wounded, or missing. "This was the most dreadful slaughter to which our regiment had been subjected during the war," Dawes penned in his memoir. A short time later, the survivors were joined by the wounded Capt. George Ely of Janesville and 18 men from the 2nd Wisconsin. The small contingent brought their flags with them. A short time later the 7th Wisconsin and 19th Indiana, powder-stained and weary, joined the line. "The roar of musketry to the front was very heavy," said Dawes. It was only perhaps 8:00 a.m. The long day of battle was just beginning.[17]

Several hundred yards to the east, long rips of musketry erupted when a fresh Union line assaulted the cornfield. Fugitives and wounded alike drifted through a variety of batteries toward surviving Black Hats. When the firing faded, it became apparent from the "tremendous number" of stragglers that the attack had been repulsed. Gibbon, who had been back at the front helping place artillery, described the "terrific fire of musketry" that filled the whole open space between the East Woods and West Woods with "a disorganized mass of panic-stricken men." Hundreds of men retreated by their right flank up the Hagerstown Pike and on both sides of it. "You must hold this woods, men," Gibbon told his Black Hats. To impress them with the importance of the moment, the general drew his sword ("a thing I never had done before in battle") only to find the hilt guard damaged by a bullet. Farther south, musketry broke out near the cornfield and Dunker Church.

The thin line of Black Hats—perhaps 500 all told—was ordered to drive back "at the point of the bayonet all men who were fit for duty at the front." Before long, large regiments hurried toward them "with their boxes half full of cartridges," wrote a disgusted Dawes. Among the tangle of confused and frightened men was Brig. Gen. Willis Gorman, the same Gorman who had refused to relieve the 6th Wisconsin at South Mountain because "all men are cowards in the dark." The fighting in the cornfield had so disorganized and shaken the man that at first he did not react when some of the Wisconsin and Indiana men in line recognized him and raised catcalls. "Make way and let my regiment pass," Gorman instructed a lone Wisconsin private standing in front of the line. The soldier shook his head. "I was put here, sir, to stop stragglers, and can't disobey orders." The red-faced general stared back and, with more heat this time, demanded he clear the way. The private refused a second time while his watching brigade comrades nodded with grim satisfaction. "The regiment went around our line," Dawes wrote with no little pride.

A new reserve formation was being pulled together behind the Black Hats. By 11:00 a.m. the fighting in the northern sector of the battlefield was all but over and

17 Dawes, journal, undated; Cheek and Pointon, *Sauk County*, 51-52.

the brigade moved farther north behind a heavy line of artillery near where they had spent the previous night.[18] The survivors were "greatly astonished" to find Lieutenant Colonel Bragg waiting for them, his wounded arm looped in a handkerchief sling. The bullet, explained Bragg, had only severely bruised him. Three cheers rent the air, for most believed he had been killed. "He was severely wounded and unfit for duty, but he was there and we had believed him to be dead," wrote Dawes. If the regiment was surprised to see Bragg, he never forgot how they looked that morning north of Sharpsburg. "What grim-looking fellows they were which came back! Powder-stained, tired and hungry, but proud of what they had done, and ready to do it over again, so far as their numbers could permit." The bloody cornfield, wrote another Badger, vomited "companies commanded by sergeants with less than a dozen men of the hundred they had gone to war with." The Wisconsin and Indiana men had been marching, fighting, or both for three days with empty haversacks.[19]

While Gibbon and his men took stock of their survival, the fighting that was already underway farther south along the Sunken Lane intensified. Early in the afternoon, a lone soldier arrived to ask after the colonel of the 6th Wisconsin. George Fink had finally caught up with the regiment. The private saluted Bragg and explained that he had eighty descriptive lists to turn over with a squad of recruits. "He asked me if I couldn't wait until after the battle, as if he were to be killed the lists would do him no good," Fink recalled after the war. "I explained I wanted to get into that battle as well as he did. . . . I do not like to tell just how profane the language used to me at the time, as I was used to it then." Some of the boys gathered around Fink to ask about the folks and any news from back home. About 4:00 p.m., orders arrived for the men to remain in the line but lie down. The fighting had moved farther south near the lower bridge. "The rebels were shelling us, but it did not last for a long time, and that was the last of the battle [for us]," wrote Fink. A short time later Bragg, who had gone to the rear to find a sutler, returned with two barrels of molasses cookies. "There were no rations left to supply the yearning, empty stomachs for food," he explained. The cookies were distributed, and the boys "were content."[20]

18 Dawes, journal, undated; Dawes, *Service*, 92; Gibbon, *Recollections*, 87-89.

19 Dawes, *Service*, 92-93; Dawes, journal, undated; Edward Bragg, letter to Earl Rogers, April 3, 1900; Watrous, *Milwaukee Telegraph*, September 26, 1896.

20 Edward Bragg, letter to Earl Rogers, April 3, 1900; Watrous, *Milwaukee Telegraph*, September 26, 1896.

The Bloodiest Day of the War

The final fighting at Antietam involved a large-scale Federal thrust on the southern end of the field directed by Ambrose Burnside against the heights around the town of Sharpsburg. It was the last in a long series of unsuccessful and largely uncoordinated Federal attacks that day. Lee's army had been hanging on by a thread facing disaster all day, but Little Mac failed to press his advantage of numbers fearing that fresh Confederates in large number were waiting in the woods just ahead or behind the next rise. For most of the day there were no additional Confederates. Lee and his officers met every challenge by stripping portions of the long Southern line, shuffling regiments from the far right to center and far left to absorb Union attacks and often to contain Union breakthroughs. By the time Burnside crossed the lower bridge, organized his attack, and set off west toward Sharpsburg late that afternoon, there were precious few Confederates standing in his way. Just then, without an hour to spare, a footsore division under A. P. Hill arrived after a seventeen mile forced march from captured Harpers Ferry. The Rebels came onto the field exactly where they were needed and launched themselves immediately into action. Their determined counterattacks threw back Burnside and ended the fighting. McClellan had large commands that had not fired a shot that day, but they did not see action and the opportunity to win the battle—and perhaps trap and destroy Lee's Army against the wide Potomac—faded with the sunlight.

"When night came it was realized not as much ground had been gained as the Federals had at 10 o'clock when Hooker's Corps was relieved," wrote Gibbon. "It was generally supposed that the battle would recommence the next morning." When the sun rose on the 18th and the hours ticked past without renewed fighting (for reasons that were not clear to the men in ranks), both spent armies maintained their positions. Despite thousands of fresh soldiers on hand, McClellan weighed the risks and saw danger in every offensive move. Robert Lee, always eager to strike a blow, was unable to do anything because his small army had been nearly wrecked. He remained in place another day only because the fighting had continued until nearly nightfall on the 17th, and there were not enough hours to retreat safely across the Potomac's single ford before dawn. After a time, white flags appeared and the day was spent gathering wounded and burying some of the thousands of dead. My men, scribbled a Wisconsin officer in his journal, were "tired and worn out and in need of rest and quest."

The cost of the single day of fighting was simply horrific. Exact numbers will never be precisely determined, but 12,500 Federals were dead, wounded, or missing compared with more than 10,000 Confederates—roughly one of every four Federals and one in three Rebels. Some 3,600 men were killed outright; many hundreds more would die in the coming days. September 17, 1862, was the bloodiest single day of the Civil War, and still stands a century and a half later as the bloodiest in American history. Of the 800 officers and men in Gibbon's brigade, more than 340 fell killed and wounded, or 42 percent. Of the four regiments, the 6th Wisconsin suffered 152 casualties out of the 315 who fought that day. The 2nd Wisconsin lost eighteen killed, 67 wounded, and six missing for a total of 91 out of 150 engaged. Battery B rolled to the cornfield with 100 officers and men and lost nine killed and thirty-one wounded—extraordinary losses for an artillery command. Twenty-six horses were killed and seven wounded. Even First Corps commander Joseph Hooker did not emerge unscathed, shot in the foot late in the action in the northern sector.

Burial details began their grisly work of tending to the dead of the Western Brigade. They found Capt. Werner von Bachelle of the 6th Wisconsin on the turnpike with "his feet crossed and arms folded, his cap drawn forward over his eyes like a soldier taking his rest, his body riddled with bullets." The German's field glass was across his shoulder, "shattered into innumerable pieces and his faithful dog . . . was lying across his body dead." Edward Bragg counted a dozen wounds and wrote home that von Bachelle "was a soldier of fortune and died as he desired—a soldier in the front of a battle." Nearby lay Lt. William Bode and four men from his German Company F.[21] The dead of the 6th and 2nd Wisconsin were buried under "a locust tree on the right of the pike . . . close to the wood." Von Bachelle's body (with his dog) was interred with his feet to the south, with the enlisted men buried in a trench dug with a drag hoe from Battery B on the reverse side of the road.

The cornfield and surrounding area offered a panorama from Hell. "When we marched along the turnpike . . . the scene was indescribably horrible. Great numbers of dead, swollen and black under the hot sun, lay upon the field," Dawes recalled. "My horse as I rode through the narrow lane made by piling the bodies alongside the turnpike fences, trembled in every limb with fright and was wet with perspiration. Friend and foe were indiscriminately mingled." A 7th Wisconsin soldier wrote home, "you could walk one mile in one straight line and not step on the ground, but on dead men and horses." If he exaggerated, it was not by much. Gibbon found the ground "literally covered with dead bodies, they being specially

---

21 The wounded in the first flurry of fire on the turnpike included four members of Company F: Michael Basel, Leo Gotsch, Jacob Mueller, and John Schilcke. Basel and Gotsch mustered out with the regiment in 1865. Mueller was discharged at the end of his three-year enlistment. Schilcke was discharged March 18, 1864, for wounds received at Gettysburg and Fitzhugh's Crossing. Fink was discharged disabled on January 9, 1865, for a wound suffered during the Spotsylvania fighting at Laurel Hill in May 1864. *Wisconsin Roster*, vol. 1, 516-519.

numerous in the open field in front of Battery 'B' along the fence bordering the turnpike. In the cornfield, the bodies, in some cases were piled on top of each other." He said it was there "many a gallant Wisconsin man met his death. They were lying side by side with the dead grey coats and the peaceful cows which were caught there between the two fires and felled riddled with bullets." The field "was too terrible to behold without a shock. I never want to see another such," a Wisconsin officer wrote home. "I counted eighty rebels in one row along the fence in front of us lying so thick you could step from one to the other, and in others, they lay in heaps, mowed down, and many of our brave boys with them. So it was everywhere." Bragg of the 6th Wisconsin said the Rebels "fought like demons—but for once, they met their equals in pluck & muscle. They are the dirtyist, lousyist, filthiest, piratical looking cutthroats a white man every saw. There are no redeeming characters that I have seen. Officers & men alike—in filth & rags." One of the dead officers was a major of the 1st Texas. The officer ("with fiery courage worthy of a State having an 'Alamo' for its nursery cradle") had fallen within the lines of the 6th Wisconsin. "He was wearing a lady's watch presumably a talisman given him by a wife or fiancé," observed Bragg. The watch was sent to headquarters "to be returned to the donor."[22]

   "Some were killed so instantly that they never changed their position," noted a Black Hat. "Some was sitting up in the very act of loading, with their cartridges in their mouth and gun still in their hands. The Rebs fight like mad men. They will not leave the field until they are badly whipped and sometimes they don't get a chance to leave them alive." It was all very "gruesome," admitted another private. "Dead men and horses lying in grotesque shapes along side each other. Now and then the rebel dead would be found lying in heaps or long wind-rows, but some would be seen scattered about our people." A third soldier wrote that the men of his regiment were "much astonished at the number of rebels lying dead in a perfect line of battle, presenting a horrible appearance and stink from the effects of the sun, their blackened corpses lying in every imaginable shape. It is hard for me to put into words what I have seen", explained a 2nd Wisconsin man. "I thought I had seen men piled up and cut up in all kinds of shapes but never anything in comparison to that field." Both Julius Murray of the 6th Wisconsin and his son Lute emerged safely, the father serving as ambulance driver while his son fought in the cornfield.

---

22 Dawes, *Service*, 94-95; Horace Currier, letter, October 16, 1862; Edward Bragg, letter to wife, September 21, 1862; Longhenry, diary, September 18-20; Edward Bragg, letter to Carman, December 20, 1894. The dead Confederate officer was probably Matthew Dale, acting lieutenant colonel of the 1st Texas. *OR* 19, pt. 1, 923. Currier enlisted at Oasis, Wisconsin, in July 1861. He died August 15, 1863, in a hospital at Annapolis of chronic diarrhea. *Wisconsin Roster*, vol. 1, 569.

"Luty has been in every fight and has fought bravely, his pants were cut open the knee and several parts of his clothes bear the marks of bullets," Murray wrote home. "I am proud of him, but he shall not go into another fight if I can prevent it, and I think I can when the whole company has been cut down to 13. I think we have run our share of risks."[23]

The magnitude of the fighting was hard to deal with emotionally. The long hours at Sharpsburg cast a shadow over the survivors of the Iron Brigade that forever marked and changed the men in ways even they did not understand. By the morning of Antietam, only 800 of the Western Brigade were left when the four regiments tramped through the misty dawn past the Miller farm buildings. Even harder for the survivors to accept was the simple realization that they too might fall in the next round of fighting. "I never want to fight there again," Dawes wrote later about Antietam. "The flower of our regiment was slaughtered in that terrible corn-field there. I dread the thought of the place."

In letters home and across the pages of diaries and journals, soldiers penned a disturbing refrain—an almost off-hand manner in dealing with death and suffering. "I have had a full realization of the horrors and excitement of the battle field, and you can hardly comprehend its horrors after the battle is over," one Badger wrote home. "It is cheering and fighting while it lasts and under the excitement you do not much mind the shells bursting over your heads, the solid balls tearing up the ground and cutting trees down around you, the incessant peal of musketry among the universal din." He went on to reveal how the horrific moment of combat changed the survivors: "You become callous to those falling around you dead or wounded, in fact, we have all become callous, and the sights of dead piled up in every direction on which we would have looked with horror a few months ago, we carefully examine now to see which is friend or foe." Private Hugh Perkins of the 7th Wisconsin wrote to a friend how he had "seen hard times and a good deal more than I expected to. My comrades and tentmates have fell on each side of me, and I am still alive and without a scratch. I have had the balls come so close they made my face smart, but it didn't break the hide. It has got so that it does not excite me any more to be in action than to be in a corn field hoeing, or digging potatoes." Another 7th regiment man, Pvt. George Partridge, tried to explain the fighting to his sister. "I took aim at one several times," he explained, "but they always fell before I could fire. . . . But to tell the truth, I could not tell whether I killed any or not as they fell so fast . . . but I know I tried as hard as I could to kill some of them." Private Horace

23 Hugh Perkins, letter, to a friend, September 21, 1862; Cornelius Wheeler, journal, September 19, 1862, Wisconsin Historical Society; Horace Emerson, letter to mother and sister, September 28, 1862; Julius Murray, letter to a daughter, September 27, 1862.

Emerson of the 2nd Wisconsin told of a man in his company left on the field thirty hours before he was taken off for medical attention. "He said the men took his canteen and haversack telling him that he may as well die one way or another," wrote Emerson. "He was mortally wounded being shot through the bowels which is sure death but slow."[24]

If the numbing sights were making them callous, the same combat was also stirring a growing sense of resentment. Earl Rogers, an officer in the 6th Wisconsin, wrote bitterly that the dead of his brigade were quickly "carried to the trench and rot." Other officers, such as Captain Dudley of the 19th Indiana, found bravery and discipline in all the carnage "except the few who found their way to the rear when danger approached." Even Gibbon tried to find solace over the horrible cost of Antietam when writing of the dead: "Lying close together in death, as they had stood elbow to elbow in the battle of life, they sleep their last sleep on the very spot consecrated by their blood." When each body was covered with dirt, his friends cut the man's name, company, and regiment into a "chestnut board" and placed it at the head. One soldier was especially troubled because "Citizens by the thousands are wandering over the battlefield picking up souvenirs."[25]

When the sun rose on the second day after the battle, the Confederates had crossed the river back into Virginia. Gibbon's brigade marched across the battlefield to bivouac in woods near the Potomac west of Sharpsburg. The respite was a welcomed one after almost three weeks of heavy campaigning and fighting. Burial details left the ranks to bury the Confederate dead. It was "decidedly unpleasant work," grumbled one soldier, "as the weather was warm, and decomposition had set in."[26] The stench was overpowering. Each house, barn, shed, straw stack, fence, and any shelter from the sun now doubled as a medical facility. "Operating tables everywhere," one Black Hat wrote home. "It was not uncommon sight to see wagons drawing off loads of legs and arms to be buried from the temporary hospitals." Citizens from surrounding communities arrived in farm wagons and other vehicles with food and to assist getting care for the

---

24 Julius Murray, letter to a daughter, September 27, 1862; Hugh Perkins, letter to a friend, September 21, 1862; Horace Emerson, letter to mother and sister, September 28, 1862. George Washington Partridge Jr., *Letters from the Iron Brigade: George W. Partridge, Jr. 1839-1863 / Civil War Letters to His Sisters*, Hugh L. Whitehouse, ed. (Indianapolis, IN, 1944), 68.

25 *Milwaukee Free Press*, September 22, 1912; Edward Bragg, letter to Ezra Carman, December 26, 1894; Gibbon, *Milwaukee Sunday Telegraph*, December 5, 1880; Longhenry diary, September 19, 1862; Earl Rogers, *Vernon County* (WI) *Censor*, November 23, 1906. Von Bachelle's body was later moved to the Antietam National Cemetery and buried in the officer's section.

26 Wheeler, journal, September 19, 1862; Longhenry, diary, September 20, 1862.

wounded. "The ladies do all they can and as every large building is a hospital they have lotts to do," one of the wounded Western boys wrote home. A Wisconsin boy on a burial detail was given a biscuit by one of the citizens. "It was a tasty bite from civilization," he wrote in his diary that night. "We have had nothing to eat for a long time except crackers and water."

For all the bodies of dead soldiers, however, it was the ghastly apparition of a dead horse that left a lasting impression on Dawes. The animal was in front of the haystacks where Battery B had made its stand. The horse seemed to be "in the act of rising from the ground," wrote Dawes. "Its head was held proudly aloft, and its fore legs set firmly forward. Nothing could be more vigorous or life-like than the pose of this animal. But like all surrounding it on the horrid Aceldama, the horse was dead."[27]

A Pile of Arms and Legs as High as a Church Window

The makeshift field hospitals were a sea of misery. Doctors and others tried their best to keep the wounded alive, but the staggering number who needed assistance overwhelmed available resources. One Wisconsin man lay on the floor of a farm building where straw had been scattered for bedding. There were about 80 wounded there, all but a handful from Gibbon's brigade. The great need, the soldier explained, was "clean clothes to take the place of those saturated with blood. Many a poor fellow was obliged to see maggots crawling about his wound, because he had no clean shirts to put on." This state of affairs ended when "The sanitary commission came and supplied their wants. Words cannot tell how much those men suffered. Many were on the battle-field for hours, with life's blood ebbing away, and no relief at hand."[28]

Sergeant Jerome Watrous of the 6th Wisconsin was horrified by what he found during a visit to Andrew Deacon of his old company. Deacon was in a "little church hospital" at nearby Keedysville, "lying in a pew, white as a sheet, with his eyes closed." One arm had been amputated, and the stump wrapped in a bloody bandage. "How are you feeling, Andy?" Watrous asked. The wounded soldier's "black eyes opened" and he looked up to see his friend. "All right; I am sorry to lose this arm, but I am glad I was in that battle." The two talked for a while, and when Watrous prepared to leave, Deacon asked an odd favor: "I wish you would go back

27 William A. Frassanito, *Antietam: The Photographic Legacy of America's Bloodiest Day* (New York, NY, 1978).

28 William Harries, "Hospital Experiences," *Milwaukee Sunday Telegraph*, November 8, 1885.

to the church and find my arm and bury it. I don't feel right to have that neglected. They threw it out the window, but I think you can find it." Watrous promised he would do so and walked around to the back of the church where he saw "a sight I shall never forget. There was a pile of legs and arms which would fill two of the largest wagons you can see in the city of Milwaukee." And that was only one of two or three dozen hospitals, added Watrous. "Of course, I could not find poor Deacon's lost arm, but I hurried around among the surgeons and attendants and got a promise that all of the arms and legs should be buried and went back and told my stricken comrade. There was a tremble on his lips and a tear in his eye when he said, 'May be I will find it in the great future, when we all come out of our graves.'"[29]

Shot in the chest, Pvt. William Harries of the 2nd Wisconsin ended up in a private home. On the blanket next to him was Uriel Olin of La Crosse, a sergeant from his own regiment. Regimental Surgeon Dr. A. J. Ward came by on a regular basis to check on the two, and on one occasion gave the wounded men a sip of whiskey. Harries watched Olin die. "The wound he received through the bowels gave him great pain early in the evening but for an hour or more before the final dissolution he made no complaint and died without a struggle," wrote Harries. His own prognosis was just as grim when told "it was considered quite probably that I would be buried in the morning with Sergeant Olin as I was bleeding frequently from the mouth." Somehow Harries survived the night, and the next morning was moved to a barn where other wounded from Gibbon's brigade were being treated. "Until the Sanitary Commission came along we were in horrible condition. I do not care to describe my own; suffice to say that I felt like a new creature when I got a clean shirt."

In every medical facility and back in the regiments was an effort to send letters home to assure loved ones they were safe or to carry the sad news of husbands, brothers, friends who were maimed or dead. "I often think our women were greater heroes than we were," a Wisconsin man said later, "because when an engagement was over our anxiety was ended until the next one, while their suspense was of continual duration, and therefore so much harder to bear." Newspapers back home

29 Harries, *Milwaukee Sunday Telegraph*, November 8, 1885; Jerome A. Watrous, *Milwaukee Sunday Telegraph*, October 5, 1890. Watrous wrote that the sight of those amputated arms and legs "would cause the generation that has grown up since the war some of whose members feel a little disposed to laugh at old soldiers and to place a slight estimation upon their services, to confess that the war cost was something." Bragg wrote his wife September 21: "Poor Deacon I hear has lost his arm, but I do not know certainly. I shall try and get permission to go to the rear this afternoon and look him up. He is not dangerous and I hear he is doing well. He was a brave boy, never flinched. This was his fourth battle." Deacon was discharged as disabled December 10, 1862, *Wisconsin Roster*, vol. 1, 494.

Sergeant Uriel P. Olin, La Crosse Light Guard, Co. B, 2nd Wisconsin

Olin enlisted at La Crosse, Wisconsin, and was mortally wounded at Antietam on September 17, 1862. *Peter Dessauer*

carried news of the great Maryland battle but few details. One example was a bold headline splashed across the *Milwaukee Sentinel* the day before Antietam: "King's Division in the Recent Battles before Washington—Splendid conduct of the Wisconsin Troops—A GLORIOUS RECORD." The details of the fighting at Gainesville, Second Bull, and South Mountain proved thin, and it was not until four days later that the headline most feared by the homefolk appeared: "The following is a list of killed and wounded in Gibbon's Brigade." The list brought joy to many homes and caused others to be shuttered and dimmed. It was not until as late as October 1, 1862, that papers such as the *Mauston Star* offered detailed news from the front. Under the headline "CAMP CORRESPONDENCE—THE KILLED AND WOUNDED" ran a typical report by an officer of the 6th Wisconsin: "Knowing the anxiety felt in your community regarding the fate of the two companies, K and I, raised in the vicinity of Mauston, I append a full list of casualties in said companies to this date, together with some incidents connected with their participation in the various battles in which our regiment had been engaged."

The letters being sent home from the brigade told the grim story. Typical of dozens and dozens of such missives reaching Wisconsin was the one from Sgt. John B. David of Company E, 2nd Wisconsin, to Mr. Lowell G. Taplin near Oshkosh. "We were the first line of battle and on the extreme right," Sergeant David wrote of Antietam. "Consequently we lost the heaviest. Our reg. Took into action 151 men, 75 of them were either killed or wounded. Our Co. Lost 12 killed or wounded." Mr. Taplin's son, Pvt. Osman Taplin, reported the sergeant, had fired just two shots when struck. Shot in the leg himself, the sergeant said, he was still able to help the private to an ambulance. "He is wounded in the right side, the ball struck him about half way between the naval and the side, passed through the body, coming out just above the point of the hip. There are no bones touched and if his insides are not hurt he will get well. That is now the question which it will take 2 days more to answer." The good sergeant said he would try to keep the father apprised of his son's condition, but he could not give any directions as to where or who to write. In closing, he added, "Osman is now sleeping very quietly says he is as well as could be expected under the circumstances." A week later came another letter, this one from the army hospital at nearby Keedyville, Maryland. If Taplin's letter offered some hope, the second proved a crushing blow: Private Taplin had died of his wounds September 24, 1862. He began to "fall away" shortly after reaching the hospital. "He asked me to write to you and his mother and tell how and where he died," wrote Sergeant David. "He also asked me to send you a fine daguerreotype that was in his knapsack." Taplin was buried in the Keedyville cemetery. "He was a noble boy. As a soldier he had no superior on the battlefield or parade ground. He was brave to a fault, kind to all, all loved him and will more his loss."[30]

Word of the terrible battle spread quickly from the small towns and villages to the backwoods farms of Wisconsin and Indiana. One tragic mix-up sent one family at Fond du Lac into tears and mourning until another telegraph brought news the loved one was in fact alive and well. The fiasco involved two prominent citizen-soldiers of the community—Edward Bragg and Edwin Brown, both of the 6th Wisconsin. On the day after the battle, a message from the Wisconsin State Telegraph Company reached Mrs. Bragg: "Your husband was shot yesterday. I will send him home by express." The telegraph was signed by a sergeant of the regiment. As it does in small towns, the news spread from neighbor to neighbor until it reached Ruth, Edwin Brown's wife. Ruth rushed to Mrs. Bragg's side to commiserate. The two wives had been left to wait and worry when their husbands went off to war in "Bragg's Rifles." Townsfolk remembered how the slight but energetic lawyer had signed on for the war and raised a company of local boys, naming the military organization after himself. Friends and business associates decided there must be a memorial service and began to make preparations. A delegate was sent to Chicago to bring Bragg's body home.

News of Bragg's demise reminded the Brown family just how worried they should be for their own husband, father, and son. No news had been received of Edwin for several days. Perhaps this was a good sign, they hoped. Isaac, Edwin's father, sent a letter to his son at the front four days after the horrendous battle: "I write to express to you how anxious we are waiting to hear the reports of casualties to our men in the late battles and yet are almost afraid to hear—our earnest prayers is that you have gone through the deadly contest safely." The news about Bragg was very sad, he wrote. It is "strange to believe there seems to be a disposition to believe the report is a hoax, we all hope it may be, but it is almost hoping against hope." The elder Brown continued:

> I notice in your last letter to Ruth that you complain of being worn down by hard service. . . . I suppose that in times such as our army's are now experiencing it is difficult to get either a furlough or a resignation accepted. But my advice is to try to get the utmost—one or the other rather than sink under the loads of sheer exhaustion. I think you have by this time proved your courage and patriotism so well as to silence all imputations of cowardice that seems to apply but too well in the case of some that have volunteered with a flourish of trumpets.

30 Sgt. J. B. David, letter, to Mr. Taplin, September 1862; Sgt. J.B. David, letter, to Mr. Taplin, September 24, 1862, Oshkosh, Wisconsin; Public Museum, Records 61/291 and 63/294.

Isaac Brown's advice never reached his son. A day after his letter was posted, a message arrived from the Fond du Lac delegate in Chicago: "The body of Capt. E. A. Brown, instead of Bragg. Will be home tomorrow. Chicago Times reports Bragg wounded in arm." Another telegraph reached Isaac Brown at home: "E. A. Brown's body is here and will be on the first train." And so it came to be that Mrs. Bragg wept in relief and joy, and Mrs. Brown reaped bitter sorrow and despaired of what would become of her and her three children. Two days later, a letter penned by Lt. Col. Bragg arrived: "He was a good soldier, a brave and chivalrous gentleman and above all he cherished a fond love for his home, and the domesticities this cruel war has severed. Believe me Madam, the Regiment . . . deeply mourns his loss and his brother officers will long cherish his memory, and through me, express to you, their kindest and heartfelt sympathies in your bereavement."[31]

While families back home waited, worried, or suffered the pain of personal loss beyond words, the soldiers at the front rested while others suffered their wounds on beds of agony. For reasons not immediately obvious to the men in the ranks, the Army of the Potomac lingered at Sharpsburg. The hours stretched into days, and the days into weeks.

Equal to the Best Troops in any Army

George McClellan was convinced his generalship at Antietam saved the nation by turning back Lee's Army of Northern Virginia. His victory, won against great odds, he reminded others, lifted the threat to Washington and Baltimore. He was thus troubled when he did not receive the public credit due him. Yes, Lee's army had fled to the safety of Virginia, but calls for the Army of the Potomac to give chase, argued McClellan, demonstrated the ignorance of non-professionals. The failure to organize a pursuit, he explained, was because his supply wagons were empty, his soldiers ill-equipped, and his command structures ruptured by sustained hard fighting.

---

31 Isaac Brown, letter to his son, September 21, 1862. "Captain E. A. Brown fell while leading his men on the field. He died nobly for his country, which he so much loved. I have often seen him point to the old starry banner and affirm that he would either live under its protecting folds or die in its defence. He was formally a student of Lawrence College, and a young man of more than ordinary ability. He left a good law business at home to serve his country, and all who knew him as a soldier and officer, knew him but to honor and respect. Every man in his Company loved him, and his loss is deeply mourned by us all." Joseph Marston, *Appleton Crescent*, October 25, 1862. Edward Bragg wrote his wife September 21, 1862: "I have the Capts sword. It was found by a New York man, in the field & I reclaimed it, & will have it sent home as soon as possible."

Many of the officers of the line agreed with him. "The regiment was now in a condition of exhaustion from the severity of its service and from its losses in battle," admitted the 6th Wisconsin's Rufus Dawes. Edward Bragg of the same regiment agreed, adding that that "weeks of inaction" after Antietam stemmed from "the shattered condition of the troops and their want or proper blankets and clothing, particularly trousers, shirts and shoes." John Gibbon took time during the respite to visit his family in nearby Baltimore; he returned to the army in an unsettled mood. Everywhere at home he was asked when McClellan would advance. "So strong had become the feeling at the delay that I returned to the army impressed with the conviction that unless a move took place very soon, McClellan would be relived from command." He mentioned his worry to a member of Little Mac's staff. "The most important reason supposed to be for delay was the lack of supplies and it is certain when the army did at least move on the Twenty-sixth of October the equipment of the men was not as complete as it should have been and might have been though Lee's army must necessarily have been worse off than we were."[32] The feeling in the ranks was much the same. "We are constantly speculating on the cause of this inaction," said one Black Hat in a letter home. "We are not as blood thirsty as we used to be that is we are not anxious for another fight, but want the ball kept in motion even if we have to take the brunt."[33]

Around their coffee fires during those long days, the soldiers in tall hats discussed what had happened on the rocky and rolling fields near Sharpsburg. "I will say this," one officer wrote home, "that if Gibbon's Brigade had of been as strong on the morning of the 17th as we were two months ago, I believe we could have succeeded in driving the Rebels into the river, for I tell you the troops that relieved us did not fight as we did for we drove them until our ammunition gave out and then held our ground until we were relieved." Lieutenant Henry Young Jr. of the 7th Wisconsin claimed the Black Hats discovered they were fighting their old foes from Gainesville. "Our brigade whipped Jackson's famous Stonewall Brigade, at the battle of Antietam in a fair and square fight," Young boasted. "It was them we met in the morning, they fought well, but we hurled them back, broken and in perfect confusion."[34]

The men in the ranks welcomed the long rest outside Sharpsburg. The fighting closed a long 45 day campaign described as the "first battle epoch" of the Western Brigade. During that period, the regiments fought four major engagements

32 Dawes, *Service*, 103.

33 *Ibid.*, 96; Edward Bragg, letter to Earl Rogers, April 3, 1900; Gibbon, *Recollections*, 92.

34 Henry F. Young, letter, October 4, 1862, Henry Young Papers, WHS.

(Gainesville, Second Bull Run, South Mountain, and Antietam) and were 11 days under fire. "I have come safety through two more terrible engagements with the enemy, that at South Mountain and the great battle of yesterday," Rufus Dawes wrote his mother on September 18. "Our splendid regiment is almost destroyed. We have had nearly four hundred men killed and wounded in the battles Seven of our officers were shot and three killed in yesterday's battle and nearly one hundred and fifty men killed and wounded. All from less than three hundred engaged." Then, Dawes added a line for the history books: "The men have stood like iron."[35]

Of course, the reference was to the name won by Gibbon's men at South Mountain—the "Iron Brigade of the West." Other soldiers also used the word "iron" in letters to the homefolk. An officer of the 7th Wisconsin reported that "Gen. McClellan calls us the Iron Brigade. By gaining this name, we have lost from the brigade seventeen hundred and fifty men. We have never turned our backs to the enemy in any engagement, although they have outnumbered us every fight we have had." The war and its fighting was "a horrid thing," Frank Haskell confirmed to his family before urging them to "believe in Genl. McClellan." To a younger brother thinking of enlisting, he wrote, "[Y]ou must not think of it—you could not begin to stand it—the losses by sickness, are far more than those of bullets. One must be made of iron to stand it—I am three fourths iron, and the rest is oak."[36]

In that clever way he had of lifting the morale of his soldiers and tying them to himself, McClellan took note of his "Iron Brigade of the West" with an endorsement to the governor of Wisconsin of his "great admiration" for the three Badger regiments of Gibbon's brigade. "I have seen them under fire, acting in a manner that reflects the greatest possible credit and honor upon themselves and their state. They are equal to the best troops of any army in the world," gushed Little Mac. A similar letter about the 19th Indiana was sent to the governor of that state. The general's remarks were read at the evening parades on October 8. "Hooray for Wisconsin! We are very cheered and encouraged," one of the boys wrote home.[37]

The mighty war name came at a steep price. At Antietam, the Western men "fought more like demons than anything else until but 400 or 500 were left of the

---

35 Dawes, *Service*, 96; Rufus Dawes, letter to his mother, September 18, 1862, written "in line of battle near Sharpsburg, Maryland."

36 Aleck Gordon Jr., letter, September 21, 1862, Wisconsin Newspaper Volumes, vol. 4, 21-22, WHS; Hugh Perkins, letter to friend, September 26, 1862; Frank Haskell, letter to brothers and sisters, September 22, 1862.

37 Cheek and Pointon, *Sauk County*, 53; Nolan, *Iron Brigade*, 174. McClellan's letter to Indiana Gov. Oliver Morton was reprinted in the *Indianapolis Daily Journal*, October 13, 1862.

Brigade that had 2500 as good men as ever carried guns, but two months before," wrote one Black Hat survivor. "Judge for yourselves whether the brigade has seen hard times or not, with three times three for brave 'Little Mac,' the man we all love, I await further movements." In the Waushara County company of the 7th Wisconsin, a private reported home there were "only eight here now fit for duty There is not many sick at present. We have no stragglers like some of the companies, but still the men are gone. They have died the soldier's death or have been wounded on the field of battle. We haven't a coward in our company."[38]

From Washington came news that would change the war. In response to the thin Union "victory" at Antietam, President Lincoln issued an "Emancipation Proclamation." As of January 1, 1863, slaves in states in rebellion would "be then, henceforward, and forever free." The document would later come to be recognized as a great turning point of the Civil War. One Wisconsin veteran called it "that great paper" and said it would always "be associated with the history of Mr. Lincoln's Administration." The proclamation accomplished little that was not already happening. The Federal army, for example, was already creating freedom wherever it marched and an end to slavery in its wake. As a political statement, the document was far-reaching and important and served to keep foreign countries that had abandoned slavery out of the war. The Proclamation received mixed reviews once printed and distributed in the camps of the Army of the Potomac. Many soldiers did not know what to make of it or where it would lead the nation. Some volunteers and officers hailed it; others feared or despised it. McClellan and many of his officers claimed with some truth that the proclamation was beyond the original aims of the war and that it would stiffen Confederate resistance. It might also threaten any negotiated settlement that could lead to the restoration of the Union.

"I don't know what effect the President's proclamation will have on the South," one officer of Gibbon's brigade wrote home, "but there is one thing certain it is just what was wanted, and if they don't lay down their arms we will have to annihilate them, niggers, cotton and all. It will make hard times for a while," he continued, "but it will forever settle the everlasting slavery question." A few days later the same man wrote, "Old Abe's proclamation [takes] well with the army here. Now the Rebs will have to die dog or eat the hatchet." Rufus Dawes discussed the proclamation while home on leave at Marietta, Ohio. Civic leaders asked him to talk about the state of the army. The presentation was "delivered in a forcible and eloquent manner," the *Marietta Register* reported. The major gave "the highest

---

38 Longhenry, diary, October 8, 1862; Watrous, *Appleton Crescent*, September 27, 1862; Hugh Perkins, letter to a friend, September 21, 1862.

satisfaction and was listened to with almost breathless interest." What he had to say was worth noting: If there "remains any one in the army, who does not like the Proclamation, he is careful to keep quiet about it. We are hailed everywhere by the negroes as their deliverers. They all know that 'Mass Linkum' has set them free, and I never saw one not disposed to take advantage of the fact." Slavery, Dawes added,

> is the chief source of wealth in the South, and the basis of their aristocracy, and my observation is that a blow at slavery hurts more than battalion volleys. It strikes at the vitals. It is foolish to talk about embittering the rebels any more than they are already embittered. We like the Proclamation because it hurts the rebels. We like the Proclamation because it lets the world know what the real issue. . . . We like the Emancipation Proclamation because it is right, and because it is the edict of our Commander in Chief, the President of the United States.[39]

All that was yet to come.

*   *   *

While the Army of the Potomac rested, reorganized, and outfitted, September slipped into October. President Lincoln decided it was high time to pay a visit to the Army of the Potomac and meet with McClellan. A review was organized to welcome the president amid camp rumors that Confederate officials were seeking a truce to end the war. "We had to forget our lunch on account of it," a soldier complained to his diary on October 2. "We waited the whole afternoon for the arrivals of the President. At sundown, there was no sight of him or his entourage. He did not arrive. We marched hungry and thirsty back to our camp."

The president arrived the next day, with the army once again drawn up for ceremonial inspection. The welcome from the men in the ranks was cool; resentment and distrust lingered. Many believed Lincoln and others in his administration were managing the war effort for political gain, and the soldiers were paying the price. This was a much different army than the one reviewed by the president outside Washington several months earlier. The regiments were "well seasoned," wrote a Black Hat, with "a record of many great battles. What changes had taken place with that army since his review of it at Bailey's Cross Roads. At least 100,000 of his partners in that one army had been killed or wounded." Despite the mistrust, despite the rumors, despite the hard words of the campfire, the soldier

39 Otis, *Second Wisconsin*, 28; Henry F. Young, letter, Wisconsin Veterans Museum, Madison; Dawes, *Service*, 126. Dawes' address was made March 19, 1863.

admitted he was touched by the president's "thin pale face and look of deep sorrow told of his aching heart at the great loss." Another Western soldier observed that "Abraham looked well and took especial interest in the Iron Brigade which was pointed out to him." Edward Bragg, a lifelong Democrat who shouted for Stephan A. Douglas of Illinois in the election of 1860, was less impressed. His wound kept him from attending, but he was well enough to write a sour description to his wife of Lincoln's "long legs, & jack knife face."

The brigade's line during the review, said an officer, was "formed in almost the position occupied by the army of General Lee at the opening of the battle. Our battle flags were tattered, our clothing worn, and our appearance that of men who had been through the most trying service.... Mr. Lincoln was manifestly touched at the worn appearance our men, and he, himself, looked serious and careworn." When the president passed the Iron Brigade, the flags dropped in salute and he "bowed low in response." Mounted in front of his regiment, Dawes "caught a glimpse of Mr. Lincoln's face, which has remained photographed upon my memory. Compared with the small figure of General McClellan, who, with jaunty air somewhat gaudy appearance, cantered along beside him, Mr. Lincoln seemed to tower as a giant."[40]

During Lincoln's October 2-4 visit, he met with the army commander several times to urge him to pursue and destroy the retreating enemy. Little Mac shook his head at what he viewed as a rash and worrisome move. His army was in disarray, he explained. He needed more supplies, more recruits, and more time. The frustrated Lincoln returned to Washington troubled but in no position to challenge the army commander. Congressional mid-term elections loomed large and the political climate uncertain, with many arguing that the administration was losing the war.

Command changes threaded themselves into the army during its month in the camp around Sharpsburg. With Joseph Hooker in Washington recovering from his wounded foot (and scheming for promotion), West Pointer John Reynolds was named to take his place at the head of First Corps. It was the arrival of the 24th Michigan, however, that created the most excitement and was most significant. Formed in Detroit, the 24th included mostly Wayne County men. As promised by McClellan, it was attached to Gibbon's Western Brigade and the Wisconsin and Indiana men watched as "the new regiment, clad in clean, bright uniforms, a thousand strong, the band playing went into camp near the remnant of the four regiments that had been together since August 1861." It was a sight not seen since

---

40 Edward Bragg, letter to his wife, October 3, 1862; Watrous, manuscript, Watrous Papers, WHS; Dawes, *Service*, 100.

the start of the war—a regiment with such full ranks, new uniforms, a brass band, and unsoiled flags. Gibbon's brigade "had been so reduced by shot, shell and disease" that the four original regiments "did not number as many as 200 of this one regiment, fresh from the chief city of Michigan," said one Black Hat. "They are a splendid looking body of men, entirely new to the service," a Wisconsin officer wrote home. "Their ranks are full now, and they are, as we were, crazy to fight." The Michigan unit had a "very good brass band," admitted one of the veterans, who could see the new regiment camped "in a small valley." One of the band's selections was "Toward God We are Mounting," he wrote home. "It is beautifully done." Gibbon liked what he saw. "From its bearing," he wrote home, "I have no doubt it will not be long before it will be a worthy member of the 'Black Hats.'"[41]

According to its own members, the 24th Michigan was formed because of a few quiet words spoken by the wife of Michigan Governor Austin Blair. The idea for a Detroit or Wayne County regiment was born in the wave of patriotic meetings organized after Southern sympathizers, draft resisters, and hooligans disrupted a war rally in downtown Detroit. The rally had been organized following President Lincoln's June 28, 1862, call for 300,000 additional volunteers. Michigan had already raised seventeen regiments, and the new quota called for six more. The rally's patriotic speeches had barely begun when angry protesters turned the crowd into a mob. Organizers and city officials ran for safety and over the next few days, amid gloomy newspaper accounts of the shameful incident, consensus was reached that the best way to prove the city's loyalty was to create a new regiment (above the quota) from Detroit and Wayne County. Faced with the seemingly insurmountable task of raising six additional regiments, Governor Blair stubbornly refused. It was not until his wife observed that the war news of late was bad, and that in her opinion the Republic needed every regiment it could get, that the governor consented.

Another rally was organized at the same place the mob had broken up the earlier meeting. The crowd swelled large enough "to cause every patriot to rejoice," boasted one witness, and included "determined and enthusiastic patriots," some armed with clubs for "any secesh rowdies who would open their blatant mouths." The two men proposed to lead the new regiment were citizens of importance and promise. Henry A. Morrow, the first judge of Recorder's Court, would soon be named colonel. The Virginia native and Mexican War veteran, whose abilities were quickly recognized, had arrived in Detroit in 1853. The would-be lieutenant colonel, 6-foot-4 Wayne County Sheriff Mark Flannigan, stood out in any crowd.

41 *Ibid., Service*, 126.

Colonel Henry Morrow, 24th Michigan Infantry

Morrow was the first colonel of the regiment and would command the
brigade during the Grand Review in Washington in 1865. *Library of Congress*

The meeting kicked off a frenzy of patriotic recruiting and the regiment was filled
by August 11.[42]

The Wolverines' welcome to the Iron Brigade was a cool one. The Badgers and
Hoosier veterans walked down to the Michigan camp and stood a handful of yards

42 Curtis, *Twenty-fourth*, 24-51.

off, small groups with hands stuffed firmly in pockets looking over the new men. The Michigan soldiers would eventually be welcomed as full-fledged brigade members, but that acceptance was still a long way off. At first, the 24th Michigan was just "the big regiment" to the veterans, or the "Featherbeds"—because they were slow to sign on for the war and brought everything from home, including their featherbeds. "They knew the record of the balance of our brigade had made," one Badger wrote, "and realized that if they were to rank with their brethren from Wisconsin and Indiana, no time most be lost in preparing for the serious work which was to come." The Wolverines had to learn "how to live upon army rations; that the first duty of a soldier was to obey all lawful orders; what was expected of them."

The cool and distant attitude was nowhere more evident than during an early drill. "Our regimental inspection over, we were drawn up in front of the rest of the brigade, whom we almost outnumbered," a Michigan volunteer recalled. "Our suits were new; their's were army-worn. Our Colonel extolled our qualities, but the brigade was silent. Not a cheer. A pretty cool reception, we thought. We had come out to reinforce them, and supposed they would be glad to see us." But, the new soldier admitted, the brigade "had already won envious fame . . . and had a right to know before accepting our full fellowship if we, too, had the mettle to sustain the honor of the brigade."[43] Adding to the discomfort was the camp rumor that the Michigan soldiers were "bounty men"—recruits paid a bonus to enlist. To the "Boys of '61," that simple fact separated them from the new men. The Wisconsin and Indiana men enlisted because of our "pure patriotism," one Badger explained. "There were no large bounties or donations as incentives to a service to the country. It was clearly a patriotic feeling of a desire for the maintenance of the Union and the preservation of our free institutions." The Michigan men were jeered as "bounty-bought" and teased to their faces that "the Government could have secured mules much cheaper." The Michigan men with their new uniforms, smart flat-topped kepis, fat wallets full of bounty money, and green ways, the Black Hats decided with solemn nods, would have to prove they could be counted on in a pinch.

The hurtful rumor, of course, was not true. The men were volunteers all—and not the green volunteers of 1861 caught up by drums and flags. The war was in its second year and illusions of glorious charges and grand marches were not as widespread as they had been during the war's early weeks. Most of these Michigan volunteers knew what they were getting into, and the ranks included steady and

43 *Ibid.*, 65.

serious men. "Not a man of us received a cent of State or county body," one Michigan volunteer argued. "Each man, however, did receive, in advance one month's pay and $25 of the regular $100 government bounty promised to all soldiers enlisting for two years; 673 of the men who were credited to Detroit received sums varying from $25 to $50 a piece as a gratuity from patriotic friends, while the remaining 354 of us never received a cent."

We Love the Old Flags

Troubles abounded in those hard days after Antietam, but one of the most frustrating issues involved the flags of the 6th Wisconsin and claims made by Lt. Col. Theodore Gates of the 20th New York State Militia. The colonel's official report for the Antietam fight claimed that Maj. Jacob Hardenbergh advanced half the small New York regiment to the support of Battery B, 4th U.S. Artillery. The 6th Wisconsin was ahead of the 20th New York in the Miller cornfield "in some disorder," Gates wrote, and the Badgers had to abandon their battle flag. One of his men, Gates continued, shot a Confederate color bearer and Hardenbergh carried the captured Confederate banner off the battlefield, "as was also the regimental colors of the Sixth Wisconsin, which they had been compelled to leave on the field."[44]

The report did not sit well with John Gibbon, a professional soldier jealous of his reputation and that of his regiments. Gibbon rode to army headquarters to personally examine the report. "I was at the Battery when the Sixth Wis. came back and helped the Major (Dawes) rally it on its colors, which were then with the Regiment," Gibbon wrote after the war. He continued:

> A half regiment (I think the Twentieth N.Y.) had been sent to aid in protecting the battery. It never went beyond the position occupied by the limbers of the guns. After the battle the Col. of that half-regiment (I am not certain of his name or the number of his regiment) turned in a Rebel color which he claimed to have captured on the field, and on the paper accompany the color stated he had brought off the field the colors of the Sixth Wisconsin. During the fight one of our men (I suppose one of the Brigade) brought me in the Battery a rebel color and in the excitement of the fight I yelled at him to throw down the flag and take his place in ranks. When the N.Y. Col. turned in his rebel flag I suspected it was the one this man had brought to me as I knew the Col. had never been in a place where he could have captured it, but when he said he had brought

---

44 *OR* 19, pt. 1, 246-247.

off the colors of the Sixth Wisconsin I knew that was not true, for I saw them come off the field myself.[45]

When Gibbon called in Gates to question him, the explanation given "was not very clear and was very weak, and I had not much difficulty in persuading him to omit all mention of the Sixth Wisconsin flag in his statement." Lieutenant Colonel Edward Bragg of the 6th Wisconsin, also a man with a reputation to be protected, responded more sharply in his own report. His regiment, Bragg wrote, "conducted itself during the fight so as to fully sustain its previous reputation; that it did not abandon its colors on the field; that every color-bearer and every member of the guard was disabled and compelled to leave; that the state color fell into other keeping, temporary, in rear of the regiment because its bearer had fallen," he continued, "but it was immediately reclaimed, and, under its folds, few but undaunted, the regiment rallied to the support of the battery." The color lance of the regiment's national color, Bragg continued, "is pierced with five balls and both colors bear multitudes of testimony that they were in the thickest of the fighting."[46]

Years later Bragg offered more detail in a letter to an Antietam historian seeking specific details about the fighting. The Confederate flag, Bragg explained to Ezra Carman, himself a Union veteran of the battle, "fell or was thrown down or dropped in the last struggle of the Sixth Wis., and was picked up as a trophy by a man of the Sixth who was carrying it, with one of the flags of the Sixth to the rear, when Gen. Gibbon, who was in the battery directing its fire, called to him, 'Put down the flags and come to the battery,' or something of that sort. The man did as commanded," Bragg added, "and both flags were laid down and were picked up by the stragglers belonging to Colonel Gates's command supporting the battery. There are the facts of the 'so-called' capture and rescue."[47]

---

45 John Gibbon, letter, to James Stewart, August 4, 1893, Antietam Studies, National Archives, Record Group 94. Gibbon was responding to a question by Stewart. The general admitted his recollections were "dim," adding the records would identify the regiment but it was his memory the "Regiment was the Twentieth N.Y. and the Col. or Lt. Col's name Gates," Lt. John McEntee of the 20th New York wrote his father that the 6th Wisconsin "broke and run, leaving their colors on the field, which our boys picked up and brought off, together with a rebel color, the bearer of which one of our men shot."

46 OR 19, pt. 1, 254-256.

47 Edward Bragg, letter, to E. A. Carman, December 26, 1894. "I cannot forbear saying that the report of this last named officer [Gates] relative to a flag of the Sixth WI. (The Regiment had two flags) which was abandoned and rescued (?) by his command, and the capture also of a Confederate flag by his regiment, going into details, naming the sergeant who shot down the bearer, smacks of 'Munchauseism.'"

Given the confused nature of combat and emotional responses penned by both sides, the truth of the incident may never be determined. Gibbon's claim that he ordered an enlisted man to put down the flags, though written long after the fact, has the ring of truth and is something easily remembered. The soldier apparently left the flags and they were picked up by men of the 20th New York. When Dawes came out of the fighting in the cornfield, he may have found the Wisconsin flag in the hands of a New Yorker. "At the bottom of the hill, I took the blue color of the state of Wisconsin, and waving it, called a rally of Wisconsin men," Dawes wrote in one account of Antietam. His second description of the same event is nearly identical: "Here, at the bottom of the hill, I took the blue color of the state of Wisconsin, and called a rally of Wisconsin men."[48] In both instances, Dawes wrote that he "took the blue color," but he did not identify from whom he took the flag, or how exactly it came into his hands. Dawes was always careful to give credit where credit was deserved. If he had grabbed it from a soldier in his brigade, Dawes almost certainly would have said so. But if it had been a solider from another organization—and a New York unit at that—Dawes may have omitted it out of embarrassment that a Wisconsin flag had somehow fallen into the hands of a stranger.[49]

The matter of the Confederate flag is also obscure. Bragg claimed the flag was picked up by a Wisconsin man in the cornfield, but several Confederate banners were captured that day. Bragg himself was not at the scene because he was being treated in the rear for his wound. In his report, he claimed the 6th Wisconsin captured two stands of colors that were "sent to the rear in charge of a wounded soldier and have become lost or fallen into the possession of someone desirous of military éclat without incurring personal danger, so that they cannot be reclaimed by the captors." To his wife, he wrote: "My regiment took a stand of colors, but it was sent to the rear by a wounded man & lost at the hospital, and somebody else will claim it, I suppose, Who cares! We took it, and many witnesses can prove it, if disputed."[50]

---

48 Dawes, *Service*, 91, 339.

49 The Confederate flag credited as being captured by the 20th New York (War Department capture No. 33) is presently in the Museum of the Confederacy in Richmond. A card is attached stating the following: "HdQrs., Doubleday's Div. Confederate Battle Flag captured at the Battle of Sharpsburg, September Seventeenth 1862, by Privt. Isaac Thompson, Co. C, Twentieth N.York S.M. He shot the Rebel color bearer, ran forward and brought off the colors. Theodore B. Gates Lt. Col. Commanding." Register of Captured Flags, 1861-65, Records of the Adjutant-General's Office (Record Group No. 94), National Archives, Washington, D.C.

50 *OR* 13, pt. 1, 255-256; Edward Bragg, letter to his wife, September 21, 1862.

The angry words used to describe these incidents demonstrate just how important these regimental banners were to the men; indeed, from the first they were as much a part of Civil War organizations as the soldiers themselves. "We are the color company of the 6th Wisconsin regiment, and carry the regimental colors," W. H. Druen of Rockville wrote home on August 1, 1861. "I feel safe in saying . . . the splendid flag entrusted to our care, shall not be dishonored by any act of ours. We shall bring it back unsullied by traitor's hands." The bright regimental flags— one national, the other state—came to represent home, duty, and cause to the Union volunteers. When the 5th Wisconsin was presented with a flag, an officer "commanded all his men to kneel down and swear to fight for the flag as long as a drop of blood remained in their veins." The order, recorded a witness, was "enthusiastically complied with." The flags were always with the regiments on the drill field, on the long march, and in battle in the very center of the regimental line. It was the movement of the flags more than the shouted commands of the officers (which often went unheard) that directed the men. The banners served to lead a charge or rally a broken regiment. It was not by chance that soldiers singled out enemy color bearers for careful aim. If the flags advanced, so did the battle line; if the flags fell back, so did the men.

The color bearer of a regiment's national flag was usually a hand-picked sergeant, with a corporal assigned to carry the state flag. The sole responsibility of the color party—usually a detail of six or eight corporals—was to protect the unit's flags and color bearers. Marching in the center of the battle line with flags was the most perilous of duties, and it was not surprising, given the sentimentalism of those days, that a popular war song called Union men to "Rally around the flag, boys, rally once again." One Wisconsin orator called the flags "sacred colors" and priceless relics—symbols of sacrifice and bravely as well as Wisconsin's "power and grandeur."

Jerome Watrous, an eloquent writer who served his four years in the Iron Brigade, described well the deep emotion the flags inspired within the hearts of the men. He spoke for all the veterans when called upon to make the dedication address for a new Grand Army of the Republic Hall in the state capitol building in Madison, where the soiled, shot-ripped Wisconsin banners were to be displayed. "Through our dim eyes, we can see these old flags as they appeared in our camps of instruction, as they went with us upon great reviews, as they went with us in long marches, as they went into battles with us, and were a constant inspiration," he told the hushed gathering. "It was in those days when we were boys or young men that we first began to understand what those flags, what our beautiful national emblem, means. It was in those early days in our experience in the war that we learned to love the stars and stripes, all of the stars, all of the stripes—everything about the dear old flag of our regiment; our flag, wherever it might be. There was a thrill whenever we saw it; it was a great part of us when the war ended."

Watrous was not finished:

> We were not vain, yet we had learned much in those four years of awful struggle—American against American—to preserve the Republic made possible by the services and sacrifices of Washington and the men who followed him in the war of the Revolution. I say we were not vain, we are not vain now, yet we realized after Appomattox that the lives of the thousands of our comrades who had died on the battlefield had in a way been woven into our colors. Then we realized that it was equally true that we have been woven into the colors. We felt, as we wended our way homeward that it was not only our flag, the flag of our country, but that we were part of it. We had helped to cleanse it; we had been given the new-born nation—for it was reborn at Appomattox—a new and clean flag; and that it is what all those old, faded, torn, furled flags that we here to-day rededicate are—sacred remnants of the new-born nation's untarnished emblem.

The old soldiers "love the old flags," Watrous concluded. "We followed them in victory and in defeat; we were with them in great demonstrations; we marched under them after the great victory had been won."[51]

That "great victory" had yet to be recognized by the soldiers who fought under those banners at Antietam in September 1862.

A Sad Good-bye to Johnny, the War Horse

Oh, how the hard veterans from Wisconsin and Indiana made "unmerciful sport" of the new volunteers from Michigan after their arrival in the Sharpsburg camps. Still, the Michigan men took to soldiering in true Western fashion. One incident long recalled involved the "poaching" of several sheep while the "Featherbeds" were on sentry duty. The Wolverines quickly "killed and dressed in fine style" the prized animals and readied them for the cooking fires. A captain in the 2nd Wisconsin, however, coveted the meat. A short time later, he appeared at the Michigan camp in his full regimentals with a squad of soldiers. After reading a "severe order" against foraging, he demanded the Wolverines deliver the sheep. There was grumbling, of course, but they turned the carcasses over. "It is hardly necessary to say that the Second boys had a fine breakfast of mutton," one of the

51 Watrous, "Program for the Dedication of Grand Army memorial in the Capitol, Madison, Wisconsin, June 14, 1918," Wisconsin Veterans Museum, Madison.

Badgers recalled with a sly smile, "and that the Twenty-fourth boys were hopping mad when they discovered how the trick had been played. They ever after held the captain in perfect contempt."[52]

After a long month outside Sharpsburg, orders arrived on October 20 for the five regiments to break camp and march seven miles to Bakersfield, Maryland. Ten days later, long blue columns pushed into Virginia, "that hot bed of secession the soldier despises above all other places on earth," was how one Black Hat put it. "At last," wrote a relieved Rufus Dawes, "the Army of the Potomac is moving." His regiment had been hard used, he added. "The feathers in our hats were drooping and the white leggings, which, as a protection to the feet and ankles, were now more useful than ornamental, had become badly soiled." The new men of the 24th Michigan found the pontoons spanning the Potomac River troublesome. "It is very unpleasant walking on them," explained one Wolverine. "They keep in constant motion, making one walk like a drunken man. He soon gets to feel drunk or seasick—very uncomfortable at least."

The march was "a long, hard and trying one," admitted one soldier. "When it did not rain and the roads were not heavy with Virginia mud, it snowed and froze." New to such hardships, the Wolverines began to "plunder nearby farmhouses" in search of anything eatable. A blowing wet snowstorm brought the column to a halt at Warrenton. "Ice half an inch thick was to be seen everywhere this morning," wrote an officer in his journal. "Stealing chickens. Snow fell all day long. It is cold, and exceedingly disagreeable campaigning now." The "weary patriots of McClellan," as one veteran described he and his comrades, "waded through mud and water up to their knees without a murmur, believe that our gallant leaders does all things for the best." Haversacks were empty. "To-day the regiment is without a cracker to eat, but our men beat it without a murmur," wrote home one officer in the 6th Wisconsin with almost certainly some exaggeration. "No regiment in the army endures privations more patiently. The new regiment (Twenty-four Michigan) does not take it so easily. They have been shouting 'Bread! Bread!' at the top of their voices all day."[53]

Whether recruit or veteran, it was hard going. "I am a fighting man no longer. The last battle was enough for me," admitted a 2nd Wisconsin man. "You folks there at home may read in the papers about the great battles and the hard marches,"

52 Otis, *Second Wisconsin*, 63.

53 Rufus Dawes, letters, October 31, November 7 and 9, 1862; Dawes, *Service*, 104-105; Lucius Shattuck, letter, cited Donald L. Smith, *The Twenty-fourth Michigan of the Iron Brigade* (Harrisburg, PA, 1962), 47; Watrous, *Milwaukee Telegraph*, October 28, 1893; Watrous, *Appleton Crescent*, November 11, 1862; Longhenry, diary, October 30-31, November 7, 1862.

a Michigan volunteer explained, "but you don't know nothing about it nor never will until you have been down here and carried a knapsack and gun 60 rounds of catriges and haversack with 3 days rations and march all day and then lay on the ground all night and perhaps in the rain at that and then march off again to go out on pickett [sentry duty] and stand all night and then march off again in the morning." He concluded: "I tell you that's what will take the patriotism away from a fellow." Another Wolverine found himself surrounded by some hard fellows from Wisconsin and Indiana: "On drill or review, if they halt to rest a minute, they have out their cards, playing poker."[54]

The spectacle of the army's march into Virginia impressed John Gibbon. His regiments crossed on October 30 at Berlin and halted at Purcellsville, where General McClellan rode through the camp and Gibbon joined the general's party. "I shall never forget the magnificent appearance presented by the vast columns of troops moving along at the foot of the mountain where a great many had already reached their camps for the night, the men being busy unloading their wagons, building fires and cooking rations," reminisced Gibbon. "No sooner did our cavalcade make its appearance than the men along the road dropped everything and rushed to the fence, commenced cheering loudly for McClellan. The marching columns, catching sight of him, took up the cheering and he reached Snickersville in the midst of a grand ovation."

The brief episode was one of those bright moments in a dark and lingering war that stands as a shining example of Little Mac's popularity with the men in the ranks. "McClellan's manner of receiving such applause added, I think, greatly to the enthusiasm," continued Gibbon. "He also seemed to appreciate so highly these demonstrations, waving his cap and smiling in every direction as he rapidly rode along, that the men appeared to think that he enjoyed the thing as much as they did. Such a feeling between the Commanding general and the men in the ranks is an immense element of strength in war and certainly McClellan possessed the confidence of his men and excited their enthusiasm in a higher degree than any commander of the Army of the Potomac ever had." One of the new Michigan soldiers caught his first (and probably his last) glimpse of the popular army

54 Lucius Shattuck, letter to his sister, November 10, 1863; Horace Emerson, letter to mother and sister, September 28, 1862; James Bartlett, letter to "Dear Brother and Sister," January 13, 1863, James Bartlett Papers, Plymouth Historical Society, Plymouth, Michigan. "I could endure it all well enough if I thought that the leaders wre trying to setle the war. But I believe that the rebels is no nearer subdued now than they were 2 years ago. But if the officers on both sides who are working for had to take up with the same force . . . as we privates I believe the thing would be settled in a hurry."

commander: "You would know him anywhere. His pictures are true—he is no ways remarkable in appearance—answering his descriptions exactly."[55]

A few days later Gibbon was summoned to Maj. Gen. John Reynolds' First Corps headquarters. Much to his surprise, Gibbon was offered command of an infantry division. "My first feeling was one of regret at the idea of being separated from my gallant brigade and some of this was allowed to appear," he confessed. He took some hours to make his decision, but by the morning of November 5 he was bidding his regimental officers goodbye. "I was to be separated, not only from the gallant little brigade," explained Gibbon, "but from my own battery which usually accompanied the brigade into battle." A pressing concern was the matter of who would replace him. The brigade was left in the hands "of a perfectly new colonel who had never been in battle and did not yet know how to command a regiment." He was describing Col. Henry Morrow of the 24th Michigan, whose commission was senior to that of the 2nd Wisconsin's Lt. Col. Lucius Fairchild. Colonel Lysander Cutler of the 6th Wisconsin was still away recovering from his wounds. "Under these circumstances feeling as averse as if trusting a cherished child in the hands of a strange and inexperienced nurse," explained Gibbon, "I sent for Col. Morrow and tried to prevail on him to waive his rank and allow the command to go to Fairchild, but although a young soldier I found him disposed to cling as tenaciously as an old one to the rights of his rank, and he declined to yield." Frustrated in his own attempt to right the matter, Gibbon raised the matter with headquarters with the same result.

The next morning a somber Gibbon sat on his horse by the roadside and watched his "gallant little brigade move from the last time from my command." It was disconcerting, wrote a Wisconsin officer coming to grips with the fact that the Western organization "shall never more be called 'Gibbon's Brigade,' but by the name of his successor." The officer whose men called him "Johnny, the War Horse," had been with them at Gainesville, Second Bull Run, South Mountain, and the horrible field of Antietam. Now he was gone. "We are sorry to lose him," lamented Dawes, "for a brave and true man, tested as he has been is a jewel here." Morrow's command lasted less than a week when Cutler returned on November 9 to assume leadership of the brigade. He was not well, still hobbled by his Gainesville wound. "He is really unfit for duty," confessed Dawes.[56]

---

55 Lucius Shattuck, letter to his sister, November 2, 1862; Gibbon, *Recollections*, 94.

56 Gibbon, *Recollections*, 95-96; P. W. Plummer, letter, November 8, 1862, to the *Wisconsin State Journal*; Rufus Dawes, letter, November 7, 1862; Dawes, *Service*, 105. In addition to Cutler, Cols. William Robinson of the 7th Wisconsin, and Solomon Meredith of the 19th Indiana were absent wounded. Meredith was given command of the brigade November 25, 1862, and held

Looking back many years later, the Western men would realize just how fortunate they were that old Cutler returned late that second year of the war. The effort to subdue the Confederacy was about to take an even harder turn. With the Congressional elections over and the Army of the Potomac on the move, Lincoln found himself in a stronger political position. It was time to remove George McClellan. It was a decision not easily reached. The president recognized the general's popularity within the Army of the Potomac and his following with the citizenry at large. But he was frustrated by the army's failure to pursue the Confederates after Antietam, embarrassed by election reverses, and tired of the persistent whispers of McClellan's presidential ambitions. Lincoln finally, once and for all, sacked Little Mac. Ninth Corps commander Maj. Gen. Ambrose Burnside was elevated to replace him.[57]

The news of McClellan's removal hit the Army of the Potomac like a "thunderclap." Word spread quickly from headquarters to regiments to company campfires. "There is but one opinion upon this subject among the troops and that is the Government has gone mad," Gibbon wrote home. "It is the worst possible thing that could have been done. . . . Every one feels gloomy and sad that a man who has done so much for the country should be treated in this manner." Angry words and threats of action against the administration swirled around the deposed leader. Some of his officers urged him to march the army against Washington and end this government interference with the war effort once and for all. Never in the history of the nation had there been such a serious challenge to the concept of the president as commander-in-chief of the military forces or a military seizure of the government. Wild rumors swept the camps with unsubstantiated tales of soldiers throwing down their arms declaring they would fight no longer. An unconfirmed story has one high-ranking officer telling McClellan, "Lead us to Washington, General. We will follow you there." Gibbon steadfastly maintained that he saw "nothing of this kind, myself, but I heard a good deal of talk calculated to produce apprehensions of the gravest character."

Something dark was at play here that tugged at the American soul. The military professional, the man trained for war as in the European tradition, was distrusted in the New World—a feeling partly due to memories of British redcoats and their

the post except for a brief period when he was removed over a mix-up of orders at Fredericksburg until he was wounded at Gettysburg July 1, 1863.

57 One of the "War" candidates defeated in the 1862 election was Lt. Col. Edward Bragg of the 6th Wisconsin, who returned to Wisconsin to recover from his Antietam wound and campaigned for Congress. "It is manifest that the cowardly sneaks who stay at home intend to sell out the country," Rufus Dawes wrote home November 10, 1862.

hired Hessians walking the streets of American cities. Accepting a leader such as George Washington as president and commander-in-chief of the nation's army was not troubling. But times had changed, and Washington the soldier-president was distant and removed. The president sitting in the White House reached that position in a fractured national election that caused civil war. He held the military reins of the country, although his own military experience was limited to a brief stint as a militia man in a minor Indian war during which he fired not a shot in anger. McClellan, son of a prominent Democrat and a respected Philadelphia family, a man trained to be a great soldier, demonstrated that he was loathe to accept orders from a backwoods lawyer with a questionable social background and scant military experience. Now the question came down to whether Little Mac and the men of the Army of the Potomac would accept Lincoln's decision to remove a beloved army commander.

The troubled hours after McClellan's removal turned the American story in a different direction. It is easy to dismiss the threat when viewed from just army headquarters or Washington. The letters and the journals and diaries from the camps, however, tell a different story: the volunteers were coming face-to-face with a military takeover of the elected government and the United States. All the hardship of two years of civil war had marched the men to a crossroads as significant as Charleston harbor or the green at Lexington. That it had reached that point at all was due in part to the European military tradition so embraced by McClellan with his bright uniforms, retinue of aides, and grand pronouncements. The Army of the Potomac created by Little Mac was a strange mix of European elan and American pluck. No American army—before, then, or since—has been quite like it.

A Foul Wrong Done to a Great and Good Man

The Iron Brigade had just finished a hard march under a steady rain, and its members were erecting their small tents when word arrived of McClellan's removal and the elevation of Ambrose Burnside. A flurry of hard words and somber headshaking coursed through the regimental camps. It was "with feelings of deepest sorrow mingled with disgust that the men heard of the displacement of Gen'l McClellan," one soldier wrote his hometown newspaper in Wisconsin. "The general query is why was he taken from us at such a time, if at all? The prevailing opinion among the officers and men is that the Administration is awfully inefficient, besides having no indication to do that which will tend to hasten the termination of the war."

On November 10, Little Mac commenced his farewell visit to the Army of the Potomac. Lieutenant Loyd Harris of the 6th Wisconsin wrote a quick letter home at the end of the day: "I feel sad. We have just parted from our late commander Genl. George B. McClellan. We had heard on the 5th that he was relieved of his command but were loath to believe it. But today we were suddenly ordered out to be reviewed. We were massed on a commanding hill near our camp and amid the sad sight of their old troops McClellan's parting 'order' was read, and soon after he appeared with Burnside and staff. He rode in advance, and came close up to our ranks, with ten feet of where I stood. Always before when passing in review he always wore a pleasant smile in the face. But today," concluded Harris, "he looked sad, very sad."[58]

According to Harris, the entire Iron Brigade stood silent at present arms.

He had already passed the 2nd and was opposite the 6th, when murmuring was heard in the 2nd. And then as if they were but one man, the old Brigade sent their rousing cheers for him. He turned way around in his saddle (I fancied I saw a tear in his eye) and slowly raised his cap, but no smile for us he used to acknowledge our cheers. No his heart was so full of sorrow. He scanned out faces again, turned, spurred his horse, and was gone. We turned home with heavy hearts. Could hear the cheers of the far off Brigades as he was passing. I feel as if it I could never forgive our nation for the insult and foul wrong they have done that great and good man. We have just got marching orders, and I must close, to get ready. We all like Burnside next to McClellan and he is a warm friend of McClellan. There is a bitter feeling on the army rising against the Administration . . .[59]

Many of the young Western officers were staunch McClellan partisans, and that night offered "considerable expression of feeling" over the general's removal. Many captains and lieutenants signed a paper resigning their commissions. Someone delivered the document to acting brigade leader Colonel Cutler, who pleaded with them to change their minds and refused to forward their resignations. Cutler visited the officers personally "and begged of us not to do so, on account of the men," recalled Harris, who was among those submitting a resignation letter. "The matter at present is at a Stand Still, but it is secretly understood among the officers that as soon as they are paid the four months pay that is due them they will

58 Loyd Harris, letter, November 10, 1862, Loyd Harris Papers, WHS. For a detailed and nuanced account of McClellan and his generalship at Antietam, see Stephen W. Sears, *George B. McClellan: The Young Napoleon* (New York, NY, 1988), and Stephen W. Sears, *Landscape Turned Red: The Battle of Antietam* (New Haven, CT, 1983).

59 Gibbon, *Recollections*, 96; *Appleton Crescent*, November 11, 1862; Edward Bragg, letter to his wife, November 16, 1862; Loyd Harris, letter, November 12, 1862.

resign in a body." Harris went on to explain the "deep feeling among both men and officers against the Administration changing Commaders so often. And the way the war is conducted. Hundreds of brave men, Aye, Thousands of our brave comrades lie buried in this state [Virginia]. Yet scarce anything has been accomplished. We feel that we are wasting our strength, wealth, and lives for nothing long as Politicians and not Generals conduct the war." The Army of the Potomac, he continued, was "dispirited" while the enemy was "confident and boasting." There was a chance to have "whipped them with McClellan, but now we have but little hope." The men generally regarded Burnside as "competent and brave," he added, but they "look daily for the order that will displace him and put in command of the army" such outspoken and notorious politicians such as Jim Lane or Cassius M. Clay.

Harris concluded his letter home:

> As long as we are here, we will fight. Don't care who commands us, for our brigade has worked to hard, fought and sacrificed to much, to let its hard earned reputation go from it now. But we want to get out of this. The officers have held a meeting last night and concluded to withdraw their resignation. We are in the face of the enemy, or else they would have let the paper stand. And we have that now our country will gather and make a combined effort to end this war. I think that both Confederacy and ourselves have on the field the last men they can raise, and now if ever our biggest effort should be made. Let there be no more changing. Let Burnside command, and give him what he wants.

Long afterward Harris wrote that the Iron Brigade served loyally through the rest of the war, but "the old enthusiasm was never seen after the retirement of McClellan from command, and the spontaneous cheers that greeted him whenever he appeared, were never afterwards heard."[60]

The incident involving the proffered resignations in the Iron Brigade regiments was little known, but after Harris talked to a St. Louis newspaper reporter in 1887 about the episode, editor Jerome A. Watrous of the *Milwaukee Sunday Telegraph* reprinted the interview under the headline "Rather Sensational." Unaware of such a confrontation during his soldiering days with the Iron Brigade, Watrous contended the resignation threat was overstated and that Harris was "misrepresented." Watrous witnessed none of the turmoil or heard threats of taking the army to Washington, although he acknowledged "whispers that there was a move to set in motion by some of the officers . . . to reorganize the army

60 Loyd Harris, letter, November 13, 1862.

according to their own notion, march to Washington and demand the restoration of McClellan." Watrous claimed a "lieutenant colonel then of the Iron Brigade was approached with a view of getting his cooperation. His emphatic answer may have had a good deal to do with the abandonment of the revolutionary scheme." In 1890, however, Lucius Dawes confirmed the incident with the publication of his war memoir and credited Cutler's "known determination of character" as the "restraining influence" in preventing the mass resignation of the veteran line officers of the Iron Brigade.

Lewis Kent of Beloit, who served in the 6th Wisconsin, wrote to the *Telegraph* to dispute Harris' account. "I was an enlisted man at the time and was as hot as any one at the removal of Little Mac, and if our officers intended to resign they took [precious] good care not to let the men know of their purposes." He added: "We would have made their exit from 'the old Sixth' one that they would have remembered all their lives." A veteran of the 2nd Wisconsin recalled veteran soldiers at the time "look[ed] depressed, and express[ed] dissatisfaction, who never did so before. Whether McClellan had been as successful as he should have been or not, he had the confidence and admiration of the best soldiers in the army to a remarkable degree. His name was referred to with an enthusiasm, and even brave men shed tears on the occasion of his leaving." A 24th Michigan man wrote home at the time saying the removal of McClellan caused a "great sensation." "Although the army had confidence in Burnside, still Mc has the hearts of the army." He continued: "They saw Mc take the army, reorganize it and two weeks from the time of its defeat [at Second Bull Run] utterly rout the victorious Rebel army in Md." McClellan's removal, "has knocked the heart of the men. Still I hope the best." A veteran Wisconsin officer wrote to his wife about the same time: "Little Mac is gone, and my heart and hopes have gone with him."[61]

Perhaps the army's officers and rank and file were ready to take the war effort into their own hands and march on Washington; perhaps not. Whether the men in company ranks would actually follow the officers once their course of action was known is another matter. "Of course, it was out of the question for McClellan not to have heard some of the discontent expressed so freely, but his bearing was admirable," wrote his friend John Gibbon. "He checked imprudent expressions, when he heard them, assuring every one about him in a cheerful tone that

---

61 Watrous, "Rather Sensational," *Milwaukee Sunday Telegraph*, August 7, 1887; Lewis Kent, *Milwaukee Sunday Telegraph*, September 26, 1887; George C. Gordon, letter, November 12, 1862; George Gordon Papers, State Archives of Michigan. Edward Bragg, letter to his wife, November 16, 1862. The "lieutenant colonel" referred to was probably Edward Bragg. Gordon served as captain of Company I, 24th Michigan.

Pvt. Watson W. Eldridge, Co. G, 24th Michigan

A resident of Livonia, Eldridge was 19 at the time of his enlistment. He was transferred into the Veteran Reserve Corps on March 29, 1864, and mustered out at Washington on June 6, 1865. *Dale Niesen Collection*

everything would come out in the end." One of the Black Hats wrote that the day McClellan left the army would be remembered "by this shamefully abused army. The last time Abraham [Lincoln] visited his children, they gave him a very cool reception, but I venture the next will be more so." Throughout the anger and debate and emotional goodbyes, however, McClellan kept his distance. Perhaps any quick and decisive action was beyond the general's temperament. In any case, he accepted the removal with proper dignity, urged everyone to support Burnside, and quietly left the army never to return. It may have been his finest moment as a soldier and as an American.[62]

Lincoln believed Little Mac's removal was necessary to hasten the war's end, but he understood the action carried with it far-reaching political implications. The president, a Republican, and the general, a Democrat, were at odds over very fundamental issues. Lincoln had radically expanded the war by attacking slavery directly with his Emancipation Proclamation, while McClellan clung to the earlier notion of compromise to restore the Union—even if it meant keeping some form of slavery. In some ways the two men had switched roles, with the general trying to dictate policy and the president driving the war effort by any means at his disposal. McClellan always worried that a crushing Federal military victory would prevent any early negotiated peace and a restored Union. What the general and many of his officers never understood was that these decisions were solely within the purview

62 Watrous, *Appleton Crescent*, November 11, 1862.

Pvt. Charles D. Durfee, Co. C, 24th Michigan

Durfee was 19 when he enlisted in the Wolverine regiment, fought through the war, and mustered out with the same regiment on June 30, 1865, at Detroit. *Dale Niesen Collection*

of the president. Statements made freely at headquarters demonstrated a belief that the army must somehow be protected against the very government that had created it—even to the point of marching on the government at Washington. When he heard similar grumbling outside of army circles, Lincoln sacked a minor officer when the careless statements became public. McClellan promptly issued a general order reminding soldiers of the necessity for military subordination to civil authority. The remedy for "political errors," said McClellan "is to be found only in the action of the people at the polls." The order was released and published in the newspapers just before the pending elections in a smug attempt by the general commanding the nation's most important army to influence the political outcome in the balloting. The general and his officers would have been astonished by accusations that such talk smelled of treason. They believed their service and patriotism had earned them a voice in the conduct of the war. That deep-rooted feeling would create a formidable obstacle in the coming months because the young citizen-soldier officers trained by Little Mac were never quite able to shake off his spell. Even Ulysses S. Grant would find it necessary to handle the Army of the Potomac with caution when he came East in early 1864 to fashion the decisive victory sought by so many.

The decision to fire McClellan and the acceptance of that removal by the soldiers was a turning point in the nation's history. It would be easy to dismiss the depth of the threat, but a casual examination of the letters, journals, and dairies tells a different story. Despite all the death and suffering and hardship, the young volunteers faced a very real choice between assisting a possible military takeover of the elected government or bowing to the supremacy of the Constitution. They admired the little general newspapers hailed as "the young Napoleon," but from the earliest days of the nation Americans looked ahead, not back. The United States was fashioned in the image of farmer-soldiers rushing from their fields to win independence against the finest professional army in the world. The men risking their lives to restore the Union understood intuitively what the nation represented, and that a large professional army of influence had no place in it. In the Old World a move against the seat of power was usually a palatable option. But these citizen-volunteers were hesitant to relinquish the hard-won freedoms to someone even as admired as McClellan. The "Republic's patriotic children" (as the fallen Edwin Brown styled his comrades) would have a government that was servant, not master. It was in those camps around Warrenton—amid angry words and hot emotions—that the soldiers decided that, despite the suffering and death yet to come, there would be no turning back. The soldiers set aside "Little Mac's" limited war for the total war Lincoln was positioning the country to accept, wage, and win. It was in those camps the citizen-volunteers turned "McClellan's Army" into "Mr. Lincoln's Army." A truly national army had been born.

The Iron Brigade is Sound to the Core

Ambrose Burnside assumed command of an army marked and changed by hard service and the sudden removal of its beloved McClellan. Gone were the cheers of innocent young citizen-soldiers. Gone were the gallant charges in the bright sunlight. Gone were the early hopes of easy glory and victory. In fact, gone were the innocent and naive "Boys of '61," replaced now by tough and seasoned veterans. The war was moving out of a shadow into a harsher light. Although distressed at the loss of Little Mac, the soldiers believed Burnside, with his tall hats and bushy side-whiskers, was competent and brave. He was McClellan's close friend, after all, from their days as cadets at the U.S. Military Academy. His development of a breech-loading carbine now in cavalry service enhanced his reputation, if not his pocketbook. His recent service at Antietam, where he was slow to capture a stone bridge and spanning Antietam Creek and attack beyond, was only a minor topic around the campfires—even as his friend McClellan whispered behind his hand that Burnside's dilatory performance denied the army a chance for an overwhelming victory.

Mr. Lincoln's Emancipation Proclamation also changed the war into a conflict not only to restore the Union but to end slavery. The letters home following McClellan's removal spoke of a hardening resolve. "The American soldier is true to his country, true to his oath, and resolved to fight the rebellion to the bitter end, no difference who commands," wrote a 7th Wisconsin man. "I am not a McClellan

Maj. Gen. Ambrose Burnside

The former commander of the Ninth Corps was appointed to lead the Army of the Potomac after McClellan disappointed President Lincoln following his strategic victory at Antietam. *Author's Collection*

man, a Burnside man, a Hooker man, I am for the man that leads us to fight the Rebs on any terms he can get."[63] George Fairfield of the 6th Wisconsin wrote a letter to his sister in an effort to explain his renewed commitment to see it all through: "I am just as ardent, and my hope of crushing the rebellion just as strong as ever. I have enlisted in the cause and without any compulsion or dissention I will go to the bitter end if I know that every pace was so much nearer the jaws of death. . . . I never want to see the North succumb." Lieutenant Loyd Harris of the same regiment, upset over the removal of Little Mac, reached a similar conclusion: "As long as we are here, we will fight." The Iron Brigade is "sound to the core," wrote Edward Bragg, and "will fight Copperheads at home, & Secesh across the lines. . . . We have no sympathy for treason anywhere, and but mighty little faith in the gilded stay at home, and talking patriotism. There can be but one peace, and that the result of victory over the Rebellious States, that will satisfy us. Compromise meets no favor here. 'Subjugation or Submission' is the doctrine," he added, "and we are ready to fight for it, as long as we have a musket & a cartridge." One soldier wrote home that the men fought "for principles far higher than the love embodied in the person of their favorite commander." The hard veterans of the Iron Brigade, one explained, had reached that point where they would "march by night and fight by day, undismayed, unfaltering. No matter whether their choice of leadership was respected, no lisp of disloyalty ever arose from their ranks. But

63 Henry Young, letter, undated.

they pushed on through the shot and the shell, across the march and the swamp, up the mountain side and against fortifications, always certain, like true fatalists that the end would come, if not to-day, then to-morrow; and if not to-morrow, some other day, and the Government would be restored."[64]

Even as the Army of the Potomac prepared to move against Lee's Army of Northern Virginia, another development unfolded with far-reaching consequences for the Iron Brigade. Colonel Sol Meredith had been home on leave recovering from his wound and politicking for promotion. His wish was granted in November when he was named brigadier general of volunteers. He needed a command to go with his new star, and none appealed to him more than the Western Brigade just then without a commander because of Gibbon's promotion. Long Sol approached Burnside and soon gained his blessing. "I have been assigned to this glorious old 'Iron Brigade,'" Meredith wrote friend and patron Governor Morton, something he considered "a very high compliment." The promotion of Meredith over Col. Lysander Cutler roused "outrage" in Gibbon, who had long been at odds with the former colonel; when he learned Burnside had made the recommendation, Gibbon intervened. "I laid the case before him, frankly telling him why I did not want this

Brig. General to have command of my old brigade, the character of the troops composing which he well knew, and ended by requesting him to apply for the officer for duty in his Grand division where he could assign him to a position where he could, at least, do as little harm as

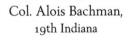

Col. Alois Bachman, 19th Indiana

Bachman, who fell while leading the charge of the 19th Indiana at Antietam, was one of several Iron Brigade officers whose place remained to be filled. *Brett Wilson Collection*

---

64 Edward Bragg, letter to Earl Rogers, undated.

possible." Burnside turned down Gibbon's request, claiming Meredith's "many strong friends" made such a move impossible. Other attempts by Gibbon to have the promotion blocked also ended in failure. At the same time, Meredith was also visiting and corresponding with his political friends in a move to fill the top positions in the 19th Indiana. Promotions were needed to replace Alois O. Bachman and Isaac May, both of whom had been killed. The appointment went to a pair of Meredith's favorites. Samuel J. Williams was elevated to lieutenant colonel and William W. Dudley to major. Meredith's assention to brigade command, however, opened a period of political maneuvering to fill the colonel's vacancy.

The army had marched rapidly and reached the Rappahannock River at Falmouth on November 17. On the far side of the river sat Fredericksburg, which had been evacuated by the Federals two months earlier. The city was lightly held by the Confederates, with most of Lee's army concentrated around Culpeper and in the Shenandoah Valley. The Army of the Potomac line was based on Aquia Creek and the Rappahannock, its artillery posted on Stafford Heights to command Fredericksburg and its approaches. It was there, opposite the historic Virginia city, that Burnside's plans to cross quickly and move against Richmond collapsed. River bridging materials failed to arrive, and the river could not be forded because of high water. On November 25, Meredith's brigade was first held at Aquia Creek, then moved to Brooks Station on the railroad between Aquia Creek and Fredericksburg. Despite a new general and changes in the regimental command positions, haversacks were again empty. A Wisconsin soldier grumbled that the "powers that be seemed to forget that the men can not live without rations. We reached the point of starvation before rations were furnished us." The Sauk County boys subsisted on a sheep foraged by Amos Johnson of Baraboo. "It was mutton or nothing," they told each other with a smile.[65]

Marching in the columns of the First Corps, the Iron Brigade (Meredith was not yet with it) moved from Warrenton toward the Rappahannock River in a movement slowed by cold weather and rain mixed with snow that made roads difficult. The army halted and the brigade went into bivouac in Stafford County by November 20. "The roads are in a desperately muddy condition, and we were all day yesterday moving the division two miles," complained one of the officers. Ten days later the army halted near Brooks Station, where there was talk about going into winter quarters. Lieutenant Colonel Dawes wrote a dark letter to his uncle, Ohio Congressman William Cutler. "There will be another bloody battle, nothing less will appease our valiant 'stay-at-home rangers,'" he predicted. "Wait and see

65 Cheek and Pointon, *Sauk County*, 54.

how much better Burnside does, before 'rejoicing' over the removal of McClellan."[66] No sooner was the brigade situated with snug cabins erected for the winter when it again received orders to move. Meredith arrived to officially take command, returning Colonel Cutler to the 6th Wisconsin. "The country is clamoring for General Burnside to drive his army to butchery at Fredericksburg," wrote Dawes before making a chilling prediction: "If General Burnside allows himself to be pushed into a battle here, against the enemy's works, the country will mourn thousands slain, and the Rappahannock will run red with blood expended in fruitless slaughter." About the same time, one of the surgeons with the 6th Wisconsin approached Bragg to ask about the prospect of whipping the Rebels. "Not by a damned sight over there," Bragg replied sharply. "After they have killed a few thousand, and ruined as many more, we'll come creeping back and be lucky if we get back at all."[67]

While Burnside waited for his pontoon bridges, a political and public storm was building in the North for the army to advance. As the days passed, Lee concentrated his arriving army on the hills beyond Fredericksburg; Burnside mistakenly assumed the Confederate army was stretched across a long distance guarding river crossings below the city. Finally, with his boats and bridging on hand, Burnside ordered the laying of pontoons directly in front of Fredericksburg. The work began early on December 11. The construction, began in the fog of morning, was hampered from the first by Confederate sharpshooters firing from ditches and houses along the riverbank. A heavy artillery bombardment was ordered to smother the fire and the bridges were completed. Union columns crossed the river, only to be met by heavy street fighting. The First Corps, meanwhile, had left Brooks Station just after midnight December 9 with each man carrying sixty rounds of ammunition. The roads were bad and clogged by wagons and marching soldiers. The Iron Brigade halted again two miles from the crossing point to await developments, and crossed the pontoon bridge on December 12 in a dense fog about one mile below town. Soldiers looking down from Stafford heights enjoyed a fine view "of the long lines being formed by our troops." At dark, the column made camp in a grove near a large stone house occupied by a man named Arthur Bernard. It was an awkward moment for the officers and men of Prairie du Chien, explained Loyd Harris, because the company's contraband cook, Matt Bernard, was born a slave there. The runaway came face-to-face with his old master when brigade officers removed "the haughty old Southern" from the house. The angry Bernard

66 Dawes, letter, November 30, 1862.

67 Dawes, *Service*, 107-108.

gave his former slave a cold look before turning away and refusing to recognize him. Old Matt returned with some sadness to his company to find the men shivering around sputtering campfires.

As the night grew colder, the soldiers cast longing glances at the plentiful old chestnut trees lining the roadway down to the main road. Permission was granted to cut a few dead limbs for their fire. When the supply was soon exhausted, the soldiers sought permission to cut one of the old trees. The request was granted. "Two stalwart men who had often felled the mighty pines in northern Wisconsin, seized their axes, but before they could strike a blow, old Matt stood before them, filled with alarm and consternation clearly depicted on his sable face," Harris wrote. "Mr. Russell, are you gwine to cut down dat tree?" old Matt asked. "Yes, Matt, we have permission, and must do it or freeze." "With a big tear starting from each eye, and with hands raised in a most imploring matter, the old slave, forgetting how his master had treated him, slowly said, 'Please, sah, don't cut down dat tree; Massa Bernard's fader planted it dar when Massa was a little boy, and if you cut it down you will break the de old man's heart.'" The axe men nodded and turned away. But the night grew colder still, and finally the order was once again given and the old tree fell to the ground. "It was by the fire made from that tree I listened to the band that played the 'Star Spangled Banner,' near the picket line," remembered Harris. "It was by that fire we passed a very uncomfortable night and awaiting for dawn to commence the great battle."[68]

A Baptism of Fire for a New Regiment

At daylight on December 13, the soldiers of the First Corps moved south of Fredericksburg along the west bank of the Rappahannock River to a point opposite the far right of a meandering seven-mile Confederate line of battle. Now assuming that Lee had anticipated his flanking move because of the delay in the Federal movement, Burnside came to the conclusion the Confederates had weakened their left and center to concentrate against him on the right near Fredericksburg. Once the town had been captured, Burnside planned an assault to drive the Confederates off the nearby heights, but his orders were vague and confusing and the attacks would go off piecemeal. The battlefield was covered by a heavy fog and little could be seen as the Iron Brigade marched in grand column by regiments with the rest of First Corps along the left wing of the army. "The artillery of the enemy was firing vigorously at us and the shot and shell whistled and shrieked about us, but owing to

---

68 Harris, *Milwaukee Sunday Telegraph*, April 8, 1883.

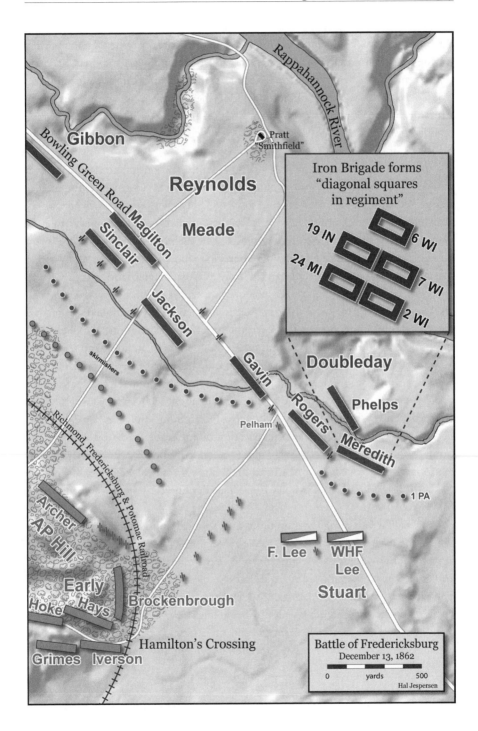

Gibbon

Pratt "Smithfield"

Rappahannock River

Bowling Green Road

Reynolds

Magilton

Sinclair

Meade

Jackson

Iron Brigade forms "diagonal squares in regiment"

19 IN   6 WI

24 MI   7 WI

2 WI

Gavin

skirmishers

Doubleday

Rogers

Phelps

Pelham

Meredith

Richmond Fredericksburg & Potomac Railroad

1 PA

Archer

AP Hill

F. Lee   WHF Lee

Stuart

Early

Hoke   Hays   Brockenbrough

Hamilton's Crossing

Grimes   Iverson

Battle of Fredericksburg
December 13, 1862

0   yards   500

Hal Jespersen

the fog, none struck our columns" wrote a Wisconsin officer. When the fog burned off the brigade found itself on a great open plain facing the Massaponax River on the extreme left flank of the army. The lines were without shelter of any kind, and Confederate artillery was lobbing shells at them from a hill near Hamilton's Crossing. When Southern cavalry was spotted massing as if to charge, the five regiments formed diagonal squares that one described "as formidable as those of Napoleon at the Pyramids."

The cavalry charge never developed. The 6th Wisconsin and 24th Michigan moved as skirmishers and found themselves engaged with enemy infantry; neither side gained an advantage. Battery B of the 4th U.S. Artillery was brought forward in a rush to duel with Confederate guns. Especially pesky were two pieces of Maj. Gen. J. E. B. Stuart's horse artillery under John Pelham. The young Alabamian pushed the guns—a Model 1857 12-pound Napoleon smoothbore and a rifled English Blakely—up close and banged away at close range before hitching up to move when Federal gunners zeroed in on them. The Blakely was eventually disabled by return fire, but Pelham and Capt. Mathias Henry continued shifting the Napoleon until the crew was too low on ammunition to continue the duel. That single gun, however, halted the Union advance for almost an hour, and it was not until it withdrew that the two divisions of the Federal First Corps commanded by Gens. George Gordon Meade and John Gibbon opened the attack against the right side of the Confederate line. The advance began about 9:00 a.m. against a portion of line held by Stonewall Jackson's veterans. The fighting intensified quickly as the Federal lines closed the distance. Meade found a soft swampy area in the Confederate line that was but lightly defended and thrust into it. Rebel reinforcements arrived to contain the breakthrough and Meade, whose division was left unsupported, was pushed back. The fighting on that front ground to a halt.[69]

On the far Union right opposite Fredericksburg, Confederate artillery opened fire on the town about 11:00 a.m. while Federal brigades prepared for an assault against looming Marye's Heights beyond. The full weight of the Confederate artillery fell upon them once the regiments emerged from the streets and buildings. The columns crossed the damaged bridges spanning a ditch and canal near the outskirts of the city and deployed into battle lines behind a low hill. Once all was ready, they advanced across open ground up a long slope toward a stone wall, where James Longstreet's infantry waited for them to step into killing range.

69 Craig L. Barry, "'The Gallant Pelham' Lead Stuart's Horse Artillery, Excelled on Field," *The Artilleryman*, vol. 31, No. 4, Fall 2010, 24-26.

Murderous volleys tore apart the formations and sent the first effort tumbling back down the slope. Another effort followed, and then another.

With the assaults against Marye's Heights underway, Confederate artillery estimated at four dozen guns opened on the exposed Union lines on the far left side of Burnside's front where the first Federal attacks had been turned back. The men were ordered to the ground as artillery shells rolled over their position. "I have never known a more severe trial of nerve upon the battle field, than this hour under that infernal fire," recalled one Wisconsin officer. The missiles would "plow deep into the ground scattering a spray of dirt and bound high over us or burst in the air, sending fragments with a heavy thud into the ground around us." The Rebel gunners could be seen working their guns "like fiends who stirred infernal fires."[70]

The new volunteers of the 24th Michigan had an especially trying baptism of fire, faced first in one direction and then another under a hot artillery fire even as the Union assault against Jackson's lines failed. It would have been a severe test even for seasoned veterans. The Michigan men initially spent some time on a hot skirmish line and found Rebel infantry and cavalry in a patch of woods. Battery B shelled the timber while the brigade formed in two lines with the 6th Wisconsin in support. The 24th Michigan was in the first line on the left, and for a time there was a sharp fight before the brigade changed front. It was mid-afternoon when the Michigan regiment found itself on the open brow of a hill fully exposed to Confederate artillery. The rain of solid shot killed several men including one ball that killed one man before continuing on to sever the head of 18-year-old Louis Hattie, a regimental favorite. Word of his death passed along the line and created some unsteadiness in ranks. "It was a most trying moment as the cannon balls ploughed through the ranks, and shells shrieked like demons in the air," wrote one Wolverine. Colonel Henry Morrow saw the wavering and moved forward to halt the regiment. While standing on the brow of an open hill under this grueling artillery fire, Morrow carefully and deliberately put the 24th Michigan through the manual of arms. His men performed with the precision of a parade. "It was a glorious sight to see nearly a thousand men standing at a 'support arms,' while the air was torn with cannon balls and the very hills seemed to rock under the reverberations," recorded one witness. The regiment moved back to find shelter in a ravine ditch to escape the plunging fire of the Confederate guns. During one of the final movements, a "single shot took off the heads of Lt. David Birrell and three others; killing also another and wounding three more, all in Company K." The regiment "nobly had . . . stood the fiery ordeal of its bloody baptism without the

70 Dawes, *Service*, 111.

poor privilege of returning an answering shot. It had won honor for itself and old Wayne County, but sorrow filled every breast."[71]

The artillery firing eased with the fall of darkness. When the regiments moved closer to a roadway, however, the noise aroused the Rebel gunners. "We could hear the sharp rattle of shot upon the ground. As the night was very dark, the firing was necessarily at random, and the danger not great, but the sound of the shot striking the ground was frightful." The night was very cold and fires were not allowed because they would give away the position. The cold and tired volunteers formed long lines of officers and men lying on their oil cloths, spoon fashion, to keep each other warm. After a few minutes, however, the command "About face!" sounded and the entire line of men rolled over as one to lie a few moments on the other side.[72]

In the Michigan regiment, Capt. William Wight struck out across the cold, gloomy, and dark battleground to "search for the trunkless head" of his 18-year-old son, Sgt. Wallace Wight. The regimental historian wrote that the younger Wight was one of the soldiers hit by solid shot. With the canister whistling above, the grieving captain located the grisly appendage and placed it with the young boy's remains for burial.

The Iron Brigade was waiting in the cold darkness when word arrived that Solomon Meredith had been relieved of command and replaced by Lysander Cutler of the 6th Wisconsin. It was later claimed the removal came about because of a mix-up involving an aide who carried an order to slightly change the line of the brigade to avoid an enfilading fire. Meredith misunderstood (or did not get the order), and when the line was not adjusted he was relieved of command by General Reynolds. The last position on the field found the 24th Michigan and 7th Wisconsin in one line with the others regiments holding a second line 200 paces to the rear. The next day, December 14, a portion of the 24th Michigan was sent forward on picket duty, but nothing of consequence arose. The Confederate position, one of the Michigan men reported, was found to be very strong "on hills covered with a thick growth of woods, protected in front and flank by creeks, marshes and almost impenetrable underbrush. The whole front was armed with batteries ready to repel any effort to storm their stronghold." At Burnside's headquarters, meanwhile, debates raged on whether the assaults should be renewed.[73]

71 Curtis, *Twenty-fourth*, 93-95.

72 Dawes, *Service*, 111.

73 Curtis, *Twenty-fourth*, 97.

A series of informal truces to care for the wounded and the dead broke out on the front held by the Iron Brigade and elsewhere. The Western dead were gathered and buried near where they fell along the banks of the Rappahannock River. That night, the veterans of the 2nd Wisconsin reached an agreement with the Confederates opposite them so both sides could get some rest: a warning shot would be fired before the contest resumed. At daybreak on Monday, December 15, the 24th Michigan replaced the 2nd Wisconsin on the picket line, where the Wolverines promptly opened fire. "This irritated the Confederates," one of the Western men recorded in understated fashion. The truce was reinstated that afternoon. The lull in the fighting led to talking, which evolved into wild claims about the war in general and the recent battle in particular. Frustrated to the point that shooting was not sufficient satisfaction, one of the Johnnies challenged one of the 6th Wisconsin men to a fist fight on the Bowling Green Road. Both sides watched as the two young soldiers slugged it out to what was regarded by all witnesses as a draw. There was some scattered cheering, and friend and enemy mingled to trade tobacco and coffee. Both sides agreed there would be no more fighting until either side ordered an advance.

A cold rain fell that night. In the darkness, said one of the soldiers, "silently and secretly, not above a breath, came the order to pack up and be ready to move." By midnight the blue columns were staggering toward the pontoon bridges. Pine boughs covered the wooden planks to deaden the rumble of moving artillery, horse hooves, and wagons.

Left behind a mile beyond what had been the brigade line was the 19th Indiana, whose job it was to watch the Rebels and keep them at a distance. General Reynolds had made the decision to abandon the Hoosiers to prevent an alarm during the withdrawal, but Colonel Cutler pleaded with the general and got permission to make an effort to save the regiment. When the Iron Brigade began marching for the bridges, Cutler sent his aide, Lt. Clayton Rogers, with an order for the commander of the 19th Indiana to call in his pickets and march for the pontoon crossing. The splendidly mounted Rogers, a man with an eye for good horses, "rushed to the extreme left with no regard to roads but straight as a bee flies." "The left once gained," a friend wrote, "he moderates his pace and whispers into the ear of each astonished officer." The order is passed by whispers and Rogers moved out to the picket line in a movement hidden by the stormy weather. A witness described the scene: "One by one our drenched boys are falling back and drawing in together. Silently as shadows the whole picket line steals across the plain. And now as the ranks closed up for rapid marching, 'double double quick' is about the pace." One bridge remained at the crossing point, and engineers were standing by with axes to cut it loose. It is only after the last of the 19th Indiana has passed that the mounted Rogers, "grimly smiling," rode onto the bridge himself. The rearguard of the regiment arrived a short time after the bridge lines were cut. They climbed into skiffs the engineers had held back for them and began paddling for the north bank. "[I]f we had been left as our head General at first designated terrible would have been our fate," a private in the 19th confessed in his diary, "or we would have known nothing of the retreat, and when the enemy advanced the 19th is not the Reg't to surrender without any fight." The consequence, he added, "would have been a wiping out of the old 19th."[74]

Horseman Lt. Clayton Rogers and his brother Earl enlisted in the 6th Wisconsin in a company named the "Anderson Guards" after the heroic defender of Fort Sumter. It was an "exceedingly fine body of soldiers" made up of pioneers "who had gone west to subdue the wilderness" of what was then Bad Ax County, now Vernon County, in Wisconsin. "Clayton Rogers was squarely built and a powerful frame. He possessed great energy and he was an indefatigable worker," said a friend. "He seemed to be absolutely fearless in battle. Earl Rogers was tall and slight, but firmly knit. He was an especial favorite in the regiment, being familiarly called "Bony" from his fancied resemblance to Napoleon Bonaparte. He had an epigrammatic manner of express that gave his sayings pertinence and force." Later in the war, after a bout of dysentery, Earl Rogers lost so much weight that his friends began to call him "Bony" Rogers. He did not like the description. Both men would be heard from in the coming year.[75]

After crossing the pontoon bridge over the Rappahannock River at the end of the fighting at Fredericksburg, the brigade marched two miles and bivouacked. Several artillery shells fired from an English Whitworth rifled cannon—which made an "unearthly scream"—were fired at random by the enemy about three miles away, but did no damage except cause Dawes and Dr. John Hall to abandon breakfast when one of the bolts swooped passed the ridge pole of their tent. The Fredericksburg losses were light because the brigade was not heavily engaged. The heaviest casualties—thirty-six—were reported from the largest regiment, the 24th

---

74 Dawes, *Service*, 112-113; Nolan, *Iron Brigade*, 186. The private was W. N. Jackson, whose diary entry was cited in *ibid.*, 187.

75 Dawes, *Service*, 113-114. Born into a Quaker family at Mount Pleasant, Pennsylvania, April 4, 1833, Clayton Rogers and his brother Earl moved to Wisconsin in 1849 in search of opportunity. They built a sawmill on the Kickapoo River at Whitestown (now Ontario) the first year and began establishing themselves on the frontier. Despite their responsibilities and Quaker background, both men enlisted in a volunteer company after Fort Sumter was fired upon. Mature and capable, Clayton Rogers was singled out for staff duty and served with Gens. Abner Doubleday and James Wadsworth. Stanley E. Lathrop, *A Brief Memorial Tribute to Captain Clayton E. Rogers* (Hayward, WI., 1900) 1; James G. Adams, *History of Education in Sawyer County Wisconsin* (McIntire, Ia.,1920), 237; Dawes, *Service*, 113-114.

Michigan, which spent much of the day under direct artillery fire. Seven Wolverines were killed outright, many others wounded, and two missing. The 2nd Wisconsin had eleven casualties; the 7th Wisconsin twelve; the 6th Wisconsin four, and the 19th Indiana six. Battery B of the 4th U.S. Artillery suffered two men and eight horses killed along with six men and five horses wounded. "We have just returned to this side of the river, after fighting for three days and nights," a Badger wrote home. "[W]e found more than our match while there. It was a big fight; ditto retreat."[76]

The building of the log houses to wait out the winter went quickly at the camp at Belle Plaine near the Potomac River. Simmering anger and dismay in the ranks spread over the conduct of the Union generals in the recent battle. "The army seems to be overburdened with second rate men in high positions, from General Burnside down," Dawes wrote home on Christmas Day. "Common place and whisky are too much in power for the most hopeful future. This winter is, indeed, the Valley Forge of the war." James Wadsworth took command of the division, replacing Abner Doubleday. His removal troubled Dawes, who described Doubleday as "a gallant officer . . . remarkably cool and at the very front of battle" near Battery B of the 4th U.S. Artillery at Antietam. New York State farmer-turned-soldier Wadsworth was generally considered a favorable choice. Regarded as a man of "strong character" and an "intensely practical commander," the old general was "indefatigable as a worker, and looking closely after details." Said one officer: "No commander could do more for the personal comfort of his men." Wadsworth was known to be one of the richest men in New York state, but the lower ranks liked the old general (it was rumored he served without pay) with his off-hand down home manner and his bushy white side-whiskers. The soldiers found it "a rare treat" to watch the old gentleman farmer overseeing the several oxen he brought into the army when mud hampered the movement of army mules. The general, often as not bespattered with grime and standing ankle-deep in mud and manure, would "Gee" and "Haw" the heavy animals as they pulled at the baggage wagons. The boys in ranks called the performance Wadsworth "whispering to his calves."[77]

The changes in higher command were far away, however, and in ranks the soldiers expressed dismay over Fredericksburg. The historian of Battery B called it "butchery" and another Black Hat wrote home, "I won't try to describe to you the

---

76 The losses from the Iron Brigade were taken from Curtis, *Twenty-fourth*, 99-100; Charlie Dow, *Portage Register*, December 27, 1862.

77 Dawes, *Service*, 129; Rufus Dawes to Mary Gates May 30, 1863; Dawes, *Service*, 146.

perfect contempt I feel for the man or men that runs us into such a place as we have just got out of."[78]

The magnitude of Fredericksburg added to a gloomy and dispirited holiday for the young soldiers far from home, but the new huts made for a comfortable camp. A large room was also constructed nearby to serve several usages. "By long association officers and men of the First Army Corps had become familiarly acquainted with each other. This greatly enlarged our social circle," Dawes said. The new building was used, he said, "for public gatherings and merry making. Here the young officers had periodical meetings, and there were hilarious songs, speeches and other amusing public performances."[79]

78 Albert Young, "His Pilgrimage," *Milwaukee Sunday Telegraph*, July 1, 1888; Dawes, *Service*, 114-115; Buell, *Cannoneer*, 44.

79 Dawes, *Service*, 115-116.

1863
Gettysburg

General Wadsworth's line atop Culp's Hill at Gettysburg.

(Left) Peleg G. Thompkins, La Crosse
Light Guards, Co. B, 2nd Wisconsin

Wisconsin Veterans Museum

An unidentified member of
the 2nd Wisconsin

Author's Collection

Part I: Worth a Man's Life

This Day of Darkness and Peril

The arrival of the New Year did little to mitigate the fact that the defeat along the Rappahannock River at Fredericksburg was a disaster for the National Army and a major setback for Abraham Lincoln's administration. Major General Ambrose Burnside's inept handling of the army nearly ruined his reputation, while the casualty list staggered a Northern population already growing tired of the war.

The effects of Fredericksburg rippled down through First Corps. Commander Maj. Gen. John Reynolds did little to burnish his record, though his rival, division leader Maj. Gen. George Gordon Meade, gained attention for his hard-fought breakthrough against Stonewall Jackson's front. Despite his new and larger command, John Gibbon had little opportunity to increase his already solid reputation because the Iron Brigade played a limited role on the army's far left flank. Still, the fighting by the new 24th Michigan established that regiment's place in an already storied unit. Brigade leader Sol Meredith's ill-advised battlefield maneuver resulted in his temporary relief from command, while his replacement, Lysander Cutler, won the respect of the men for rescuing the 19th Indiana; Cutler's aide, Clayton Rogers, once again proved able and fearless under fire. The uncle of Maj. Rufus Dawes, Ohio Congressman W. P. Cutler, summed up the situation in his memorandum book: "This is a day of darkness and peril to the country—The great trouble is the loss of confidence in the management of the army. Under [George] McClellan nothing was accomplished. Now Burnside fails on the first trial. McClellan's friends chuckle and secretly rejoice over the result—The Democrats cry peace and compromise clamor for McClellan, denounce the radicals, do everything to embarrass the government."[1]

---

1 Dawes, *Service*, 114.

After Fredericksburg, the Iron Brigade settled into its winter camp at Belle Plain to replay an endless routine of reveilles, drills, and inspections. "This Jan'y 1st finds 'Iron Brigade City' about complete and quite 'scrumptious,'" said a Wisconsin soldier. "My Chimney was not looking quite up to date somehow, so the boys capsized it and set up a new one and in the eve I treated them to a sugar-candy pull." The January weather was mild and duty light. "At nine p.m., Tattoo is sounded and the evening roll-call is made, and at ten p.m. Taps are beaten, all lights put out and the day is done." The health in the 19th Indiana was "tolerable good," one Hoosier wrote, but morale was down with the "soldiers discouraged, tired of the war and about the proclamation freeing the damed negroes." The army, he added, "has one third playing cards, the other going the duty and the last third deserting as fast as they can." The men in his regiment, however, were "playing there hands out."[2]

The Westerners expected to wait out the winter in camp, but orders on January 18 dashed that hope. Burnside intended to march around Lee's left flank and drive the enemy away from his strong fortifications. Two days later at noon, January 20, the Iron Brigade marched toward Stoneman's Switch on the railroad between Aquia and Fredericksburg. The weather was dry, the roads good, and the marching generally easy. Late in the afternoon, however, a "cold and driving storm penetrated the clothing and cut the faces of the men as they staggered along," wrote one who suffered under the intense weather changes. The column reached the railroad after dark and the troops made a wet camp in a sloppy field of Virginia mud as the storm "raged and howled" around them. "The mud, the cold winter rain, the wild wind and smoke of camp fires of wet wood, had inflicted discomforts, even miseries, upon our men not easily described," was how one officer put it.

The march resumed early the next morning, but the rain and muddy conditions nearly froze the column in place. Colonel Henry Morrow of the 24th Michigan wrote in his journal that the movement was miserable with "every foot of the road was a slush." The regiments struggled in ankle-deep mud. Sick and ill soldiers sought out the surgeons, but there was only one ambulance for each regiment. One "poor fellow" who was turned away marched about half the distance to camp, lay down in the mud in a fence corner, and died. "It was only another form of the casualties which in a thousand ways destroyed human life in the war," said Dawes. Wagons and artillery pieces were dragged and shoved through the quagmire while drivers whipped and cursed mules while wet and mud-covered companies of soldiers pulled on long ropes to move heavy guns sunk hub-deep. Dead horses and mules lined the roads. Individual soldiers sank into the mud, in some cases up to

2 Amos Rood, diary, January 1, 1863; A. W. Galyean, letter, January 6, 1863.

their waists, and comrades had to "build bridges of rails to get them out. It sometimes took four men to help one out of the mud."[3] Jerome Watrous of the 6th Wisconsin, an old newspaperman, came across Theodore R. Davis, the well-known artist for the *Harper's Weekly Illustrated News*, who had fallen in with a battery. The "boyish looking fellow, beardless, slim, straight as an arrow," was a great favorite among the troops because he had worked under fire with the soldiers watching. Davis was so completely worn out and discouraged by the mud march, however, that "he gave his horse away, together with all of his baggage except a blanket and struck for New York."[4]

The effort, waxed Watrous, was "one of the nastiest, stickiest and most disagreeable of all marches ever made by troops. . . . It rained and rained and rained, and then turned from raining to pouring. All the worlds above seemed to have had a washing day and were emptying their tubs right on that particular part of Virginia." Colonel Morrow watched a dozen horses trying to draw a 12-pound artillery piece. When the column finally halted, the Iron Brigade bivouacked in lines of battle facing the Rappahannock River. The regiments remained there all of the next day and into the next morning, January 22. Any hope of stealing a march on the Confederates was "stuck in the mud." Burnside ordered his army to return to its winter camps. Left behind were the floundered horses and mules to die in the mud, along with stalled artillery and wagons that had to be dug out after the ground dried. Later, the boys would say with smiles that they were willing to make their stand in Dixie, if it was not mud instead of land.[5]

The weary Western men reached their old camp only to find their snug huts occupied by infantry from the 55th Ohio. Angry words and raised fists followed until Col. John C. Lee, the Buckeye commander, invited the original inhabitants to come in and share the quarters with his men. The fault is not ours, explained the colonel, but the general who ordered us to take these quarters. "The greatest hilarity and good feeling prevailed between the two regiments after this," admitted a Wisconsin officer, "and the men of the fifty-fifth, pitying our forlorn condition, gave up the best they had for supper." When orders moved the Ohio regiment the

---

3 Dawes, *Service*, 116-117.

4 Jerome A. Watrous, *Milwaukee Sunday Telegraph*, January 10, 1886. "Davis was one of the army artists who knew what he was sketching. He was there and saw it. There was not a great battle in the Army of the Potomac up to the time he left it in '63, which he did not see, and when he was not under fire. He made the same sort of record in the western army. After he went west the Potomac boys were always anxious to see Davis' sketches, for they knew they were truthful; they knew Davis had been right there and looked on and had sketched from life." *Ibid.*

5 *Ibid.*; Dawes, *Service*, 117; Henry Morrow, diary, January 21-22, 1864.

following day, the Western men settled in for "the monotonous routine of camp duty."[6]

Despite the pleasant winter camp, the Army of the Potomac passed the days under a cloud almost as thick as the mud of the recent march. The early weeks of 1863 comprised one of the darkest periods of the war for the Union's Eastern army. After McDowell's failure at Bull Run in July 1861, McClellan's followed up his dismal performance outside Richmond the next summer with a campaign that barely turned aside the latest offensive of the Confederate army at Antietam. Now, newspaper headlines described in bold type faces how the Army of the Potomac was defeated and almost ruined at Fredericksburg, before being stuck in the mud. The war effort in the Western Theater was making somewhat better progress, though at a slow and brutal cost. William Rosecrans' army rang in the New Year with an important hard-fought victory at Stones' River that cleared Middle Tennessee of the enemy. Just days earlier farther west along the vital Mississippi River, however, Maj. Gen. U. S. Grant's army suffered another setback in its attempt to seize Vicksburg when a quick thrust at Chickasaw Bluffs was bloodily repulsed. Still, the twin Fredericksburg-Mud March disaster dominated headlines in the major media centers in the East. Congressman Cutler described the situation in his journal on January 26: "to-day it is said that Burnside has been relieved at his own request, and [Joseph] Hooker put in his place. Our Potomac army is so far a failure, and seems to be demoralized by the political influences that have been brought to bear upon it. All is confusion and doubt. The President is tripped up by his generals who seem to have no heart in their work. God alone can guide us through the terrible time of doubt, uncertainty, treachery, imbecility and infidelity."[7]

On February 15, Colonel Morrow traveled to Washington to find a distressed Brig. Gen. Solomon Meredith with orders to report to General Hooker under arrest for leaving camp without authority. Meredith asked Morrow to intercede on his behalf. Two days later Morrow found Hooker alone in his tent. The talkative commander told Morrow that he was "proud to be at the head of so noble an army as the Army of the Potomac—that it was the finest army in the world," and that his only fear was that the Rebels would get away before he could get a chance at them. As for politics, Hooker told Morrow he wanted nothing to do with it, and would "be prouder of a high position in the United States Army" than to be president. When Morrow advised Hooker to get rid of all the officers who would only fight

6   Dawes, *Service*, 117-118; Nolan, *Iron Brigade*, 190-191.

7   Dawes, *Service*, 118.

under McClellan, the commander replied "that was being done very fast and that all such officers would have to go." As for Meredith, Hooker promised to make an inquiry and, "if he was found not guilty of disobedience of orders he would be reinstated." Morrow left what he called "a most pleasant and interesting" interview with an elevated view of the commanding general's ability. Hooker's remarks were "shrewd, sagacious & pointed—He has great firmness of will, great goodness of heart & clearness of judgment."

Morrow met later that day with Senators Ben Wade and Morton S. Wilkinson, from whom he "learned enough to satisfy me that the intention of the government is to get rid of all the McLellan officers in the Army of the Potomac. [William B.] Franklin & [William F.] Smith have been removed & [John] Reynolds will be . . ."[8]

The Return of Mickey, of Company K

The naming of former First Corps leader Joe Hooker to replace Ambrose Burnside was greeted with favor in the Iron Brigade. The colorful and outspoken general had used his weeks in Washington recovering from his minor Antietam foot wound to plot with the powerful and influential for command of the army. Because of a pressman's error, newspapers called him "Fighting Joe" (Hooker disliked the name), and he was written up as a general of stout reputation. His promotion brightened the short days of the dismal winter of 1862-1863. Unaware of Hooker's political scheming, Rufus Dawes wrote home that the "Apollo like presence of General Hooker . . . his self-confident, even vain glorious manner, his haughty criticism of others and his sublime courage at the battle front have combined to make his impressions upon the public judgment that obscure his most valuable traits of character and his best qualities as commander." He went on: "With indefatigable zeal he addressed himself to the task of re-organization, and if I may so express it, re-inspiration."[9]

Despite an unsavory personal reputation, Hooker proved surprisingly apt when it came to running an army. Rations improved, new equipment and accouterments arrived, and long overdue furloughs were granted. The army was reorganized and camps of instruction resumed. Competent officers were promoted. Recognizing the merit of unit identity and pride, Hooker assigned a different woolen badge to each corps to be affixed to the hat or cap. Because divisions within a corps were designated by color, the First Division of the First

---

8 Morrow, journal, February 17, 1863.

9 Rufus Dawes to Mary Beman Gates, April 13, 1863; Dawes, *Service*, 118, 132.

Corps was marked with a red sphere or circle. The Iron Brigade received their new badges in mid-April. Hooker understood "the true Napoleonic idea of the power of an Esprit de Corps," remarked a Wisconsin officer, and the red badges became the "almost worshipped symbols of a glorious service." Another morale enhancement arrived with the paymasters. "Nothing is more disheartening and demoralizing to the soldier than to feel that his family is suffering at home for want of his small and richly earned wages," confessed one volunteer. For the first time since the days of McClellan, the men felt confident in their commander.[10]

More important to the men of the 6th Wisconsin was the reappearance of Pvt. James Patrick Sullivan. The return of the regimental favorite everyone called "Mickey, of Company K" was greeted along the company streets with shouts of happiness and welcome. The private had been shot in the foot at South Mountain on September 14, 1862 while fighting on the skirmish line with a silk handkerchief wrapped around his cheeks to ease a bad case of the mumps. Mickey's reputation for fearlessness peaked after an incident just before South Mountain. Worn out by a hard march, lack of food, and the heat, the Irishman stopped to rest. Burnside arrived on a "powerful black horse" and used the animal to force stragglers to back onto the road. Burnside, explained Mickey, was out of sorts, and when he reached the slight Irishman he ordered the resting private to get up. Sullivan paid no attention to the command, "as I considered I did not belong to his command and he was not my 'boss,' and with an exclamation that he'd make me leave there, he spurred his horse towards me." Sullivan said his Irish temper was aroused and he jumped up at the thought of being ridden over like a dog. He cocked his musket and brought it to a ready, "determined to let the results be what it would, to kill him right there." Burnside reined in his mount. "Whether he was struck with shame at the thought of riding down a tired and worn out boy, or that he saw death in my look, he stopped." When Burnside asked of his regiment and Sullivan answered, the general replied, "You are one of the Western men." After conferring briefly with an aide, Burnside advised Sullivan to hurry along before riding away. Sullivan was wounded a few days later at Turner's Gap on South Mountain.

The question put to him on his return to the regiment after being discharged was a simple one: "Why did you return?" After leaving the battlefield, he explained around camp fires that night, he was treated at a field hospital and eventually landed in Washington and the makeshift facility in the House of Representatives. There, surgeons removed the ball as well as the second toe of his right foot. Sullivan was

10 *Ibid.*, 125, 132. The order sent to the First Division detailing the shape of the badges and colors can be found in the regimental papers of the 7th Wisconsin Infantry, Wisconsin State Historical Society.

up and about by mid-December, when he was ordered to report to an examining board. "After some scientific stares through their eye-glasses and some scientific talk about 'cuspal,' and 'flexious' and a good deal more intelligible jargon," he was discharged and told to go home. When he objected, the Irishman was told he did not belong to the hospital any longer and must leave. Not having been paid in six months, Sullivan found himself on the streets of Washington flat broke except for carfare borrowed from a 56th Pennsylvania soldier to get him to the paymaster's office, which was locked with a card on the door that read "Closed for want of funds." It was a fine fix, Sullivan continued, "turned loose in a strange city, crippled, unknown, no money, and a thousand miles from home." When other ex-soldiers in the same circumstance told him of "a patriot, who, for patriotic considerations and a discount of 10 percent, would cash our papers, provided we accepted state currency, and considering that his patriotism and state currency were better than none," he and the boys "closed on his offer" and set off for home.

Once back in Wisconsin, however, boredom set in. The home folks welcomed and fed him well, but no one really listened when he tried to tell them about the war and soldiering. He also found it troubling that while he was eating his fill and sleeping in a soft bed, the friends in his old company were back in Virginia breaking teeth on hardtack and sleeping on the ground. "There was no company" back home, he said, "only discharged invalids that had killed half the rebel army, and men who were growling about the draft, the army, the scarcity of money . . ." Sullivan lasted six weeks before traveling to Madison to see if a fellow missing a middle toe could join the army once again. When a sergeant told him that "Anyone owning a name can enlist," Mickey found himself on his way to the war front, this time with a nine month enlistment "or sooner 'killed.'" It was the second of the three times he would sign a 6th Wisconsin muster roll. Sullivan reported for duty in the middle of February, 1863.[11]

To be Shot like Sheep in a Huddle

It all seemed to be going well for the enlarged and revitalized Army of the Potomac under Hooker. The regular arrival of the pay officers, better rations, additional furloughs, and other improvements lifted morale. An example of improving attitude was found in a tongue-in-cheek letter by Col. William Robinson of the 7th Wisconsin to Wisconsin officials. A commission had been received for

11 Sullivan, *Telegraph*, November 4, 1883, and May 13, 1888; U.S. Pension Office, James P. Sullivan file, affidavit of April 18, 1891. Born in Ireland around 1841, Sullivan and his family came to the Wisconsin Territory in the early 1840s.

Capt. A. Bean of Co. D, wrote the colonel, but his name was misspelled as "McBean." The captain, continued Robinson, wanted it known that his correct name was "Alexander W. Bean— 'and a very good quality of Bean it is'—and by the way, he wishes to go home on a short leave, for the furlough purpose, he says, of sowing the seed for another crop, as he thinks the service will need more of the store, perhaps before the present war closes." When the brigade's regiments marched from their camps during the last days of April, they did so with a new enthusiasm that "Fighting Joe" Hooker would deliver them a victory. This general knew his business, was a common campfire refrain.[12]

Joe Hooker's bold plan called for his 130,000-man army to envelop the enemy from west and east. George Stoneman's large cavalry corps would open the operation with a deep strategic raid in Lee's rear to cut supply lines in the hope that Lee would abandon his fortified position opposite Fredericksburg. Simultaneously, three of Hooker's seven infantry corps (Fifth, Eleventh, and Twelfth, about 40,000 men all told) would cross the Rappahannock well upriver, slip south across the Rapidan, and march around Lee's exposed left flank while another large component of the Second Corps crossed the Rapidan to join up in the movement. The third leg of his double-envelopment thrust two corps (First and Sixth, also about 40,000 men) under the overall command of Maj. Gen. John Sedgwick across the Rappahannock below Fredericksburg to threaten Lee's right flank. Sedgwick's wing included Maj. Gen. John Reynolds at the head of First Corps. Reynolds was under a political cloud because of his friendship with McClellan, and his role in this secondary operation was partially designed to keep him from winning too much acclaim. The infantry—including the Iron Brigade—would hit Fitzhugh's Crossing opposite a local landmark known as the Smithfield House. Hooker's remaining Third Corps and additional infantry (about 25,000) would remain in reserve and in camp (for a time) as a diversion to confuse the enemy. Hooker reasonably believed that if he could steal a march on Lee, the Confederate general would have no choice but to retreat—in which case Hooker would pursue aggressively and perhaps catch him in motion—or force him to fight without the initiative on unfavorable terrain.

The Black Hats broke camp at Belle Plain and reached the Rappahannock River below Fredericksburg about midnight on April 29, when they deployed to a ditched fence to wait for army engineers to lay a pontoon bridge. The plan was simple enough, but tactically complicated. Thousands of men and mule-drawn pontoon wagons would move to the water's edge. One brigade would cross on

---

12 The letter is dated March 11, 1863, and can be found in the 7th Wisconsin Regimental Letter and Order Book.

boats under the cover of darkness while engineers constructed a pontoon bridge. The boats did not reach the river until dawn. Despite a heavy fog, Confederates on the opposite bank opened with muskets and artillery. The shell fire panicked the Federal mule train hauling the pontoons and some of the animals bolted in a "grand skedaddle" for the rear, carrying off pontoon boats and extra duty men. Watching infantry scattered in front of this "frantic and ludicrous flight," only to be met with laughter and catcalls from their stationary comrades.[13]

The seriousness of the situation ticked up a notch when Confederate small arms fire drove back the engineers. The 6th Wisconsin, 24th Michigan, and 14th Brooklyn were dispatched to the water edge to suppress the fire. The ground was against them. The bank on the Union side of the river sloped gradually down to the water with little cover, while the Confederates on the higher opposite bank were in "a thriving growth of young timber down the side of the hill to the water. The copse was full of rifle pits, arranged for sharp-shooters." Beyond the bluff was "an elaborate system of breastworks." The Rebels, continued Mickey Sullivan, were "entirely concealed and all we could see was puffs of smoke, and our fire and a heavy cannonade had no effect on them."[14]

For thirty minutes both sides traded fire across the Rappahannock River without apparent effect. Something else had to be done. Reynolds withdrew the men from the bank. Already hours behind schedule, the general decided to storm the far shore. The honor of spearheading the assault fell to the veterans of the 6th Wisconsin and the new men of the 24th Michigan, together with a trio of companies from the 2nd Wisconsin, in boats described by one witness as "clumsy, flat bottomed, square-bowed institutions, about 25 feet long, 4 feet wide and 3 feet deep." The other regiments of the brigade—joined by the 14th Brooklyn—would deliver a covering fire. The first out were the 2nd Wisconsin men, using ropes attached to the pontoons to pull the boats to the river. One company was assigned to each boat with four men to man the oars. It was a bold and daunting situation, and the practical men of the frontier could see immediately that several things might go wrong. "I confess," admitted one officer, "that a shrinking from the proffered glory came over us to be shot like sheep in a huddle and drowned in the Rappahannock appeared to be the certain fate of all if we failed and of some if we succeeded."[15]

13 Dawes, *Service*, 136.

14 James P. Sullivan, "Charge of the Iron Brigade at Fitzhugh's Crossing," *Milwaukee Sunday Telegraph*, September 30, 1883; Sullivan, *Irishman*, 74-79.

15 Dawes, *Service*, 136.

It was Col. Edward Bragg who brought news of the planned assault to his regiment. Slight and always sharp-spoken, he bluntly laid out the situation in his usual bitten-off manner. He ordered the men to drop their knapsacks, haversacks, canteens, and other equipment and keep in mind their "western breeding and . . . skill as oarsmen . . . rush down to the river and each company take two boats and launch them and paddle and pole over as fast as possible." While the Black Hats stripped away excess gear, one volunteer joked loudly, "good-bye, vain world, farewell, knapsack, haversack and canteen." Others tore letters many times read and scattered the pieces before tucking photos into pockets. Only weapons and cartridge boxes remained. One Badger remembered how his comrades "seized the muskets with a firm grip and with teeth set as firm." Bragg ordered the percussion caps removed from the musket cones to prevent accidental firing. "We looked over the river with thoughts of what will be the destiny of the Sixth in the next half hour," wrote a soldier.[16]

As his regiment formed by fours, Bragg moved to the front to look over the situation. What he saw was not encouraging, and he later said that he expected to lose one-half of his men during the crossing. One of General Wadsworth's aides arrived, presented the general's compliments, and delivered the message to Bragg: "You are slow, Sir." The little colonel gave the rider a long hard look, pulled down his hat a little firmer, looked around, and replied, "Come on boys." That was the "all the orders we got," said one Wisconsin soldier. The regiment broke for the river on the run while behind them another officer shouted, "Keep your heads down, boys!" It was just after 9:00 a.m.[17]

Ahead of the 6th were the men of the 2nd Wisconsin, working the ropes dragging the pontoons from behind a small hill while yelling as "only soldiers can." When they cleared the rise with the heavy boat in tow, the Badgers were "met by a volley from the rifle pits on the opposite bank; but the balls mostly passed over our heads, lodging in and making the splinters fly most beautifully from the pontoons we were hauling." The regiments left behind put down a heavy fire, and "woe to the gray back that showed his head long enough for an Austrian rifle to be trained him," wrote one eyewitness. "The boats reached the river—were shoved in; some of them were so riddled as to be rendered useless; but others were soon filled with the boys."[18]

16 Earl Rogers, "Fitz-Hugh Crossing," *Milwaukee Sunday Telegraph*, August 7, 1887.

17 Edward Bragg to Rufus Dawes, no date; Sullivan, *Telegraph*, September 30, 1883.

18 Walter Rouse to the *Oshkosh Northwestern*, "Camp near White Oak Chapel, Va., May 15, 1863."

Colonel Edward Bragg, 6th Wisconsin

Bragg led the 6th Wisconsin in the Fitzhugh Crossing attack at
Fredericksburg, Virginia, during the Chancellorsville Campaign. *Author's
Collection*

The running men of the 6th Wisconsin passed Bragg, "who being small and short-legged, and having an immense pair of military boots and spurs on, was not able to keep ahead." When the colonel and his men reached the river all was a jumble, with officers and soldiers yelling while manhandling heavy boats into the water and doing their best to climb aboard. Behind them, 2nd Wisconsin men pulled additional boats to the river's edge. Some 6th men climbed into one boat only to discover the oars were still in the bottom of the pontoon. A mad scramble ensued to pull them up while men shouted "Shove her off!" again and again. One private yelled, "The first man up the bank shall be a general," while another called back something about showing "the Army why the old 6th was chosen to lead them." The boat was loaded amid a shower of bullets that ripped the river bank and chipped off large splinters. "It was no time to quail or flinch, one halt or waver was destruction," recalled Major Dawes, who climbed to the bow of his boat to swing his sword in one hand and cheer the oarsmen, while holding his pistol in the other to shoot them if they hesitated. Nearby, Capt. Thomas Kerr pressed the barrel of his revolver against the head of a frightened soldier to force him to climb into a boat or die on the wrong side of the Rappahannock.

Mickey Sullivan was in the second boat carrying the Company K men. "The Johnnies opened on us a deadly fire," he wrote. "Hoel Trumbull was one of our company who assisted in pushing our boat off, and he waded into the water and made a spring to get in, and some of us were assenting him when a bullet hit him in the head and he let go his hold and sank." Mickey kept his eyes glued on the spot "until we were more than half way across," but the unfortunate soldier did not resurface. "[B]eing on the upper side of the boat, I commenced firing on the rebels," continued the Irishman. "[T]he water fairly boiled [from Confederate bullets] . . . and it is a mystery to me now how our boat escaped being sunk." The men were piled three deep in some boats. "The scene of wild excitement which then ran high is indescribable," reads one Wisconsin report of the crossing. "Whiz-whiz-spat- spat, their bullets struck around us. Our men rose in the boat and fired." One of the Sauk County boys stood at the edge of his nearby boat, shouting at the top of his voice. "I half expected to see him fall into the river and drown," related a friend.[19]

The heavy Confederate fire splashed alongside the boats, pinning down the oarsmen. "The balls from the rebels came skipping over the water and occasionally crashing through the boat amongst the men's legs and musket stocks," said one

---

19 Cheek and Pointon, *Sauk County*, 64-65. The private was Bodley Jones of Baraboo. Trumbull enlisted May 10, 1861, from Lemonweir and was killed in action on April 29, 1863.

Wisconsin officer, "while the regiments in the rear were firing over our heads at the rebels in the work beyond the river had good effect in keeping the Johnnies down." According to Dawes, fifteen of his men were shot before they even reached the boats. Colonel Henry Morrow of the 24th Michigan, in one of the first boats, was "so impatient . . . [he] could hardly keep himself in the boat." Ahead on the opposite shore, amid the shouting and paddling, "shaggy-backed butternuts began to climb for the top of the rugged bank" only to be hit and tumble back down again. A Michigan man told his home folks that his regiment crossed under "a heavy fire, but we came at them like so many wild men. They were scared and left their holes in a hurry as soon as we struck the shore."[20]

Every Man for Himself and a Rebel

When the first wave of boats drew near the contested shore, "We tumbled into the mud or water, waist deep, wade ashore, crawled and scrambled up the bank," wrote a Badger. "Nobody could say who was first." Once bayonets sheathed on the crossing were pulled out and fixed into place with a metallic snap, with a yell and very little shooting it was "every man for himself—and a Rebel." According to Colonel Bragg, "The 24th Michigan were ordered across at the same time & did their duty nobly, but the 6th were in for a fight, and they led the run, and flung out their flag, first on the enemies [sic] shore, and then, such cheering & shouting that you never heard—Everybody was crazy— we had been ordered to do it—had done it in the face of the enemy & gallantly—that old soldiers 'behaved foolishly in the exhibitions of joy.'"[21]

The boat carrying the Anderson Guards of Company I, 6th Wisconsin, claimed to be the first to reach the Confederate-held bank. "The men were quickly on land and without waiting for any formation, as quickly rushed up the tangled slope, through grape vines and brush on to the works," remembered Lt. Earl Rogers, "when the rebels ran in great confusion, our men shooting and in such great excitement were as unmanageable as wild men, made so by the complete victory under such disadvantage." The unlucky Cpl. Gabriel Ruby of De Soto fell dead when a ball fired by fellow Federals from across the river struck him. When a Confederate leveled his musket and mortally wounded Pvt. Charles Conklin of Viroqua, Pvt. Sam Wallar returned the favor by lifting his own weapon and killing the man. Private Levi Stedman of Brookville, "a big, overgrown boy of 17, standing

20 *Ibid.*, 64-65.

21 Dawes, *Service*, 136; Sullivan, *Telegraph*, September 30, 1883; Bragg to Dawes, no date.

Captain Alexander Gordon, Jr., Wisconsin Rifles, Co. K, 7th Wisconsin

Gordon was mortally wounded at Fitzhugh's Crossing at Fredericksburg, Virginia, during the Chancellorsville Campaign. *Wisconsin Historical Society 25643*

on the right of the company and 6-feet-6 [dislocated his knee jumping out of the boat and] was left sitting in the mud with his feet in the water, and crying because he could not go on with his company."[22]

The 7th Wisconsin landed on the left of the 6th. They were organizing for an advance when a volley knocked down Capt. Alexander Gordon, Jr. and killed Lt. William O. Topping. "Boys, I am struck!" exclaimed Gordon, who pulled open his accouterment belt and sat down with a surprised look on his face. When one of his privates told the officer that he appeared to be hit in the arm, Gordon replied that he could feel the bullet in his chest. Both men were right: The ball entered his arm first before passing into his body. The wound proved mortal and his death a short time later was especially troubling. Gordon was much admired and his marriage to his childhood sweetheart while the regiment mustered at Madison was a great celebration with the men of his new company. His subsequent burial in Beloit drew a mournful assembly much larger than the First Congregational Church could accommodate.[23]

The 6th Wisconsin moved right and left of the Smithfield house and cleared the immediate area of enemy. There was some laughter and excitement when one of the Sauk County "little fellows"—Charles Kellogg of Baraboo— "brought in a large, burly fellow about twice his own size," and Bill "Nosey" Palmer chased down a Rebel, gaining on him at every step until he finally caught him with his bare hands.[24]

The first boats returned to pick up more Federals to secure the beachhead and were about to return when old General Wadsworth, caught up in the moment, yelled, "Hold on!" to the men in one boat. The general tossed the reins of his horse over the animal's head and jumped into the stern of the boat, pulling at his horse as the boat pushed off. When the horse balked, Wadsworth ordered a nearby officer to "Push him in lieutenant." With the horse in the water and swimming, Wadsworth struck a pose much as we imagine George Washington had some nine decades earlier. When the boat reached the far bank, Wadsworth jumped into the water and made his way to the bluff, where he moved from "company to company,

22 Rogers, *Telegraph*, August 7, 1887. Conklin enlisted on June 1, 1861, and Ruby on the same date. Ruby had also been wounded at Antietam on September 17, 1862. Stedman also enlisted on June 1, 1861, and was also wounded at Antietam. He would die on July 17, 1863, from wounds received on the first day of battle at Gettysburg west of town. *Wisconsin Roster*, vol. 1, 529, 531, 532.

23 *Wisconsin Newspaper Volumes*, vol. 8; 408; Thomas Walterman, *There Stands "Old Rock:" Rock County, Wisconsin, and the War to Preserve the Union* (Friendship, Wisconsin, 2001), 254.

24 Cheek and Pointon, *Sauk County*, 64-65, 212.

Fitzhugh Crossing

A drawing depicting the crossing of the pontoon boats under fire at Fitzhugh Crossing.
Institute for Civil War Studies

thanking the men for their brave assault." The old general's cap showed two new bullet holes.[25]

By 10:30 a.m., the pontoon bridges were complete and the rest of the First Division crossed the river and secured the bridgehead. "Without discredit to any regiment, I have the honor to report, without the fear of contradiction, that the 6th Wisconsin Volunteers first scaled the bank and their colors first caught the breeze on the southern bank of the Rappahannock on the morning of April 29," Bragg boasted in his after-action report of the crossing and fight. Colonel Morrow, however, disagreed. He claimed it was his 24th Michigan "in the lead, its flag landing first."

To the historian of the Wolverines it mattered not: "It was a neck and neck race, between two friendly regiments of the Iron Brigade . . . and there were bullets and glory enough for both." The Michigan regiment led the casualty list with twenty-two killed and wounded, the 6th Wisconsin lost sixteen from all causes, the 7th Wisconsin nine, and the 2nd Wisconsin just six. Slightly fewer than 100 Confederates were captured and two or three dozen more killed and wounded. It only took about fifteen minutes from the time his company ran toward the river until the bluff was seized, or so Mickey Sullivan remembered, but it was the

25 John A. Kress, "At Gettysburg," *St. Louis Missouri Republican*, December 4, 1886.

"grandest fifteen minutes of our lives!" In the end, the successful river crossing was for naught.[26]

While the Iron Brigade moved on Fredericksburg, Hooker moved west and then south with the bulk of his army in his attempt to get around the left flank of Lee's army. Once alerted by his cavalry that Hooker had flanked the army and was advancing to strike him, the Southern general did not panic and withdraw, as Hooker hoped he might. Instead, Lee violated a principle of military tactics by splitting his army in the face of a superior enemy. He sent a large part of his command west under Stonewall Jackson to confront the main Union column, leaving a smaller segment at Fredericksburg to watch Sedgwick. When Jackson's divisions met the Union advance a bit before noon on May 1, a surprised Hooker stopped, fell back into the heavy woods, and consolidated his position. After executing a brilliant plan that fooled Lee, Hooker turned over the initiative to his aggressive counterpart. Later that night when he found that Hooker's right flank was subject to being turned, Lee sent Jackson with about 26,000 men on a daring 16-mile march over backwoods roads to strike it. The decision left Lee with only 16,000 men to face the bulk of Hooker's army. Jackson followed up his legendary march with a bold late afternoon attack on May 2 that crushed Hooker's right and reunited the wings of the Southern army the following day. (Jackson had been mortally wounded by his own men the evening of his attack, and died on May 10.) On May 3, Hooker was concussed by an explosive shell that landed near him. Although his army substantially outnumbered Lee and had erected stout breastworks across much of its front, Hooker ended the operation on the evening of May 5 and began withdrawing across the river.

The Shooting of a Deserter

When Joe Hooker halted his advance and prepared a defense near Chancellorsville, the Iron Brigade and the First Division was hurriedly withdrawn from the hard-won far bank of the Rappahannock and gathered with other commands as a reserve. Thereafter the Western men (and many thousands more) did not fire another shot. On May 6, the brigade joined the rest of the defeated army moving back across the river crossings to safety. Somehow, the Army of the Potomac suffered another stunning reverse at the hands of the Army of Northern Virginia. The high hopes, well-executed early marching, and desperate fighting produced nothing but the loss of 17,200 Union men killed, wounded, and captured

26 Cheek and Pointon, *Sauk County*, 65.

(compared with Lee's 13,300) and one of the army's most humiliating defeats. Only Jackson's fatal wounding dimmed the Confederate success.

As the Federal brigades trudged back to their old camps, no one—from Joe Hooker to the lowest private—could explain how they had been whipped. The unexpected defeat shook the nation's confidence just as surely as it squeezed the resolve of the officers and men. "Never an army had such confidence as we when we gave battle," asserted an officer. "In no single instance were we outfought, but we gained nothing, and in a great degree lost our confidence in the head of affairs." Hooker abandoned the offensive not because his army lacked the ability to fight on, argued another officer, but "because he was outgeneraled and defeated—a humiliating confession, I own, but I believe true."[27]

If Chancellorsville dashed hopes in the North, it little affected morale within the ranks of the Iron Brigade. Although disappointed about the defeat, the veterans of some of the hardest fighting of the war were convinced their brigade accomplished one of the battle's most stunning feats of soldiering—a river crossing under heavy fire in wooden pontoon boats against a strongly posted and determined foe.

The Westerners spent the waning days of May much as they had the previous five months—waiting to see what was going to happen next. Many speculated that Lee would march his battalions north once more, just as he had the previous September of 1862, to feed and supply his soldiers as well as to lure the Federal army into a decisive battle on Union soil. Union officers spent the long days readying their companies and regiments for the next round of fighting certain to come, whenever or wherever it occurred.

Of more direct importance was the lack of faith the men felt in Joe Hooker. The army had fought well at Chancellorsville despite the outcome, and would do so again if only given the chance to meet the enemy on something approaching equal footing. After the string of defeats and near-misses, the soldiers understood the next fight was more important than the last. "To speak it plainly the Army of the Potomac was mad clear through; every man's pride was touched," one soldier complained. "There had been successive changes in the general command, and a heap of marching, with defeat after defeat emblazoned on our banners; the few victories were either not appreciated by those high in authority, or passed over so lightly as to be the subject of little or no concern." Catcalling Rebels only added to the embarrassment and growing anger of the men in blue. "Where is Hooker now, I haven't seen him for some time?" shouted an enemy picket from across the

---

27 Bragg to his wife May 22, 1863; Dawes, *Service*, 142.

Rappahannock River. The Federal response was quick, but not nearly as satisfying: "Oh, he's gone to Jackson's funeral."[28]

How could the situation have changed so quickly? Just weeks earlier the consensus was that the war's turning point was at hand. After two bloody years of trying to suppress the Southern rebellion, the National armies were on the move. Middle Tennessee was solidly in Union hands, Vicksburg and Port Hudson were the targets of two large Union offensives, and a new commander was preparing to lead the veteran soldiers of the star-crossed Army of the Potomac to Richmond. So much had changed in so little time.

On June 3, 1863 the head of Lee's army left camp to begin a long march northwest toward the Shenandoah Valley and then north toward the Potomac River. Lieutenant General Richard Ewell's Second Corps led the march, followed by James Longstreet's First Corps men. A. P. Hill's Third Corps waited in place above Fredericksburg to protect the army's rear and to deceive the Federals into thinking that Lee's army was still in place. Hooker learned of the move a couple days later, challenged Hill on the Fredericksburg line, and believed Lee was still in place. After the large cavalry battle of June 9 at Brandy Station, and Ewell's stunning victory well down the Valley at Winchester, however, Hooker realized Lee was making a serious stab north and acted accordingly. The army moved cautiously, shielding Washington and Baltimore while Federal cavalry tried to figure out exactly where Lee's army was located. The Southern leader had seized the initiative, striking out north determined to relieve a Virginia torn by war, feed his men and horses on Northern food stocks, and hopefully force the Union to abandon the growing threat against Vicksburg. Lee knew the recent Federal reverses had dampened Union war spirit, and hoped a decisive Confederate victory on Northern soil might bring a political end to the war. If successful, perhaps the Republicans supporting the war would be defeated in upcoming elections and enemies of the war would "become so strong that the next administration will go in on that basis."

The Iron Brigade and other elements of the First Corps left their camps on June 12 on the march that would carry them into Pennsylvania. It got off to a grim start when the columns halted at noon to shoot a deserter. His name was James Woods, a private in the 19th Indiana. Woods walked away from his regiment before the fighting at Fredericksburg in December 1862 and then again in May just before Chancellorsville. When caught, he begged one more chance. The verdict was

---

28 Otis, *Second Wisconsin*, 83; Walker S. Rouse to *Oshkosh Northwestern*, June 11, 1863, cited in Mark R. Karweick, editor, *Ever Ready: A History of the Oshkosh Volunteers—Co. E, 2d Regiment of Wisconsin Volunteer Infantry, 1861-1865*, unpublished manuscript.

swiftly delivered: death by firing squad.[29] The execution was set for June 12, a Friday, but marching orders reached the division the night before and the regiments were on the road before daylight. Handcuffed and shackled, Woods was brought along in an ambulance sitting on the wooden coffin that would be his final resting place. Condemned men "were shot as we marched so that the sentences of the court-martial could not be mitigated by telegrams from Washington," explained one officer. "Desertions had become so frequent that only the extreme penalty of death would put a stop to them."[30]

The tough veterans of Gainesville, Second Bull Run, South Mountain, Antietam, Fredericksburg, and Chancellorsville understood the execution was more than just the final punishment for a soldier who had failed his duty, and more than a warning for the men still in the rank. This was a purging. Men like Wood weakened every battle line into which they were forced. "No man can fight when surrounded by cowards, who are easily panic stricken, and who are unrestrained by any consideration of pride from ignominiously running way to save their lives," one soldier observed.[31]

The quick execution in an open field was just one more stopping point on the long dark road of civil war. Yet, the incident haunted the hard veterans who witnessed it. One soldier writing two decades later understood what had happened that June day in 1863 in Virginia: "I can still see that poor trembling, moaning fellow drop back into the coffin. It seemed hard, but it was just."[32]

Tired, Sore, Sleepy, Hungry, Dusty and Dirty as Pigs

The First Corps and the Iron Brigade were in the advance of the Union march that roughly shadowed the Confederates. The twisting columns flowed slowly northward over the dusty roads in a dull tangle amid the din of shuffling feet, rolling wheels, creaking harness, animal cries, and, as usual, cursing and shouting. The soldiers, and even the animals, were out of sorts over the column's hurry and wait.

29 Clayton E. Rogers, "Shooting a Deserter," *Milwaukee Sunday Telegraph*, May 24, 1885; Howard J. Huntington, *Milwaukee Sunday Telegraph*, March 1, 1885; E. R. Reed, "Shooting a Deserter," *Milwaukee Sunday Telegraph*, April 12, 1885; James P. Woods court-martial record, citied in Gaff, *Bloody Field*, 248-249.

30 Kress, *Republican*, December 4, 1886.

31 Frank Wilkeson, "Coffee Boilers," *Milwaukee Sunday Telegraph*, August 1885; Dawes to Mary Beman Gates, August 6, 1863; Dawes, *Service*, 197.

32 Jerome A. Watrous, "Three of a Kind—Reminiscences," *Milwaukee Sunday Telegraph*, April 6, 1882.

The marching men were jolly in rainy weather and quiet and sullen in hot. When temperatures reached uncomfortable levels, exhausted soldiers dropped out of the columns. Some marchers collapsed of sunstroke. Officers carried the muskets and knapsacks of used-up men as the regiments, thinned by straggling, slogged on muddy roads or cut through immense clouds of dust. Dead men and those unable to keep up were left by the roadside. The soldiers were "tired, sore, sleepy, hungry, dusty and dirty as pigs," was how one Wisconsin man described himself and his comrades. "Our army is in a great hurry for something." The march was hard and getting harder.

People who saw them those days recognized the men of the distant frontier were somehow different, with a certain dash and sense of themselves as they moved along roads with a quick stride, eyes bright and watching under their big hats. The open land, deep woods, and good water of Wisconsin, Michigan, and Indiana attracted ambitious and active men interested in making a name and a future. It was not a place for the weak. Those who came were the hardy sons of New England and Pennsylvania and Ohio and New York as well as steady fellows from Germany, Ireland, and Norway. "They were young men and youths in their very prime; a sturdy, stalwart, self reliant element such as push out to develop a new country," wrote one observer. "Their superiority was noticeable." Whenever a Western regiment appeared, the "fine physique, the self-reliant carriage of its men at once challenged attention." One Badger put it plainly, "We would have died rather than have dishonored the West. We felt that the eyes of the East were upon us."[33]

It was a reorganized Army of the Potomac that marched north that mid-June of 1863. The command shuffles touched even the proud "Old First Corps." The organization dated its existence to 1861, when McClellan created an army. Major General Irvin McDowell was the first to lead the corps, followed by Joe Hooker. The famous unit was now under West Pointer John Reynolds, an officer with a solid military reputation even though some in the Lincoln Administration questioned his politics. It was going into the third summer of the war reduced by hard service as well as the muster out of the two-year New York regiments and the brigade of nine-month New Jersey volunteers who had temporarily replaced them. As a result, two of the three divisions of the First Corps were down to two infantry brigades instead of the usual four. More important to the Wisconsin, Indiana, and Michigan men was their redesignation as the First Brigade of the First Division of

33 Ed. E. Bryant, "Our Troops!" *Milwaukee Sunday Telegraph*, October 26, 1879; Curtis, *Twenty-fourth*, 466. The quotation is from Phil Cheek of the 6th Wisconsin to a Grand Army of the Republic meeting in Detroit.

Maj. Gen. John Reynolds First Corps, Army of the Potomac

Reynolds was killed just west of Gettysburg during the opening of the fighting on July 1, 1863. He was directing the 2nd Wisconsin men into the Herbst woodlot atop McPherson's Ridge when he was struck in the back of the head. *Howard Michael Madaus Collection*

the First Army Corps. The news triggered a loud though harmless round of boasting. An officer wrote to his best girl that his 6th Wisconsin was now "by designation, the first regiment in the volunteer army of the United States. As a brigade, we are one of the oldest in the army and deserve the title."[34] If Lee will give us a "good opportunity," asserted one soldier, the Black Hats were ready to pitch into him."

The Iron Brigade regiments marched twenty miles on the first day of the pursuit of the Confederate army, a dozen miles the second, and a long thirty miles on the third. The march to Leesburg, Virginia on June 17 was especially severe with little water and "heat like a furnace." The "sun poured down," reported a Wisconsin soldier, and along the road "you could see the boys laying, given out. Perhaps one fainting, a sun struck man and others you would see pouring water on their heads. The heat and dust is awful." A Michigan man wrote home: "I hardly think I shall ever again think water too muddy to drink—not in the Army at least." Another soldier claimed the dust was a "foot deep" in some places and when "the wind blows the dust flies so that it is impossible to see the sky." At Centreville, the First Division halted to rest. Fresh newspapers reached the column bringing "bad news about the rebs in Maryland & Penn. Some . . . within 16 miles of Harrisburg [Pa.]." The sketchy reports claimed the Confederates were threatening not only Harrisburg, but Philadelphia and Baltimore, gathering up anything that could be

---

34 Nolan, *Iron Brigade*, 20-21, 223-224.

used or carried off—wagons, fodder, horses, mules, and various foodstuffs both on the hoof and off.[35]

In Maryland, as the Iron Brigade neared the Pennsylvania state line, 6th Wisconsin company commander Lt. Loyd Harris noticed a "beautiful girl, scarcely twenty" at the gate of her home waving a large American flag. The mounted officers doffed hats and bowed and the men in ranks were smitten. "Every last man seemed ready to give his life if necessary for that fair patriot, yet did not seem to know just what to do." Taking matters in his own hand, Harris ordered his men take up the step and bring rifle-muskets to "Right shoulder, shift." The boys "caught the idea, every head was up; the fours perfectly aligned—then as we just opposite the maiden, I commanded, 'Carry arms!' Down came the very bright shining muskets. The next company did the same and all the companies . . . gave her a salute as if she were general of the army."[36]

The long blue columns were moving in areas untouched by war; foraging became a problem. Headquarters sent down a circular to establish a camp guard. On June 22, Brig. Gen. Sol Meredith issued an order forming a "Brigade Guard" to be "mounted at the same hour each day when circumstances will permit until further orders." The detail of 100 men under the command of two officers was made up of privates and noncommissioned officers from each of the five regiments. Meredith's order also contained a curious paragraph that raises the impression that the old stump-speech politician now in uniform might just like the pomp and show of military life. Each day from the detail, he ordered, would be selected "one Sergeant, three corporals and fourteen privates for special guard duty at HeadQrs." These men would be picked "with special reference to cleanliness and soldierly bearing," and would be brought to the guard formation about 9:00 a.m. with the brigade "band playing." No official reason was given for the special headquarters detail.[37]

The commander of the First Division, James Wadsworth, seemed to be everywhere those days trying to lift the burden of his marching soldiers. The general reached into his own pocket to buy fence rails to build roadside fires so his men could boil coffee, secured straw from a farmer to make beds, and ordered the valises of the officers serving on his staff thrown from an ambulance to fill it with

35 Dawes to Mary Beman Gates, June 15, 1863, June 18, 1863, and June 21, 1863; Shepard to his mother, June 11, 1863.

36 Grayson, Loyd G. Harris, "Fredrick City to Gettysburg," *Milwaukee Sunday Telegraph*, January 25, 1885.

37 General Order No. 24, Order Book, First Brigade, First Division, First Army Corps, 7th Wisconsin, Records, National Archives.

the knapsacks and muskets of the exhausted men. The 55-year-old's kind gestures impressed the men, but one action in particular endeared the old gentleman to the rank and file. When his route carried him past a large flour mill, Wadsworth noticed the proprietor and his employees sitting on the front step watching the marching soldiers. The general guided his mount to offer a greeting and ask if there was any source of footwear available for his men. The proprietor's "surly and ungracious" reply aroused the general's ire. "You have a good pair of boots on your feet, give them to one of my soldiers!" Wadsworth ordered. When the miller sputtered a refusal, the division leader instructed an orderly to take possession of the footwear. "It was quickly done," wrote one of Wadsworth's staff.[38]

Another sign of the hard marching manifested itself at Broad Run. Lieutenant Harris was finishing breakfast when one of his privates, worn out by the long miles and lack of water, was brought in under guard. Dick Marston, a farm boy from Crawford County, was found sleeping on a guard post. Ironically, Marston was known in the ranks as "Sleepy Dick." Harris knew that sleeping while on picket duty "in the face of Lee's Army, meant a drum head court-martial and death; for the discipline of the army was being enforced in a most vigorous manner." The lieutenant was convinced it would be "like murder to have this young man, only twenty-one years of age, shot like a deserter or a traitor." He explained his position to Lt. Col. Rufus Dawes, who was just then in command of the regiment with Edward Bragg off in Washington recovering from the vicious kick of a horse. (Bragg was promoted to colonel when Lysander Cutler was given a brigade command and Dawes had been moved into the number two position.) Dawes was still getting used to making command decisions and was steadfastly against releasing Marston with a just warning. Harris "stormed considerable; then begged" until Dawes relented and visited brigade headquarters to see what could be done. A short time later "Sleepy Dick" was released from arrest. He had heard it all, he told relieved friends—how Dawes enlisted General Meredith and the two went to headquarters to see Wadsworth ("Three warm hearts," was how Harris described the trio of officers), and how Wadsworth ("glorious old man that he was") ordered the young soldier be given a stern warning and released. When he finished his story, Marston shook his head in thanks as the "tears started in his eyes, and his voice failed him; but we all felt happy that he was with us, safe and sound." That night, a pleased and relieved Dawes wrote in a letter to his sweetheart, "I had a chance to do

38 Dawes, *Service*, 183; Kress, *Republican*, December 4, 1886; Sullivan, *Irishman*, 77, 78, 95-97, 102. When it was discovered that the division headquarters' papers and the general's own valise had been abandoned, men were dispatched to recover them.

a good thing this morning and it gave me pleasure." The march was hard and getting harder.[39]

In Maryland on June 25, a group of school children stood solemnly by the roadside watching the Western regiments pass. The youngsters were a "most beautiful sight," wrote a Michigan man, a reminder of home that "brought tears to many an eye."[40] By the 27th the advance column was at Middletown, not too far from the old fighting ground at Antietam. That evening, Dawes and Meredith rode to the old battlefield of the previous September. "The grass has grown green over the graves of our brave boys, who lie buried there," Dawes remembered. "The inscriptions on the head boards are already scarcely legible and with their destruction seems to go the last poor chance that our sacrifice these men have made for their country shall be recognized and commemorated."

The next day was a Sunday and Lts. Orrin D. Chapman and Loyd Harris of the 6th Wisconsin were in command of the picket line. There were no enemies within miles, and Chapman "scraped an acquaintance" with a nearby farmer. The family had a "very good parlor organ" the men carried outside to the porch. Hymn books were found and passed around as the Crawford County boys clustered around the porch. The farmer's daughters sang soprano, the old man boomed a deep bass, and Harris and Chapman joined in "on the still quiet air of that bright sunny morning." Here is what the impromptu group sang:

> The morning light is breaking—
> The darkness disappears.
> The sons of earth awaken
> To penitential tears;
> Each breeze that sweeps the ocean,
> Brings tidings from afar.
> Of Nations in commotion,
> Prepare for Zion's War.

Buttermilk at 25-cents a Glass

When the dusty First Corps column tramped past Emmitsburg, students of St. Joseph's Catholic College turned out to welcome the Black Hats. Several of them

39 Grayson Loyd Harris, "Asleep at his Post," *Milwaukee Sunday Telegraph*, June 6, 1880; Rufus Dawes to Mary Beman Gates June 24, 1863; Dawes, *Service*, 155-156.

40 Curtis, *Twenty-fourth*, 150.

with "great enthusiasm" kept pace with the column well beyond the town. "They were much interested in watching the movements of our advance guard and flankers, the feelers of the army," observed one of the Black Hats. "They wanted to see us 'flush the enemy.'"[41]

The next day word coursed rapidly through the ranks of the army: Hooker was out as commander of the Army of the Potomac and Maj. Gen. George Gordon Meade of the Fifth Corps had been named his successor. There was some talk in the ranks that John Reynolds, commander of First Corps (like Meade, a Pennsylvania man) should have gotten the post. "Meade lacked the martial bearing and presence of Hooker," one officer argued. "Few of our men knew him by sight. He was sometimes seen riding by the marching columns of troops at a fast trot, his hat brim turned down and a poncho over his shoulders. The only sign of rank was a gold cord on his hat." Meade added to the sense of unease by producing a clumsy first official communication to the army. In it, he reminded the soldiers that the "whole country looks anxiously to this army to deliver it from the presence of the foe." It was the final sentence that caused the trouble: "Corps and other commanders are authorized to order the instant death of any soldier who fails to do his duty at this hour." As one Michigan man put it, a simple appeal to the honor of the men in the ranks "would have sufficed." After the 6th Wisconsin was mustered for pay on June 30, Dawes read Meade's address to the regiment without comment. Before he bedded down for the night, Rufus Dawes wrote a letter to his sweetheart. Scribbled near the top was this line: "Bivouac in Pennsylvania, On Marsh Creek, near Gettysburg."[42]

The march from Emmitsburg into Pennsylvania the next day was an easy one. The Iron Brigade was in the advance, and it was the 6th Wisconsin that first crossed into the Keystone State. At the halting point at midday at Marsh Creek, the Second Brigade camped in a cultivated field south of the sluggish creek while the Iron Brigade regiments erected their small shelter halves along the north bank. They had only covered about five miles. When the 19th Indiana was designated to picket the road ahead, four companies of the Hoosiers pushed on, stopping just short of the small crossroads town of Gettysburg. The Confederates were also operating in the vicinity, but no one knew exactly where.

The Westerners used the warm afternoon to wash clothes or get rid of the dust and dirt with a swim in a nearby millpond. It was also an opportunity to gather in a

41 Dawes, *Service*, 158.

42 Rufus Dawes to Mary Beman Gates, June 18, 22, 24, 27, 1863; Dawes, *Service*, 157; Ray, *Iron Brigade*, 184.

decent meal. Farmers brought in chicken, fresh bread, and pies for the soldiers and a Michigan soldier said that foragers who slipped through the picket line came back with an "abundance of chicken, geese, pigs, mutton, milk, butter, honey." Private James Sullivan filled his canteen with milk given to him by a Dutch farmer, while Charles Walker of the 7th Wisconsin, assigned to the Brigade Guard, rested in a barn. Another member of the detail, Pvt. William Ray of the 7th Wisconsin, got "a good supper & some milk for which we paid 25 cts a piece." Lieutenant Amos Rood of the 7th Wisconsin rode about until he found a tavern. "I went in and said, 'Boss, fill my three canteens for the General.' I got the stuff. Kept one for myself and distributed the others to brother officers and men." The satisfied officer spurred his horse back to Emmitsburg to find a home in which he could complete his monthly company returns.[43]

Other soldiers were less fortunate. A Wisconsin man attached to Battery B of the 4th U.S. Artillery scuffled with a Pennsylvania farmer who demanded a high price for fresh milk. When the soldier shrugged off the protests and milked the cow himself, the farmer followed him back to camp to demand the officer in charge punish the thief. The soldiers expected to be welcomed as "deliverers of the country from a hated foe, to live on the fat of the land, milk, chickens, honey, eggs, butter and potatoes in profusion, without much money, and not at very high price," explained one officer. "Butter was the disappointment and sour the buttermilk doled out at 25 cents a glass, and other things in proportion."[44] Lieutenant James Stewart, a career officer in command of the battery, regarded the milk thief to be a good soldier. But if he did not punish the offender, the farmer might take his complaint elsewhere and the man's punishment might be worse. The old Regular ordered the citizen-soldier lashed spread-eagle on the extra wheel of an artillery caisson. The private's friends gathered around him, muttering against the punishment. One called the farmer nothing more than an "Adams County Copperhead" out to cheat a poor soldier. Stewart ordered the men to disperse, but

43 Lucius Lamont Shattuck to family June 24, 1863; Charles Walker, diary, Carroll Institute for Civil War Studies; *Iron Brigade*, June 30, 1863; Amos Rood, diary, Wisconsin Historical Society. Rood, who enlisted at Milwaukee, wrote the memoir between 1889 and 1892 and recopied it with added remarks in 1918 based on the diaries he kept during his service. Inside Walkers' journal book is a thin pamphlet from one of the Christian societies concerning a matter close to the soldier heart—letters from home: "Keep him posted in all the village gossip, the lectures, the courtings, the Sleigh rides, and the singing school. . . . Tell him every sweet and brave and pleasant and funny story you can think of. Show him that you clearly apprehend that all this warfare means peace, and that a dastardly peace would pave the way for speedy, incessant and more appealing warfare."

44 Kress, *Republican*, December 4, 1886. Kress was an aide to Maj. Gen. James Wadsworth.

they remained where they were. For a few moments it seemed there might be trouble. When the lieutenant, with more force this time, ordered them away, the men heeded his order.[45]

That night south of Gettysburg, Loyd Harris entertained his tent mate, Orrin Chapman, with music from a harmonica he purchased passing through Frederick. His last song that night was "Home, Sweet Home."[46]

One of the mail sacks that reached the army at Marsh Creek contained a letter for Ord. Sgt. Jerome Watrous of the 6th Wisconsin: his brother Henry had been killed by an artillery shell serving with the 4th Wisconsin at Port Hudson in Louisiana. The surviving brother stood alongside an army wagon a few miles south of Gettysburg, letter in hand and with a great battle in the offing. It was a long night of memories.

The Michigan Boys Get Their Black Hats

The Wisconsin, Indiana, and Michigan soldiers camped at Marsh Creek were much changed since being called to Washington. Later, it was said to be a sight never seen again—the Black Hat brigade swinging along with an easy stride toward the Marsh Creek camp, their famous headgear now more serviceable than showy. One who saw them said they "looked like giants with their tall black hats," and recalled how they moved with a "steady step [filling the] entire roadway, their big black hats and feathers conspicuous."[47] After two years of service, their letters, journals, and diaries reveal the bright hopes of 1861 were long gone for the veterans of the original four regiments. Survivors gather in close and tight messes to share food and coffee and memories and gossip. While they marched, died, and endured unspeakable hardship, the homefolk "growled" about high prices, short money, and hard times. The army tossed out the used-up soldier and the "patriotic" speculators fleeced them of their pay. The soldiers fought well, but were denied victory by incompetent generals. Only one of every three soldiers was still in the ranks from the '61 regiments; the others dead from battle or illness or even homesickness. Scores of the early volunteers were sent home sick and disabled. The survivors were dependent first on the men around their campfires and then to their

45 Buell, *Cannoneer*, 62. The private was Frank Nobels, Stoughton Light Guard, Company D, 7th Wisconsin. He enlisted from Rutland on August 10, 1861, and served in the battery from June 8, 1862, until January 1864. *Wisconsin Roster*, vol. 1, 553.

46 Charles Walker diary; Ray, *Iron Brigade*, 191; James P. Sullivan, *Mauston Star*, March 22, 1883.

47 Charles A. Stevens, *Berdan's U.S. Sharpshooters in the Army of the Potomac, 1861-1865* (St. Paul, MN, 1892), 277-278. Stevens' brother George was an officer in the 2nd Wisconsin.

small companies and then to their regiments. They are isolated now from the homefolk, misused by their generals and the country's leaders, cheated by sutlers, and snubbed by Easterners because of their Western origins. They trust only their comrades and the few brave and skillful officers still among them. They are a hard lot, good soldiers, and proud of their reputations.

Only the men of the 24th Michigan, even after ten months in service, marched toward Gettysburg feeling they still had something to prove. The Wolverines and their famous brigade saw only limited service at Fredericksburg. It was there they first came under fire and their colonel called out, "Steady, men, those Wisconsin men are watching you." The Michigan regiment joined in the spirited river crossing during the Chancellorsville Campaign, but it was nothing like the fighting endured at Gainesville, Second Bull Run, South Mountain, and Antietam. It was only after Chancellorsville that the Michigan regiment's coveted black hats arrived. As one approving Wolverine put it, "They made our appearance, like the name of the brigade, quite unique."

Corps commander John Reynolds caught up with the First Division as it readied to leave Marsh Creek. The general had spent the night at Mortiz Tavern six miles south of Gettysburg, where he was joined late by Maj. Gen. Oliver O. Howard of Eleventh Corps. Reports were coming in from cavalryman John Buford at Gettysburg. One body of Confederate infantry, perhaps as much as one-third of Lee's Confederate army, was massed near Cashtown farther northwest. Another Confederate body was operating near Carlisle, and a third force was operating close to Chambersburg, farther west of Cashtown. The Army of Northern Virginia was still widely dispersed, and Buford's information was reliable. Reynolds understood its import: General Lee and his veteran battalions were not yet aware of the Federal army's positions and had no idea much of it was concentrating near Gettysburg.[48]

Reynolds was up at 4:00 a.m. His first order was to Wadsworth's First Division: push ahead to Gettysburg. Major General Abner Doubleday with the rest of First Corps would follow with Howard and his Eleventh Corps behind First Corps. Other riders galloped to Third Corps commander Dan Sickles near Emmitsburg, Maryland, with orders to also move toward Gettysburg. Reynolds rode ahead to confer with Wadsworth before pushing his black horse "Fancy" up the Emmitsburg Road toward Gettysburg.

The soldiers of the Iron Brigade finished a "hearty breakfast of coffee and hardtack" at daybreak. "The Pennsylvania line had been reached and the forces of

---

48 Otis Howard, "The Campaign and Battle of Gettysburg," *Battles & Leaders of the Civil War*, vol. 5, Peter Cozzens, ed. (Chicago, 2005), 323-324. The article first appeared in the July 1876 issue of the *Atlantic Monthly*.

the enemy must be met very soon," a Michigan man later wrote, "though none suspected that the foe was within a few hours march." On the previous day, Devin's Union brigade of cavalry, part of John Buford's division, had leaned from their saddles to warn the infantrymen that they had run into Johnnies just ahead near Gettysburg. Lee's whole army was gathering there, they warned. The men on ordnance wagons parked nearby heeded the prior warnings on this first morning of July by passing out the required "60 rounds of ammunitions in the boxes and upon the person." There was an awkward moment in the 24th Michigan while the men drew cartridges and the chaplain did his best to complete his morning prayer.[49] In appearance, the Western men carried knapsacks (or an occasional bedroll) and common to all were the famous big black felt hats marked by the red wool badges of the First Corps. Most of the men wore the dark blue four-button sack or fatigue coats, but the Regular Army nine-button blue frocks were still plentiful—especially in the 6th Wisconsin, where they were favored. Over the shoulder each soldier carried a haversack and canteen and in each knapsack (in addition to personal items) a rubber or woolen blanket. On the top straps of the knapsack, soldiers tied a shelter half where overcoats usually were carried. Two soldiers combined shelter halves and buttoned them together to form a common tent and share their woolen and rubber blankets.

A Strangely Reticent Man

As the men formed their companies, some observed the 6th Wisconsin's former colonel Lysander Cutler with his new Second Brigade already on the roadway. The soldiers also saw Reynolds conferring with General Wadsworth.[50] Hall's 2nd Maine Battery was moving behind Cutler's brigade. The Second Brigade's 7th Indiana was left behind to guard the division wagons. Sol Meredith was slow getting his Black Hats into formation, so Cutler ordered his brigade to push off. It was nearly a mile ahead before Wadsworth sent a rider with orders for Meredith to "close up." The 2nd Wisconsin led the way, followed by the 7th Wisconsin. A short distance ahead, the soldiers of the 19th Indiana waited to file in behind the 7th. The 24th Michigan closed up behind the Hoosiers. The 6th

---

49 Curtis, *Twenty-fourth*, 155; Sullivan, *Telegraph*, December 20, 1884; *OR* 27, pt. 3, 416-417. An ammunition study determined the 8,700 men of the First Corps expended about 68 rounds per man. Dean S. Thomas, *Ready . . . Aim . . . Fire . . . Small Arms Ammunition in the Battle of Gettysburg* (Biglerville, PA, 1981), 13.

50 R. K. Beecham, *Gettysburg: The Pivotal Battle of the Civil War* (Chicago, 1911), 120. Beecham was with the 2nd Wisconsin.

Sgt. Guilford (Gilford)
Smith, Bragg's Rifles
Co. E, 6th Wisconsin

Described by a friend as a
"nice, clean-faced boyish
fellow" and a "splendid
soldier," He was also lucky.
Three bullets passed through
Smith's uniform without injury
at Gettysburg. *Brett Wilson Collection*

Wisconsin was last in line,
followed by the Brigade Guard
of 100 men and two officers.[51]

The weather was pleasant
and the Western men, well
rested and looking forward to a
friendly reception in the town just ahead, moved with an easy route step. They were
in "high spirits" and a Milwaukee company lifted up a "soul stirring song as only the
Germans can sing." The 6th Wisconsin took up the step of the music. When the
Milwaukeeans finished, others responded with three rousing cheers. The Juneau
County company ("with about as much melody as a government mule") began a
song about "a heifer wild" that stole cabbage "in the moonlight mild" and that
everyone knew she should be "killed and quartered and issued out for beef." It
went on verse after verse with the whole column joining the chorus, "On the
distant prairie, Hoop de dooden doo," until the song broke down in laughter.
Another soldier began the scandalous "Paddy's Wedding." One soldier recalled he
found it "odd for men to march toward their death singing, shouting and laughing
as if it were parade or holiday." After a time the Western men settled down and the
column "plodded along" in a march of "unusual quietude." The peaceful moment
was broken when cavalry clattered up the roadway, scattering the infantrymen to
the left and right. An Irishman in a Wisconsin regiment raised a fist and called after

---

51 Earl M. Rogers, "The 2nd, of Fifty-sixth Which?" *Milwaukee Sunday Telegraph*, June 22, 1884.
Rogers quotes his brother, Clayton, an aide to Wadsworth, as saying the gap was "one mile"
due to Meredith's "delay in giving orders."

them, "May the devil fly away with the roofs of your jackets; yez going now to get us into a scrape and thin walk off and let us fight it out like you always do."[52]

Staff Officer Capt. Hollon Richardson of the 7th Wisconsin had been in the saddle most of the morning. He anticipated a warm welcome by the loyal citizens of Gettysburg and, as usual, kept an eye out to avoid his estranged father-in-law—Col. William Robinson of his own regiment. The two were still at irreconcilable differences over his secret elopement with the colonel's daughter several months earlier. Now, riding toward Gettysburg, young Richardson was about to face a trying day on two fronts.[53]

One of the officers the young lieutenant passed that morning was John Reynolds, who was about to make an important decision. A Pennsylvanian, Reynolds faced an enemy army on his native soil with his family less than a day's hard ride away. The 1841 graduate of West Point saw service in Florida, on the frontier, and during the Mexican War, during which he was twice cited for bravery. He was commandant of the cadet corps at West Point when Southern guns opened on Fort Sumter. Although he sought a Regular Army position he was offered (partly due to the efforts of his friend George McClellan) the First Brigade of the Pennsylvania Reserve Division. Reynolds demonstrated ability and was advanced to command of First Corps, succeeding Joseph Hooker. Although offered command of the Army of the Potomac that June, he refused when operatives of President Lincoln—hampered by political whispers of Reynolds' connections to the Democratic Party and friendship with McClellan—were unable to assure him a free hand. One who saw him about that time described the general as "tall, dark, and slender [with] a wild look a rolling eye. Very nervous to all appearance." When his rival, George Meade, was named instead to command the army, Reynolds put on his best uniform and offered congratulations. Afterward, to Col. Charles Wainwright of his Artillery Brigade, Reynolds confided that he had refused the command because he was "unwilling to take Burnside and Hooker's leavings." "For my part, I think we have got the best man [Meade] of the two, much as I think of Reynolds," Wainwright wrote in his diary. "He will do better at carrying out plans than devising them, I think."[54]

52 Grayson, Loyd Harris, *Milwaukee Sunday Telegraph*, February 15, 1885; Fairfield, diary, July 1, 1863.

53 Jerome A. Watrous, "A Badger Traveler," *Milwaukee Sunday Telegraph*, December 22, 1878; *Soldiers and Citizens Album*, vol. 2, 578-582; Hollon Richardson family records.

54 Edward J. Nichols, *Toward Gettysburg: A Biography of General John F. Reynolds* (College Station, PA, 1958), 75-76, 220-223; Edward P. Adams to his father from Washington, July 3, 1863, Edward R. Adams Papers, Carroll Institute for Civil War Studies; Charles S. Wainwright, *A*

To the men in the ranks of the Iron Brigade, Reynolds was a distant and formal Old Army Regular, respected for his ability and "common sense" but not a great favorite. They remembered how the general was ready to abandon the 19th Indiana at Fredericksburg.[55] In manner, Reynolds was a tough disciplinarian with a hands-on manner of command (one artillery officer complained the general sometimes got caught up in the minor details of running an army corps) and not the officer of the colorful uniform or quick remark. He lacked colorful personality, dress, and nickname, and there were few camp stories about "that dark, silent, alert man," as one Wisconsin soldier described him.[56] As a soldier, Reynolds had not been lucky. He led his Pennsylvania brigade with promise in the Seven Days fighting of 1862 only to be captured one night when his horse became mired in mud. The praise his division won at Second Bull Run was lost in the sour wrangling and finger pointing following the defeat. Reynolds missed South Mountain and Antietam while away on a political assignment in Pennsylvania that advanced neither his career nor his reputation. At Fredericksburg he led the First Corps, but it was his rival Meade who won attention with his break through on Stonewall Jackson's front. At Chancellorsville, Hooker—aware of the political forces arrayed against Reynolds—gave the general an assignment that would win no headlines. Finally, Lincoln offered him command of the army, but it came at a time when the president and the administration were unable to give the assurances the general needed. Now, as Reynolds moved toward Gettysburg with the command of three army corps in hand, he was being handed a chance to play a significant role in shaping the campaign. When he saw the general that morning, a 2nd Wisconsin soldier said Reynolds looked "careworn, sad and stern, but the high purpose of his patriotic sprit was stamped upon every lineament."

A Show on the Streets of Gettysburg

The survivors left no record of any haste or undue concern those first miles from the Marsh Creek bivouac toward Gettysburg. The 2nd Wisconsin, the oldest and most famous of the five regiments, was at the head of the Iron Brigade column.

Diary of Battle: The Personal Journals of Colonel Charles S. Wainwright, 1861-1865, Allan Nevins, ed. (New York, 1962), 227.

55 Lance J. Herdegen, "John Reynolds and the Iron Brigade," in Giants in Their Tall Black Hats: Essays on the Iron Brigade, Alan T. Nolan and Sharon Eggleston Vipond, eds. (Bloomington, 1998), 101-112; Lance J. Herdegen, "The Lieutenant Who Arrested a General," Gettysburg Magazine (January 1991), 25-32.

56 Wainwright, A Diary of Battle, 218; Beecham, Gettysburg, 120.

It was one of the first three-year organizations to reach Washington in 1861. The regiment enjoyed a reputation for hard fighting even though it was an organization with a troubled record of leadership and marked by a wont of discipline. Just ahead and out of sight, Cutler's brigade halted for a time near an orchard to rest. The last regiment in the Iron Brigade column was the 6th Wisconsin, with Lt. Col. Rufus R. Dawes commanding it this morning as Colonel Bragg was away at Washington recovering from a kick by a horse. Dawes, enjoying "a beautiful morning," decided "to make a show in the streets of Gettysburg."[57]

Orders were given to close up and the hood was pulled off the national flag. It was a stirring moment, and the drummers and fifers moved to the head of the regiment. With the sharp command of Drum Maj. R. N. Smith, the musicians struck up "The Campbells are Coming," the fierce rallying song of the clans. Dawes selected the song, he said, "through a fancy that the people would infer that the 'rebels are running,' or would run very soon after so fine a body of soldiers as the 6th Wisconsin then was, confronted them." Just moments later, over the shrilling of fifes and the rumbling of drums, came a distant "boom . . . boom . . . boom." For some reason "the sound was very dull," Dawes recalled, "and did not attract our attention as indicating any serious engagement." Lieutenant Loyd Harris with the Brigade Guard leaned over to Lt. Levi Showalter of the 2nd Wisconsin and smiled: "The Pennsylvanians have made a mistake and are celebrating the 4th [of July] three days ahead of time." Back along the column came word that the cavalry had "found the Johnnies over at York or Harrisburg."[58]

A mounted staff officer caused a stir a few minutes later as he rode along the column swinging his hat and shouting over and over, "Boys, Little Mac is in command of the Army of the Potomac!" In an instant, the uncertainty over Hooker and the promotion of Meade gave way to joyous shouts. The talk just the day before was that McClellan was marching from Harrisburg with a force of Pennsylvania militia and when he reached his old army he would again assume command. "Our

---

57 Harris, *Telegraph*, December 20, 1884; Fairfield, diary; Rufus R. Dawes to John B. Bachelder, March 18, 1868; Dawes, *Service*, 164; John W. Bruce, "Lieutenant Bruce Relates His Experiences at Gettysburg After Being Shot Through the Body," *Milwaukee Sunday Telegraph*, January 23, 1881; Rufus R. Dawes, "Align on the Colors," *Milwaukee Sunday Telegraph*, April 27, 1890. Bruce was a second lieutenant with Company K, 7th Wisconsin.

58 This National flag is held by the Wisconsin Veterans Museum in Madison. The regiment carried only one flag that day because the badly damaged state blue banner had been returned to Wisconsin to be replaced. A proud letter accompanied the returned banner: "History will tell how Wisconsin honor has been vindicated by her soldiers, and what lessons in Northern courage they have given Southern chivalry. If the past gives an earnest of the future, the 'Iron Brigade' will not be forgotten when Wisconsin makes up its jewels." Dawes, *Telegraph*, April 27, 1890; Harris, *Telegraph*, February 15, 1885; Sullivan, *Telegraph*, December 8, 1884.

fellows cheered like mad," one private said. Of course, it was not true. McClellan was not returning to the army, and later some in ranks grumbled that the officer used the rumor as a calculated ploy to boost the fighting spirit of the soldiers. A 2nd Wisconsin officer admitted that the soldiers had "a lighter and more elastic step. Our hearts were full of gratitude." Thousands of the marching men fought the opening of the battle of Gettysburg believing that McClellan was restored to command. Major Cornelius Otis of the 2nd Wisconsin said the announcement created the "greatest enthusiasm" because Little Mac was the "idol" of the army and "one in whom our confidence remained unshaken."[59] Even before the Little Mac cheers faded, the pattering of small arms fire added to the noise ahead. However, they were approaching the town of Gettysburg, one private wrote, so "our fellows straightened up to pass through it in good style." The brigade band stopped alongside the roadway and was playing "Red, White and Blue" when "all at once, hell broke loose . . . in front."[60]

The respite Cutler's men of the Second Brigade were enjoying near an orchard was cut short by the distant gunfire's discordant strains. Without waiting for instructions, Cutler ordered his men to their feet. The Second Brigade was already well ahead of the Iron Brigade when the old officer directed his new command to move briskly toward the sound of rising battle. Cutler was already moving when Reynolds found Wadsworth and ordered him to hurry forward his entire division.[61]

The Confederates seen the day before by Buford's men belonged to James J. Pettigrew's brigade of Henry Heth's division, part of A. P. Hill's Corps. Heth believed shoes were to be found in Gettysburg, and told Pettigrew to get them. The brigadier returned without additional footwear and without setting foot in Gettysburg after discovering it was occupied by Federal cavalry. More ominous was the fact that some of his officers heard what they believed were infantry drums beating on the far side of town. A. P. Hill dismissed the intelligence out of hand: "The only force at Gettysburg is cavalry, probably a detachment on observation. I am just from General Lee, and the information he has from his scouts corroborates

---

59 James P. Sullivan, *Mauston Star*, February 13, 1883; Otis, *Second Wisconsin*, 83-84; Cheek and Pointon, *Sauk County*, 70.

60 Sullivan, *Mauston Star*, February 13, 1883; Otis, *Second Wisconsin*, 83-84; Cheek and Pointon, *Sauk County*, 70; Watrous, in the August 15, 1880, *Milwaukee Sunday Telegraph*, wrote of the McClellan incident: "This news had the effect to bring out as hearty cheers as that army ever indulged in. It is doubtful any army commander in our late war was more popular with his men than George B. McClellan, and yet when he became a candidate for president—the candidate of a party that said the war was a failure, his old soldiers did not give him their united votes." Sullivan, *Telegraph*, December 20, 1884.

61 Sullivan, *Mauston Star*, February 13, 1883.

what I have received from mine—that is, the enemy are still at Middleburg, and have not yet struck their tents." When Heth asked Hill whether he had any objection about marching his infantry division into Gettysburg the next morning, Hill replied, "None in the world."[62]

Henry Heth—Harry to his friends—was well-liked. He had served as a quartermaster for Lee in the Virginia Provisional Army early in the war and was one of the few soldiers Lee continued to call by his first name. Heth was remembered in the Old Army for several things, and two in particular: getting stabbed in the leg with a bayonet at West Point, and finishing at the bottom of his class in 1846. His cousin, Gen. George Pickett, led a division under James Longstreet.

At 5:00 a.m. on July 1, Heth ordered his division to move from Cashtown along the Chambersburg Pike toward Gettysburg. The head of his column reached a high ridge about a mile northwest of town four hours later. Under orders not to bring on a general engagement, he halted and shelled the woods to the right and left of the pike. When no reply was forthcoming, he deployed one infantry brigade north of the pike and a second on the south side of the road and pushed forward. As he discovered a short time later, Buford's dismounted Federal cavalry stood in his way. Although the horsemen were outnumbered, they used their fast breech-loading carbines to advantage.[63] The weight of the advance was with the gray infantry, however, and Buford's line slowly fell back, using the rolling ground as best they could until Gettysburg was but a short distance behind them. It was about 10:00 a.m. The matter came down to a decision by wing commander Reynolds: fight or fall back.

The undulating ground around Gettysburg is a good position, Buford pointed out to Reynolds, and an in-depth defense could be mounted here. The town could also be used to advantage if the Union soldiers were forced to retreat. High ground south of Gettysburg, where a small cemetery was located, also appeared promising for defensive operations. Wadsworth's two infantry brigades were near at hand to make a firm stand, but the next closest division was still a good hour behind them. Advance elements of Howard's Eleventh Corps could not arrive until noon or thereafter, and the Third Corps under Dan Sickles was at Emmitsburg. Later, it would be said that Reynolds had already made up his mind to fight because he

---

62 Henry Heth, "Why Lee Lost at Gettysburg," *Battles and Leaders*, vol. 5, 364-373. The article first appeared in the September 22, 1877, issue of the *Philadelphia Weekly Times*.

63 Although it is often claimed these troopers were using the multi-shot repeating Spencer carbine, they were in fact armed with single-shot breech loading carbines made by Sharps, Burnside, Smith, and others. They could fire two or three times faster than a muzzle-loaded weapon, but their effective range—only 200 to 300 yards—was much shorter.

believed an engagement might force decisive action from Meade, whom he thought hesitant in gaining firm control of his army. It was also whispered that Reynolds acted because he was a Pennsylvania man facing an invading army with his home and family but fifty miles distant. Here, then, was his long-awaited chance to strike a blow and win glory.[64]

Regardless of when Reynolds made his own decisive decision, he did so and told Buford to hang on. Riders galloped off with orders for Wadsworth's division to come on the run and to hurry on the other First Corps divisions as well as Eleventh Corps and Third Corps. Another galloper was sent to find Meade: "Tell him the enemy are advancing in strong force and that I fear they will get to the heights beyond the town before I can," directed Reynolds. "I will fight them inch by inch and if driven back into town, I will barricade the streets and hold them back as long as possible."[65]

Wadsworth's division would be the first Union infantry on the field, and through nothing but chance it included two of the army's finest brigades. The First Division had led the march the previous day, and ordinarily would have brought up the rear in the regular marching order. Because it was the closest to Gettysburg, however, Reynolds told Wadsworth to lead the column that morning. Leaving his position near the Lutheran Seminary building, Reynolds rode back into town, where he lost his way for a short while on a back street. When the general found his infantry column south of Gettysburg near the Codori farm, he ordered fences lining the Emmitsburg Road knocked down so the men could march cross-country rather than through town. He watched as Cutler's Second Brigade angled northwest off the road at a quick pace, and waited until the First Brigade reached the turn-off point to wave them to follow Cutler. Satisfied the men were moving quickly and in the right direction, Reynolds spurred his horse ahead toward the fighting.

They are Coming, Give it to Them!

Cutler's column moved over the low ridge marked by a large stone building housing the Lutheran Theological Seminary toward a second parallel crest farther west called McPherson's Ridge. Just behind this second rise, Reynolds placed three regiments north of the road leading to Chambersburg and two others south of it.

64 Charles H. Veil, *The Memoirs of Charles Henry Veil*, Herman J. Viola, ed. (New York, 1993), 28-30.

65 George Meade, *The Life and Letters of George Gordon Meade*, 2 vols., George Gordon Meade, ed. (New York, 1913), vol. 2, 35-36; Edwin B. Coddington, *The Gettysburg Campaign : A Study in Command* (New York, 1968), 267.

The left of the brigade's line rested against a stand of trees called Herbst Woods. After placing Hall's battery on the roadway, Reynolds told a staff officer he would hold the Chambersburg Pike and that General Doubleday, who was bringing up the rest of First Corps, should extend the line to the south to prevent being flanked. It was about this time when Reynolds spotted a heavy line of enemy skirmishers followed by at least a brigade moving toward the woods on McPherson's Ridge. If the Confederate line gained the crest and seized the woodlot, Reynolds realized, it could threaten the whole Union position. Reynolds pivoted in his saddle and watched as the Iron Brigade, marching en echelon in lines of battle, crossed through the swale to McPherson Ridge at the double-quick. It was going to be very close.

Faces turned skyward when scattered artillery shells clattered through the treetops and showered the 2nd Wisconsin at the head of the Iron Brigade with dancing leaves and spinning branches. The fighting was closer than expected. Colonel Lucius Fairchild slid from his horse to yell, "Non-combatants to the rear!" Extra baggage was tossed aside. Officers dismounted and sent away their horses. Without orders the veterans began snapping percussion caps to clear firing vents of moisture and then set about loading their short Austrian rifles. Bayonets clanked into place as the column pressed forward toward to the prominent seminary on the ridge just ahead.

The line of Alabama and Tennessee Confederate infantry approaching McPherson's Ridge from the west belonged to Brig. Gen. James J. Archer. The Rebels were not in a great hurry. The ridge to their front was wooded, with Willoughby Run cutting a meandering swath along its western slope. Thick brush and clumps of willow trees along the rocky bank made it more difficult for a mounted man to make his way over, so Archer swung from his saddle and went forward with his infantry on foot. Like so many Confederates that morning, the veteran brigadier of slight frame and prone to dysentery had little anticipation of meeting serious enemy resistance. The result was a careless push into the unknown. Archer was well regarded in the Confederate army and much admired. A graduate of Princeton (where his friends called him "Sally"), he practiced law after graduation in 1834 and served in the Mexican War and cited for gallantry. One of his old Army friends was Stonewall Jackson, who served as his second in a duel with another officer in Mexico that left Archer with a minor wound. Archer's brigade was under strength on July 1 with just three regiments and part of another, something fewer than 1,000 men in line. When the Southern infantry reached the creek they pushed across with a yell and a shout to mount the wooded ridge just ahead. Herbst Woods was used as a pasture, and the grazing animals had kept the weeds and brush between the trees to a minimum. The Confederates pushed on more briskly now against what they believed was nothing more than a scattering of blue troopers.[66]

Meanwhile, north of the Chambersburg Pike, three regiments under Brig. Gen. Joseph Davis—the 2nd and 42nd Mississippi and the 55th North Carolina—reached the ridge crest more quickly and caught Cutler's New Yorkers and Pennsylvanians just getting into line. Davis, the likeable but inexperienced nephew of Confederate President Jefferson Davis, was still new to brigade command. He was practicing law at the start of the war in 1861, was elected captain in the 10th Mississippi Infantry, promoted to colonel, and became an aide-de-camp to his uncle. When he was nominated to be a brigadier general, the president's political opponents in the Confederate Congress delayed the commission under charges of nepotism.

The 56th Pennsylvania was still forming when Col. John W. Hofmann saw Davis' approaching line, but was unable to determine the color of the uniforms. "Is that the enemy?" Hofmann called to Cutler. The old general lifted a pair of field glasses. "Yes," Cutler replied in a rather casual voice. Hofmann gave orders to his small regiment: "Ready—Right Oblique, Aim. Fire!" To the right of the Pennsylvanians, the 76th New York also let loose a ragged volley. The Confederates fired back, hitting the Union line with a "shower of bullets." Although later disputed by some Wisconsin men, this was the first exchange of infantry fire at Gettysburg.

About the same time, the 2nd Wisconsin moved up the eastern slope of McPherson's Ridge just as Archer's Confederates were slashing across Willoughby Run and leaning forward for the climb up the western slope. Union cavalry skirmishers pulled out of the tree line on the jump. In the ranks of the 2nd regiment, Pvt. Elisha R. Reed was dealing with a "feeling of dread" and other undefined horrors. "I now began to wish that I had never been born, or, having been born, had died in infancy. I could distinctly feel the blood receding from my face, and I know I must be looking very white. I was so sure that my face would betray my cowardice I dared not raise my head." Someone bellowed "Double quick, Load!" followed with "By the left flank, double quick, Charge!" The regiment swung into a line of battle toward the ridge where the Union troopers were falling back amid scattered firing. The following Iron Brigade regiments began shifting into lines of battle, moving en echelon to the left and behind the advancing 2nd Wisconsin.

---

66 Marc and Beth Storch, "What a Deadly Trap We Were In," *Gettysburg Magazine*, January/1992, 13-27; John W. Busey and David G. Martin, *Regimental Strengths and Losses at Gettysburg* (Hightown, NJ, 1986), 291.

(Long afterward, a Wisconsin man carefully stepped off the distances. It was 500 paces from Seminary Ridge to the edge of McPherson's Woods.)[67]

Sergeant Burlington Cunningham carried the national colors in the 19th Indiana. The national flag presented to the regiment back in 1861 was used up and had been sent back to Indiana the previous winter, so Cunningham carried a banner requisitioned from the Quartermaster Department but marked with the regiment's number and state. A staff officer riding along the Indiana line, fearful of attracting fire, cautioned, "Do not unfurl the flag." Cunningham, who had been singled out for rescuing his regiment's colors at Antietam, shook his head and called to A. J. Buckles, "Abe, pull the shuck." Cunningham swung open the flag with a series of swirling motions as he and the regiment pushed off. Just ahead on the right, Union cavalry troopers were yelling to the advancing infantry, "They are coming, give it to them!"[68]

Those Damned Black Hats!

The 2nd Wisconsin was the first regiment to reach McPherson's Ridge. Just behind the Badgers was Reynolds on his big horse. "Forward Men!" he shouted. "Forward for God's sake, and drive those fellows out of those woods!" As soon as the Wisconsin men reached the crest, a line of Confederates on the other side opened "a most murderous volley" that tore "great gaps" in the Union line. [69] "Charge men, I mean charge!" Colonel Fairchild screamed in a loud voice over the shooting. Private Reed escaped his premonition and a serious wound, at least in the first flurry of bullets, when the ball that hit Virgil Helmes of Madison in front of him passed through the body and lodged in his Helmes' knapsack. The wounded man staggered out of line. "One ball carried away my cap box and glanced on my belt," said Reed. "It produced a sensation in my abdominal regions very much like the kick of a mule and I was uncertain for a moment whether I was summoned to the courts above or only a little frightened; but a hasty examination disclosed the fact that I was in a pretty good state of preservation yet and I resumed my place in

67 E. R. Reed, "A Private's Story," *Milwaukee Sunday Telegraph*, June 12, 1887; Beecham, *Gettysburg*, 62. Reed was captured at First Bull Run and returned to the army several months later.

68 "The 19th Indiana at Gettysburg: The Thrilling Story of a Great Regiment in a Great Battle. Deathless Glory of its Color Bearers," Indiana State Library; Howard Michael Madaus and Richard H. Zeitlin, *The Flags of the Iron Brigade* (Madison, WI, 1997) 32-33.

69 Otis, *Second Wisconsin*, 72.

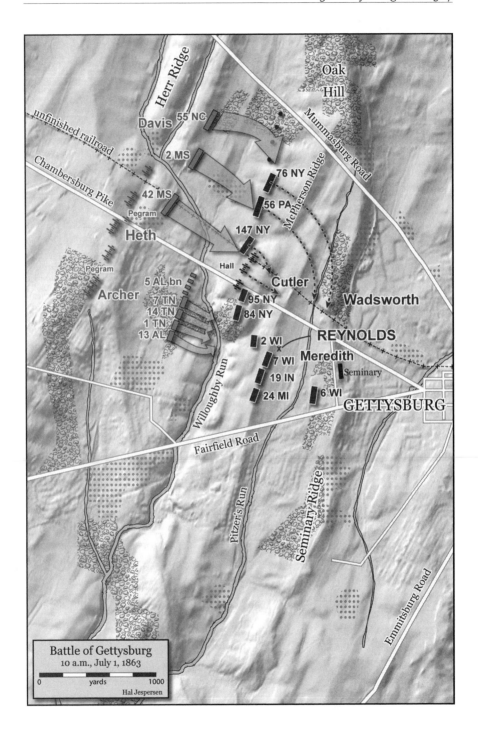

Battle of Gettysburg
10 a.m., July 1, 1863

0   yards   1000

Hal Jespersen

line."[70] Within a moment one-third of the Badger line had been shot down, but the survivors plunged forward with a yell. "We held our fire until within 10 yards of Archer's line and then gave them a volley that counted," boasted one. Disorganized and surprised by the sudden appearance of a heavy line of infantry, the Confederates tumbled down the slope through the trees toward the creek, many with empty muskets. "There are them damned black hatted fellows again," one Rebel called out. "Taint no militia, it's the Army of the Potomac!" Another shouted, "Hell! Those are the big hat devils of the Army of the Potomac."[71]

Not far behind the 2nd Wisconsin, just about the time the two lines crashed together, Reynolds toppled from his saddle when a bullet "entered the back of the neck, just below the coat collar, and passed downward." His aides believed he was looking backward when struck and there was from the very first speculation that the bullet was fired by a Confederate sharpshooter in a nearby tree and that it was, somehow, an unfair and cowardly act. Sergeant Cornelius Wheeler claimed the general was "struck by a stray ball" immediately after the volley his regiment received as it "charged over the top of the ridge." Unsaid was the grim possibility the fatal shot could have been fired by a federal infantryman or retreating cavalryman behind the general.

In the woods ahead, meanwhile, Archer's small brigade found itself on the receiving end of a broad and wholly unexpected counterattack. The 7th Wisconsin reached the ridge on the left side of the emerging Union line, where Col. William Robinson ordered his regiment to halt to allow the Indiana and Michigan regiments to come up on his left. When the colonel spotted Confederate flags dancing in the gun smoke, however, he ordered his regiment to charge. The line pushed into the ravine with a shout. "Our skirmishers began to fire [on seeing the Confederates]," explained Pvt. William Ray. "Soon we see the top of a rebel flag. We still advance. As soon as a man sees a reb he shoots. We fix Bayonet still going on. Pass right over their dead and wounded." Lieutenant Amos Rood said the "cusses skedaddled, or tried to" under the "roaring volleys" fired by his 7th Wisconsin. Private Alexander Hughes, one of the regiment's boy soldiers (he was but fourteen when he enlisted from Columbia County), suffered his third battle wound of the war when a bullet hit his cartridge box and passed into his side. Slowed for an instant by the "painful,

70 Reed, *Telegraph*, June 12, 1887. Helmes survived his wound.

71 Cheek and Pointon, *Sauk County*, 73; Lucius Fairchild, unfinished manuscript, Lucius Fairchild Papers, Wisconsin Historical Society; Jerome A. Watrous, *Richard Epps and Other Stories* (Milwaukee, 1906), 10; C. Tevis and D. R. Marquis, *The History of the Fighting Fourteenth: Published in Commemoration of the Fiftieth Anniversary of the Muster of the Regiment into the United States Service* (New York, 1911), 132.

but not serious wound," Hughes gathered his wits about him and ran ahead to catch up to his company.[72]

The unsuspecting Alabamians and Tennesseans were struck by a series of blows—the first delivered by the 2nd Wisconsin, which took the brunt of the opening volley, and then by Robinson's 7th Wisconsin, the 19th Indiana, and finally the 24th Michigan, which swung around to overlap the exposed Confederate right flank. In the smoke and confusion, it seemed to the surprised Confederates that the Black Hats were approaching from every direction. The series of blows tumbled them down the slope, across the creek, and crowded them northwest. "It seemed to me there were 20,000 Yanks down in among us hallooing surrender," recalled one Southern survivor, "and of course I had to surrender."

The firing in the smoky woods was fast, furious, and sustained. Color Sgt. Abel G. Peck of the 24th Michigan was killed and tall Lt. Col. Mark Flannigan wounded. Corporal Andrew Wood of the 19th Indiana was engulfed in a whoosh of smoke and fire when a ball struck his cartridge box, hit a twist of percussion caps, and ignited his cartridges. Lieutenant William Macy stripped off Wood's equipment and patted out the burning uniform before, ordering him to the rear. The first rounds to hit the 19th Indiana also wounded Sgt. Burlington Cunningham. Corporal Abe Buckles was ordered to "take the flag" Cunningham had been carrying and push on. The flurry of fighting, intense as it was, was over in a few minutes. As Colonel Robinson put it, "the enemy—what was left of them able to walk—threw down their arms" and fled west toward the safety of Herr Ridge.[73]

Lieutenant Colonel John Callis of the 7th Wisconsin, on foot in the powder smoke after his horse was struck and wounded with buckshot on his side and hip, was confronted by a wild-eyed Confederate officer running toward him shouting "I surrender!" while pointing his drawn sword at him. "That is no way to surrender," yelled Callis before knocking the sword away from the Rebel's hand with his own blade. The Wisconsin officer took a swipe at the Confederate's neck, but missed. The two men were now face-to-face. "If you surrender," said Callis, "order your men to cease firing, pick up your saber and order your men to go to the rear as prisoners." The officer did as instructed. There were so many Southern captives, recalled Callis, that "we had more prisoners than men of our own." A few yards

72 Alexander Hughes, "A Sketch of a Wisconsin Solider Who Has Won a High Place in Dakota," *Milwaukee Sunday Telegraph*, May 20, 1887; Rood, diary, 60. Hughes enlisted May 24, 1861, and mustered out September 1, 1864, his term expired. *Wisconsin Roster*, vol. 1, 546.

73 For more information as filed in the official battle reports see: Mansfield's report, *OR* 27, pt. 1, 273-274; Robinson's Report, *ibid.*, 279; Morrow's report, *ibid.*, 267; Andrew Wood Pension file, cited in Gaff, *Bloody Fields*, 256; Ray, *Iron Brigade*, 191.

ahead Callis spied an escaping Confederate trying to wrap a flag around its staff. He called out to a private in his old Grant County company named Dick Huftill to kill the Rebel. Huftill stepped forward, steadied his rifle-musket on the shoulder of his friend, Webster Cook, and squeezed the trigger. His "unerring aim" knocked down the man and the colors. The shooter ran ahead, picked up the flag, and handed it to Callis. Nearby, Abe Buckles of the 19th Indiana was so far ahead of his line—well beyond Willoughby Run—that Lt. William Dudley had to order him to "Come back with that flag."[74]

Knocked to the right by the first devastating storm of bullets, the 2nd Wisconsin crossed Willoughby Run in pursuit of the fleeing Confederates. The 2nd's flag was well to the front even though the regiment's two original color bearers were down. Sergeant Philander Wright entered the woods carrying the National flag while an unidentified corporal waved the regimental flag of blue silk, commercially made and featuring a painted representation of the Great Seal of the United States on one side and the 1851 version of the Wisconsin seal on the other.[75] As the regiment ran down the slope, a bullet punched through Wright's black hat, quickly followed by another. He continued toward a Confederate flag bearer just fifty yards ahead and a third bullet splintered his flagstaff, almost knocking it from his hand. His luck ran out when a fourth round slammed into his left leg and flipped him over. "When I looked for the guards—not one was there—all shot. I guess—sure not a man would lag at such a time—I know I wondered where one might be," recalled Wright. "I might have known each had been halted leaving me alone."[76]

Nearby, Colonel Fairchild was down with serious wound. "My regiment . . . became hotly engaged the moment they passed the [Hall's] battery. We pushed forward slowly, loading and firing as we went, down a slight incline which was thickly studded with trees of a large growth, toward the enemy who seemed to be posted at the foot of the incline behind a small stream [Willoughby Run]," reported the colonel. "My officers and men fell, killed or wounded, with terrible rapidity—

---

74 John B. Callis to John Bachelder, *The Bachelder Papers: Gettysburg in Their Own Words*, David L. and Audrey J. Ladd, eds., 3 vols. (Dayton, OH, 1994), vol. 1, 616; "Dick Hutfill and the Flag," *Lancaster* (WI) *Herald*, reprinted in the *Milwaukee Sunday Telegraph*.

75 Madaus and Zeitlin, *Flags*, 9-12. The blue regimental banner was forwarded to the 2nd Wisconsin in late 1861.

76 Morse, *Grandad*, 39, 121-123. Morse was in Company F of the 7th Wisconsin. Wright was Morse's cousin. Wright's information is taken from a memoir he wrote and presented to family members in 1921. He had been wounded at Gainesville in 1862. He was discharged May 25, 1864, for disability. *Wisconsin Roster*, vol. 1, 356.

Col. Lucius Fairchild, 2nd Wisconsin

Fairchild was wounded in the attack on Archer's Confederate brigade on
McPherson's Ridge on July 1, 1863. His arm would be amputated in
Gettysburg. *Wisconsin Veterans Museum*

from the instant they arrived at and passed the highest point of the ridge. We had
gone but a short distance after becoming engaged," he continued, "when I was
struck by a rifle ball which struck my left arm and made amputation necessary."

Wounded flag bearer Wright watched as the first of the Confederate prisoners were herded past him to the rear. Corporal Rasselas Davidson collected the downed colors, passed one to Cpl. Paul V. Brisbois, and together the two men pushed off after the regiment. The outspoken Davidson, a veteran of several battles, "swor[e] that he would never go into another fight if he could find any honorable way of dodging it." Now, in the early stages of what would become the largest battle of a very large war, he was rushing ahead hoisting the regimental flag ten to fifteen yards in front of the 2nd Wisconsin shouting for the Badgers to follow him. "That struck me as being a very singular way to dodge a fight," observed one of his friends, "but it shows how little a man knows of how he is going to act when he goes into the fight. [Davidson] continued to carry those colors through to the end and brought them home. . . . He seemed to have borne a charmed life."[77]

Wright, meanwhile, crawled over to his friend, Daniel Burton of his own Company C, who was propped up against a tree bleeding from a fatal wound. Despite Wright's best efforts to save him, Burton soon bled out. Otto W. Ludwig, "sweating and swearing in a spluttering yell" while still wearing his glasses, was a handful of feet away. "Without specs at fifty feet he couldn't tell a man from a stump," said Wright. Ludwig was also beyond help and soon died. "[B]lood smeared, dust stained [and] feeling dizzily like," Wright put elbows and knees to the ground and began the long crawl back to town and safety. When the regiment reformed a short time later, Wright was one of 116 of the 302 men the 2nd Wisconsin carried into the fight who had been killed or wounded in the opening minutes.[78]

Private Elisha Reed, his premonition of death and fear of cowardice apparently behind him, was still with the 2nd Wisconsin line halted in the ravine. When his cap box was shot off his belt at the top of the hill, Sgt. Alexander Lee gave him a handful of replacements and he joined the line, only to be hit on his left hip by a partially spent ball. The leg slug left a terrible bruise, but broke no bones. Reed limped after the line as it moved through the woods firing. At the bottom of the ravine Reed was struck on the ankle by yet another spent ball. "The line now halted and I came up into my place. After halting, with no rebel in sight anywhere, a stray shot came from somewhere, and struck Jonathan Brian [Jonathan Bryan] in the breast and he fell dead, being killed almost instantly," Reed recalled. "We had killed and wounded many rebels, taken a great many prisoners . . . and had driven the rest from the

---

77 Lucius Fairchild, unpublished and undated manuscript, Fairchild Papers; Morse, *Grandad*, 122-123; Madaus and Zeitlin, *Flags*, 31-32; Reed, *Telegraph*, June 12, 1887.

78 Morse, *Grandad*, 122-123; Beecham, *Gettysburg*, 69.

woods. We now about faced and moved back into the woods and reformed our line. It was with difficulty that I executed this movement with my lame ankle." The men were ordered to lie down, and an orderly sergeant took a head count: Reed's Company H had ten men left. "We struck that charge with thirty-three men." Of the survivors, he observed, "many of those left were more or less battered or bruised. . . . The rest of the brigade lost as heavily as we did." The Confederate prisoners told the Black Hats they were in A. P. Hill's Corps and, more ominously, "reported Lee's army was close by, massed to overwhelm us before our entire army could get together."[79]

The surprise collision between the advancing 2nd Wisconsin and Archer's 7th and 14th Tennessee regiments threw the gray line into a tangle just as the three other Iron Brigade regiments slammed into it. Without a horse to help him control the situation, Archer and some soldiers from the 1st Tennessee and 13th Alabama, firing as they moved, slipped into the cover of trees along the northern base of the ridge or moved into the open ground leading back to Herr Ridge. About thirty yards west of the run, Archer was pushing his way through a patch of weeds and willow trees when a soldier in a black hat named Pvt. Patrick Mahoney of the 2nd Wisconsin ran out of the smoke and grabbed the general. The exhausted Archer struggled for naught and was soon on his way to the rear with hundreds of his soldiers. Archer was the first general officer to be captured since Robert E. Lee took command of the Army of Northern Virginia in early 1862. On his way to the rear, Archer—"a trim, neat looking man," observed one Wisconsin soldier—met his old Army friend Abner Doubleday. "Good morning, Archer! How are you? I am glad to see you!" exclaimed the Union general. "Well, I am not glad to see you by a damn sight," Archer spat back.

Pat Mahoney would not enjoy his brief celebrity. He would be killed later in the day.[80]

It was about the time when Mahoney was snagging Archer that Sgt. Jonathan Bryan of the 2nd Wisconsin, while waving his hat and cheering wildly, was shot through the heart. He was the only man in the regiment killed west of Willoughby Run.

79 Reed, *Telegraph*, June 12, 1887; Rood, *Memoir*, 62.

80 Mahoney enlisted at Madison on May 22, 1861. *Wisconsin Roster*, vol. 1, 366; Beecham, *Glory*, 72-73; "Osseo," "The Surrender of Gen. Archer," *Milwaukee Sunday Telegraph*, February 4, 1883.

Go Like Hell!

The 6th Wisconsin was the last regiment to reach the field, followed by the Brigade Guard of 100 men. Ahead, the four other Iron Brigade regiments were advancing toward the wooded ridge where Union cavalrymen were running out of the tree line. Farther to the right (north) on the far side of the Chambersburg Pike was a "stake and rider" fence, clouds of smoke, and the sound of heavy fighting. A Union battery—Hall's 2nd Maine—was firing near the road. The 6th Wisconsin was moving forward when an aide from General Meredith reached Rufus Dawes: "Colonel, form your line, and prepare for action." Dawes swung his horse around and looked to the wood line where he saw "a line of rebel skirmishers, running back from my own front." He shouted a series of orders: "By Companies into line!" "Forward into Line! By Companies, left half wheel, double quick, March!" Schooled for hours on the drill fields of a dozen camps, the regiment ("that unequalled body of skilled veterans," was how Dawes described them) made the "intricate evolution" into a line of battle, the soldiers struggling to keep their alignment while they loaded their rifle-muskets on the move. Before the regiment could advance to the flank of the Iron Brigade, another rider brought orders for Dawes to halt and wait where he was as a reserve. The running soldiers pulled up in some disorder, quickly dressed the line, and waited.[81]

The 6th regiment was down in the swale between the two ridges, southwest of the seminary building with the left of the regiment almost touching the Fairfield Road. Heavy crashes of musketry ahead told the broad strokes of the tale as the men of the 2nd and then the 7th Wisconsin followed by the 24th Michigan plunged into the woods and down the slope toward an unseen enemy. Lieutenant Loyd Harris of the 100-man Brigade Guard came up for orders. Divide the guard into two companies of fifty men each, instructed Dawes, and place one on each flank of the regiment. Harris did as ordered, assuming command of the left company while the guard's other officer, Lt. Levi Showalter of 2nd Wisconsin, took charge of the right. During that moment before he moved his detachment up, while the soldiers were still trying to catch their breath after the hard half-mile run in knapsacks, Harris stepped in front of the makeshift force and admitted he was "feeling keenly my situation," commanding veterans who "no doubt felt a novel sensation in fighting under a strange officer, and away from their companies and regiments." He continued: "I know how much you would like to be with your own commands, and

---

81 Rufus R. Dawes to John Krauth, April 20, 1885. Krauth later served as secretary of the Gettysburg Association.

I am just as anxious to join company C over there on the right of the 6th, but it cannot be so. Do the best you can and I will do my duty toward you." The company moved forward on the left of the 6th Wisconsin.[82]

Another rider brought word to move forward once again. Before Dawes could execute the order, a "very boyish looking staff officer" came up on the gallop. "Colonel," he said with a salute, "General Doubleday is now in command of the First Corps, and he directs that you halt your regiment." Dawes ordered his men down and the Badgers flopped into the grass in a tangle of equipment and arms. To the regiment's right front, the other regiments of the Iron Brigade were busy exchanging long rips of musketry with Archer's men, and the wounded were already trickling back.[83] The staff officer returned a few minutes later and pointed north to the Chambersburg Pike: "General Doubleday directs that you move your regiment at once to the right." Dawes ordered his regiment to its feet and to face right, forming a column of fours. "Double-quick, March!" he shouted. Ahead, the "musketry fighting along the whole front of the division was very sharp." Only the 6th Wisconsin remained unengaged. His regiment was tramping along the swale when an officer from Meredith's staff guided his mount alongside Dawes and the moving column. The fighting north of the pike has gone badly, he said, and Cutler's brigade was in trouble. The staff officer pulled off to the side and yelled, "Go like hell! It looks as though they are driving Cutler!" In the ranks, Capt. Earl Rogers of Company I spotted his brother Clayton, an officer on Wadsworth's staff, talking with Dawes. The orders from Wadsworth were the same: help Cutler and stem the breach in the division's line north of the road.[84]

This was the first time Dawes had led the 6th Wisconsin into battle, although he had fought the command with skill at Antietam after Col. Edward Bragg was wounded there. Dawes was about to keep a promise to his sweetheart that he would do something brave.

82 Grayson, Loyd G. Harris, "The Iron Brigade Guard at Gettysburg," *Milwaukee Sunday Telegraph*, March 22, 1885.

83 Sullivan, *Telegraph*, December 20, 1884; Albert V. Young, "A Pilgrimage," *Milwaukee Sunday Telegraph*, April 22, 1888; Watrous, "Some Premonitions," *Milwaukee Sunday Telegraph*, July 27, 1895.

84 Rufus R. Dawes to John B. Bachelder, March 18, 1868; Earl Rogers to Jerome Watrous, undated; Dawes, *Telegraph*, April 27, 1890.

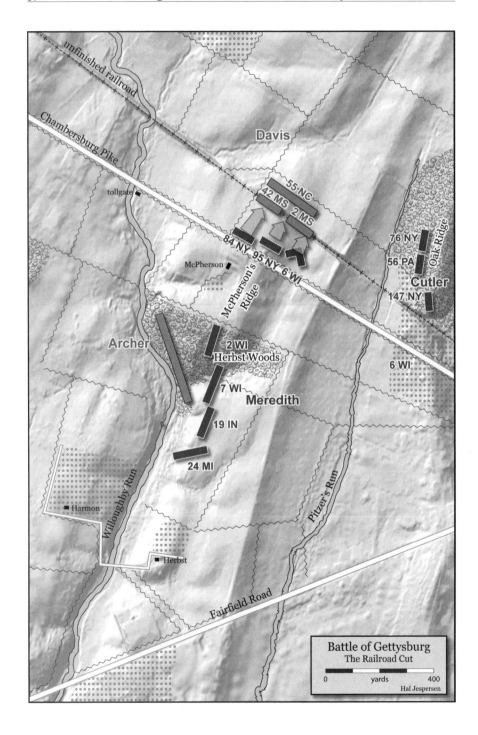

Battle of Gettysburg
The Railroad Cut

0   yards   400

Hal Jespersen

Part II: An Unfinished Railroad Cut

A Long Line of Yelling Rebels

As the 6th Wisconsin moved in columns of four toward the Chambersburg Pike, Rufus Dawes could see Hall's battery "driving to the rear" and Cutler's men "falling back toward town." Lieutenant Harris recalled seeing the Confederate line in "hot pursuit." The Federal infantry, said another Badger, "not enough to make a heavy skirmish line . . . flying before the enemy [and] scattering like sheep, leaving the . . . artillery . . . and outrunning the enemy." His was an unfair remark. The New Yorkers had orders to retreat with the rest of Cutler's brigade, but the commanding officer was wounded before the order could be carried out. Assailed on the front and right (bullets "flying thick and fast," reported an officer), the regiment hung on until a rider from Wadsworth slipped "through the leaden hail like a whirlwind across the old railroad cut" with orders to retreat. The New Yorkers "ran, pursued pell-mell by the enemy" to the relative safety of Seminary Ridge. They would later sharply deny any claim that they had to be "rescued" by the charging Wisconsin men—or any other regiment.[1]

As they moved toward the road and fence, some of the Black Hats saw Federal soldiers carrying John Reynolds's corpse in a blanket.[2] In the days following the fighting, it was said Reynolds made his stand northwest of town because he saw an opportunity to save the deep defensive positions south of Gettysburg. Other officers complained that Reynolds was the victim of his own rashness, heedlessly and impetuously engaging a powerful enemy even though his main infantry force

---

1 Capt. J. W. Pierce, *New York at Gettysburg*, 3 vols. (Albany, NY, 1900), vol. 3, 990-994, 1,004.

2 Dawes, *Telegraph*, April 27, 1890; Harris, *Telegraph*, March 22, 1885; Fairfield Diary, July 1, 1863; George Fairfield to Jerome A. Watrous, undated; Dawes, *Service*, 166; R. L. Murray, *First on the Field: Cortland's 76th and Oswego's 147th New York State Volunteer Regiments at Gettysburg* (Wolcott, NY, 1998), 27.

was not on the field, when what he should have done was fall back to a more defensible position. The whispers were lost in the eulogies for the fallen commander. General officers killed near the front with their troops, even rash ones, escape the double-sided questions of Congressional committeemen, the sharp pens of newspaper editors, and the snide remarks of jealous officers. In the present, as his still warm body was being borne from the field, it was up to the men of Wadsworth's division to confirm the general's decision was indeed the right one.[3]

The 6th Wisconsin and the Brigade Guard companies ran in formation toward the Chambersburg Pike through the smoke, noise, scattered bullets, and backwash of wounded soldiers pouring out of the woods. To their left front, the 14th Brooklyn and 95th New York, both of Cutler's brigade, were slowly falling back. Ahead, across the road, a heavy line of yelling Confederates rolled east, chasing other men from Cutler's command running for Seminary Ridge. The 147th New York was north of the pike when Joe Davis' large brigade (composed of the 2nd and 42nd Mississippi and 55th North Carolina) swept down upon it. After a gallant but brief stand, the Union line collapsed. The 76th New York and 56th Pennsylvania were caught just as they formed battle lines. The Rebel front extended well beyond the exposed Union right, and the converging fire from both front and flank was too much for any soldiers. Although surging in pursuit, Davis' line was piling up and the officers were slowly but surely losing firm tactical control.

Now in command after Reynolds' death, Abner Doubleday described this as the "critical" moment of the opening infantry fight. Four regiments of the Iron Brigade were collapsing and driving Archer's brigade, but three of Cutler's regiments were on the run and two others were in retreat. Davis' line was slowly reaching a place from which it could pour volleys into the right and rear of the makeshift Union line. Doubleday said he ordered the 6th Wisconsin ("a gallant body of men, whom I know could be relied upon") to the right to prevent "the defeat, perhaps the utter rout of our forces."[4]

With each passing second the Badgers of the 6th Wisconsin were closing the distance on the rail fence lining the Chambersburg Pike. Ahead, wrote Dawes, "a long line of yelling rebels" spilled over the ridge beyond what he later found to be an unfinished railroad cut. The ridge had been gouged for the track, but no rails were laid and the bed was strewn with boulders and piles of dirt and stone. It was nearly impossible to see the cut from the Union position. The Confederates were moving east past Dawes' approaching column and slowly drifting right. The young

3   Herdegen, "The Iron Brigade and John Reynolds," in *Tall Black Hats*, 101.

4   Abner Doubleday's report, *OR* 27, pt. 1, 246.

officer realized the opportunity and set about to make it so. "File right, March!" he ordered. His column swung to move alongside the flank of the Rebels pursuing Cutler's retreating regiments. Dawes barked another command: "By the left flank!" This order, he explained, "threw my line parallel to the turnpike and the R.R. cut, and almost directly upon the flank of the enemy."[5]

By this time some of the Confederates saw the approaching blue line and turned south to fire into the Wisconsin soldiers, who bowed into "the leaden storm and dashed forward."[6] Dawes had just turned his horse to the fence when the mare was "struck in the breast" and began rearing and plunging. The bullet struck the shoulder bone and moved around it before stopping fourteen inches from the entry wound. Unaware of the injury, Dawes savagely spurred the animal until she fell heavily on her haunches, tumbling him to the ground just as his line swept past in the double-quick.[7] "I am all right boys!" the young officer shouted. Those who heard responded with a friendly yell of their own. Not far away, an officer of the 147th New York watched as the Wisconsin men and the Brigade Guard—only "a little band," he said, but every "man of that band was a host in himself. Steady, swiftly and furiously they charged upon the enemy's flank." From behind his line Dawes yelled, "Fire by file, fire by file!" "I could see the enemy coming over the hill now by the railroad cut in a heavy line. I looked back and saw that my gallant old mare was on her feet and was hobbling sturdily to the rear on three legs." (The horse was found later among the brigade's wagons.) The 6th Wisconsin men reached the fence, rested their rifle-muskets on the rails, and fired by file from right to left. The staggered but effective fire from "our carefully aimed muskets" convinced many of the heretofore victorious Confederates to seek cover in the unfinished railroad cut.[8]

Mickey Sullivan and his Lemonweir Minute Men were just left of center when the regiment reached the fence. "The Johnnies were so intent upon following up their advantage that they did not for some time discover what was going on [on] their right," said one Badger. On the left of the line, Lieutenant Harris saw the Confederate line wheeling to face the new fire. "I could not help thinking, how, for once, we will have a square stand up and knock down fight. No trees, nor walls to protect either, when presto! Their whole line disappeared as if swallowed up by the

5 Dawes, *Telegraph*, April 27, 1890.

6 Young, *Telegraph*, April 22, 1888.

7 Dawes, *Telegraph*, April 27, 1890; Dawes, *Service*, 167.

8 Dawes, *Telegraph*, April 27, 1890; Dawes, *Service*, 167; Watrous, "Gettysburg," *Milwaukee Sunday Telegraph*, November 26, 1879.

earth." The Confederates had moved into the unfinished railroad cut, which from Harris' vantage point was essentially invisible. To Sullivan, it seemed "as if the ground had opened and swallowed them up; but we soon found that they were still on top if it—as they opened a tremendous fire upon us."[9]

Sullivan quickly discovered he was in serious trouble: His musket would not fire. The frustrated Irishman withdrew another percussion cap from his pouch, put it in place, aimed, and pulled the trigger. Nothing. While he fumbled with his musket, Rebel bullets splintered rails along the long fence and ripped furrows in the tall grass. "In the road our fellows straightened up their lines and waited for all hands to get over the fence," recalled Sullivan. A few moments later they were over a second fence and standing in an open field facing the musketry from the railroad cut about 175 yards away. It was "a galling fire," admitted one 6th Wisconsin man. "Several of our poor boys are left dangling on the fence." Dawes agreed, calling the fire "murderous" and said that "to climb that fence in the face of such a fire was a clear test of mettle and discipline."[10]

The Wisconsin regiment and two companies of the Brigade Guard, shooting as fast as possible in an attempt to beat down the Confederate fire, began to slowly move into the smoke-filled field. Still waging his own battle with his musket at the fence, Sullivan concluded his firearm must be double-loaded. Try as he might, however, he could not get the weapon to discharge. Seeing Adj. Edward Brooks, he shouted, "Brooks, my gun won't go off!" Brooks handed him a musket he had picked up and Sullivan crossed the fence to rejoin his company—only to find the second musket would not fire. "I knew my caps were bad," he concluded. The private ran up to Capt. John Ticknor of his own Company K, who pointed to a downed soldier "We rolled him over [Cpl. Charles Crawford] and I took the cartridge box and buckled it on myself." Sullivan turned around and watched "Ticknor start for the rear in a spread out, staggering sort of way. After a few steps, he fell." Sergeant Erastus Smith saw the same thing and yelled to Sullivan, "I think he is killed and I am going to see about him." The stricken captain was indeed mortally wounded. A sawmill worker in Juneau County when Fort Sumter was fired upon, Ticknor was one of the first to sign the roll. In camp the regimental favorite was known as "Jerky," for reasons never discovered. Ticknor was carried up and down his company street when his commission as lieutenant was approved, his

9 Dawes, *Telegraph*, April 27, 1890; Harris, *Telegraph*, March 22, 1885; Sullivan, *Telegraph*, December 20, 1884.

10 Sullivan, *Telegraph*, December 20, 1884, Rufus Dawes to Bachelder, March 18, 1868; Young, *Telegraph*, April 22, 1888; Harris, *Telegraph*, March 22, 1885.

men laughing and singing all the while. He was six feet tall, "straight as an arrow," and incredibly brave.[11]

In the Bloody Railroad Cut

The Wisconsin line lurched toward the railroad cut with Lt. Col. Rufus Dawes shouting "Forward! Forward charge! Align on the Colors! Align on the Colors!" The color bearer was Sgt. Thomas Polleys of Trempealeau, and the regiment went into battle under just the National flag. The blue state regimental banner that would normally accompany the men had been used up and sent back to Wisconsin. Before midday, all eight men of the color party would be dead or down. The firing from the railroad cut was "fearful" and "destructive," said Dawes, crashing "with an unbroken roar before us. Men are being shot by twenties and thirties and breaking ranks by falling or running. But the boys . . . crowded in right and left toward the colors and went forward." The advancing line moved quickly deeper into the field. On the left of the line, Harris saw the flag stagger forward and knew the order to charge had been given. As he passed the stationary 95th New York, he ran to the New Yorkers and shouted at an unnamed officer, "For God's sake why don't you move forward and join our left?" But the New Yorkers did not advance, and Harris ran back to his command. The 6th Wisconsin and the Brigade Guard, he said, "charged, singly and alone."[12]

Halfway into the field a bullet struck Sgt. Michael Mangan in the ankle. He was hopping to the rear when Francis Deleglise of the color party came to help him. Deleglise was shot in the calf of his right leg, and then in the right knee. Dropping down beside Mangan, Deleglise tried to bandage the sergeant's ankle, but found his muscles rigid from his own injuries. Captain Joseph Marston ordered Pvt. Harry Dunn to take Mangan to the rear. A few yards away Lt. Orrin Chapman, who had listened to a harmonica playing "Home, Sweet Home" the night before, was down and dying. The officer, who had blown the melancholy tune, Loyd Harris, was struck in the neck by buckshot, but still managed to rush forward toward the railroad cut. Private Dick Marston, just a few days earlier spared for sleeping while on guard duty, was killed here by a Southern bullet. The National flag went down, but was picked up. It fell again, and again went up. Captain Earl Rogers watched

---

11 Sullivan, *Telegraph*, December 20, 1884, and May 9, 1886.

12 Harris, *Telegraph*, March 22, 1885. Harris wrote: "The Ninety-fifth N.Y. did rally and re-form their regiment and deserve great praise for it, but they never joined the left of the 6th. That place was occupied by the 'Iron Brigade Guard.' . . . They failed to respond and the 'truth of history' compels me to state that 6th, with the brigade guard, charged, singly and alone."

Capt. Joseph Marston, Bragg's Rifles, Co. E, 6th Wisconsin

Marston captured a sword at Gettysburg and tried later to reach the Confederate officer who had surrendered it so he could return the blade to a worthy foe. *Buck Marston*

Dawes pick up the banner only to be shouldered aside by one of the color party still standing.

By this time the battered Wisconsin line was a "V-shaped crowd of men," related Dawes, "with the colors at the point, moving hurriedly and firmly forward, while the whole field behind is streaming with men plunging in agony to the rear or sinking in death to the ground." The young officer saw his wounded men "leaving the ranks in crowds."[13] Rebel bullets were taking a heavy toll. A ball smashed Sgt. George Fairfield's canteen and slashed his hip, but he plunged forward. Private Amos Lefler of Eden was shot in the face, spitting blood and teeth and he fell. Sergeant Henry Schildt, a native of Prussia and one of the older men in the regiment, was putting a percussion cap on his rifle when a charge of buck and ball struck him. Two buckshot entered his left side between the fourth and fifth ribs, about one inch apart.[14]

---

13 Rufus R. Dawes, "Sketches of War History," in *Military Order of the Loyal Legion of the United States, Commandery of the State of Ohio, War Papers*, reprinted in Dawes, *Service*, 351; Dawes, *Telegraph*, April 27, 1890.

14 Sergeant Henry Schildt was knocked out of active service for several months, but joined his German Company F as a captain near the end of the war. Born in Prussia in 1820, Schildt's family moved to Brunswick and Henry served six years with the Brunswick army. He migrated in 1847 to Canada and finally to New York state before traveling in 1858 or 1859 to Iowa County in Wisconsin, where he took up farming. Henry moved his family (at 41, he had several small children) to Mazomanie in Dane County and enlisted as a private in the German Milwaukee Citizens' Corps, Company F, 6th Wisconsin. His son Andrew, who enlisted in the

Pvt. Amos Lefler,
Bragg's Rifles,
Co. E, 6th Wisconsin

The young farmer enlisted in
1861. He was wounded at
South Mountain and shot in
the face at Gettysburg in the
charge on the railroad cut. He
transferred to the Veteran
Reserve Corps in November
1863. *Larry Lefler*

Less than thirty yards from
the bloody cut, Private
Fairfield with the wounded hip
somehow maintained enough
presence of mind to realize that
the Confederates were holding
their fire, "and it became
evident we should get a volley."
When it came, the wall of flame
and lead delivered at point-blank range could not miss. In the smoke and noise,
recalled Fairfield, "it seemed half our men had fallen."

Not too far distant, Cpl. Frank Wallar was running forward in a "general rush
and yells enough to almost awaken the dead." According to Harris, the "fire was the
worst ever experienced, yet not a man failed to move promptly forward and closed
in to the right as the men fell before the murderous fire of the rebels in the railroad
cut." It only took the Wisconsin men a short time to reach the equally determined
enemy infantry waiting for them above the unfinished tear in the earth, but when it

same regiment in early 1864, told the enlisting officer he was 15 and a farmer, but in truth he
was only 14. Andrew fought in all the major battles of 1864 and 1865 and mustered out with his
regiment as a 16-year-old veteran. Young Schildt did not return home. From 1866 to 1872, he
worked as a cowhand in Texas before moving to work in mining camps in Nevada and
California. By 1882 he was living on the Blackfoot reservation in Montana Territory, where he
courted a young Blackfoot girl named Nellie. According to Schildt family history, the two were
"married by a Methodist minister when he was on a buffalo hunt with a party of hunters from
Fort Benton, Montana," and the couple had seven children. Andrew died October 21, 1925,
and is buried at his ranch home west of Browning, Montana. His father is buried at Mazomanie.

Capt. Henry Schildt, Milwaukee Citizens Corps, Co. F, 6th Wisconsin

A veteran of the Prussian Army, Schildt was still a noncommissioned officer when wounded in the charge on the unfinished railroad cut at Gettysburg on July 1, and again at Gravelly Run in Virginia in 1864. He mustered out on July 14, 1865. *Brett Wilson Collection*

The Unfinished Railroad Cut

This postwar view shows the installed railroad ties and iron rails, which were not present during the fighting in 1863. This image was included by the Dawes family in a 1936 edition of Rufus Dawes' 1890 memoir.

happened, the opposing lines crashed together in a cacophony of screaming humanity near a Confederate flag fluttering on the edge of the depression, the historic encounter punctuated by a tangle of bayonets, musket butts, fists, and other implements of war.[15]

When he saw a chance to capture the Confederate flag, Lt. William Remington moved to his right behind his battle line and ran through a break toward the enticing banner. A bullet nicked the left side of his neck as he closed on the prize. He transferred his sword to his left hand, which was holding his revolver, so he could reach out for the staff. "I saw a soldier taking aim at me from the railroad

---

15 George Fairfield to Jerome Watrous, undated; Frank Wallar to Earl Rogers, in *Milwaukee Sunday Telegraph*, March 22, 1885.

cut," he said. "I threw my right shoulder forward and kept going for the flag. He hit me through the right shoulder and knocked me down." Remington got up and walked backward through his line where he "got d——-d" by Maj. John Hauser for going after the flag. He started for the rear at his best run, admitted later that "Flag-taking was pretty well knocked out of me." The wounded lieutenant was just 20 feet from the Confederate flag when he got hit, and two other soldiers with the same idea passed him: Cornelius Okey of Cassville and Lewis Eggleston of Shiocton. According to Okey, he reached the flag ahead of Eggleston and, "bending over grasped the staff low down, but he was so close to me that before I could draw it from the ground, the staff having been driven well down in the dirt, Eggleston had also got a hold of it. I noticed a rebel corporal on his knees, right in front of men in the act of firing, his bayonet almost touched me; as quick as thought almost I made a quarter face to the left," Okey continued, "thus pressing my right side to him and bringing Eggleston, who still retained his hold on the flag, as well as my self, at my back." The Rebel fired and his buck and ball charge passed through the skirt of Okey's frock coat and lodged in his left forearm and wrist. Eggleston also fell, shot through both arms.[16]

Also in the tangle of soldiers was John O. Johnson, who did his best to save Eggleston, a member of his mess "whom I loved as a brother." Johnson's musket ramrod, however, jammed halfway down the barrel. "Seeing other rebels raising their guns as if to shoot or bayonet Eggleston, I stepped in front of him and raised my musket to defend him as best I could. While thus in the act of stroking, I received a wound that disabled my right arm. Poor Eggleston also went down, and I think from the same bullet that wounded me."[17] As Eggleston fell, David "Rocky Mountain" Anderson of Minneapolis[18] swung his musket like a club, crushing the skull of the Rebel who fired the fatal ball. Nearby, John Harland was shot as he moved toward the Confederate flag, his body sliding into the railroad cut at the foot of the soldier who killed him. Private Levi Tongue aimed his musket pointblank at the Rebel. "Don't shoot! Don't kill me," yelled the Johnny. "All hell can't save you now," replied Tongue, whose discharge knocked the grayback onto the body of his friend. In the tangle of "shooting, thrusting and parrying thrusts," Cpl. Frank

16 William Remington, *Milwaukee Sunday Telegraph*, April 29, 1883. His account was dated December 17, 1882; Cornelius Okey, *Milwaukee Sunday Telegraph*, April 29, 1883.

17 John O. Johnson, "One Rebel Flag," in *Milwaukee Sunday Telegraph*, July 17, 1887.

18 Lewis Eggleston of Shiocton came into the regiment as a drummer, but quickly assumed the duties of a soldier. His friend David Anderson of Minneapolis was remembered as a "rough looking man with a shaggy head of hair" nicknamed "Rocky Mountain" because of his pre-war travels.

Wallar, his brother Sam at his side, closed on the embattled Confederate flag.[19] Along the edge of the railroad cut, the Wisconsin men pushed musket barrels into the upraised faces of hundreds of Confederates who now fully realized they were trapped in the deep portion of the long gouge. "Throw down your muskets! Down with your muskets!" the soldiers in big hats shouted over and over. "The men are black and grimy with powder and heat," recalled one Wisconsin officer. "They seemed all unconscious to the terrible situation; they were mad and fought with a desperation seldom witnessed."[20]

Holding the flag of the 2nd Mississippi was Cpl. W. B. Murphy. "My color guards were all killed and wounded in less than five minutes," he would somehow live to report, "and also my colors was shot more than one dozen times, and the flag staff was hit and splintered two or three times." A group of Federals rushed toward him, "but all were killed our wounded." Others, he added, "still kept rushing for my flag and there were over a dozen shot down like sheep in the mad rush for the colors." He saw Captain Remington shot down along with a dozen or so others. "Then a large man [Frank Wallar] made a rush for me and the flag. As I tore the flag from the staff he took hold of me and the color. The firing was still going on, and was kept up for several minutes after the flag was taken from me."[21]

A Confederate leveled his musket at Wallar's side, but his brother Sam knocked the barrel aside as the gun went off, reversed his own musket, and clubbed the unnamed Johnny. "[S]oon after I got the flag," continued brother Frank, "there were men from all the companies there. I did take the flag out of the color bearer's hand." He thought about making for the rear with the trophy, but "then I thought I would stay, and I threw it down and loaded and fired twice standing on it. While standing on it there was a Fourteenth Brooklyn man took hold and tried to get it,

19 Earl Rogers, *Milwaukee Sunday Telegraph*, July 29, 1883; Cheek and Pointon, *Sauk County*, 47. According to Pointon and Cheek in their invaluable history of the Sauk County Riflemen, Wallar added a selfless account of what happened and how he ended up with the Mississippi flag: "Bodley Jones of A Company had made for the flag in the charge and had captured it and had it in his possession when killed. I grabbed it as Jones fell and carried it back and surrendered it to our proper officers, and I got the medal of honor for the capture. But if he had not been killed he and not I would have the medal." *Ibid.*

20 Earl Rogers to Jerome Watrous, undated.

21 W. B. Murphy to Dr. F. A. Dearborn, Nashua, New Hampshire, June 29, 1900, Edward S. Bragg Papers, Wisconsin Historical Society. "I was about fifty paces East of the cut, and on the side toward Gettysburg, and I and my color guard were about ten paces south of the railroad," recalled Murphy after the war. "There was no cut there at all; the ditch was not more than two feet deep where I passed over the railroad. Our regiment stopped in the railroad for protection." *Ibid.*

Sgt. Frank Wallar,
Anderson Guards,
Co. I, 6th Wisconsin

Wallar was still a corporal when he captured the flag of the 2nd Mississippi at the railroad cut at Gettysburg. His accomplished earned him a Congressional Medal of Honor in 1864. *Scott D. Hann Collection*

and I had threatened to shoot him before he would stop. By this time we had them cleaned out."[22]

They Got You Down, Mickey, Have They?

Lieutenant Colonel Rufus Dawes reached the edge of the railroad cut and called for the Confederates trapped inside to surrender. "I found myself face to face with hundreds of rebels, who I looked down upon in the railroad cut, which was, where I stood, four feet deep." Farther west, the cut grew much deeper and steeper. To his right, Adj. Edward Brooks threw a dozen men across the east end of the cut and they began firing into the Confederates. Those hundreds deep in the cut were unable to calculate the number of their attackers. Many of the Rebels held up their hats as a signal of surrender. "Where is the colonel of this Regiment?" shouted Dawes. Major John Blair of the 2nd Mississippi replied, "Here I am. Who are you?" Dawes jumped into the cut, pushing and pulling aside armed enemy soldiers as he cut a path toward the major. "I command this regiment. Surrender or I will fire." Blair handed over his sword without a word. The Confederates around the pair of officers began dropping their muskets. "The coolness, self-possession, and discipline which held back our men from pouring in a general volley saved a hundred lives of the enemy," reported Dawes, "and as my mind goes back to the fearful excitement of the moment, I marvel at it." Echoing Dawes, another Wisconsin soldier recalled that the Union men "would have made a great slaughter down the cut had they not surrendered." Dawes accepted Blair's sword and other blades offered by additional Southern officers. They made for an awkward bundle. Brooks made his way into the cut to assist him. "It would have been a handsome thing to say, 'Keep your sword, sir,' but I was new to such occasions and when six other officers came up and handed me their swords," explained Dawes years later, "I took them also." Loyd Harris heard later that when the two officers confronted each other, Blair demanded Dawes' surrender and that Dawes replied, "I will see you in hell first!" Harris admitted that he doubted the veracity of the story and Dawes did not remember it that way. A Wisconsin private who was there claims that when the Confederate major was told he faced a Wisconsin unit, he answered, "Thank God. I thought it was a New York regiment."[23]

The fight at the railroad cut devastated Joe Davis' brigade as surely as it crippled his reputation as a combat leader. The depression looked enticing as a natural breastwork, but once crowded inside the Rebels "could neither fight nor retreat . . . on account of the high banks." Some ran for it out of the western end, "as the cut was too deep for them to see the scarcity of our numbers or make attack. The 2d Miss. lay in the water, mud and blood at the east end of the cut where the cut was coming out to a grade."[24] Not far from where Dawes accepted the surrender, Mickey Sullivan captured his own sword. The Irish private jumped into the railroad cut to help gather prisoners when an officer handed him a sword. "Some of the Johnnies threw down their guns and surrendered. Some would fire and then throw down their guns and cry 'I surrender,' and some broke for the rear," wrote Sullivan. Another soldier, Pvt. Augustus Klein, claimed every Rebel who "fired after we asked them to surrender got either a bullet put through his head or a bayonet through his breast. We didn't show them no mercy." Sullivan was climbing up the far side of the embankment when "a big rebel broke for the rear and I called on him to halt, to which he paid no attention, and I flung the rebel sword at him with all my might." But as Sullivan was turning to throw the blade, "a bullet hit me on the left shoulder and knocked me down as quick as if I had been hit with a sledge hammer."

23 Harris, *Telegraph*, March 22, 1883; Dawes, *Service*, 169; I. F. Kelly to Rufus Dawes, August 2, 1892; Howard Huntington, letter, July 2, 1863.

24 George Fairfield to Jerome Watrous, undated; Joseph Marston, *Milwaukee Sunday Telegraph*, April 24, 1881.

Sgt. Albert Tarbox, Lemonweir Minute Men, Co. K, 6th Wisconsin

Tarbox was shot and killed at the railroad cut at Gettysburg while talking with his wounded comrade, Mickey Sullivan. *Institute for Civil War Studies*

His first thought was that he had been struck with a musket butt, "for I felt numb and stunned, but I was not long in finding out what was the matter." If he had not tried to throw the sword, he said, he would have been shot square in the body." Sergeant Albert Tarbox stood over the prone private to ask, "They got you down Mickey, have they?" before falling forward dead, shot by a Rebel who had already surrendered. "They did a good deal of that kind of work that day. I never saw so many men killed in such a short time, as it was not more than fifteen or twenty minutes from the time we saw the rebels, until we had them officers, colors and all."[25]

On the left of the bloodied and exhausted 6th Wisconsin, the 95th New York and then the 14th Brooklyn fired into the Confederates trying to escape the cut. Fighting along the whole line once again erupted, but it soon sputtered to a halt amid cries of "Surrender!" and "Throw down your muskets!" The captured included seven officers and 225 enlisted men, including Major Blair, and the regiment's torn and trampled battle flag.[26] Of the roughly 300 men in ranks, the 6th Wisconsin lost two officers killed and six wounded, 27 enlisted men killed, 105 wounded and 20 missing.[27]

---

25 Sullivan, *Telegraph*, December 20, 1885. The target of the thrown sword was probably Alfred H. Belo of the 55th North Carolina, who documented what was almost certainly the same incident this way: "One officer, seeing me, threw his sword at me and said: 'Kill that officer, and we will capture that command.' One of my men, however, picked him off and we were able to get out of the railroad cut after a severe struggle." Alfred Belo, *Confederate Veteran* (1900), clipping, Carroll Institute for Civil War Studies, 165-168.

26 Dawes, *Service*, 173. According to Dawes, about 1,000 dropped muskets lay in the bottom of the railroad cut, and that the 95th New York "took prisoners, as did also the 14th Brooklyn."

27 *Ibid.*, 168. Rufus Dawes to August Gaylord, Adjutant General, State of Wisconsin, July 19, 1863: William W. Dudley, 19th Indiana, in his "official report" on the Iron Brigade at Gettysburg, listed 22 soldiers in the Brigade Guard as wounded, including the two officers. William W. Dudley, *The Iron Brigade at Gettysburg: 1878, Official Report of the Part borne by the First Brigade, First Division, First Army Corps* (Cincinnati, OH, 1879), 15.

The 6th Wisconsin's Capt. John Kellogg, serving on the staff of his former colonel Lysander Cutler, watched his regiment overcome the Rebels from his position on Seminary Ridge. It was "three minutes" after the 6th Wisconsin reached the unfinished railroad cut, he said, before the 95th New York and 14th Brooklyn arrived to fire into the fleeting enemy. Nearby, an excited James Wadsworth and his staff watched the same historic charge. When the National flag was hoisted high in victory, Wadsworth swung his hat and cheered.

The early morning fighting finally sputtered to a fitful halt along the length of McPherson's war-torn ridge. Dawes was trying to organize what was left of his command when Corporal Wallar bought him the square red battle flag of the 2nd Mississippi. On it was the names Manassas, Gaines Farm, Malvern Hill, and Seven Pines. Dawes passed the flag to Sgt. William Evans, who was shot through the upper legs and on his way to the rear using two muskets for crutches. Dawes wrapped the flag and tied it around Evan's body under his coat, urging him to keep it safe. Adjutant Brooks arrived at this time with a bundle of captured swords that he gave to another wounded man. The swords were delivered to Surgeon A. W. Preston in Gettysburg, but were lost when Confederates overran his temporary hospital later that afternoon.

Wounded Mickey Sullivan was having a hard time staying on his feet. General Wadsworth, who had come up by this time, noticed the Irishman's distress. "My man, you are too badly hurt to be here," observed the division commander, who ordered a cavalry sergeant to mount Sullivan onto his horse and take him to a hospital being set up in Gettysburg. The sergeant was told not to leave the wounded private "until he saw me in care of a doctor."[28] Sullivan was leaving the field when Dawes released members of the Brigade Guard to return to their regiments, which were now moving to a defensive position in the woods along McPherson's Ridge. Battery B also arrived and unlimbered along the Chambersburg Pike and the railroad cut, where it was supported by the 6th Wisconsin, 14th Brooklyn, and 95th New York. The three other regiments of Cutler's brigade extended the Union line north along the ridge. Cutler's command and Iron Brigade's 2nd and 6th Wisconsin had been shot to pieces. The 6th Wisconsin lost one of every two men in the rush for the railroad cut. The 2nd Wisconsin lost one of every three soldiers in line in the initial exchange of musketry on McPherson's Ridge. The other regiments of

---

28 Dawes, *Service*, 170-172; Sullivan, *Telegraph*, December 20, 1884; I. F. Kelly to Rufus Dawes, August 21, 1892. In his letter, Kelly told Dawes: "How you ever got through without being killed is more than I can understand, as you were always in front in every fight. . . . Always looking after the interests of your men and officers. Never asking them to go where you did not lead. Perfectly cool under fire. A brave leader of as noble a band of patriots as ever wore the blue and fought under the stars and stripes."

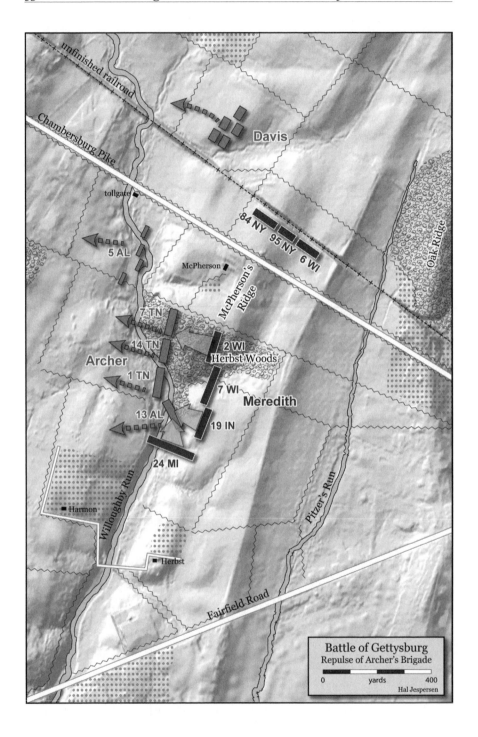

unfinished railroad

Chambersburg Pike

Davis

tollgate

84 NY 95 NY 6 WI

5 AL

McPherson

McPherson's Ridge

7 TN

14 TN

Archer

1 TN

2 WI
Herbst Woods

7 WI

Meredith

13 AL

19 IN

24 MI

Harmon

Herbst

Willoughby Run

Pitzer's Run

Fairfield Road

Oak Ridge

Battle of Gettysburg
Repulse of Archer's Brigade

0   yards   400

Hal Jespersen

Meredith's brigade suffered fewer immediate casualties in the morning fighting, but the totals would change dramatically during the afternoon.

We Fight a Little and Run a Little

The opening action at Gettysburg involved just four infantry brigades: Archer and Davis on the Confederate side, and Cutler and Meredith on the other. Both sides took advantage of the lull that followed to move heavy reinforcements to the field. The Confederates spent the time preparing for a renewal of the assault after the bloody and unexpected setback. Major General Henry Heth, whose rash thrust that morning had cost him a pair of brigades, brought up additional artillery batteries to rake the Federal position as he readied his two remaining brigades—a large outfit under James Pettigrew and an unreliable collection of Virginia regiments under John Brockenbrough—to renew the combat.

With John Reynolds down, Abner Doubleday—a First Corps division commander and now senior officer on the field—assumed command of the Union forces on and near the battlefield. He arrived only minutes before Reynolds was shot, and so had no instructions of what the fallen general planned. "Upon taking a retrospect of the field, it might seem, in view of the fact that we were finally forced to retreat, that this would have been a proper time to retire," Doubleday explained in his official report. Given Reynolds' decision to fight northwest of Gettysburg, he continued, "I naturally supposed that it was the intention to defend the place." Because Doubleday believed the key to the entire position was woods on the McPherson's Ridge line, he kept the four Iron Brigade regiments in the trees (the 6th Wisconsin was still north of the pike by the railroad cut). Sol Meredith protested to no avail that the position was not strong enough to hold. Doubleday also placed two brigades from his own division that had just reached the field under Cols. Chapman Biddle (Brig. Gen. Thomas Rowley's outfit) and Roy Stone on the ridge, the former on the left of the Iron Brigade, and the latter on the right near the Chambersburg Pike. Two other brigades from John Robinson's division under Brig. Gens. Henry Baxter and Gabriel Paul marched north across the pike to extend the line north along Oak Ridge. Doubleday also ordered Cutler's battered regiments to once again move forward to McPherson's Ridge. "It's just like cock-fighting to-day," Lysander Cutler told his men. "We fight a little and run a little. There are no supports."[29]

---

29 Sidney G. Cooke, "The First Day at Gettysburg," *War Talks in Kansas*, 280, as reprinted in *The Gettysburg Papers*, Ken Bandy and Florence Freeland, compliers (Dayton, OH, 1986), 239.

A short time later, Maj. Gen. Oliver O. Howard of Eleventh Corps reached the battlefield and assumed command because of his senior commission. Howard ordered Doubleday to hold Seminary Ridge at all hazards if driven off McPherson's Ridge. Howard left an Eleventh Corps' division under Brig. Gen. Adolph von Steinwehr along with some artillery in reserve south of Gettysburg on Cemetery Hill and ordered his two other divisions under Maj. Gen. Carl Schurz and Brig. Gen. Francis Barlow through the town to meet any Confederate threat coming from the north.

The fighting west of Gettysburg and the movement of soldiers and artillery through streets and yards sent civilians scurrying for safety. The excitement aroused the fighting spirit of former Town Constable John Burns, a 68-year-old cobbler and veteran of the War of 1812. Burns was present when a Confederate column occupied the town on June 26 after scattering a makeshift force of home guards and militia. The Rebels burned a nearby iron foundry owned by Congressman Thaddeus Stevens, an outspoken abolitionist and hard-line proponent of putting down the rebellion by force. An advance party of enemy cavalry ("the filthiest looking pack of men we had ever seen," said a town girl) galloped through Gettysburg yelling and firing revolvers, scaring citizens off the streets before looting barns, stores, and chicken coops and stealing pet horses. Confederate Maj. Gen. Jubal Early arrived from nearby Mummasburg a short time later to find about 100 captured local militia under guard in the town square. He lectured them about the consequences of rash action, told the old fellows they should have used more sense, and that the younger ones should have stayed with their mothers. Early paroled the lot of them.[30]

Now the Confederates were back, and old Burns was restless and eager to take a hand. What happened over the next few hours was a story retold so often no one was sure of the exact truth. Gathering his old musket, Burns went out on the streets in an effort to rouse his neighbors to action. Despite his curses (one pious lady claimed Burns berated a neighbor as a "damned coward, a chicken hearted squaw, a tallow faced sissy"), he had little success. He finally declared that he "must have a hand in the fight," and the old cobbler put musket to shoulder and marched in what must have been a unique fashion toward the fighting on the rolling ridges northwest of Gettysburg.[31]

---

30 "Recollections of John L. Kendlehart Written for his Sisters, Mary and Sarah," February 1916 (Privately held). He was twelve years old at the time of the battle. His father was David Kendlehart, president of the Gettysburg Town Council. Margaretta Kendlehart McCartney, "A Story of Early's Raid," *Gettysburg Compiler*, June 30, 1923.

31 Timothy H. Smith, *John Burns: The Hero of Gettysburg* (Gettysburg, 2000), 43-45.

I Both Respected and Feared Him

Four regiments of the Iron Brigade—the 2nd and 7th Wisconsin, 19th Indiana and 24th Michigan—were posted in the center of the Union line on McPherson's Ridge along a low wooded crest running east of Willoughby Run. To the south and slightly to the east were Biddle's 121st Pennsylvania, 80th New York, 142nd Pennsylvania and 151st Pennsylvania. To the north, Stone's 150th Pennsylvania, 143rd Pennsylvania, and 149th Pennsylvania held the line, but they were in the open and susceptible to attack from the north. It was apparent there were not enough men to hold the Union position against a determined effort to take it.

What none of them realized was that a new storm was approaching from north of Gettysburg. Two divisions from Richard Ewell's Corps reached Cashtown and turned south on the Carlisle and Harrisburg roads toward Gettysburg. They would arrive squarely on the Union right flank and rear. Some of Howard's units from his Eleventh Corps were spilling through town and into line farther north, but they were arriving strung out and piecemeal; the Confederates were already arriving in heavy numbers and good order. In the early afternoon, one of Ewell's divisions under Robert E. Rodes attacked off Oak Hill northwest of town and struck the Federals on Oak Ridge. The effort was poorly coordinated, however, and Edward O'Neal's and Alfred Iverson's brigades suffered especially heavy losses against the First Corps brigades defending the wooded terrain. The Southern advance stalled. Directly north of town, Jubal Early's division attacked Howard's Eleventh Corps in the largely open ground, where there was too much terrain and not enough blue uniforms and guns to hold it. Barlow's division was in an especially weak formation and was overrun. The right flank of the entire Union line of battle unraveled.

Farther south and west, in the woods on McPherson's Ridge, the Black Hats watched as Confederates massed to their front on Herr Ridge. The Union position along the east bank of Willoughby Run was slightly up the slope. It was apparent the brigade could be overlapped on both flanks, and that the left side was almost invisible from the right because of the contours of the land and the trees and brush. Colonel Henry Morrow of the 24th Michigan found his right flank awkwardly turned back to unite with the 2nd Wisconsin while his left went down a hillside to a hollow to reach the 19th Indiana. Morrow believed the Federal line should be moved back to the ridge crest. Three times he sent off aides to ask permission to correct his line, and three times his requests were refused. The Confederate buildup lasted until mid-afternoon, when the Confederates stepped of Herr Ridge and began moving in heavy lines down into a wooded area halfway down the slope, where they halted. The Wisconsin, Indiana, and Michigan veterans could see at least three brigades (and behind those others as well) arrayed against them. Only three small Union brigades would face them—the Iron Brigade in the center, Rowley's

Sgt. George Eustice,
Lancaster Union Guards,
Co. F, 7th Wisconsin

Eustice was one of the Iron Brigade soldiers who caught up with citizen John Burns on the firing line on McPherson's Ridge that terrible first day at Gettysburg. *Institute for Civil War Studies*

brigade under Biddle on its left to the south, and Stone's brigade on the right to the north. Farther north and behind their right shoulders, the Western men listened to the heavy sound of fighting where the men of the Eleventh Corps were being systematically crushed and outflanked.

It was approaching 3:00 p.m. when some 3,000 soldiers of Heth's two brigades and some of Archer's survivors stepped off to clear McPherson's Ridge and open the way to Gettysburg. Colonel John Brockenbrough's Virginians held Heth's left near the pike facing Stone and the right side of the Iron Brigade, Brig. Gen. Pettigrew's North Carolinians marched in the center against the left side of the brigade and well beyond, and Archer's regiments under Col. Birkett Fry held Heth's far right. Behind Heth's division formed another under Maj. Gen. William D. Pender. Brigadier General Edward Thomas' Georgia regiments formed north of the Chambersburg Pike, with the brigades of Brig. Gen. Alfred M. Scales, Col. Abner Perrin, and Brig. Gen. James H. Lane deployed south of the road. The front lines of advancing Confederates, muskets at the shoulder, moved down into the swale with a swaying step. The Black Hats held their fire, watching as the gray infantry stepped over a weak rail fence into a field of oats. Once there, the Johnnies came on with that chilling and wild yell heard on so many battlefields.

Heading directly toward the 24th Michigan and the 19th Indiana was the 26th North Carolina, with 800 men in line. The huge and well-trained 26th was led by Henry King Burgwyn Jr., who at just 22 was perhaps the youngest colonel in the Confederate army. The 26th North Carolina held the left of Pettigrew's brigade line, with the 11th North Carolina, 47th North Carolina, and 52nd North Carolina stretching farther right (south). The four regiments were midway through the field when the Western men fired their first volley. The noisy shower of bullets mostly fell short. The Confederate line stopped to fire a largely harmless volley of its own. A second Union volley, this time high, did nothing to stop the Confederates, who sprang forward at the quick-step. The third Federal volley opened holes in the line, though the determined Southerners, in a great swirl of shouts, gunfire, and swarming bullets, leaned into the effort and pushed ahead. Once the distance closed, the 24th Michigan and 26th North Carolina locked themselves into one of the most brutal close-range firefights of the war, a bravely waged combat that made both units famous and forever linked them by blood.[32] Morrow knew his 24th Michigan was at the very point of attack in the enemy effort to clear McPherson Ridge. His soldiers fired steadily, and the smoke gathered in the low ground around the creek limiting visibility. The bowed Michigan line, however, made it difficult for his men to concentrate fire against the advancing Rebels. The distance was now point-blank: just 50 to 80 yards. The Wolverines in their new black hats had done little to throw up any protection. It was a time when Iron Brigade men still believed there was a certain honor in a "stand up and knock down" fight against a brave foe—a prideful notion that was about to be knocked out of them in the next 60 minutes. It was a terrible time, the air full of bullets and the boys going down at a fearful rate. "Yelling like demons," the 26th North Carolina pressed forward without hesitation and the 24th Michigan men stood firm in their path.[33]

The battle flags of the opposing regiments were clearly visible in the smoke and noise and the bright banners became the target of soldiers on both sides. The Michigan regiment carried only the magnificent and beautifully embroidered National colors made by Tiffany & Co. of New York. It was presented to the regiment in August of 1862 on behalf of F. Buhl & Co. of Detroit. At the time, Color Sgt. Abel G. Peck was handed a $100.00 check from a Detroit citizen that he could keep if the banner was returned unsullied. Peck would not live long enough to collect the reward, for he was killed earlier that morning—the first of at least nine Michigan color-bearers to fall.[34] Opposite the Michigan men, the red Confederate flag went down, and then up again. The underbrush around Willoughby Run slowed the Confederate advance. The Rebels splashed across the shallow stream in fairly good order and halted briefly to reform. Michigan soldiers watched in wonder

---

32 Rod Gragg, *Covered with Glory: The 26th North Carolina Infantry at Gettysburg* (New York, 2000), 110-116.

33 Sullivan, *Telegraph*, December 20, 1884; Young, *Telegraph*, April 22, 1888.

34 Curtis, *Twenty-fourth*, 225-227; Madaus and Zeitlin, *Iron Brigade Flags*, 34-35.

when a Southern officer riding a mule behind the main line had his hat knocked off by a bullet and caught it in the air with one hand, all the while yelling "Give 'em hell, boys!"

Farther south, Confederates were flanking the 19th Indiana, bending the Hoosier line back bit by bit. The Federal regiments under Biddle, formed behind the 19th Indiana's left-rear en echelon, could not prevent a heavy fire from tearing into the flank of the Hoosiers.

By this time, the four Iron Brigade regiments had been heavily engaged and ammunition was running dangerously low. The 19th Indiana, with at least 20 men already dead and another 100 or so wounded, slowly fell back as bullets swept the Union line from the front and the left. Farther north along the line, the 2nd Wisconsin and 7th Wisconsin were also heavily engaged, as were Stone's Pennsylvania regiments in the open field farther north near the pike, where Brockenbrough's Virginians were approaching. The entire front was once again full of smoke, shouting, shooting, and blood.

Shot to pieces and now face-to-face with a heavy line of Tar Heels, the 24th Michigan found itself in a deadly crossfire. With muskets fouled, hot to the touch, and hard to load, the Wolverines took a step backward. And then another. The Johnnies, just as determined, took a step forward, and then another. Somewhere in the noise and confusion, the 26th North Carolina's gallant Colonel Burgwyn picked up his regiment's red battle flag from a downed color bearer. Just after he passed it to another soldier, a bullet hit the young officer in the side and passed through both lungs, knocking him to the ground. John Randolph Lane, a 27-year-old farmer who rose from the ranks to become lieutenant colonel, assumed command and continued shoving what was left of his regiment into the woods toward the wavering line of Wolverines. Lane was tall with a solemn manner that made him seem older. With the regiment from the beginning, and a steady leader, he too would be shot down within a few short minutes.[35]

The Flag is Down!

The 19th Indiana, standing tall in the face of the 26th and 11th North Carolina regiments, carried two flags that day—a blue regimental presented by the ladies of

---

35 George C. Underwood, *History of the 26th Regiment of North Carolina Troops in the Great War, 1861-'65* (Goldsboro, NC, 1901), 351. The report of Col. Samuel Williams of the 19th Indiana is in Alan D. Gaff, "Here Was Made Our Last and Hopeless Stand—The 'Lost' Gettysburg Reports of the 19th Indiana," *Gettysburg Magazine*, January, 1990, 25-32; Curtis, *Twenty-fourth*, 182.

Indianapolis in 1861, and a National color requisitioned from the Quartermaster Department when a complementary National flag from 1861 was retired. The National flag was carried first that morning by Sgt. Burlington Cunningham, who fell wounded in the opening flurry of bullets. Abe Buckles picked up the flag, only to be surprised at midday when Cunningham reappeared to take up the banner again despite a wound in his side.

The Hoosiers were fighting for their lives with the line bending under a heavy flank fire. (Captain Hollon Richardson described the Indiana regiment as disappearing "like dew before the morning sun.") Cunningham was wounded a second time in the leg and Buckles was struck in the shoulder. Lieutenant Colonel William Dudley grabbed the National flag while Sgt. Maj. Asa Blanchard looked for another color bearer. The round that smashed into Dudley's right shin before a replacement could be found would cost him a portion of his leg. "Colonel, you shouldn't have done this. That was my duty!" exclaimed Blanchard as he took the flag from the downed officer to hand to another soldier. "I shall never forgive myself for letting you touch that flag." Two soldiers picked up Dudley and carried him to the rear. The Indiana flag fell yet again. Eight Indiana color bearers had been shot down and the regiment's loss in killed and wounded climbed to about one of every two on the field. Unable to hold against the heavy fire from front and left, the surviving Hoosiers began moving backward.[36]

Corporal David Philips, who was carrying the Indiana regimental banner, scooped up the fallen National flag and was waving it with one hand when he was wounded and collapsed on both bloodied banners.

"The flag is down!" someone shouted.

Captain William W. Macy ordered a nearby private to "Go and get it!"

"Go to hell, I won't do it!" shot back the soldier.

Macy, Lt. Crockett East, and Cpl. Burr Clifford rolled Philips off the flags. Aware the bright silk was attracting bullets, East furled the banner, slipped it into its case, and was trying to wrap the tassels when he was shot and killed. Macy and Clifford finally got the two flags in their respective cases only to be confronted by an angry Sgt. Maj. Blanchard, who demanded the banners be uncased. "No, there's been enough men shot down with it," shot back Captain Macy. When Blanchard appealed to Col. Samuel J. Williams, the colonel directed Macy to turn over the flags. Blanchard pulled out the National colors, tied the case around his waist, and yelled "Rally boys!" Blanchard was waving the banner when a bullet entered his thigh and severed his femoral artery. The officer fell in a gush of unstoppable blood

---

36 William W. Dudley, "Sgt. Mjr. Blanchard at Gettysburg," *Indiana Magazine of History*, June 1939, 215-216.

Lt. Col. William Dudley
19th Indiana

Dudley took a painful wound to the leg on the afternoon of July 1. He was unable to get off the field and was captured. His right leg was amputated and he was left behind when the Rebels evacuated the town. *Institute for Civil War Studies*

---

and died almost immediately. Clifford picked up the National colors and made a mad dash for the town and safety.[37]

Not far away, Iron Brigade commander Sol Meredith was also down, struck on the head by a piece of shell just as his large horse was killed by a bullet. Meredith was pinned under the kicking and dying animal. Someone pulled him out from under the horse and arranged for his transport to the rear. Meredith was out of the battle and, although it was not known at the time, out of the war. A staff rider rode into the woods to find Col. William Robinson of the 7th Wisconsin and tell him he was now in command of the Iron Brigade. The entire line was now collapsing. The 19th Indiana was already coming apart, and the 24th Michigan had already folded back its left companies against the flanking Confederates. The 7th Wisconsin and 2nd Wisconsin were also under a "galling fire," and Stone's Pennsylvania regiments fighting in the open field to the right were also just about played out. Grimly did these men fight on, convinced as many of them were that the fate of the Army of the Potomac rested on holding McPherson's Ridge.

Somehow, and at some point in the line, citizen John Burns and his old musket came up to join the Black Hats. The recollections of old soldiers make it seem as though he was everywhere that day. Veterans claimed the old gent was given a new musket and cartridges that he stuffed in the pocket of his old-fashioned coat. Amos

---

37 Dudley, "Blanchard at Gettysburg"; Madaus and Zeitlin, *Flags*, 33-35.

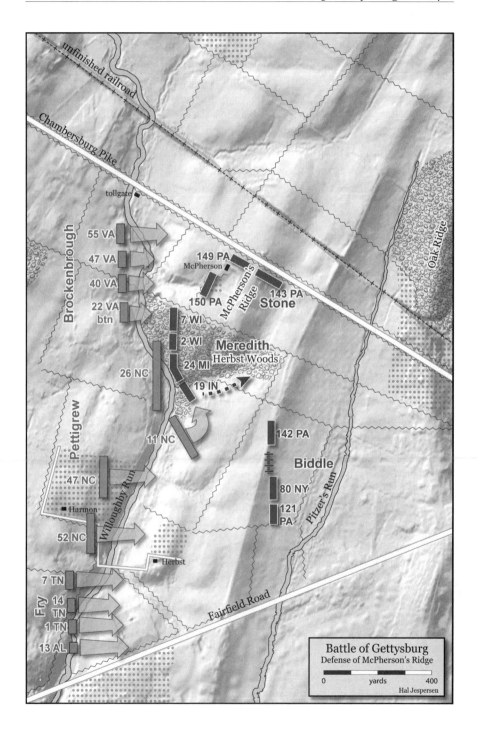

Battle of Gettysburg
Defense of McPherson's Ridge

0   yards   400

Hal Jespersen

D. Rood of the 7th Wisconsin long afterward claimed that he formally swore Burns into Federal service by asking, "Do you solemnly swear that you will obey all orders you may receive from any and all commanders placed over you until we knocked hell out of them?" Burns replied, "Now that's just what I'll do," or at least that was the way Rood remembered it. One soldier claimed the old citizen was first on the skirmish line of the 150th Pennsylvania in the open field near the McPherson farm buildings. Another soldier recalled Burns close to the 7th Wisconsin. Lieutenant Colonel John Callis of that Badger regiment said he saw Burns shoot a Confederate officer off a white horse, and that "the old man loaded and fired away" until he retreated with the skirmish line. When the line moved back, wrote a Wisconsin man, Burns "was as calm and collected as any veteran on the ground." Hollon Richardson said he saw Burns fighting from behind a tree at the edge of the woods. Another Badger said the men around him watched Burns in action and remarked, "Ain't he a triumph," "See how cool he is," and "Look at my old man." They also observed that Burns "did not slight a friendly tree, no more than we did." Like so many others that day, the old man was soon wounded. According to various accounts, he was hit three, five, or seven times, but the ball that felled him struck his leg. He was on the ground in some pain when the fighting moved off. Worried about his status as a combatant in civilian clothes, Burns discarded his musket and used his pocket knife to bury musket cartridges still in his pockets, rolling over the ground several times to mask the hole. When finished, he waited for Confederate soldiers to discover him.[38]

The McPherson's Ridge line was nearing collapse. Fouled and hot muskets made firing ever more difficult, fresh Confederate units were pouring in from several directions, and the line was now completely flanked. Only one of every four Michigan men was still on his feet, recalled Colonel Morrow, who was doing his best to try and swing a portion of the left part of his line around to face the flanking fire. Before the difficult move under fire could be executed, Confederate pressure forced Morrow and his men to fall back and take up a new position a short distance farther east. One of the Michigan officers killed trying to restore the collapsing flank was Lt. Gilbert Dickey, a member of Michigan State's first graduating class. At the new rally point, the Wolverines offered what one witness described as "desperate resistance" to slow the advancing Confederates. Their cartridge boxes were just about empty.

---

38 Smith, *John Burns*, 50-67. One of the locations at which John Burns fought was just east of where the 7th Wisconsin monument now stands. Smith's account, *ibid.*, is the best available on Burns' role at Gettysburg, and it makes a good effort to resolve the many conflicting details surrounding his participation that day.

A Mule Train Charge of Wagons

Ordnance Sergeant Jerome Watrous of the 6th Wisconsin had spent an anxious few hours south of Gettysburg. The Badger was assigned to a line of ammunition wagons stretched alongside the Emmitsburg road belonging to the First Division of First Corps. Unable to stand it any longer, Watrous rode ahead to higher ground and found artillery, infantry, and excited officers preparing a defensive position around a small cemetery. Explosions of musket and artillery fire spread out in a wide arc north, northwest, and west of his position. The roads leading out of Gettysburg were crowded with civilians and their buggies and wagons and tens of hundreds of wounded and demoralized soldiers. Word from the front was mixed. The Confederate army was coming down hard on the regiments and brigades of the First Corps and Eleventh Corps west and north of Gettysburg. It was common talk now that General Reynolds was down and likely dead, and that Watrous' own First Division was heavily involved in the fighting.[39]

Watrous returned to his wagons to make sure that, if needed, they would be ready. The division's ordnance officer, who had orders to stay with the train, waved his hat and told Watrous to take charge before galloping off toward the sound of the fighting. A few minutes later a rider arrived from the front, helloing for Watrous while carrying orders to bring 10 wagons of ammunition to the front as quickly as possible. Watrous rode along the wagons, selecting the best teams and drivers. One of the chosen was Bert O'Connor, a steady experienced man from the 7th Wisconsin: "Bert, you run your team to the front." Within a short time Watrous had the wagons in a line and two men on each seat. His orders were straightforward: each driver was to whip the mules into a "keen run" and do not stop until the order came to do so.[40] The road into Gettysburg was a good one, remembered O'Connor and "you can bet we made those 10 mule teams spin along." The train rolled and bumped along at reckless speed, and it "seemed as those mules knew that glorious old Wadsworth's gallant men were getting short of ammunition, and that we must get it to them without a moment's delay." Watrous spurred his mount alongside the moving wagons shouting over and over for the drivers to go faster.[41]

39 Jerome A. Watrous, "The Mule Train Charge at Gettysburg," *Milwaukee Sunday Telegraph*, July 30, 1882.

40 Albert O'Connor enlisted Company A, Lodi Guards, from West Point, Wisconsin, June 12, 1862. He was wounded at the Wilderness in 1864 and was mustered out with his company on July 3, 1865. *Wisconsin Roster*, vol. 1, 542.

41 Jerome A. Watrous, "Major General Winfield S. Hancock, Memorial Meeting, March 3, 1886," *War Papers*, vol. 1, 298-300; Watrous, *Telegraph*, July 30, 1882.

Watrous and his ammunition wagons threaded their way past clots of retiring soldiers and scampering civilians and cleared Gettysburg on the run while the crippled Iron Brigade clung to the McPherson's Ridge line. The wagons moved into an open field west of town beyond the Seminary building, well within range of at least a dozen Confederate artillery pieces, and a few minutes later reached the east edge of the woods on McPherson's Ridge. The second man on each wagon shoved off one wooden box of ammunition after another as the wagons shook and rolled along the uneven fringe of timber. Behind the rumbling wagons and tumbling crates ran Watrous, who had ditched his horse and, axe in hand, used the blunt end to splinter each box so the bundles of cartridges could be quickly distributed to the men. According to O'Connor three wagons full of ammunition, almost 75,000 rounds, were distributed in this manner. "All this time the rebels were shelling us to kill. Nearly every wagon cover was hit with a shell, solid shot or minnie ball while we were there."[42] With his task complete, Watrous now faced the challenge of getting his wagons, teams, and drivers out of danger. He ordered the train back to town and told his men to issue the remaining rounds to any soldiers in need.

When the wagons turned onto the Chambersburg Pike, Confederates infantry appeared on the ridge and swept the roadway with "a perfect storm of shot, shell and bullets." O'Connor watched a solid shot take off the hind legs of the saddle mule of the team next to him. The driver of the wagon was a man everyone called "Indiana." "I shall never forget the look [he gave] . . . when the poor mule fell down on those stumps of legs," said O'Connor. Someone cut the unfortunate animal from the harness before killing it with a shot from a revolver. At that instant, another artillery shot grazed the other wheel mule while another round smashed the rear wheels of the same wagon. Nearby Federal infantry unloaded the wagon, which was then dragged into town "with three mules hauling the front wheels and box. Two other wagons were also hit, but none of the ammunition was lost."[43]

Lieutenant Clayton Rogers of Wadsworth's staff watched the event, including young Watrous unloading the wagons under a heavy fire and returning down the pike near the unfinished railroad cut. "The sergeant had a very warm gallop across the railroad embankment into Gettysburg," said Rogers. "It seems impossible that a single man should have escaped through such a narrow passage."[44]

By now the streets were jammed with wounded and fleeing soldiers, wagons, and debris of all sorts. O'Connor's wagon was at the rear of the train with Watrous

42 OR 27, pt. 2, 643.

43 Watrous, *Telegraph*, July 30, 1882; Watrous, *War Papers*, vol. 2, 299-300.

44 Clayton E. Rogers, "Gettysburg Scenes," *Milwaukee Sunday Telegraph*, May 13, 1887.

riding at his side. "The rebels were shelling the town right lively" when the wagons turned right on the town square, wrote O'Connor. Collapsed and broken, large elements from Howard's Eleventh Corps moved along the streets in a desperate effort to escape the pursuing Southerners. The "zip, zip and zipping of a shower of bullets" from a line of Confederate infantry less than 100 yards distant endangered the wagons. When he saw several Federal officers responding with revolvers, O'Connor stood on his wagon bed, drew his own, and added to the snapping pistol fire. A nearby New York regiment unleashed a sharp volley that broke that part of the enemy advance. "The street was packed with troops, mounted officers, artillery and cavalry, and such confusion I never saw," O'Connor admitted. "But there was method enough in the confused crowd to push forward at a good pace" for the rally point.

When he reached Cemetery Hill, Watrous discovered that each of his wagons had been hit "one to a dozen times with solid shot, shell or bullets." The first general officer he came across was General Howard, "sitting upon his horse with as much coolness as though he was watching a Fourth of July parade." Just beyond, where the wagons cleared the ridge and moved to safety, was Maj. Gen. Winfield Scott Hancock, commander of Second corps. Hancock had just arrived with orders from General Meade to assume command of the spreading battlefield. The corps leader was "young and fresh and bright and constantly active," recalled Watrous, who guided his mount through the confusion, offered a crisp salute to the corps leader, and asked for orders. The general looked him over and soaked in the damaged wagons.

"Good God!" exclaimed Hancock. "What have you got here? What have you got a wagon here for? You haven't been into action?"

Watrous nodded. "Yes sir, just came back with the rear guard."

Hancock shot him another hard look. "Well, did you lose all your ammunition?"

"No sir, distributed nearly all of it."

"Lose any of your wagons?"

"Well, I got back with some of them," replied the Badger.

Hancock appreciated this sort of battlefield courage and cracked a wide smile. "Good. But it is the first Mule Train Charge I ever knew anything about. You did well, Sergeant. Just move your wagons down there and report to me in half an hour."

Five mules and three of Watrous' men were wounded during the "Mule Train Charge," which O'Connor later remembered as said the hottest place he experienced during the war. Watrous' bold wagon thrust provided ammunition to soldiers fighting with four different Union divisions. The ammunition played a key role by extending the fighting long enough for the Union to strengthen the high ground south of Gettysburg—the same ground many would later argue proved the key to victory in the three long days of fighting.[45]

Watrous always gave credit for the Gettysburg victory to Hancock. Twenty years later, in a speech to veterans in Milwaukee during a memorial service on the death of the general, Watrous recalled his chance meeting with Hancock on the field that day. It was the only time in his four years in uniform that he met the general. "It did me lots of good—I don't suppose it did the general any. I think I grew about a foot and a half [on seeing Hancock], and it was after a hard day's work too."[46]

God Damn 'Em, Feed it to 'Em!

The advancing waves of Confederate infantry continued, the distribution of ammunition notwithstanding. Exhausted Southern infantry paused at the crest of McPherson's Ridge to let fresh brigades from Maj. Gen. William Dorsey Pender's fresh division move forward about the time the remnants of the tired members of the Iron Brigade reached the rally point along Seminary Ridge. They found there a low barricade "of loose rails, which . . . had been thrown together by some of our troops in the earlier part of the day, behind which I threw the regiment," reported Colonel Robinson of the 7th Wisconsin, who assumed command of the brigade when Meredith fell wounded.

The torn Western organizations formed along the ridge as best they could. They didn't have long to reorder themselves and prepare for the heavy combat everyone knew was coming. The 19th Indiana ("now reduced to a mere squad") formed just west of the seminary on the left of the Iron Brigade front, the crippled 24th Michigan streaming into position on its right. A few 2nd Wisconsin men also joined the formation, with the 7th Wisconsin holding the right brigade front. On their left was Biddle's brigade, with Gamble's Union cavalry holding the far left below Fairfield Road. Roy Stone's Pennsylvanians formed on the right of the Iron Brigade on and beyond the Chambersburg Pike, with Cutler's remnants extending the line northward. The 6th Wisconsin remained with some of Stewart's guns beyond the railroad cut. All told, the Iron Brigade and other infantry on the Seminary Ridge line numbered no more than 2,300 men. The exhausted Westerners

---

45 Some of the ammunition ultimately fell into the hands of the Confederates. An officer of the 26th North Carolina said in his report that his men collected ammunition from the enemy's dead as his men were very low on ammunition. *OR* 27, pt. 2, 642-644.

46 Watrous, *War Papers*, vol. 2, 299-300; Watrous, *Telegraph*, July 30, 1882.

watched as a fresh heavy Confederate line lurched forward; the final push was coming.[47]

The new Confederate line was composed of two veteran brigades. Brigadier General Alfred Scales' North Carolinians advanced on the left just below the Chambersburg Pike, moving against the right side of the Iron Brigade and Stone's Pennsylvanians. On the Rebel right, Col. Abner Perrin's South Carolinians drove forward against the balance of the Black Hats and Biddle's exposed left flank. The Union position was not particularly strong, and there were not enough men and guns to hold it against nearly twice their number. "Every man on the fighting line supposed there was unity in this action and that Gen. Meade, with his whole army would soon be with us," wrote one. As the new Confederate advance stepped down into the swale, those Federals still in the fields between the ridges realized Union artillery that studded the ridge behind them was preparing to fire, but would not be able to sufficiently elevate the tubes to fire safely above them.[48]

Battery B of the 4th U.S. Artillery formed by half battery on both sides of the railroad cut abreast what would become known as the Thompson house. The right half battery under Lt. James Stewart (supported by the 6th Wisconsin) was deployed on the north side of the cut slightly forward and facing west. The left half battery, under Lt. James Davidson, was in open order along the space between the turnpike and the railroad and faced southwest. In a small grove to the north were soldiers of the 11th Pennsylvania and the 6th Wisconsin.[49] The 5th Maine Artillery and a battery of the 1st Pennsylvania Light Artillery deployed near the Seminary building. Battery B opened the defense with case shot on the Confederates on the ridge before switching to murderous shotgun blasts of double-canister when the gray infantry moved more deeply into the swale. The hail of iron ripped through the advancing lines, which staggered and slowed but continued eastward step by step.

Colonel Robinson held his survivors tightly as the Confederate infantry tramped into killing range. "It was with some difficulty I restrained the men from firing until the enemy got as near as I wanted them," he reported. "When they were within easy range, the order was given, and their ranks went down like grass before the scythe . . . very few, if any, of that brigade escaped death or wounds," Robinson continued with some excusable exaggeration. The view from the opposite side was

47 The arriving Confederates comprised Dorsey Pender's Division. Alfred Scales' Brigade was on the left, Abner Perrin's Brigade in the center, and James Lane's Brigade on the right. Edward Thomas' Brigade was held in reserve.

48 Beecham, *Glory*, 75.

49 Stewart's report, *OR* 27, pt. 2, 566.

in general agreement with Robinson's assessment. According to Colonel Perrin, the Union line erupted at 200 yards with a fire he called "the most destructive fire of musketry I have ever been exposed to." Near the Lutheran Seminary at the head of the 7th Wisconsin, Lt. Col. John Callis found himself fighting soldiers from his home state under Scales. A native of North Carolina, Callis and his family moved to Wisconsin when he was 10 and, despite his father's warning that he was going to war against his own "flesh and blood," he decided to do "battle for the Nation's safety." Now he found his regiment "in a tight place."[50]

The heavy brass Napoleons of Battery B were firing with a fury equaled only by the fighting near the cornfield at Antietam the previous September when the guns were almost overrun. "Feed it to 'em! God damn 'em, feed it to 'em!" Davidson yelled through the choking smoke and confusion. The battery was one of the best in the army, and the volunteers and Regulars manning it that day stood to their duty. "Up and down the line men were reeling and falling," one battery man wrote of Gettysburg. "Splinters were flying from wheels and axles where bullets hit in the rear, horses were rearing and plunging, mad with wounds or terror, shells were bursting, shot shrieking over, howling about our ears or throwing up great clouds of dust where they hit; the musketry crashing on three sides of us; bullets hissing everywhere, cannon roaring, all crash on crash and peal on peal, smoke, dust, splinters, blood, wreckage and carnage indescribable; but the brass guns of old B still bellowed and not a man or boy flinched or faltered."[51]

Scales' Confederates, "creeping toward" the battery "fairly fringed with flame," were slaughtered during this approach and began to go to ground. The soldiers of the 6th Wisconsin and 11th Pennsylvania crawled over the bank of the railroad cut behind the caissons and added their musketry to the storm of iron rounds. When Davidson was twice wounded, including a shattered ankle, he grew so weak that one of his men had to hold him up. The Rebels fired volley after volley into the half-battery killing and wounding men and horses alike. Unable to remain in command, Davidson turned over the guns to Sgt. John Mitchell, who, "moving calmly from gun to gun, now and then changing men about as one after another was hit and fell, stooping over a wounded man to help him up, or aiding another to stagger to the rear." The buckets of water used to sponge out the hot tubes looked "like ink." Another gunner was smeared with burnt powder and "looked like a

50 Walter Clark, ed., *Histories of the Several Regiments and Battalions from North Carolina*, 5 vols. (Goldsboro, NC, 1901), vol. 5, 615, as cited in Roger Long, "A Gettysburg Encounter," *Gettysburg Magazine*, July 1992. The quotations are from a letter Callis wrote September 3, 1893, from Lancaster, Wisconsin.

51 Buell, *Cannoneer*, 65.

Sgt. John Mitchell
Battery B,
4th U.S. Artillery

The Regular Army sergeant took over command of a half-battery at Gettysburg when Lt. James Davidson was wounded in the afternoon fighting on July 1, 1863. *Scott D. Hann Collection*

demon from below." North of the railroad cut, Stewart's three artillery pieces from the other half-battery "flashed the chain-lightning . . . in one solid streak."[52]

Lieutenant Colonel Rufus Dawes of the 6th Wisconsin watched the fighting some distance from his regiment from amidst the smoking guns of Battery B. When the Confederate assault slowed under the heavy rain of canister and musketry, one of his infantrymen jumped forward waving a fist while calling over and over, "Come on, Johnny! Come on!" It was going to be a very close affair, Dawes concluded. Unable to withstand the carnage, Scales' Tar Heels fell back westward.

Yelling at us to Halt and Surrender

Farther south below the Chambersburg Pike, meanwhile, the fighting along Seminary Ridge reached a fever-pitched crescendo. By now it was late in the afternoon, perhaps 4:30 p.m. Perrin's Palmetto soldiers closed the distance on the right side of the Southern line just above the Fairfield Road, moving around Biddle's exposed left flank to unhinge the entire Union position. Their assault turned the Pennsylvania and New York regiments and began folding up the line. The 7th Wisconsin's Pvt. William Ray recalled how he and his stalwart comrades "got behind it [the barricade] and just mowed the rebs, all in front of our Regt was

52 *Ibid.*, 67-71

1st Lt. William Sloat,
Citizens Corps, Milwaukee,
Co. F, 6th Wisconsin

Said one soldier: "I can never forget how Brave the officers was at Gettysburg, especially Lieut. Sloat. He gave the cowards and stragglers no Peace at all, kept driving them to their Regts. And them that there Regts was too far away he put them in our regiment." Sloat resigned September 13, 1864, because of wounds at Bethesda Church in 1864.

Author's Collection

just mowed down. But their line being the longer," he observed, "they kept swinging around the end and getting crossfire on us."[53]

By the time Ray and his comrades realized they were being flanked on their left, the Hoosiers of the 19th regiment and the Wolverines of the 24th Michigan were already falling back. A short distance south of Ray's position, a captain in the 2nd Wisconsin named Nat Rollins spotted gray infantry to his south with Biddle's men falling back. In the opposite direction, looking north toward the Chambersburg Pike, was a roadway jammed with Union men moving quickly east toward Gettysburg. "There was no time to waste," wrote Rollins, "so we stood not on order of our going, but went at once."

Lt. Col. John Callis of the 7th Wisconsin, already twice wounded by buckshot, had been afoot since his horse was killed under him earlier that morning on McPherson's Ridge. He was now fighting along the rough barricade lining part of Seminary Ridge in a position that was no longer tenable. It was time to fall back. Moving by right of companies to the rear toward the Lutheran Seminary building, Callis halted the 7th Wisconsin to fire at the pursuing Rebels before moving farther east while reloading. "We executed the same movement with terrible effect," he

53 Ray, *Iron Brigade*, 191.

later reported. He was directing his men when he went down with a shot in the chest. The heavy ball pierced his right side and broke a rib before lodging in his lung. In the 24th Michigan, which was fighting a short distance to the left, only one of every five men taken into the fight was still standing, and many of those were wounded.

Once again Colonel Morrow found himself with the regimental flag. "Rally, rally!" he screamed before a bullet sliced through his scalp. With blood streaming down his face and obscuring his vision, Morrow turned command over to Capt. A. M. Edwards, the senior officer still on his feet, and made for the rear. Edwards searched for and found the regimental flag locked in the crook of a dead soldier's arm. The officer wrested the banner free and carried it to safety. He never determined the identity of the dead soldier.[54]

And so that Union line, pried out of position in an almost methodical fashion one regiment after another regiment, reached Pvt. Ray's position. "We had to abandon that Place," the 7th Wisconsin private would soon scribble in his journal. "Battery B was just in the [right] rear of us when we lay behind the Rails and every gun poured in the grape which swept the rebs. But there being no Battery on the left to help the Boys so they couldn't hold up under double their number." Ray turned to run for the town when he was hit "by a Ball on the top of the head, came near knocking me down. But I straightened up, went on, another Ball hit the sole of my shoe cutting it nearly in two, it only making my foot sting a little." Ray limped his way toward Gettysburg.[55]

The 7th Wisconsin was less exposed than the other regiments, but was raked with fire as it made its way eastward, the pursuing Confederates just 200 yards behind them advancing in a long determined and victorious line of battle. Men "were falling at every step, many of our men that had fought gallantly all day, were taken prisoner by not keeping on the road." When the small column reached the town, Sgt. Daniel McDermott, carrying the regiment's national colors, was severely wounded by a piece of shell that also splintered the flag staff. Alexander Hughes used a folding knife to cut the flag from the damaged pole. He handed the banner to McDermott, who clutched it to his chest, soaking it with his blood as he was placed on a caisson rolling ahead of the regiment. The wounded color bearer did his best to feebly wave the flag in defiance even as he moved away. "He has carried this color through every battle in which the regiment has been engaged," Col. William Robinson attested in an official report. A few hours later on nearby Culp's Hill,

54 Curtis, *Twenty-fourth*, 165.

55 Ray, *Iron Brigade*, 191.

soldiers of the 7th Wisconsin cut and trimmed a sapling to replace the shattered staff that had so proudly held the National colors aloft.[56]

During some of the heaviest shooting in the retreat, Hollon Richardson of the 7th Wisconsin was seen on his horse waving the flag of one of Stone's Pennsylvania regiments while calling on the men to "do their duty." He did so in vain. "But the captain, left alone and almost in the rebel hands," wrote the correspondent for the *Cincinnati Gazette*, "held on to the flaunting colors of another regiment, that made him a conspicuous target, and brought them safely off."[57]

The 6th Wisconsin's Lt. Col. Rufus Dawes was watching the fighting from a point near the half-battery of guns north of the railroad cut when Capt. Clayton Rogers from Gen. Wadsworth's staff reached the regiment and was directed to Capt. Rollin Converse. The two officers shouted at one another in an attempt to be heard; Rogers brought orders for the regiment to retreat. Converse ordered the men to their feet and to about face. When Dawes spotted the men facing the rear, he rushed through the ranks, jerked the National flag from the hands of color bearer I. F. Kelly, and halted the regiment. Once Captain Converse explained the order, Dawes nodded in understanding. The Wisconsin men turned one more time to pour a volley into the Confederates who were so close, Kelly said, "we could hear them yelling at us to halt and surrender."

The orders from Wadsworth were for Dawes and his regiment to retreat beyond the town and "hold your men together." The directive astonished Dawes because the cheers of defiance ringing along the Seminary Ridge line "had scarcely died away." When he looked north and behind him, however, he understood: "There the troops of the eleventh corps appeared in full retreat and long lines of

---

56 OR 27, pt. 1, 281; Henry Young letter to his father, July 11, 1863; McDermott, who enlisted at Clinton, was wounded again at Petersburg in 1864. He mustered out with the regiment in July 1865. *Wisconsin Roster*, vol. 1, 573. Hughes was born in Canada and was an infant when his parents came to Wisconsin in 1846. He was only fourteen when he enlisted in Company B, 7th Wisconsin. Jerome A. Watrous, "Alexander Hughes," *Milwaukee Sunday Telegraph*, March 20, 1887. The sapling flag staff is held by the Wisconsin Veterans Museum in Madison. Young said it was difficult if not impossible to tell who was dead or wounded or a prisoner "for men were falling thick and fast around us and there was no time to pick them up or even see who they were."

57 Cited in William DeLoss Love, *Wisconsin in the War of the Rebellion* (Chicago, 1866), 413. Whitelaw Reid of the *Cincinnati Gazette* wrote that Richardson "seized the colors of a retreating Pennsylvania regiment and strove to rally the men around their flag. It was in vain; none but troops that have been tried as by fire can be reformed under such a storm of death; but the captain, left alone and almost in the rebels' hands, held on to the flaunting colors of another regiment, that made him so conspicuous a target, and brought them safely off." Whitelaw Reid, *A Radical View: The 'Agate' Dispatches of Whitelaw Reid, 1861-1865*, James G. Smart, ed., 2 vols. (Memphis: Memphis State University Press, 1976), vol. 1, 31.

Pvt. Ernst Schuchart, 2nd Wisconsin

Here, Schuchart poses with his new Austrian Lorenz rifle at Fredericksburg, Virginia in 1862. He was wounded at Gettysburg on the first day and died on July 4, 1863. *Tim and Mary Spellman*

Confederates, with fluttering banners and shining steel were sweeping forward in pursuit of them without let or hindrance. It was a close race which could reach Gettysburg first, ourselves, or the rebel troops." The survivors of the 6th Wisconsin marched away with flag high and with a steady step, wrote one, but another of the big hats remembered a different order: run for it. "We obeyed this literally, and how we did run! As we came out of the smoke of the battle what a sight burst upon our gaze! On every side our troops were madly rushing to the rear. We were flanked on the right and on the left. We were overwhelmed by numbers. My heart," he admitted, "sank within me. I lost all hope."[58]

With his infantry supports retreating, Stewart of Battery B ordered his guns to limber up. The left half-battery withdrew along the Chambersburg Pike with the enemy as close as fifty yards, losing more men and horses. Stewart had to move his three guns across the railroad cut. When his three guns were clear, he rode back to check on the left half-battery below the road only to find it was already gone and the place full of Rebels. The enemy yelled for him to surrender and fired, but Stewart jumped his horse over a fence and escaped with only two bullet holes in his blouse. Along the way he was struck in the thigh by a shell fragment that left him so nauseated he stopped and dismounted. In severe pain, Stewart wet his face and drank water from a furrow in a nearby field before searching for and finding his battery. The 6th Wisconsin was also on hand. The men opened ranks to allow the guns to roll through. According to Stewart, the Wisconsin regiment and his battery were the last to leave the field.[59]

The famous Iron Brigade of the West, which marched to the fighting with such a confident step at mid-morning, was wrecked.

Mangled Forms of Tall Westerners

In the streets of Gettysburg, the retreating soldiers found panicked citizens and tens of hundreds of wandering soldiers, some wounded but most not. Artillery shells exploded amid homes and buildings as the sound of the fighting moved closer and the angry buzz of nearly spent bullets sailed past. The town square and railroad depot were jammed with wounded men in blue sporting blood-soaked bandages. The river of misery swept more injured into the town with each passing

---

58 I. F. Kelly to Rufus Dawes, August 2, 1892; Dawes, *Service*, 175; Young, *Telegraph*, April 22, 1883.

59 Buell, *Cannoneer*, 73-75; Herdegen and Beaudot, *Railroad Cut*, 219; Dawes to the *National Tribune*, December 5, 1889.

minute. Army surgeons set up make-shift hospitals before midday to deal with what were already an overwhelming number of causalities.

Civilians hid their horses and cows. Entire families, grim-faced men with nervous eyes, terrified women, and frightened children, clogged the streets carrying their valuables or riding in wagons and carriages loaded with possessions in a macabre scene accompanied by a hellish orchestra of bellowing artillery and ripping musketry. A 13-year-old boy watched his sisters and mother "making bandages and drawing lint for the wounded." Passing by his front door on stretchers, he added, were "borne the bloody, mangled forms of tall Westerners, bearing on their black felt hats the red circular patch denoting their membership in the first division of the First Corps, many of them of the 'Iron Brigade.'"[60]

Among the first of the wounded to enter Gettysburg while the fighting north and west of town was still raging was the 6th Wisconsin's Mickey Sullivan, who did so in style atop a cavalry horse ordered up for him by General Wadsworth. Civilian panic had not yet set in, so many townsfolk "had wine and refreshments of all kinds on tables and trays, and in their hands, urging them on every wounded man, and assisted them in every way." Mickey was dropped off at the courthouse, where he found Dr. John C. Hall and Dr. O. F. Bartlett of his regiment, along with a large number of civilians, "busy cutting up and patching up the biggest part of the sixth regiment." Sullivan was put back together "with sticking plaster and bandages" and handed a cup of coffee. Exhausted and feeling faint, he lay on the floor to rest. When some strength returned he rose to look around. "I found nearly every man in the company was in the same fix I was, and some a great deal worse." He also was told there were more wounded from his company in the nearby rail depot, "though there were enough here out of the little squad of a company that went into the fight that morning." He found his uncle, Hugh Talty, among the injured. Talty (called "Tall T") was not feeling his wound because a citizen had filled his canteen with whiskey.[61]

Later that afternoon, with the sound of heavy firing north and west of the town approaching, Doctor Hall glanced out a north window and spotted elements of Howard's Eleventh Corps in full retreat. "Away went guns and knapsacks, and they fled for dear life, forming a funnel shaped tail, extending to the town," wrote Hall. "The rebels coolly and deliberately shot them down like sheep. I did not see an officer attempt to rally or check them in their headlong retreat."[62]

---

60 Robert McClean, "A Boy in Gettysburg—1863," *Gettysburg Compiler*, June 30, 1909.

61 Sullivan, *Telegraph*, December 20, 1884.

62 John C. Hall, journal, July 2, 1863; Dawes, *Service*, 176.

Consternation spread through the ranks of the wounded men, confessed Sullivan before adding that "solid shot and shell began to crash through the courthouse and burst in the yard." The doctor ordered all who could walk to leave and a hospital flag be placed in a prominent location. The artillery fire dwindled after a time, and a Confederate officer entered the building to demand a mass Federal surrender. "The doctor told him there were none there only medical men and the severely wounded, and the band men who were nurses," wrote Sullivan. "After some palaver and a drink or two of hospital brandy, the rebel told our doctors to have the nurses tie a white string around their arm and the wounded to keep inside and they would not be disturbed. I was mad as the devil that all our hard fighting that morning had went for nothing and here was over two hundred of our brigade all smashed to pieces."[63]

No Wonder You Men are Called the Iron Brigade

One of the wounded being treated in Gettysburg was Lt. Loyd Harris of the 6th Wisconsin. Young Harris was sitting in a chair with a surgeon about to probe for a buckshot lodged in the fleshy part of his neck. His assistant was a "good old lady" from town who "declared her nerves" would now allow her to witness such a sight. Harris pulled his harmonica from his pocket. "Madam, the surgeon will be so gentle that while he is operating I will pay on this little musical affair," he said. "So, while he in no delicate manner probed around with his torturing instrument, [I] recklessly played 'Tramp, Tramp the Boys are Marching,' until he finished, when the old lady . . . explained, 'No wonder you men are called the "Iron Brigade."'

Just after Harris was bandaged, an orderly appeared to announce to Dr. Andrew J. Ward of the 2nd Wisconsin that wounded Lt. Col. Lucius Fairchild was waiting for him. "Doctor, Col. Fairchild of the Second, sends his compliments, and wants ye in a devil of a hurry to cut off his left arum." Harris and some other officers asked Fairchild's orderly whether there were "pleasant quarters" to be had. The aide left but was soon back to announce he had "found a splendid place, wid such kind and beautiful ladies." The officers moved to the home of "Mr. Hollinger, a true Union man." His wife was an invalid, added Harris, but his daughters, "two very pretty and sensible young ladies, assumed charge of the house-hold affairs, and we were soon made to feel that for the first time in two years of the hardest kind of campaigning, we were to enjoy a peaceful rest; under a roof, with comforts that too forcibly reminded us of home, sweet home."

63 Sullivan, *Telegraph*, December 20, 1884.

The Wisconsin officers were surprised to discover Sgt. William Evans in the same house with the captured flag of the 2nd Mississippi. The sight of "that crimson rag" brought a surge of emotion. "We had fought the bloodiest fight of the war to win it . . . and thirty brave comrades lay unburied on the field and one hundred and fifty more were maimed and crippled, all sacrificed to trail that haughty flag under ours; yet we had the esprit du corps to hold it before our new found young lady friends, and in a modest manner told the story of the charge [of the 6th Wisconsin on the unfinished railroad cut.]." It was a moment treasured and remembered. "No Desdemona ever listed with more heartfelt sympathy than those two young ladies," Harris said later, "and the story finished, we felt that in their eyes every man of the old Sixth was a hero." Heavy cannonading swept the town and "a shell went tearing through a grape-arbor just in front of the house." Harris looked out a window and never forgot the sight of the Union retreat: "My emotions were sickening, as I vainly gazed for the First Army corps, that Spartan band who had routed all before them in the morning fight. They were no where in sight—Brave men, I know they would sell their lives dearly: almost bewildered by the maddening scenes that were happening in rapid success, but a rifle shot distant."

Back in the kitchen, Harris advised the other officers to make a run for it. "We have lost," Harris concluded, "and the rebels are in the next street." Sergeant Evans was too badly wounded to be moved, and was left in his bed. The invalid mother fainted and her two young daughters cried as they fluttered around her. Harris was about to bolt himself when he saw the despair lining the father's face. "Have you a cellar?" he asked. When one of the daughters nodded, Harris told her, "Then we must carry your mother there." Harris and the father struggled with the wheelchair down a narrow staircase to the cellar. With the family settled, it was time for Harris to leave. "Good-bye, many thanks for your kindness," he began, "I shall always—" One of the young ladies cut him short. "Oh, hurry away or you will be lost!"

With Rebels crowding the front street Harris made for a board fence and went over "as a dozen bullets rattled on it." He crossed another backyard, slipped through a vacant house, and emerged into a street crowded with fleeing Union soldiers. Visible in the surging crowd was an army ambulance with Lt. John Beely and Capt. William Remington of the 6th Wisconsin inside, who pulled him into the wagon. A Federal artillery battery was deployed on the street. As soon as the crowd cleared the muzzles the guns fired and the Rebels pulled back as the ambulance rolled to safety. "Oh, misery and shame, comrades forgive us," Harris wrote later, "We left behind the rebel flag, that dearly bought prize."[64]

64 Loyd G. Harris, "Advances of a Rebel Flag," *Milwaukee Sunday Telegraph*, January 29, 1880.

"Mickey, of Company K" Sullivan

After his Gettysburg wound, once he recovered Mickey made time on the
way back home to pose in civilian clothes. *Author's Collection*

Part III: Retreat, Then Victory

We Know Nothing about a Cemetery Hill

The retreat from Seminary Ridge to the rally point on Cemetery Hill passed through Gettysburg. Lt. Amos Rood of the 7th Wisconsin said his regiment stayed behind until the Federal artillery was gone before pushing toward town. Artillery fire raked the retreating Black Hats and a canister ball thumped off Rood's left shoulder blade. "But as I was moving rapidly it did not knock me down nor go thro me. It had struck the ground and was rising or I would have been torn and killed. I did not give up tho, and limped and hobbled along."

The Rebels were also entering Gettysburg, with men from Richard Ewell's Corps firing along the left cross streets and those from A.P. Hill moving and shooting along the right cross streets. "I lost one-half of my men getting through town and to Cemetery Hill," wrote Lieutenant Rood. "Moving, fighting, best as I could!" No men were in sight, he continued, but there were "lots of women and some children" pumping fresh water for the passing soldiers into tubs resting in the gateways. "Our men were suffering with thirst. Hot as hell too!" Behind the 7th Wisconsin were scores of 6th Wisconsin survivors also trying to work through the streets of Gettysburg. "We know nothing about a Cemetery Hill," Rufus Dawes noted later, referring to the rally point he had been ordered to reach. "We could see only that the on-coming lines of the enemy were encircling us in a horseshoe."

On the porch of one of the houses they passed was Col. Lucius Fairchild, standing with the support of Doctor Ward. Stretcher bearers had carried the wounded officer to the home of Rev. Charles F. Schaeffer, the principal of the Lutheran Theological Seminary. Throughout the painful journey the colonel assured them that once his arm was dressed he would return to his regiment. Surgeon Ward cut off Fairchild's vest, examined the wound, and amputated the crippled limb above the elbow. When Fairchild awoke to find a bandaged stump he announced, "Thank God! I still have one left." The maimed regimental leader sat in the parlor and watched through the window while Reverend Schaeffer buried his amputated arm outside in a tin box in a small garden. A Confederate officer would later search the house and find Colonel Fairchild's sword hidden in the coal bin. Fairchild's condition prompted him to scribble out a parole before leaving. And so, with his left arm freshly amputated, Fairchild raised his good arm and called out to the passing Westerners in a faint voice, "Stick to 'em boys! Stay with 'em! You'll fetch 'em finally!" The colonel's appearance was simultaneously heartening and sorrowful.[1]

The buildings of a small college helped shelter the retreating 6th Wisconsin and Battery B of the 4th U.S. Artillery, at least for a time. Dawes admitted his soldiers were just about played out. "The sweat streamed from the faces of the men. There was not a drop of water in the canteens, and there had been none for hours." Farther on the streets were "jammed with crowds of retreating soldiers, and with ambulances, artillery and wagons. The cellars were crowded with men, sound in body, but craven in spirit, who had gone there to surrender," added Dawes with distain. "I saw no men wearing badges of the first army corps in this disgraceful company." Some of the men hiding in the cellars mistook the passing Black Hats for advancing Confederates. "Don't fire, Johnny, we'll surrender," they called. When the regiment halted again in the crowded street, Rebels opened fire on them from houses and cross-lots. At that desperate moment, an old man appeared with two buckets of water. "The inestimable value of this cup of cold water to those true, unyielding soldiers—I would that our old friend would know," said Dawes. The cheers raised by the thirsty Black Hats attracted more Confederate shooting. The Wisconsin men returned fire and the exchange of bullets soon cleared the street. "The way open, I marched again toward the Cemetery Hill. The enemy did not pursue." Just ahead was a line of blue and a fluttering National flag. It was the 73rd Ohio, part of Eleventh Corps. The 6th Wisconsin had reached Cemetery Hill.[2]

Others who moved through town that afternoon also left accounts of what they saw and experienced. "As we passed through the streets, pale and frightened women came out and offered us coffee and found and implored us not to abandon them," reported Maj. Gen. Abner Doubleday, the officer who had assumed command of First Corps upon the fall of Reynolds. The corps, he admitted, "was broken and defeated, but not dismayed. There were but few left, but they . . . walked leisurely from the Seminary to the town, and did not run." Lt. James Stewart of

---

1 Ross, *Empty Sleeve*, 49-50; Rood, diary, 63. Fairchild's vest is among the holdings of the Wisconsin Veterans Museum in Madison.

2 Buell, *Cannoneer*, 73-74; Rood, diary, 63; Dawes, *Service*, 177-179.

Battery B found one of his caissons abandoned in the street with a broken rear axle. A private was busy working on the chest in an effort to destroy the charges, just as the regulations called for, so they could not be used by the enemy. When Stewart asked if he had been given an order, the private replied "No, but the Rebs are following us up pretty hard and if the caisson fell into their hands they would use the ammunition upon us." Stewart waited until the soldier finished, mounted the man behind him on his horse, and spurred toward safety.[3] Colonel Charles Wainwright of the artillery brigade remembered the confusion of crowded streets and retreating men. "There was little order amongst them, save that the Eleventh [Corps] took one side of the street and we the other; brigades and divisions were pretty well mixed up," he scribbled in his journal. "Still the men were not panic stricken; most of them were talking and joking."[4]

First Corps Brig. Gen. Thomas Rowley was experiencing a particularly bad day. Rowley, the acting commander of the Third Division, was suffering from boils on his inner thigh, the largest "about the size of hen's egg." Although physically unable to manage an engagement from horseback the veteran of the War with Mexico was well aware that serving in a great battle would have political advantage back home in Pittsburgh. His mistake was taking a drink or two to ease his suffering. By midafternoon he was red-faced and reeling in the saddle. His aides claimed he fell from his horse because the animal refused a ditch, and not because of the general's drinking. During the fighting later in the day, the fleshy general was seen on horseback once again rallying his men. "Here is for the Key Stone!" he shouted again and again while riding behind his fighting troops.

During the retreat, however, Rowley appeared confused and out of control, brandishing his sword and cursing retreating officers and privates alike as cowards. Wainwright encountered Rowley on a street. "He was very talkative, claiming that he was in command of the corps" recalled the artillery officer. "I tried to reason with him . . . but soon finding that he was drunk, I rode on to the top of Cemetery Hill, the existence of which I now learned for the first time. Whether Rowley would have handled his division any better had been sober, I have my doubts."[5] According to Doubleday, by the time he reached Cemetery Hill Rowley was so intoxicated he was unable to do his duty. "His face was very red and he enunciated slowly." What troubled him most, Doubleday continued, was Rowley's mistaken insistence that

---

3   Stewart,"Battery B, 4th U.S. Light Artillery at Gettysburg," *Sketches of War History* (Ohio), vol. 4, as reprinted in the *Gettysburg Papers*, 363; Buell, *Cannoneer*, 73-76.

4   Wainwright, *Diary*, 237.

5   *Ibid.*

he was now in command of the corps. "If I had succeeded General [John] Reynolds, General Rowley could not have succeeded me."[6]

A Confused Rabble of Disorganized Regiments

The 6th Wisconsin reached Cemetery Hill to find officers there frantically trying to establish a defense. Everything was in "disorder," observed Rufus Dawes. "Panic was impending over the exhausted soldiers. It was a confused rabble of disorganized regiments of infantry and crippled batteries." Confederates fired and yelled as they closed in around the rally point. The "confusion and peril" only increased with the arrival of General Rowley, remembered Dawes, who described the officer as "positively insane." The general "was raving and storming, and giving wild and crazy orders." Still, added the young officer, amid the confusion, "cool, courageous and efficient men, at that supreme crisis in the history of our country, brought order out of chaos."

Staff Officer Clayton Rogers, without hesitation, placed Rowley under arrest and asked Dawes for a detail to enforce the order. "This was perhaps the only instance in the war where a First Lieutenant forcibly arrested a Brigadier-General on the field of battle. I saw all that transpired and during the half hour of confusion, Rogers, who was well mounted, by his cool, clear-headed and quick-witted actions did more than any other one man to get the troops in line of battle," lauded Dawes.[7] According to Rogers, Rowley was "giving General Wadsworth's troops contradictory orders, calling them cowards, and whose conduct was so unbecoming a division commander and unfortunately stimulated by poor commissary [whiskey]. Not having seen General Wadsworth since the retreat commenced, the writer did not hesitate to arrest the crazy officer, on his own responsibility."[8] And so Rowley moved to the rear under guard. It had been a long

---

6 Transcript of the Court-Martial of Brig. Gen. Thomas A. Rowley, Edmund L. Dana Papers, Wyoming Historical and Genealogical Society, Wilkes-Barre, Pennsylvania, Folder: 1864 B. A typed copy of the original is on file at the Gettysburg National Military Park. Dana served as Rowley's defense counsel during the proceedings.

7 Dawes credited Rogers' action with helping save the position on Cemetery Hill: "History now shows us that the whole fate of the battle turned on rallying those troops on Cemetery Hill and Culp's Hill, and forming them at once in line of battle." Rufus Dawes, "Gallant Officer," *Milwaukee Sunday Telegraph*, February 3, 1884.

8 Dawes, *Telegraph*, February 3, 1884; Rogers, *Telegraph*, May 13, 1887. Rowley was charged with drunkenness on duty on the battlefield, conduct prejudicial to good order and military discipline, conduct unbecoming an officer and a gentleman, and disobedience of orders. Secretary of War Edwin M. Stanton, however, disapproved the sentence and reassigned the

Lt. Col. Rufus R. Dawes, 6th Wisconsin

Dawes was a seasoned veteran when he commanded the regiment at Gettysburg. July 4, 1863 was his twenty-fifth birthday. *Author's Collection*

hard day for any soldier, and Rowley, suffering from boils, a veteran of two wars, and perhaps too old for active service, had been in the thick of it—drunk or sober.

The survivors of the Iron Brigade reached the confusion that was the rally point on Cemetery Hill exhausted. "[O]vercome by heat . . . almost dead with thirst," they threw themselves on the ground to rest. Captain A. M. Edwards arrived carrying the flag of the 24th Michigan in company with about two dozen of his men. He planted the banner beside a battery to attract other Michigan men to him, and then sat down on a tombstone. Other Black Hats gathered around the flag. A sergeant in the 6th Wisconsin counted only five men around his regimental colors. Two hours later, about 65 men answered the roll.[9]

With Confederates gathering in large numbers around the hill, the final outcome of the day was still in question. When Maj. Gen. Winfield Scott Hancock saw the enemy moving northeast, he ordered Doubleday to send a division to support a battery he had ordered to nearby Culp's Hill, a wooded eminence that dominated Cemetery Ridge and extended the Union line to the east. My men are just about played out, Doubleday cautioned, but Hancock insisted, more sharply this time, and the survivors of the Iron Brigade began moving toward the wooded

general to command the District of the Monongahela until the cessation of hostilities. Ezra J. Warner, *Generals in Blue: Lives of the Union Comanders* (Baton Rouge, LA, 1964), 414.

9   Dawes, *Service*, 179; I. F. Kelly to Rufus Dawes, August 2, 1892; George Fairfield to Jerome Watrous, undated.

high ground, taking up a position on the Union left flank next to Brig. Gen. George "Pap" Greene's brigade. A short time later the rest of the 6th Wisconsin and Battery B arrived on Cemetery Hill. After a brief rest, Rogers arrived with orders for the Badgers to join the rest of the brigade on Culp's Hill. Battery B deployed near a stone gate near the town cemetery, where it would remain for the next three days.[10] The battery was in rough shape. Of the 145 or so men who served the six guns, two were killed, two mortally wounded, and thirteen confirmed as seriously wounded. Two guns were disabled, but brought along. One caisson was blown up and three others abandoned with axles or wheels destroyed. Twelve battery horses were killed outright and several more so injured they had to be shot with revolvers. Most of the losses occurred in the fifteen to thirty minutes of fighting late that afternoon. Only four of the heavy Napoleons were serviceable, and they were placed on each side of the Baltimore Pike, the main approach from Gettysburg.[11]

Friendly helloes greeted the arriving Wisconsin men when they finally reached the brigade about 500 yards northeast of the Pfeffer farm and Baltimore Pike. When a regimental wagon disgorged a dozen spades and shovels, the soldiers began constructing earthworks. Some in the army believed breastworks made a man cautious and sapped his will to fight, but that notion was knocked out of the Black Hats on McPherson's Ridge. "The men worked with great energy," remembered one officer. "A man would dig with all his strength till out of breath, when another would seize the spade and push on the work." The spades were also passed to men from the other regiments and before too long a respectable defensive line was in place. The Iron Brigade occupied the far left of the line along Culp's Hill facing almost north. The 24th Michigan was on the far left not far from Cemetery Hill. The 7th Wisconsin was on the right of the Wolverines and moving up the slope were the 6th Wisconsin and 2nd Wisconsin and finally the 19th Indiana. A 7th Wisconsin officer remembered the "rocky faced hill" as "not hard to hold against attack. We piled stone along our front. Dandy for defence, and got water . . . from springs at the foot of the hill." Rations were issued, but coffee fires were banned and men ate sugar and hardtack and "water was our helper with the cold grub." With the work finished, the men settled in and reflected on what had been accomplished. Dawes tried to put the day into words: "Our dead lay unburied and beyond our sight or reach. Our wounded were in the hands of the enemy. Our bravest and best were numbered with them."[12]

---

10 Dawes, *Service*, 176-178.

11 Silas Felton, "The Iron Brigade Battery at Gettysburg," *Gettysburg Magazine*, July 1994, 63.

12 Rood, diary, 63; Dawes, *Service*, 179.

Pvt. Peter L. Foust, Winchester Greys, Co. C, 19th Indiana

Foust is pictured here with the Iron Brigade uniform (circa 1863). The linen leggings are long gone and his Black Hat is mostly untrimmed. Like so many in his regiment that day, Foust was mortally wounded on July 1, 1863. *Civil War Museum of the Upper Middle West*

Great Men are Apt to Make Great Mistakes

In Gettysburg, meanwhile, Pvt. William Ray of the 7th Wisconsin rested after having his head wound treated. "Night comes on and we lay on our straw, some dying, some heaving their limbs amputated, others waiting," he wrote in his journal. "I threw away my knapsack when hit and lost my haversack so I lost both Bedding & food. But can get along for that."[13] Not far away rest the 6th's Mickey Sullivan, his shoulder wound bandaged. Along toward night, said Sullivan, he began "to skirmish around for some better place to sleep than the floor of the court house where having no blankets or knapsack for a pillow, I was not very comfortable." He and Cpl. William Hancock discussed what to do. Hancock observed, "our fellows had a good place in the railroad depot." They found the place crowded with wounded soldiers, but made the best of it. "I slept with a dead officer who had been mortally wounded in the cavalry fight," recalled the Irishman. "[S]ome citizen had brought out a feather bed and some bed clothes and had fixed him on it; not being able to roll him off I lay down with him and some time in the night I went to sleep."[14]

Robert Beecham of the 2nd Wisconsin was captured at Gettysburg and sent to a Confederate prison, but exchanged several months later. He returned to Gettysburg in 1900 and spent two weeks walking the battlefield, carefully stepping off the distance from McPherson's Ridge to Seminary Ridge. He first wrote at length about Gettysburg in "Adventures of an Iron Brigade Man," a serialized memoir printed between August 14 and December 18, 1902, in the *National Tribune*, a weekly newspaper published in Washington aimed primarily at veterans. Beecham also published a battle history in 1911 called *Gettysburg: the Pivotal Battle of the Civil War*. The book was praised, although one ex-Confederate claimed it was prejudicial against General Lee.[15] According to Beecham, the Confederates could have won Gettysburg if they had pushed ahead and seized Cemetery Hill. He called it Lee's "great mistake" of the campaign. Up to 5:00 p.m. on July 1, he wrote, Lee "had

---

13 Ray, *Iron Brigade*, 191.

14 Sullivan, *Telegraph*, December 20, 1884. William Hancock enlisted from Mauston on June 25, 1861. He would be wounded and captured at Petersburg, Virginia, in 1864. Hancock died after being shot by a guard at the prison in Salisbury, North Carolina, on November 27, 1864. *Wisconsin Roster*, vol. 1, 534.

15 Robert K. Beecham, *Gettysburg, The Pivotal Battle of the Civil War* (Chicago, 1911); Robert Beecham, *As if it were Glory: Robert Beecham's Civil War from the Iron Brigade to the Black Regiments*, Michael E. Stevens, ed. (Madison, WI, 1998), xviii. A full record of Beecham's service was included in editor Michael Stevens' Introduction, *ibid.* The book was compiled from Beecham's *National Tribune* articles.

everything going his way" except for the surprising resistance by the First Corps and Eleventh Corps of west and north of Gettysburg. Union forces had been driven from their first position and "fully expected to be attacked in their second," claimed Beecham. But the attack never came.

The Confederate Army of Northern Virginia was exhausted and disorganized after the day's marching and fighting, Beecham explained, but the Union First Corps had lost 5,500 men and the Eleventh Corps, which had been only partially engaged, another 2,600. Facing most of Lee's army, the Federals only had slightly more than 21,000 men, including cavalry, still available. "Why he did not follow up the advantage gained with his wonted vigor is beyond the comprehension of everyone familiar with conditions," Beecham wrote after his 1900 visit to the battlefield. Lee was a "man of genius, a great man. Great men are apt to make great mistakes. . . . It would seem that the finger of God had paralyzed his brain in the very moment of victory."[16] In fact, Lee recognized the strength of the Union position, but believed "it was only necessary to press those people in order to secure possession of the heights." His orders to General Ewell were to take Cemetery Hill and Culp's Hill should his corps commander deem it "practicable." Ewell was new to corps command, most of his own troops were exhausted, and he was dealing with the confusion of Gettysburg itself and the coming darkness. Several subordinates pressed him to go forward. He hesitated. It was the first time Ewell had served under Lee, whose custom and practice was to give wide discretion to his top lieutenants (hence the word "practicable" in Lee's message). Stonewall Jackson, under whom Ewell had served as a division leader, was never vague in his orders. Ewell could see a strong line of the enemy and numerous batteries of artillery. Despite some repositioning in front of Cemetery Hill and Culp's Hill, Ewell kept his victorious Confederates in place. The high ground would remain in Union hands, at least for now.

The Iron Brigade welcomed the onset of darkness without having to repel another attack. When the regimental officers called the rolls on Culp's Hill, the final numbers spoke for themselves. The brigade took 1,883 men into the fighting that morning. By sundown, only 691 were left to answer. The 6th Wisconsin escaped the heavy fighting on McPherson's Ridge, but still sustained losses totaling 48 percent. The 7th Wisconsin lost 42 percent, the 19th Indiana 71 percent, and the 2nd Wisconsin 77 percent. The newest and largest regiment of the brigade, the 24th Michigan, suffered an astounding 80 percent loss—the largest number of casualties sustained by any Union regiment at Gettysburg. Three of the five regimental

16 Beecham, *Glory*, 78-79.

commanders had been either wounded or captured: Fairchild of the 2nd Wisconsin, Callis of the 7th Wisconsin, and Morrow of the 24th Michigan.[17]

The artillerymen manning the four guns of Battery B near the cemetery gate began taking stock of the day's fighting. It was generally agreed that most of the deaths and wounds came during the battery's retreat into town. A whisper passed among the men that Lt. James Stewart had used his pistol to escape capture, but the Regular Army officer never verified the story. Their new position, thought the old battery veterans, was "much stronger than the old." Union reinforcements were also coming up. Most of the men agreed Howard's Eleventh Corps "had behaved well enough to redeem themselves from their disgrace at Chancellorsville," and the "Old First had covered itself with glory and every man in ranks knew it." They didn't think they had been whipped, for they had long held the ground outside Gettysburg against superior numbers. They also knew they "had punished the enemy terribly" and made "an orderly and respectable retreat to a much stronger and better position." Around the four guns of Battery B and in the line of the five Iron Brigade regiments, the men in the ranks "knew that we had done as desperate work as ever befell an army corps, and we were almost as proud of the record as we would have been of a victory."[18]

Dawes would one day look back from a distance of three decades on that awful day and night of July 1, 1863 and conclude: "We had lost the ground on which we had fought, we had lost our commander and our comrades, but our fight had held the Cemetery Hill and forced the decision for history that the crowning battle of the war should be at Gettysburg."[19]

In the darkness on Culp's Hill, along the makeshift zigzagging breastworks, the Black Hats ate what hardtack remained in their haversacks and tried to sleep. About 1:00 a.m. a soldier in the nearby 7th Indiana "cried out so loudly in his sleep" that it woke the sleeping soldiers around him. Shooting erupted in the darkness when happy trigger fingers squeezed too tightly when confronted by shadows and trees.

---

17 The Iron Brigade's opponents were also in some disorganization. In Harry Heth's Confederate division, the general himself was slightly wounded in the head, and James J. Archer's and Joe Davis' brigades had been battered by the heavy fighting, as was John Brockenbrough's brigade. Two of four colonels in J. Pettigrew's brigade were killed and wounded. The 26th North Carolina carried 800 men into the fighting, from which 216 emerged. In Dorsey Pender's division, Abner Perrin's brigade counted 500 men killed and wounded, and Alfred Scales' brigade suffered 545 killed, wounded, and missing. Nolan, *Iron Brigade*, 253-254.

18 Buell, *Cannoneer*, 80-81.

19 Dawes, *Service*, 179.

Two hours later officers roused soldiers on the Culp's Hill line to assume their firing positions in case of a renewed Rebel attack.

Separated from his comrades by thousands of Ewell's veteran gray infantry, Mickey Sullivan remained in Gettysburg and watched Rebels plunder stores and houses, "carrying away pails of sugar, molasses, and groceries of all kinds, clothing and bales of goods, silks, calico and cloth." Except for a surly officer or two the Confederates were generally friendly to the Union wounded and shared "whiskey, tobacco and baker's bread freely." When an officer directed a Rebel soldier to take Mickey's "good pair of balmoral shoes," the Badger bristled. "[T]there would be an Irish row first," he warned, "and the fellow said they could not fit him, that they were too small."[20]

You Have Refused a Kind Act

An injured Wisconsin soldier, Francis Deleglise of the 6th, was resting in a cellar in Gettysburg with other wounded when a Confederate officer entered. The stranger looked around in the gloomy darkness, taking in the situation with a grim face. When his eyes settled on two seriously wounded men lying under a quilt, he inquired about their regiments. The first answered he was with a Georgia regiment. "I belong to the Federal army," replied the second man. According to the watching Badger, the officer "drew from his pocket his canteen filed with milk punch and first gave a drink to the Union soldier and afterward to the man who belonged to his own side."[21]

The news was read at morning roll call that Abner Doubleday had been replaced as commander of First Corps by John Newton of Sixth Corps. The announcement was met with "instant disapprobation by the men." Doubleday was not the sort of officer "to excite much enthusiasm," admitted one Westerner, but the men believed the general had handled First Corps well, displaying "skill and courage which the dullest private could not help commending." The ranks were "disgusted when they learned that a stranger had been put over them."[22]

The Army of the Potomac organized itself into a giant fishhook during the darkness. The right side of the line on Culp's Hill wound from near the Baltimore Pike across the wooded rocky crest to Cemetery Hill below Gettysburg, where the line turned south to run south along Cemetery Ridge (the shank of the hook). The

20 Sullivan, *Telegraph*, December 28, 1884.

21 *Ibid.*, December 28, 1884; *Soldier's and Citizen's Album*, 171.

22 Buell, *Cannoneer*, 80.

Black Hats waited on the battle line atop Culp's Hill, but except for an occasional shelling nothing of consequence developed. The high ground offered the Western men a good vista from which to view other parts of the field. Troops "were hurrying to different points of the field to take the positions assigned them," wrote one. "Batteries were being placed in advantageous positions as fast as the already jaded horses could be lashed into drawing them. Ammunition wagons came to the front on a keen gallop. Cartridge boxes were replenished. All was, noise, hurry and confusion." As one soldier put it, each man "felt that a desperate struggle was to come and that the result no one could foretell. All felt they must nerve themselves for the ordeal."[23]

The day passed in relative quiet until about 4:00 p.m., when heavy artillery firing erupted a couple miles to the south on the far left of the Union line. The Westerners would not know until much later that James Longstreet's First Corps was attempting to roll up the Union line, an attack that other Confederate brigades along Seminary Ridge would take up, one at a time, until the fighting wrapped itself around town. Other troops from Ewell's Corps opposite their own position, meanwhile, would demonstrate against the high ground south and southwest of town, and launch a full attack if circumstances warranted. The fighting escalated quickly and crushed much of the Third Corps, which in turn required Meade to pull reinforcements (almost 20,000 soldiers, all told) from other parts of the line to stabilize the position. The fighting at Devil's Den, Little Round Top, the Wheatfield, and the Peach Orchard was some of the most savage of the war.

"We could plainly see that our troops were giving ground," recalled a Wisconsin officer. "Our suspense and anxiety were intense. We gathered in knots all over the hill watching the battle. . . . As the sun was low down a fine sight was seen. It was two long blue lines of battle, with twenty or thirty regimental banners, charging forward into the smoke and din of battle. To all appearances they saved the field." About 7:00 p.m., as the light was fading, the Rebel Yell went up in front of Culp's Hill. Within minutes the far right side of the Meade's hook-shaped Union line was under an attack led by Maj. Gen. Edward "Allegheny" Johnson. The Confederates doggedly ascended the timbered rock-strewn slope, slugging their way ahead to reach the crest and dislodge the defenders. Johnson's men enjoyed some success on the far right of the Union line, which had been stripped of troops for service elsewhere. Only a brigade of New Yorkers under Brig. Gen. George S. Greene remained in position. Greene's insistence that his men construct defensive

---

23 Young, *Telegraph*, April 22, 1888.

works proved the difference, although a portion of the abandoned Federal works on the lower part of Culp's Hill were lost.

The musketry fighting was one long incessant roar when an officer came looking for Lt. Col. Rufus Dawes with orders to report to Greene. The 6th Wisconsin and the 14th Brooklyn (84th New York) assembled and moved to the right to assist in repelling an attack. Wisconsin color bearer I. F. Kelly remembered how awkward it was struggling through the brush and trees in the darkness with his 11-foot flag staff. The first mounted officer Dawes encountered was Greene himself, who took a card from his pocket and wrote his name and command, handing it to the young officer. He ordered Dawes to take his regiment into the breastworks and hold them. With the New Yorkers on his right Dawes pushed his men ahead: "Forward—run! March!" When the 6th Wisconsin reached the line, however, Virginia Rebels perched among the dark rocks rose to fire a volley directly into their faces. Greene was unaware that Confederates occupied the breastworks, and the Rebels seemed just as surprised by the arrival of the Wisconsin men. After the volley, the gray infantry made their way down Culp's Hill. "This remarkable encounter did not last a minute," admitted Dawes. "We lost two men, killed—both burned with the powder of the guns fired at them." One of the wounded was color bearer Kelly, who was struck by a spatter of lead that ricocheted off a rock and cut his neck. The wound bled freely. His comrades soaked a rag before wrapping it around his neck. The 6th Wisconsin remained in the line until midnight, when they were relieved by returning Twelfth Corps troops. The Wisconsin and New York regiments marched back to their original positions without further incident.[24]

In town that night, two surgeons set up a mess in a saloon where the wounded Union soldiers were served coffee, tea, and hardtack. They shared some of it with wounded Confederates. Mickey Sullivan and William Hancock, both of the 6th Wisconsin, looked for a place to sleep and decided to use the bed Sullivan had slept in the night before. The dead Union cavalry officer was still there, so the two Black Hats simply rolled him off and took possession. "I did not enjoy our conquest very much," admitted Sullivan. "What added to our uneasiness was the fact the Rebs might clean out the Army of the Potomac and take Washington, then 'Old Abe' and the country was gone for certain."[25]

24 Dawes, *Service*, 171-172; I. F. Kelly letter to Dawes, August 2, 1892.

25 Sullivan, *Telegraph*, December 28, 1884.

They Meant to Make Trouble Pretty Soon

The third day of fighting at Gettysburg arrived even before dawn broke when a flurry of artillery and musket fire exploded about 4:30 a.m. on Culp's Hill. Edward Johnson's Confederate division had made a solid lodgment on the wood slope the previous day, though at high cost. Reinforcements in the form of several brigades from other divisions in Ewell's Corps arrived early that morning in preparation to renew the attack. It was imperative for the Federals to push the Confederates from the captured trenches on the far right side of Culp's Hill and elsewhere to interrupt another Southern drive to capture the high ground. During the night, twenty Union artillery pieces were placed to enfilade the enemy. When the Northern guns opened, Johnson had little choice but to begin his own assault. Because the Iron Brigade was facing almost due north on the far left of the line, it escaped much of the bloody action to follow. For almost six hours the fighting surged and ebbed along Culp's Hill as the Southern infantry launched one attack after another, reformed, and attacked again. None of the efforts were successful. One Confederate survivor always claimed he stood in an ankle-deep stream of blood while he fired up the slope. By 11:00 a.m., the murderous fire had ripped apart every Southern effort to capture Culp's Hill and the gray infantry was too exhausted and disorganized to continue. A failed Federal countercharge on the far Union right brought the fighting to a fitful close.

The battlefield fell quiet once again, and except for an occasional flurry of artillery or exchange of musketry along the picket lines, nothing much happened for the next couple of hours. Still, great anticipation coursed through the Western ranks as the minutes passed. Nothing had been resolved. The Southern failures the previous day—Longstreet's attack against the far left, A. P. Hill's against southern Cemetery Ridge, and Ewell's inability to hold Cemetery Hill after dusk and seize Culp's Hill on the far right—left the Union line unbroken. None in the ranks knew who would make the next move.

The third day of July, a Friday, moved to noon with no heavy action. The thin regiments of the Iron Brigade manned their breastwork along the top of Culp's Hill and waited. One officer remembered the "zip of the sharpshooter's bullet, the 'where is you' of cannon shot and the ringing whistle of the ragged fragments of bursting shell." The Western men continued throwing up branches, stones, and earth to strengthen their position, a firm indication the desperate fighting and heavy losses of two days earlier had unsettled them.[26]

26 Dawes, *Service*, 182.

In Gettysburg, scores of Union prisoners and walking wounded moved about more or less freely. Many of them learned in advance that something big was in the offing. Stymied in his attempt to turn the Union left and seize the high ground on the far right, General Lee decided to attack the right-center on Cemetery Ridge to break Meade's army in two and drive it from the field. Major General George Pickett's fresh Virginia division of Longstreet's Corps would spearhead the effort, supported by six brigades from A. P. Hill's Corps. About 150 to 170 Confederate guns would bombard the Union position to drive away many of the defenders and enemy guns and pave the way for the infantry. Federal prisoners in town had a lookout in the observatory of the train depot and called to the captured Union men below that Confederate infantry and artillery was massing on the right side of town. "We knew they meant to make trouble pretty soon," said Mickey Sullivan. After the midday meal, the observer announced the Johnnies were on the move. "Just then 'bang, bang' went a couple of guns, and then such a roar of artillery as I have never heard before or since," remembered the Irishman. "[T]he ground shook and the depot building fairly trembled. Our fellows answered just as loud, and it seemed as if the last day had come."[27] On Culp's Hill, General Wadsworth and his staff were sitting around "a cracker-box table" when the first artillery shells from "a furious cannonade" swept the position. A dozen shells burst near the officers, covering their meal with dirt. The division commander and other officers moved to a safer location that gave them what staff officer John Kress described as "a fine view of the whole field of battle."

Despite a lack of adequate artillery ammunition, the Confederate guns increased their rate of fire and about 80 Union guns answered. How long the bombardment lasted is up for debate, for eyewitness accounts vary wildly. Most agree it began about 1:00 p.m. and probably ended about an hour later. Once the Southern fire died away Wadsworth, Kress, and the other officers peered through the drifting gun smoke. Soon, they spotted "lines over a mile long of gray coats forming on the opposite ridge, saw them move across the valley and the low ground under the terrible fire of our artillery, posted as thickly along our lines as the ground permitted, blowing great gaps in the ranks." The heavy Confederate battalions appeared an irresistible wave, tramping steadily toward the ridge with their bright red battle flags waving all the while.[28]

Afterward, the Black Hats would discover that the portion of the Union line about to confront the historic attack included two former Iron Brigade men now

27 Sullivan, *Telegraph*, December 28, 1884.

28 Kress, *Republican*, December 4, 1886.

serving with the Second Union Corps: Brig. Gen. John Gibbon and Lt. Frank Haskell. The former commander of the Iron Brigade was about to be wounded, though he would survive and continue fighting through the war. His aide would live to write about the fighting in a long letter sent within two weeks to his brother at Portage, Wisconsin. In time, Haskell would become Wisconsin's most widely known Civil War soldier—not for his service with Gibbon's Black Hat Brigade but as "Haskell of Gettysburg," the officer who rallied the Union line in the final Confederate attack at Gettysburg on July 3, 1863. His lengthy letter would be published long after Haskell's death at Cold Harbor in June 1864, his description of the action so important that no historian writing of Gettysburg would be able to ignore it.

In Gettysburg, Mickey Sullivan found one of the Iron Brigade band members to help him up the stairs to the cupola of the rail depot. "I saw [what appeared like the whole Rebel Army in a chunk start for our lines with their infernal squealing yell. It seemed as if everything stood still inside of me for a second or two, then I began to pray." Staff officer Kress, watching from Culp's Hill, called it an irresistible sight: "On they came, banners waving in the battle smoke, cannon roaring, men shouting, horses neighing, small arms crashing in volleys! Still they came on . . . nothing stops them. . . . They almost reach our main line of battle with a fairly well-filled line of their own, as it seemed from our location." Sullivan's prayer (though he admitted he "was, and am not yet noted for the frequency and fervency of my prayers"), was that the Confederates would "catch h——l." It seemed as "if the fire from our lines doubled and doubled again, and I could see long streaks of light through the Rebel columns, but they went forward. I was afraid they would capture our guns." Another Wisconsin soldier watched the Confederates fall by the score and later said that he "felt bad for the poor cusses who went down, but it had to be."

Watching from Culp's Hill, Wadsworth could "keep quiet no longer" and sent Kress off at the gallop to "ask him [Meade] if he did not want our division." The young officer rode through sheets of bullets and exploding shell fire before finding the army commander "close in rear of our main line where the enemy had but a moment before pierced it, and a large body of the brave fellows who had charged so recklessly, were just surrendering by individuals and detachments." Meade received Wadsworth's offer with a smile and shook his head. "Tell the general I am much obliged for this tender of service, but we are all right and do not need his troops here."

Mickey Sullivan watched the same thing from his distant perspective in the rail depot cupola; the Confederate infantry wave seemed to be melting away. "[W]e could hear the Northern cheer. We knew that the rebs were scooped, and the old Army of the Potomac was victorious," was how he later put it. The dozen or so

Iron Brigade Band, Gettysburg

This composite photograph of members of the Iron Brigade Band was
taken by the Tyson Brothers of Gettysburg. The band remained in
Gettysburg after the battle, and probably took part in the dedication of the
soldier cemetery in November 1863. *Author's Collection*

wounded soldiers around Sullivan "were wild with joy, some cried, others shook
hands, and all joined in with the best cheer we could get up. I forgot all about my
wound and was very forcibly reminded of it when I went to shout as I had to sit
down to keep from falling." A Confederate officer arrived to see what the clamor
was all about. "[W]hen told that Lee was cleaned, he growled out if we d——d
Yankees were able to cheer we were able to go to Richmond," recalled Sullivan,

who admitted, "our fellows felt good anyway, and the reb went out and we saw no more of him."[29]

West of town on Seminary Ridge, a dozen wounded and captured Federal soldiers—including Elisha Reed of the 2nd Wisconsin—watched the charge from the Lutheran Seminary's cupola. The failure of the attack brought shouts and cheers, and when the viewers climbed down to share the news, more yells and rejoicing ensued. A Rebel lieutenant came in "slowly, sadly, and silently," recalled Reed, and walked around the room looking at no one. Finally, the officer— "like the pent-up thunder in the earth beneath"—poured out "a raging torrent of long suppressed wrath. Imagine if you can an enraged Southern fire-eater pouring out volcanic clouds of vigorous and vehement volumes of profanity." The lieutenant argued that General Lee was "a fool [for] undertaking to dislodge Meade" from Cemetery Ridge. "He can't do it—and he knows he can't do it; then why in hell does he try to do it?" After cussing once more, the Confederate officer added, "there was not a private soldier in the whole Confederate army but would know better than to undertake to dislodge Meade from such a position." With that, the lieutenant turned and left the chapel.[30]

All the Rebs Gone Someplace

Not far away, Col. Henry Morrow, also a prisoner, watched the failed charge from a church steeple. A short time later down on a street he met up with Confederate Brig. Gen. John B. Gordon and his staff. Morrow saluted and said, "General, I am informed that the wounded of our first day's battle lie uncared for where they fell, and I ask your assistance in having them attended to." A surprised Gordon turned to his staff. "Is this so, and if so, why is it?" A surgeon replied that the wounded of both armies had been cared for, but they had been unable to visit that extreme part of the field. Gordon promised help. That evening, a train of twelve Confederate ambulances arrived on the scene of the first day's fighting. With lanterns held high in the darkness, hospital stewards and nurses moved among the "blackened and swollen corpses" seeking the survivors who had suffered on that ground for two days and a night. "The moans and cries for assistance and water were heart rendering," confessed one eyewitness. "Some were delirious and talked of home and friends and wondered that they neglected them so long, while others,

29 Sullivan, *Telegraph*, December 28, 1884; Sullivan, *Irishman*, 104. Kress, *Republican*, December 4, 1886.

30 Elisha Rice Reed, "General Lee at Gettysburg, Pa.," Elisha Reed Papers, Wisconsin Historical Society.

in their wild delirium cheered on their comrades as they fought over in imagination the terrible battle." One of the wounded was Cpl. Andrew Wagner of the 24th Michigan, who had been shot through the breast while carrying the colors. While he lay helpless, a small party of Confederates stole his shoes and money. Thinking Wagner was dying, they made a pillow for his head. He was the only survivor from the two entire color guard detachments of the 24th Michigan that marched into the first day's battle. Nearby they found Lysander Trent of Co. I, 19th Indiana, the Spencer Greys. He had been shot in the "hip, limb and leg" and was somehow still alive although most of his possessions were stolen. All three of the Bush brothers in the same company from Owen County, Indiana, were wounded. Private John Bush, the youngest of the trio, was shot through the right breast with the ball exiting below the shoulder blade. Corporal David Bush was shot through the back part of the neck and Sgt. George Bush was thumped on the left breast and bruised by what probably was a spent bullet. It was not until after midnight that these wounded survivors were finally taken to hospitals. By then, after so long on the field, one soldier explained, "the maggots began to crawl and fatten in their festering wounds."[31]

Except for some Union men the streets of Gettysburg were almost empty when the wounded Private Ray stepped outside the morning of July 4, 1863, to take a look around. "All the Rebs gone someplace, ambulances, wagons & all," he wrote in his journal. A Confederate cavalryman clattered down the street at a dead run yelling to the Union men, "keep in your heads, your skirmishers are coming!" A moment later a gun went off and a bullet whizzed down the street past him. Union cavalry followed and infantry from Howard's Eleventh Corps "searched every Barn & horse taking a great many prisoners right in the town," Ray continued. "I guess nearly as many as they took of our Boys when they could." Within minutes the streets were full of walking wounded who "scratch & hobbled along" in a painful effort to return to their regiments.[32]

A pre-dawn rain woke Rufus Dawes after a long gloomy night filled with "troubled and dreamy sleep of the battlefield." Half awake behind the makeshift breastworks manned by his regiment on Culp's Hill, Dawes wondered whether the

---

31 Smith, *Twenty-fourth Michigan*, 148; Bush family records compiled by Brett Wilson; Curtis, *Twenty-fourth*, 190-192. John Bush was not taken to a hospital until July 6. He never remembered who found or cared for him. The ball that hit David Bush entered the left side of his neck, passing through and exiting on the other side. All survived and would be back in ranks in the next few months. Company I went into battle with thirty-five officers and men, but only three reached the rally point. One burial party found nineteen Indiana men lying dead in a well-ordered row.

32 Ray, *Iron Brigade*, 193-194.

fighting would be resumed. More fully awake now, he realized that it was Independence Day 1863—his 25th birthday. As the day brightened, he withdrew a letter from his pocket begun the night before and added a few lines: "I am entirely safe through the first three of these terrible days of bloody struggle. The fighting was the most desperate I ever saw. O, Mary, it is sad to look now at our shattered band of devoted men. . . . Tell mother I am safe."

The horrific sights of the battlefield challenged the mettle of the men who moved across it on the fourth day. Colonel Morrow located his 24th Michigan and told stories of his grim night trying to find the regiment's dead and wounded northwest of town. The Confederates treated the wounded well, he added, but stripped and robbed "the bodies of the dead who still lie there so bloated as to be unrecognizable." Jerome Watrous of the 6th Wisconsin found the farm fields "covered with unburied dead, hospitals," the homes, sheds, and barns "crowded with bleeding, dying men." Moving out of the town toward the Union position was a "wounded squadron with broomsticks for crutches, and any means of assistance they could lay their hands on"—men trying to find their regiments. Several of them wore the black hat of the Iron Brigade. "I have seen more of awful, terrible suffering and misery. . . at Gettysburg then I ever did before," a Wisconsin man wrote home, "used as I have been to mangled corprses and revolting sights general—and no one living can form the faintest idea of the horrors of war, until he or she has seen a battle field immediately succeeding a fight, and for weeks after in the hospitals."[33]

William Ray discovered only 19 men were left in his company of the 7th Wisconsin. "They all seemed as glad to see me as if I were their Brother and I assure you I was just as glad to see them." Mickey Sullivan found his 6th Wisconsin "about the size of a decent company . . . in the center of the horseshoe in which our line was formed." His Company K, down to "seven or eight men" with a sergeant in command, had marched north to Gettysburg with 34 bayonets. The 6th Wisconsin carried 340 soldiers into the battle and more than 160 were down, dead, or missing. Six of a dozen company officers fell with two killed outright. The 19th Indiana was in sad shape as well, he observed, and most of the officers were down or wounded.

33 William P. Taylor, letter to Mrs. J. S. Taplin, July 20, 1863, from Washington, Oshkosh, Wisconsin Public Museum Record 65/294. Taylor was writing to the mother of Pvt. Osman Taplin of the 2nd Wisconsin, who had been mortally wounded in the fighting at Antietam on September 17, 1862. Taylor, who was a member of the same company, had been captured at First Bull Run while serving as a fifer. Later in the war he worked in the office of the Wisconsin Soldier's Aid Society in Washington, and mustered out of service with the regiment in June of 1864.

The five regiments of the Iron Brigade, realized the stunned Irish soldier, "would not make one."[34]

One of the arriving wounded from the 6th Wisconsin was Sgt. William Evans, who presented Dawes with the captured flag of the 2nd Mississippi. The banner had been hidden beneath the mattress in his bed in town during the Confederate occupation. Another wounded soldier handed the young officer a bouquet of flowers and a note with the compliments of "Miss Sallie Paxton," who had watched the regiment's charge against the railroad cut on the morning of July 1. "The day for us was fearful and our thoughts turn to those at home whose dear ones lie on yond field," one Michigan soldier wrote home, "some in their last gory sleep, others suffering from wounds and no aid near them."[35]

After a time the wounded made their goodbyes and began walking to the First Corps hospital two miles distant. The next morning most of them made it to Littletown, and from there to Harrisburg and Philadelphia for treatment. Sullivan and about two dozen others spent the night in a barn, where "The old Pennsylvania farmer furnished us with quilts, supper and breakfast." The next morning the farmer hitched a wagon and hauled them to Littletown. From there, Mickey and his comrades were sent to an army hospital at Germantown, Pennsylvania. "It was a long time before I was able to go back to the regiment."[36]

Back on the Culp's Hill early that evening Dawes added another few sentences to his letter. It was 6:00 p.m. on July 4: "What a solemn birthday. My little band, now only two hundred men, have all been out burying the bloody corpses of friend and foe. No fighting to-day. Both armies need rest from the exhaustion of the desperate struggle. My boys until just now have had nothing to eat since yesterday morning. No regiment in the army did better service than ours." According to a Michigan man, the Union wounded soldiers "were full of enthusiasm, though unable to move with limbs crushed and swollen, and without food."[37]

Independence Day at Gettysburg in 1863 was "chiefly a day of gloom," recalled a Badger. "Nearly every survivor had lost from one to a dozen of his

---

34 Curtis, *Twenty-fourth*, 184; Watrous, *Richard Epps*, 102; Ray, *Iron Brigade*, 194; Sullivan, *Telegraph*, February 13, 1883; Sullivan, *Irishman*, 101-102.

35 Sullivan, *Telegraph*, December 28, 1884; Sullivan, *Irishman*, 102; Dawes to Mary Beman Gates, July 4, 1863; Dawes, *Service*, 159-160; *Soldiers' and Citizens' Album*, 171; Sullivan Green, letter, July 2, 1863, in Curtis, *Twenty-fourth*, 184.

36 Sullivan, *Telegraph*, December 28, 1884; Sullivan, *Irishman*, 102; Sullivan Green, letter, July 2, 1863.

37 Dawes to Mary Beman Gates, July 4, 1863; Dawes, *Service*, 159-160; Sullivan Green, letter, July 4, 1863.

company comrades. It was a day like a funeral, a quiet day, save the labor called for in burying the dead and caring for the wounded." William Ray represented the feelings of most of the Black Hats when he noted in his journal, "This has been rather a dull fourth to me as well as a hard one." It was about sunset when Meade "ordered all of the bands to move up close to the men who had fought and won one of the greatest victories that any army had ever won and play the patriotic airs. At first the music had but little effect upon the victorious army, said a Wisconsin sergeant, but when the bands came to 'America' and the 'Star-spangled Banner' hearts were touched . . . and by and by a cheer started. It was taken up and went along the five mile line of battle and was repeated several times, and the old army had come to itself again and the next day was ready to start in pursuit of Gen. Lee and his brave army in gray."[38]

The small regiments of the Iron Brigade left Culp's Hill the morning of July 5 for nearby Cemetery Ridge, not far from what a Michigan man called "the scene of the rebels' desperate and final charge." Evidence of the struggle was everywhere: "the ground trampled down; buildings riddled with shot or in black ruins, trees cut and fences splintered with grape." Here and there, in a growing stench under the hot sun, details of soldiers pulled dead Confederates into piles for mass burials. Civilians were also moving about on the fields in small groups on foot or in wagons and buggies. Some were curious to see the battlefield, but others arrived deep in the grieving process. Some carried shovels to open fresh Union graves looking for a missing loved one. An entry in a Badger diary read simply, "There is an unusual stillness everywhere."[39]

When further orders did not arrive, the Western men put up what small tents they had and rested through a rainy night. Much of the campfire talk centered on whether the Confederate army was making a run for Virginia and safety. There was also some discussion about Meade's handling of the battle. Having been thrust into command of a scattered army less than a week before Gettysburg, Meade, they agreed, had fought well enough to at least avoid disaster. Few realized the

38 Ray, *Iron Brigade*, 195; Jerome A. Watrous, untitled manuscript. A fifer in the 7th Wisconsin, Ludolph Longhenry, described it as a "serenade of pretty music." Ludolph Longhenry diary, July 4, 1863. The literature of the Gettysburg campaign is deep and interesting. For good single-volume accounts see Edwin B. Coddington, *The Gettysburg Campaign: A Study in Command* (New York, 1968), and Stephen W. Sears, *Gettysburg* (Boston, 2003). The battle as seen by the Confederates: Clifford Dowdey, *Death of a Nation: The Story of Lee and His Men at Gettysburg* (New York, 1958). For an analytical look at the photography of Gettysburg, see William A. Frassanito, *Gettysburg: A Journey in Time* (New York, 1975).

39 Longhenry, diary, July 5, 1863; Fairfield diary, July 5, 1863; Neff, manuscript, cited Smith, *Iron Brigade*, 184; Otis, *Second Wisconsin*, 88; Curtis, *Twenty-fourth*, 193-194.

significant nature of their victory or how history would come to see their achievement. The Army of the Potomac was nearly as disorganized in victory as was the Army of Northern Virginia in defeat, however, and mounting a quick pursuit was easier said than done. Steady rains had turned the roads into mud and the army was short on nearly everything, including rations, ammunition, and shoes. Still, Meade had fresh brigades on hand. Most of the Sixth Corps, for example, had hardly pulled a trigger. However, the general, an engineer by training, was cautious by nature and not about to lose what he worked so hard to gain. He was having "great difficulty in getting reliable information," he wired Washington, but he believed "the enemy is retreating, very much crippled and hampered by his trains." When the delay finally ended the following morning, a Michigan man wrote home, "The army is in motion towards the retreating invaders."[40]

The main portion of the Army of the Potomac took to the roads "very early" on July 6 with the telegraph line from Washington (unmindful of "knee-deep mud" slowing the soldiers) frantic with messages to press the retreating Confederates. It was raining again. "[T]he very heavens seemed to weep at the dreadful carnage just past," waxed a soldier in the 24th Michigan. The regiments halted near Emmitsburg. There was little coffee and many of the men did not have blankets. A Wisconsin officer scribbled to the folks at home, "May God save me and my men from any more such trials." The columns reached Bellville by nightfall on July 7 after a march of 24 miles. The Black Hats tried to sleep under yet another hard rain that lasted through the dark hours. Lieutenant Rood "sat up against a nice big tree. Pulled hat rim down around. Poncho over my feet, and, by George, I never slept sounder. . . . Everybody else too, I reckon."

Vicksburg has Fallen

The column halted once it moved through Middletown, Maryland. The Iron Brigade bivouacked on the west slope of South Mountain. Having been in a hard place or two, explained a veteran Wolverine, the soldiers piled rails knowing that "a rail fence properly disposed, and covered with a few shovelfuls of earth, doubles the defence of the troops as well as gives strength to their confidence." As the hours passed without any orders to move, one Wisconsin soldier told his diary, "never was [the rest] more welcome." Word reached the Union column that the Confederate stronghold at Vicksburg, Mississippi, had finally fallen. "Hooray!

---

40 Rood, diary, 68; OR 27, pt. 1, 80, 84; Sullivan Green, letter, July 5, 1863, cited Curtis, *Twenty-fourth*, 184-185.

Hooray!" a Wisconsin officer penned in his journal. "[W]e celebrated as best we could."[41]

"We have marched night and day and we have beaten the rebel army," Dawes wrote home during the pursuit. "At last the Army of the Potomac has done what, well-handled, it might have done long ago, out-marched, out-maneuvered, and defeated the great rebel army of General Lee." He continued his letter from Boonsboro on July 9: "Oue men have toiled and suffered as never before. Almost half of our men have marched barefooted for a week. . . . We have had severe rains since the battle. I have not slept in a dry blanket or had on dry clothing since crossing the Potomac [River] before the battle. If we can end this war right here, I will cheerfully abide the terrible risk of another battle." And later that day: "We are again near the rebel army and unless they escape over the river, we may expect a battle. . . . General Meade has shown himself equal to the emergency." He had troubling news to share as well: The oldest of the Iron Brigade regiments, the 2nd Wisconsin, "cannot muster fifty muskets." What was left has been with the advance since the battle, "and will probably open the next fight as it did the last."

About a week after leaving Gettysburg, on July 12, the Union columns caught up with the retreating Confederate army at a crossing of the Potomac River at Williamsport. The river was running high and fast because of the recent rains, and for a time it appeared as though General Meade had Lee's men trapped. The Confederate line was a strong one, with powerful earthworks studded with artillery. Gray infantry aggressively manhandled Union skirmishers trying to ascertain the strength and depth of the line. The hours slipped away. The cautious Meade, an engineering officer who knew the power of strong defenses, was worried that an ill-planned assault would end in failure and sacrifice the hard-won gains at Gettysburg. By the time an attack was ordered, the Potomac had fallen enough for the Confederates to begin crossing the wide river on a pontoon bridge to safety. Advancing Union skirmishers on the morning of July 14 found the earthworks empty. Later, the survivors of the 24th Michigan learned that one of the last Confederate units to escape was the 26th North Carolina, which had fought "such a terrible duel" with the Wolverines on July 1. When President Lincoln read Meade's telegram that Lee's army had escaped, he said in bitter disappointment, "We had them within our grasp. We had only to stretch forth our hands they were ours." In truth, it was not that easy.[42]

41 Rood, diary, 68.

42 Curtis, *Twenty-fourth*, 195; Rood, diary, 68; Longhenry, diary, July 14, 1863; John Hay, *Lincoln and the Civil War: Letters and Diaries of John Hay*, Tyler Dennett ed. (New York, 1939), 667.

Citizens across the North celebrated the twin victories of Vicksburg and Gettysburg, despite the sour muttering over how Meade and the Army of the Potomac had allowed Lee to escape. The Iron Brigade men, by and large, were not of the same mind. Dawes and a group of other officers examined the Confederate works and proclaimed them strong and well-constructed. "I think General Meade would have certainly failed to carry them by direct assault," concluded Dawes. "Both flanks of the works were on the Potomac River. We had no other alternative than direct assault. I take no stock in the stuff printed in the newspapers about demoralization of the rebel army after Gettysburg," he continued. "They were worn out and tired as we were, but their cartridge boxes had plenty of ammunition, and they would have quietly lain their rifle pits and shot us down with the same coolness and desperation they showed at Gettysburg." A Michigan man agreed when he wrote that many in the North "seem to think that Meade's army should have annihilated" the Confederates. The Army of the Potomac "won a great victory in defeating and turning back the invaders, but the opposing armies were too nearly equal, both before and after the Gettysburg battle, for each to destroy the other. Our victory had cost us too dearly to be rash."[43]

The Iron Brigade, indeed the whole Army of the Potomac, asserted Dawes, needed rest. "The incessant and toilsome marching from Fredericksburg to Gettysburg, the terrible battle, and the hurried pursuit of the enemy to their point has been the most trying campaign of this army," he wrote home. "Our men have become ragged and shoeless, thousands have marched for days barefoot over the flinty turnpikes. The army has shown a willingness and alacrity under its toils, sufferings and privations, that entitle it to the gratitude of the Nation and I think for once we will receive it."[44]

And so the Gettysburg Campaign ended at the Williamsport and Falling Waters crossings. The hard-luck and politically-infested Army of the Potomac had finally triumphed over the Army of Northern Virginia. It was a victory forged in noise and smoke and suffering and death of unexpected magnitude. It was a victory despite, or perhaps because of, the unlikely situation of a new general thrust into command just days before the battle. And it was the victory the survivors of the

---

43 Dawes to Mary Beman Gates, July 14, 1863; Dawes, *Service*, 186; Curtis, *Twenty-fourth*, 194.

44 Dawes, *Service*, 187. John A. Kress, who served as a staff officer for James Wadsworth, voiced the same conclusion in 1886: "After three days' fighting, marching and indescribably hard and exhausting work for the whole army, reserves included, it seemed as if we had just about reached the limit of human endurance and must have rest." He added, however, that he believed if U.S. Grant or Phil Sheridan had commanded the army at Gettysburg, Lee's army would never have been allowed to cross the Potomac River.

Iron Brigade believed was a turning point on the long hard road of civil war. "I think the backbone of the rebellion is broken, or soon will be," a Wisconsin private wrote home. "They have played their hand long enough."[45] Gettysburg, as they would discover in the coming months, was the last great battle for the bright volunteers who had flocked to the Union banners in 1861. The days of stand-up battle lines and bold charges were passing. The war to come would take on a grim and harder face, and the letters, diaries, and journals would take note of the change. Throwing up hasty earthworks at almost every halt would become common place. Without orders, the Wisconsin, Indiana, and Michigan men would gather logs and brush and pile ground on top using bayonets, shovels, canteen halves, tin plates, and even bare hands. It was as if they knew instinctively that by conserving themselves, their small regiments and famous brigade might continue to exist.

For that was the question many were afraid to consider: What would become of the Old Iron Brigade of the West? Each of the four original regiments delivered 1,000 volunteers to Washington in 1861, and the 24th Michigan added 1,000 more in late 1862. Now, after Gettysburg, fewer than 700 of the 5,000 were still in ranks. The brigade was used up. "It is awful to soldier in this kind of way, only five or six men in a company, and were we N.Y. troops, we would be taken home, or at least relieved from the front," complained 2nd Wisconsin man Charles Dow to the folks back home. "But we have no friends at home to speak for us, and our Generals know very well that the Wis. Boys will fight and not run, they just shove them ahead like a lot of cattle going to slaughter. Well," he added with unshielded bitterness, "it will take but one more shove for the Second, and the 'jig is up.' Then, some man who saw us fight will be promoted to Brigadier General as a reward for our gallantry."[46]

The "shove" came July 16, though in a manner Charles Dow or the others did not expect. In complete disregard for tradition and morale, the high command added the 167th Pennsylvania to what was once the all-Western brigade. The Keystone unit counted 800 men—more than all the survivors of the five original regiments combined—but had seen no serious fighting. What most angered the veterans from Wisconsin, Indiana, and Michigan was the simple fact the new arrivals were nine-month men. In other words, they were draftees. The Pennsylvanians were also sulky and mutinous because they believed their nine months had expired and they were entitled to go home. The first "little difficulty" with the new regiment wrote a 7th Wisconsin man in his diary came on July 30

---

45 George Fink to his brother, *Milwaukee Sentinel*, July 20, 1863.

46 Charles Dow to *Portage Register*, August 1, 1863.

when the Pennsylvanians refused to go on guard duty. They did so only after two or three of the mutineers were arrested. Two days later the drafted men refused to march. The acting commander of the Iron Brigade was now Lysander Cutler, a grim and serious New Englander with little patience. Cutler, Dawes explained:

> ordered the rest of the Brigade to fall in and to load their guns. They formed in line of battle on two sides of the Reg. And they had 5 minutes given them to fall in and take their arms. The 2nd and 6th [Wisconsin] were marched up in a line of battle and the order was given to them to halt and right dress. Then the Gen. gave the order to make ready and then to aim, and quick as that was done the whole of the 167th fell in double quick time and they got out of that camp quicker than any Regt I ever saw go out of camp.

A company of the 6th Wisconsin followed the reluctant soldiers with orders to shoot any man who fell out of ranks. A final report dated August 5 read thusly: "The 167th drafted Regiment started for home. The brass band belonging to the Iron Brigade serenaded them part way to the R.R." [47]

The departure of the Pennsylvania regiment and the return to all-Western status lasted only a few more days when the four companies of the 1st Battalion New York Sharpshooters were added to the brigade. The New Yorkers were three-year men and would stay with the brigade for most of 1864. As veterans the Empire State men were generally welcomed, but the old brigade was not the same as the one that had performed for so well for so long on so many fields. Perhaps some in ranks were beginning to realize the Iron Brigade's greatest days of service were behind it.

A New Flag and a New Song

The twin Union victories at Gettysburg in Pennsylvania and Vicksburg on the Mississippi River rocked the Confederacy. Its armies were still in the field, however, and the war was moving now into a darker stage. In the East, General Meade worried that what his army accomplished at Gettysburg might be undone. He maneuvered his forces here and there without major result. Confederate Robert E. Lee and his army remained a major and threatening force. Farther west Maj. Gen. William Rosecrans scored a major strategic and nearly bloodless coup in the Tullahoma Campaign when he forced Gen. Braxton Bragg's Confederate army out

---

47 The Pennsylvanians joined the brigade on July 16, as they were halted on the north bank of the Potomac River. Dawes, *Service*, 194; Nolan, *Iron Brigade*, 367.

of Tennessee and into northern Georgia and seized the important rail and river town of Chattanooga. Bragg routed Rosecrans at Chickamauga that September, but was unable to capitalize on the victory. Two months later, with a new Union commander named U. S. Grant in charge, the Federals drove Bragg's Army of Tennessee away from Chattanooga and set the stage for a campaign to capture Atlanta.

In the Army of the Potomac, meantime, the staggering losses suffered by the First Corps at Gettysburg triggered a series of wholesale command changes through the organization from top to bottom. Its commander John Reynolds was dead, and John Newton permanently replaced him—despite objections that he was an outsider. The active campaigning exhausted and sickened the First Division's commander, James Wadsworth, and the aging general left on extended leave beginning July 17. Medical leave was also the fate of injured Iron Brigade commander Sol Meredith, who went home to Indiana to recuperate only to return that November to find that field service was too much for him. Meredith was ordered to light duty at posts in Illinois and Kentucky. Colonels Lysander Cutler of the 6th Wisconsin and William Robinson of the 7th Wisconsin shared brigade command in Meredith's absence.

At the regimental level, the 2nd Wisconsin's Lucius Fairchild left the army to begin a long and controversial political career helped by the empty sleeve of his coat—a never-ending reminder to voters of his service at Gettysburg. John Mansfield replaced him. Rufus Dawes remained in day-to-day command of the 6th Wisconsin in the place of the injured Edward Bragg. Samuel Williams led the 19th Indiana, Col. Henry Morrow the 24th Michigan, and William Robinson the 7th Wisconsin. An unexpected bit of trouble hit them all when a new War Department policy was enacted that cut off officer promotions when rosters fell below a certain level. One officer called the decision a far-reaching "blunder" that damaged the spirits and efficiency of the volunteer army.

Despite the outstanding ability he had demonstrated at Gettysburg, Lt. Col. Rufus Dawes was no longer eligible for promotion because his regiment had suffered such heavy losses. The governor of a state could commission a colonel in case of vacancy, but the United States' mustering officer could not muster a colonel for the bloodied 6th Wisconsin. As Dawes put it, "an honorable promotion [was a] reward and recognition of perilous service [and] an inestimable prize to a true soldier."[48]

---

48 Nolan, *Iron Brigade*, 266-267; Dawes, *Service*, 189. See Nolan for a full listing of promotions and other changes in the brigade.

Two shining moments helped the brigade pass through those long days after the harrowing experience of Gettysburg: The arrival of a new song, and the presentation of a new flag. The former was the effort of young Lt. Loyd Harris. Always fond of music, he became convinced the now-famous Western Brigade needed a quickstep to match its prowess in battle. Harris contacted H. N. Hempsted in Milwaukee, the composer of the celebrated Milwaukee Light Guard Quickstep, about composing a special march for his outfit. Hempsted agreed, but only if subscriptions for 300 copies at .50-cents each could be obtained before he wrote a note. The deal was struck, the money sent off, and the promised sheet music soon reached camp. The Iron Brigade Quickstep was presented with a brilliant title page featuring lithographs of Sol Meredith, Edward Bragg, Lucius Fairchild, William Robinson, and Sam Williams. The 24th Michigan had just joined the brigade, explained Harris, "and had I known then how bravely they would have sustained the fighting reputation of the brigade, I would have added their gallant Col [Henry] Morrow's good looking features to the group."

The sheet music found the brigade on the march near the Rapidan River, "destitute of wrappers, postage stamps, in fact all that was necessary to forward them to our homes, sweet hearts and wives," complained Harris. Nonetheless, many of the copies found their way back to Wisconsin, Indiana, and Michigan in "all sorts of self-made envelopes," wrote Harris, who went on to admit that "the music was not so pleasing to the ear as the Light Guard Quickstep. But the name sold it, and I understand that it has the second best record on sales of all of Hempsted's compositions. . . . I regret that the publisher has allowed the title page to be changed, for the piece is now published simple and unadorned by the galaxy of stars."[49]

The new flag was the effort of citizens proud of brigade's record at Gettysburg and elsewhere ("one of the most glorious organizations in the entire army," was how a *New York Times* correspondent described the brigade). The civilians raised $1,000 and commissioned Tiffany & Company of New York to produce a banner of the richest construction "as a testimonial of the appreciation in which the Brigade is held for its bravery, gallantry and valor." Mounted on a special staff with a massive silver spear head, the flag carried the names of all five regiments together with their various well-earned battle honors. The plan was to present it on September 17, 1863, the one-year anniversary of Antietam, with dignitaries including Alexander Randall, Wisconsin's first war governor, in attendance. A "beautifully decorated bower" was prepared by regimental work details suitable for

49 Grayson, Loyd G. Harris, *Milwaukee Sunday Telegraph*, January 18, 1880.

Iron Brigade Tiffany Flag

Funds for this Tiffany & Co. presentation banner were raised by citizens in Wisconsin, Indiana, and Michigan. It is presently housed in the Wisconsin Veterans Museum in Madison. *Wisconsin Veterans Museum*

such a "grand affair." Marching orders, however, arrived before the proposed date of the event.[50]

50 The flag is presently held by the Wisconsin Veterans Museum at Madison. For more information on this, see Madaus and Zeitlin, *Flags*, and Iron Brigade correspondence, 1200 series, Wisconsin Historical Society.

Nevertheless, on the appointed day W. Yates Selleck of Milwaukee, Wisconsin's military agent at Washington, caught up with the brigade at Culpeper, Virginia. The regiments drew up in a square. The presentation had "no splendid bower nor distinguished guests," observed one officer, but "victuals" were on hand, as were "the liquors." Selleck gave a brief speech and presented the flag to Col. William Robinson of the 7th Wisconsin. As befitted its stature as the oldest regiment, the 2nd Wisconsin, served as the official escort for the new colors. One of the highlights was the reading of a letter by Selleck from the army's former commander George B. McClellan: "My heart and prayers are ever with them, and that, although their new colors can witness no more brilliant acts of patriotism and devotion than those which the old torn flags have shared in, I know that on every future field, they and the whole Army of the Potomac, will maintain their part, and the honor of their country and their colors."[51] Afterward, officers made for the full tables. A Wisconsin officer noted for his temperance views wrote his sweetheart the next day that it had turned into "an affair that conferred little honor on the brigade, as gentlemen. I feel glad to say there were a few exceptions." He also reported that the brigade officers and visiting generals "and staff officers within any convenient distance of us were almost unanimously drunk last night. We will see an account of the presentation in the *New York Times*, as I saw the 'graphic and reliable' correspondent of that paper guzzling champagne and wine with the rest of them." Another Badger labeled the drunken affair "a most disgraceful thing that spoiled the whole." The officers had several barrels of whiskey on hand, and "most all got drunk." A guard was posted by the whiskey barrels, the soldier said, but 'the guard got drunk and the tables kicked down and the result was that most of the whole Brigade was drunk and the supper that was prepared for us was spoiled." The spree of epic proportions went on for two days and disturbed the sleep of the enlisted men. The rank and file, admitted one private, "got what they could swipe, which was not a small amount." Another private called it "a gala day."

The new flag had no official place with the brigade, however. The men could not keep it because regulations forbade all but official banners, so the officers of the

---

51 State legislatures provided state agents whose duties attached them to regiments to serve soldier needs. Duties included distributing mail and goods sent from home, visiting hospitals to see the soldiers received adequate care, and helping to administer the state's new voting-in-the-field law. Democrats contended the agents were in fact "political commissars" interested in "manufacturing Republican votes from camp and battlefield." Governor Lewis Harvey directed Selleck, of Milwaukee, be attached to the Washington area rather than regiments. Selleck was often praised for his work. The criticism of state agents is found in the *Madison Daily Patriot*, September 9, November 8, 12, 1862. Frank L. Klement, *The Gettysburg Soldiers' Cemetery and Lincoln's Address*, "A Milwaukeean Witnesses Lincoln's Gettysburg Address: W. Yates Selleck and the Soldiers' Cemetery at Gettysburg," (Shippensburg, PA, 1993), 122-123.

five regiments resolved to send the flag to Washington with Wisconsin Agent Selleck.[52]

Home and the Veteran Question

Private William Ray returned to his 7th Wisconsin on September 25, 1863, nearly three months after being wounded in the head at Gettysburg. Pronounced fit for service by the surgeons, he made his way back to the army at Culpeper, Virginia, and reached his regiment about noon. Most of the men of his Grant County company were out on picket duty when he arrived. The boys were generally okay, he was told, although two of the men wounded and probably captured at Gettysburg had not yet returned. Captain Henry F. Young was sick, and "looks bad as he has for a number of weeks," Lt. Alphonse Kidd was still lame from his Gettysburg injury, and Lt. Col. John B. Callis was at home recovering from his chest wound—the Rebel ball that had lodged in his lung. Ray told his journal that he found the boys "well situated and living well." There was mutton and pork thanks to nearby farmers, and the country around camp did not show the scars of war so much as in most places of Virginia.

Also comforting, Private Ray continued, was that his company was "living like brothers [and] very much attached to each other." The fighting at Gettysburg had touched the survivors of the original 107 volunteers (Ray called them the "essence" of his company) who had left Grant County so long ago. "They are or seem to be well satisfied with their lot. They seem to be more devoted with their work than I ever saw them." The "brotherly feeling" also extended to the officers. "It does my very soul good to see it. I can never forget how Brave the officers was at Gettysburg especially Lieut [William] Sloat. He gave the cowards and stragglers no Peace at all, kept driving them to their Regts. And them that their Regts was too far away he put them in our Regt." Across the Rapidan River, not far from the peace and harmony in camp, Ray and his comrades could see Confederate pickets.[53]

The weather was good and Ray and the other Western men settled into a soldierly routine. The men appreciated the light duty and their new Springfield

52 Dawes, letters of September 6, September 13, September 17, and September 18, 1863, to Mary Beman Gates; Dawes, *Service*, 202-204; Cheek and Pointon, *Sauk County*, 80; Rood, diary. Walker wrote: "The presentation came off this afternoon. The whole brigade was out and also Battery B. The presentation speech as made by Mr. Sellick [sic]. After that Col. Robinson made a speech. The regiments were all marched to their own quarters and the officers went and got drunk, some of them." Charles Walker, diary, September 17, 1863.

53 Ray, *Iron Brigade*, September 25, 26, 27, 1863.

rifle-muskets, issued to replace the regiment's Austrian Lorenz shoulder arms. Ray called the new weapon "a splendidly finished piece [too nice] to use in the field. The finish on them would entitle them to a rack in a gentlemans Parlor. The boys are very proud of them and take the best care of them."

A week after Ray's return, excitement swept the regiment when a proposal arrived for the soldiers to enter a "Veterans Corps." The question was whether the boys who enlisted in 1861 were willing to see the war through to its conclusion. Many of the volunteer regiments were reaching the end of their three-year enlistments—just at a time when victory seemed possible. The men and boys who were the first to volunteer and who had borne the brunt of the fighting might just pack up and go home. In the Army of the Potomac alone, the enlistments for more than 75 regiments were set to expire before the end of August 1864. Worried Army officials had published an order on June 25, 1863, giving authority for veteran re-enlistments of "all able bodied men between the ages of eighteen and forty-five years, who have heretofore enlisted and have served not less than nine months." If three-fourths of the men on the regimental roster of a volunteer regiment re-enlisted, the order continued, each soldier would receive a $402.00 bounty paid in six installments over the three years (this at a time when privates collected $13 a month) and a 30-day furlough—the "veteran volunteers" to be sent home as a regiment to enjoy it. The order caused quite a stir, not only in the 7th Wisconsin, but the other Iron Brigade regiments as well. "There seems to be a good many that will go," said Ray.

There was much to support such a "veteranization." Approaching was their third Christmas away from home in this long, grim civil war. To the common soldiers of the Iron Brigade it seemed that, despite the thousands of deaths and other hardships told and untold, there was still much to be resolved. Lee's Rebel army lay just across the river, and there was quiet coffee fire talk of a possible Confederate invasion of Kentucky or Ohio, or even another offensive against the Army of the Potomac onto Northern soil. Some Black Hats argued that the war had turned at Gettysburg, and the hope of the Confederacy now rested on a political end to the war or the success of a peace candidate over Abraham Lincoln in the upcoming presidential election of 1864.

It was not the usual weather or winter duty or progress of the war that filled soldier talk, but the vexing "veteran question" and the warm prospect they might be going home, if only for a short time. The matter was discussed in quiet serious tones and with boastful shouts and wild laughter. After almost three years of the harshest service, death, illness, and suffering, even the thought of seeing home was almost beyond comprehension. It had been some thirty months since the Wisconsin and Indiana regiments left their states amid shouts and cheers and the music of town bands. Home to most of the men was now a few pictures, a packet of folded letters, and dim memories of the places and loved ones left behind. Now, at least for those willing to re-enlist, there was the promise of warm homecomings, soft beds, and kitchens with good smells and full tables. But there was more to going home than the expected welcome. They had marched off full of innocent patriotic zeal caught up in the great crusade for the Union. They would return as heroes in one of the most famous organizations of the Union armies, veterans of the Iron Brigade of the West.

There was more to the issue than just going home, of course. Some Black Hats argued the war could be successfully concluded within the year, and that re-enlistment would allow them to "share the glory of a continuous service to the end of the war." If the month-long furlough was a most "tempting bait," however, other matters were just as important: "Down in the hearts of the men there was the manhood of patriotism," one veteran Jerome Watrous explained, "the feeling that the country needed them, and that they would not be contented at home while armies were contending."

The elements of the Army of the Potomac were still marching here and there and engaged in some of the last skirmishing of the 1863 summer campaign, but Ray's journal entries contained his thoughts on the veteran issue:

October 5, 1863: They got up considerable excitement [over the veteran question] and I believe it will work. But as for me, I don't know what to do with it. For Mother requests that I shouldn't enlist again. And I shall hate to see the Boys all go and me go into some other Regt. I consider a Mothers wish should be complied with. But I think she would rather see me coming home with the Co than go amonst strangers . . .

October 6, 1863: Great excitement about reenlisting. The papers were drawn up and most of the Co signed. But I wouldn't at first until I had a little talk with Cap . . . who advised me to go. He said that when they got back to the State and got furlough to go home and when he come to see Mother she would want to know why William didn't come. . . . This going home & getting a furlough and getting the Big Bounty and more than all this, we will belong to the Veterans Corps and have the Badge of Honor to wear. The honor of belonging to the Veteran Corps is something. Taking it all together I must go and the more effective it will have on the war will be as good as a hard Battle and perhaps many Battles. Just think the old troops going in again after having such hard times, it shows our hearts are in the work. The thought will make the Rebels tremble.

October 7, 1863: The excitement continues unabated about reenlisting. There are a few that try to put a damper on the thing. But I guess they will fail. The Boys generally want to go. . . . They say the 6th [Wisconsin] and the 2nd [Wisconsin] don't go into it so strong as we do. They are between a Hawk and a Buzzard about it. I want to go the more I think about it. Going in under the same officers is what just suits me. Our Co officers are good and well liked in the Co . . .

October 30, 1863: Our going home has played out. We cant go, so the War Department say. So the Veteran Business is played out and we stay 10 months more and go home for good. The President has called for 300,000 more men to be raised by Volunteering by the 4th of Jan next. And if not raised by that time there will be a draft to fill it up. All those are designed to fill up old Regt. Go ahead old Abe, I will support you in that.

There was other news as well:

October 31, 1863: We were mustered at 10 A.M. today for 2 months more pay, $26.00 by Maj. Finnecum [Mark Finnicum]. We had no Inspection as we used to. He only called out names. The Regt is small, the largest Co. is only 26 men for duty & we are next. We have 23 for duty . . .

November 2, 1863: Today there was a detail sent out of each of the Regts that were in the fight at Gainesville to rebury the dead. They found them almost naked, many of them quite naked . . .

That November, while members of the brigade discussed the veterans' question, President Lincoln made a trip to Pennsylvania to dedicate a soldier cemetery at Gettysburg. A number of Iron Brigade men were on hand for the ceremony. In addition to the members of the Iron Brigade band, Gen. John Gibbon, still recovering from his Gettysburg wound, and his aide, Frank Haskell, traveled to the battleground as representatives of the Army of the Potomac. They brought with them the new Tiffany Iron Brigade flag to display for visitors. "How different from the time we were there before," Haskell wrote home November 20, 1863. "The sights and sounds were all changed. Then it was sultry July—now it is somber November. The leaves and harvests were then green and luxuriant—now they were yellow and sere. Then the sound of hostile cannon shook the earth—now the voices of women and children filled the air."

The bright new flag of "very heavy blue silk, with yellow silk fringe" included the names of the five regiments and the battles in which the brigade was engaged—Gainesville, Bull Run, Antietam, South Mountain, Fredericksburg, and Gettysburg. "That Brigade is known to everybody and the flag was much noticed," Haskell wrote home. Haskell found the ceremonies and the president's brief "Gettysburg Address" of little interest and did not bother even to describe them.

Gibbon and Haskell toured the battlefield after listening to the start of the main oration, explained the general, but returned to the grounds in time to hear what he described as "Mr. Lincoln's touching speech."[54]

The neat arrangement of the cemetery troubled Haskell. The dead, he argued, should be buried where they fought at "the spot where he died nobly fighting the enemies of the country, where perhaps the shout of victory went up with his spirit to Heaven—where his companions in arms, his survivors, had lovingly wrapped him in his blanket, and wet with brave men's tears, had covered him with the earth his blood had consecrated. . . . But no, these things were not to be. The skeletons of these brave men must be handled like the bones of so many horses, for a price, and wedged in rows like herrings in a box, on a spot where there was no fighting—where none of them fell! It may be all right," Haskell added, "but I do not see it . . . but as it is now . . . we have instead a common, badly arranged grave yard, in which names, and graves, if designated at all, are as likely to be wrong as right. But read the newspapers, every body says this is splendid, this making the 'Soldiers' Cemetery,' and I suppose it is."[55]

Haskell would be promoted to colonel and command of the 36th Wisconsin the following February. On June 3, 1864, near Cold Harbor, Virginia, he was killed in action with a shot through the temple. "My God! I have lost my best friend, and one of the best soldiers in the Army of the Potomac has fallen!" exclaimed Gibbon when he heard the news. Haskell's body was transported for burial to Portage, Wisconsin—far from his native Vermont and far from the field on which he fell.[56]

In early December, the Iron Brigade crossed Mountain Run and camped near Kelly's Ford. The column spent much of the day marching past other regiments putting up winter quarters. It looked as though active campaigning was at an end for the year. The next day the Western men reached woods near Kelly's Ford and established camp. Good water and plenty of wood were nearby. Despite rumors the brigade might be moved again, the soldiers went to work and by dark had gathered logs to build shanties. The small huts were laid out in company streets, logs laid along a foundation, floors dug to an acceptable depth to allow a man to stand, and makeshift mud chimneys added. Details went out to cut wood for the construction

---

54 Gibbon, *Recollections*, 184.

55 The full text of the letter is included in *Haskell of Gettysburg*, 232-236.

56 Frank Haskell's body was returned to his brother Harrison at Portage and buried in Silver Lake Cemetery. His long account of Gettysburg was privately printed by his brother about 1881. In 1898, it was included in a history of the Dartmouth Class of 1854, and reprinted in 1908 by the Massachusetts Commandery of the Military Order of the Loyal Legion and that same year by the Wisconsin History Commission.

of the shebangs and stack woodpiles. With the camp well established, soldier thoughts turned to the approaching holidays and memories of faraway homes and loved ones. The homesickness was especially sharp during the quiet times. The mail calls were greeted with more than the usual excitement and the gloom was deeper for those with no letters to read. A few parcels reached the front from Wisconsin and Indiana and Michigan, but were as often as not already ransacked by strangers.

A tough Iron Brigade officer was discovered looking with sadness at a page torn from *Harper's Weekly* tacked to the wall of his hut. It showed a family in a Christmas scene—mother, father, and children, all smiling and happy. The veteran admitted to the visitor his thoughts were of home and loved ones. Another soldier sunk into deep longing for home and what he called "the pleasant country across the great Lake Michigan."

Home seemed a far way off.

1864

The Overland Campaign

to Petersburg

Amos Bissett, Company B, 7th Wisconsin

Brian Hogan

Part I: Into the Wilderness

Sally had a Baby, and the Baby had Red Hair

The Army of the Potomac made its own music. Thoughts of the long marching columns evoked faint echoes of singing soldiers or tooting brass bands. Sometimes it was the stern song about abolitionist John Brown and other times more scandalous airs, such as the one about an unexpected baby with "red hair." The brass bands performed for morning formations and evening tattoos, and during inspections and reviews. The Western men sang as they marched to Gettysburg, and the Iron Brigade band played "Hail, Columbia" and other stirring marches when the Black Hats left the Emmitsburg Road for the long trot to McPherson's Ridge. Music was an integral, if overlooked, part of a Civil War soldier's life. Soldiers sang in camp. They played violins, harmonicas, and other instruments. Songs from those days still have an ability to connect a listener to those men of long ago. "How often on the long weary march," wrote Lt. Loyd Harris, "when it seemed as if our sore and tired limbs almost refused to go on—it was then the full swelling notes from a good band rallied us from the roadside 'into line,' flag unfurled, muskets at a right shoulder shift, gleaming in the bright sun, and the regiment appeared infused with new life and energy."

A native of New York who came into the ranks at Prairie du Chien as a Union volunteer in 1861, Loyd Harris rose to become an officer of the 6th Wisconsin. Long after the war, he wrote a series of memoirs for the *Milwaukee Sunday Telegraph*, light-hearted sketches of marches and camp life and much about the music of those days. Editor Jerome Watrous described Harris as "genial, patriotic, kindly," a writer of "more than ordinary merit, whose articles in this paper have always been read with interest."[1] Harris was eight when his family migrated to Wisconsin from

---

1 Jerome A. Watrous, "The Singing Master," *Milwaukee Sunday Telegraph*, August 29, 1896.

Buffalo, first to Sheboygan and then to Milwaukee. In 1856, when he was sixteen, Harris marched with a volunteer fire company in the funeral of Solomon Juneau, Milwaukee's founder. Rufus King, who was also in the party as foreman of Engine No. 1, was the editor of the *Milwaukee Sentinel*. The foreman of Engine No. 6 in that same parade was Irishman Thomas Kerr, who would also make a name for himself in the Iron Brigade. By age nineteen, Harris was on his own working as an express agent in the Mississippi River community of Prairie du Chien. He was one of the first to "shoulder a musket and enter the ranks as high private."[2] Wealthy industrialist Norman Wiard, who invented an ice boat that ran from Prairie du Chien to Winona, Minnesota, and later designed a rifled artillery barrel, gave the new recruit a gold watch that Harris would show to President Abraham Lincoln.

Soon after reaching Washington Harris was advanced to sergeant and on October 31, 1861, to second lieutenant. One of his comrades remembered that Harris "made something of a reputation as a singer of old airs as well as the newly published army songs." After he put on "the shoulder straps, wore better clothes, and had more leisure than a first sergeant has," he organized a body of singers ("all young, brave and handsome," said one soldier). It was "during the long, dreary winter of 1861-62" when the officers and men of the regiment and brigade were serenaded by the 'Harris quartette or singing class.'" His friend concluded: "I am fully conscious that Captain Harris and his associate singers saved many a man from homesickness that undid men, even strong men, that first winter in camp."[3]

One of those singers was Capt. Edwin Brown, who would die at Antietam and leave a wife and young orphans behind. Two other singers were Lt. Orinn Chapman of the Crawford County Jayhawkers and Capt. John Ticknor of the Lemonweir Minute Men; both were shot down at Gettysburg. It was Captain Brown those long winter nights who would call out in a bright voice, "Let's do 'Benny Havens!'" How the men enjoyed the young officers singing the old West Point drinking song in the quiet of a dark army camp. After Brown's loss at Antietam, however, and the loss of Chapman and Ticknor in Pennsylvania, the regimental singers refused to lift their voices to "Benny Havens, O"—for it brought memories too painful to bear. "I shall be killed in battle," Brown told his singing friends one night in a solemn voice that echoed his homesickness. He escaped South Mountain only to fall in the Miller farm yard at Antietam. Two days after his body was sent home in a metal casket, an officer arrived with an item found

2 L. G. Harris, "All about Old Times," *Milwaukee Sunday Telegraph*, September 1, 1894. Butterfield Consul Willshire, *History of Crawford and Richland Counties, Wisconsin* (Springfield, Ill., 1884), 497-499, 515.

3 Watrous, *Milwaukee Telegraph*, August 29, 1896.

Lt. Loyd Harris, 6th Wisconsin Infantry

Harris brought his violin to war and wrote afterward of the music of the camps and marches of the Iron Brigade and the Army of the Potomac. *Wisconsin Historical Society 10699*

on the body of a dead Rebel officer: Brown's identification medal, a small brass coin-shaped device with his name and regiment on one side and an embossed eagle and the words "War of 1861" on the other. Brown had given the brass ID to a pair of children a few weeks earlier in the kitchen of a Virginia home where he, Rufus Dawes, and Harris begged and bought a meal. The children reminded Brown of his own. They were shy and he won them over (as well as their mother) by showing them the medal and then giving it to them. How the Confederate soldier acquired the medal remains a mystery.[4]

During marches long or short when the bands ceased playing, Harris said, a chorus of voices would lift from the columns. The Prairie du Chien boys especially liked to sing:

> *O never mind the weather, but get over double trouble,*
> *For we are bound for the happy land of Canaan.*

Then the Juneau County boys (despite "religious warnings" from the pious Rufus Dawes), would add:

---

4   Grayson [Loyd Harris], "A War Medal," *Milwaukee Sunday Telegraph*, February 5, 1884. The song refers to a tavern near the U.S. Military Academy at West Point, N.Y. operated by Benny Havens. It was a favorite hangout for the cadets.

My name it is Joe Bower
I have a brother Ike,
I came from old Missouri
Just all the way from Pike.

After several verses of "Joe Bower" the company would conclude with the
sequel where "Sally had a baby, and the baby had red hair." That always brought a
roar of laughter, recalled one man, and then the Irish "Skull-crackers" of the 6th
Wisconsin would pitch in with a song endorsed by them:

Here's a health to Martin Hannegan's aunt,
And I'll tell ye the reason why;
She eats bekase she is hungry,
And drinks bekase she is dhry.
And if ever a man
Stopped the course of a can,
Martin Hannegan's aunt would cry—
Arrh, fill up your glass,
And let the jug pass
How d'ye know but your neighbor is dry.

The songs of the Milwaukee Germans were a special favorite, said Harris.
"How often . . . did I steal quietly to their camp-fire and, perhaps concealed by the
shadow of a friendly tree, listen . . . as in the bright fire-light, their voices in pure
harmony rang out on the quiet scene." In quiet times, the Germans sang:

Blue is the flower called the forget me not,
Ah, lay it on their heart, and think of me.

Or, in happier times:

The Pope he leads a happy life.
He knows no care or married life.

It was Harris, of course, who listed the favorite songs of that army of long ago,
from "Ever of Thee" to "John Brown's Body." Others included "Sweet bye and
bye," "Tramp, Tramp, Tramp, the boys are marching," and "Rally Round the flag."
The Rebel bands could be heard across the rivers playing "Bonnie Blue Flag,"
"Dixie," "My Maryland," and "Stonewall Jackson's Way."

The violin he carried east as an enlisted man from Prairie du Chien traveled in the field officer's regimental mess chest, thanks to Lt. Col. Ben Sweet, a lover of music who was later promoted to the 21st Wisconsin and left the regiment. Sweet's favorite was "Ever of Thee."[5] Harris played for others, but when alone "gratified my own taste in playing a variety of operatic airs a little too select for a mixed audience of my army friends." He was playing a favorite air from "Norma" when two rough-looking soldiers from another brigade approached and listened at the door. "Stranger, while yet got yar hand in jes' play us the 'Rankensack Traveler,'" one suggested. Harris shook his head. "No." "Wall then, shake out 'Pork Packin' in Cincinnati." Harris ignored the request. "How about 'Sally in Our Alley,' eh! Can't play that? Then give me 'Hell on the Wabash.'" When there was no response, the requester turned to his friend and said, "Come pard, let's move on; when we come back, that fellow may have his fiddle tuned and shake out something for us."[6]

It was not only the soldiers who sang in the camps, but the contraband cooks, strikers, and other former slaves who gathered with the soldiers. On one occasion, said Harris, one such singer astonished his listeners by singing a favorite of his old master:

"I'll load my gun wid ball and lead,
And shoot old Linkum in the head."

After the laughter subsided, the boys "assumed the most virtuous indignation and informed the singer that he was 'guilty of treason in the most corrugated form.' (that word made him tremble all over), and as punishment he must be 'loaded into a cannon and fired back to the tobacco factory of his old master.'" The camp striker begged another chance and when told to go ahead, with "a broad grin extending from ear to ear, he roared . . . "

---

5 Sweet was promoted to colonel of the 21st Wisconsin and was severely wounded in the battle of Perryville. When a group of Wisconsin citizens appeared on the scene to care for the wounded and dead it included Otis B. Hopkins of Milwaukee, an aide to the governor and the brother-in-law of Loyd Harris. Harris had sent a note to Hopkins to see about his friend. Recovering at Chilton, Wisconsin, Sweet, who lost the full use of his right arm, wrote Harris a letter, telling how Hopkins brought "dainty food, underclothing for change, and what was better kind, hopeful, cheering words. So you see that a thousand miles away from me you yet did much to soothe the pains and sorrows of my sick couch. Such is the power and far-reaching benefits of friendship . . . . Remember me kindly to the old Sixth. I have watched its career since the June day when I left it at Fredericksburg with never-failing pride and interest. What changes have come over us since then, Yours, Ever, Truly, B. J. Sweet." B. J. Sweet, "Grayson" [Loyd Harris], "Music in the Army," *Milwaukee Sunday Telegraph*, November 26, 1882.

6 Harris, "Music in the Army," November 26, 1882.

I'll load my gun wid ball and lead,
And shoot Jeff Davis in de head.

That verse brought even more cheering, more laughter, and then lengthy applause.

One story never forgotten involved the fine band of the 24th Michigan, fresh from Detroit and Wayne County. The new regiment was moved forward into position at Fredericksburg just in front of the 6th Wisconsin under the cover of a dense fog. The band was playing "Hail Columbia, Happy Land," when the sun broke through the fog and the trained guns of a half-dozen Confederate batteries opened. One of the first shells landed "in the midst of the band, scattering them right and left." The survivors made for the sheltering bank of the river as Col. Henry Morrow held his regiment under the guns, shouting, "Steady, men, those Wisconsin men are watching you." The teller of the story admitted, however, he could not remember ever again seeing the band of the 24th Michigan again in any hard-fought battles thereafter.[7]

Much of the music of the Army of the Potomac faded after Gettysburg. Many of the singers were dead or gone by the time the calendar turned to 1864. The war was taking on a harder edge, and the soldiers were stripped down for hard fighting. The winter camps were not as pleasant, and the long quiet times unmarked by fighting. The music had been all but beaten out of the army.

Going Home on 30-Day Furlough

The new year did offer one bright spot for some members of the Iron Brigade. It did not matter that the last week of 1863 in Virginia proved the stormiest of the year. It did not matter that a strong wind carrying a wet snow swept in from the northwest and covered the Rappahannock River camps to the depth of a man's boot tops. It did not matter that Christmas Day, an uncertain holiday for a lonely soldier in the field, arrived with cold and stillness. All that mattered was the Wisconsin and Indiana boys were going home. By the end of December 1863, the votes on the veteran question were taken and counted. No one realized it at the time, but the individual decisions cast within the regiments brought about the end of their storied association. The mustering of the new veteran volunteers came December 31, with the pay officers appearing on New Year's Day. "Signed the

---

7   Harris wrote of army music in four articles in the *Milwaukee Sunday Telegraph*. They appeared November 12 and 26, and December 12 and 31, 1882.

payroll and got my pay amounting to $194.50," one happy Black Hat wrote in his diary.[8]

The results were surprising. The 7th Wisconsin, with 249 on the rolls, re-enlisted 218 as veterans. The 6th Wisconsin, with 290 men, signed 237. The 2nd Wisconsin, however, used up by hard service, mustered only forty veteran enlistments with the remaining 170 on the rolls to be sent home in June. The 19th Indiana re-enlisted 213 men, but in some mix-up never explained, was ruled short of the goal of three-fourths of the roster; the unit was not recognized as a veteran volunteer regiment. Unlike the 6th and 7th Wisconsin, which were declared veteran regiments, the Indiana re-enlisting men would have to leave behind their muskets and accouterments. The 24th Michigan's three-year enlistment ran until 1865. The vote convinced one Wisconsin veteran to write home with pride: "The men, who have stood by the old flag through fair and foul weather, and through many bloody battles, almost to a man dedicated their lives and services anew to their country."[9]

The month of veteran furlough during the early weeks of 1864 was remembered with fondness. The regiment's first colonel, Lysander Cutler, who paraded the 6th Wisconsin through Milwaukee on its way to the front in 1861, wrote a proud letter January 9 to the Milwaukee Chamber of Commerce about the return. "More than half of the thousand young and old men who followed me from your midst have been killed or wounded, and many of them have been wounded several times," wrote Cutler. "What are left of the regiment have enlisted as veterans and will soon visit the State in a body, and it is expected they will come by way of your city. The object of this is to bespeak for them such a reception as is due to such a body of men. Out of over a thousand, but few more than two hundred will return: every one a hero. You can not do them too much an honor."

The start for home began on a hard note for the 6th Wisconsin. The 227 soldiers suffered from cold in unheated freight cars on the first sixty-mile leg of their journey. One man was so frozen he was left behind in an Alexandria, Virginia, hospital. At Washington, the veterans "replenished their wardrobe with fine suits of clothes and new hat trimmings." A member of the 2nd Wisconsin working as a clerk in the Wisconsin Soldier's Aid Society remembered the visit in a letter home. "They (the 6th) have left behind them a name not soon to be forgotten, for sobriety, manly bearing and fine appearance. They were here [in Washington] three days ago and not a single man was put in the guard house." Colonel Edward Bragg engaged seats at Ford's Theater for "all 220 of his men," the clerk noted, "and it was

---

8   Charles Walker, diary, Institute for Civil War Studies.

9   Dawes, *Service*, 235; Quiner, *Military History*, 482.

a good triumph for Wisconsin, and enough to make the heart of a Badger Jump for Joy to see those war worn veterans, just from the battle, and from the rough camp life of over two years, where they were deprived of everything pertaining to civilization and not one single unbecoming remark made." Famed tragedian Joseph Proctor had the lead role in "Lion of the Forest" at Ford's and upon "being cheered" by the soldiers at the end of the performance, waved and shook his head to show that the clapping was misdirected and should go instead to the veterans, and then he "complimented them highly."[10]

Colonel Bragg visited the War Department for the flag of the 2nd Mississippi captured at Gettysburg and a few days later, on January 13, the regiment would carry it down Milwaukee's main street in a foot of snow. It was to be nailed to a wall in the Chamber of Commerce hall for the month of furlough so citizens could come look at it. The regiment's parade was accompanied by six companies of the 30th Wisconsin, now under the command of Col. Daniel J. Dill, formally a captain in the 6th regiment, and the Milwaukee Light Infantry militia company. "At a few minutes past one o'clock the cortege made its appearance [at the Chamber Hall]," reported the *Milwaukee Sentinel*, "headed by Christian Bach's excellent band playing: 'The Year of Jubilee.' The veterans marched into the hall and the escort was dismissed. As the regiment entered, they were greeted with a salvos of cheers. They formed in the center of the room in close column by company, and at the command of Colonel Bragg, brought their pieces to an order with a thud that elicited rounds of applause." It was the first parade of veterans the city had witnessed, and it included members of two Milwaukee companies—the Irish Montgomery Guard and the German Citizens' Corps. "Their long service had so perfected them in drill that they marched as one man, giving more the impression of a homogeneous mass of military force, controlled by one will. . . . The whole city was out to welcome them with continuous cheers along the line of march."

Singled out for attention was Frank Wallar, who had captured the displayed Confederate flag. A breathless report dated January 16 in the *Milwaukee Sentinel* described how Wallar sprang "out in advance of all the rest, and rushing among the rebel host with a ferocity of a thousand tigers, wrested the standard from the color bearer." A number of prominent men were also on hand, but the one received with the most warmth and applause by the returning veterans was one-armed Lucius Fairchild, late of the 2nd Wisconsin and now Wisconsin's secretary of state. The *Sentinel* also noted the returnees "all look rugged and hearty." A military ball

10 William P. Taylor, letter to Jane S. Taplin, January 11, 1864, Washington, DC, Oshkosh, Wisconsin, Public Museum Record, 68/294.

followed at the Newhall House, where festivities were described by one soldier as "gay beyond measure for the veterans who had just emerged from the hardships and dangers of many campaigns."

It was during this joyful time that Lt. Loyd Harris got the sad word that Matt Bernard, the runaway slave who had walked into his regiment and became a cook for the officers, was dying of smallpox. Bernard was famous in the regiment for his steadfastness and display of courage under fire. He was one of the first men to jump up and pull down the rail fences at Gainesville to allow Battery B of the 4th U.S. Artillery to reach the field. He had marched with the regiment up the main street of Milwaukee in the January snow after the long ride back to Wisconsin. "Human skill and good treatment were of no avail," lamented Harris, "and in a retired spot in the outskirts of beautiful Milwaukee lies buried a once poor old slave who, freed by the pen of Lincoln and the sword of McClellan, proved his gratitude in more than one way by faithful service to his country."[11]

The new veteran volunteers of the 7th Wisconsin left their camp on a cold and windy January 4 for the capital and were put up for the night in No. 4 Barracks of a holding area. "There being good fires in the stoves, it was somewhat comfortable," one Black Hat wrote in his journal. The next two days the boys used passes to shop in Washington to buy clothing and other items for the trip home. Private William Ray got an overcoat, dress coat, knapsack, and haversack, plus a new hat, vest, and pants. The soldiers roamed freely, Ray added, "all the pass needed was to have the figure 7 on their hats." Three days later the new "veteran volunteers" got on trains for Baltimore. In Pittsburgh, many of the veterans went to an evening performance at a local theater, where their knapsacks were stolen by thieves. Chicago was reached on January 11 and Madison, Wisconsin, the next day. The regiment formed and marched up and around the capital square with the drums beating. The capitol building was opened and Gov. James T. Lewis gave a welcome speech ("short and to the point," one said), the paperwork was completed, and the boys released for their furloughs.

Private Albert Morse reached his home in Lancaster on a Sunday and found his family seated at the dinner table with his older brother, Edward, at the head. He had been away almost three years as had two other soldier brothers, and was much changed from the boy who left home in 1861. Edward stood up and pushed the table over to make room. "Welcome brother. Come on in," he offered with a smile. "I don't know which one of you it is but welcome anyhow. Welcome home." It was his only furlough during four years of service. Pvt. William Ray and friends took the

---

11 Details of the Milwaukee welcome are found in Frank A. Flower, *History of Milwaukee, Wisconsin* (Milwaukee, WI, 1881); Harris, *Telegraph*, April 8, 1883.

express train to Bridgeport, where Ray made an acquaintance with Reuben R. Wood of La Crosse, late captain of the 2nd Wisconsin Cavalry. Wood gave them a ride to Patch Grove for .25 cents each. Ray hitched a ride with a teamster (cost $1.60) who carried him to within half a mile of his home, where he found his mother with four other members of his family. "I will leave it to the reader to imagine how happy we were," he wrote in his journal.[12]

During those free and easy days at home, reported a weekly newspaper in central Wisconsin, the veterans monopolized all "horses, cutters, sleighs and young lady's to be found in the vicinity." There were also several social notices: Lt. William S. Campbell wed Millie Pixley in Portage City, and William Palmer of the Sauk County Riflemen "took a wife in the person of Miss Clara Kern of Sumpter." George Bush of the 7th Wisconsin also married his sweetheart, Charlotte Gard.[13]

Lieutenant Colonel Rufus Dawes left the 6th Wisconsin at Pittsburgh to go home to Marietta, Ohio, where he married Mary Beman Gates in a 5:30 a.m. service Monday morning, January 18, 1864. Besides family, there were only a handful of guests because of the early hour. The young officer and his new wife then left by train for Milwaukee to join the regiment. At one point a strike by locomotive engineers delayed the journey and the couple rented a sleigh for a twelve-mile drive across country to another rail connection to continue in a freight train. "Of course under such circumstances," Dawes remembered, "the trip was in every respect delightful." The new Mrs. Dawes never saw her husband's regiment except to see in a hall the "stacks of muskets with belts and cartridge boxes hanging upon them, as left by the column when broken for the men to visit their homes." Dawes' mare, wounded at Gettysburg, had been shipped with the regiment by train. He was riding her along an icy Milwaukee street when the animal slipped at a corner and dislocated the new bridegroom's ankle. He was unable to return to active duty for several weeks. "This accident," the young husband admitted, "was regarded as a great piece of good fortune."[14]

The 19th Indiana veterans left Virginia on January 13, arrived in Indianapolis on the 17th, and formed the next day for a public reception. "The men are happy to get home again; they want to see their friends; they expect to see them; let them not be disappointed," suggested the *Indianapolis Daily Journal*. The Masonic Hall was

12 Morse, *Grandad*, 15. The details of the return of the 7th Wisconsin are in Ray, *Iron Brigade*, January 2-14. Morse enlisted from Tafton on August 19, 1861. He mustered out with his regiment in July 1865. *Wisconsin Roster*, vol. 1, 560.

13 Cheek and Pointon, *Sauk County*, 86-87; Watrous, *Milwaukee Telegraph*, February 25, 1899; Bush family records as provided by Brett Wilson.

14 Dawes, *Service*, 237-238.

packed. A warm welcome greeted Gov. Oliver Morton, but it was "Long Sol" Meredith's appearance that raised his old boys to greet him with cheer after cheer. These men, the tall general told the crowd, shared in all the honors won by the Army of the Potomac and the welcome they received "at the hands of friends at home compensates for all they have endured."[15] The Hoosiers were dismissed and made for home. The reunion with his old regiment turned sour the next day when Meredith's son, Lt. Samuel Meredith, wounded in the neck at Gainesville in 1862, fell ill and died of lung fever on January 19 at age twenty-five. Sol Meredith buried his son and was confined to his room with fever and exhaustion. He was also spitting up blood from his Gettysburg injury.

The thirty days ended much too quickly. The 6th Wisconsin gathered at Milwaukee and the 7th Wisconsin at Racine to catch trains to Washington. At Crestline, Ohio, Lt. Amos Rood and Capt. Fred Warner of the 7th Wisconsin left the train to find a saloon. "I knew orders forbid this, but we sailed on along . . . . Charged into a place, and there sat Col. Robinson and Lt. Col. Callis taking their quiet drink!" wrote Rood. "Oh me! Oh my! I had my cheek on; so I said, 'Col., Capt W and I thought we'd drop in and grab some pizen [whiskey].'" Robinson gave the two a long look. "Rood—I see you boys won't obey orders! You are regular . . . foragers, but you had better sit down and have a snort of grog." It was too good an invitation to resist, admitted Rood, since all four were en route "to see old Mars, Bobby Lee and his Confederates."[16]

The train carrying the 7th Wisconsin left the track in Pennsylvania and "sent ties & railroad iron in every direction for about 20 rods." Fortunately, the only injury was the smashed leg of a brakeman. The 19th Indiana men rendezvoused at Indianapolis on February 18, but paperwork and other issues kept them there until the 24th, when loaded aboard a train for the trip back east. The parting from home and family was difficult. "I never hated any thing in my life as bad as I did to leave my dear old mother," one Hoosier admitted. "I had to keep whistling, singing, all the way to Selma to keep it off my mind." The returning soldiers stayed at the Soldiers Home at Baltimore during the night of February 27, and reached the capital at Washington the next day. They did not reach Culpeper Court House until March 5, where reception and music waited "to Meet the Returning Braves of Indiana."

15 *Indianapolis Daily Journal*, January 18, 1864.

16 Rood, diary. Warner enlisted at Stanton on August 5, 1861. He mustered out September 17, 1864, term expired. Rood enlisted September 13, 1861, at Milwaukee and resigned December 9, 1864, wounded. *Wisconsin Roster*, vol. 1, 561, 572. For a detailed account of the Wilderness, see Gordon C. Rhea, *The Battle of the Wilderness, May 5-6, 1864* (Baton Rouge, LA, 1994).

Grant Wants Fighters

The three were back in their old camps by early March to face several important changes. The most important was the appointment of Ulysses S. Grant, famous for his victory at Vicksburg on the Mississippi River and his pronouncements of "unconditional surrender," as commander of all the Union armies. Although George Gordon Meade remained in command of the always politically charged Army of the Potomac, Grant decided to travel with the Eastern army and made his new headquarters not too far from the Iron Brigade camps.

Cold miserable weather lingered well into late March of 1864. Dawn on the 29th arrived overcast and damp. A six-inch snowfall two days earlier was still slushy and made walking muddy ground a tricky affair. The Black Hats and other veterans of the old First Corps marched to a railroad track near Culpeper, where the small regiments formed into ranks under a drizzle of rain. The soldiers were members of the First Corps no more. During the effort to reorganize the army that winter it became apparent the five understrength corps could no longer function effectively. Accordingly, on March 23, 1864, in Order 115, the War Department consolidated the five corps into three. Fifth Corps survived, merged into two divisions and combined with two divisions created by the consolidation of three First Corps divisions. The Third Corps also disappeared when it merged into Second Corps. The orders specified that veterans of First Corps and Third Corps could retain "their badges and distinctive marks," and expressed the hope "that the ranks of the army will be filled at an early day, so that those corps can again be reorganized." It was not to be, however, for the horrendous casualties these organizations were about to suffer during the 1864 campaigns would forever seal the fate of the old First and Third Corps.[17]

Why were First Corps and Third Corps selected for demise? Army politics may have played a role. Neither Maj. Gen. George Sykes, commander of the army's Regular contingents and the Fifth Corps after Meade's elevation to lead the Army of the Potomac on June 28, 1863, nor John Newton, who replaced John Reynolds at Gettysburg, performed well during the fall 1863 Bristoe Station and Mine Run campaigns. Moreover, G. K. Warren, who had been serving as interim commander of the Second Corps while Winfield Scott Hancock recovered from his Gettysburg wound, needed a corps of his own to command now that Hancock was ready to return to the army. Warren, one of Meade's favorites at the time, was tapped to

---

17 The Second Corps was merged into two divisions and combined with two divisions of the Third Corps; the other division of the Third Corps was transferred intact to the Sixth Corps, which was likewise consolidated into two divisions.

command the consolidated Fifth Corps on March 25. The appointment was generally met with approval. Warren's performance at Gettysburg, where he realized the importance of Little Round Top just in time to save it, enhanced his reputation, as did his solid showing during the fall 1863 endeavors. Dawes, who was introduced to the general some weeks later, left a description: "He is a keen-looking fellow of small stature, about my own complexion, black eyes and hair, and quite young looking. His address is gentlemanly and pleasing." Another Iron Brigade officer proclaimed later that "no more efficient and patriotic officer than Warren ever wore a star."[18]

Under these changes, the Iron Brigade was now the First Brigade, Fourth Division, Fifth Army Corps, though it retained the distinctive First Corps red discs as well as the plain white triangular flag bearing the same badge.[19] The loss of First Corps was a bitter disappointment to the soldiers, who had been with the famous old unit organized by George McClellan in the Washington camps of 1861. Lost was the proud designation of the three "firsts": First Brigade, First Division, First Corps—an identity, one Black Hat said, "purchased with blood and held most sacred."[20]

The regiments were being formed on that late wet March day so General Grant could review them. They had been mustered twice before only to have the general fail to appear. As Dawes waited with his regiment under the cold rain, he was reminded of another review in November 1861. On that occasion, a party including President Lincoln, McClellan, and other dignitaries rode along the line at a dashing gait while cheer upon cheer filled the air and soldiers flung caps into the air. In those innocent days of new soldiering, the young officer recalled, it was regarded that perfect silence—not wild cheering and throwing caps—was evidence of the true and well-disciplined soldier. Thus, when McClellan and Lincoln passed, the new brigade of Westerners had stood silent and made only the proper salutes. McClellan did not acknowledge them.

Now there was a new commander and another review. Grant was two hours late when he and his escort finally appeared. The small party, which included Fifth Corps Commander Warren, passed slowly along the line. Cheers erupted, but

---

18 Dawes, letter to his wife, April 15, 1864; Dawes, *Service*, 245; John Azor Kellogg, *Capture and Escape: A Narrative of Army and Prison Life, Wisconsin Historical Commission: Original Papers, No. 2* (Madison, WI., November 1908), 1.

19 Howard Michael Madaus, "Army Reorganization," *The Blackhat, Occasional Newsletter of the 6th Wisconsin Volunteers*, Issue No. 9, William J. K. Beaudot, ed., May 1984, Wisconsin Historical Society.

20 Curtis, *Twenty-fourth*, 222; Cheek and Pointon, *Sauk County*, 89.

Grant offered no recognition of the compliment. For most of the men it was their first look at Warren. One described the general as "a small man, about thirty-five years old, dark complexioned, with black eyes and long, straight black hair; he has a little of the look of an Indian, and evidently is a nervous temperament." Grant rode in "a slouchy unobservant way," wrote another soldier, "with his coat unbuttoned and setting anything but an example of military bearing to the troops." Another thought "Old Grant" not "so hard-looking a man as his photographs make him out to be, but stumpy, unmilitary, slouchy and Western-looking; very ordinary in fact." A third soldier wrote home that the new commander (perhaps comparing him with the dashing Little Mac) "is a pretty tough-looking man for Lieutenant General but I guess he is all right on the fight question." An Indiana boy thought the future president took on "a sort of shy, half-embarrassed, half-bored look" as he rode the lines. Grant and the old Iron Brigade veterans were getting their first look at one another and, in that steady way of Westerners, taking each other's measure.[21]

Dawes' impression was both favorable and prescient: "He looks like a plain common sense man, one not to be puffed up by his position nor abashed by obstacles." Still, the twenty-five-year-old Dawes, who had learned his soldiering in McClellan's army, was a bit miffed by Grant's presence. There was, he admitted, some resentment that the government turned to a general not from the Army of the Potomac. Some soldiers welcomed the appointment because they hoped and believed Grant would force the issue, while others were fearful Grant never had confronted Robert E. Lee and the Army of Northern Virginia on a battlefield. It was in this swirl of conflicted emotions that Dawes turned, faced his regiment, and announced: "As General Grant does not seem to think our cheering worth notice, I will not call for cheers. Maintain your position as soldiers."

When Grant reached the 6th Wisconsin, he was met with military salutes performed with exact precision and the hard veterans as motionless as statutes. The lieutenant general was pulled up by the silence and he understood it all in an instant. Grant took off his hat and made a slight bow. His Westerners understood the gesture immediately, and regimental colors dipped in salute. "It was to say, 'I did not come here for a personal ovation.' It was a genuine Grantism and our men were highly pleased at it," related Dawes. Afterward, the Wisconsin soldiers said that "Grant wants soldiers, not yaupers."[22]

Old Grant would need all the soldiers he could get.

---

21 Dawes, *Service*, 239; Wainwright, diary, 339.

22 U. S. Grant recalled the incident while attending a reunion of Civil War veterans in Milwaukee. *Milwaukee Telegraph*, May 1, 1897.

Lieutenant General Ulysses S. Grant

Ulysses S. Grant journeyed east to command all the armies in early 1864 after a string of successes in the Western Theater. He attached himself to the Army of the Potomac and reviewed portions of First Corps, which included the Iron Brigade. *Author's Collection*

The Ominous Forebodings of War

The Iron Brigade reviewed by U. S. Grant that March of 1864 was not the Iron Brigade of Gettysburg. The old associations dating back to 1861 were forever changed by the hard fighting on McPherson's Ridge coupled with the never-ending sickness, desertions, and promotions that shaped and changed each company, regiment, and so the brigade. For example, nine of the brigade's fourteen field officers were killed or wounded in a single day at Gettysburg; new men stood in their places. Also lost in the reorganization of the army was the brigade's all-Western makeup. The change came when the undisciplined 167th Pennsylvania, about 800 drafted men, was attached for a four-week period after the Pennsylvania fighting in 1863. These Keystone troops were replaced by the 1st Battalion New York Sharpshooters, a capable though Eastern regiment, which would serve with the Black Hats almost to Appomattox. The 76th New York was also temporarily attached for a few weeks in early 1864 before the veteran 7th Indiana under Col. Ira G. Grover became part of the brigade. The Western 7th included old friends from First Corps.[23]

The Army of the Potomac of 1864 also evolved when a flood of conscripts arrived to fill the ranks of the old regiments. There were a few real volunteers, but most of the new men had been drafted or accepted bounties to join the army. These new men sparked Gen. Lysander Cutler to pen a strange letter to President Lincoln. They are worthless, he complained. Many were "aged paralytics, scorbutics, imbeciles, &c." He concluded, "I am most firmly convinced that not two-thirds of the conscripts and substitutes ever reach the army, and I think a thorough investigation would show that not half of those who did were ever available as soldiers for the field."

The tough veterans of the Iron Brigade were troubled by the new men, described by one veteran as "cattle." "Conscripts are beginning to come to this army, and a sorry looking set they are," concluded a Wisconsin officer. "Many are substitutes who have received large sums of money, and who are old soldiers discharged or deserted, who have come with the deliberate intention of deserting, and again speculating in the substitute money. They are closely guarded." What struck the officer most was the contrast "between such hounds and the enthusiastic and eager volunteers of 1861." The bounty men were the most suspect and despised. The drafted men were given a grim acceptance by the veterans as fellows who had the bad luck to be conscripted, but were there doing their duty and making

23 OR 27, pt. 3, 795.

the best of it. One soldier explained it this way: "No man can fight when surrounded by cowards, who are easily panic-stricken, and who are unrestrained by any consideration of pride from ignominiously running away to save their lives." The hard veterans of many fields understood that safety in battle was had by "steadiness, persistence in fighting, and most of all by holding together." Colonel Edward Bragg wrote to his wife of an early drill for the new arrivals: "It was cold, but the recruits were on the ground and we set them at work with muskets, for the first time. They are fearfully awkward, humpbacked, bowlegged & and all that sort of thing but we shall make something of them yet."[24]

The ranks of the regiments reviewed by Grant may have been full, but they were in many ways not the same as those sent to Washington in 1861. No longer were the companies made up of hometown boys—brothers, cousins, schoolmates. A radical change in the makeup of the regiments was underway with soldiers from the same state but different communities, strangers in many ways, serving in each company. There were also changes among the brigade's officers. Many wearing the shoulder straps were in the ranks in 1861. The veterans, distrusting the new men, clung to themselves in small messes even as they attempted to get the companies and regiments ready for the campaigns of 1864. "We have to drill almost all the time to teach these awkward recruits," a Black Hat wrote home. "There is some of them that take hold and try to learn, but most of them are as awkward as mules." The veterans especially enjoyed telling the new arrivals "big bear and bull stories, which they listen to with eyes & ears open, and believe as implicitly as if they read them out of the Bible." One example of low morale occurred when General Cutler reached a picket line just as a private in the 7th Wisconsin called out, "Oh, my greenbacks, how I do suffer for thee." Cutler approached the soldier with a stern look. "Boys, that's pretty rough you had ought to say 'country' instead of 'green backs.'" "I know it," replied the cheeky private, "but, General, I can't. It was greenbacks that I enlisted for." The surprised Cutler stood for a second or two and then walked on.[25]

In addition to the bounty and draft men, among the new arrivals from Wisconsin were members of Indian nations previously barred from military service. No one knew quite what to make of them. Back home in Wisconsin and Michigan, tribal members were initially considered members of an alien nation and not allowed to enlist in the Union army. They were also not subject to the draft. Some French-Indian "mixed bloods" or *metis*, seeking adventure and to avoid hard times

---

24 Frank Wilkeson, "Coffee Boilers," *Milwaukee Sunday Telegraph*, August 1885; Rufus Dawes, letter to Mary Beman Gates, August 6, 1863; Dawes, *Service*, 197, 202; Bragg, letter to wife, March 5, 1864.

25 Matrau, *Letters Home*, 75; Perkins, letter to a friend, April 14, 1864.

at home, enlisted early in the war by claiming to be "French Canadians." The need for soldiers soon ended the restriction on Native Americans in uniform, and unscrupulous agents looking for substitutes to replace drafted white men worked the Wisconsin reservations with a promise of $100 to any young male tribal member willing to sign the muster roll. This effort came at a time when the agents were getting up to $300 for substitutes and disease and starvation were a common part of reservation life. "A lot of recruits came in for our regiment and 13 were Indians for Co. G," a 7th Wisconsin man wrote home in April 1864. "They were from up above the Chippewa Falls and are a very intelligent looking set of men. Only one or two can speak a few words of English. Quite a crowd of men was around their tents till dark. . . . The Indians were out drilling this morning in Co. G and they did very well for the first time." The new arrivals proved such an attraction, in fact, that thousands of soldiers from the Eastern regiments came out to watch them perform a "regular war dance" on the eve of the battle of the Wilderness.[26]

When the cold weather of the winter months eased, national attention once again centered on the star-crossed Army of the Potomac. The Hero of the West— U. S. "Unconditional Surrender" Grant—was preparing an offensive against Confederate forces strung along an imaginary line stretching 1,000 miles across the country from Virginia to the Mississippi River. It did not go unnoticed that the new commanding general decided to stay with the Army of the Potomac and face Robert E. Lee even though steady George Meade remained the army's commander. Many believed the upcoming months would decide the course of the war. Unanswered in the discussions and debates by the coffee coolers was whether the new general would be up to the task of facing Lee. Grant probably wondered whether the Army of the Potomac would fight as well as his Western soldiers.

When dawn broke on May 4, the Army of the Potomac confronted the Army of Northern Virginia along opposite banks of the Rapidan River. In the consolidated Fifth Corps resided Lysander Cutler's Iron Brigade in a division commanded by "gray-haired and noble" Maj. Gen. James Wadsworth. Like the rest of the army, the brigade had been reorganized, equipped, and fitted, and then roused just before midnight on May 3 to move to the parade ground in heavy marching order. It tramped away to join Fifth Corps' line of march, passing through Stevensburg, across the Rapidan on a spongy pontoon bridge, and then up the Orange Court House Turnpike before turning east to the old Wilderness Tavern.

---

26 George Eustice, letter, April 26, 1864. The arrivals were probably members of the Ojibwa tribe.

By dusk on May 4—after a march of twenty-five miles—the brigade had crossed the Rapidan River at Germanna Ford and bivouacked. The 2nd Wisconsin was strung out on the Chancellorsville Pike as far as Chancellorsville for the purpose of keeping open communication with Winfield Hancock's Second Corps. The crossing had gone well. The enemy, apparently surprised, made only a token resistance at the river before falling back to its entrenchments at Mine Run. "Word passed over the land that General Grant was moving," a Wisconsin officer wrote long afterwards, "and with almost breathless anxiety our people awaited the result."[27]

Your Work this Morning will not be Play

The sleeping soldiers were roused early the next morning by calls of "Turn out! Turn out! Ten minutes to cook coffee and prepare for marching!" One officer remembered the scene in the gray dawn light: "Staff officers and orderlies were galloping hither and thither, the ammunition wagons were ordered to the front, general officers could be seen inspecting the ground, and all those grim preparations were being made that to the soldier were recognized as the precursors of battle." The line was formed and the old soldiers began to throw up breastworks before dropping to the ground to wait.

Captain John Kellogg was in command of the "Anderson Guards," Company I of the 6th Wisconsin. He was told to bring his men and report to Lysander Cutler for skirmish duty. Kellogg was a familiar figure in the regiment and even the brigade. He had been with the regiment from the very first, helping raise the Lemonweir Minute Men of Juneau County and later assuming several staff positions. He was an officer known for steady leadership as well as a sharp temper that showed itself when he fell into a latrine during an alarm at Patterson Park in Baltimore early in the war. He was tall and erect and well-liked. A native of Pennsylvania, Kellogg's grandfather served in the Revolutionary War before the family moved west to the Wisconsin Territory about 1840, settling in Prairie du Chien to farm. John Kellogg began reading law at eighteen and was admitted to the bar in 1857 at twenty-nine. He was also one of the founders of the Republican Party and attended an organizing meeting in Madison in September 1855. Four years later he opened a law office in Mauston and the next year was elected district attorney of

---

27 Henry B. Harshaw and Richard Lester, "Operations of the 'Iron Brigade' in the Spring Campaign of 1864," Oshkosh, WI, Public Museum, Record 44/294; Dawes, *Service*, 251. The "operations" report was compiled by Sgt. Richard Lester and 2nd Lt. Henry B. Harshaw of Company E, 2nd Wisconsin, from their diaries while clerks in Madison, Wisconsin.

Juneau County. Although married with children, he resigned in April 1861 to enlist.[28]

When he reached the makeshift brigade headquarters, Captain Kellogg found a group of officers standing near General Cutler's tent. They were, he said, "evidently pleased that this unwelcome message should have come to some one besides themselves." Duty on the skirmish line came with all the dangers of lethal combat without an opportunity for military glory. It required an officer's best efforts, all of which were sure to be overshadowed by events to follow and seldom made the official reports. Many of the young officers were old friends, and Kellogg put on a smile to conceal "my distaste for the duty." The captain called out, "Good bye! I expect you fellows will all be wiped out before I get back." Once the laughter died down, Maj. Philip Plummer asked with a grin, "What word shall I send to your wife?" "Never mind my wife," replied Kellogg, "Look after Converse's girl!" Capt. Rollin Converse laughed as well, saying, "Plummer will be shot before either of us, leave your messages with Dawes, he is the only man they can't kill." Another officer joined the bantering. "Better 'shake' before you go," he advised, "for it's the last we'll see ever see of you." "Shake them up lively, my boy!" said another officer. "Never mind me," Kellogg replied. "Look out you don't get run over by the line of battle, when they follow me in."[29]

Cutler was pacing up and down before his tent. Kellogg had served on Cutler's staff and the two were well acquainted. The general invited Kellogg into his tent. "Captain, your work this morning will not be play. Out in front—I do not know exactly how far, but probably within a mile—you will find the sharpshooters deployed as skirmishers," Cutler explained. "You will join them. Use your own company as you think best; take command of the line and advance until you raise the enemy and bring on an engagement."

It was not unusual work, and more like a simple reconnaissance. Kellogg deployed his company. Once in the woods, he ordered a cautious forward movement, the thin line of blue finding heavy going in the thick brush and stunted

---

28 Rufus Dawes tried to talk Kellogg out of enlisting: "I argued with Kellogg, who was ten years my senior and a married man, that young men, without families, could crush the Rebellion, but he could not brook the thought of being deprived of sharing in the satisfaction and glory of that service, and feeling that this would be his only chance, he joined in the work of making up the company with utmost zeal." Dawes, *Service*, 6.

29 Dawes, *Service*, 259; Kellogg, *Capture and Escape*, xi-xii, 5-6. Phil Plummer and his brother, Thomas, were Englishmen who came to America with their father in the years before the war. Both served as officers in the Prairie du Chien Volunteers, Company C, 6th Wisconsin, before Phil Plummer was promoted to captain of the Beloit Star Rifles, Company G, 6th Wisconsin. Lysander Cutler's August 13, 1864, report can be found at *OR* 36, pt. 1, 610-611.

growth. The area was known locally as "the Wilderness," some eighty square miles of second and third growth trees, dense shrubs, heavy underbrush, ravines, and winding creeks. "Our progress was necessarily slow," recalled Kellogg, "the ground being broken and heavily timbered with a kind of scrub pine." After about a mile, he found the 1st New York Sharpshooters and then moved on to "discover a long line of 'graybacks' moving slowly forward in line of battle, without the precaution of throwing forward a skirmish line." Kellogg halted and ordered his men to commencing firing. "If ever a set of men were astonished, those Confederates were the men. The nature of the ground was such that neither party saw the other until within thirty-five or forty yards of each other." Posted between trees, stumps, stones, and anything that might afford concealment and protection gave the Federals an initial advantage. The Confederate line responded with a volley that filled the woods with bullets and smoke, but the enemy did not advance farther.

After a short time, Kellogg heard the cracking and thumping of moving soldiers behind him—the main Union line coming up with a cheer. "Cold steel, boys!" he heard Cutler call out in a loud voice. "Give them the bayonet!" The woods erupted with shooting and yelling. The Confederate line gave way in confusion and the Federals pressed them for several hundred yards with loud yells. The Union advance, however, was about to come tumbling back.[30]

A Strange and Terrible Struggle

Unlike previous drives into Virginia, Grant's objective was Lee's army, not the capture of Richmond. Lee's army is your objective, he informed Meade. Wherever he goes, so would the Army of the Potomac. Grant had no desire to fight the Confederates in the tangled thickets, which would negate his advantage in manpower and artillery. Instead, he intended to press through the rough terrain on a couple major roads, break free to the southeast, and then meet Lee in battle. Warren's Fifth Corps followed by Sedgwick's Sixth Corps crossed the Rapidan at Germanna Ford, with Burnside's Ninth Corps moving behind the supply trains, with the goal of reaching Wilderness Tavern. The remaining Second Corps under Hancock crossed farther east at Ely's Ford to advance on Spotsylvania Court House. Stretched out and vulnerable to attack, the Federals had little choice but to move as fast as possible before Lee could react and strike.

Any early Federal advantage gained by the quick passage of the Rapidan gave way when Confederates appeared from the west along both sides of the Orange

30 Kellogg, *Capture and Escape*, 7-9.

Turnpike on the morning of May 5. Unbeknownst to the Federals, Lee realized what Grant was doing and ordered his three dispersed infantry corps to drive east and hit the enemy during their march along the tight roads. When Warren's corps encountered the enemy, Grant—unaware Rebels were on hand in force—ordered an attack and Meade complied. What no one knew (but prudence should have at least suggested) was that Richard Ewell's entire corps was bearing down on Warren.

One of the units deployed to brush aside the Southern infantry was Cutler's Iron Brigade, which moved south of the Orange Turnpike into position on the right side of Wadsworth's divisional line. The brigade formed in two lines of battle south of Saunders Field in the center of the Fifth Corps front, with Brig. Gen. Joseph Bartlett's brigade (Griffin's division) on its right and Col. Roy Stone's to its left. The 7th Indiana was in the front line on the right flank of the Iron Brigade, followed by the 6th Wisconsin at a distance of 100 paces. The 6th Wisconsin had only 370 men in line, and it was "with the greatest difficulty that we could keep the 7th Indiana in sight," said Dawes. "We soon lost connection on our right, but we followed the colors of the seventh Indiana." The 7th Indiana pressed forward and disappeared into the trees. The regiments moved through "entangled woods" by companies for about one mile, formed lines, and with a yell went forward at the double quick. The 19th Indiana and 24th Michigan extended the line left. The surprised Confederates retreated quite a distance. Because of the difficult terrain, no one realized the Union line had drifted left and a crash of musketry erupted. "Look to the right!" Major Philip W. Plummer yelled to Dawes, who spotted "the enemy stretching as far as I could see through the woods, and rapidly advancing and firing upon us." Dawes tried to order a change of front on his color company, ordering the major to take the left wing while he gave orders to the right. Plummer was shot and killed almost instantly, and the attempted maneuver left the 6th Wisconsin in an awkward position. Forty or fifty men were shot down in a few minutes, including Plummer, Capt. Rollin P. Converse, and Lt. James L. Converse.

The heavy underbrush now proved an advantage. Within minutes all the regiments were engaged with Stonewall Jackson's former veterans, front, rear and flanks. Organization and control melted away. "Our little band, as always under fire, clung around its colors," reported Dawes. "We rallied and formed twice or three times and gave the enemy a hot reception as they came on." Captain Kellogg painted a different recollection when he wrote the Confederate flanking fire caused confusion and then panic: "Our line, vigorously pressed in front and rear at the same time became demoralized. Officers made desperate efforts to rally the men, but it was of no use; they could not endure the bullets coming from the front and rear at once, and away they went." Kellogg felt "a sensation akin to being struck by lightning" when a bullet struck him. He fell hard and was left behind. The brigade was breaking up and down the line. What began as a slow retreat turned into a great

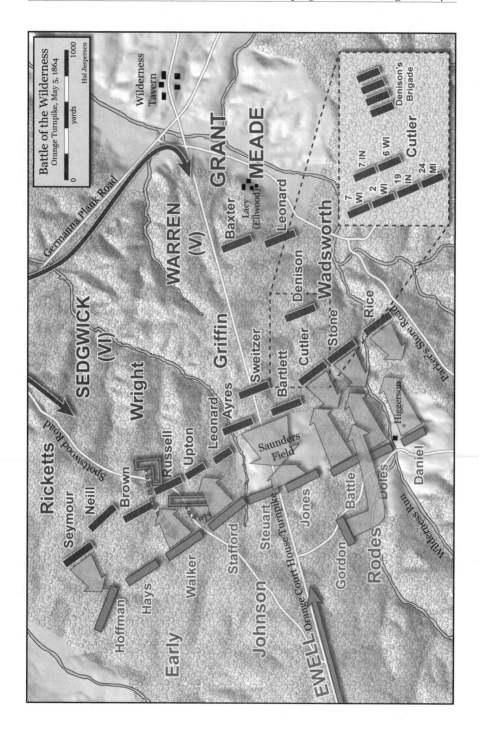

Battle of the Wilderness
Orange Turnpike, May 5, 1864

Hal Jespersen

yards

0   1000

skedaddle with the men fleeing as fast as the brush and trees allowed. "The men here gave way in confusion, each trying to outrun the other," said a Wisconsin soldier, "the reason for this or who or what was to blame, I have not learned. I have heard a good many surmises as to the cause," he continued, "one was that one of the Officers told his men to run if they wanted to save themselves, but I do not believe it."[31]

It was the kind of fighting never before experienced—in a thick, almost impassable woods that held the gun smoke and obscured vision. The 2nd Wisconsin was in the rear of the brigade as a reserve. When the fighting erupted General Wadsworth ordered the unit to the left with orders "to fire on some Penn. regiments in its immediate front if they broke." With some relief, one of the Badgers reported, "no necessity arose for executing these instructions." Then the regiment, in the confusion and noise and the battle turning against the Federals, was moved by the right flank to the right of the brigade and ordered to advance to the front and support the Union line. No sooner had this been done when the 2nd was brought to a halt "by a terrific volley in its front." Stunned by "such an unexpected reception," the regiment was in confusion and hesitant to return fire fearing some Union forces were ahead of them. Men fell "thick and fast" from the enemy firing, and then through the smoke could be seen a line of Confederates some seventy-five yards distant and a "proper" return fire was made. It was all for naught, however. A quick look around disclosed other Federal units had retired. The 2nd Wisconsin made what the soldier called "a hasty withdrawal."[32]

In the tangle of fighting during the brigade retreat, Pvt. William Ray of the 7th Wisconsin was struck by buckshot in the calf of his right leg. "They fired into us pretty brisk for a while," he said. "But we outrun them & got back to some breastworks & here the officers, what there was there, and a few of the Bravest Privates got a few to rally. And they of course gave confidence to the others so it was not long till we had a line of battle 1 mile long." The makeshift line fell back to a rally point being organized by the balance of the Fifth Corps. The buckshot lamed Ray and knocked him out of the rest of the fight, but he told his journal with satisfaction that "they couldn't catch me."[33] When the Rebel pursuit broke off, the men of the 6th Wisconsin discovered they were lost in heavy woods. "[W]e lay flat

---

31 Dawes, *Service*, 261; Kellogg, *Capture and Escape*, 10; John O. Johnson, letter to John Hauser, July 2, 1864, Wisconsin Historical Society. Johnson enlisted at Stevens Point, July 16, 1861, and served as corporal and sergeant in the 6th Wisconsin before being promoted to 2nd lieutenant in the 45th Wisconsin. *Wisconsin Roster*, vol. 1, 526.

32 Harshaw and Lester, *Spring Campaign*.

33 Ray, *Iron Brigade*, 269-270.

on the ground, not knowing certainly which way to go to join our troops," admitted one officer. "We were in the woods between the hostile lines and we felt our way cautiously back to the open ground around the Lacy House, where our corps was being formed after this repulse."[34]

While the Iron Brigade regiments did indeed break in the face of these attacks, despite later writings of other witnesses, the situation was not as bleak as the tangled wilderness setting may have made it appear at the time. The regiments were full of recruits, and it was these inexperienced and frightened new men who led the wild-eyed panicked retreat while the veterans tried to hold together around their battle flags. Dawes himself grabbed the regimental colors to rally his men. A member of General Warren's staff said he saw the Parker's Store Road "crowded with stragglers and large crowds of soldiers pouring out of the woods in great confusion and almost panic-stricken." However, Cutler's Iron Brigade, he admitted, "came back in good order bringing a number of prisoners." Wadsworth's divisional front, however, was in severe disarray and offered several enticing flanks begging to be struck.[35]

When the Federal advance stalled, General Ewell ordered a counter-thrust. Brig. Gen. John B. Gordon, one of the rising stars of the Rebel army, led the attack by moving up from his reserve on the turnpike and tramping 300 yards into the smoky thickets. When the Georgia veterans slammed into the exposed right flank of the Iron Brigade, serious Federal resistance ended. Perhaps only then did the Black Hats discover that the Federal brigades on their right and left were no longer in position. Within minutes the woods below Saunders Field was littered with dead and wounded. Smoldering sparks from musket firing ignited dry grass, leaves, twigs, and overgrown bushes. The flames consumed the bodies of the maimed and the dead. "Thus ended this brief but fierce engagement, being the first, after crossing the Rapidan, in which infantry took part," said one participant. "On account of the difficulty of getting out of the woods a large loss in prisoners was sustained."[36]

Among the wounded left behind were Wisconsin privates Jim Whitty and Mark Smith (each of whom would lose a leg within the next couple days), who were resting on the grass on the southern edge of the field watching Rebels empty the

34 Dawes, *Service*, 261; Kellogg, *Capture and Escape*, 9-10.

35 Washington A. Roebling's Report in the Gouverneur K. Warren Collection, New York State Archives, Albany, NY, quoted in Sharon Eggleston Vipond, "A New Kind of Murder," in *Tall Black Hats*, 130.

36 Harshaw and Lester, *Spring Campaign*.

pockets and knapsacks of the Iron Brigade dead. A tall Confederate officer with a star on his collar rode in their direction. The two Black Hats pulled themselves up, saluted, and asked his name. "My name is Gordon, boys," he replied. "We are badly wounded General, would you get us a drink?" one of the Western men asked. Gordon dismounted and gave each a pull from his canteen. Once back in the saddle Gordon turned in his saddle and said, "I am sorry for you, boys, but such is the fortune of war."[37]

Another of the severely wounded early that day was Sgt. Abe Buckles of the 19th Indiana, who was shot through the body while carrying the regimental color he had defended with such bravery at Gettysburg. A shoulder wound during the Pennsylvania fighting was still bothering him that morning when the Iron Brigade stopped to throw up light breastworks before its first advance. The exertions, Buckles said, irritated "some loose bones in my shoulder." The sergeant sat down and pulled his coat open to use a small pair of pincers to remove bone fragments out of his seeping wound. Just as he finished the advance began, pushing back the Confederate line to a clearing where the Union line reformed under an enemy fire from a dense thicket. "Up to this time I had been unable, because of the bushes and trees, to unfurl my colors, but on coming into the clearing I loosened its folds and shook the regiment's flag free to the breeze," explained Buckles. "From their covered position the enemy had begun to pour a withering fire into us, comrades were dropping at every hand and delay was fatal." Taking it all in with a veteran's understanding, the sergeant concluded a quick charge would "force the rebels to flee." Buckles ran to the front of his regiment waving the flag and calling for the line to follow him before rushing forward into "the troublesome thicket." The Hoosiers were hollering and shouting in good style when he was shot through the body. "I fell, but managed to keep the flag up until . . . one of the color-guard . . . took it out of my hands, to be killed a few minutes later." Buckles was ultimately carried to an army hospital where a doctor mistakenly pronounced his wound mortal. He would survive the war and be awarded a Congressional Medal of Honor.[38]

Regimental flags were the source of three additional incidents in the Wilderness. Private John N. Opel of the 7th Indiana captured the colors of the 50th Virginia, and Maj. Albert M. Edwards of the 24th Michigan captured a flag from the color-bearer of the 48th Virginia (both from Brig. Gen. John M. Jones' brigade, Ewell's Corps). The latter flag was taken to the rear, and when wounded Col. Henry

---

37 Watrous, "Some Short Stories," *Milwaukee Telegraph*, September 1, 1894.

38 "He Kept His Colors Flying," in *Deeds of Valor: How America's Civil War heroes Won the Congressional Medal of Honor*, W. F. Beyer and O. F. Keydel, eds. (Detroit, MI: Perrien-Keydel Company, 1903), 316-317.

Morrow was found on a stretcher, Maj. Edwards stuffed the flag into his haversack. The third flag incident involved the colors of the 6th Wisconsin, which were at first thought lost. When the regiment rallied after the first retreat, the soldiers looked around and realized their banner might have been left behind or captured. Several soldiers prepared to go back into the woods to search for it when Sgt. Maj. Culyer Babcock appeared. "Sergeant Major, where is our flag?" someone asked. The weary and dirty Babcock smiled and unbuttoned his coat to reveal the tattered emblem wrapped around his body.[39]

My God, No One Could Stop Him!

The fortunes of war had turned against Wadsworth and his men that morning. That afternoon, the division leader convinced both Grant and Meade to let him go forward a second time to support elements of Hancock's Second Corps, which were engaged somewhere off to the southeast below Wilderness Run and the Orange Plank Road against A. P. Hill's Confederates. Later it would be said that the old hero of Gettysburg was embarrassed by the retreat of his division and wanted to restore its (and his) honor. By 6:00 p.m., the division was again moving forward with the brigades of Roy Stone and Henry Baxter in the first line with the Iron Brigade following in close support. James Rice's brigade formed a reserve. The line was advancing cautiously when Wadsworth and his staff heard Colonel Stone shooting his revolver in the air and yelling. He and other officers had been seen earlier that day "swilling whiskey as they would water."[40] Wadsworth sent his aide, Lt. Earl Rogers, to stop Stone, but Stone refused and continued calling for his men to cheer for Pennsylvania. Nearby, a group of about 150 men from the 5th Alabama Battalion were guarding Federal prisoners. Caught up in the uproar and excitement of the moment, they left their post to charge into Stone and Baxter's lines. Still shaken from the morning combat, Stone's brigade scattered and the colonel fell when his horse reared. He was carried from the field. Efforts by the Iron Brigade to halt the fugitives with bayonets met only limited success. The advance of Wadsworth's division, however, was over and the Federal line had to be reformed.

---

39 Watrous, "Some Short Stories," *Milwaukee Telegraph*, October 6, 1894; Curtis, *Twenty-fourth*, 231. Edwards did not receive credit for his capture of a flag. See "Report of Colors Captured From the Enemy by the V Army Corps from May 4 to Nov. 1, 1964," *OR* 36, pt. 1, 1,020-1,021. Babcock enlisted from Beetown on June 22, 1861, from Company F. *Wisconsin Roster*, vol. 1, 494. Morrow took the 48th Virginia flag with him to Detroit, where it was displayed before being returned to the War Department.

40 Survivor's Association, *121st Regiment Pennsylvania Volunteers* (Philadelphia, PA, 1906), 76-77, as cited in Vipond, "A New Kind of Murder," *Tall Black Hats*, 130-132.

When darkness brought the fighting to a close, the lines were a tangle of formations pointing wildly this way and that. Here and there, opposing skirmish lines barely separated by handfuls of yards in some places, exchanged flurries of musket fire while adjusting their lines. Several men from the 24th Michigan fell on the skirmish line. The calls of the maimed and the dying only added to the unfolding nightmare. "The sufferings of these poor men, and their moans and cries were harrowing," one officer recalled. "We gave them water from our canteens and all aid that was within our power." One hurt Confederate called out again and again: "My God, why hast thou forsaken me!" In the darkness, staffer Rogers left Wadsworth to check on the men in his former company in the 6th Wisconsin. He became especially troubled when he could not find Pvt. Pete Markle, a company favorite with a reputation beyond his own regiment. Markle had walked from a farm field in 1861 to stop a passing recruiting wagon and inquire about signing the roll. The recruiting officer looked him over and asked his age. "Twenty years. Peter Markle, of Coon Slough." The recruiter gave him a second look, taking in the "bright eyes, good head and fair physical development," then wrote on the roll: "Pete Markle, Coon, age 17." And so began a fabled military career.

"Pete was careless of his clothes and of his personal appearance," Rogers said. "His pants were baggy and slouchy; his coat too large and ill fitting; usually a sleeve partly torn out and seams rent, a button missing in one place and a button hole torn out in another." If a coat seam was repaired, it was overlapped with white thread and the buttons replaced upside-down. "His shoes were seldom blackened even for a review." What the young man did possess, Rogers said, was an independent spirit and unerring sense of direction. He always was on hand for duty, but while on a march, Markle would "quietly and mysteriously, unbidden and unknown; even in disobedience of orders," slip away and "straggle" among the nearby farms and woods. He always returned at dusk with something on his bayonet to share. Markle, added Rogers, "had the instincts of a hunter, a scent keen as a hound and could trail the regiment as a dog trails his master." Now, "Markle, the Straggler"—always on hand when there was shooting to do—was not with his company in the dark smokey woods of the Wilderness. The worried Rogers returned to Wadsworth wondering what had become of the boy.[41]

---

41 Earl M. Rogers, "Markle, Straggler," *Milwaukee Sunday Telegraph*, October 8, 1887.

I am a Prisoner, Sir!

By the time the wounded Capt. John Kellogg opened his eyes, he was behind enemy lines. "I found myself with a badly-swelled head and great confusion of ideas," he wrote, "and I was bleeding profusely from ears and nose. On all sides were the maimed, the dying and the dead. I tried to stand, but then became dizzy and collapsed." When he awoke a second time, he tried to make his way to the Union line and safety, but the going was slowed by his "giddiness and partial blindness." Within minutes he found himself looking into the barrel of a 13th Georgia musket, part of a squad of Georgians lost in the dense woods. A Confederate officer looked over the wounded Union officer.

"Captain, were you in the skirmish line out yonder?"

"I am a prisoner, sir, and must decline to answer any questions touching our position or forces," Kellogg replied.

"That's all right, Captain, but I would like to know whether you have any skirmishers in there. Do you know where Gordon's brigade is?"

"Gordon's brigade! Why, I don't know where I am myself."

The enemy officer smiled. "Then there are two of us in the same fix. To tell the truth, I am lost. I got through an interval in your lines, I think; at all events, I found myself in your rear without knowing how I got there, and was trying to get back when you-uns run us over. We just lay still, and the yanks passed us."

"In what direction did they go?" asked Kellogg.

"Out yon."

"Then it strikes me that your rear is in an opposite direction."

"Well, yes, I reckon so," answered the Southerner. "Corporal, take this officer to the rear and find the Provost Marshal and report him."

An hour later Kellogg and his guard found a huddle of captured Federals. One was Cpl. Frank Hare, whose partially amputated leg had already felt the sting of a surgeon's saw. Kellogg was surprised to see Hare holding a cocked pocket revolver in an effort to keep Confederate surgeons at bay. Next to him was Capt. Rollin P. Converse resting under a large tree on a blanket, shot through the body and both thighs. "He knew that his moments were numbered, and the end was nigh. He only asked to be permitted to die in peace," Kellogg remembered, "but the surgeons were desirous of experimenting upon him by what is known as the 'hip amputation.'" Converse had a small pistol hidden in his coat, and gave it to Hare with these words: "Frank, I'll die soon. Don't let them cut off my leg." When the Confederates came to remove Converse to an operating location, Hare "in quiet, yet firm tones, warned them that he would shoot the first man that laid a hand" on the captain. Muskets were raised and the private was told he would be shot if he did not surrender. "Hare only laughed at them, asking them what they supposed he cared for life, with one leg gone?" A Confederate officer watching the exchange told the soldiers around him, "I would like a regiment of such men!" The comment roused the wounded Converse, who lifted his head and told the officer he had the honor to lead a hundred just such men— "The North is full of them." Converse fell back and was soon dead. When the fighting resumed the next day, the Union prisoners were marched away. [42]

About 1:00 a.m. on May 6, word reached General Wadsworth that a new advance would be made against A. P. Hill's corps at dawn, and that his brigades would join the Second Corps assault. Wadsworth's regiments would need ammunition for the effort. Captain Robert Montieth of the 7th Wisconsin found Ord. Sgt. Jerome Watrous, who packed up twenty-four mules with more than 20,000 rounds and brought them to the regiments in the darkness.[43] When a signal gun exploded about 5:00 a.m. Hancock's Second Corps rushed against Hill's jumbled lines straddling the Orange Plank Road while Wadsworth's division angled southeast to strike Hill's exposed left flank. No one had a good clear idea of what, exactly, was happening where because of the limited visibility. Riding with Wadsworth that morning was his aide Lt. Earl Rogers, who remembered the general seemed anxious to redeem the reputation of his division. Much as it had the day before, the fighting erupted all at once. Hill's Confederates held for a time before giving way, but when they did the front collapsed all at once. The chaotic Federal pursuit became entangled in the woods and it was only with some effort that Wadsworth's division was reformed in something of a stack along the Orange Plank Road. The smoke, woods, and confusion made even the smallest effort difficult, and the jumbled lines were reforming when a Confederate counterattack roared out of the woods from the west. Lieutenant General James Longstreet's Corps had come up without an hour to spare, and it was later learned that General Lee himself had urged the attack forward and would have led it except for the demands that he move to the rear. The Confederates slammed into the disorganized Union line, crumpled it, and sent it reeling. "We were in oak openings,

---

42 Kellogg, *Capture and Escape*, 15-16; "Captain Rollin Converse and Corporal Hare," *Milwaukee Sunday Telegraph*, July 27, 1879. Converse, a native of New York State, was working as a clerk in Prescott, Wisconsin, when he enlisted on May 10, 1862 in the Prescott Guards, which became Company B of the 6th Wisconsin. He was promoted to captain on July 28, 1862, and cited for "conspicuous bravery" at Gettysburg. Frank Hare, from Beetown, enlisted in the Prescott Guards on May 10, 1861, and was discharged because of wounds. *Wisconsin Roster*, vol. 1, 499, 502.

43 Robert Montieth, "The Battle of the Wilderness and Death of General Wadsworth," *War Papers Read Before the Commandery of the State of Wisconsin, Military Order of the Loyal Legion of the United States*, 3 vols. (Milwaukee, WI, 1891), vol. 3, 414.

Adjutant Robert Montieth, 7th Wisconsin

Montieth enlisted at Liberty as a 2nd Lieutenant in Company H (Badger State Guards). He was promoted to captain on October 13, 1863, and to adjutant on December 29, 1862. He mustered out on September 26, 1864, term expired. *Author's Collection*

trees, but no underbrush," said a soldier in the Iron Brigade. "Just in front of our first line, the brush was thick, hiding the view to the front. Just as the command was given for the first line to advance, to our surprise, the rebel line burst forth from the brush and poured a volley into our ranks, killing and wounding many of the first line and a few of the second." The attack was unexpected and the Federals were wholly unprepared to receive it. "The second line was ordered to lie down and allow the first line to pass over us and to the rear of us where they could recover from the shock." In the flurry of shooting brigade commander Lysander Cutler suffered a minor wound on his upper lip that left his face covered with blood.[44]

In a stunning repeat of the first day's fighting, Longstreet's yelling soldiers again broke the Federal line and sent the Iron Brigade men in a run-and-shoot retreat through the woods and brush and even down the roadway. Sergeant John Johnson of the 6th Wisconsin was struggling to keep one of his veteran privates in the line, to no avail: "There was a very heavy fire in front about 10 o'clock and then all at once the front line broke, and came running right into us. I worked hard to stop them and being file closer, I took my musket in both hands to hold them there, but they forced me back till I fell and they passed over me like an avalanche, carrying everything before them." The retreat lost all organization as squads of soldiers from the 24th Michigan, 6th Wisconsin, and 7th Wisconsin found themselves fighting here and there with soldiers from other regiments. After falling back 200 yards, Johnson found the 6th reforming behind a makeshift breastworks. "Col. Bragg and Dawes were there and a little squad of us men, maybe 75. Bragg made a little speech here exhorting the men not to disgrace the name we had so nobly won for the Iron Brigade."[45]

Two other brigades from Wadsworth's command under Baxter and Rice were forced through the woods to the Orange Plank Road, where they began reforming. Wadsworth's division had broken in full retreat for the second time in as many days. All he could do now was try to rally the men and keep it from becoming a complete disaster. Earlier that day, during a lull in the fighting, the general told Captain Montieth that "he felt completely exhausted and worn out; that he was unfit to command, and felt that he ought, in justice to himself and his men, to turn the command of the division to Gen. Cutler." Now, with his division again in trouble, he ordered Montieth to find Cutler's brigade and extend his right. The aging general had two horses shot from under him and was mounted on a third when he passed soldiers of the 56th Pennsylvania and 149th Pennsylvania. "Come on Bucktails," he

---

44 Cheek and Pointon, *Sauk County*, 92.

45 John O. Johnson, letter to John Hauser, July 2, 1864.

Major General James Wadsworth

The wealthy New York state farmer-turned-officer was mortally wounded trying to rally his men in the fighting during the second day at the Wilderness on May 6, 1864. *Library of Congress*

called out, holding his hat in his hand and waving them forward. Wadsworth jumped his horse over some logs in an attempt to organize a counter-charge himself into the smoke-filled woods, but found himself alone with Rogers on the roadway. In the gloom and haze, a line of Alabamians from Abner Perrin's brigade rose and fired a point-blank volley. Wadsworth's horse careened forward. Some said later the frightened animal was out of control, while others claimed the general refused to rein in his mount. "Bona" Rogers rode alongside Wadsworth to within twenty feet of the enemy in a vain effort to halt the general's horse. The general was turning to escape when a ball slammed into the back of his head, spattering his blood and brains onto Roger's coat. Wadsworth tumbled to the ground. Rogers, whose own horse was hit and dying, kicked free, dismounted, and ran to assist the general. Seeing it was too late, he tried to secure his papers and personal property. "During my endeavor to take a watch from his outside coat pocket a rebel ball passed in close proximity to my head, and a rebel bayonet thrust toward me admonished me that I had better go," Rogers recalled. "I ran but a few yards, when I found the horse the General had fallen from, the rein caught on a dry limb of a pine tree." He jumped into Wadsworth's saddle and rode back to the Union line with bullets zipping around him. Asked later by a friend why he did not stop the old general from riding into the Confederate line, Rogers replied, "My God . . . nobody could stop him!"[46]

With Wadsworth missing and presumed dead, command of the division fell to Lysander Cutler, who reported to General Hancock before reorganizing the survivors of his fractured new command. Colonel William Robinson of the 7th Wisconsin moved up to command the Iron Brigade. Thankfully, however, the fighting flared off to the south and involved other troops, so Cutler's men escaped further action.

One of the mortally wounded Westerners was Isaac Vandecar of the 24th Michigan. The Wolverine was serving as a volunteer gunner with Battery B, 4th U.S. Artillery, when exploding case shot struck him in the face, breast, abdomen, and groin. "Van, my poor boy," inquired a batteryman. "What can I do for you?" Vandecar, who had grown quite fond of "Old Tartar," the famous bobtail horse in

---

46 Earl Rogers, "How Wadsworth Fell," *National Tribune*, December 24, 1885; Rogers, *Telegraph*, October 2, 1887; Robert Montieth, "Battle of the Wilderness and the Death of General Wadsworth," *War Papers*, vol. 3; John F. Krumwiede, *Old Waddy's Coming: The Military Career of Brigadier General James S. Wadsworth* (Baltimore, MD, 2002); Wayne Mahood, *General Wadsworth: The Life and Times of Brevet Major General James S. Wadsworth* (Cambridge, MA, 2003), 250-255. Sadly, General Wadsworth was still alive, though lingering in a near-vegetative state. When Confederate officers found the critically wounded officer unresponsive, they erected a tent over him made up of a blanket supported by muskets. Someone wrote "General Wadsworth of New York" on a piece of paper and posted it nearby. The dying general was eventually carried to a field hospital, where the curious came to stare at him. It took thirty hours for the old patriot to finally expire.

the battery, shook his head and replied, "Nothing. I know I must die and I want to see that 'Old Tartar' gets good care after I am gone."[47]

It was a Hot Place, I Can Tell You

Confederate counterattacks against both ends of the long Union line scored tactical successes on the second day of fighting without affecting the outcome and cost the Southern army the services of James Longstreet, who fell severely wounded by the accidental firing of his own men. Once the fighting ended on May 6, the bloodied armies found themselves in essentially the same general positions, though with 18,000 fewer Federals and 11,500 fewer Rebels. The first meeting between Grant and Lee ended as a bloody stalemate.

The sheer numbers lost and the ferocity of the combat left the soldiers of both sides numbed and uncomprehending. One combatant described it as the beginning of "a new kind of murder," and it was now understood by the men in ranks that the war had taken an even harder turn and the fighting might go on and on, day after day, until one side or the other was exhausted or exterminated.[48] The heavy woods and impassable terrain and the advances of weaponry prevented either side from forging a significant victory. The meeting in the tangled brush of the Wilderness, however, was a turning point and that became clear to the soldiers of both sides when Grant made his decision to order his columns south to Spotsylvania Court House in another attempt to get around Lee's right flank.

Ordnance Sergeant Jerome Watrous spent many of those frightful and anxious hours of Wilderness fighting guiding a train of thirty wagons with Federal wounded to Fredericksburg for medical treatment and returning with ammunition. He called the dozen-mile run "the most sorrowful experience" of his four years of service. His orders were to keep moving and make the quickest possible time: the army could move at any hour, and ammunition was sorely needed. "The roads were rough, stony and full of ruts, and in places it was necessary to go through fields and woods when fence rails and small trees had to be passed over. The joltings . . . kept that train loaded with hundreds of wounded, mangled human beings groaning, crying and loudly demanding help," lamented Watrous. "Not less than a dozen men died on that journey." At Fredericksburg, citizens helped unload the wounded and a contingent of volunteers from New York led by a man "here, there, and

---

47 Curtis, *Twenty-fourth*, 239; Buell, *Cannoneer*, 182.

48 *Ibid.*, 184-185. The "new kind of murder" quote was from William A. Holland of the Pennsylvania Reserves, as cited in Vipond, "A New Kind of Murder," in *Tall Black Hats*, 130.

everywhere at about the same minute, giving orders, speaking words of encouragement, offering a swallow of wine to this one and something stronger to the man who needed it." The New Yorker approached the wagons while they were being reloaded with ammunition to shake hands with the young sergeant. Watrous never forgot the man: Theodore Roosevelt, a New York merchant whose son would make a name for himself.[49]

The armies remained in place when dawn broke on May 7. The Iron Brigade spent most of the day in their rifle pits and saw no action. No one knew what would happen next. At 8:00 p.m. on that very dark night, the brigade fell into line and moved out with the rest of Fifth Corps, heading south along the Brock Road toward Todd's Tavern. What they did not know was that Grant had decided against attacking fresh enemy earthworks, and decided instead to maneuver around Lee's right flank to reach Spotsylvania about ten miles to the southeast. There would be no withdrawal north of the Rapidan River.

Later, there would be stories and memories of the movement as one of the most significant moments in the Civil War, and how soldiers cheered Grant and his watching staff when the columns turned south down a road toward more fighting.[50] That was not the case in the Iron Brigade regiments. There was no wild cheering for a passing general and no sense the war was about to change. There was just a memory of hard marching in the dark over narrow roads clogged with vehicles and cavalry. "Before setting out on this campaign," the historian of the 24th Michigan wrote later with much hindsight, "General Grant had resolved upon the 'left flank movement' to Richmond, by which was meant that in case of failure to defeat or rout the enemy in one place, he would flank him out of such position and compel him to fight on another field." He continued: "This was done by moving by night one corps, usually the right, around the left of the army, and so on. About 9'o'clock Saturday night, May 7, Grant began his first left flank movement toward Spotsylvania Court House, about thirteen miles distant. Lee discovered the movement and started his army by a parallel road about a mile south, for the same place, he moving on the chord and Grant on the arc of the circle."[51]

When the marching men truly understood what was happening is open to some debate, but there would be no return to the old camps as had happened after

49 Watrous, *Richard Epps*, 156-158. Roosevelt's son would also be a soldier of some reputation and would become president of the United States.

50 Horace Porter, *Campaigning With Grant*, Wayne C. Temple, ed. (Bloomington, IN, 1961), 78-79.

51 Curtis, *Twenty-fourth*, 238.

other battles. Now would be no period of rest and refitting and training. There would be only fighting, and it was going to be fighting as not seen or imagined— attacks here and there where the line would advance one or two miles, then retreat a mile or two, followed by the construction of defensive works or building roads slashed through near impassable woods and brush. Those days in early May began what would become almost forty days of continuous contact between the Army of the Potomac and the Army of Northern Virginia.

It had been a horrifying three days for Cutler's old Iron Brigade. The returns for May 5-7 showed 724 men killed, wounded, captured, or missing.[52] Only 740 remained in the ranks of some 1,464 engaged. The 7th Wisconsin suffered the most with seven officers and 148 killed or wounded and another thirty-five missing for a total of 217. The 7th Indiana reported 162 casualties; the 2nd Wisconsin forty; the 1st New York Sharpshooters thirty-five; the 24th Michigan 104; the 19th Indiana 103, and the 6th Wisconsin sixty-three. "Many of my comrades are laying cold, and ghastly corpses unburied some unmarked," one of the Black Hats wrote in a grim letter home. In the ranks of killed officers, the toll took some of the best: Capt. George Clayton of the 7th Indiana; Lt. James Converse, Capt. Rollin Converse, and Maj. Philip Plummer of the 6th Wisconsin; Capt. Jefferson Newman and Lt. James Holmes of the 7th Wisconsin; Lt. William B. Hutchinson and Capt. George Hutton of the 24th Michigan; Capt. John R. Spoerry and Lt. William Noble of the 2nd Wisconsin, and perhaps saddest of all, Col. Samuel J. Williams, that doughty old fighter of the 19th Indiana who was killed when struck in the chest by a cannon ball. In him, an Indiana officer, wrote, the regiment has "lost an able and loved Commander." These men would be hard to replace.[53]

There were more names. In addition to General Wadsworth, who was shot and believed dead or dying, Capt. John Kellogg was missing and presumed dead. General Cutler suffered a minor wound, and Col. Henry Morrow of the 24th Michigan was again injured, this time in the leg. He would not return to the brigade until November. Lieutenant Colonel John Mansfield of the 2nd Wisconsin was also wounded and temporarily captured. He would not return until August, and then only to be mustered out of the army. Colonel Ira Grover of the 7th Indiana was wounded and missing. Farther down in the ranks, Pvts. Jim Whitty of the 6th Wisconsin and Mark Smith of the 7th Wisconsin were left in the woods and

---

52 "Return of Casualties, Union Forces, Battle of the Wilderness, 5-7 May 1864," OR 36, pt. 1, 125. The report for Wadsworth's division can be found in *ibid.*, 615.

53 Matrau, *Letters Home*, 77; "Return of Casualties, Union Forces, Battle of the Wilderness, 5-7 May 1864," OR 36, pt. 1, 125. Plummer was called "Tip," and one friend called him a "general favorite" and "a man of unquestioned bravery." *Milwaukee Sunday Telegraph*, November 4, 1885.

Colonel Samuel J. Williams, 19th Indiana Infantry

Williams was struck in the chest and killed by a shell fragment during the
Wilderness fight. He was described as an "able and loved commander."
Institute for Civil War Studies

captured. Both survived. Each soldier had a leg amputated by Confederate
surgeons following their encounter with Gen. John Gordon. Once placed in an
ambulance for wounded prisoners, the determined duo overcame a careless driver
and took the reins of what they later told their friends was a "one-legged brigade"
that made its way to Union lines near Fredericksburg. Both men were out of the
war. It was Whitty's third battle wound. The self-styled "Wild Irishman" had

suffered a minor wound at Gainesville, was shot in the chest at South Mountain (the ball never removed), and had now lost a leg in the Wilderness. "Poor Jim!" said a friend in the Sauk County Rifles, "he was a great soldier." Smith was also a veteran, having enlisted at Linden in 1861. A 7th Wisconsin man from his hospital bed at Philadelphia in a letter to a friend tried to make sense of what transpired in the Virginia thickets. "It was a hot place, I can tell you, but we all done our best and drove the rebels about three miles through the thickest woods you ever saw. The recruits," he added, "fought like tigers"—high praise for the drafted and bounty soldiers used to fill his regiment.[54]

The tragic shooting of Wadsworth and his narrow escape left staff aide Earl Rogers shaken. The young officer was even more troubled when he learned the soldier he called his "straggling diamond"—Pete Markle—had not returned to his company. Rogers visited dismal field hospitals and medical stations to call over and over, "Pete Markle of Coon Slough?" They were places of horrible suffering and smells, and that worried him even more. No one answered his calls. Finally, while walking along a row of hospital beds, he called again, "Pete Markle of Coon Slough?" After a pause, a faint voice replied, "Aye aye, sir." Markle's leg had been amputated at the hip. The marching and hot weather had only made things worse, and the rough trouser wool chafed his wound, which became infected. When gangrene spread, amputation followed. Death was "stamped in his pallid features." Rogers shook Markle's fevered hand and wished him well, promising to see what could be done. Of course, nothing could be done. The Wisconsin farm boy who had walked out of a field to join the Anderson Guards and earn a reputation as the Iron Brigade's best straggler was soon dead—a victim of what would become known as Grant's Overland Campaign.[55]

---

54 Cheek and Pointon, *Sauk County*, 91; *Wisconsin Roster*, vol. 1, 567; Perkins, letter to a friend, May 17, 1864. Cheek and Pointon claimed the South Mountain ball finally killed Whitty in 1906. The report of Lt. Col. Rufus R. Dawes can be found in *OR* 36, pt. 1, 618.

55 Rogers, *Milwaukee Sunday Telegraph*, October 8, 1887.

Part II: Our Once Splendid Brigade

A Shout and a War Whoop

After the fighting in the Wilderness, the Iron Brigade regiments marched south some fifteen miles with the rest of Warren's Fifth Corps toward Spotsylvania Course and reached the grounds of the Alsop farm north of Laurel Hill as early as 8:00 a.m. on May 8. What none of them knew was that they had been in a very tight foot race with Longstreet's First Corps veterans (now under Maj. Gen. Richard Anderson). What they found when they arrived was Confederate artillery posted ahead of them. Perhaps they learned that the leading elements of the corps had already been repulsed. The new Union battle line formed in a woods, with Wadsworth's former division now under Lysander Cutler west of the road and Brig. Gen. Samuel Crawford's division east of the road. "This was perhaps the most formidable point along the enemy's whole front," thought a Wisconsin officer. The crest was crowned by earthworks, the approach swept by artillery and musketry. The line eased forward into the trees and brush. The two lines were only a few hundred yards apart. A house burned between them.[1]

The Iron Brigade, now under Col. William W. Robinson of the 7th Wisconsin, stepped into the attack with Brig. Gen. James Rice's brigade on its left. Colonel Edward Bragg of the 6th Wisconsin now commanded a Pennsylvania brigade on the right. The Westerners were quickly flanked on both sides when Rice did not advance at the same time and Bragg's men angled to the right to avoid artillery fire before crumbling backward. "I could plainly hear the Reb Commander give the command by the left flank and we soon were aware of it," wrote a Wisconsin man. In an effort to prevent a regiment of Alabamians under William C. Oates from flanking them, the 2nd Wisconsin moved at a right angle to the 7th Wisconsin just

---

1   Dawes, *Service*, 263-264.

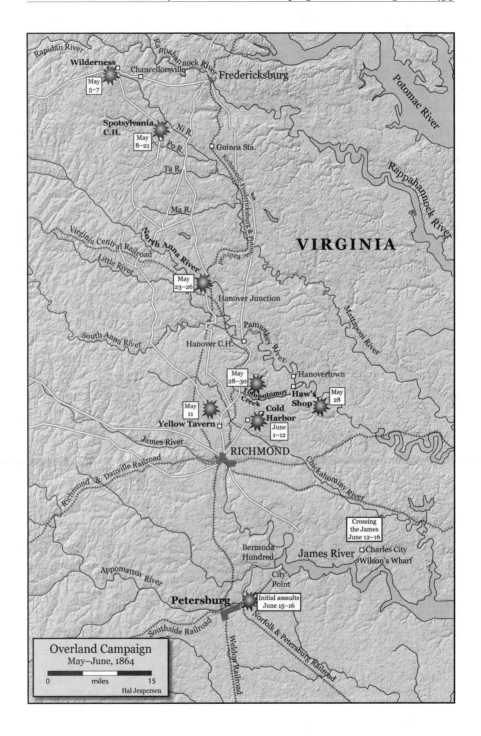

Rapidan River

Rappahannock River

Wilderness
May 5–7

Chancellorsville

Fredericksburg

Potomac River

Spotsylvania C.H.
May 8–21

Ni R.

Po R.

Guinea Sta.

Ta R.

Richmond, Fredericksburg & Potomac Railroad

Rappahannock River

Ma R.

VIRGINIA

Virginia Central Railroad

North Anna River
May 23–26

Little River

Hanover Junction

Pamunkey River

Mattaponi River

South Anna River

Hanover C.H.

May 28–30

Hanovertown

Totopotomoy Creek

Haw's Shop
May 28

May 11

Cold Harbor
June 1–12

Yellow Tavern

James River

RICHMOND

Chickahominy River

Richmond & Danville Railroad

Crossing the James
June 12–16

Bermuda Hundred

James River

Charles City

Wilson's Wharf

Appomattox River

City Point

Petersburg

Initial assaults
June 15–16

Southside Railroad

Norfolk & Petersburg Railroad

Weldon Railroad

Overland Campaign
May–June, 1864

0   miles   15

Hal Jespersen

1st Lt. Howard F. Pruyn, Sauk County Riflemen, Co. A, 6th Wisconsin

Pruyn was wounded on July 1 at Gettysburg in 1863, and killed at Laurel Hill on May 8, 1864. Virginia. *History of the Sauk County Riflemen, Company*

moments before the gray infantry seemingly poured out of the ground. "They came marching right up a ravine which was running at right angles of our line about 50 steps from our right wing, and they poured a volley into our men." A sharp musket fight erupted and the Black Hats held for a time. "The rebels came on with their fiendish yell, but our boys poured such a fire into them that they had to stop and fall back," said one Badger. But not for long. "Outflanked both ways and pressed by the enemy on both sides, the line broke in disorder," reported Rufus Dawes of the 6th Wisconsin. Among the killed was the 6th's Lt. Howard F. Pruyn. He was trying to rally the line when he was shot and fell forward onto his hands and knees, arose, staggered into the timber and died. He had been promoted from the ranks for bravery and had fought in every battle and was "loved by all." Cutler's staff rallied the Western Brigade and Bragg's men, who drove the enemy to the higher ground, and then retired. The brigade built a strong "log breastwork" along their rally point, where they would remain for the next five long days. Pruyn was buried beneath a group of pine trees by the side of the road.[2]

Throughout the day and night additional troops from both armies gathered, extending the lines that would soon fight one of the longest and bloodiest

2   Cheek and Pointon, *Sauk County*, 94. "His death was a great loss to the company, for he had, by his soldierly qualities and kindness of heart, won the love and esteem of every member of the company."

engagements of the entire war. The next day, May 9, opposing skirmishers filtered into the no-man's land that was the tangled brush and woods to keep up "a ceaseless and deadly fire." Gray sharpshooters perched in the trees and high ground offered constant and fatal harassment. A thirty-man detail under Lt. William Golterman of the 6th Wisconsin ("that nervy little German," was how one officer described him) went forward to clear the area with a flurry of shooting. Also remembered that day was the appearance of the new Ojibwa recruits attached to the 7th Wisconsin. "They covered their bodies very ingeniously with pine boughs to conceal themselves in the woods," remarked Dawes. "When skirmishers advanced from our lines, they would run across the open field at the top of their speed, and numbers of them were shot while doing so. Upon this run the Indians would give a shout or war whoop."[3]

May 10 would witness an astonishing assault tactic and heavy bloodshed, but the morning passed quietly for the Western men. General John Gibbon, now with Second Corps was moving troops into position past some resting soldiers when the prone men jumped up with a cheer. "At first I did not realize what it meant but on looking around I discovered the smiling faces of the men of my old brigade, who took this method of testifying their feeling for their old commander," said the general. It was an "inopportune" gesture, he admitted, because the yelling caused heavy artillery fire from the enemy.

Gibbon was moving up a division to assist Warren in a fresh assault against Laurel Hill. Later there were murmurs that Warren had been careless and slow in planning and executing the attacks. Cutler's division, with Robinson's Iron Brigade in the ranks, held the left side of the assaulting front. It was 4:00 p.m. Most of the jagged line lurched forward in fits and starts. Cutler's seems to have stepped off in fine style until meeting a choked ravine, where all semblance of order vanished. A "terrific and continuous fire" ripped through the Western ranks. It was "sure death to stand up there and a waste of powder to fire," wrote a 2nd Wisconsin man. Most of the men dropped to the ground, some reached the outer abatis, and a slim handful made it to the parapets. But the "terrific and continuous fire" proved an insurmountable obstacle.[4]

Dawes was reorganizing his 6th Wisconsin when he came upon Fifth Corps commander Warren straining for a better view. "To have exposed himself above the hill was certain death," wrote Dawes. "I seized his yellow sash and pulled him back." When Dawes spotted Pvt. Aaron Yates of his former Company K creeping

---

3 Dawes, *Service*, 264-265.

4 Harshaw and Lester, *Spring Campaign*, 1-3.

up the hill to get a shot at the enemy, he sharply ordered the young man to seek safety. Yates was the last man to sign the roll to fill out the Lemonweir Minute Men in 1861. When Dawes returned a short time later, Yates was dead. "He was a fine looking fellow, with sandy hair. He had grown during his two years and a half of service to be tall and strong," remembered Dawes. "He was a good soldier and a fearless fighter. . . . Poor fellow, his body was burned by the forest fires that mercilessly raged after that battle. He was a victim of his boyish eagerness and lack of fear for himself." Captain Robert Hughes of the 2nd Wisconsin was also dead above the brow of the hill, the flames in the burning grass crackling toward his corpse. Lieutenant William H. Harries made a "rope" out of suspenders gathered from the men, crawled forward, and tried to cast the loop over the Hughes' upturned foot. The attempt failed. Another creative soul used a dead body for protection, rolling it slowly inch by inch until he reached safety. Out of momentum, without reserves, and with the strong works manned by Rebel veterans supported by batteries of flaming artillery, Dawes finally convinced his superiors to pull back.[5]

Robinson reorganized the Iron Brigade about 100 yards from the enemy lines at the bottom of the slope, where they remained under musketry fire. The Western men watched in horror as sparks fanned into flames, and the fire consumed the maimed and the dead. "Three dead bodies within forty feet of my position were now enveloped in the red mantle of flames, the smoke of which came drifting madly into my face," said a Badger man, who braved enemy fire to pull several wounded to shelter. Culter reported his losses as "quite heavy." Another failed attack.[6]

The attacks of the Iron Brigade regiments near Laurel Hill made no progress except to add to the list of killed and wounded. The latest victims included Lt. Oscar Graetz of the 6th Wisconsin, killed outright, and the severe wounding of Capt. William Remington and Lts. Howard Huntington and John Timmons of the same regiment.

Privates Bill Palmer and Mair Pointon of the Sauk County Riflemen were among the last to leave the exposed field. They fell back slowly together, loading and firing. During the withdrawal, a bullet hit a glancing blow on Palmer's jaw and cut off the lobe of his ear. Bleeding profusely, he asked Pointon whether he was

---

5   Dawes, *Service*, 266-267. Dawes' description of Yates was in a letter in response to an invitation to the January 1885 reunion of Company K in Mauston. He was unable to attend. Yates had been the last volunteer needed to complete the ranks of the forming Lemonweir Minute Men in 1861.

6   For a full detailing of the fighting, see Gordon C. Rhea, *The Battles for Spotsylvania Court House and the Road to Yellow Tavern, May 7-12, 1864* (Baton Rouge, LA, 1997).

Captain Oscar Graetz, Citizens Corps Milwaukee,
Co. F, 6th Wisconsin

Graetz was killed on May 10, 1864, at Spotsylvania Court House. He is
buried at Fredericksburg, Virginia. *Michael Keller*

seriously hurt. Pointon looked him over with a practiced eye of a hard veteran and said he better go to the rear. The two were tent mates. With Rebel bullets zipping between them like angry wasps, Palmer peeled off his knapsack, opened it, and passed their frying pan and shared tin pail to Pointon, who pulled out his pocket book and divided the money with his friend. There was no great show or fuss about the exchange of items under fire. It was just one more example of how far the men had come since leaving Wisconsin. Pointon continued firing until struck by two bullets. The first entered his knapsack and the other cut him on the upper left arm—the latter a painful but not serious wound. Pointon, too, headed for the rear but refused to go to the hospital. "We have had terrible fighting, and more of it than ever before crowded into so short time," was how one Wisconsin man remembered that blur of hellish days. The men in ranks and officers were worn out. Chaplain Samuel Eaton of the 7th Wisconsin claimed those days of fighting aged the young and healthy officers, who were now "older by years than before the campaign." One of the newly aged was Lt. Earl Rogers of the 6th Wisconsin. According to Eaton, Rogers' cheeks were sunken and he "can but just hang on his horse."[7]

Grant launched another major attack later that evening, farther left opposite a giant bulge in the Southern line later dubbed "the Mule Shoe." The creative formation, the brainchild of brigade commander Col. Emory Upton, called for a narrow but deep assaulting column to storm a single point along the Confederate works. The thrust penetrated the front, but was unsupported and beaten back with heavy losses. The initial success, however, helped put in motion another attack two days later.

Especially troubling those hard days of early May—at least to the old hands—was the formal detaching of the 2nd Wisconsin from the brigade on May 11. The move ended an association with the original Western regiments that began in the Washington camps of McClellan in 1861. The 2nd was now so reduced by hard service that it had fewer than 100 men present for duty. The proud regiment was detailed as Provost Guard for the Fourth Division, Warren's Fifth Corps.[8]

The morning of May 12 began what Dawes called "the most terrible twenty-four hours of our service in the war." The brigade was "worn and exhausted" by five days and nights of continuous service under the fire of the

---

7   Dawes, *Service*, 252-253. "Major Plummer, Captain Kellogg, Captain Converse, Lieutenant Pruyn and Lieutenant Graetz are in their graves," he wrote in a letter to his wife on May 11, 1864. "Captain Remington, Lieut. Timmons and Lieut. J. L. Converse are wounded. The perils of the last week have been fearful," *ibid.*, 266-267. Gibbon, *Recollections*, 218; Cheek and Pointon, *Sauk County*, 96; Wheeler, papers; Samuel Eaton, papers, Wisconsin Historical Society.

8   Quiner, *Military History*, 466-477.

determined enemy. Another charge against Laurel Hill involving the Western men kicked off about 10:00 a.m. Cutler's division advanced alone, both flanks exposed with the Iron Brigade in the front next to Ed Bragg's mixed brigade. The front dropped into a ravine before stalling below the enemy abatis in front of a brigade of Georgians. The attack, complained one disgusted Iron Brigade man, was "almost a farce for we scarcely got but a few paces beyond our lines." Dawes' 6th Wisconsin in front paused to allow the second line to close. "It was plain that no body of troops could pick its way through such a formidable obstruction as long as the works were properly manned." Dawes urged Cutler to withdraw, and after some doing, Warren agreed. "The assault was manifestly hopeless at the outset," complained Dawes. "Gettysburg is a skirmish compared to this fight," marveled one of the Western men. One Southern division had easily beaten back an entire Union corps. The result more close to home was the death and wounding of several of the Iron Brigade's "best and truest men," including 1st Sgt. Nicolas Snyder of Co. H, 6th Wisconsin.[9]

Many hours earlier before the final botched Laurel Hill assault, well off to the left, Hancock's Second Corps stormed out of the pre-dawn darkness to overwhelm the stunned Confederate defenders of the Mule Shoe. The fighting along the breastworks was the most bitter, sustained, close, and deadly of the entire war. And it would continue for nearly twenty hours as both sides poured in thousands of men to either break open the line or seal the breach. The epic combat raged in the Mule Shoe that afternoon when orders pulled the Iron Brigade out of line from in front of the much despised Laurel Hill position. The Western men shifted more than one mile to the left (east) to assist John Sedgwick's embattled Sixth Corps. Horatio Wright, elevated to lead the corps after Sedgwick's death on May 9, was attacking the northwest face of the Mule Shoe in an effort to punch through. He could do so with Warren's help, he assured Grant. It was about 3:00 p.m. Held in reserve, the Black Hats watched "this dreadful struggle, one of the fierce and most deadly of the war." The 7th Wisconsin and 7th Indiana were sent to relieve some in the Second Corps, and were in turn relieved by the 6th Wisconsin and the 24th Michigan.[10]

The two regiments were holding a position near what would become known as the "Mule Shoe" or "Bloody Angle." The lines of colors of both armies "stood waving within twenty feet of each other and there was a continual roar and crash of musketry," said one eyewitness. A while later orders recalled the Iron Brigade, which trudged away in "a driving rainstorm," only to be sent back to the same

9   For details, see Rhea, *Spotsylvania Court House*, 53-59.

10 Harshaw and Lester, *Spring Campaign*.

general position where "the unbroken roar of musketry continued into the darkness of the night." The evening was dark as pitch and the roads muddy from rain. A ravine marked the course for the regiments, which formed a battle line behind the embattled Sixth Corps before orders arrived to move forward. The night's work was "very hard," admitted Dawes, who recalled the soldiers of his regiment standing and firing all night into the Confederate earthworks. The men went in near the spot where Hancock's Second Corps had breached the enemy works and then rushed in artillery. Now Hancock could not get his guns out again, so the Black Hats attempted to keep the Confederates down in the area of "disputed ground." It went that way all night in the rain and mud. "We stood perhaps one hundred feet from the enemy's line, and so long as we maintained a continual fire they remained hidden in their entrenchments," Dawes explained. "But if an attempt to advance was made an order would be given and they would all rise up together and fire a volley at us." The mud was "half boot top deep and filled with the dead of the battle, over whom we stumbled in the darkness."[11]

On the left of the Wisconsin regiment, the 24th Michigan added its fire into the angle from a distance of just fifty feet. A "large oak tree stood [to their front] just inside the Confederate entrenchments within the Salient between his lines," remembered a Wolverine. The Michigan regiment had replaced the 7th Wisconsin about dusk with orders to fire on each side of the oak tree to prevent the enemy from moving their artillery. "The night was very dark and the flash of the enemy's muskets over their second line showed their line of earthworks at the Salient, and the oak tree was used as a guide to fire by," said one soldier. "Standing in deep mud and keeping up a constant fire for hours and till after midnight, the men's muskets became so foul that details were made to clean the guns while their comrades kept up the fire. The men were so weary (having been under fire night and day for a week) that some lay down in the mud under the enemy's fire and slept soundly amid the thunders of battle, despite all efforts to arouse them." The historian of the Wolverine regiment claimed the 24th alone fired 5,000 rounds into the angle.[12]

The Confederate entrenchment was about four feet deep and filling rapidly with water and mud because of the continuing rain. On top was a "head log," which allowed infantry behind it to fire beneath it or through chinks to protect their heads. In the darkness, however, the protective log was a hindrance. Heavy bullets fired over the long hours shredded and destroyed the head logs. When the Wisconsin

---

11 Dawes, *Service*, 267-268; Cheek and Pointon, *Sauk County*, 97-98; Curtis, *Twenty-fourth*, 243-244.

12 Curtis, *Twenty-fourth*, 242-243.

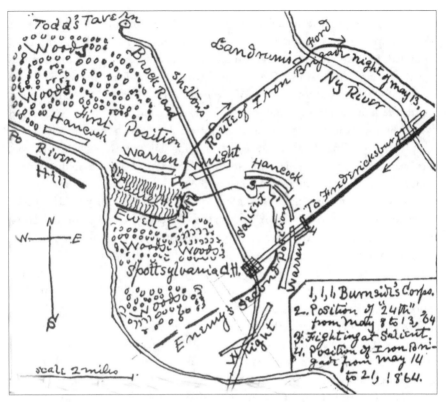

The Iron Brigade in the Spotsylvania Campaign

This map, drawn by a veteran of the 24th Michigan, depicts the brigade's movements around the Bloody Angle during the Spotsylvania fighting. *History of the Twenty-fourth Michigan*

men quickly emptied their cartridge boxes, Dawes systematized the firing from right to left by company. Some of the soldiers each fired 300 rounds during the long ordeal. Squads of men made for the rear for ammunition as the rain poured down "in torrents," but only one returned with a wooden box of packed cartridges. "To wade through the mud on that awful night, stumbling over the dead and carrying that heavy box was a labor of heroic faithfulness," said Dawes. "Sometime in the night I suspected the enemies were retreating. I then ceased firing and my exhausted men lay down as best they could and some laid their heads upon the dead and fell asleep."[13]

13 Dawes, *Service*, 267-268; Cheek and Pointon, *Sauk County*, 97-98.

The grisly spectacle troubled even the hard veterans of the Iron Brigade. "Rebel works presented an awful spectacle [at dawn] . . . crowded with dead and wounded, lying in some cases upon each other and several inches of mud and water," remembered Dawes. "I saw the body of a rebel soldier sitting in the corner of one of these cellars in a position of apparent ease, with the head entirely gone, and the flesh burned from the bones of the neck and shoulders. This was doubtless caused by the explosion of a shell from the small Coehorn mortars within our lines." The Iron Brigade men had seen everything during this long war, but even they were appalled by the slaughter the sun revealed. "Wounded soldiers at the bottom of the trench were pinned down by the dead bodies of their comrades and those of the enemy," one said. "On the slope in front of the angle lay dead bodies of men and horses so riddled with bullets that they flattened out on the ground. Not a blade of grass, twig or shrub left standing; the face of the gun carriages and caissons towards the enemy was sheeted with lead from the striking bullets." A Badger counted thirteen artillery caissons and eight cannon in the rebel works with the horses dead in their traces. It was "a hard looking field . . . the dead laid in profusion. Ours and the Rebs mixed as thick as I ever saw them in any place." Of special interest was a large oak tree that had been cut down entirely by musket fire. A portion of the tree was later saved. It measured "five feet six inches in height and twenty-one inches in diameter." The section was eventually displayed during the Centennial Exhibition in Philadelphia in 1876, and there were many claims ("Second Corps regiments, of course," scoffed one of the Black Hats) about which regiment or regiments shot off the tree. But there was no doubt in the minds of the Black Hats. "[I]t is a historic fact that the tree fell about midnight after several hours of shooting at it by the Twenty-fourth Michigan and Sixth Wisconsin," argued one of the Michigan men. "These two regiments stood nearest to it, fired at it longest, and were shooting away at it when it fell."[14]

My regiment, explained Dawes was "in a deplorable condition of exhaustion" when he marched his men away from the "Bloody Angle" to find them a patch of ground to rest for a while before moving to join the other regiments of the brigade at their former position near Laurel Hill. At 10:00 p.m. that evening, the brigade was roused again to march from the extreme right side of the Union line to a position on the extreme left—part of Grant's new flanking swing to the south around Lee's right flank. The Fifth Corps's tramp over muddy and broken roads in the darkness was an "immense difficulty." The route led to the Ny River, which had to be waded. The columns traversed open fields and stumbled along paths cut through woods,

14 *Ibid.*; Curtis, *Twenty-fourth*, 243-244.

with not a clue as to where they were going. A dense fog masked fires built to guide the column. Some of the men fell asleep during the march—but kept moving.[15] The brigade went into position on the morning of May 14 behind a line of works. The Black Hats would remain there, enduring occasional artillery duels and lively skirmishes, until May 21. "We have been fighting for 10 days now & I think on the whole the Rebs have got rather the worst of it," Henry Matrau of the 6th Wisconsin wrote home. "We have lost 160 men in our Regt killed and wounded. We have got six men in my company. I am well, but I almost wonder how I have stood it as well as I have."[16]

Finally, on May 21, Robinson's exhausted Iron Brigade marched with the balance of Cutler's skeleton division in a southeasterly direction following the shifting Confederates. Lee had the inside track south. With most of Grant's men tramping the arc, Lee won the race to the North Anna River. Warren's Fifth Corps moved into position on the right side of the Federal line on May 23, crossed the river unopposed at Jericho Mills, and deployed his divisions in line of battle. The last to move into place were Cutler's men, who filed into position on the right side. The Iron Brigade held the left of Cutler's front next to Griffin's division. Dawes' 6th Wisconsin was on the left of the brigade, with the 7th Wisconsin and 2nd Wisconsin, 24th Michigan, and 19th Indiana extending the line toward the river. Cutler's other brigades were moving behind the Black Hats to anchor the flank, which was still exposed. General Lee had misread the situation and thought Warren's presence was a feint. As a result, A. P. Hill thrust only a single Confederate division against Fifth Corps. Despite being heavily outnumbered, the Southern attack broke apart Warren's front, though without inflicting heavy losses.

Edward Thomas' Georgia brigade struck the right front of Black Hats, who had just taken up their position when the hammer fell. The Black Hats were not expecting trouble and were at their coffee fires when a sharp attack "with great fury" caught them by surprise. Another Confederate brigade was moving to overlap their exposed right while clots of animals, including cattle and sheep, ran amok and added to the confusion. The spring campaign had exposed the Western boys to one terrible predicament after another, and now another wave of bad luck was heading in their direction. Although he could not see well from his position on the far left, Dawes ordered his men to fire at the right oblique toward the west. Within minutes he learned that the other Black Hat regiments extending the line in

---

15 Stine, *Army of the Potomac*; Dawes, *Service*, 268-270; Henry Matrau, letter to mother, May 15, 1861; John O. Johnson, letter to John Hauser, July 2, 1864.

16 Quiner, *Military History*, 467-468.

1st Lt. Burns Newman, Grand Rapids Union Guards, Co. G, 7th Wisconsin

Newman enlisted at New Lisbon and worked his way up from the ranks. He was killed on May 24, 1864, at Jericho Ford, Virginia, during the fighting along the North Anna River. *Author's Collection*

that direction had either broken or were in the process of doing so. Hit front and flank, Robinson's men cracked again and fled, some back across the North Anna River. The 6th Wisconsin remained in place. Dawes turned his line to face west and protect his own now exposed flank. When Thomas' Georgians enfiladed his now-exposed left flank, Dawes held his men together and performed an orderly withdrawal.

Warren's line was unraveling, one unit at a time and fell back in some disorder toward the bluffs. Only well positioned Union artillery and Hill's failure to follow up his success drove back the attackers and stabilized the line. Warren ordered his corps to dig in. Later Brigade Commander William W. Robinson would be criticized for his performance in the setback, but what happened to the weary and exhausted men of the Iron Brigade regiments on May 23, an artillery officer noted in his journal, was an indication of how panic at times can seize a whole command. "No brigade in the whole army had a higher reputation than the 'Iron Brigade.' Its pre-eminence in the old First Corps was very generally acknowledged, yet one-half of it ran clear across the river without firing a shot . . ."[17]

"We came near being driven into the river, but the enemy has lost vigor in attack," one Western man wrote home. "Their men are getting so they will not fight except in rifle pits." Dawes wrote his wife the next day, "I have had not a full night's sleep since May 7th when I took command of the regiment. Day after day, and night after night we have marched fought and dug entrenchments. I have not changed my clothing since May 3rd." A Michigan soldier said the two weeks since the start of the campaign were "but a tale of blood." His regiment had been reduced from 320 to 149, and the bright new battle flag presented just three weeks earlier by the citizens of Detroit (the first flag used up and sent home) "was now tattered and riddled with bullets."[18]

In the 6th Wisconsin, there were two bright moments that gloomy night as the regiment waited in the woods. Out of the darkness, came a call, "Whar's the sixth Wisconsin? Whar's the sixth Wisconsin?" It was Rufus Dawes' young servant, William Jackson, who had waded across the waist-deep river and, almost exhausted, stumbled along the lines in the dark with a coffee pot and "a full supper" for the officer's mess. "To him the officers of the sixth Wisconsin owed this comforting relief from hunger and exhaustion," said Dawes, "for I shared it with them all." The other occurred when a man appeared out of the darkness to ask the pickets of the 6th Wisconsin, "What regiment is this?" The reply "Sixth Wisconsin" puzzled the

17 OR 3, pt. 3, 651; Wainwright, *Diary of Battle*, 386.

18 Cheek and Pointon, *Sauk County*, 102-103; Curtis, *Twenty-fourth*, 246.

man, who asked if the speaker meant the 6th Mississippi. The picket confirmed the regiment was of Badger origin. The stranger announced that he was a Confederate surgeon, and could not understand how a Wisconsin regiment could be here since he had been told the Yankees had been driven into the river. The pickets scooped him up and sent him to the rear.[19]

By the time the balance of the Army of the Potomac arrived along the North Anna, General Lee realized a major battle was about to take place and erected an inverted V-shaped series of entrenchments that would separate the Federals should they attempt to cross the river. Warren pushed his corps forward on May 24 to the Virginia Central Railroad, and the next day felt out Lee's extensive earthworks. In the end, the North Anna was the showdown that wasn't, a series of small-scale combats that never escalated into a full-scale engagement. Each side lost about 2,500 men to all causes. Once again Grant shifted the army around Lee's right flank, his goal the crossroads of Cold Harbor about twenty-five miles southeast. On the evening of May 26, Warren's Fifth Corps and Wright's Sixth Corps pulled back over the North Anna and moved eastward the next day toward the Pamunkey River crossings at Hanovertown.[20]

The Prince of Soldiers

By June 2, the two armies were once again dug in along a series of winding entrenchments stretching some seven miles. Warren's corps held the right-center of the Union line, with Cutler's division west of Bethesda Church mostly below the Old Church Road. Luckily for the Western boys, they had missed most of the bloodshed for which Cold Harbor is known. Two days earlier on June 3, Grant—frustrated in his many failed efforts to destroy the Army of Northern Virginia or gain a march to flank it, ordered the three army corps left of Warren to assault Lee's line. The effort failed within an hour and left the attackers pinned down with heavy losses. Additional efforts to renew the attack failed. Exact losses are not known, but estimates stretch as high as 7,000 Federals and perhaps 1,500 Confederates. Grant would one day admit the attack was the only assault he made during the war that he wished he had never ordered.

The Black Hats escaped the horror of that senseless fight, but the old Iron Brigade veterans were troubled when word arrived that Frank Haskell, who had

19 Dawes, *Service*, 277.

20 For a full description, see Gordon C. Rhea, *To the North Anna River: Grant and Lee, May 13-25, 1864* (Baton Rouge, LA, 2000).

shaped the first Western regiments with John Gibbon, had been killed. Haskell was finally leading his own regiment—the 36th Wisconsin—in Gibbon's Second Division, Hancock's Second Corps. When his brigade commander was killed, Haskell succeeded him. Although his line was pinned down by a heavy fire, Gibbon ordered the attack pushed. When the soldiers stood up, they were shot down by the dozens. Haskell ordered his men to lie down while he alone stood alone, leaning on his sword, to set an example. Just weeks earlier in Madison, he had told a friend that he fully expected to be killed. "You see, I have a green regiment," he explained. "I cannot get behind the lines as I might do in the case of seasoned troops. I shall be obliged always to lead, and of course I shall be shot." He was standing tall in the storm of lead and iron at Cold Harbor when a heavy musket ball struck his temple. The "Prince of Soldiers" and hero of Gettysburg was dead.[21]

Just before the army left Cold Harbor, the Iron Brigade left behind the brave old 2nd Wisconsin, which had been with it from the first days of the war. Its three-year term of enlistment filled, the regiment was released to finally go home. The soldiers of the 2nd Wisconsin who had not "veteranized," together with recruits whose terms had not expired, were organized into an independent battalion of two companies. It was with heavy hearts that the old Black Hats formed for the last time on June 11, 1864. A brief farewell ceremony unfolded and the small remnant that was the 2nd Wisconsin faced right and began marching to a landing on the James River for transport. Its blue regimental banner was about used up, remembered one, the flag staff shattered by musket balls and the colors "unfurled at the first Bull Run, now in tattered streamers." Eight hundred had stood in the ranks when the 2nd joined the 6th and 7th Wisconsin and 19th Indiana at Washington in 1861; fewer than 200 remained—"a little body of bronzed veterans." When the brigade band struck up "When Johnny Comes Marching Home," the old hands lifted their hats for the "Ragged Assed" 2nd Wisconsin one more time and offered three loud cheers as it marched away from the Army of the Potomac for the last time. It was soon out of sight.[22]

Back at army headquarters, it was again time for hard decisions. Unwilling to lay siege to Richmond with its strong network of defensive works, and out of room

21 Byrne and Weaver, *Haskell of Gettysburg*, 244. Haskell's body was returned to Wisconsin and buried in the Silver Lake Cemetery at Portage, the home of two brothers. Haskell would not become famous until after the publication of his long letter describing the battle of Gettysburg.

22 Earl Rogers Papers, Wisconsin Veterans Museum. Richard Lester of the 2nd Wisconsin said of the return to Wisconsin: "I shall never—nor will, I think, any member of the command present—forget the splendid and hearty manner in which the 'Old Second' was greeted on its return to the Capitol of the State it had for three long years represented on the battle field in as good a cause as ever soldiers fought and died for." Harshaw and Lester, *Spring Campaign*.

to maneuver above the James River, Grant set in motion one of the grand movements of the war: the army would slip south to the wide James, cross as fast as possible, and capture the vital logistical center of Petersburg. Without Petersburg, Lee could not feed his army; Richmond would fall. The army began moving on the evening of June 12. The Iron Brigade regiments crossed the Chickahominy River, marched to the James River, and crossed at Wilcox's Landing. A series of botched attacks followed, bogging down the army east of Petersburg. The Iron Brigade took up a position in breastworks with the rest of Warren's Fifth Corps on the left side of the developing line just above the Norfolk and Petersburg Railroad. The Badgers of the 6th Wisconsin noted with some pride and wonder that the regiment was on the left of the brigade, and therefore constituted the extreme left flank of the Army of the Potomac.[23]

On the afternoon of June 18, the Black Hats moved against the enemy's fortifications on the west side of the railroad about two miles outside Petersburg. With the 6th Wisconsin on the left and the 7th Wisconsin on the right, the 24th Michigan, 7th Wisconsin and 19th Indiana in the center, the line reached a point 100 yards in front of the enemy's works before the attack faltered when Federal units on their left gave way—exposing the 7th Wisconsin. While the other regiments fell back, the men of the 7th sought shelter in a ravine. Musketry and artillery fire pinned them there for nearly ninety minutes. Union batteries firing above their heads to prevent the Rebels from advancing added to the brigade's losses when some of the shells fell short. Some of the men of the 7th found a few shovels and began constructing an earthwork to protect their left flank while others used bayonets and tin plates to throw up the red earth. Major Hollon Richardson ran "the gauntlet of fire" to report the terrible fix to brigade headquarters. No help could be sent, however, unless a general assault was made. Before the earthworks could be completed, a Rebel line moving beyond the exposed left flank of the 7th Wisconsin advanced within seventy-five yards. At the same time, a heavy Southern skirmish line advanced against the right flank. The Badgers divided their firepower, some against each threat. The threat was too great, however, and it was no use standing still. The embattled Badgers ran to the right and rear though a heavy and destructive fire to the position they had left that morning. Sergeant Calvin G. Parker, who was carrying the regimental banner, was killed. The flag was recovered but his body was left between the lines.[24] As expected, the 7th Wisconsin had the brigade's heaviest losses with fifty-one killed, wounded, and missing, followed by

---

23 Quiner, *Military History*, 472-473.

24 *Ibid.*, 474; Ray, *Iron Brigade*, 286.

forty-four in the 6th Wisconsin. The entire series of attacks failed that day. Works were constructed within 500 yards of the growing enemy line. A Michigan soldier called the day "a great disaster." Little was gained, he said, except "to gain positions very near the lines of the enemy which were intrenched, and the lines of the two armies remained about the same till the close of the war."[25]

And so began the long and deadly trench warfare that would slowly curl around Petersburg in the south and Richmond in the north and consume so many more lives. "It is awfully disheartening to be ordered upon such hopeless assaults," Rufus Dawes wrote home the next day. What he didn't know was that he could reuse that sentence and again and again in the coming months. His 6th Wisconsin suffered five killed and 35 wounded.

A Young Boy Seeking Freedom

It was during that June of near-continuous fighting that Sgt. Jerome Watrous finally won his lieutenant's shoulder straps and began serving as adjutant in the 6th Wisconsin.

The new officer was in the regiment's camp outside Petersburg when he first became aware of a young teenage male with a quick smile and bright eyes. In the fashion of the day, Watrous romanced the account just a bit, carefully quoting the young boy's words in what he perceived as the broad dialect of the Virginia slave and using descriptions that would be insensitive, even harsh, to modern readers. But the story he wrote was one of admiration, pride, and even affection for the young man who would become his servant and then his friend.

The youth stood off for a while, watching, but soon enough stepped forward with some hesitation to ask in a quiet voice, "Does you want a boy, suh?" He was a "contraband"—a name given in hard army fashion by a Union general to the hundreds of former slaves who fled plantations and farms to go into the Union lines to become servants, cooks, and common laborers. "The boy was sixteen, black as night, with a pleasant smile and a set of teeth which any one might be glad to possess," Watrous wrote long afterward. "I knew that he was a newcomer, and was getting away from his master—reaching for freedom. Why did I know? Because an old hand would not have applied for a job in a line of battle." Watrous himself was young and a newly promoted lieutenant who had "plodded my way up from the prized rank of a private in the back file." He had also been without a servant for a week—the last one ran away after Cold Harbor.

25 OR 40, pt. 1, 475; Curtis, *Twenty-fourth*, 263.

Officer Servant

This unusual image of his camp servant was found in the personal photo album of a 5th Wisconsin officer and is an example of the friendship that developed between Wisconsin officer and former slaves. *Institute for Civil War Studies*

"What can you do?" asked the officer.

"Ise dun helped old massa with de hosses and old misses in de kitchen."

"Can you make coffee, fry pork and boil beans?"

"I never did massa, but I kin get de habit."

Richard Epps was his name, added the teenager, but he was called Dick. Questions about salary led to confusion, the young Epps unsure what Watrous meant. When he explained the concept of pay for work, the young man answered quickly, "Jes zactly what you wants to give me, suh, only let me wuk and get away from ol' massa. I wants to be free, suh." Watrous gave the boy a steady look before he finally said, "Mr. Richard Epps, of Petersburg, or vicinity, Virginia, you are engaged." It was the beginning of a long relationship between the boy, Watrous, and the soldiers of Company E of the 6th Wisconsin. And it would last through the war and beyond.[26]

---

26 A large home owned by a Dr. Richard Eppes, a physician, was located nearby at City Point, Virginia, but it is not known if there was a connection to the young boy and the slaves who lived on the plantation. When the Union army arrived in the area in 1862, the family moved to

Dick took care of "Charlie," the lieutenant's horse, cooked, washed, blacked boots, and was "handy, generally." Watrous did his own mending. "I will call you Mr. Epps," Watrous announced. There was one other thing: "[H]old up your right hand and swear that when the big guns begin to boom and the bullets come around hinting for scalps, you will not desert your post and fly to the rear with the shirks and some other servants."

"Ol' mammy dun said I mustn't never swear, suh."

"Well, then, do you promise to stay by me in the hour of danger?"

"Oh, yes, suh, I dun makes dat promise."

The arrangement worked from the very first. Mr. Epps was busy frying fat pork and making coffee when fighting opened on June 18—his first battle. Watrous took to his saddle. "Mr. Epps, remember your promise?" he called with a smile. The boy nodded. "I'll be yer, suh, dead or 'live, suh, and dinner'll be ready when you dun come back."

Watrous rode off into the fighting and came upon Gen. Edward Bragg, his first company captain. A shell had knocked the general from his horse by a shell. After a time, the stunned Bragg climbed back into the saddle with enough presence of mind to ask Watrous if the old Iron Brigade was "all right." Watrous assured him it was. Hollon Richardson of the 7th Wisconsin came out of the fighting with a wounded arm, followed by Capt. Earl Rogers of the 6th Wisconsin. "I'm hit bad," grimaced Rogers as he moved to the rear. A canister ball had ploughed through his thigh and left a terrible wound. Much later, in the dusk with the battle behind them and the fighting a draw, Watrous returned to where he had left young Mr. Epps. A smile and a cheerful hello greeted the returning officer. "I'se dun got supper rady, suh"—fried pork, a cup of coffee, and hardtack. The next morning he set "a breakfast fit for a corps commander," exclaimed Watrous. After he had eaten, the boy approached slowly to ask, "Massa, does yo' want me to stay?" "Yes, Mr. Epps, I am well satisfied—well satisfied."[27]

One of those in the ranks who took Mr. Epps under his wing was Pvt. Jake Deiner. (According to Watrous, the association resulted because the quiet private missed his younger brothers and sisters.) The two were unlikely friends—quiet, large-hearted and brawny Jake Deiner, the farm boy who left home to defend the Union, and the slight Mr. Epps, a Virginia slave boy bound for freedom. Deiner was "always the same good natured, gallant, brave soldier," Watrous said. "Fellow

---

Petersburg for safety. Two years later, Ulysses S. Grant took over the Eppes' home as his headquarters.

27 Watrous, *Richard Epps*, 7-12.

soldiers can recall such men with whom they served. No one ever saw Jake Deiner shirk a duty or try to escape a danger." When the former slave expressed surprise that runaway slaves and freed men in Wisconsin could read and cipher, Deiner bought a primer and began giving the boy reading lessons. Never was there a more willing student. The young runaway and the man he called "Massa Big Jake" were often seen working with the reader in the evening hours. The soldier friend was "frequently quoted and discussed by the colored boy," explained Watrous. "What Deiner did was just right in the eyes of the young contraband." The friendship and learning, however, never got in the way of his other duties, and Mr. Epps was always on hand when the regiment moved and whether supper or breakfast, the meal and coffee were ready when needed.[28]

The young "contraband" suffered his first wound just a few weeks later. He was standing near the earthworks when a bullet zipped in and the boy collapsed with a groan. Private Jake Deiner was the first to reach him. The lead slug had clipped a patch of hair from the boy's head. "Where is Jones, our temperance man?" yelled Deiner. "I want a little commissary whisky to rub on this boy's head. Jones is the only man in the company who is likely to have any. Send him here, quick." Soon Cpl. Edwin Jones arrived "with his long, awkward, shambling step." He always carried a canteen of whiskey, although everyone in the company knew it was only for emergencies as he never drank himself. Someone rubbed the whiskey on the small wound and a "a gill of it and more" was swallowed by Mr. Epps. The stunned boy came to his senses after a time and was soon on his feet.

"Who—who—who dun struck me?" the boy asked. "I never dun hurt none of you alls."

"Why, boy, none of the white folks stuck you; you were shot."

"What's dat? Me shot? Who shot me? What does da want to shoot me for? I ain't hurt nobody.

"Why, a Johnny shot you boy," said Watrous.

"Is I goin' to die, Massa Ag'tant?"

"Oh, no, Mr. Epps, but you had a narrow escape. A sharpshooter has undoubtedly been watching for a chance to kill you ever since you became my servant. He came very near it this time. You must be exceedingly careful, hereafter."

It was the first wound for Mr. Richard Epps, though not his last.[29]

---

28 *Ibid.*, 16-19.

29 Jacob Deiner, Ellington, enlisted on June 28, 1861, *Wisconsin Roster*, vol. 1, 513. When he wrote the account at the turn of the century, Watrous misspelled Deiner as "Diener."

Whiz, Whiz, the Bullets go Over Our Heads

Private William Ray of the 7th Wisconsin finally left the hospital where he was being treated for his Wilderness wound to return to his regiment in July. His outfit was in the front line. Only twenty men were left in his company. "Whiz, whiz, the bullets go over our heads," he wrote in his journal shortly after his arrival. "But we don't fire. Our breastworks are high enough that they cant hit us if we keep in them. Occasionally a shot from the Artillery. We have some morter on the right & they throw shell occasionally which fairly makes the earth quake. Some light right in the Reb works, play havoc with them." Trench warfare was completely foreign to Ray, who was surprised at how easily his comrades took to it. "We lay in the ditches all day. Cook & eat. We can have a good liberty by way or stirring around if we are of mind to risk our lives which the Boys do to a great deal. A ball whizzing past never stops anything unless it hits the man. Never stops conversation at all. I was amazed to see how indifferent the Boys are to things passing." The gunfire was ceaseless, explained another Wisconsin boy to the folks back home. "The sharpshooters are popping away all the time on both sides and the hiss of the big gun comes in to sing bass." The artillery fire and mortar shelling went on day and night, confirmed Henry Matrau of the 6th Wisconsin. "But we have become so accustomed to this sort o' thing that we don't mind it and sleep as sound at night with shells bursting around and over us as we would at home out of range of hearing of cannon or bomb-shells." A huge 13-inch mortar he called "the Petersburg Express" was stationed nearby, Matrau continued, "and keeps belching away, occasionally throwing the shells directly over our heads."

The constant exchange of mortar fire was something one never forgot, recalled one officer. "How vividly the experience . . . when the mortars began their work comes back to me, and how plainly I can hear the dull roar of the monsters as the charge of powder exploded and the big, round iron shell started upward on its journey of destruction; how plainly it could be seen as it went up like a great black bird, and then turned and came rapidly towards our lines. A few seconds later there was a mighty explosion and a scattering of dirt and dust; then came a glad hurrah, for the black monster had only frightened the veterans of Cutler's division." A Union mortar returned fire with "the great shell slowly climbed up a thousand feet or more, and then slowly swung over toward the Confederate line and started down like a shooting star. It exploded twenty or more feet in the air. There was a flying of timbers and gray uniforms, and the groans and cries were like those in a railroad accident." The brass coehorn mortars were becoming a regular feature of the siege. The coehorns operated in six-gun batteries. Each tube and platform could be carried by four men, and the short barrels fired a 24-pound shell. "We have Artillery

Captain Henry Sanford, Belle City Rifles,
Co. F, 2nd Wisconsin

Sanford became captain of the company from Racine on May 4, 1864, and
was mustered out on June 28, 1864, term expired. *Wisconsin Veterans Museum*

enough here to shell the whole Southern Confederacy, if it was in range of our guns," boasted an Indiana soldier.[30]

The brigade rotated on and off the front line, three days up and three days back. Once in the rear, the weary soldiers found what shade they could, cooked, and tried to get some real rest. Ray and a friend walked to divisional headquarters, found a sutler, and bought a bottle of mustard and .25 cents worth of lemons. The Badger was disappointed that night to see so many of the brigade's officers getting drunk. The three days sailed past, and the Black Hats returned to the front line. Sometimes the steady shooting across no-man's land would fall away to silence, and the soldiers on both sides would get up to take a look at one another. On one occasion where the lines were very close, a man from each side ran out to trade newspapers, but a Union soldier off to the right squeezed his trigger. As the two men scurried back to their earthworks, the Iron Brigade men began hollering that someone should shoot the man who fired that cowardly shot. "Most everybody seems to think he deserved death for shooting on such an occasion," grumbled Ray. After two or three minutes of quiet, the two men were again racing across the ground between the lines. This time they solemnly shook hands and exchanged their papers. Once they were safe in their own trenches, the scattered shooting started all over again.[31]

The end of June 1864 marked an infamous event in the history of the Iron Brigade known as the Brooks' Raid. A special detail of thirty-two men from all the regiments under the command of Adj. Edward Brooks of the 6th Wisconsin was sent out to destroy some bridges on the Danville Railroad. The men were well armed and mounted. On the morning of June 22, they found a Confederate officer inside a house and captured him. He was paroled and the party rode on. At midday, Brooks dismounted his command at a farm house and stacked arms for supper, though without throwing out any guard. Soon after, the Confederate officer they had just paroled arrived to demand their surrender. The Southerner, who had gathered area farmers armed largely with shotguns to pursue the Union column, deployed his ad hoc command beyond a small hill so that only the heads of their horses and men could be seen. They appeared more numerous than they were in reality. Brooks complied, and the Union horses, accoutrements, and arms were taken from them and the entire command made prisoners of war. Some later said

30 George Eustice, letter to his mother, June 15, 1864; Watrous, *Richard Epps*, 12; Henry Matrau, letter, July 25, 1865; John Hawk, letter to father, July 11, 1864. The large mortar mentioned was the famous "Dictator." It was mounted on a railroad flatcar and could throw a 200-pound shell about two and one-half miles.

31 Ray, *Iron Brigade*, 286-287; Watrous, *Richard Epps*, 22.

Brooks was drunk at the time. The news was especially troubling to those waiting back at the front because the men selected for the raid were among the brigade's finest.[32]

The Iron Brigade spent July with the rest of Warren's Fifth Corps southeast of Petersburg, sandwiched between the Norfolk and Petersburg Railroad on the right and the Jerusalem Plank Road on the left. In late June, Second Corps launched an attack beyond Warren's right to break and capture the Weldon Railroad. Heavy fighting drove the Federals back without significant damage to the logistical line, but the result managed to extend the Federal lines westward, which forced Lee to do likewise.

The Western boys spent the long hot weeks of July engaged in the myriad but routine duties of siege warfare. They were in the front works on July 30 when a large mine exploded under the Confederate earthworks to their right in a major effort to rip open a gap in the lines and drive through to capture the city. A group of Pennsylvania miners-turned-soldiers had tunneled more than 500 feet before placing 8,000 pounds of powder under a Confederate fort. The dawn blast lifted 500 yards of Confederate trench. "Slowly, the great heaps of earth, timbers, cannon, a regiment of men, its tents, gun carriages and caissons climbed higher and higher," wrote one witness. "Then there was a parting, Timbers, men, guns, tents were scattered to the right and to the left; to the front and the rear. Oh. What a sight! At least one poor fellow was thrown clear over the Union lines."

Rufus Dawes wrote his wife that he was inside a bomb proof "taking a nap, when I felt a jar like an earthquake. I jumped out in time to see probably the most terrific explosion ever known in this country." Private Ray did his best to describe the indescribable scene in his journal:

> Half past 4:00 arrived and with it the shaking of the ground awakened me. I rocked to and fro, looked at the ground to see the crack that might engulf me . . . the mine had burst. There were . . . parts of things whirling and whizzing in the area. It was a grand sight. . . . Just as soon as the thing burst, hundreds of pieces of artillery and different kinds and thousands of small arms belched forth Death and Destruction into the enemy's lines. I fired as fast as I could . . . Five minutes after the fort blew up, our men piled over and into the fort and we see rebs coming in. Oh how our boys cursed and damned them and damned the officers for not reinforcing our brave fellows when the rebs would charge on them. There is something wrong says the boys. The boys yell too much commissary allowed meaning of this the officers was too drunk on commissary whiskey. For last night when our brigade ammunition train came up with ammunition

32 Curtis, *Twenty-fourth*, 267.

they brought a barrel of whiskey. I supposed think that it would be needed to insure success. But the rank and file did not get a smell.

A special detail of sixty Iron Brigade men manned a series of picket pits about 150 yards from the Confederate entrenchments and opened fire to support the attack, but to no avail. The picket holes were about ten yards apart and the day was very warm. One of the Sauk County boys on the advanced line, Cpl. Cyrus Macy, realizing the heat would be unendurable without water, called out for the boys to throw him their canteens. Then Macy, after taking off all his clothing except for trowsers and shirt and with a dozen canteens strapped to his back, braved the Confederate shooting to dash to the Union line where he was "upbraided soundly for the needless exposure." He was urged not to return, but filled the canteens and again crossed the open space in a flurry of enemy bullets. The Black Hats would stay in the open pits until dark.[33]

"The firing continued throughout much of the day and in the end nothing was accomplished except a growing list of killed and wounded," wrote Dawes later that same day. He witnessed the attacks and counterattacks from atop a log house behind the front. "Our men gained the enemy's works and took their line, and the position held would have broken the rebel army. But victory stands with the enemy, who drove our men out and regained all they had lost." The Western men escaped the carnage with only three men wounded on the skirmish line.[34]

It was an event the day the Battle of the Crater, a Sunday, that touched on the strange war between these people who shared so many things—language, history, culture—but were so far apart on others. A truce was called from noon until dark so sides could bury the dead. About 6:00 p.m., a remarkable site greeted the watching Federals: "For more than a mile along the Confederate front stood men, women and children on the enemy's breastworks, not soldiers, but men in citizen's clothes, their wives, their children." The two sides stood quietly looking across the field over the heads of the burial parties working on the field. When a Confederate band struck up "Dixie," the enemy soldiers and civilians raised a cheer and waved handkerchiefs. The last notes were dying away when Union bands responded with the "Star Spangled Banner." And so it went for many minutes, this back-and-forth musical duel. When the Confederates counterattacked with "Bonnie Blue Flag," the Federals answered with "Yankee Doodle." Just as the "shades of night" were

33 Stine, *Army of the Potomac*, 718. Macy had been wounded in the left knee in the fighting at the Wilderness. He would be hit again in the head at Hatcher's Run on February 7, 1865, a serious wound that took away the sight in his left eye and left him deaf in his left ear.

34 Dawes, *Service*, 302.

appearing, said one witness, Federal bands—as many as two dozen—began to play "Home, Sweet Home." Not a cheer was heard. "Within a few minutes from the time our bands ceased to play," the watcher said, "the Confederate bands, a great number of them, took up the same beautiful, impressive strains, played 'Home, Sweet Home,' as our folks had played it, and then there was a mighty cheer along both lines of battle." After a time, the citizens left the front and "our forces settled down to their old modes of living; the next day the cannon began to roar, the mortars to heave their shells and shot back and forth, and the sharp shooters to pick off the unwary."[35]

Oh, Lord, Da Dun Shot Massa Big Jake

Part of Mr. Richard Epps' world collapsed with the Virginia soil in the fighting south and west of the bloody scar that was the mine crater. One of the picked squad of Black Hats who ventured into the exposed picket pits to fire on the Confederates early that historic July 30 was Pvt. Jake Deiner. His young contraband friend was not far away, eyes fixed on his friend he so admired. When Lt. Watrous passed, Mr. Epps called out, "Massa Ad'tant, see over yondah, how Massa Big Jake dun chuck it to um. He's dun shot mor'n forty times a'ready. He's jes killin' em like bootcher day." The officer admired Deiner's shooting before inquiring, about how the private was getting along. "Oh, first rate, Adjutant, first rate, but why in hell don't our folks charge? I don't believe that there are many of those fellows in line; we can take their works; why in hell don't our folks charge?" Watrous called back that the generals were probably waiting for just the right moment. "I don't care if they are," Deiner replied shaking head. "I don't care if Lincoln is there. I know that if our boys would charge we could take that line of works and capture Petersburg." Deiner then turned back to his steady shooting and Watrous was a step or so away when he heard Mr. Epps cry out in alarm, "Oh, Lord, da dun shot Massa Big Jake."

Watrous looked just in time to see Big Jake Deiner sink to the ground. Despite a hail of bullets, the soldier's young friend was soon at his side, trying to give him a drink from a canteen. "Deiner tried to get upon his feet but could not," said Watrous. "Then I saw the colored boy get down on his hands and knees and heard him tell his white friend to get upon his back . . . . With a mighty effort the young lad straightened up and started with his precious load for the Union line." Willing hands pulled Deiner to safety. Mr. Epps followed his friend to an army hospital where he waited on him, nursed him, "held his hand, talked to him, cried over him

---

35 Watrous, *Richard Epps*, 18, 28.

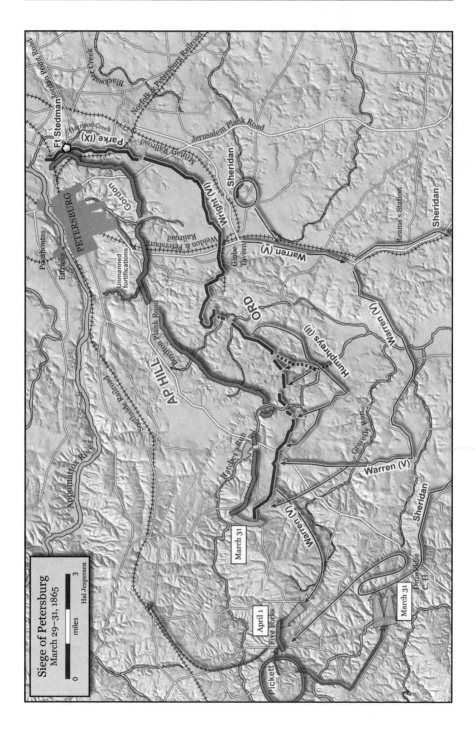

Siege of Petersburg
March 29–31, 1865

0   miles   3

Hal Jespersen

Appomattox River

Petersburg

Southside Railroad

Boydton Plank Road

A P HILL

Hatcher's Run

March 31

April 1
Five Forks

Pickett

March 31

Dinwiddie C. H.

Sheridan

Warren (V)

Warren (V)

Gravelly Run

Humphreys (II)

ORD

Warren (V)

Globe Tavern

Weldon & Petersburg Railroad

Reams's Station

Sheridan

Sheridan

Sheridan

Jerusalem Plank Road

Wright (VI)

Military Railroad

Gordon

Unmanned fortifications

Fort Stedman

Parke (IX)

Ft Stedman

Harrison Creek

Jordan Point Road

Norfolk & Petersburg Railroad

Blackwater Creek

Pocahontas

Ettricks

and prayed for him." Deiner, however, who was shot through the body, died about midnight August 2 with "the colored boy sitting by his side and holding both of his big hands and crying as though his heart would break," said Watrous. "He sat there and cried himself to sleep, having had little or no sleep from the time his friend was wounded until his spirit had flown to the other shore, and he did not wake until daylight."

The next day Mr. Epps borrowed a shovel and dug a deep grave next to a maple tree. When he finished he asked for a coffin, but there were none to be had. He settled on the next best thing: a long rough wooden box used to haul muskets. "He was assisted in placing the remains in it," continued Watrous, "and that hero of more than a score of great battles, in none of which he failed in any duty, was given a military burial with sincere mourners from his company; but there were none who mourned him more deeply than Mr. Epps."[36]

The Iron Brigade regiments remained on the front southeast of Petersburg until August 18. Although the weather was hot, the soldiers escaped serious duty except for being on a picket line. The break was welcome and the construction of shelters from the sun was much the order of the day. "Occasionally, we hear a burst of cannon and mortars in the distance, but we are out of the way of things," Lt. Col. Rufus Dawes wrote home August 5. Somewhere Dr. John Hall had found a milking cow and Dawes noted that he and the good doctor "were very popular with our friends." Then on August 9, Dawes received official notice that he and Lt. William Golterman of his 6th Wisconsin were being mustered out of the army. Two days later Dawes left the Army of the Potomac for good and headed for Ohio and home.

The twenty-six-year-old Dawes may well have been one of the best volunteer officers of the Union armies. At the start of the war, he enlisted as a private and was at once made captain of his Lemonweir Minute Men at Mauston in Juneau County, Wisconsin. He became major of his regiment in 1862 and lieutenant colonel in 1863. When Col. Edward Bragg was promoted, Dawes took command of the 6th Wisconsin, but was never mustered as colonel because the regiment—due to hard service—was below the numbers needed for such promotion. A friend noted that Dawes was in all the battles involving the Iron Brigade from Gainesville in August 1862 until he left the army in 1864, and that his "record is one of which any officer might well feel proud." During his last engagement," the friend added, "I saw one of our men being brought in from the field with a fractured thigh. By his side on the stretcher was his musket and equipments. When asked why he attempted to save his gun, and he so badly wounded, his answer was: 'Captain is a bully little fellow,

36 *Ibid.*, 23-25.

and the Ordnance Department isn't going to stop his pay on account of carelessness on my part.'" Now Dawes, with the regiment from the first, was gone.[37]

By mid-August, the Iron Brigade regiments marched with the rest of Warren's Fifth Corps to the Yellow House near Ream's Station on the Weldon Railroad. The move initiated a fresh attempt to sever the Confederate supply line running from Petersburg through Weldon to Wilmington, North Carolina, with a lateral connection running west to Raleigh and into South Carolina to Florence. Warren's men moved through rain and slogged along muddy roads to reach the area. One division set about destroying track, while another deployed to confront any potential Confederate attack from the north. Cutler's division, with the Iron Brigade in its ranks, remained in support. Confederates from Lt. Gen. A. P. Hill's Corps counterattacked that afternoon, driving the Federals to within a mile of Globe Tavern. Warren recovered and rallied, drove the Rebels back, and entrenched. "The Boys drive & are driven &c for a couple of hours when our line, all but a strong skirmish line, fall back & same in front of us," remembered a Wisconsin soldier. The brigade moved left to prevent a potential breakthrough, the soldier continued, and "we march up in as pretty a line as ever I seen to the edge of the woods & halted and built works. The fighting is over."

Rain hampered activities operations the next day, August 19. Late that afternoon, a Southern division under William Mahone advanced through a ravine and crashed into the right flank of the Union line, rolling up Crawford's division. Fired on in the front and right, the Federals scattered in disorder. Part of the attack landed between the 19th Indiana and 24th Michigan. Casualties were heavy, and hand-to-hand fighting ensued along parts of the front. Night and rain ended the day's fighting. Heavy rains prevented significant fighting August 20. Warren pulled back two miles that night to a new line of fortifications connecting with the main Union lines.

Major William Hutchinson of the 24th Michigan, who had been in a hospital recovering from a wound, arrived back with his regiment on August 19. Within fifteen minutes he was hit again while drinking coffee with Lt. Col. Albert Edwards. Also recalled around coffee fires was how in the middle of a salvo of artillery fire,

---

37 Dawes, *Service*, 303-304. Dawes noted in his memoir that the 6th Wisconsin lost some of its best officers to resignations in 1864 and 1865. In addition to Dawes, they included: Capt. Thomas W. Plummer, July 25, 1864; Capt. Charles H. Ford, July 29, 1864; Capt. William N. Remington, October 11, 1864; 1st Lt. Loyd G. Harris, July 23, 1864; 1st Lt. John Beely, July 25, 1864; 1st Lt. William S. Campbell, October 11, 1864; 1st Lt. Earl M. Rogers, March 10, 1865; 2nd Lt. Howard J. Huntington, July 23, 1864; 2nd Lt. William Golterman, August 10, 1864, and 2nd Lt. Hiram B. Merchant, September 6, 1864.

one of the new Wisconsin recruits was taken by the sight of a solid shot sailing through the air. The soldier belonged to a "nine club" back home, and as the iron ball angled down the Federal line he yelled, "Look out there 3rd base!"[38]

Under fair skies the next day the Confederates attacked again, but the advance stalled in front of strong Union breastworks. "They were allowed to come up pretty close when a general rattle of musketry and artillery cut them to pieces," said a Michigan Black Hat. A large number of prisoners were taken along with the flag of the 12th Mississippi. The Wolverines had often built earthworks, but just as often moved in front to do their fighting. "On this occasion," one explained, the Michigan men "welcomed the enemy's attack." When a Michigan officer asked one of the prisoners what regiments he had been fighting., the captive replied, "The troops that have whipped you so often—Mahone's Division—but they did not do much of that to-day." By the time the fighting ended, the vital Weldon Railroad was blocked, the objective largely complete. The Confederates would have to carry supplies thirty miles by wagon to bypass the new Union line extending south and west. The noose had been squeezed a little bit tighter.[39]

A Perfect Storm of Bullets

Long afterward, the historian of the 24th Michigan explained that a full history of the war could never be written. "Each soldier's experience is a volume in itself, portions of which are related in country stores in winter, at noonings in harvest and around veteran camp-fires." His pronouncement was literally true, of course, but historians nonetheless worked as best they could to share the stories of what the men had endured, and why. Some cases were harder than others. For example, much of the material written about the fighting at Globe Tavern (Second Weldon Railroad)—this brigade moved here, that brigade moved there, attacking here, firing there—provided little or no context to replicate the clear and distinct lines that appear on battle maps of the action. As far as Pvt. James Patrick "Mickey" Sullivan of Company K, 6th Wisconsin, was concerned, his "volume in itself" was a confusing pastiche of sights, sounds, rumors, and hardship. His personal battle of "Globe Tavern" began on August 18 when Fifth Corps pulled out of its lines southeast of Petersburg for yet another march into the unknown. Rumors ranged from the Iron Brigade shipping north to enforce the draft to Fifth Corps becoming a separate command. One whisper with legs had the soldiers moving off to catch

---

38 Curtis, *Twenty-fourth*, 263; *Milwaukee Sunday Telegraph*, January 24, 1886.

39 Ray, *Iron Brigade*, 305-306; Curtis, *Twenty-fourth*, 273.

ships south to the Gulf of Mexico for an attack on Mobile Bay. As usual, the rumors proved false. The men were moving south and west to break the Weldon Railroad. With Dawes gone, Maj. Thomas Kerr commanded the 6th Wisconsin. The discharge of non-veterans, deaths, wounds, illness, and other reasons left only about 1,000 men in the ranks of the old Iron Brigade. Warren's entire Fifth Corps scarcely mustered 10,000 souls. Still, morale remained reasonably high, and the belief within the ranks was that they could hold their own against "any reasonable amount" of Confederates. "I noticed, though, that the buoyant feeling that used to characterize the brigade on the march was absent," explained Sullivan, "and there were no songs and jests as there had been in the earlier years of the war. The almost continual fighting since spring, and so many defeats and disappointments had a depressing effect on the hilarity of our fellows." During the march to the army's left flank, he said, "we trudged along in almost absolute silence."

The day was very hot and it was about 11:00 a.m. when the marching Western men heard heavy firing in the distance. The brigade arrived in a large cleared area called the Yellow House (or Yellow Tavern). Warren, recalled Mickey, rode up "with a pleasant express on his face and in his cheery tone" told brigade commander Edward Bragg that the Weldon Road had been captured. Bragg had been in command of the Black Hats since June 7, 1864, when Col. William W. Robinson left the army exhausted and under a cloud from what had happened at North Anna. The regiments could stop for twenty minutes to boil coffee, he explained, but had to be ready to support Romeyn B. Ayre's division. A. P. Hill's Confederates made a counterattack against Ayre's front about 3 p.m., drove back Warren, but were eventually repulsed. The next morning, August 19, the Iron Brigade was deployed as skirmishers. Rebel sharpshooters began taking a toll. Adjutant Culyer Babcock, who had saved the regimental flag at the Wilderness, was sitting at the foot of a tree wrapped in a poncho when an unnamed Southerner drew him into his sights. The bullet hit a tree limb above Babcock, deflected downward, and struck him on the top of the head. The deadly wound was not discovered until the regiment began to move and he did not get up to move with it.[40]

The brigade, Mickey continued, was ordered to another position at a right angle to a line of breastworks. The Black Hats were in that position when General Mahone's men burst from a ravine on the brigade's left flank and attacked in force.

---

40 Sullivan's account of the three-day engagement was published in the *Milwaukee Sunday Telegraph* in two parts on June 28 and July 5, 1885; Dawes, *Service*, 310; Cheek and Pointon, *Sauk County*, 132. Babcock, Beetown in Grant County, enlisted in 1861 and became sergeant major in April 1863. He was promoted to regimental adjutant a year later and killed in combat along the Weldon Railroad on August 19, 1864. *Wisconsin Roster*, vol. 1, 494, 495, 505.

"The 7th Wisconsin had been sent to the right, and the 19th [Indiana] and 24th [Michigan] were on the left . . . and there was nothing to meet that torrent of graybacks but our diminutive regiment, less than two hundred strong," remembered Mickey. Fighting erupted up and down the line. "[W]e were in a cul-de-sac of fire . . . [and] Gen. Bragg said that if we would save ourselves we would have to get out of that, and we stood not on the order of our going, but went at once, and lively, too." Bragg tried to rally the men along a fence with a ditch on each side of it, but the Johnnies were soon on the left and rear and tore up the Western men with a volley in the flanks. "Bragg shouted for every man to break for a barn that was in sight, and we rallied around it and again opened fire on the rebels who were coming up on three sides of us, but one might as well try to dam the Mississippi with a chip," continued Mickey, "and before they surrounded us Bragg ordered us to run for the Yellow House, which we did." A Union officer running close to the Irish private was shot in the back of the head, "and it seemed to me it knocked the whole top of his head off." Bragg saw it too, and shouted, "There goes Billy Campbell, shot through the head!"[41] Sullivan and brigade commander Bragg were now running alongside Sgt. Frank Wallar, who was doing his best to carry the regiment's national color out of harm's way. Near the Yellow House, they found "a fellow who was crouching in a ditch that was half-filled with water. [He] ordered him [Wallar] and Bragg and myself to halt, saying he was provost guard and was stationed there to stop runaway stragglers." The order brought the three men up short and raised their tempers. Wallar, who had captured the flag of the 2nd Mississippi at Gettysburg, had but little tolerance for fools. In one fluid motion he turned the flag staff and jabbed the fellow with the sharp finial while "Mickey" added the point of his bayonet. The provost guard jumped out of the ditch, his prodders "telling him to go where we had been and see if he would stay there as long as we had." It was about that time Parke's Ninth Corps with elements of Charles Griffin's division rallied and caught Mahone's men in crossfire. "Mahone and his Johnnies had a good chance to show their speed and they were sent back jumping, with severe loss," boasted Sullivan.

When the fighting ended, Sullivan searched the field to find Billy Campbell's body and retrieve his papers to send to his friends back home. Along the way he found a dying 11th Pennsylvania soldier who begged for water while urging Sullivan

---

41 Bragg was mistaken. The dead officer was actually Capt. John Timmons of Company G. Timmons, of Beloit, enlisted as a private in the Beloit Star Rifles, Company G, in June 1861, was promoted lieutenant in December 1862, and to captain in August 1864. Timmons was wounded at Laurel Hill and killed at Second Weldon Railroad (Globe Tavern) on August 19, 1864. *Wisconsin Roster*, vol. 1, 520. Timmons was one of two regimental officers killed that day, the other being Capt. William Hutchins of Company B.

to take his diary with a tintype of his wife and two children and "something over $11," along with his watch, and send it all home to his wife. (Sullivan grumbled later about receiving "a regular caustic letter" from the wife complaining there was "not more money"). When he reached the area where Campbell fell, Mickey discovered it was not Billy at all but Lt. John Timmons who had caught the unlucky bullet. A nearby officer and squad of New York artillerymen had taken Timmons' watch and papers, but when they learned Sullivan belonged to the same regiment, they handed over the personal effects. Night "set in cold and rainy." Private Jim Rhoades retrieved his old copper-bottomed coffee pot (which held two or three gallons) from a regimental wagon and hung it over a sputtering fire. Each man furnished coffee and water. "Bragg, whose culinary department had disappeared in the melee, shared the coffee as well," Mickey remembered. "The boys felt good and were as jubilant as though we had won a victory, for they felt that though we had been overpowered and compelled to run it was better than to lie down and surrender." The sad news spreading through the regiments along the coffee fires, however, was that the 7th Wisconsin had been "gobbled up entire" and was missing. "Our boys felt very sorry for the loss of our good 'Huckleberry Regiment.'"[42]

In truth, the soldiers of the 7th were alone in a stand of timber on the battlefield trying to figure out where they were and what to do. Two officers conducted a reconnaissance early that night only to return with twenty-three Rebels they had surprised and captured from a picket line. Once they had their bearings, the Badgers and prisoners fell back in the general direction of the Union line and met up with elements of Hancock's Second Corps. "We bivouac for the night," Private Ray scribbled in his journal. "We get supper through the rain & go to bed, making the best of things as we can. Get no tidings from the Brigade or the rest of the Corps. This has been a hard old day for us."[43]

Not far away, the rest of the Iron Brigade spent the night in the mud and rain. The next morning, the men marched across the railroad bed and took up a position in some Union field works. "The day was very cold and the rain came down in sheets and our fellows sat on their knapsacks and haunches with rubber blankets over their heads in vain efforts to keep dry," wrote Sullivan. "Every thing was soaking wet so that we could not make fires and were obliged to do without our much needed coffee; we passed a very uncomfortable day and night." The next morning dawned fair and bright, the wet soldiers hanging out blankets and shirts to

---

42 Rhoades, of Middleton, enlisted in 1864. A corporal, he was wounded during the Spotsylvania Campaign and mustered out of service in July 1865. *Wisconsin Roster*, vol. 1, 535; Matrau, *Letters Home*, 94; Hutchins was leading his men as captain for the first time when killed.

43 Ray, *Iron Brigade*, 306.

dry. Late in the morning, the 7th Wisconsin marched into camp with their prisoners. The brigade men gathered around them with welcoming yells and questions. The Wisconsin men had been given up for lost. "[G]lad we were to see each other," Ray confirmed to his journal.[44]

At mid-morning the Confederates attacked again, first shelling the Union position and then moving out of the woods. The 15th Battery, New York Light Artillery, was nearby, but the gunners had all been killed or wounded and the 12-pound Napoleons stood silent. The frantic artillery officer ran to the 6th Wisconsin seeking replacement gunners. When told some old Battery B men were in ranks, the officer exclaimed, "For God's sake, send them to my guns!" Sergeant C. A. Winsor of Company A, a veteran of service in Battery B, stepped forward to volunteer. Within minutes Winsor was placed in command and assigning the new gunners to positions. His first shot exploded in front of the Rebel colors in the center of the charging line and swept away the color guard and the colors. The Confederates closed ranks and came on again. Winsor fired again and again with uncanny accuracy. The artillery officer went "wild with delight" cheering every shot, noted an observer, patting the men on the back as he moved around the gun twirling a "black thorn stick" between his fingers. Despite heavy losses the Johnnies—a brigade of Mississippians—continued into easy rifle-musket range, "with their heads down and arms at a trail." When the men in the Iron Brigade pulled their triggers, said one Badger, "It was a continuous snapping of caps with here and there a p-i-s-h until the exploding caps had dried the powder sufficiently to burn and generate gas enough to blow the ball out of the gun." The muskets had been left loaded during the night and the powder was damp. "We got orders to fix bayonets to repel charge," said Mickey Sullivan, but the Union muskets began to fire, and "when they were within a few rods of us they threw themselves down in a small ravine and surrendered." According to a 24th Michigan man, the Rebels in the ditch "dropped their guns and, waving their hats or anything they had in token of surrender, rushed pell-mell over the Union works as if Satan would get the last man." The Wolverines, he continued, "took them by the hand in many instances and helped them over the works."

When Union artillery and small arms fire raked the enemy support columns the Confederate soldiers broke and ran despite the best efforts of their officers to rally them. Some of the Rebels tried unsuccessfully to get around the flank, but the 7th Wisconsin ventured out and in the shooting Cpl. Horace A. Ellis of the 7th Wisconsin captured the battle flag of the 16th Mississippi and a Congressional

44 *Ibid.*, 307.

Medal of Honor. In the end, Nathaniel H. Harris' Mississippi brigade was just about used up and 339 men and officers were taken prisoners.[45]

While that fighting was being played out, Johnson Hagood's South Carolina brigade struck a part of the Union line where the troops were in echelon. The Rebels soon found themselves in serious trouble and nearly surrounded. Thinking they were about to be captured, some of the Johnnies stopped shooting. During the ensuing confusion, Capt. Dennis Dailey, who was in command of the division provost guard made up of the 2nd Wisconsin, rode his horse into the enemy ranks at the head of some thirty men. Dailey had taken Confederate James Archer's sword at Gettysburg a year earlier and now seized one of the flags belonging to Hagood's brigade. He was demanding the banner's surrender when the forty-five-year-old Hagood arrived on foot in a great excitement asking his soldiers around him why a mounted Union officer was holding their colors. Some men along part of the line had already surrendered, while others were refusing. It was a near thing, and for a time seemed as if the whole Confederate brigade might yield. Hagood grabbed the bridle of Dailey's horse. "Give me that flag, sir!" shouted the general.

"Who are you," demanded Dailey.

"I command this brigade," replied the South Carolinian. "I admire your bravery. Give me the flag, and you shall be returned unmolested to your own lines."

Dailey stared at Hagood and said, "General, you had better surrender to me yourself. Look behind you!"

The Confederate looked around at the knots of men making up the Wisconsin Independent Battalion and replied, "Once more, sir, will you give up that flag?"

The Wisconsin officer shook his head. "Never."

The frustrated Hagood raised his revolver and shot Dailey in the chest, knocking him from his horse with a ball lodged in his spine. Hagood, meanwhile, swung into the saddle from the opposite side and ordered his men to the rear. The fighting was over, and Hagood was convinced that he had not only saved his brigade from capture but had killed the Federal officer.[46]

---

45 Cheek and Pointon, *Sauk County*, 133-134; Curtis, *Twenty-fourth*, 27; General Warren's report can be found *OR* 42, pt. 1, 431. Nathaniel Harris' brigade included the 12th, 16th, 19th, and 48th Mississippi regiments. Ellis enlisted from Chippewa Falls on July 10, 1861. He served for a time as a volunteer in Battery B, 4th U.S. Artillery before returning to his regiment in January of 1864. Ellis mustered out with his regiment in July 1865. *Wisconsin Roster*, vol. 1, 541.

46 Wm. J. K. Beaudot, "The Bravest Act of the War," *Virginia Country's Civil War Quarterly*, vol. VI, 6-13; Stine, *Army of the Potomac*, 692; *OR* 42, pt. 1, 536. Years later Dailey contacted the South Carolinian, who was delighted he had not killed the Northern officer. The pair exchanged the warm letters of two old soldiers. Johnson Hagood, *Memoirs of the War of Secession From the Original Manuscripts of Johnson Hagood, Brigadier-General C.S.A.* (privately printed, 1989), 294-295.

1st Lt. Charles Weeks, Columbia County Cadets, Co. B, 7th Wisconsin

Weeks enlisted at York, Wisconsin. He was wounded at Bethesda Church, Virginia in late May 1864 and later promoted to captain, but not mustered. Weeks mustered out of service on December 3, 1864, term expired.

Author's Collection

"Mickey" Sullivan had taken a good position alongside a gate post he used as a rest while shooting at the Rebels. It was here, while in the act of firing, that he was injured a fifth time. His first wound came in 1861 when he was struck by a ramrod fired accidentally by a rear rank 7th Wisconsin man during a camp celebration of Washington's Birthday. He was shot in the foot at South Mountain on September 14, 1862, again in the shoulder at Gettysburg on July 1, 1863, and lost his finger in an accident while laying logs to corduroy a roadway in 1864. This time he was knocked unconscious when a shell burst over his head. When awoke, two of his friends were busy pouring water on him from their canteens in an effort to rouse him. One of the soldiers pulled a sliver of metal from the back of Sullivan's neck. As Mickey put it, "my head felt as though a band of iron was tightening about it."

Each time the Confederates were driven back they were rallied by an officer riding a white horse—despite the efforts of Union "sharpshooters with their telescope rifles [to] give him a quietus but could not succeed." The frustrated Western boys talked it over before calling up Pvt. Jared Williams of Ontario, a noted marksman of Company K, 6th Wisconsin. Williams carefully put the powder from two cartridges into the muzzle of his gun and patched the "minnie-ball" with part of his shirt tail. The private rested his musket on a rail post, aimed, and fired. "The Reb tumbled out of his saddle, and the horse dashed off behind the woods," Sullivan said. That ended any belligerence by the Confederates to their front, or so the story goes.[47]

The enemy skirmishers were soon back, however, using the shelter of some willow trees along a creek to take a toll of artillery battery horses. Union skirmishers fanned out to meet them, but stopped a short distance away in a small triangular earthwork. Colonel Bragg called for volunteers to drive off the enemy skirmishers. Mickey Sullivan offered himself as corporal to lead them. "We made those Rebs skip for the woods in a hurry," the Irish private boasted with satisfaction. He also noted that he was promoted that night to sergeant by order of Bragg and Maj. Tom Kerr for good conduct. His regiment had suffered heavily during the three days of fighting for the Weldon Railroad. "The old sixth Wis has been terribly decimated in these fights and we now number 75 men, rank and file, in the regt," a private wrote home. On August 27, the regiments called the rolls to discover that Company A of the 6th Wisconsin—the Sauk County Riflemen—numbered only six men present

---

47 Williams enlisted February 1, 1862, from Ontario in Bad Ax County and served until war's end. The standard load for a .58-caliber rifle-musket was sixty grains of musket black powder. Doubling the load to 120 grains would have flattened the bullet's trajectory dramatically. *Wisconsin Roster*, vol. 1, 536.

for duty: Mair Pointon, C. A. Winsor, John Moore, Cyrus Macy, Hiram Palmer, and William A. Perkins.[48]

Even though he had resigned and was no longer in command of the 6th Wisconsin, Rufus Dawes still had not escaped the weight of command responsibility. He was in Washington on his way home when news arrived that both Capt. William Hutchins and Lt. John Timmons had been killed. "I am safely here to-night, somewhat tired from the journey. I am fairly heart-sick at the stories of blood I hear from the old regiment," he wrote his new wife on September 1. "Captain Hutchins was killed. Full of the satisfaction of his new commission, he met death in his first battle." His next few lines revealed just how battle-weary Dawes had become: "But the saddest of all, Timmons was killed. Poor, murdered Timmons! His legal right to be discharged was as clear as mine and just the same. It seems almost certain to me that I could never have lived through another such carnival of blood. Only eighty men are left in the ranks for service."

Timmons' enlistment had already expired. He was waiting for the mustering officer when the regiment was ordered to the front, and decided to accompany his outfit into battle rather than remain idle in camp with his comrades in danger. Some days after his death, his application for discharge reached brigade commander Edward Bragg. The application asked whether Timmons (one soldier remembered him as "an Irishman, quiet, but full of humor and brim full of pluck") had taken his veteran furlough. Bragg endorsed the document and returned it: "This officer has taken his long furlough. He was killed in the battle."[49]

Grab a Root!

In mid-September, Dr. John Hall of the 6th Wisconsin sent a long letter to Rufus Dawes, now discharged and home in Ohio. The doctor filled the pages with information about what had happened to the regiment since his resignation. U. S. Grant, he wrote, "seems to be giving a look of permanency to our occupation of this line. He has nearly completed a railroad from City Point to Yellow Tavern, Warren's headquarters and the extreme left of our line on the Weldon Road." The new Union line, he continued, "makes a loop around the tavern, and back upon itself for six or eight miles. This, of course, is to protect our rear and the new railroad." Dr. Hall concluded, "Well, Colonel, how does the war look to you from

48 Matrau, *Letters Home*, 94; Cheek and Pointon, *Sauk County*, 136.

49 Dawes, *Service*, 305-308, 309.

the standpoint of civil and domestic life? Have you joined the grumblers who severely ask, 'Why does not the Army of the Potomac move?' I think not."[50]

The brigade's monotonous siege duties dragged through September and into the last days of October—long hours with heat and rain, trenches that always seemed muddy, whizzing bullets, and the occasional wounding of a soldier. When death arrived it was usually swift and at the hands of an unseen sharpshooter. On one occasion, a federal battery some yards behind the line responded to the pesky hidden enemy. As some of the Western men discovered, friendly artillery could be more trouble than sharpshooters. A handful of Black Hats were sitting in a trench about two feet deep eating dinner when the guns opened fire. "The wind from the [artillery] explosion swept the ground . . . clean of all loose dirt, leaves and rubbish, nearly burying us and filling the pail containing our dinner of soup with dirt of all description," complained a hungry Wisconsin man.

Sharpshooting or sniping began at first light. "If we could see the smoke from the rifle we could drop under cover before the bullet could reach us," explained one man. Such was not always the case, however. Two schoolmates of a Wisconsin soldier stopped by from another regiment for a visit. The men were talking about days long ago when another soldier saw a puff of smoke along the enemy line. "Look out!" Lawson D. Finton of the 6th Wisconsin turned just in time to be struck in the head. He lingered several days before dying. The sniping started at first light. On one occasion, a Rebel sharpshooter took a position in a tree near a brick chimney in the works opposite the brigade. A shot rang out and a Wisconsin soldier threw himself to the ground behind a large cracker box. "That-son-of-a-gun is shooting at me!" he exclaimed. A second shot slammed into the cracker box. And so it went, day after day, often with the call "Grab a root!" A shot was "fired at every one who exposes their person in the least."

One story that eased some tension was how Sgt. Robert Gibbons of the 24th Michigan managed to escape capture after being taken by half a dozen Confederates while scouting the enemy position. The sergeant, known as a persuasive man, began telling his guards they should consider themselves his prisoners and head for the Union line "where their safety and good feeding were assured since the war was lost. "Yank, if you don't stop that kind of talk, I'll blow the top of your head off," replied one of the graybacks. Gibbons turned, walked up to the man, and said they were all going to get their heads shot off if they kept wandering around the woods. The Johnnies puzzled over his argument for a time and "were persuaded their cause was going up sure and their prisoner's advice was

---

50 *Ibid.*, 309. The letter was written September 10, 1864.

Private Alfred Thompson, Anderson Guards,
Co. I, 6th Wisconsin

Thompson was wounded at Gettysburg, taken prisoner at the Wilderness in
early May the next year, and died of disease on December 12, 1864, while
being held at Charleston, South Carolina. *Wisconsin Veterans Museum*

wise for them, and they consented to go with him." Gibbons was lost himself,
however, and unsure how to get to his lines. "Presently he heard the loud 'Baw—
baw—baw' of some of the enlisted Indians in one of the Wisconsin regiments of

the Iron Brigade, and turned in the direction of their familiar whoop." The Confederates surrendered their arms to members of the 7th Wisconsin, who were reconnoitering the area.[51]

The Iron Brigade, meanwhile, involuntarily surrendered more of its organizational integrity. That fall the brigade became part of Samuel Crawford's Third Division. The old Fourth Division, which had been led by James Wadsworth and then Lysander Cutler at the start of the Overland Campaign, disappeared off the army rolls. What was left of the Iron Brigade was now officially First Brigade, Third Division, Fifth Corps. It included the 6th and 7th Wisconsin, 24th Michigan, four companies of the 1st New York Sharpshooters, and the 143rd, 149th, and 150th Pennsylvania. The 19th Indiana, which failed to veteranize, was merged with the 7th Indiana on September 23. Both units were combined into the 20th Indiana three weeks later and left the brigade for good. "It was a sorrowful day," one veteran said when the Indiana boys marched out at Reverse Arms. "The friendships that are formed in camp and on the field of danger are Stronger than they are in civil life," explained a Wisconsin soldier. "I seen officers and men of the gallant Old 19th Shed tears this morning in parting with us, and I have Seen those same men Stand firm and swing their hats, and cheer when charging on the enemy amidst a perfect Storm of bullets. Thus they go," he added in a somber postscript. "There will Soon be nothing of our once Splendid Brigade left together." The two companies in the Independent Battalion of Wisconsin Volunteers—the final remnants of the 2nd Wisconsin—merged into the 6th Wisconsin on November 30 as Companies G and H.[52]

Although mobile cavalry and infantry strikes above and below the James River continued with consistent regularity, the Army of the Potomac was firmly bogged down around Richmond and Petersburg. No one expected any sudden end to the fighting. Elsewhere, however, other Federal armies were driving the war effort with all eyes on the national election campaign that November. When Union forces marched south threatening Lynchburg on the Confederate supply line, General Lee stripped Maj. Gen. Jubal Early and 10,000 men from the Richmond defenses in a desperate attempt to drive them back. Early brushed aside the threat and marched north down the Shenandoah Valley over the Potomac River to pause before

51 Cheek and Pointon, *Sauk County*, 100, 106; Curtis, *Twenty-fourth*, 279. Finton of Merrimac enlisted May 11, 1861, veteranized, and was killed near Cold Harbor. *Wisconsin Roster*, vol. 1, 497.

52 "Dissolution of the Iron Brigade," *Milwaukee Sentinel*, July 1, 1865; Henry Young Papers. Fifteen officers and 288 men were still in the ranks with the 19th Indiana when it was consolidated.

Washington itself. President Lincoln came out to see the Rebel army, which was not strong enough to seriously threaten the capital. Once Early returned to Shenandoah, Grant ordered cavalryman Maj. Gen. Phil Sheridan to take command of Federal forces in the Valley (about 48,000 strong) and defeat Early. He crushed the Confederates at Third Winchester that September, and again a few days later at Fisher's Hill. Early, however, returned with a stunning surprise attack a month later on October 19 that put Sheridan's army to rout at Cedar Creek. The Federals rallied later in the day and counterattacked, clearing the field in one of the decisive victories of the war.

In the Western Theater, Union forces drove Joe Johnston's Confederate Army of Tennessee deep into Georgia in an effort to crush the Rebels and capture the major rail and industrial hub of Atlanta. When Grant was made a lieutenant general and went east to the Army of the Potomac, he left William Sherman—a familiar figure to 2nd Wisconsin men—to carry out the offensive. Following a series of deep maneuvers and combats large and small, Johnston retreated beyond the Chattahoochee River just north of Atlanta and President Davis fired him. John Bell Hood, Johnston's replacement, did his best in a doomed situation to drive Sherman back, to no avail. After several bloody battles at Peachtree Creek, Atlanta, Ezra Church, and Jonesboro, Hood abandoned the city on September 2. When an effort to lure Sherman west failed, Hood moved north into Tennessee in a desperate effort to get Sherman to follow him. Sherman refused to take the bait. He sent Maj. Gen. George Thomas to deal with Hood and moved his army group (some 60,000 strong) eastward from Atlanta to Savannah on the coast—cutting a wide swath of destruction through the heart of Georgia. While Sherman's March to the Sea was underway, the Federals won a major tactical victory in late November at Franklin, Tennessee, and all but destroyed what was left of Hood's army outside Nashville in mid-December 1864.

The evolving military situation sealed Abraham Lincoln's re-election. When the Overland Campaign opened that May Lincoln looked like a one-term president. Grant's horrendous casualties, coupled with his failure to quickly capture Petersburg shocked the North and dimmed resolve to press the war effort. Failures elsewhere, including along the Red River in Louisiana, hardened sentiment against the war. Voices in and out of the army were raised against the Emancipation Proclamation, which had changed the effort from a war to preserve the Union to one calling for an end to slavery. Lincoln's opposition for president on the Democratic ticket was none other than George B. McClellan, who still had the loyalty of a large number of his soldiers in the Army of the Potomac. And then the Union military situation changed. The port of Mobile Bay fell to the Union Navy in August, Sherman captured Atlanta in September, and Sheridan cleared the Shenandoah Valley in October. Lincoln carried all but three states (Kentucky, New

Jersey, and Delaware) with 212 electoral votes to just 21 for McClellan. The fact that the election occurred at all was significant. "We can not have free government without elections," said Lincoln, "and if the rebellion could force us to forego, or postpone a national election, it might fairly claim to have already conquered and ruined us."

The deep Union military advances, significant victories, and the national election doomed the Confederacy.

All that is Left of the Old First Corps

One unexpected development in the presidential election of 1864 was that seventy-one percent of the vote in the Army of the Potomac went to Lincoln and not its old commander McClellan. The result was not surprising to the men in ranks. "The soldiers are generally going to vote for 'Old Abe,'" a Black Hat wrote before the election. "If they are willing to support him the officers ought to be." Democrats claimed some of the one-sided vote was the work of state Republican political operatives who drafted and passed legislation to allow soldiers in the field to vote, thereby affecting state and county elections. In Wisconsin, for example, the 1864 election was close and especially contested, and no Democrat was more outspoken than editor "Brick" Pomeroy of the *La Crosse Democrat*, who wrote in his columns: "May God Almighty forbid that we are to have two terms of the rottenest, most-stinking, ruin-working, small-pox ever conceived by fiends or mortals in the shape of two terms of Abe Lincoln." On August 23, he published a picture of Lincoln on his front page with the caption: "The Widow Maker of the 19th Century and Republican Candidate for the Presidency." McClellan carried twenty-two of Wisconsin's fifty-eight counties and trailed Lincoln by only 6,000 votes.[53]

The 1864 election was also a source of conversation for the soldiers on both sides of the trench lines at Petersburg. Many of the men in the Iron Brigade regiments were for McClellan until just before the balloting. "The Rebs & our Boys got into conversation this evening, our boys cheering for Abe and they for Jeff [Confederate President Jefferson Davis] & our Boys for Little Mac & they the same," a Wisconsin soldier wrote on October 11. "They seemed to be pleased we cheered him. Then our boys cheered for [Union Gen. Ben] Butler & they said to hell with him &c&c, And so on, things to numerous to mention." It was something after the unusual exchange of political views between the soldiers that troubled

---

53 Frank Klement, *Wisconsin in the Civil War: The Home Front and the Battle Front, 1861-1865* (State Historical Society of Wisconsin: Madison, 1997), 120-121; Mair Pointon, letter to a friend, September 18, 1864.

some of the Badgers. "[W]e all agreed that what the Rebels liked was just what we had no right to like, and if it was going to do them so much good to elect McClellan, we just wouldn't do it. Since that, you hardly hear McClellan's name mentioned in our regiment," a private in the 7th Wisconsin wrote home. "McClellan is played out in the Army. . . . you may bet it now lays with the citizens of the North." Two weeks later, he wrote again: "The Reb prisoners say they should stand it four years longer if Abe was elected, and we told them we could stand it for forty years, and anyway, as long as Abe lived he should stay at the white house. They are pretty spunky. They are just as good soldiers as us, but not better, but we slightly outnumber them."

"The Election goes off quiet but with considerable sport with some McClellan men," Pvt. William Ray of the 7th Wisconsin wrote in his journal on November 11. "Our Co went 22 for Lincoln & 3 for Mac and the Regt. went about the same proportionally, Lincoln getting 4 fifths majority. . . . My hope is that Lincoln will be Elected and I believe I shall realize it." Company I, the 6th Wisconsin's very satisfied Sgt. Frank Wallar noted in his diary, was "unanimous for Abe. I am going to have two canteens of whiskey tonight." In the end the old Iron Brigade regiments voted 749 for Lincoln and 147 for McClellan. The 2nd Wisconsin voted 70 to 1, the 6th Wisconsin 121 to 37, and the 7th Wisconsin 137 to 30—all for Lincoln. In the 24th Michigan, the tally went for Lincoln 176 to 50. The men of the 19th Indiana did not vote because the Democratic-controlled Indiana legislature deemed it "inexpedient" for Hoosier soldiers to vote in the field. During the day-long balloting a lone Confederate deserter stepped into the Michigan picket line to announce that he, too, wanted to vote for Lincoln. It was not recorded whether he was given that opportunity.

"There is many Deserters from the Rebs coming in," noted Private Ray. "Most everyday some come into our Brigade. The Boys with the Big hats wont fire on them they say, & in fact our boys & them are very friendly on the Picket line. They say they cant trust the others."[54] The Lincoln victory triggered a flood of fresh desertions from Lee's army. "They say when Abe is elected their last hope dies forever," was how one Badger put it. It was becoming apparent to the men in ranks on both sides that the end of the war might be drawing close. It troubled many in the ranks of the Iron Brigade that so many of the soldiers who helped shape the Union war effort would not be on hand to see the final victory. James Wadsworth, Alois Bachman, Frank Haskell, Edwin Brown, Edgar O'Connor, and so many

54 Ray, *Iron Brigade*, 227, 336; Perkins, letter to a friend, October 16, 1864, November 1, 1864; Frank Wallar, diary, November 8, 1864; Cheek and Pointon, *Sauk County*, 143; Curtis, *Twenty-fourth*, 280. The election figures are found in the James Perry Diary at the Wisconsin Historical Society.

others were in soldier graves. Many more were the victims of disease that killed as surely as a Rebel bullet. Others soldiers went home physically broken and often emotionally scarred. Grim old Lysander Cutler, shot in the leg at Gainesville in 1862, was wounded again at Globe Tavern and left the army August 21. He was remembered for opposing the elimination of the Fourth Division. "I cannot help remember that it is the oldest division and about all there is left of the First Corps," he wrote headquarters on July 26. "I am the only general left in what was the First Corps, and I believe about the only one who entered the service with rank above captain."[55] The division was not eliminated until after Cutler's wounding. He would finish the war on draft duty in New York and Jackson, Michigan.

Henry A. Morrow of the 24th Michigan, wounded in the leg May 5 at Bethesda Church and returned to duty on November 13, was given command of the brigade only to be severely wounded again carrying the colors at Hatcher's Run. Exhausted and still suffering from his earlier battle wound, Col. William Robinson of the 7th Wisconsin had resigned in July 1864. He returned to Wisconsin to farm and was named some years later U.S. Counsel to Madagascar. Conspicuously absent from the 6th Wisconsin was stalwart Col. Rufus Dawes. The veteran resigned on August 10 completely worn out and suffering from what then was called "Soldier's Heart," but now recognized as combat fatigue. "About the most demoralized man I have ever seen in the Army was Dawes before he got his discharge," a soldier in his regiment wrote a friend. "With him the Government was everything but what it should be. And there is some more here yet that for the good of the service they ought to be discharged." Dawes was also carrying something else inside: "I wonder if a man can go forever without being hurt in battle," he had written his new wife. Out of all the officers of the regiment, only Dawes had never suffered a wound except for a bullet burn on the calf of his leg at Antietam.[56] In his place was his former lieutenant from the Lemonweir Minute Men of Mauston, John A. Kellogg, who had been wounded and captured at the Wilderness, but returned to duty after his escape from a rebel prison. Lt. Col. Hollon Richardson was promoted to command the 7th Wisconsin in place of his father-in-law, but in that strange way with veteran regiments of those days, was never mustered as colonel. Also noted in the 6th Wisconsin was that the slight young soldier called the "Baby of the Regiment" in 1861—Henry Matrau—was promoted to lieutenant of Company G. He wrote home for a quick loan of $30 to "enable me to get a respectable outfit

55 OR 43, 1, 470-471.

56 Fairfield Papers.

such as a sword and belt, Officers uniform, &c, &c . . . as my clothes are rather seedy now."[57]

Kellogg's story of his capture and escape was an interesting one. Following his wound in the Wilderness in early May, he and other prisoners were taken first to Gordonsville and then Lynchburg, where 200 officers were stuffed into one room. "The floors of the building were filthy, and the ceilings swarmed with vermin," Kellogg said. He and others began working on an escape tunnel, but the prisoners were taken to Danville before it was completed. He described the rations at Danville as pea soup and cornbread of such poor quality "the very recollection is nauseating." He and other captives rode the rails to a prison camp at Macon, Georgia. The haggard appearance of the prisoners there shocked him: "Who were these gaunt skeletons, clothed in rags, covered with dirt . . . wild, eager eyes were peering into our faces — eyes from which had departed all expression except that of hopeless misery." One ragged man pressed through the crowd to call Kellogg by name and "listlessly held out his hand." He did not recognize the man. "His hair and beard were long and neglected, he was barefooted, a coarse blue shirt and a pair of overalls were his only clothing. . . . The expression on his face . . . mirrored the soul of man from whom hope had forever departed. "I don't know you," Kellogg answered in shock. The ragged prisoner laughed and said, "I used to be Captain Rollins." The news horrified Kellogg. He had last seen Nathaniel Rollins of the 2nd Wisconsin at Gettysburg. The camp held 1,500 prisoners. Once settled, Kellogg discovered and joined an effort to construct an escape tunnel. The effort was foiled when a Union prisoner told the guards about the shaft.[58]

A short time later Kellogg was moved by rail to Charleston, South Carolina, but he and five others jumped off the train in the dark and made their way through swamps only to be recaptured by a slave catcher using bloodhounds. He was imprisoned in Charleston until a yellow fever outbreak convinced Confederate authorities to move the prisoners to Columbia. Kellogg and others again jumped from the moving train and traveled mostly at night to elude pursuers. Finally, near the Savannah River, they approached a slave cabin seeking help. The slaves fed the escapees and helped them across the river in a boat. "They were faithful to every trust imposed upon them by us, even to the imperiling of their lives," wrote a thankful Kellogg. "They were not only willing to divide their final crust with us, but to give us the last morsel of food in their possession." The Federals finally reached

---

57 Henry Matrau, letter, October 30, 1864; Matrau, *Letters Home*, 98-99.

58 Kellogg, *Capture and Escape*, 24, 28, 35. Kellogg identified the man who betrayed the tunneling as "a Lieutenant of a cavalry regiment, by the name of Silver."

Gen. Sherman's lines near Calhoun, Georgia, where the ragged and thin escapees were sharply questioned by Union officers who suspected they might be Confederate deserters. The suspicions ended when an officer of the nearby 1st Wisconsin Cavalry recognized Kellogg. After having traveled 300 miles to safety, Kellogg was taken to Chattanooga, and orders were cut for his return to Wisconsin.

After a short visit at home, Kellogg went to Madison for orders to take a detail of drafted men to fill out the skeletal 6th Wisconsin. Back in Virginia he located his regiment on the Jerusalem Plank Road near City Point. So much had changed. "The regiment was commanded by Major [Thomas] Kerr, who was a Lieutenant when I left," he said. "Nearly every officer on duty when I left the regiment the previous May, was either promoted, killed, or mustered out. It seemed lonesome." Kellogg presided that night at dress parade. "When it was dismissed, there were many anxious inquires by the men, who wanted to know who 'that white-headed old fellow' was, that was commanding 'our regiment?' Six months of Southern prison life had turned my head white, and reduced my weight from a hundred-and-seventy-five to a hundred-and-fifteen pounds."[59]

Ripping up Track and Winter Camp

In early December, elements of Warren's Fifth Corps (including the Iron Brigade regiments) made one last foray to tear up track on the Weldon Railroad. The move ended weeks of picket duty, winter camp preparation, and drilling new recruits. One significant change involved the reshuffling of the 6th Wisconsin. Companies G and H merged with Companies D and F. The Independent Battalion of the 2nd Wisconsin was consolidated into the regiment as Companies G and H. "The Grand old Second," as one soldier called it, ceased to exist as an organization and left the army rolls forever. New recruits—drafted and bounty men—were being added almost daily to all the regiments, and that set off a heavy schedule of drills to "put the new men in shape." Those arrivals that had spent time in the armies of Europe quickly picked up the drill. For those with language difficulties, especially Germans, countrymen were found and explanations were made in their native tongue.[60]

The expedition included Fifth Corps and a large force of cavalry and several batteries. Camp was broken on December 6 and the regiments moved to the rear

59 Kellogg, *Capture and Escape*, 199. The reference to Kerr as a lieutenant was an error as Kerr was appointed captain in 1863.

60 Cheek and Pointon, *Sauk County*, 143-144.

Cpl. George W. Bunch, Richmond City Grays, Co. B, 19th Indiana

Bunch began the war as a private in the19th Indiana, and ended it as a lieutenant in Company C of the 20th Indiana. He served at Gettysburg, Antietam, and Appomattox. *Civil War Museum, Kenosha, Wisconsin*

and then about two miles southeast. "The weather was good and it was comfortable marching, the new men stood the march like veterans," one of the old hands said later. Whenever there was a halt the companies were put through drills. Finally, the march continued the next day along the Jerusalem Plank Road and then on a road heading to Weldon, North Carolina. The columns crossed the Nottoway River on a pontoon bridge and pulled up about four miles from Sussex Court House after moving about fifteen miles. A heavy rain delayed movement the next day, December 8, and the wet weather made it "quite hard, rather rough on the men fresh from the comforts of home," snickered a Badger. "The 'old vets' did not mind it so much."

The column halted at the Weldon Railroad while the cavalry escort drove off a small force of Confederates. The infantry was stopped past Jarratts Station where the soldiers could see fortifications and a bridge the Federal cavalry had set afire. About 6:00 p.m., the column moved again and came upon parties of soldiers burning ties and bending hot rails along the rail bed. The 6th Wisconsin was placed on a skirmish line covering the front of the division while other soldiers worked well into the night destroying track. It was quite a sight, recalled one soldier. The "regiments formed in line along the track, stack arms, advance to the edge of the track, stoop over, take hold of the rails and ties and at a given signal turn the track bottom side up." The rails were knocked off and put into piles, which were set on fire. Once the iron was red hot in the center, "half dozen men would take hold of each end and twist it around a tree of telegraph pole. The damage we did was beyond the resources of the enemy to repair," claimed one soldier. Some of the Wisconsin boys "captured a cow," butchered it, and—in hard soldier fashion— "some got & some didn't." A camp was made in the woods as the weather turned cold, freezing the mud and turning the rain to snow. The soldiers tied their shelter halves together to provide large covers over wood poles. A rubber blanket was placed on the windy end and a fire built in the front, the warmth keeping them comfortable. The veterans showed the new men how to sweep the wet leaves and snow from the ground inside the enclosures and make a "nice bed of pine needles." It was still a miserable night, one Badger said: "All is quiet with the pickets & so we make bed & lay down but cant sleep for the cold."

The column returned to Sussex Court House the next day with the Confederates following closely. Several minor engagements broke out as the Rebels pressed the rearguard. At one point, Union soldiers lay in the brush and fence corners alongside the road and the Union cavalry was ordered "to fall back in disorder & let the rebs come on & when they got well in between our fellows, our Boys fired, killed 4, wounded 5 & captured several. So this made them mad & and saucy & and watchful." Despite the fighting, muddy roads, and biting cold, the column was back in the old camp by December 12. "The new men stood the march splendidly," boasted one of the Wisconsin veterans.[61]

He has got a Load on and Going West to Start a Snake Farm

One of the favorite stories of the old veterans, told and retold at the Camp-fires of the Iron Brigade Association, involved the so-called Applejack Raid. In fact, editor Jerome Watrous told it on himself. The raid unfolded in December 1864 when the brigade was near Yellow House destroying railroad tracks. Snow fell while the troops prepared to return to their old camp. Five inches covered the ground and it was biting cold. "It's a shame to start men out on a long march through this snow without something with which to brace them up," observed Maj. Tom Kerr, a man known for taking a drink or two. "But we can't get any thing down here," replied the colonel. When Kerr responded that Adjutant Watrous had offered to take a squad to a nearby plantation to get some applejack, the colonel smiled and nodded. Watrous and four men on good horses galloped away.

The woman at the large plantation house said she would only sell the liquor by the barrel—for $1,000.00 Confederate money or $18.00 in greenbacks. Since the barrel could not be carried, the men broke it open with an ax and filled a dozen canteens. The task was no sooner completed than a large squad of Confederates was spotted. "Hang to your canteens and ride for your lives!" shouted Watrous. The chase was a wild one over ditches and fences, the five bluecoats turning to fire at the pursuers until they dropped back and stopped. The five riders slowed to a

---

61 Cheek and Pointon, *Sauk County*, 146-148; Ray, *Iron Brigade*, 341.

walk. They had missed breakfast, but had plenty of applejack. Canteens passed freely from one man to another. When they reached the brigade, the five "planted a canteen of the stuff where it would be wisely used, not forgetting to hang one on to the colonel and give another to the major." The sipping of the canteens continued. "It was as smooth as oil and had an enticing taste—did that treacherous applejack," Watrous said. "It went down wonderfully easy, and on empty stomachs, too. The stuff was loaded, loaded heavy, and so were we ten minutes later." He approached the colonel to tell him of the adventure, but "his tongue ran crosslots at such a place that the colonel laughed. 'Hang onto your horse and don't try to talk. You are not well.' There is nothing like silence when a fellow is as sick as you are."

"What's the matter with the adjutant?" asked a passing soldier. "He's got a load and is going west to start a snake farm," joked another. Watrous did not object to the waggish remark because he was so sleepy. Another swig from the canteen revived him, he said, and now there was no more sociable man in the brigade. He offered a drink to the brigade commander. "I never drink on duty, a practice I advise you to take up," the officer replied. When Gen. Samuel Crawford passed, Watrous waved at him with a friendly hand and offered him the canteen. Crawford looked on sternly and advised the colonel, "You better put that officer in a wagon." Come morning, Watrous remembered, he was "full of aches" and facing rear guard duty. He never touched the sweet drink after that, he claimed, and "has ever stoutly maintained that people who would make such deceiving stuff deserve to have their Confederacy upset—even as it had upset him."[62]

Not in Accordance with Civilized Warfare

Colonel Henry Morrow of the 24th Michigan was troubled by the destruction of private property and other matters during the December marching. "The same worthless destruction of property was carried to day beyond all bounds," he wrote in his diary on December 11. "Even churches were given to the flames. It is no exaggeration to say our march could have been traced by smoking & smoldering homesteads, churches, barns, stables, hay & fodder stacks &c. In every direction solitary chimneys alone mark the homes of many families—It is proper I should say that I know no well authenticated instance where an occupied house was burned," implying that rumors to the contrary were heard. The expedition, however, could be called a success if the object was to destroy the railroad from Nottoway River to Hicksford, for "hardly a tie escaped the flames & scarcely a rail was unwarped and

---

62 Watrous, *Richard Epps*, 138-141.

unhurt." The destruction haunted the colonel. "The burning of private dwellings, churches &c deserves to be reprobated as nether politic nor in accordance with civilized warfare—It exasperated the People & and makes the struggle more cruel & bloody." Sometime after writing that, Morrow had a conversation with Rev. Alfred Roe, chaplain of the 104th New York, a staff officer for General Crawford (commanding Third Division of Fifth Corps). "He tells me that the hideous crime of rape was perpetrated in several instances on both white and black women, and in one instance on a woman far advanced in pregnancy." According to Morrow, the chaplain had not witnessed the crimes, but heard of them from "lips of the victims their declaration it had been committed." Morrow concluded, "He even goes so far as to say that more than one brutal wretch wearing the Federal uniform committed this crime on the person of the same woman—I record the facts and blush for the men who could even tolerate such acts."[63]

As Morrow struggled with his misgivings, a winter camp was established four days later near the Jerusalem Plank Road. Each company had its own street with quarters built on both sides, facing inward. Using pine logs from the site, one soldier said, the shebangs "were about seven by eleven feet in sides . . . dovetailed at the corners. The spaces between the logs were filled with chinking and plastered with mud. The sites were about six feet high." A ridge pole was covered with shelter tents and fastened at the eaves. A fireplace was built on one side by building a framework of wood branches and packing them in mud. The soldiers built a fire and burned the wood out, baking the mud "similar to a brick." Double bunks were built, "one above the other . . . making good sleeping quarters for four men." Some of the arriving new soldiers were assigned to the Sauk County Riflemen, placed with veterans in the various cabins. Finally, a parade ground was leveled and cleared to keep up the needed drills. One Wisconsin soldier said later that his state "made a mistake in organizing new regiments instead of filling the ranks of the veteran regiments, where the new men could receive the necessary training from veteran officers and touch elbows in the ranks with veteran soldiers, giving to them the benefits derived from years of drilling and campaigning."[64]

Christmas Day was a quiet one for the Iron Brigade regiments. Many of the soldiers spent the day resting and writing letters. Sergeant Frank Wallar of the 6th Wisconsin finished his winter shanty and noted in his diary and he was now ready "for the Christmas dance." Three days later he finally received his Congressional Medal of Honor for capturing the flag of the 2nd Mississippi at Gettysburg. "It is a

63 Henry Morrow, diary, December 12, 1864, 15.

64 Cheek and Pointon, *Sauk County*, 148-149; Ray, *Iron Brigade*, 342-345.

big one," he wrote in his diary. There was also news from the West: Sherman and his armies had captured Savannah, Georgia, and Maj. Gen. George Thomas had defeated the Confederate Army of Tennessee under John Bell Hood outside Nashville. "All is well all around & the goose hangs high," Private Ray of the 7th Wisconsin wrote in his journal. "The last Herald N.Y. [newspaper] has a full & graphic account of the operations of both armies which was very interesting. I & my tentmates have read it. It is many columns long." There was a final entry on the last day of 1864: "Well this as everybody knows is the last day of the year & the last day of the week & last day of the Month &c as also being New years eve. There is nothing transpiring to note but I expect if I were home there would be. How are they that are in civil life tonight. Well I cant say as I am unhappy. I enjoy myself very well, sitting & chatting with my good tentmates."[65]

---

65 Ray, *Iron Brigade*, 346.

Major General
George G. Meade

Although Grant gets most of the credit, Meade handled the Army of the Potomac as well as anyone had and better than most. He deserves a better hand than history has thus far dealt him. *Library of Congress*

1865
Victory

Major General
Gouverneur K. Warren

The commander of the Fifth Corps turned in a solid performance in 1864-1865, and was well-liked by the Western men. His treatment at Five Forks angered the Black Hats.
Library of Congress

President Abraham Lincoln

The president's assassination shocked and angered the Black Hats, as it did so many in the North. *Library of Congress*

Part I: They Wish to Remain

Kissing the Pine River Belles

It was three days into the new year of 1865 and the soldier was busy writing to a friend back home in Wisconsin. He had been in the service more than three years and had veteranized a few months earlier for another three years or the war. It was a time for true reflection, and he wondered in the letter what his life would have been like had he not once again signed the roll. "I was just thinking . . . that had I not reenlisted I would likely have been going to school this winter, hugging and kissing the Pine River belles, sleigh riding, and having all the fun imaginable." I am not complaining, he added. "Here I am, well and hearty after three years' hard service, and only one year and a bit of a chunk to stay; while there is hundreds of others who have not stood the racket of one campaign, and now they lay deep down in the Virginia mud, taking their last sleep. . . . I have no reason to complain, even while comparing my fare with that of the regiment." And there was the future to think of after the war. "[W]hat say you to going west after I get home?" he continued. "I think we would like it where the game is plenty. The boys are all talking strong of it here."

The letter writer was Hugh Perkins, and his words were meant for his friend Herbert E. Frisbie. Perkins was just seventeen when he enlisted in the summer of 1861 in the 7th Wisconsin. Now he was a battle-hardened veteran of some of the heaviest fighting of the war, still suffering the effects of his Wilderness wound from back in May 1864. Hugh was excited about the prospect of war, as evidenced by his first letter home in 1861 just after leaving Pine River: "We expect to move further on toward Dixie in a few days. Our men are all anxious for the big fight to come off." By late September 1862 he was a veteran who understood the hardships and inconveniences of war: "Herbert, you spoke about me forgetting an old friend. That can never be so long as I live, but we have been under fire for 28 days at a time and had to keep our cartridge boxes on all the time. So we didn't much chance to write." By that time combat had become second nature: "It has got so that it does not excite me any more to be in action than to be in a corn field hoeing, or digging potatoes." Late in 1864 it was obvious to he and his comrades that the war was inexorably drawing toward a conclusion: "Rebel deserters come to here by the hundreds every day. They say it is common talk with both officers and privates that as soon as they hear for certain of Lincoln's re-election, they will desert if it is a possible thing. They say when Abe is elected their last hope dies forever."[1]

The quiet of the Iron Brigade's winter camps near the Weldon Railroad outside Petersburg was routinely interrupted by the weekly arrival of new recruits—draftees and bounty men—to flesh out the old regiments to levels not seen since the beginning of the war. The small winter huts and "shebangs" meant for three or four soldiers were now jammed with five or even six, the new men sleeping on the wood floors. Out on the picket posts facing the trench lines of the still defiant Army of Northern Virginia, a steady flow of ragged, starved, and played out men trickled into the lines.

The Federal regiments were much changed since a year earlier. Most of the line officers had been privates or in the non-commissioned ranks in 1861. Major Thomas Kerr, a private at the start of the war, was superseded in command of the 6th Wisconsin when Col. John Kellogg returned after his adventures as a prisoner of war. Lieutenant Colonel Hollon Richardson finally rose to command the 7th Wisconsin, taking the place once held by his father-in-law, Col. William Robinson, who had resigned and gone home worn out and still suffering from an 1862 wound. The lingering differences between the two men over Richardson's elopement with the colonel's young daughter were a thing of the past. The two men were sharing a tent when Robinson rolled over to offer his hand in friendship, saying something along the lines that he had been a damned fool in his long and bitter opposition to the match. Richardson was the fourth man to command the regiment.

The seeming possibility of the end of the war also brought thoughts of home and the future to the old hands such as Pvt. William Ray of the 7th Wisconsin. "And happy New Year to all is my best wish & God grant it," he wrote in his journal on January 1, 1865. "Last night as the old year was going out & the new one ushering in, the Brigade Band played a number of good & sweet airs around the camp, the night being clear & still. The sweet strains of music . . . made me think of home & how it would be to be there, but I didn't allow myself to think too long on such Pleasures for fear that I might get homesick & that is a disease I have been so fortunate as not to have much while I have been in the service." An officer in the 6th Wisconsin wrote about the possibility of getting a furlough. To get a pass to

---

1   Hugh Perkins, letters, October 14, 1861, September 21 and 26, 1862, November 22, 1864, and January 3, 1865. Perkins enlisted from Leon, August 2, 1861. He mustered out with the regiment in 1865. *Wisconsin Rosters*, vol. 1, 570.

return home required a close relative be dangerously ill, he wrote. "So I wish you to take the enclosed envelope and put it in P.O. and send it to me." He would then take the envelope with the postmark from back home and put it in a letter "stating that my wife Mary, Jane, Sally, or Polly are very sick & and not expected to live," and "carry it to Army headquarters." His effort to get home proved unsuccessful. The soldiers talked and wrote of peace, home, and possible furloughs with the ring of distant musket firing in their ears.

While Private Ray avoided homesickness, Col. Henry Morrow of the 24th Michigan could not. "The last day of the year 1864—gloomy, stormy, cheerless!" he wrote in his diary. "The late glorious Union victories are being beclouded by the failure of [Gen. Benjamin] Butler at Wilmington [N.C.] and the defeat of [George Armstrong] Custer in the [Shenandoah] Valley." A visit to the headquarters of corps commander Warren slightly lifted his sour mood. It was the first time he had met the general, whom Morrow described as "about 38 years of age insignificant in appearance, dark complexion, nothing striking in his face or features, full of ambition and energy, intelligent in his profession, ivory in his conduct & and has a broad lack of conceit with all in his character—He is thought to be the best, ablest Corps Commander in the Army and I concur in this opinion—Both officers and men have great confidence in him."[2]

When they looked back to where they had been as the summer campaign of 1864 opened, many wondered aloud at how much they had accomplished during the intervening months. The Army of the Potomac left the old camps along the Rapidan River in early May and was now tightly wrapped around Richmond and Petersburg. The two armies had been in almost daily contact since the horrific fighting in the Wilderness. New names adorned tattered battle flags—Saunder's Field, Jericho Mills, Henagan's Redoubt, The Bloody Angle, and Yellow Tavern just to name a few. Northern hopes faded when Lee's army rebuffed the best Grant could throw at it, and the re-election of Lincoln seemed in doubt. Major General William Sherman's capture of Atlanta that fall, followed by his stunning march across Georgia, coupled with a string of victories in the Shenandoah Valley exposed the weakness of the Confederacy, re-elected Lincoln in a landslide, and guaranteed the war would continue until final victory was secured. The arriving new recruits were part of that final push to success. The men drilled every day, despite the cold weather, as regiments readied the rookie soldiers for the rigors ahead.

The war resumed in earnest that 1865 on the morning of February 5 when a Union cavalry division rode out in an attempt to intercept Confederate supply

---

2 Henry Matrau, letter, January 15, 1865; Henry Morrow, diary, December 31, 1864; "The Last of the Iron Brigade, The H. A. Morrow Diary: Conclusion," *Civil War Times, Illustrated*, 17.

trains operating near Dinwiddie Court House. Soldiers of Warren's Fifth Corps—including the old Iron Brigade— left their winter camps in light marching order to cross Hatcher's Run and take up a blocking position along the Vaughan Road. Two additional divisions of the Second Corps (now under Maj. Gen. Andrew Humphrey's command after Hancock retired from active field command in November 1864 because of his lingering Gettysburg wound) covered Warren's right flank. Late in the day, Confederates moved on the Union right near Armstrong's Mill, but were turned back after sharp fighting. When the cavalry raid proved unsuccessful the Union horse soldiers reached Gravelly Run and found themselves under attack. Warren pushed some of his brigades forward and was soon engaged with two enemy divisions, one each under Brig. Gen. John Pegram and Maj. Gen. William Mahone. The February 6 shooting flared up for a time and did not halt before Pegram fell and the Southern attack was repulsed. The two days of movement extended the Union front to the Vaughan Road on Hatcher's Run—another step closer to the encirclement of Petersburg to the Appomattox River.

The official reports presented the engagement as contained and orderly—the units moving this way and that, and the end result another positive advance for the Army of the Potomac. The view from the ranks, on the wet and often muddy roads, was different. In the late afternoon fighting on the 6th, for example, the left of the Fifth Corps line was driven back and the 6th Wisconsin found itself flanked and almost overrun. "We could get no artillery into position & therefore the rebs had a gay time cracking the spherical case and canister shot to us blue coats," Capt. Henry Matrau wrote home. "Our regt did remarkably well considering that we had nearly 400 drafted men in the fight. Well, we had it backwards & forward, alternatively driving the rebs & then getting [driven], our regt losing heavily all the time, on acct of being in an open field most of the time while the rebs were in thick woods."[3]

The soldiers hung on with a flurry of shooting until the attack got around a flank. "Our regiment did not give ground nor cease to engage the enemy until the order to retreat was given, which was after the enemy was in our rear to the left," one Badger said. Especially troubling for the Sauk County boys was the death of Sgt. Allison Fowler, who was shot while reporting to Lt. Mair Pointon about clearing the brush from an area in front of the company. The bullet that "entered his brain" killed him instantly. A friend mourned the sergeant as one of "the brave, moral young men of our company." The oft-wounded Fowler's luck had simply run out. He had been hit at South Mountain in 1862, Gettysburg in 1863, and again

---

3   Henry Matrau, letter, February 13, 1865.

Montgomery Guard, Co. D, 6th Wisconsin

Matrau enlisted in the Beloit Star Rifles, Company G and was promoted to captain on March 7, 1865. He was called the "Baby of Company G" because of his youth and stature. At war's end, a friend labeled him "The Smallest Captain in the Iron Brigade." *Brett Wilson Collection*

along Weldon Railroad in August of 1864.[4] Also long remembered was when the Federals caught the Confederates in a deadly crossfire and an officer on a white horse rode along the lines to rally his men. "Lieut. Pointon told us that if the officer

4   Fowler enlisted from Kingston, Wisconsin, May 10, 1861. *Wisconsin Roster*, vol. 1, 498.

on the white horse was disposed of, the enemy's line would break and give way, [and] he cautioned us to aim low and at the man on horseback," recalled one Black Hat. "We fired volley after volley by front and rear rank, but the man passed through it all apparently uninjured."[5]

After the fighting ended on February 5 the night turned cold and the men slept on their muskets. The next day dawned with a chilling rain that turned to sleet and clung to hats, coats, and muskets. The men had set out with only rubber and woolen blankets, and so were ill-equipped to deal with the freezing weather. The troops formed a line to the right of the Second Corps and moved into the wet woods only to be halted by enemy artillery fire. The 6th and 7th Wisconsin changed front and swung to the right of the brigade to check an enemy advance from that direction. Just before dark the regiments joined an assault on the Confederate position near Dabney's Mill. The charge was repulsed with loss. During the confused retreat, Maj. Thomas Kerr of the 6th Wisconsin snarled his canteen strap in the thick brush. He was "frantically trying to break away from his fastenings" when he called out to some passing Black Hats to help him avoid capture. "Someone cut the string and he struck a two-forty gait and was soon out of danger."[6]

At one point during the combat, Lt. Col. Albert Edwards of the 24th Michigan noticed that some of his men had ceased firing. When he looked closer, he discovered they were helping a few 7th Wisconsin men bury their beloved pet dog. The animal had known no fear, and had followed them from camp to field, sharing his chances in battle with the masters. When a ball killed him, his collective owners suspended firing to give their pet dog "an honorable but hasty burial amid showers of bullets from the enemy." The fighting also resulted in another battle wound for Colonel Morrow. When the 6th Wisconsin gave way in front of Morrow, who was commanding the Third Brigade during Brig. Gen. J. William Hofmann's temporary absence, the Wolverine went forward to steady the line. A few minutes later when one of his own regiments "broke and fled to the rear," the colonel took up the brigade colors to rally his men. "The lines were so close that I could see the flash of the enemy's guns tho' it was not yet 5 Oclock in the afternoon," wrote Morrow. "I received at [that] moment & place a wound from a musket ball which passed in my right side & out near the back bone, making a flesh wound some five and a half or six inches long—the wound though severe is not dangerous."[7]

5   Cheek and Pointon, *Sauk County*, 152-153.

6   *Ibid.*, 153; Ray, *Iron Brigade*, 357.

7   Curtis, *Twenty-fourth*, 292; Henry A. Morrow, diary, February 8, 1865.

Lt. Col. Albert Edwards, 24th Michigan

The colonel was surprised when he discovered some of his Wolverines had stopped firing to help members of the 7th Wisconsin bury a pet dog killed during the fighting. *Dale Niesen*

The regiments ultimately reformed, but the expected counterattack did not develop. The columns again moved to the right and threw up some earthworks. Later that night, the columns crossed Hatcher's Run and went into bivouac. The lines were too close to permit fires, and a small whiskey ration did little to ease the cold. "We passed it as best we could but suffered intensely," recalled one soldier. A new man, Pvt. John Vinz, was put out on the picket line among some pine trees. Lieutenant Pointon went out to check on the recruit and found the frightened private trembling so badly he was unable to hold his musket still. When the officer asked after him, a Confederate sentry heard him and fired. The bullet that struck a tree near Vinz unnerved him even more, prompting Pointon to caution the scared private to remain at his post. "Lieutenant, I no leave my post, I die first," Vinz replied in broken English. It was an example of "true bravery," was how a man in his company later described it.[8] After midnight, the brigade pulled back to the east side of Hatcher's Run and began fortifying the line between the stream and Vaughan Road. At daylight, a detail was sent to corduroy the road with felled trees

8   Vinz was a Milwaukeean drafted in September of 1864. He mustered out with the regiment June 8, 1865. *Wisconsin Roster*, vol. 1, 550; Cheek and Pointon, *Sauk County*, 154.

2nd Lt. Anthony Barberich, Buffalo County Rifles, Co. H, 6th Wisconsin

While still a sergeant, Barberich was cited at Hatcher's Run on February 7, 1865, "for coolness and bravery in urging forward the men and by strenuous exertions to keep the ranks closed and the lines unbroken, while exposed to a severe fire from the enemy; stimulating the bravery of the men by [his] conspicuous gallantry and courage." He was promoted to second lieutenant a few weeks later. *Brett Wilson Collection*

while the rest of the Wisconsin men strengthened the new line. Another whiskey ration was issued that night. The brigade began returning to its former camp at 6:00 a.m. on February 10, corduroying roads as it went because of the muddy conditions. They arrived about seven that evening, "awfully tired and nearly played out." The old camp, wrote one soldier, "looked like home." The returning 7th Wisconsin men were especially pleased to find that the men left behind on camp guard duty had started fires in their shebangs.

Although left unmentioned in the official reports, the nights spent in the woods and on the line were remembered by the survivors as among the most uncomfortable during the regiment's four years of service. "No shelter or fires and the weather bitter cold," complained one veteran. "We were near to the enemy; if we conversed in ordinary tone of voice the bullets would come singing at us, making it dangerous to speak aloud." On duty with the camp guard of the 7th Wisconsin, Private Ray wrote in his journal: "As near as I can find out only 3 have been killed out of the Regt and some 10 or 12 wounded. But tis said that our Regt has lost the least of any in the Brigade by them being on skirmish line most of the time." There was also a bit of good news to report: "There was 64 recruits come this evening for Regt & a sett of good looking men too."[9]

The General was Too Drunk for Business

What happened next to the regiments of the old Iron Brigade marked a significant turning point in the organization's annals and was recalled with bitterness. It began February 11 when the War Department asked for a brigade of reliable troops to take charge of draftee camps farther north. When Grant asked Meade to select several under-strength units from the Army of the Potomac, he picked the brigade containing the three Iron Brigade regiments and three Pennsylvania regiments. The reformed and reinforced brigade—presently under the command of Brig. Gen. Edward Bragg—showed a total roster of 78 officers and 1,261 enlisted men. Division commander Samuel Crawford objected. "If Bragg's brigade may not return, I earnestly desire to retain the Twenty-fourth Michigan, with the Sixth and Seventh Wisconsin," urged Crawford. "I have a surplus of regiments which can much better be spared. . . . The three regiments mentioned have served together from the beginning of the war and are identified with the Army of the Potomac. They desire to remain and I ask the privilege of sending other regiments in their place." Crawford sent the same plea to General Warren. "I have many regiments better fitted for service out of this army," pleaded Crawford, "and have asked that I be allowed to . . . retain my Western regiments. They wish to remain."[10]

The brigade prepared to move on February 10 amid wild and unsubstantiated rumors, including one that they were being sent to fortify a new line of trenches. It was 10:00 a.m. the next day when orders arrived to take railroad cars to City Point, and then a boat for special duty at Baltimore. One soldier believed the change was being ordered for "our daring bravery at Hatchers Run & and other times before." When they arrived at City Point, officers were informed only 1,200 could board the waiting steamer *George Weems*. The recent recruits were stripped away and the six regiments climbed aboard, the new men taking a second vessel. When a delay ensued because of missing baggage, however, the extra hours allowed Crawford's entreaties to bear fruit. Just prior to weighing anchor, for reasons never fully explained, the 6th and 7th Wisconsin were ordered to disembark. As the "downhearted" men of the Wisconsin regiments tramped down the gangplanks

9   Cheek and Pointon, *Sauk County*, 154-155; Ray, *Iron Brigade*, 358.

10   *OR* 46, pt. 1, 532-553.

and stood watching from land, the *George Weems* pulled away with Bragg and their old comrades of the 24th Michigan still on board and no chance for goodbyes. A sour Wisconsin soldier told his journal that they had "bunked on the Boat & lay there all night. But were ordered off in the morning & and could not go to Baltimore but no orders to go anyplace." General Bragg and the rest of the regiments suffered a splintered fate unbefitting their valorous records. Bragg and the 24th Michigan, along with the 143rd, 149th, and 150th Pennsylvania regiments, moved to Baltimore via Fortress Monroe. The general would remain there to the end of the long war. The 24th Michigan, however, found itself on the way to the draft rendezvous at Springfield, Illinois, where the Featherbeds would play a part in one of the closing (and saddest) chapters of the war. The 143rd Pennsylvania was ordered to New York City, and the 149th and 150th Pennsylvania to Elmira, New York.[11]

In the end, the 6th and 7th regiments returned to Crawford's division on the Petersburg front, climbing aboard railroad cars about 1:00 p.m. on February 12 for the dreary return to Crawford Station and the war. They were dropped off about a mile from their old camp and went into the woods to hunt for a new place to bivouac. "We are likely to be put into other brigades & and we know not where," surmised Private Ray. "Loud are the curses against old drunken Bragg. We think he is to blame for us not going to Baltimore." The "downhearted" soldiers end up tramping about five miles before finally making camp near the old division. And there they sat, awaiting new orders. It was very cold and the soldiers put up windbreaks and built fires. The Badgers were soon as comfortable as possible, said Ray, "but nothing compared, says the boys, to what we would have been in Baltimore. But we must abide by our fate. But old Bragg. Oh dear, what Blessing is showed on his head by most of the Boys. He has played truant to the men that won him his star."[12]

The 24th Michigan's Colonel Morrow learned about the mix-up while recovering from his wound at Niles, Michigan. His detailed diary entry evidenced his disgust with the confused affair and his simmering anger with Bragg: "During the night orders by telegraph were received from Army head Quarters directing Genl Bragg to disembark the Wisconsin Regts. & send them back to report to Genl Warren for orders. Bragg was beastly intoxicated [drunk] & and did not know what he was about. Had he been sober this order could have been changed so as to send the Penn. Troops back, because the 24th Mich & and Wisconsin Regts. have always

11 Nolan, *Iron Brigade*, 279.

12 Ray, *Iron Brigade*, 359.

Sgt. Charles Walker, Co. B, 7th Wisconsin

Walker was wounded at South Mountain in 1862, again in 1864 in the Wilderness, and mustered out with his regiment in 1865. He kept a careful diary of his soldier days from 1861 to 1865. *Mary Rieder and Dale Walker*

been together. However, the General was too drunk for business & and he contended himself with sending back incoherent and drunken messages."[13]

The rest of February passed quietly for the Black Hats still at the front, with rumors from other war theaters arriving daily— including one that General Sherman had been captured. Pay officers visited the regiments on March 1, bringing the vouchers up to date. "There is a great many Deserters coming into the lines now," one Badger wrote. "They average 125 daily in the Army of the Potomac." Among other developments, Lt. Col. John Kellogg, who had returned with a large party of recruits in November 1864, was given the 6th Wisconsin. He was subsequently promoted to full colonel and placed in command of the all-Wisconsin provisional organization. The 91st New York, a heavy artillery regiment converted to infantry for the final push on Lee's army and Petersburg, was assigned to Kellogg's brigade on March 3. Together the trio of

13 Henry A. Morrow, diary, February 28, 1865.

regiments had a total strength of about 3,000. The term "provisional" was dropped on March 15.[14]

One story making the rounds of the brigade campfires involved Sgt. James "Mickey" Sullivan of Company K. He had returned to the 6th Wisconsin a few months earlier after being hospitalized because of his Gettysburg wound. He arrived with surprising news: he had married a local girl there who worked as a nurse. During the winter came word that Sullivan was about to be a father. He was granted a quick furlough and sent off with good wishes for Pennsylvania to visit his wife and new son. He left with a smile and a shout. When the period covered by his furlough ended, Mickey failed to report. It was also discovered about the same time that his uncle, Pvt. Tommy Flynn, was also out of camp without authorization. Both were listed in the day book as deserters. Happily, the two turned up together a few days later to the jeers and calls of his friends. Unrepentant as usual for any infraction of the regulations, Sullivan was reduced to private for his spree. It was only during the closing days of the war that Kellogg—who had served as one of the lieutenants of the Lemonweir Minute Men in 1861—returned the stripes so Sullivan could go home to Wisconsin as a veteran sergeant.[15]

"De Bes' Man Fat Eber Libed

As the weather improved, the Army of the Potomac prepared to extend the Union line against the right flank of the Army of Northern Virginia. Before that could happen, however, Robert E. Lee sprang his own surprise on March 25. A large and compact column of his lean and hard soldiers attacked from the left side of his line to break through the front east of Petersburg and capture Fort Stedman and a large number of prisoners. The fighting was intense, but the Union troops rallied and drove the Confederates back with heavy losses in killed, wounded, and prisoners. Two days later Kellogg's brigade was ordered from its camp about 7:00 a.m. without waiting for breakfast and marched to City Point and army headquarters. "They took 2 of our forts & the works between & as was just playing hob & our fellows come in their rear & gobbled up the lot of them," a Badger wrote in his journal. Instead of going back to camp, however, the brigade was marched to a nearby open field for a hurriedly organized review of Fifth Corps by what one soldier called "all the big ones," including President Lincoln.

14 Ray, *Iron Brigade*, 363. The report of the Wisconsin Adjutant General for 1865 shows Kellogg was commissioned major October 19, 1864, and made lieutenant colonel December 10, 1864.

15 Beaudot and Herdegen, *Irishman*, 135.

The president had traveled to City Point just two days after the forlorn fight at Fort Stedman to meet with Gens. Grant and Sherman, as well as Rear Adm. David Dixon Porter. The discussion centered around how to forge a quick end to the war that seemed to have no end. The three military men and lone politician met for two days aboard the USS *River Queen*. All were in agreement that the long war would be over soon. What was recalled of the sessions was Lincoln's desire to return the rights of citizenship to the defeated Confederates. "I want submission and no more bloodshed," he advocated. "I want no one punished; treat them liberally all round. We want those people to return to their allegiance to the Union and submit to the laws."[16]

No one in the old Iron Brigade regiments was more excited about Lincoln's visit to the Army of the Potomac than Richard Epps, the young runaway serving just then as a cook and striker for Adjutant Jerome Watrous. The boy was told the president would pass right in front of the 6th Wisconsin as it was drawn up in a line. "Den I'se goin' to see Mass Linkun, bress de Lawd," Watrous quoted Epps as saying. "I'se gwine ter stand wid de men in de company and look at de bes' man dat ever libed." Watrous shook his head and told Epps it was not possible. "It will not do to have you in front of the men or standing with them when the President passes," Watrous said. The slight lad took it in, looked up and replied sharply, "Massa Ag'tant, is it any worser fo' me to stan' wid de boys when Massa Linkun comes down dan it was when Massa Mahone dun come down at the Weldon Railroad?" Epps was referring to an incident in which the former slave picked up a musket and bravely fought with the 6th Wisconsin against Confederate William Mahone's vicious counterattack. "The colored diplomat made me blush for myself," Watrous recalled. Perhaps, he relented, Epps could fill in an odd file in Company E.

The moment of Lincoln's appearance approached with the young contraband in his place next to his friend Private Jones. "When President Lincoln reached the right of our brigade, the command was to give three cheers. What hearty cheers those were," remembered Watrous. "It seems as if I can hear them now; it seems as if I can see Father Abraham lift that plug hat and show his high forehead." Lincoln rode along the lines in a carriage with other dignitaries as his son Tad, mounted on a black horse, trotted close to the carriage while talking with his father. The presidential entourage passed about twenty yards in front of the soldiers. When the president's carriage was immediately in front of the Wisconsin company, young Epps "dropped upon his knees, raised his hands as if in prayer and said in a voice

---

16 David Eicher, *The Longest Night: A Military History of the Civil War* (New York, NY: 2002), 806.

Captain Jerome Watrous, Adjutant, Iron Brigade

After enlisting in the 6th Wisconsin in 1861, Watrous served most of the war as the regiment's quartermaster and later the brigade's quartermaster. This photograph was taken a short time after he was promoted. He became editor of the *Milwaukee Sunday Telegraph* after the war, where his valuable contributions chronicled the story of the Iron Brigade and other regiments. *Milwaukee County Historical Society*

Pvt. Valentine Eckenrod,
Citizen Corps Milwaukee,
Co. F, 6th Wisconsin

Eckenrod was in Dodgeville
when he was drafted. He was
wounded in the fighting at Five
Forks, Virginia, on April 1,
1865, and mustered out July 7,
1865. *Wisconsin Veterans Museum*

that was heard by nearly every man in the company, 'de Lawd bress date good man."[17]

After the review the brigade marched off to the sound of distant fighting that played out before it arrived. The men arrived back to camp about 9:00 p.m. "all tired out."

The next morning they were told to be ready to march at a moment's notice, but nothing developed. The Black Hats had witnessed Lincoln's last review of an army corps.

It was Proved the Draft Men Could Fight

It was widely understood within the ranks of the Western men that the end of the war might be at hand. A great veteran force is arrayed against General Lee and his small army and the failure of the attack against Fort Stedman signaled the desperate nature of the situation. Now Grant was thinking of a final flanking effort to make Lee's position untenable. Under the command of Maj. Gen. Philip H. Sheridan, Warren's Fifth Corps, and some 13,000 horsemen, marched south and then west to turn Lee's right flank and sever the Southside Railroad line into Petersburg, the last line supplying the city. Lee countered the effort by dispatching Maj. Gen. George E. Pickett with his division of infantry and Maj. Gen. W. H. F. "Rooney" Lee's cavalry. Pickett and Lee struck and stalled the Union advance in

17 Ray, *Iron Brigade*, 367; Watrous, *Richard Epps*, 45; Watrous Papers, Wisconsin Historical Society.

Pvt. James Feight,
Anderson Guards,
Co. I, 6th Wisconsin

Originally from Watertown,
Wisconsin, Feight was
wounded on June 18, 1864,
and was absent sick when his
regiment mustered out in
1865. *Dale Niesen Collection*

fighting around Gravelly Run at Dinwiddie Court House on March 31 before falling back to entrench around and protect the vital crossroads at Five Forks. Lee ordered Pickett to hold Five Forks "at all hazards." The situation was becoming desperate for the Army of Northern Virginia and the Union rank and file knew it. "Sheridan is on hand with his cavalry. The army of the James is ready for the end. The army of the Potomac wants the finish," one veteran said.[18]

As part of this flanking effort, the Iron Brigade left its camps at sunrise March 30 and marched toward Hatcher's Run, forming a line of battle near the Boydton Plank Road. As the line advanced, heavy skirmishing developed and "quite a number of prisoners were brought to the rear." Once across the Boydton Plank Road the Union regiments built breastworks and bivouacked. It snowed that night for a time before the flakes "turned to rain, making it very muddy under foot," recalled a Western man. The two Wisconsin regiments and the 91st New York halted with "mud and slush . . . over our shoe tops and raining very hard."[19]

The weather cleared that night but rain fell again the next morning. The brigade column crossed Gravelly Run with the rest of Crawford's division, angling northwest past the Butler house massed "in column of regiments." The Iron

18 Earl Rogers, "A Well-Told Story," *Milwaukee Sunday Telegraph*, February 24, 1889.

19 Cheek and Pointon, *Sauk County*, 159-160.

Pvt. Herman Hoffman, Marquette County Sharpshooters, Co. E, 7th Wisconsin

Herman Hoffman enlisted at Springbrook, Wisconsin, on October 20, 1861. He veteranized, and mustered out on July 3, 1865. *Wisconsin Veterans Museum*

Brigade regiments were shaking out a line of battle when a Confederate attack by Bushrod Johnson's division of Anderson's Corps hit Maj. Gen. Romeyn Ayres' Second Division advancing in front of Crawford's command south of the Claiborne Road. Union fugitives "who were flying in confusion from the field" struck the forming Iron Brigade men like a whirlwind. Brigade commander John Kellogg struggled to organize a battle line with the 91st New York deploying on the 6th Wisconsin, but Confederates burst through a 200-yard gap between the regiments. Within minutes the Wisconsin men were being attacked in the front, flank, and rear as artillery showered their position. The Union front began to break as men sought safety in the rear. "I never ran so in my life," admitted one Badger. "The trees was knocked endwise with shot and shell. The flying Yankees could be seen biting the dust in every direction. Twas a horrid sight." Like they had on so many fields, parts of the Reb and Yank lines met and mixed. A Rebel sergeant attempted to grab one of the 6th Wisconsin men, but was felled when a nearby Badger clocked him with a swing of his musket. When the 7th Wisconsin fell back across the river, Sgt. Albert O'Connor saw a Confederate stand of colors that might be taken. He and Sgt. William Sickles splashed back across the river to go for them, but soon came under fire and the effort fizzled. When they spotted Capt. William L. Herwerth of the 91st New York in the process of being taken prisoner, the two attacked the group of Confederates holding him, killing some and dispersing the rest.[20] In the ranks, the veterans shook their heads and said it was just the kind of thing O'Connor—who was regarded as one of the regiment's daredevils—was expected to do. Previously, he had dressed in a Confederate uniform to prowl behind enemy lines for information. Once he was captured and sentenced to death as a spy, but jumped a guard and escaped. Both he and Sickles would be awarded Medals of Honor for their actions on this day and the next, but the awards were not announced until 1917.[21]

The three regiments rallied at one point to fire "rapidly on the advancing enemy until both flanks were turned and the enemy firing upon both flanks and rear of the command," reported Kellogg, who tried to put the best face on the situation. "I then directed Lt. Col. [Hollon] Richardson of the 7th Wisconsin to change front so as to meet the fire on his flank, which was executed, but the enemy appearing in so large a force in my rear, I directed the brigade to retire across Gravelly Run in as good order as possible. In retiring to this position my command was somewhat broken up, owing to the fact that the enemy was in their rear, compelling them to fight their way back."[22]

One of the Black Hats caught up in this desperate late-war fight was Jerome Watrous, the adjutant of longstanding for the 6th Wisconsin. For the first time in his four years of service he had a premonition that something bad was going to happen to him. Kellogg had not helped the uneasy feeling when the colonel

20 E. A. Paul, "Conspicuous Part Taken by the Iron Brigade at Gravelly Run, March 31," *New York Times*, April 1, 1865. This fight is also called White Oak Road or Gravelly Run. General Robert E. Lee was on the field watching the Confederate attack and making tactical adjustments accordingly. Edwin C. Bearss and Chris Calkins, *Battle of Five Forks* (Lynchburg, VA, 1985), 59.

21 W. K. Wright, *We Band of Brothers: The Record of Company B Seventh Wisconsin Volunteer Infantry*, unpublished and undated manuscript, Wisconsin Historical Society; Quiner, *Military History*, 480. O'Connor was breveted captain on March 31, 1865. He mustered out on July 3, 1865, *Wisconsin Roster*, vol. 1, 542. According to the U.S. Army Center of Military History, O'Connor's citation reads as follows: "On 31 March 1865, with a comrade, recaptured a Union officer from a detachment of 9 Confederates, capturing 3 of the detachment and dispersing the remainder, and on 1 April 1865, seized a stand of Confederate colors, killing a Confederate officer in a hand-to-hand contest over the colors and retaining the colors until surrounded by Confederates and compelled to relinquish them." The citation for William Sickles states: "With a comrade, attempted capture of a stand of Confederate colors and detachment of 9 Confederates, actually taking prisoner 3 members of the detachment, dispersing the remainder, and recapturing a Union officer who was a prisoner in hands of the detachment."

22 Hugh Perkins, letter to a friend, April 19, 1865.

Col. John A Kellogg
6th Wisconsin

The last field commander of the Iron Brigade regiments, his hair partially white after his harrowing time as a prisoner of war. He signed the final muster out at Madison, Wisconsin, in 1865.

Capture and Escape

announced with a smile before the fighting, "Gentleman, in less than an hour we shall be in the midst of the hottest kind of fight. Do any of you want to send word to your families? You may not be able to write after the battle is over." Thirty minutes later the three regiments of the Iron Brigade were being overpowered by Johnson's attack. During the retreat Kellogg realized the 91st New York was cut off and surrounded. "Mr. Watrous!" he called out, "we must get out of this. Do you think you can reach [Jonathan] Tarbell [colonel commanding the 91st]?" "I can do it if any live man can," Watrous yelled back, or at least that is the way Kellogg liked to remember the exchange long after the war. According to Watrous, he replied, "I will go, general, and order the 91st to fall back." Watrous (who also could tell a good story) said he wheeled and "put spurs to my horse and dashed through that thicket with bullets flying like a hive of bees stealing away, expecting at every bound to drop from the horse, but uppermost in my mind was the desire to reach the right and order it back—to give the order that would save it from capture." In the swirl of fighting, however, Watrous found the New Yorkers gone and he and his mount within Confederate lines. When his horse Charlie dropped to its knees, Watrous thought he had stumbled and spurred him. The horse lurched forward a few steps and fell again. Watrous dismounted and Charlie thrashed about, blood spurting from both sides of his neck from a bullet wound. When the young officer looked about, he found a dozen muskets leveled in his direction. "Surrender, Yank." Watrous lifted his hands.

"I watched him with such anxiety as only those in like circumstances can appreciate—rebs in front of him, rebs in rear of him, and yet he rode on," remembered Colonel Kellogg. "A rebel party threw themselves in front of Watrous, who "wheeled to the right and dashed on. Again they crossed his front, and he wheeled to the left. How many times he was shot at, God only knows. I could see the gallant Tarbell and the remnants of his regiment holding their position. I knew he would stay until ordered to return, and I knew Jerry would carry that order if he could. But my God, what chances where against him!" Kellogg looked away for an instant, but turned back just in time to see Watrous "throw up his arms; his horse fell at the same time; the rebs were all round him by the score." Colonel Tarbell had heard Watrous calling for him to retreat, so he swung his New Yorkers about to fight their way from the encirclement in an effort to join the brigade south of Gravelly Run. Watrous, however, never returned.[23] The brigade's losses in the brief but intense battle were eight officers and 290 men killed, wounded, or missing. Among the seriously wounded was Lt. Col. Tom Kerr of the 6th Wisconsin, who was shot while "cheering on his men." Kellogg proudly noted in his report, "I claim that my command were the last organized troops to leave the field."

When Union reinforcements from Humphrey's Second Corps arrived from the east, the outnumbered Confederates retreated. Around sundown, Warren massed his Fifth Corps in a large field. The waiting infantrymen could hear Sheridan's cavalry "pounding away to our left." "We bivouacked for the night, very tired and weary and sad; that sadness which comes from the loss of those dear comrades we had learned to admire and love," one said. The day's fighting had proved one thing to the veterans—the drafted men had stood fire and "could fight."[24]

There was one additional troubling report, at least to the old Iron Brigade hands who spent time serving Battery B, 4th U.S. Artillery. Lieutenant John Mitchell, who rose from the ranks to finally command the six guns, had been wounded again in the fighting at Gravelly Run. Rebel infantry had pushed within

---

23 Watrous, *Richard Epps*, 54-57.

24 *OR* 46, pt. 1, 884; Cheek and Pointon, *Sauk County*, 161-162. During the fighting, noted Pointon and Cheek, some soldiers in the 6th Wisconsin watched two gunners working at the muzzle of an artillery piece ramming home a charge. The gun accidentally fired, blowing the two men "from the gun almost into the creek." The man thumbing the vent on the artillery tube had raised his thumb during the loading, one soldier explained, allowing the passing air to fan a glowing ember inside the barrel and ignite the powder." Union losses for White Oak Road (also called Gravelly Run) were reported as 177 killed, 1,134 wounded, and 554 missing, the bulk coming from the ranks of Warren's Fifth Corps. Crawford's division reported 51 killed, 380 wounded, and 127 missing. Kellogg reported his losses were eight officers and 260 men. *OR* 46, pt. 1, 885.

200 yards to sweep the battery with musketry, knocking down horses and men. Poor Mitchell was hit in four places, bullets smashing his arm, tearing his neck, left shoulder, and thumping off his right side. The last shot broke some ribs, but did not penetrate his body. Mitchell, who was in his eleventh year of service, refused to leave his guns. He fought on for nearly another four hours until a brigade surgeon warned him that to remain at his post would cost him his life.[25]

We Believed a Great Wrong Had Been Done Him

The broad Union advance continued the next morning—April Fool's Day. It was a Saturday. The exhausted men marched in the dark not long after midnight while before and after that hour General Warren and Army headquarters exchanged a series of messages that demonstrated the confused nature of the fluid state of affairs. Fifth Corps moved south and then west to Dr. Boisseau's, where it remained waiting for orders. When Sheridan's horsemen moved aggressively north later that morning, what had been light and fitful firing increased in intensity as the minutes slipped past. His troopers were developing a new Confederate line of battle running along White Oak Road. Orders finally reached Warren about 1:00 p.m. to attack north and envelop west with his entire corps, striking and rolling up the exposed enemy left flank. Crawford's division took the lead and arrived at Gravelly Run Methodist Episcopal Church, where Warren formed his corps. Crawford's division formed in the middle of Warren's three-division front, with Ayres to his left and Griffin to his right. Kellogg's brigade was on the left front of the division, with the 6th and 7th Wisconsin regiments in the front, the former regiment's left flank on the Gravelly Run Church Road. Kellogg's third regiment, the 91st New York, formed behind the Badgers. The ground was rough, muddy, and cut by ravines.[26]

The advance began about 4:15 p.m. Kellogg led his three regiments with the rest of Crawford's division north and slightly west, driving enemy skirmishers before them. The Sauk County men were surprised when they spotted what appeared to be about two dozen Confederate cavalrymen trotting along the road to their rear. "We started to about face and give them a volley when we recognized the leader as being our chief of scouts, and his followers army scouts belonging to our Corps," explained one soldier. "They were dressed in Rebel uniforms and rode with

---

25 According to Buell, *Cannoneer*, 338-339, Mitchell thereafter "could never pass examination for active service, having one arm, one leg and one hand crippled, together with a wound in the side which never completely healed." He died three years later at Fort Leavenworth.

26 Bearss and Calkins, *Five Forks*, 87-88; *OR* 46, pt. 1, 831,880, 885, 889-890, 897.

short stirrups. The chief asked us to open our ranks and let them pass through, which we did; they rode through the Rebel line of skirmishers and were soon out of sight in the woods."[27]

The Union men reached the White Oak Road and continued north. Warren had been led to believe Crawford's men would strike near the left flank of the Confederate line that stretched along White Oak Road, but instead his men punched nothing but air. After driving well beyond the road Warren ordered his infantry to wheel left. The sounds of fighting swelled to the west, and after a march of a few hundred yards they came in on the flank and rear of the Confederate earthworks. "The enemy was busy fighting the cavalry in their front," one Badger said, "they did not see us or know of our presence until we gave a cheer and charged into their ranks. They jumped over their works and fought us from the other side." In the thickest of the fighting, the soldiers watched General Warren jump his horse over the works, and lead the effort to capture a portion of the breastworks. A heavy fire tore into the advancing Union line from the right, and an officer called Warren's attention to that fact. "Never mind. Charge them! Charge them!" the general called.

A Union cheer went up as the men went forward, one said, and "were soon in possession of all the works and the enemy, who had fought like demons, using bayonet and musket clubbed, were made prisoners." One Badger recalled that the "Rebs flew like chaff, but night closed the ball or we would have had the whole force. . . . They were April-fooled, although they have just the best kind of breastworks." In the 7th Wisconsin, Sgt. Albert O'Connor and five others from various commands rushed a Confederate stand of colors. The fighting soon became hand-to-hand. With his comrades already killed or wounded, O'Connor shot the color bearer and went after an officer who picked up the downed flag. The sergeant seized the flag with one hand and used the butt of his musket to knock down and kill the Confederate officer. But it was to no avail. Surrounded by the enemy, he dropped the captured banner and "took shelter behind a friendly tree until rescued by the advancing Union line.[28]

Among the Wisconsin wounded was Lt. Col. Hollon Richardson, who was shot trying to shield General Warren. "During my last charge my horse was fatally shot within a few paces of the line where the enemy made his last stand," wrote Warren in his official report. "An Orderly by my side was killed and Colonel

27 *Ibid.*, 844; Cheek and Pointon, *Sauk County*, 162-163; Hugh Perkins, letter to a friend, April 19, 1865.

28 Wright, *We Band of Brothers*, 260. O'Connor is sometimes listed as from Decorah, Iowa, but he was a farmer in the township of Dekorra (Columbia County, north of Lodi), Wisconsin. *Ibid.*, 261.

1st Lt. Solomon B. Holman, Prescott Guards, Co. B, 6th Wisconsin

Sol Holman was promoted through the ranks to lieutenant on December. 21, 1864, and was later made quartermaster of the regiment, but never mustered. He mustered out with the regiment on July 14, 1865. *Brett Wilson Collection*

Richardson of the 7th Wisconsin, seeing my danger, sprang between me and the enemy, saving my life and receiving a severe wound." It was the sixth time Richardson had been wounded. Pressed from the front by Sheridan's cavalry and overwhelmed on their left and rear by most of Warren's corps, the Rebel line collapsed. The Federal cavalry drove north and captured the Southside Railroad, cutting the communications from Petersburg to the rest of the Confederacy. While the Union commands reorganized, the soldiers were pleased to discover that they had captured a large portion of George Pickett's famed division, the "troops that made the 'Grand charge' at Gettysburg," wrote one Western man. The Iron Brigade regiments bivouacked for the night listening to what one man described as "heavy fighting" coming from the direction of Petersburg.[29]

The firing in front of Petersburg continued through the night and escalated the following morning on April 2. Although the massive battle being fought farther east was of interest to the men, of more immediate concern was the stunning news that General Warren had been removed as commander of Fifth Corps. As was later determined, Sheridan expected Warren to arrive sooner and attack with more alacrity and accuracy to crush Pickett's command early enough to capture or

29 Cheek and Pointon, *Sauk County*, 163-165.

destroy it before nightfall. However, roads were muddy, maps were inaccurate, and a bridge at Gravelly Run had to be rebuilt before Fifth Corps could cross. All of this delayed Warren's attack until after 4:00 p.m. When Fifth Corps finally moved out, it struck too far to the east and missed Pickett's line entirely. Warren was working desperately to realign his men when an enraged Sheridan arrived to take command of a portion of infantry under Romeyn Ayres and charge the Confederate left, which quickly gave way. Farther north, Samuel Crawford's division wheeled left and helped envelop the enemy line and score a stunning victory. As soon as the shooting stopped, however, Sheridan replaced Warren with Maj. Gen. Charles Griffin.

The men in the ranks were not happy about this turn of events. Many believed Warren was sacked because he did not press his disorganized command all the way north to the Southside Railroad. "We felt that a great injustice had been done him, as his troops were not in shape to meet an organized force of the enemy," complained one Badger. Yet, when Sheridan passed along the road some time later the men of the Iron Brigade regiments lifted a hearty cheer. "Although we felt that he was in the wrong as to Warren," explained a Wisconsin man, "we admired him as a soldier. In the afternoon we received the news of the evacuation and capture of Petersburg."[30]

The great chase to defeat Lee's army was now underway.

Let Them Alone, They are Going Home

Elements of the Fifth Corps (now under Maj. Gen. Charles Griffin, one of the division commanders) moved to the Southside Railroad about fifteen miles west of Petersburg on April 2. Kellogg's Iron Brigade men and the New Yorkers halted at the Burkeville Road about sundown to build coffee fires and rest. It was learned that the enemy had reached the road about an hour earlier and the chase resumed before the coffee was ready, the columns pressing on until they reached the Confederate rearguard well after dark. The 7th Wisconsin deployed as skirmishers with the 6th Wisconsin forming a first line of battle and the 91st New York a second behind the Badgers. Intrepid Sgt. Bert O'Connor of the 7th Wisconsin was again at the point of contact and was moving through the brush in the darkness when he was challenged.

"Who goes there?"

O'Connor froze. "Friends," he finally whispered.

---

30 *Ibid.*, 165.

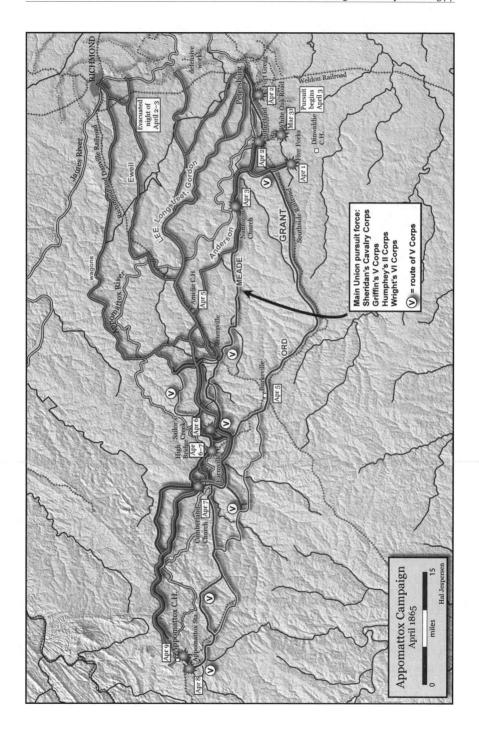

Appomattox Campaign
April 1865
Hal Jespersen

0   miles   15

Main Union pursuit force:
Sheridan's Cavalry Corps
Griffin's V Corps
Humphrey's II Corps
Wright's VI Corps

Ⓥ = route of V Corps

"Who be you all's, be you Pickett's men?"

"Yes," came his reply.

The Confederate sentry told O'Connor to step into a clearing for a better look. The moon broke from under a cloud just as the two men stepped into the open. "You all's Yanks!" spat the Confederate. A second Rebel picket fired at O'Connor but missed. A hidden Badger leveled his own rifle and fired at the flash and struck the enemy in his hand. The ball spun the Johnny around. The wounded soldier ran a few steps before slamming into Capt. Ole Graseley, who slapped his new prisoner on the shoulder and said, "Come in out of the wet!" The Rebel replied in a complaining voice, "This is a damned Yankee trick!"

Colonel Hollon Richardson determined the 7th Wisconsin was deploying along the enemy's picket line. When O'Connor continued forward and was halted a second time by the same questions, the colonel whispered, "Bert, tell him who we are." When he did, "a sheet of flame filled with bullets" erupted from the Confederate line. The 7th Wisconsin men dropped to the ground and returned fire. Behind the 7th and 6th Wisconsin, the 91st New York opened fire and refused to stop even while the Badgers hollered that they were firing into their own kind. The New Yorkers did not stop pulling triggers until a Wisconsin stretcher-bearer named Tom Anderson used his stretcher as a club to knock down a dozen or more men. Once the shooting ended, both sides settled down in the dark.[31]

The next morning, April 3, the enemy was gone from their front and the columns marched west toward the Appomattox River and halted. "The roads were very muddy, the streams were all swollen with continued rain," one soldier said. During the rest a mail wagon arrived, an occurrence one soldier described as "a very welcome thing." The march resumed about midday, the Western men and their comrades tramping along a road "strewn with limbers and ammunition chests, broken wagons and the things thrown away by the retreating enemy." The Army of Northern Virginia was in full retreat.

The pursuit was dubbed by one veteran as a "fox hunt." The soldiers marched on roads "ankle deep in mud, and in rain more than half the time." As soon as it was realized that Lee's army was running, he said, "our fellows just stretched their necks forward and loped off like bloodhounds on a fresh track, determined to get across Lee's path and wind the thing up then and there." It was marching of the kind never before seen. "Talk about light marching order, it was flying!" explained one Western man. "Knapsacks had long ceased to exist in the Fifth Corps. A rubber blanket was considered 'baggage' and a woolen blanket 'freight.'" The only things

---

31 *Ibid.*, 166.

the soldiers took with them were "haversacks, canteens, rifles and cartridge-boxes. We were right after old Lee that time. We knew we had him at last, and did not propose to let him get away."[32]

The march resumed the next day, April 4, without breakfast. Enemy stragglers began to appear alongside the roadway. One of the played-out Confederates told the passing Wisconsin men that the war would be over in six weeks. "We thought it wouldn't last that long," recalled one Badger, "judging by the way our cavalry was knocking them and the number of stragglers that could be seen going home from his army." The end was obviously drawing closer. Now and then a small squad of Confederates could be seen resting in the woods. "See that squad of 'Johnnies,' we ought to pick them up!" one man exclaimed. But another Badger would reply, "Let them alone, they are going home; the war is ended for them! and they would be allowed to go." The brigade reached the Danville Railroad just before dusk, formed a battle line, and threw up light defensive works.[33]

At daylight on April 5, the commissary department reached the column and rations were issued to fill haversacks that had been empty for some time. That afternoon, cavalry trotted past the marching Western men escorting about 1,000 prisoners and horses and mules that once pulled Confederate wagon trains. "Our cavalry did great work; the enemy never knowing when or where they would strike them," gloated one soldier. That night, Humphrey's Second Corps arrived to join forces in the pursuit of Lee's fleeing army. One Badger remembered in ranks there was a feeling as the hours passed that the Confederates were used up. "Everyone felt that the end was near at hand."[34]

The brigade halted near Jetersville and the Second and Sixth Corps came up in the afternoon, the Second Corps extending the line toward Amelia Court House, and the Sixth halted nearby. The Fifth Corps led off the next day in a great hurry to reach the courthouse or Amelia Springs, about three miles beyond, in an attempt to attack Lee, but no enemy was found. A burned Rebel wagon train was passed at noon and by 3:00 p.m. the column was moving through Deatonsville. Friendly former slaves told the marching men the Confederates had been there two hours earlier and were "on the run." Ligonton Ferry was reached and the Second Corps moved toward Lynchburg. The Fifth Corps (with Crawford's division in the van) kept marching westward, forcing the Confederate rearguard to continue its retreat. The column pushed on until 11:00 p.m. Despite the hard march of some thirty

32 Buell, *Cannoneer*, 361.

33 *Ibid.*, 168.

34 Cheek and Pointon, *Sauk County*, 168.

miles in about ten hours, the men remained in good spirits as they gathered at nightfall around fires of rails and limbs of trees boiling coffee in their tin cups and roasting salt pork on sticks or ramrods. We were "fat, ragged and sassy," wrote one of the men. One of the topics discussed over coffee that early April was whether "Old Billy" Sherman and his bummers might reach Lee's army first. It would never do, they pronounced with solemn nods. Lee and his men "are our meat, and we must have them ourselves."[35]

At sunrise, April 7, Fifth Corps columns left the road to begin moving cross-country. Word coursed through the ranks that some of Second Corps and Sheridan's cavalry had captured 13,000 prisoners, seventeen pieces of artillery and hundreds of wagons. The north branch of the Appomattox River was reached and the soldiers found regiments of the Second Corps crossing. Fifth Corps men moved up the river, crossed at High Bridge, and marched to Prince Edwards Court House before going into camp. The next day the Iron Brigade regiments moved out on the Lynchburg Road near the rear of the corps. It was a hard slow slog through the woods and fields. General Sheridan appeared on a big horse and announced to the marching soldiers that if they could reach Appomattox Court House, which was not far ahead, they "might expect glorious results, for it was the door that closed old Lee in on all sides; and retreat was impossible." No one recorded whether the men cheered the news or kept quiet. Long after dark, about 2:00 a.m., they finally halted and bivouacked.[36]

The next day was April 9, 1865—Palm Sunday. The men of the old Iron Brigade regiments roused themselves at daylight and shuffled along a railroad. Ahead came the sound of steady artillery fire. News flashed along the marching column that 20,000 Rebels had surrendered, but the hard veterans smiled, shook their heads, and told the newer men to disregard the story—it was too good to be true. When the firing ahead stopped altogether, the brigade halted to make camp. Word arrived that the men could erect their tents—something that had not been done in many days. Even the veterans furrowed their brows at the odd news. In the distance, white flags were seen hoisted from every tree, and word spread that

---

35 Buell, *Cannoneer*, 365.

36 The rumors were indeed true. Phil Sheridan, together with elements of the Second Corps and the Sixth Corps, fought the last major battle of the campaign (and the war in the Eastern Theater) at Sayler's (Sailor's) Creek on April 6, trapping and then breaking apart about one-quarter of General Lee's Army of Northern Virginia. Nearly 8,000 Confederates were captured in the confused fighting, including nine Southern generals. The number of Rebel killed and wounded was never reported.

Lt. Earl Rogers

This photo was taken shortly after Rogers returned home to Wisconsin following the end of the war. The staff officer was with Maj. Gen. James Wadsworth when that beloved officer was mortally wounded in the Wilderness.

Kim J. Heltemes

General Lee wanted an interview with Grant because he did not want to surrender to Sheridan, preferring instead a man of his own rank.

Was it true? Was the end of the war at hand? wondered the Western men. Lieutenant Earl Rogers would later note that in the "army at Appomattox [stood] the remnants and shattered battalions" of Rufus King's old division of 1861—the same men who had fought the battles of their country for nearly four years. "Many had fallen by the wayside, while others had pressed forward to the end."[37]

The hours passed slowly and quietly on that last day. Private Hugh Perkins of the 7th Wisconsin later recalled that he climbed to the top of a nearby house and watched Generals Lee and Grant meeting under an apple tree. Of course Perkins was mistaken—the apple tree conference involved lesser officers from both sides. The "Appomattox Tree," as it would become known, would soon disappear, the victim of souvenir hunters.

Before too long, recalled a Baraboo soldier, "We saw an officer come riding down the lines, his horse wet and covered with lather. As he passed along we saw the boys' caps went up in the air—the shout rang with cheers. . . . As he came in front of us, he shouted, 'Gen. Lee and army had surrendered to Gen. Grant.' Cheer—Oh, no! We yelled for joy for we know the war was ended."

---

37 Rogers, *Milwaukee Sunday Telegraph*, February 24, 1889.

Officers of the Sauk County Riflemen,
Company A, 6th Wisconsin

1st Lt. Mair Pointon (left), 2nd Lt. Nels Moore (right), and Maj. Lewis A. Kent (standing) posted for this picture while in Richmond, Virginia, in mid-April 1865, shortly after General Lee's Army of Northern Virginia surrendered at Appomattox. *History of the Sauk County Riflemen, Company "A," Sixth Wisconsin*

That night, one of the Indiana men later admitted that it was very hard to comprehend that the long and bloody Civil War that had cost all of them so much was really over. "It seems all like a dream to us," was how he put it. "Can it be that Peace is declared? Glory to God."[38]

"You All Kick up a Row with Johnny Bull and We Alls Will Help You."

The last march of the Army of Northern Virginia has been well documented. When it left the Petersburg line, Richmond was left undefended and fell a short time later. Confederate President Jefferson Davis and what was left of the Rebel government was already on the run. Lee's army, whittled down to about 30,000 men, marched west toward Amelia Court House in search of a promised food train that never arrived. His only hope was to get around Grant's aggressive corps and hard-riding cavalry just to the south and join with Gen. Joseph E. Johnston's reduced army operating in North Carolina. Lee continued marching his veterans toward Farmville, where he found rations shipped from nearby Lynchburg. Lee's rearguard was attacked at Sayler's Creek and some 8,000 men and most of the wagon train captured. Then the last of the Confederates marched to Appomattox Court House where more supplies were supposed to be waiting. Sheridan's cavalry and Union infantry got there first. His small army trapped and starving, Lee sent a note under a flag of truce to Grant asking about terms. He surrendered on April 9, 1865. Johnston surrendered later that month in North Carolina. The last major Confederate force operated under Gen. Edmund Kirby Smith in the Trans-Mississippi Theater. Its arms fell silent on May 26.

All that was yet to come. At Appomattox, the soldiers on both sides wondered what the end of the war would mean for them. Duties were light, although the formal paroling of the Confederates occupied many officers and clerks. "The rebel army is now camped with ¼ of a mile of us with their arms stacked," a Wisconsin officer wrote home. "I don't know how many men there are in the army of Gen. Lee, but from where we can see them they look like a pretty big squad. They are mostly Virginia troops & will be allowed to go to their homes after taking the oath of allegiance to the U.S." The Iron Brigade's former commander, Maj. Gen. John Gibbon, was one of the commissioners appointed to arrange the details of the enemy surrender. "They had made a splendid and heroic fight for what they firmly believed to be right—and lost," was how one Badger put it. "The victors, that had

---

38 Cheek and Pointon, *Sauk County*, 167-170; Hugh Perkins, letter to a friend, April 19, 1865.

1st Lt. David O. Davis Citizens Corps Milwaukee, Co. F, 6th Wisconsin

Davis enlisted in 1861 and rose through the ranks. He fought through the war and mustered out with the regiment on July 14, 1865. *Brett Wilson Collection*

as firmly believed they were right, had said that this Nation should remain one, not two, and they bowed to the will of the majority and most of them accepted the result as final." The Union men divided rations with their former enemies and "as they left us, the friendly feeling existed between the men of the two armies."[39]

Major Lewis A. Kent of the 6th Wisconsin, one of the officers taking the surrender, received the arms of a regiment from the Virginia county where he lived as a boy. Some of the Confederates recognized him from days long gone. "Hello Kent. What are you doing here?" one asked. He replied, "Just now I am busy taking the guns of your regiment." That night, he visited the Rebel campsite with some of his Badgers to share food with his boyhood associates. A few days later, paroled North and South Carolina soldiers walked past the Wisconsin camp on their way home. Some of the Black Hats went out on the road to shake hands with their old foes and wish them "God speed" and a safe return to their homes. Just before one group passed from view, a ragged Confederate called back with a smile, "You all

---

39 One of the officers involved in the surrender was Brig. Gen. Joshua Chamberlain, a former professor at Bowdoin College in Maine whose reputation has grown in the century and a half since the war. He had been cited for gallantry at Gettysburg and elsewhere, and was well known for his bravery on the field, but may not have been well liked: "Chamberlain was a cold, unlovable man, very brave and all that, but not dashing either in appearance or manner. He always reminded me of a professor of mathematics we had in college. Still, he was a gallant officer, and had more than once been desperately wounded while leading his troops in the most deadly assaults." Buell, *Cannoneer*, 322.

kick up a row with Johnny Bull and we alls will help you." The Black Hats waved back and nodded in agreement, knowing the Johnnies would be there if needed.

It was a strange kind of war.[40]

A Grave Blot on an Otherwise Great Victory

One continued topic of campfire discussion was Gouverneur K. Warren's removal as commander of Fifth Corps. An outraged soldier called it the "one grave blot upon this otherwise great victory." It was later learned there had been misunderstandings between Meade and Warren. The latter had a way of modifying the plans of operations prescribed by orders, and Meade "sometimes did not approve." The disagreements led to a sharp exchange of messages that only made the situation worse. With the closing days of the war at hand and aware of the tension between Warren and Meade, Grant gave Sheridan permission to "relieve General Warren if, in his judgment, it was for the best interests of the service to do so." Roused by the fighting around Gravelly Run and Five Forks, a frustrated and angry Sheridan did just that, and then, in a report dated May 16. 1865, criticized Warren for not moving as quickly as he could have, giving the "impression that he wished the sun to go down before dispositions for the attack could be completed."

After the war, Warren, who was sent to other duty stations on engineering assignments, pressed for a court of inquiry, but it was not until 1879 before a panel sat to begin hearings, and its findings were not published until 1882—against Sheridan. The exoneration came too late for Warren, who had died three months before. According to the 24th Michigan's historian, the entire Fifth Corps believed Sheridan acted "impetuously." Warren's corps, he explained, had been "marching and fighting for three days and nights and their speed could not approach to that of cavalry." To add to the insult of removal, Sheridan "evinced a jealousy in merging the four days' fighting under the one name of Five Forks, claiming the whole honor himself, after dishonoring the General who did far more than himself to obtain this victory." The "pen of history" is a great adjuster, he added, and will "insist that his name and the General who successfully directed the Fifth Corps shall be accorded the honor and credit of the victory. It was General Warren and the Fifth Corps who

---

40 Henry Matrau, letter, April 10, 1865; Watrous, *Richard Epps*, 114. There was a sad moment at Appomattox in Battery B of the 4th U.S. Artillery when a young mare, born in camp near Fredericksburg in 1862 and kept as a pet, died. She had been taught many tricks and there was a desire to see her grow into a battery horse. The Appomattox Campaign had been too much for her, however. The "Child of the Battery"—as she was called—was buried and the hard veterans fired their revolvers over her grave in salute." Buell, *Cannoneer*, 384.

Capt. Alexander Lowrie, Anderson Guards, Co. I, 6th Wisconsin

Alexander Lowrie succeeded John Kellogg as captain of Company I. He was wounded at Second Bull Run and mustered out with the regiment on July 14, 1865. *Brett Wilson Collection*

won the battle of White Oak Road. For three days had this corps been fighting and paved the way for the sweeping victory the next day at Five Forks." Another Iron Brigade man, writing of the removal, said there "is no man who fought under Warren but will say he possesses the love and esteem and confidence of the rank and file of the Fifth Corps."[41]

Lincoln Dead, and the Assassin Would Have Been Torn Limb from Limb . . .

The news of the assassination of President Lincoln reached the Iron Brigade regiments the morning of April 16 after they marched to Farmville and made camp. "We received official notice of the assassination of our beloved Lincoln," said one. "We could hardly believe it. It cast a deep gloom over the army." A Wisconsin officer called the act what it was—"murder"—and added, "Isn't that a burning shame? They didn't want him to live to enjoy the glory of having crushed the rebellion." Other soldiers "wept as at the loss of a father." It was the manner of the president's death that was most troubling, explained a Michigan man, coming "just as the silvery lining appeared on the dark war cloud that had enveloped his country, and which gave promise of a lasting peace and joy to his burdened heart, was particularly sad. It was horrible to contemplate the deed. The assassin would have

41 Curtis, *Twenty-fourth Michigan*, 300; Stine, *Army of the Potomac*, 706.

been torn limb from limb, could the soldiers have meted out his punishment." A soldier in the 7th Wisconsin wrote a friend, "Oh! Herbert, isn't it awful about old Abe. I would like to have the killing of old Wilkes Booth." There were burning tears on the cheeks of hundreds of soldiers, a Wisconsin officer said, but hardest hit by the news was Richard Epps, the ex-slave working as a cook in the 6th Wisconsin. He had a "keen appreciation of what President Lincoln and the soldiers had done for him," recalled a friend. "[That] poor colored boy fell upon the ground in terrible agony, and wept aloud for more than hour."[42]

In Springfield, Illinois, at Camp Butler, the 24th Michigan began preparing to serve as the honor guard for the burial of the assassinated president. A detachment met the train bearing Lincoln's body and escorted the coffin to the State House, outfitted with "new Iron Brigade black hats, feathers, brasses and white gloves" for the event. One of the officers present was Maj. Gen. Joe Hooker, who "seemed pleased again to meet the Regiment whose acquaintance he had made in the early stages of the war." The rest of the 24th arrived from Camp Butler by train on May 4 and was given the place of honor directly behind the hearse. The regiment marched "at slow time, company front, reversed arms," said one Black Hat. "The day was very warm and it was rather hard work." Lincoln was buried with great ceremony in Oak Ridge Cemetery and members of the Michigan regiment were posted as guards until a permanent tomb and reinforced vault doors were installed.[43]

Colonel Henry Morrow had left his regiment before the burial to assume command of what was left of the old Iron Brigade. His orders came on the day of the assassination. When he reached the army, he caught up with the brigade on the march sixty miles from Petersburg. Though it was only early spring in Illinois, he found the roses in "full bloom, and the fruit such as apples, peaches, etc., was as large as peas." It was a march of triumph, Morrow said, and when the Iron Brigade tramped through the streets of Petersburg on May 2 "by platoon front, closed en masse, at right shoulder shift, with banners flying and music playing," the soldiers "felt proud of his country and its deeds." One of the men standing quietly alongside the street was the disgraced General Warren. "As we passed him, the men cheered him heartily; we wished to convey to him our sympathy and loyalty," one Badger explained. Two days later the brigade was camped outside Richmond. "Every eye was strained to catch the first view of Richmond, so long the object of our hopes," continued Morrow. Of special interest was Libby Prison "(a large, low, three-story

42 Cheek and Pointon, *Sauk County*, 172; Ray, *Iron Brigade*, 367; Watrous, *Richard Epps*, 45; Curtis, *Twenty-fourth*, 311; Watrous Papers, Wisconsin Historical Society; Hugh Perkins, letter to friend, April 19, 1865.

43 Alfred Noble, diary, May 6, 1865, Bentley Historical Library, University of Michigan.

brick building with the upper story painted white & the lower two story's the red color of the brick," one soldier wrote home), Castle Thunder, the Capitol, and the "residence of the late Jefferson Davis."

The march through the enemy capital came May 6. The weather was perfect as the Army of the Potomac marched along streets lined by the Army of the James. The tread of the Iron Brigade men was firm as they passed through the Richmond streets—the "sun shone splendidly . . . the soft music floating through the pure air, the gay flags waving in all directions, the bright sunshine flashing on the guns of the long lines of infantry." The soldiers of their sister army lifted "shout after shout" as the veterans swung by. The men tramped past Gen. Lee's "plain substantial brick dwelling [but] we do not insult a fallen enemy," explained Morrow. The young officers of the company of Sauk County men of the 6th Wisconsin—1st Lt. Mair Pointon, 2nd Lt. Nels Moore, and Capt. Lewis A. Kent—took a moment in Richmond to have their likenesses captured for posterity. Other officers tried to find black crape to wear as a badge of mourning for President Lincoln, but none could be had.

On the fourth day after leaving Richmond, the brigade reached Fredericksburg and Morrow rode out to view the field where his new regiment fought its first battle. He found the "maundering head-board" marking the grave of 18-year-old Pvt. Louis Hattie—"our first offering to the grim God of War." An artillery shell had severed the boy's head from his body. Other graves were nearby. Morrow sought the answer to the question asked by every battle survivor: "'Why was I spared?' I asked myself. Here I was mounted on the same horse which I rode in the first battle of Fredericksburg!" When no satisfactory answer presented itself, he turned the head of his mount in the direction of his brigade and set his spurs.[44]

The Iron Brigade reached Washington on May 12 and went into camp. The men performed routine duties in addition to company, battalion, and brigade drills. One surprise was the reappearance of Jerome Watrous. Richard Epps was carrying water when he saw the officer coming into camp. "He hurled the camp kettle to the ground and started toward me on a run," Watrous wrote. "He was not satisfied with one hand, but seized both and shook them vigorously, and then gathered me in his arms. His eyes were swimming tears." At headquarters, Col. Kellogg came out and threw his arms around the lieutenant's neck. "Old boy, we are mighty glad to see you back." Sergeant Samuel Vincent, a boyhood friend and comrade from his old company in the 6th Wisconsin, followed suit. At mess that night, Kellogg told the

---

44 Henry Matrau, letter, April 19, 1865; Curtis, *Twenty-fourth*, 307-310; Cheek and Pointon, *Sauk County*, 176. The account was taken from a letter by Morrow on May 19, 1865, upon reaching Arlington, Virginia.

story how he, Vincent, and young Epps had gone out on the battlefield after the fighting with a lantern in search of Watrous' body. "We found many of our dead, and still more of the Confederate dead, as well as many new graves," Kellogg related. "We searched for you more than two hours, but in vain. Dick was moaning most of the time. He flew from soldiers to soldier, anxiously looking into the white faces and gloomily proclaiming 'dat ain't he.'" The trio returned to camp "in the firm belief" Watrous was among the buried. His name was given to the New York and Chicago news correspondent as one of the killed. Only later did they learn the adjutant was among the prisoners at Annapolis and was in the process of being released.

Anxious to hear his story, the men gathered around the returned officer to hear how when his horse Charlie was hit, Watrous dismounted just as the animal fell, his clothing pierced by three bullets. He was marched to the White Oak Road in a group of other dejected prisoners, where he "sat down on a stone-pile with my face in my hands." By noon on the 2nd of April they were "at Richmond and marched to Libby Prison. Before night we had been paroled and placed on boats for transportation to a landing a little above City Point, to which we marched and boarded a steamer for Annapolis." When he told the story long after the war at the reunion meetings and campfires, Watrous always added with a smile that he had never been regularly exchanged and assumed he was "still a paroled prisoner."[45]

More important than Watrous' return was the ongoing work of cleaning up and preparing for what was being called a "Grand Review." Captain Henry Matrau of the 6th Wisconsin admitted that he was "a sorry looking object" at Appomattox. As he told the folks back home, he had "waded creeks, plunged into swamps & morasses, laid in the dirt until I look more like a gopher than a human being." All through the old Iron Brigade regiments new uniforms and hats were issued. Colonel Dennis Dailey procured white gloves for the men and all arms and accoutrements "were made clean and bright." On May 23, 1865, the Army of the Potomac marched in triumph through the streets of Washington. The Iron Brigade regiments were in column of the Third Division of the Fifth Corps, the 6th Wisconsin at the head of the brigade. "Our boys marched splendidly while coming down the [Pennsylvania] Avenue in column by companies, and were cheered many times by the people who lined the housetops, windows and sidewalks by the thousands," one Badger said. "One could see the bronzed faces of the men, their muskets at a right shoulder shift, and interspersed in the line were the commanders

45 Watrous, *Richard Epps*, 54-57; William H. Washburn, *The Life and Writings of Jerome A. Watrous, Soldier-Reporter Adjutant of the Iron Brigade* (privately published, 1992), 113-115. Washburn was the grandson of Jerome A. Watrous.

Boys of Company K

These original members of the Lemonweir Minute Men, Company K, 6th Wisconsin, gathered for a final picture during the Grand Review period in Washington, DC, in 1865. The soldier seated on the far right is John St. Clair. *Institute for Civil War Studies*

of corps, divisions, brigades, and regiments in their staffs, superbly mounted. Above floated the flags under which they fought bearing the historic names. . . . It was a sight that will never fade from one's memory."

In ranks of the 6th and 7th Wisconsin were the veteran volunteers who had been there from the first days of the war. Old hands from the 2nd Wisconsin marched with the 6th Wisconsin and probably looked for "Bull Run" painted on the worn and tattered flags of the veteran regiments. At the head of the brigade rode Henry Morrow of the 24th Michigan and nearby, in the 20th Indiana, marched some of the old 19th Indiana men. The heavy guns of Battery B of the 4th U.S. Artillery rolled along the avenue as well, with "Tartar," the bob-tailed horse famous throughout the army, in one of the teams. The brigade's second commander, John Gibbon, rode at the head of his own corps. Remembered by the veterans as they marched to cheers along the streets were all the old fights—Gainesville, Second Bull Run, South Mountain, Fredericksburg, Fitzhugh's Crossing, Gettysburg, Mine Run, Spotsylvania, Wilderness, Laurel Hill, Cold Harbor, North Anna, Petersburg, Weldon Railroad, Hatcher's Run, Gravelly Run, Five Forks, and finally, Appomattox. "The whole thing went off quietly & without a blunder," Willie Ray of the 7th Wisconsin wrote in his journal of the Grand Review. [46]

The soldiers of Maj. Gen. William Tecumseh Sherman—old 2nd Wisconsin men always boasted he was their first brigade commander—marched the next day. One Wisconsin man said at the head of each corps "marched, or straggled" a band of foragers called "Sherman's Bummers." It was a magnificent body of men and made an enviable record, the Iron Brigade man said with a literary sniff, but "they lacked that soldierly bearing which characterized the Army of the Potomac." A Wisconsin man said Sherman's army was larger than the Army of the Potomac and noted as "remarkable" the flag of one of Sherman's units—"the badge on it is the cartridge box & the two words written in a circle over it, forty rounds." And then the grand review was over. Said Earl Rogers of the 6th Wisconsin—"Now, finally, all was quiet on the Potomac."[47]

The last great gathering of the Union armies was a spectacle never forgotten. Now it was time for the soldiers to go home. On June 16, the 24th Michigan at Camp Butler was ordered to proceed to Detroit to be mustered out. The city's formal welcome came on June 20 at the place where the regiment departed nearly three years before. Fewer than 200 of the original 1,026 men returned. "Of all the brave troops who have gone from our State," reported the *Detroit Free Press*, "few, if

46 Henry Matrau, letter, April 18, 1865; Cheek and Pointon, *Sauk County*, 178-180.

47 Ray, *Iron Brigade*, 373-374.

any, regiments can point to a more brilliant record, to more heroic endurance, to greater sacrifices for the perpetuation of the priceless legacy of civil liberty and a wise and good government." There were speeches, full tables of food, and the sad realization that many of those who left with the 24th Michigan in 1862 would never be welcomed home. The regiment was formally mustered out on June 30. "You will soon return to your homes and families, and engage in civil pursuits," wrote Lt. Col. Albert M. Edwards in his farewell order. "You can carry with you the sweet reflection that you have done your duty, and a restored and happy country will applaud the heroic sacrifices you have made in its defense. Let no act of your future life sully the fair name you have won in the field."

And with that, the "Featherbeds" from Michigan were gone.[48]

Old Boo, and Then Home

The two Wisconsin regiments were held at Washington into mid-June, the muster-out process seeming to take forever—especially to the veterans of the Lemonweir Minute Men of the 6th Wisconsin. The paymaster was late, as usual, and rations, complained Pvt. Mickey Sullivan, "became very scarce, whether owing to the fact that the war being over the government wished to economize or that expecting soon to be out of a job, the commissaries were trying to feather their nests, was not known." When a company discussion was held by the old hands, someone brought up the subject of "Old Boo," an animal acquired somewhere, by means no one fully understood, who had appeared at the end of the company street late in the war. Named for Confederate Gen. P. G. T. Beauregard, "Old Boo" was unusual in appearance, and so the talk centered on whether he was a mule, donkey, large goat, or small horse. As usual in such discussions, Pvt. Hugh Talty settled the matter, declaring the animal was "not a horse at all, that's in it, but a rare jackass."

The boys of company K were "mighty hungry," Sullivan recalled. They were also without pay, which made them unable to partake of the plenty that was available in Washington. Various schemes involving peddler wagons and women selling pies came to naught, and after dismissing various projects, one was declared by all as acceptable. The next morning "Old Boo" was missing and a Company K delegation called on Capt. Andrew Gallup to declare their animal stolen. Reports reached Gallup's tent that such an animal had been seen in a certain stable owned by a man ready to "buy anything on which 500 percent could be made in a single

48 Curtis, *Twenty-fourth*, 312-314; Smith, *Twenty-fourth Michigan*, 260-261. Edwards' order was dated June 28, 1865.

Sergeant James P. Sullivan, Lemonweir Minute Men,
Company K, 6th Wisconsin

"Mickey, of Company K," had this likeness taken late in the war when the Hardee hat was no longer part of the standard issue for the Iron Brigade regiments. The dark shadow of war is already visible. *Robert and Pat Sullivan*

day." A detail of soldiers was dispatched, and "Old Boo" was found and recovered amid hot words and raised shaking fists. Along the way to make the recovery, the detail met members of Company K carrying "various and numerous parcels and packages" back to their camp. The old veterans were quick to point to a sutler where the animal could be found. That night, oysters, sardines, canned fruit, fine-cut tobacco and plug were plentiful on the Company K street, and outstanding pie debts settled. The luxuries were gone soon enough, of course, and not long afterward "Old Boo" was again declared missing and probably stolen—and once again brought back to camp in triumph, his return celebrated with another feast. The affair was repeated a third time, but shortly thereafter orders to move the regiment were circulated and "Old Boo" was sold a fourth and final time. This time the deal stuck.[49]

Finally, on June 16, the two Wisconsin regiments left Washington for Louisville, Kentucky, traveling by rail over the Baltimore and Ohio to Parkersburg, Virginia, where they were loaded on steamers for a trip down the Ohio River to Louisville. They arrived on June 22 and went into camp on the Indiana side of the river. Ten western regiments—from Wisconsin, Indiana, Michigan, Ohio, and Minnesota—were organized into a provisional division under the command of Gen. Henry Morrow. An uneasy rumor swept the camps that an effort was underway to have certain regiments retained in the service. "The men wanted to go home and were vexed we were not mustered out," one Badger said. The talk proved false, and the process of mustering out began.

In the 7th Wisconsin, Lt. Col. Hollon Richardson gathered his soldiers for a few concluding remarks. The orders had come to muster the regiment out of service and head for Wisconsin to be paid off and discharged. He cautioned his men that he wanted none of "this drunkenness" he had seen earlier, and that he wanted the soldiers to go home better than they came back to the army from the veteran furlough the previous year. "He said he would tie up the man that was disorderly, let him be a private or officer, to which the Boys say bully," one of the listeners wrote. "He advised them to brush up & get shaved & hair cut &c &c. Go home like men." The colonel was given "three rousing cheers" and the regiment dismissed.

The departure for Wisconsin came July 2 with "a great shaking of hands" with the old 6th Wisconsin boys who came to see them off. The regiment formed and found the division drawn up for farewell honors, "which they did in good style

---

49 James P. Sullivan, Mickey, of Company K, "Company K's Mule," *Milwaukee Sunday Telegraph*, January 4, 1885.

cheering us lustily as we passed." Madison was reached on July 5 and the regiment marched under a large banner—"Boys, we welcome you home!"—into Capital Park for a formal ceremony. During the series of farewell speeches, Richardson got the biggest laugh with a clever line how everyone is welcoming the regiment home—families, friends, the loyal, and especially the anti-war copperheads because we have "quit fighting their friends." On July 16, the paperwork completed, the regiment gathered for a final speech. The colonel said he wanted to simply say goodbye, and they should always remember they belonged to the old 7th Wisconsin. He cautioned them against "intemperance, Idleness & Bad women, those either separately or altogether would spoil any Man." Goodbyes were said and the boys—no longer soldiers—started for home.[50]

The homecoming was played out in many hundreds of communities and backwoods farms. William Ray made his way to Prairie du Chien and caught a Mississippi River boat downriver for Cassville for two bucks. "Soon as the Plank touches shore, I leap on & am ashore which I find overgrown with grass & weeds and only one dim path up to the Beach to the street," he said. "I start for home & on reaching the gate see Mother standing in the door. I tell you I felt a thrill of joy run through my whole frame when I opened the gate & approached the house. I thought everybody is not Blessed with such a home, a kind Mother to greet them with a Kiss."[51]

The old Black Hat Hoosier veterans of the 19th Indiana were also at Louisville, though now in the ranks of the 20th Indiana. They mustered out July 12 to head for home. The regimental reports show the 20th Indiana numbered 23 officers and 390 men. It reached Indianapolis the same day, given an official welcome, and mustered out.

The return of the 6th Wisconsin was delayed by a shortage of blank discharge papers. This interminable delay, as its members waited opposite Louisville, explained of the Badgers, was "a very unpleasant state of affairs." Lieutenant Mair Pointon rode to Camp Chase at Columbus, Ohio, for a supply of the forms and upon his return the discharge process began. The 6th Wisconsin started for Wisconsin on July 14 and arrived in Madison two days later to "an enthusiastic public welcome." One of those on hand for the welcome of the 6th Wisconsin with its two companies of 2nd Wisconsin men was one-armed Lucius Fairchild, the hero

---

50 Original strength of the 7th Wisconsin was 1,029; gained by recruits in 1863, 74; in 1864, 343; in 1865, 12; gained by substitutes, 189; gained by draft, 67; veteran re-enlistments, 218; total 1,932. Losses by death, 385; missing 12; by desertion, 44; by transfer, 106; discharged, 473; mustered out 912. Quiner, *Military History*, 482.

51 Ray, *Iron Brigade*, 386-388.

of Gettysburg, who was just at the start of a long political career. "Should our country be again in danger," he told the hushed assembled crowd, "we'll raise another 2nd, 6th and 7th, and Indiana will furnish another 19th and we'll send to Michigan for a 24th and we'll have another Iron Brigade." Then, at the conclusion of the welcome, "the words of command were given," one of the old Black Hats recalled, and "the bronzed veterans wheeled to the right, drums and fifes struck up their stormy music and, with guns at right shoulder shift and bayonets gleaming in the slant sunbeams, under the green arches of the summer trees, the last organized fragment of the old 'Iron Brigade' of the Army of the Potomac . . . passed on, to dissolve and disappear from men's eyes forever, but to live immortal in history and in the memory of a grateful people." It fell to Col. John Kellogg to write the last formal order "dissolving the organization of the 'Iron Brigade,' and the gallant corps . . . ceased to exist."

A correspondent for the *Milwaukee Sentinel*, writing on July 1, 1865, tried to put the record of the storied Western unit into a perspective others might understand: "Wisconsin, Michigan and Indiana can say with truth that they have furnished the bravest soldiers of the war and they have had their shoulders to the wheel ever since the rebellion broke out. Their soldiers have never faltered . . . [and] they were confident that Right would be vindicated—and the result proved they were not wrong."

But the fame of serving as a soldier in one of the five regiments of the Iron Brigade of the West came at a cost almost beyond understanding. Once the powdersmoke disappeared and the numbers tallied, it was found that a greater percentage of these men had been killed and mortally wounded than in any other brigade in all of the Federal armies.[52]

---

52 Fox's *Regimental Losses* lists the 1st Vermont Brigade (six regiments) with the highest loss of 1,172, as compared with 1,131 for the Iron Brigade, 116-117; Beaudot and Herdegen, *Irishman*, 31; Cheek and Pointon, *Sauk County*, 180-182; Quiner, *Military History*, 481. Fairchild was secretary of state and would be elected governor the next year. Members of the 2nd Wisconsin who re-enlisted in 1864 were temporarily designated the Wisconsin Independent Battalion. The unit was consolidated with the 6th Wisconsin as Companies G. and H. *Wisconsin Roster*, vol. 1, 379-1,391; Dawes, *Service*, 311; Original strength of the 6th Wisconsin, 1,108; gain by recruits in 1863, 58; in 1864, 171; in 1865, 18; gained by substitutes, 79; gained by draft in 1864, 411, in 1865, 61; veteran re-enlistments, 237; total 2,142. Losses by death, 322; missing, 7; by desertions, 7; transfer, 75; discharged, 513, mustered out, 1,147. Quiner, *Military History*, 482. Nolan, *Iron Brigade*, examined the official numbers listed in Fox's *Regimental Losses*. In a comparison of the percentages of all Federal regiments, first on the list was the 2nd Wisconsin with a loss of 19.7 percent; sixth on the list was the 7th Wisconsin with 17.2 percent; eleventh on the list was the 19th Indiana with 15.9 percent; the 6th Wisconsin was thirtieth with 12.5 percent, and the 24th Michigan with 11.4 percent. Nolan, *Iron Brigade*, note 66, 381.

And at the very top of this unforgiving list of fighting regiments was the first regiment of the Black Hats—the 2nd Wisconsin.[53]

53 War Department records list the 7th Wisconsin first on the list of regiments that lost the most men killed in battle. It had 280 men killed outright or mortally wounded, compared with 278 for the 83rd Pennsylvania and 277 for the 5th New Hampshire. The records were later revised by the various states when soldiers listed as missing were found to have been among those killed in action. As a result, the 5th New Hampshire moved to the top of Fox's list with 296 killed or dead of wounds, compared with 282 for the 83rd Pennsylvania and 281 for the 7th Wisconsin.

Alfred Rolfe, Company K, 6th Wisconsin

The old solider attending the 1913 fiftieth anniversary reunion at Gettysburg. *Lance Myers*

Postscript: Thereafter and Evermore

Glorious Remembrance

The great armies that saved the Union faded away quickly, the one-time soldiers returning to various pursuits of civilian life. They faced an uncertain future. The war had changed them in ways they did not understand. Tens of thousands of men returned to farms and hometowns in Wisconsin and Indiana and Michigan missing an arm or leg or some other body part, or carrying diseases of which they were unaware. Even more veterans returned troubled in mind and spirit by what they had seen and done. Home was also a different place. Wives, younger sisters and brothers, and aging fathers and mothers had been tending crops and livestock and running shops and businesses. In some cases they found it hard to step aside for the returning soldier; just as often it was harder still to return to the old life for which they had longed. Uneasy and restless, many of the soldiers made plans to head west to make new lives. Nothing was ever going to be the same again.

The veterans also brought home a new sense of nation. They had seen the country and marched over it. They shared a common view of the future of the United States and would spend the rest of their lives trying to shape it. In many ways, the American Civil War was never going to end. The issues that caused the conflict of 1861 to 1865 are still being debated 150 years later—the civil rights of individuals, what it means to be an American citizen, the rights of states in a strong central government, and the role of the president in times of war. In so many ways, the nation would always be working on what President Lincoln in his little speech at Gettysburg called "a new birth of freedom." His words would remind the veterans as they went about their lives in a world of growing complexity that freedom was bought with sacrifice, hard work, and understanding.

At first the veterans, young men still, turned aside thoughts of the war and what it cost. They had little time for reunions or military matters, and attempts to organize meetings of former soldiers were outright failures or modest successes at

Lucius Fairchild, Edward Bragg, and John Gibbon

The trio of former officers sat for this portrait during an 1880 soldier reunion in Milwaukee, where the veterans formed an Iron Brigade Association. Fairchild is on the left (note his empty sleeve), Bragg is standing in the center, and Gibbon is seated on the right. *Author's Collection*

best. Dr. Benjamin F. Stephenson, former surgeon of the 14th Illinois Infantry, was one of the first to call for a veteran's organization, and after the war was among several individuals pushing such an effort. Exactly how the label "Grand Army of the Republic" came to be attached to the largest of such organizations is unknown, but it was a mighty name that was a force in its own right. In Wisconsin, for example, the first GAR post was started in Madison in 1866 and named for Lucius Fairchild. It had only eighteen members. A call by former Gen. John A. Logan of Illinois, then president of the fledgling GAR, for a special "Decoration or Memorial Day" each May to decorate the graves of fallen soldiers was met with favor. Following an initial period of enthusiasm, however, the GAR experienced waning interest. By 1879, for example, only three posts were still in operation in Wisconsin. "We were too occupied building lives and families and businesses that had been neglected by our years in uniform," said Jerome Watrous, now editor of a newspaper in Milwaukee. "Then one day we looked up from our work and saw dimming eyes and graying hair. Suddenly we wanted to talk again with our old comrades and of our soldier days when we were young."

With the rekindling of interest in soldier days came plans to organize a great reunion at Milwaukee on June 8, 1880. "Comrades! Attend to this at once, or we shall not know whether you are dead, proud, or gone to Texas," proclaimed the circular published in Watrous' *Milwaukee Sunday Telegraph* and dozens of other newspapers. Edward Bragg called on commandeers of former Iron Brigade regiments to shepherd their men to Milwaukee. Tom Allen of the old 2nd and 5th Wisconsin asked veterans from those regiments to attend. Other calls were made to soldiers who had fought at Shiloh, Vicksburg, Atlanta, Chattanooga, and the March to the Sea. From Wausau, John Kellogg issued the call to any former prisoners of war to contact him about the reunion, and to his old comrades of the 6th Wisconsin, he announced, "Let us do honor, if we can, to the memories of those who gallantly fell, as well as to exchange hand-clasps with those that remain." City leaders swung into action fashioning a welcome and providing $40,000 for entertainment. Under a headline "Coming Afoot," the *Milwaukee Sunday Telegraph* on March 14, 1880, quoted a *Stevens Point Piney* newspaper column that soldiers there were talking about marching to Milwaukee to attend the Soldier Reunion. "They will start about a week previous to the opening of the exercises at the Cream City, will have their route published, and all farmers are hereby notified to leave their chicken coops open." The *Telegraph* added: "That's right! It will be like old times. Left, left—left—left." Former Cpl. William H. Dow of the 2nd Wisconsin sent a note to the newspaper that "if any of the boys want to know what he proposes to pack in his haversack when he starts for Milwaukee, they can address him at Weyauwega."[1]

---

1 *Milwaukee Sunday Telegraph*, March 8, 1880.

Hattie Aubery, Daughter of the Iron Brigade Association

Hattie Aubery was named daughter of the Iron Brigade Association and poses here with an association banner. She was the daughter of Doc Aubery, a newspaper boy with the Army of the Potomac who later moved to Wisconsin. *Recollections of a Newsboy in the Army of the Potomac*

The week-long reunion was a great success. As many as 150,000 people flocked to the city to play a role in the event. The veterans brought with them tin cups, plates, utensils, and blankets, sometimes the very items they had with them in war and took home when the shooting stopped. They paid fifty cents a day for food. Prospect Hill was covered with tents large and small. Hotels and private homes filled to overflowing. Special trains brought former general and president Ulysses S. Grant and General Warren's old Five Forks nemesis Phil Sheridan.

Wisconsin's famed war eagle, "Old Abe," the longstanding pet of the 8th Wisconsin that had fought so long and well in the Western Theater, was a major attraction of the grand parade as the veterans marched under their old bullet-ripped battle flags. It was the famed eagle's last parade, for the grand old bird died the following year. Long remembered was how the parade halted at one point and a young woman ran out to Grant's carriage to have the old general kiss her baby. "The general not only enthusiastically kissed the baby, but the mother as well," exclaimed a reporter. The Milwaukee reunion set off a flurry of GAR organizing and "Camp-Fires" among the old veterans.

Just as important for the Iron Brigade men was the appearance of John Gibbon. Their former commander took time from the celebration to pose for a likeness with Edward Bragg from the old 6th Wisconsin and Lucius Fairchild of the 2nd Wisconsin, and there was talk about forming a special veteran organization for the Black Hats—the Iron Brigade Association. The veterans held their first formal meeting as an association in 1882 during the Army of the Cumberland reunion. Represented were the 2nd, 6th, 7th Wisconsin, 19th Indiana, 24th Michigan, and Battery B, 4th U.S. Light Artillery. Gibbon was selected president, but as he was still on active duty and unable to attend regular meetings, the first vice president, Edward Bragg, became the de facto leader who selected the sites and speakers. The fact that Bragg was a Democrat would lead to political infighting with Republican members like Fairchild, but the association organized large, well-attended Wisconsin "Camp-Fires" at La Crosse in 1883, Lancaster in 1884, Madison in 1885, and Oshkosh in 1886.

Gibbon also attended the reunion at Muncie, Indiana, in 1892. "It was pathetic to see a company of old, gray-haired men form Friday evening after dark and move to the station to meet General Gibbon," a reporter wrote. "A rousing cheer was given just as he stepped from the train." *Milwaukee Telegraph* editor Jerome Watrous was on hand, as was Abe Buckles of the 19th Indiana (now "Judge Buckles of California") and Nathaniel Rollins of Colorado, who had served in the 2nd Wisconsin. In 1896 during a meeting at Devil's Lake, Wisconsin, brigade veterans voted full membership to their children and to their grandchildren. As was to be expected, as the years passed, the number of attendees diminished. Time and old age were together achieving what Southern powder and shot and disease and grit could not.[2]

One of the last highlights for the Black Hats was the 50th anniversary gathering at Gettysburg in 1913, where a huge Iron Brigade tent was erected in the camp grounds and paid for by Charles H. McConnell, one-time color bearer of the 24th Michigan. It was decorated with large placards for the 24th Michigan of the Iron Brigade and the 26th North Carolina of Pettigrew's Brigade—"First at Gettysburg." A large American flag served as the backdrop for the stage. Entertainment included John Pattee, a veteran of the 24th Michigan now billed as "Colonel John A. Pattee," and his band "Old Soldier Fiddlers of the Blue and Gray." The reunion was a grand success. More than 400 Iron Brigade survivors

---

2   "After Many Years, Indiana, Michigan and Wisconsin Clasp Hands at Muncie," *Milwaukee Telegraph*, September 24, 1892.

registered during the week. Meetings were held twice a day during the reunion and 1,200 to 1,400 attended each session. Hollon Richardson from Washington state was there for the 7th Wisconsin. George Fink, who fought at Gettysburg as a 20-year-old newlywed was there for the 6th Wisconsin, as was Levi L. Tongue of Hillsboro, a former county sheriff from back home in Vernon County. Editor Watrous enjoyed every minute of the large gathering, scribbling copious notes for his newspaper and talking with old friends and enemies alike. George Eustice of the 7th Wisconsin, who fought beside citizen John Burns a half-century earlier, bought souvenirs to take home to Gilroy, California, including a commemorative badge, a reunion book, and a chair whose wooden arms had been carved from a tree containing bullets from the battle.[3]

Iron Brigade Association meetings became less frequent as the years passed one after another, the survivors of the old Black Hat Brigade reported to what they called the "Last Muster." One of the last gatherings came in 1928 at the Grand Army of the Republic, Wisconsin Department's sixty-sixth meeting held at Madison.[4] It was dubbed the "Lucius Fairchild Encampment" in honor of the late governor who had lost an arm fighting with the 2nd Wisconsin at Gettysburg. And then, finally, the meetings stopped altogether. It was not until decades later, in 1990, that two sons of Iron Brigade veterans—William H. Upham of Milwaukee, and James F. Sullivan of New Port Richey, Florida—issued a formal call for a "Reunion of the Iron Brigade Association." As members of the original association, the two passed a resolution opening membership in the Iron Brigade Association to all persons interested in the brigade and its history. The two men turned the operation of the association over to the Civil War Round Table of Milwaukee. Sullivan was the son of Sgt. James P. "Mickey" Sullivan, the popular rapscallion of the 6th Wisconsin, and Upham's father was William Upham, who served in the 2nd Wisconsin and was severely wounded at First Bull Run. Both men recalled the pride

3 Levi Tongue was captured in 1864 and spent nearly four months at Andersonville and other Confederate prison camps before being released on March 5, 1865. He weighed 190 pounds on his enlistment and emerged from the Southern prison system a skeletal seventy-three pounds. Tongue died on March 9, 1918; George Eustice family records.

4 The last survivor of the famous brigade may have been Josiah E. Cass of Eau Claire, Wisconsin, who stepped forward in November 1949. He said he was fifteen at the time of his enlistment in the 7th Wisconsin in 1864, and quoted the examining officer as telling him: "I think you are lying to me. I don't think you are 18 years old. But I think you'll make a darn good soldier. Go in and sign up." Cass told the *Milwaukee Journal* in an interview that appeared on November 24, 1940, that he was probably overlooked as an Iron Brigade survivor because he never joined the Grand Army of the Republic or other patriotic organizations. "There were too many parades," he said, "and I didn't care for them." He died a few months after making his appearance.

their fathers had as veterans of an effort to save the Union during the Civil War. "I believe that this renewal of interest in the Civil War is presaging a more or less revival of patriotism," explained Sullivan, who was born in 1901 when his father was sixty. Mickey, the elder Sullivan, died in 1906. "The war was the high point in their lives in many respects," Upham said of his father and other members of the Iron Brigade. He remembered his father and other veterans "talked constantly" of the war.

Redemption and Absolution

Typical of the old soldier gatherings of the Upper Middle West during those glory days of the early reunions was the one held at Mauston in Juneau County, Wisconsin, on January 1, 1885. The host was Angus S. Northrup Grand Army of the Republic, Post 59. Despite temperatures well below zero, it was by all accounts a grand success. The veterans, their families, and their friends came in by rail, sleigh, and foot from the neighboring towns of Lindina, Summit, and Wonewoc for the festivities. The *Mauston Star* reported the event was, "as advertised, an interesting one." A state GAR dignitary offered a rousing speech; a solo was performed by "little Arthur Patterson, upon a drum carried from Atlanta to the sea"; a six o'clock supper offered a "good, substantial repast"; and a "beautiful solo by Miss Addie Parker" pleased everyone.

However, it was a public reading of a letter from an old comrade and friend that "received the closest attention." The missive was written five weeks earlier on November 23 by Rufus R. Dawes from his home at Marietta, Ohio. Regretfully, he began, as he had attended the Iron Brigade Reunion the previous August at Lancaster, he was unable to again make the long journey to Wisconsin. However, he added, he did wish to write "'a proper acknowledgement" to his old comrades and their families. Twenty-one men of the old company—the Lemonweir Minute Men, Company K, 6th Wisconsin—had been killed in battle and another fifty-one wounded. Many of those soldiers, Dawes continued, "are now your plain fellow citizens, but they were heroes tried and true as ever offered life on a field of battle. The young generation can hardly realize that their modest neighbors are soldiers who have fought on more fields of battle than the Old Guard of Napoleon, and have stood fire in far greater firmness." And Dawes—who had mustered the backwoods volunteer company at Mauston in 1861, served as its first captain, and who commanded the regiment in its most famous fight at Gettysburg—wrote of many bloody fields, including Gettysburg, of fallen comrades, of farm boys, shopkeepers, river men, piney camp boys, and the others who made up the Iron Brigade.

William H. Upham and James F. Sullivan

William Upham's father served with the 2nd Wisconsin and was wounded at
First Bull Run. James Sullivan (right) is the son of James "Micky" Sullivan of
the 6th Wisconsin. The two officially called a meeting of the Iron Brigade
Association in 1990 specifically to turn over operations of the organization
to the Milwaukee Civil War Round Table. *Author's Collection*

The old soldiers pressed in to catch the words. Dawes was touching upon a
concern that grew more important to them with each passing year. There was a
touch of Wisconsin pride in all this, as shown in letters written during the war, to
each other afterward, and the articles prepared for publication—a festering
resentment that they had been cheated of a full share of the credit for their service
in the multitude of battle accounts (mostly penned by Eastern writers and officers).

Dawes also wrote of those who had paid the ultimate price: "They lie scattered over the land, and their names should be gathered upon around campfires, and their character and deeds presented."[5]

The Dark Shadow of War

Rufus Dawes walked in the dark shadow of his war experiences the rest of his days. He returned to his new wife and Marietta, Ohio, in 1864 and set about building a future for himself and his family. Even though he was discharged, he was breveted a brigadier general in 1865. Over the years he returned to Wisconsin only three times—once at war's end when his father died, again the next year to settle the estate, and a final time to attend the 1884 reunion of the Iron Brigade Association at Lancaster. There was much to do those first months after the war. The young veteran worked around the clock to build a promising iron works and other investments. But the financial panic of 1873 claimed his resources and only his wholesale lumber business kept him and his family from more difficult times. A son, Charles Gates Dawes, was born in 1865, the first of the couple's four sons and two daughters.

Dawes returned home from the war with his army servant William Jackson. Back in Ohio, Jackson worked as a waiter and later as a station baggage master, accumulating along the way a small house and other property of value. In 1866, Jackson asked Dawes to help him find his mother, who was still believed to be in Virginia. Jackson's brother Moses, who was working in Washington, DC, was sent to Spotsylvania County, Virginia, where he discovered his mother still being held as a slave "by a brute named Richardson." Moses pulled out a revolver and held the loathsome Richardson at bay until the man produced his mother and sister. Once free, Moses saw them safely aboard a train bound for Ohio. William Jackson was waiting when they arrived.

The son was only able to recognize his mother by the name card pinned to her dress. The meeting was one of great distress. "She had been whipped and choked, so that her power of speech was almost gone, owing to injury of the throat and palate," reported a bitter Dawes. "The daughter was an idiot, rendered so by blows upon her head. Poor William! He could not bear to take this bitterness to my wife, with whom he had so often talked and planned in joyous anticipation of this event, but he went to my mother, and saying: 'Mrs. Dawes, see what slavery has done!' He

5 *Mauston Star*, clipping undated; Rufus R. Dawes, letter, November 23, 1885. The post was named for Angus Northrop, 1st Lt., Company F, 16th Wisconsin, who was killed at Corinth, Mississippi, on October 3, 1862. The post was established on January 10, 1883.

broke down in an agony of grief and disappointment." The story has a better ending, for the mother lived the rest of her days free, outliving both her sons who provided enough to see that her last days were lived in comfort and security.[6]

Public duty called in 1880. Now 42, Dawes ran successfully for Congress as a Republican. In Washington he found old friends, including Gen. Edward Bragg, now Congressman Bragg. He also got a chance to help out an old comrade. One day, on the floor of the House of Representatives, Dawes was asked by another member of the Wisconsin delegation whether he knew Capt. Bill Remington of the 6th Wisconsin. Of course he did. Remington had been shot in one shoulder at Gettysburg and the other shoulder at Laurel Hill before leaving the army. Now he was having a hard time getting a pension because he had lost contact with his old commander. Dawes made for the U.S. Pension Office to call up the case and "swear it through." It gave him pleasure to do so.

Dawes was narrowly defeated for re-election two years later, partly due to his vote against the Chinese Exclusion Action, which angered organized labor in Ohio. He returned to private life to work at his lumber business and pen his war memoir in the midst of growing health concerns brought about mostly by the dark shadow of war. The emotional impact of what he had seen and done lingered. The defeated Congressman penned a letter to his wife on December 18, 1881, just before he left Washington for home. He had been out of the service for seventeen years:

> "I have to-day worshiped at the shrine of the dead. I went over to the Arlington Cemetery. It was a beautiful morning and the familiar scenes so strongly impressed upon me during my young manhood were pleasant. Many times I went over that road, admiring the beautiful city and great white capitol, with its then unfinished dome, going to hear the great men of that day in Congress. . . . Now at middle age, with enthusiasm sobered by hard fights and hard facts, I ride, not run with elastic step over the same road. . . . My friends and comrades, poor fellows, who followed my enthusiastic leadership in those days, and followed it to the death which I by a merciful Providence escaped, lie here, twenty-four of them, on the very spot where our winter camp of 1861-1862 stood. I found every grave and stood beside it with uncovered head. I looked over nearly the full 16,000 head-boards to find the twenty-four, but they all died alike and I was determined to find all. Poor little Fenton who put his head above the works at Cold Harbor and got a bullet through his temples, and lived three days with his brains out, came to me in memory as fresh as one of my own boys of today, and Levi Pearson, one of the three brothers of company "A" who died for their

---

6 Dawes, *Service*, 314-316. Dawes added: "The gratitude of Mrs. Jackson was amusing as well as touching. She put Abraham Lincoln as the first man and myself as the second."

country in the sixth regiment, and Richard Gray, Paul Mulleter, Dennis Kelly, Christ
Bundy, all young men who fell at my side and under my command. For what they died,
I fight a little longer."[7]

By 1889, his illness more acute, Dawes worked with some effort to finish his
war memoir entitled *Service with the Sixth Wisconsin Volunteers*. He published the book
the next year and sent copies to all of the surviving veterans of his regiment that he
could find. One of his last public appearances came on Decoration Day, 1899.
Already in an invalid's chair and marked by a white flowing beard, he was wheeled
into Marietta High School where he spoke of patriotism and duty. He died on
August 1, 1899, and is buried at Marietta, Ohio. He was 61.

Left behind were his beloved Mary Beman Gates, the "My Best Girl" of his
war letters, and his six children. One of them, Charles Dawes, would be Vice
President of the United States, but his father did not live to see it.

Was the War Worth its Horrible Cost?

Many of the old veterans struggled to make sense of their role in the war and
how it affected their lives. "We old soldiers tell stories in our camp-fires, and laugh
at the same old jokes, even when we have heard them a hundred times or more.
This seems ridiculous to other people, but you'd laugh as heartily yourself if you
had gone through what the soldiers have experienced," explained one-armed
Lucius Fairchild. Behind the tears and smiles, he continued, were hidden tears and
grieving hearts. "How plainly we recall the old camps, the old marches, the old
hardships, the old battles, the old forces of the times," wrote Jerome Watrous
following the 1884 reunion at Lancaster. Those who attended the reunions, he
continued, were "Boys—gray-haired boys—stoop-shouldered boys—bullet-
riddled boys—spectacled boys—glorious old boys." The anniversaries of the old
battles, he added, brought "an almost boundless grist of memories; and they are not
such memories as to make us gleeful; not such as to set us to cheering; not such as
smooth wrinkles and add greater freedom to our heartbeats." Unspoken in those
troubling memories of war, sacrifice, destruction, maimed comrades, and those

---

7 *Ibid.*, 316. Dawes' reference to "Poor little Fenton" was Lawson D. Finton, who was killed
near Cold Harbor on June 2, 1864; Richard Gray died May 25, 1864, from wounds received at
Laurel Hill (Spotsylvania); Dennis Kelly died June 23, 1864, from wounds sustained at Laurel
Hill; Christian Bundy died June 17, 1864, also from wounds sustained at Laurel Hill; Levi
Pearson died July 21, 1864, of wounds received on June 21, 1864. *Wisconsin Roster*, vol. 1, 499,
526, 530.

who died too young was an unanswered question: Was the war worth its horrible cost?

The world around them was changing. Old war injuries and aches and pains from wet camps reminded them of soldier days. Attending farewell services for dead comrades was now commonplace. The memories of 1861-1865 somehow seemed sharper and more vibrant, more immediate, and even the country itself seemed to be moving in troubling directions with their old battlefield enemies from the Southern states back in Congress and moving into places of authority and power. What had transpired over the intervening years?

With a few exceptions, most of the veterans of the Iron Brigade believed the war started as a great cause to save the Union forged by their forefathers. It most certainly was not a crusade to end slavery. "I can come to no other conclusion that should the Gen. Government be overpowered there will be but one continued scene of anarchy and confusion for the future," one new soldier wrote at the time. A captain of infantry explained during those early days in a letter to his wife that a Union victory would cement a country "purified of this blighting breath of treason and corruption, and history will record of the Republic, that in the year 1861 her patriotic children rallied around the emblem of the early fathers, and purged the land of the great curse of secession."[8]

During those years in uniform, however, the young soldiers came to see the hard face of slavery up close and personal. Some turned away from the human enslavement with hardly a thought. "I did not come from the grand west to wrangle over the Virginia niggers and South Carolina niggers and other niggers," admitted one Western man. An Indiana Black Hat admitted that he was troubled by an Emancipation Proclamation that freed only the slaves in territories still in rebellion: "There is no good news, everything is sad, soldiers discouraged, tired of the war and about the proclamation freeing the damned negroes. . . . A man that wasn't used to this country [in Virginia] would think it rained negroes, the way they come in." Other soldiers from the Western frontier, however, saw in slavery a great injustice and unfairness—where a man's work belonged to another who owned him—and came to understand that an end to slavery would hasten the end of the war. "You are right," one soldier admitted to his brother and sister. "The Union or Slavery will have to be knocked under. I am glad [General] M'Clellan has been removed. He tried to keep slavery just as it was."

---

8   Julius Murray, letter to his father, undated; Edwin A. Brown, letter to his wife, September 8, 1861; Mair Pointon, letter to brother and sister, December 8, 1862.

While working to destroy slavery, however, many of the young soldiers backed away from the idea that one of the major goals of the war had changed. "I for one deny it being an Abolition war. It is the same now as ever, a war for the Union," insisted one soldier to his parents in 1863. "The Nigger is in the road and must be removed come what will. If it was an Abolition war why was not the niggers in the loyal states set free?" He went on: "No, that is not what the proclamation strikes at. It is for the main support of our enemies from them, their slaves who does all their work. They are now and have been to work since the breaking out of the war in throwing up entrenchments at different points in rebeldom. . . . I came to fight for Uncle Sam. If he see fit to free darkees it is all right. I believe in whipping the rebes some way or the other."[9]

"How intense your interest is, in the cause of the Negro!" a soldier wounded at Gainesville during the Second Bull Run Campaign wrote from his hospital bed to an abolitionist friend. "Stronger than mine, I confess; but I can have no controversy with you, or with any other sympathizer with the down-trodden. For, however, good men may differ with regard to the policy which should be pursued in dealing with our great national evil, all who ever felt a single heart-beat for the good of humanity, are anxious that the great wrong should be righted and the African placed upon his proper footing as a man and brother."[10] By 1864, a Wisconsin officer recorded that the army camps were "now flooded with negroes, with packs on their backs, and bound for freedom. No system of abolition could have swept the system away more effectually than does the advance of our army. Behind us the slaves, if they choose, are free. . . . Let us thank God, and take courage."

By the middle of the war, many Iron Brigade men came to understand that the fight to end slavery was a way to save the Union and destroy secession. They returned to their homes victorious in 1865, sure of the rightfulness of their cause. The passing years, however, made it more difficult to accept the results when measured against the death, destruction, sacrifice, and things they had seen and done as young men—and how it had changed them. Now, as some of them looked back across the decades, it was to seek an understanding they hoped would lead to a kind of personal redemption. Was the war really worth it? The answer finally

9 Mair Pointon, letter to brother and sister, December 8, 1862; George Eustice, letter to mother and father, 1863.

10 Watrous, *Milwaukee Sunday Telegraph*, September 28, 1879. Watrous quoted from a series of letters written by Edward Kellogg of the 2nd Wisconsin, a former newspaperman. Kellogg was wounded at Gainesville and taken prisoner. He returned to the army and regained strength enough to travel back to Wisconsin, but died at his father's house in Boscobel (Grant County) on October 9, 1862. *Wisconsin Roster*, vol. 1, 342.

accepted by many, but not by all, was that the four years of fighting not only saved the Union, but that they had marched to history's drum in the great moral crusade of their lifetimes. The victory once and for all ended human bondage in the U.S. and brought forth the "new birth of freedom" martyred President Lincoln called for in his brief speech at Gettysburg in 1863. This view was on full display four decades later when Jerome Watrous wrote in the *Milwaukee Sunday Telegraph* about his young camp cook and servant, Richard Epps, and when Loyd Harris told with obvious affection the story of old Matt Bernard, the runaway who walked into the camp of the 6th Wisconsin. After the war, Epps accompanied his soldier friends back to Wisconsin. Rufus Dawes took his servant William Jackson back to Marietta, Ohio.

Veteran Albert Young of the 6th Wisconsin was experiencing the same reawakening. Two decades after the war, he made a long tour of his old battlefields. While writing about his experience in a series of stories in the *Milwaukee Sunday Telegraph*, he observed how his view of slavery changed during the war and afterward. "I had never thought I had entered the army in the interest of the slave," he explained until he had a mid-war encounter with a carpenter who was a slave. As they talked, he realized with somewhat of a start that all of the carpenter's work was owned by his master. It was all so unfair that a man's work should belong to someone else, Young continued. It was then he "came to feel that I wished the war might result in the freeing of the colored people." This end of slavery, Young wrote in the newspaper columns (perhaps as much for himself as for his old comrades) "finally became our work, and we were permitted to accomplish it—and it was granted me to see it. . . . Surely we were serving God in this, for He loves good and hates evil. . . . He hates slavery and loves freedom. He hates sin—what a monstrous evil, what a monstrous wrong, what a monstrous sin was this accursed institution."[11]

Their Fame Cannot be Mustered Out of the Memory of Men

Wisconsin celebrated its 150th year as a state on May 29-30, 1998. One of the highlights of the busy weekend was a living history re-enactment of the 1864 return of the 2nd Wisconsin to Madison at the end of its three-year enlistment. It was fitting that the regiment was singled out for the special honor on a special weekend. The 2nd Wisconsin was not only a member of the famed Iron Brigade, but the first

11 A. W. Galyean, letter, January 6, 1863; Rufus Dawes, letter, April 26, 1862; Albert Young, "His Pilgrimage," *Milwaukee Sunday Telegraph*, July 1, 1888. Edward P. Kellogg, *Milwaukee Sunday Telegraph*, September 28, 1879; *Green Bay Advocate*, December 19, 1861.

regiment to leave Camp Randall for the war front. It was also the first regiment to return after three years of hard service. As noted earlier, the original organization left the city in June 1861 with more than 1,000 young men in ranks and returned with fewer than 200.

Just as it was during its original welcome in June 1864, the city was in a festive mood in 1998 as the re-created 2nd Wisconsin camped again on the old grounds at Camp Randall with its large athletic stadium looming nearby. Organizers of the event carefully selected re-enactment units from around the state to represent the original companies. The number of participants in uniform (wearing the famous black hats) was restricted to the actual number of returnees. On the grounds, tents were carefully erected along company streets. Field kitchens were established. Drills were held. Thousands of visitors flocked to the camp, some carrying dim photographs as they looked for individuals representing their kinsmen of long ago along the company streets. One "private" among the re-enactors was surprised to find an officer escorting a man, his wife, and two small children, to the small tent where the soldier was eating off a tin plate. "Private," the officer began with a smile, "Here is your great grandson and his family to visit." The soldier blinked several times as he came to understand the true meaning of those few words. Overcome by the moment, his eyes went suddenly wet. "Geewillikens," he said jumping up, spilling his plate. His great-grandson stepped forward to embrace him. "Grandpa, you don't know how long I have been looking for you."

Later that day, thousands of citizens turned out under rainy skies to watch the 2nd Wisconsin parade around capital square accompanied by the cheers and shouts of the onlookers. Some in ranks recalled it was the return of the thinned ranks of the 2nd Wisconsin men in 1864 that first brought home the consequences of the Civil War to those left behind. The full regiment had left in 1861 to the music of brass bands and the cheers and farewells of friends and family. A reporter wrote in 1864 the regiment was "a splendid body of men—strong, brave, and full of ambition. They left Madison amidst the shouts of the people, and the small remnant of them, after three years of hard service, have returned to be greeted with shouts of welcome from the same people. Would that all who went might have been here, to have heard those shouts, and to have been gladdened by the sound of those ringing bells, and that roaring cannon, which welcomed home their living companions. Hundreds of those absent ones are gone where 'no sound can awake them to glory again.'"

Then he tried to compare the joyous departure of 1861 with the troubling return of 1864: "As we beheld their shattered decimated ranks marching around the public square of our city . . . we turned gloomily away to meditate upon the horrid consequences of war." The 2nd Wisconsin would soon disappear, he said, "but its history will still survive. It will share in the glory which has shed to pure luster upon the fame of the long abused but now vindicated McClellan. It has stood the brunt of the fierce onset of battle under Meade, Hooker, Burnside and Grant. . . . [I]ts fame cannot be mustered out of the memory of men." He concluded: "God speed the day when peace shall muster out all of our gallant soldiers. May that day bring with it a resorted Union, a vindicated constitution, and a government of laws under which civil liberty and the rights of the people will find a secure shelter from the encroachments of power. God speed the day!"[12]

In June of 1864, that day was still to come.

Others

"Mickey, of Company K"—James P. Sullivan of the 6th Wisconsin—came home to Bad Axe (now Vernon) County with a new wife and son where he became a farmer near Hillsboro. Two other children soon followed, but his war years had taken a heavy toll and by the 1880s he was wearing a special truss to ease a bad back as he worked his 40-acre field. The meetings of the Iron Brigade Association spurred him to begin writing about his war experiences for local newspapers and Jerome Watrous's *Milwaukee Sunday Telegraph*. But times were troublesome and the farming unsuccessful.

An epidemic swept Wisconsin in 1885 and claimed his two youngest children, Anna (called Fannie), and her brother James. Mickey abandoned the farm as a failure and moved to nearby Ontario, where he read law. He was admitted to the State Bar of Wisconsin on September 1, 1897. One of his examiners was Gilbert Woodward of the old 2nd Wisconsin of the Iron Brigade. Five months later Mickey bought a vacant lot for $65.00 in downtown Ontario and opened his law office, which he painted a patriotic red, white, and blue. He was soon a major figure in the small community, joining the Ontario cornet band and carrying the U.S. flag to lead Independence Day parades. A woman who was a child when she saw Sullivan said she was always afraid of him because of his "loud voice and gruff manner."

Mickey's life took yet another unexpected turn a few years later when his son George shot a neighbor to death and was sentenced to ten years in Waupun State Prison. A short time later, Mickey divorced Angeline, his wife of thirty years, and on January 18, 1899, married widow Bessie Gorham of Ontario—whose husband George Sullivan had shot and killed. Despite local gossip, the new couple and her three young sons lived in the building housing Sullivan's law office. That same year, Mickey won a judgment of $5.00 plus costs against the Chicago and Northwestern

12 *Wisconsin Newspapers*, vol. 10.

J. P. Sullivan, Law Office, Ontario, Wisconsin. James P. Sullivan, "Mickey of Company K," sits in his law office at Ontario, Wisconsin, in the 1890s. He painted the establishment a patriotic red, white, and blue. His dog, Pom, sleeps at this feet. *Author's Collection*

railroad for the loss of his dog "Pom." The second marriage produced a son, James Fitz, who would become a soldier of some reputation himself.

Old war injuries left the elder Sullivan stooped and lame. He died on October 22, 1906. It was said that one of the causes of death was a piece of shell fragment lodged near the base of his skull, a souvenir from the fighting at Weldon Railroad in 1864. Sullivan's grave was first marked by a simple government headstone until sometime later when a more prominent marker was ordered, probably by his son George. It is fair to state that the epitaph would have satisfied old Mickey:

James P. Sullivan
Sergt. Co. K
6th Wis. Vet. Vol. Inf.[13]

Edward Bragg returned to Fond du Lac and began a long political career that included thirty years in Congress. In 1884, seconding the nomination of Democrat Grover Cleveland for president, he coined the phrase, "We love him for the enemies he has made." Bragg died in 1912 and was buried at Fond du Lac.

Lysander Cutler served as a division commander in the Army of the Potomac until August 1864, when he was severely wounded. He finished the war in command of the draft rendezvous at Jackson, Michigan. He resigned from the army on July 1, 1865, and returned to Milwaukee. He died there the following year from a stroke, which doctors claimed was the result of wounds sustained during the Petersburg Campaign.

Dennis Dailey, shot by Confederate Gen. Johnson Hagood at Weldon Railroad in 1864 in what was called "the bravest act of the war," rose to major of the 6th Wisconsin. At the end of the war he migrated to Council Bluffs, Iowa, where he practiced law. He died there on March 24, 1898.

Despite the loss of a leg at Gettysburg, **William Dudley** of the 19th Indiana remained in the army until 1866, when he resigned and returned to Richmond, Indiana. In 1881, he was named Commissioner of Pensions in Washington DC, resigning two years later to engage in business and practice law. He died in 1909.

Richard Epps returned to Wisconsin with Dr. C. C. Ayres of Green Bay, a surgeon with the 7th Wisconsin, where he completed his formal education and worked briefly in a lumber camp. It was said he returned to Virginia where he worked in Negro education. His ultimate fate remains unknown.

---

13 For information on Sullivan's wife and writings, see Beaudot and Herdegen, *Irishman*.

Lucius Fairchild returned to Wisconsin after Gettysburg and served as Wisconsin secretary of state. He was nominated in 1864 as governor and served three two-year terms. A major reunion figure, he died in 1896. He was buried in Madison with his amputated arm.

John Gibbon rose to lead a Federal corps after Gettysburg and remained in the U.S. Army after the war. In 1876, units under his command discovered the bodies of George Armstrong Custer and the men of the 7th U.S. Cavalry at the Little Big Horn. Gibbon died on February 6, 1896.

Loyd Grayson Harris served three years in the army and then three years in the U.S. Marine Corps. Thereafter he lived in St. Louis, where he was engaged in the lumber business and was active in reunion meetings. He was a regular contributor to the *Milwaukee Sunday Telegraph* after the war.

John Kellogg returned to Mauston and his family and his law practice. In 1866, he was appointed U.S. Pension Agent at La Crosse and moved there. He resigned in 1875 and moved to Wausau, where he practiced law and served one term as a state senator. He died in Wausau in 1883. He was 55.

Thomas Kerr joined the Irish Montgomery Guards in Milwaukee as a private in 1861. He returned to Milwaukee after the war and worked as a carpenter. He was active in local politics and was a regular attendee at Iron Brigade reunions before his death in 1893.

Rufus King was relieved of division command September 14, 1864, and resigned from the army the next year due to ill health. He became minister to the Papal States and served in Rome until 1867, when he returned to the U.S. He spent the rest of his life in New York and died there in 1876.

Henry Morrow mustered out and served as Collector of the Port of New York. He resigned and re-entered the army in 1867. He served in several duty stations and was cited in 1877 for his conduct during the Pennsylvania railroad riots. He died in 1891 and was buried at Niles, Michigan.

Hollon Richardson settled in Baltimore in 1865 and practiced law. He was a delegate to the Republican convention that nominated U. S. Grant for president. He returned to Chippewa Falls in 1870, and thirty years later moved to Washington state in 1900, where he settled near Keyport. Hollon attended the 50th Gettysburg Reunion in 1913.

Earl Rogers joined Company I of the 6th Wisconsin and was promoted ultimately to lieutenant, serving on the staffs of Gens. Wadsworth, Cutler, and Bragg. Rogers was with Wadsworth when the general was mortally wounded. He lived in Viroqua until his death January 3, 1914.

Frank Wallar of the 6th Wisconsin was awarded a Congressional Medal of Honor for capturing the flag of the 2nd Mississippi on July 1, 1863, at Gettysburg in the fight at the Railroad Cut. The medal was stolen from the

Hollon Richardson, late of the 7th Wisconsin

Hollon returned to Gettysburg in 1913 to participate in the battle's 50th
Anniversary. His father-in-law, Col. William W. Robinson—who had so
vigorously disagreed with Hollon's marriage to his daughter—had died a
decade earlier. The hatchet between them was buried near the end of the
war. *Steve Victor*

Vernon County Historical Museum in 1977, and was discovered fourteen years
later in a collection of artifacts being offered for sale in New Hampshire. It was
returned to Wisconsin.

Appendix A

The Iron Brigade Companies and Counties

The 2nd Wisconsin Volunteers		
Company	**Name**	**County**
A	Citizen Guard	Dodge
B	La Crosse Light Guards	La Crosse
C	Grant County Grays	Grant
D	Janesville Volunteers	Rock
E	Oshkosh Volunteers	Winnebago
F	Belle City Rifles	Racine
G	Portage City Guards	Columbia
H	Randall Guards	Dane
I	Miner's Guards	Iowa
K	Wisconsin Rifles	Milwaukee
K*		Dane and Milwaukee
* Replaced original Company K in January 1862 after the original company was detached and converted to heavy artillery.		

The 6th Wisconsin Volunteers

Company	Name	County
A	Sauk County Riflemen	Sauk
B	Prescott Guards	Pierce
C	Prairie du Chien Volunteers	Crawford
D	Montgomery Guards	Milwaukee
E	Bragg's Rifles	Fond du Lac
F	Citizens' Corps	Milwaukee
G	Beloit Star Rifles	Rock
H	Buffalo County Rifles	Buffalo
I	Anderson Guards	Juneau and Dane
K	Lemonweir Minute Men	Juneau

The 7th Wisconsin Volunteers

Company	Name	County
A	Lodi Guards	Chippewa/Columbia
B	Columbia County Cadets	Columbia
C	Platteville Guards	Grant
D	Stoughton Light Guard	Dane
E	Marquette County Sharp Shooters	Marquette
F	Lancaster Union Guards	Grant

Company	Name	County
G	Grand Rapids Union Guards	Wood
H	Badger State Guards	Grant
I	Northwestern Tigers	Dodge/Waushara
K	Badger Rifles	Rock

The 19th Indiana Volunteers		
Company	Name	County
A	Union Guards	Madison
B	Richmond City Greys	Wayne
C	Winchester Greys	Randolph
D	The Invincibles	Marion
E	Delaware Greys	Delaware
F	Meredith Guards	Marion
G	Elkhart County Guards	Elkhart
H	Edinburgh Guards	Johnson
I	Spencer Greys	Owen
K	Selma Legion	Delaware

The 24th Michigan Volunteers		
Company	Name*	County
A		Wayne
B		Wayne
C		Wayne
D		Wayne
E		Wayne
F		Wayne
G		Wayne
H		Wayne
I		Wayne
K		Wayne
* The companies of the 24th Michigan did not have formal company names.		

Appendix B

The Iron Brigade Regiments

The First Army Corps (Army of the Potomac) disbanded on January 23, 1864. Its units were absorbed into the First Brigade, Fourth Division, Fifth Army Corps under Maj. Gen. Gouverneur K. Warren. The Fourth Division became the Third Division on August 24, 1864.

2nd Wisconsin: October 1861 – June 11 1864

Became the Wisconsin Independent Battalion on June 11, 1864, and served as division provost until November 30, 1864, when its survivors merged into the 6th Wisconsin as Companies G and H.

6th Wisconsin: October 1861 – July 1865

7th Wisconsin: October 1861 – July 1865

19th Indiana: October 1861 – October 18, 1864

The 7th Indiana merged into the 19th Indiana on September 23, 1864, and the 19th Indiana merged into the 20th Indiana on October 18, 1864, and left the Iron Brigade.

24th Michigan: October 8, 1862 – February 10, 1865

Battery B, 4th U.S. Artillery: October 1861 – April 1865

The battery accepted volunteers from the 2nd, 6th, and 7th Wisconsin, 19th Indiana, and 23rd and 35th New York regiments in January 1862. All these volunteers had been returned to their respective regiments by August 1864.

167th Pennsylvania Infantry: July 18, 1864 – August 1863
Organized November 11 – December 6, 1862. Mustered out on August 12, 1863.

1st New York Sharpshooters: August 1863 to October 1864
Composed of four companies: A, B, D, and H.

7th Indiana: August 1863 – September 1864
Organized on September 13, 1861, and mustered out on September 20, 1864. Veterans merged into the 19th Indiana on September 23, 1864.

76th New York Infantry: January 1865 – February 1865

143rd Pennsylvania Infantry: August 25, 1864 – February 10, 1865
Organized on October 18, 1862, and mustered out on June 12, 1865.

149th Pennsylvania Infantry: August 25, 1864 – February 10, 1865
Organized on August 1862, and mustered out on June 24, 1865.

150th Pennsylvania Infantry: August 25, 1864 – February 10, 1865
Organized September 4, 1862, and mustered out June 23, 1865.

91st New York Infantry: March 3, 1865 to May 1865
Organized September 12, 1861, and mustered out July 3, 1865.

Bibliography

Newspapers and Periodicals

Appleton Crescent
Appleton Motor
Baraboo News-Republic
Baraboo Republic
Beloit Free Press
Beloit Journal
Chetek Alert
Chicago Chronicle
Chicago Times
Chilton Times
Chippewa Herald
Christian Science Monitor
Cincinnati Daily Commercial
Columbus Republican
Delaware County Free Press
Detroit Advertiser and Tribune
Evening Wisconsin
Fond du Lac Reporter
Gettysburg Compiler
Goshen Democrat
Grant County Herald
Green Bay Advocate
Indianapolis Daily State Sentinel
La Crosse Chronicle
La Crosse Morning Chronicle
La Crosse Republican and Leader
Mauston Star
Milwaukee Daily News
Milwaukee Free Press
Milwaukee Journal
Milwaukee Sentinel

Milwaukee Sunday Telegraph/Milwaukee Telegraph
Mineral Point Tribune
Missouri Republican
Plymouth Reublican
Portage Register
Prescott Journal
Richmond Palladium
National Tribune
Vernon County Censor
Virginia Country Civil War
Wisconsin Newspaper Volumes
Wood County Reporter

Manuscripts and Collections

Antietam National Battlefield, Sharpsburg, MD

A. O. Bachman Papers, 19th Infantry file
Edward S. Bragg letter
Elisha B. Odle Papers, 19th Indiana file
Ezra Carman Papers
Ludolph Longhenry, 7th Wisconsin file

Burton Historical Collection, Detroit Public Library, Detroit, Michigan

Asa Brindle letters, Ward Family Papers

Carroll University, Waukesha, WI

Charles King Papers
Rufus King Papers

Chicago Historical Society, Chicago, Illinois

James L. Converse letters

Chicago Public Library, Chicago, Illinois

Charles McConnell Papers

Detroit Public Library, Detroit, Michigan

Mark Flanigan diary
Henry Morrow journal

Fredericksburg-Spotsylvania National Military Park
Abel G. Peck letter

Gettysburg National Military Park, Gettysburg, Pennsylvania
Iron Brigade files, various

Gordon, Alexander Family Collection
Alexander Gordon Jr. Papers

Heltemes, Kim Collection
Chester A. Wyman Papers

Indiana Historical Society, Indianapolis, Indiana
Henry C. Marsh Papers
John C. Jessup letters
Sam Nasmith letters
Solomon Meredith Papers
Thomas H. Benton letters
William N. Jackson diary
William R. Moore letters

Indiana State Library, Indianapolis
19th Indiana file
A. J. Buckles Papers
Solomon Meredith file

Institute for Civil War Studies, Civil War Museum, Kenosha, WI
Charles Walker diary
Edwin A. Brown Papers
George Eustice letters
George W. Downing letters
John St. Clair letters
Levi Raymond diary
Ludolph Longhenry diary
Karweick, Mark R., ed. "Ever Ready: A History of the Oshkosh Volunteers—
Co. E, 2d Regiment of Wisconsin Volunteer Infantry, 1861-1865"
Unpublished manuscript.

Johnson, Paul Collection
   William Robinson Papers,

Library of Congress
   James Wadsworth Papers

Manassas National Battlefield Park
   Second Wisconsin Infantry file

Michigan State Archives, Lansing, Michigan
   Regimental Records, 24th Michigan Infantry

Michigan State Library, Lansing, Michigan
   Abel G. Peck letters

Milwaukee County Historical Society, Milwaukee,
   William Lindwurm Papers

Newberry Public Library, Chicago, Illinois
   Dr. John Hall Papers
   Rufus R . Dawes Papers

National Archives and Records Service, Washington, D.C.
   Descriptive Books, Second, Sixth, and Seventh Wisconsin Infantry
   Morning Reports, Sixth Wisconsin Infantry
   Order Book, First Brigade, First Division, First Army Corps
   Order Book, Sixth Wisconsin Infantry

Oshkosh Public Museum, Oshkosh, Wisconsin
   Henry B. Harshaw and Richard Lester, "Operations of the Iron Brigade in the
   Spring Campaign of 1864"
   William P. Taylor letters

Mr. and Mrs. Robert Sullivan Collection
   James Sullivan Papers

University of Michigan, Ann Arbor, Michigan
   Alfred Noble Papers

Horace Emerson diary
Lucius L. Shattuck letters
Luther Hemingway letter

U.S. *Army Military Institute, Carlisle Barracks, Pennsylvania*

Civil War Times Illustrated Collection
Elon F. Brown journal
Frank Wallar diary
Henry A. Morrow journal
John F. Neff Papers

U.S. *Pension Office, Washington, D.C.*

James P. Sullivan file, and various

Wisconsin Historical Society, Madison, Wisconsin

A. W. Galyean Papers
Alured Larke letters
Amos Rood Papers
Andrew Gallup Papers
Andrew J. Langworth Papers
Caleb B. Clark letters
Chandler B. Chapman Papers
Cornelius Wheeler Papers
Edward S. Bragg Papers
Emerson F. Giles Papers
Frank Haskell Papers
George Fairfield Papers
Henry F. Young Papers
Henry W. Beecham letters
James M. Perry Papers,
Jerome A. Watrous Papers
Jesse M. Roberts letters
John H. Cook Papers
John O. Johnson letters
Julius Murray Papers
Loyd Grayson Harris Papers
Lucius Fairchild Papers
Nathaniel Rollins Papers
National Guard, AG's Office, Regimental Descriptive Rolls, Sixth WI. Infantry
Peter Larsen Papers
Reuben Huntley letters

Robert Hughes Papers
Robert Monteith Papers
Rollin P. Converse letters
Samuel Eaton Papers
State Militia, AG's Office, Regimental Muster and Descriptive Rolls
Thomas Barnett letter
William H. Church letters

Wisconsin Veterans Museum, Madison, Wisconsin

Earl M. Rogers Papers

Victor, Steve, Collection

Hollon Richardson Papers

Periodicals and Newsletters

Artilleryman, The
Blue and Gray Magazine
Civil War Times Illustrated
Columbiad
Confederate Veteran
Gettysburg Magazine
Milwaukee History
North-South Trader
The Blackhat, Occasional Newsletter of the 6th Wisconsin Vols.
Wisconsin Magazine of History
Wisconsin Necrology (Wisconsin State Historical Society)

Government Publications

Alphabetical List of Soldier and Sailors of the Late War Residing in the State of Wisconsin, June 20, 1885. Madison, Secretary of State, 1886.

Annual Report of the Adjutant General of the State of Wisconsin. Madison, WI, 1866.

Annual Reports of the Adjutant General of the State of Wisconsin for the Years 1860, 1861, 1862, 1863 and 1864. Madison, WI, 1912.

Biographical Directory of the American Congress, 1774-1960. Washington, DC, United States Governement Printing Office, 1961.

Confederate States Ordnance Bureau, Field Manual. Richmond, VA, 1862.

Military Order of the Loyal Legion of the United States, Commandery of the State of Wisconsin, War Papers, vol. I. Milwaukee, WI, 1891.

Military Order of the Loyal Legion of the United States, Commandery of the State of Wisconsin, War Papers. Vol. II. Milwaukee, WI, 1896.

Military Order of the Loyal Legion of the United States, Commandery of the State of Wisconsin. Vol. III. Milwaukee, WI, 1903.

Revised United States Army Regulations of 1861. Washington, DC, United States Governement Printing Office, 1863.

Roster of Wisconsin Volunteers, War of the Rebellion, 1861-1865. 2 vols. Madison, WI, 1886.

War of the Rebellion, Official Records of the Union and Confederate Armies. Washington, DC, United States Government Printing Office, 1889-1900.

Ordnance and Technical Manuals

Coggins, Jack. *Arms and Equipment of the Civil War*. Garden City, NY, 1962.

Coppee, Henry, *Field Manual of Evolutions of the Line*. Philadelphia, PA, 1862.

Fuller, Claud E., *Springfield Muzzle-Loading Shoulder Arms*. New York, NY, 1930.

Hardee, W. J., *Rifle and Light Infantry Tactics*, 2 vols. Philadelphia, PA, 1861.

McClellan, George B., *Manual of Bayonet Exercise*. Philadelphia, PA, 1862.

Reilly, Robert M., *United States Military Small Arms, 1816-1865*. Eagle Press, 1970.

Thomas, Dean S., *Ready . . . Aim . . . Fire*. Bilgerville, PA, 1981.

U.S. Infantry Tactics. Philadelphia, PA, 1863.

Books

Adams, James G. *History of Education in Sawyer County, Wisconsin*. McIntire, IA, 1902.

Aderman, Ralph M., ed. *Trading Post to Metropolis, Milwaukee, Wis*. Milwaukee, WI, 1987.

Aubery, Doc [Cullen B.]. *Recollections of a Newsboy in the Army of the Potomac*. Milwaukee, WI, 1900.

Bak, Richard. *A Distant Thunder: Michigan in the Civil War*. Ann Arbor, MI, 2004.

Bandy, Ken, and Freeland, Florence, eds. *The Gettysburg Papers*. 2 vols. Dayton, OH, 1978.

Bates, Samuel P. *The Battle of Gettysburg*. Philadelphia, PA, 1875.

Bearss, Edwin C., with Bryce A. Suderow. *The Petersburg Campaign: Vol. I: The Eastern Front Battles, June-August 1864*. El Dorado Hills, CA, 2012.

Bearss, Edwin C., and Calkins, Chris. *Five Forks*. Lynchburg, VA, 1985.

Beatie, Russel H. *Army of the Potomac: McClellan Takes Command, September 1861-February 1862*, vol. 2. New York, NY, 2004.

Beaudot, William J. K., and Lance J. Herdegen. *An Irishman in the Iron Brigade: The Civil War Memoirs of James P. Sullivan, Sergt., Company K, 6th Wisconsin Volunteers.* New York, NY, 1993.

Beecham, Robert K. *Adventures of an Iron Brigade Man.* Washington, DC, 1902.

———. *Gettysburg: The Pivotal Battle of the Civil War.* Chicago, IL, 1911.

———. Michael E. Stevens, ed. *As If It Were Glory: Robert Beecham's Civil War from the Iron Brigade to the Black Regiments.* Madison, WI, 1998.

Bruce, William G. *History of Milwaukee, City and County.* 3 vols. Chicago, IL, 1922.

Buell, Augustus. *The Cannoneer: Recollections of Service in the Army of the Potomac.* Washington, DC, 1897.

Busey, John W. and David G. Martin. *Regimental Strengths and Losses at Gettysburg.* Hightstown, NH, 1986.

Byrne, Frank L., and Andrew T. Weaver, eds. *Haskell of Gettysburg: His Life and Civil War Papers.* Madison, WI, 1970.

Carman, Ezra A. *The Maryland Campaign of September 1862. Vol. 1: South Mountain,* Thomas G. Clemens, ed. El Dorado Hills, CA, 2010.

———. *The Maryland Campaign of September 1862. Vol. 2: Antietam,* Thomas G. Clemens, ed. Savas Beatie, El Dorado Hills, CA, 2012.

Catton, Bruce. *Grant Takes Command.* Boston, MA, 1968.

Cheek, Philip, and Mair Pointon. *History of the Sauk County Riflemen, Known as Company "A" Sixth Wisconsin Veteran Volunteer Infantry, 1861-1865.* n.p., 1909.

Clark, Walter, ed. *Histories of the Several Regiments and Battalions from North Carolina.* 5 vols. Goldsboro, NC, 1901.

Coddington, Edwin B. *The Gettysburg Campaign.* New York, NY, 1968.

Conard, Howard L. *History of Milwaukee From its First Settlement to the Year 1895.* 3 vols. Chicago, IL, 1895.

Cox, John D. *Culp's Hill: The Attack and Defense of the Union Flank, July 2, 1863.* New York, NY, 2003.

Cozen, Kathleen Neils. *Immigrant Milwaukee, 1836-1860.* Cambridge, MA, 1976.

Cozzens, Peter, ed. *Battles and Leaders of the Civil War,* Vol. 5, Chicago, IL, 2005.

Current, Richard N. *The History of Wisconsin . . . The Civil War Era, 1848-1873.* Madison, WI, 1976.

Curtis, Orson B. *History of the Twenty-Fourth Michigan of the Iron Brigade.* Detroit, MI, 1891.

Damon, Herbert C. *History of the Milwaukee Light Guard.* Milwaukee, WI, 1875.

Davis, William C. *Battle at Bull Run: A History of the First Major Campaign of the Civil War.* Garden City, NY, 1977.

Dawes, Rufus R. *Service with the Sixth Wisconsin Volunteers.* Marietta, OH, 1890.

Dawes-Gates Ancestral Lines, *A Memorial Volume Containing the American Ancestry of Mary Beman (Gates) Dawes.* Chicago, IL, 1943.

Doubleday, Abner. *Chancellorsville and Gettysburg.* New York, NY, 1886.

Dougherty, James J. *Stone's Brigade and the Fight for the McPherson Farm: Battle of Gettysburg, July 1, 1863*. Conshohocken, PA, 2001.

Dowdey, Clifford. *Death of a Nation: The Story of Lee and his Men at Gettysburg*. New York, NY, 1958.

Dudley, William W. *The Iron Brigade at Gettysburg. Official Report of the Part Borne by the 1st Brigade, 1st Division, 1st Army Corps*. Cincinnati, OH, 1879.

Dunn, Craig L. *Iron Men, Iron Will: The Nineteenth Indiana Regiment of the Iron Brigade*. Indianapolis, IN, 1995.

Dyer, F. H. *A Compendium of the War of the Rebellion*. Des Moines, IA, 1908.

Eicher, David. *The Longest Night: A Military History of the Civil War*. New York, NY, 2001.

Fitch, Michael H. *Echoes of the Civil War as I Hear Them*. New York, NY, 1905.

Flower, Frank A. *History of Milwaukee, Wisconsin*. Chicago, IL, 1881.

Frassanito, William A. *Gettysburg: A Journey in Time*. New York, NY, 1975.

Freeman, Douglas A. *Lee's Lieutenants: A Study in Command*. 3 vols. New York, NY, 1942-1944.

Furgurson, Ernest B. *Chancellorsville 1863: The Souls of the Brave*. New York, NY, 1992.

Gaff, Alan D. *Brave Men's Tears: The Iron Brigade at Brawner Farm*. Dayton, OH, 1985.

———. *If This is War: A History of the Campaign of Bull's Run by the Wisconsin Regiment Thereafter Known as the Ragged Ass Second*. Dayton, OH, 1991.

———. *On Many a Bloody Field: Four Years in the Iron Brigade*. Bloomington, IN, 1997.

Gaff, Alan D., and Maureen Gaff. *Our Boys: A Civil War Photograph Album*. Mt. Vernon, IN, 1996.

Gallagher, Gary W., ed. *The First Day at Gettysburg, Essays on Confederate and Union Leadership*. Kent, OH, 1992.

Gates, Theodore B. *The "Ulster Guard" [20th State Militia] and the War of the Rebellion*. New York, NY, 1879.

Gibbon, John. *Personal Recollections of the Civil War*. New York, NY, 1928.

Gottfried, Bradley M. *The Maps of Antietam: An Atlas of the Antietam (Sharpsburg) Campaign, including the Battle of South Mountain, September 2-20, 1862*. El Dorado Hills, CA, 2012.

———. *The Maps of First Bull Run: An Atlas of the First Bull Run (Manassas) Campaign, including the Battle of Ball's Bluff, June–October 1861*. El Dorado Hills, CA, 2010.

———. *The Maps of Gettysburg: An Atlas of the Gettysburg Campaign, July 3–July 13, 1863*. El Dorado Hills, CA, 2008.

Gragg, Rod. *Covered With Glory: The 26th North Carolina Infantry at the Battle of Gettysburg*. New York, NY, 2000.

Gramm, Kent. *Gettysburg: A Meditation on War and Values*. Bloomington, IN, 1994.

Grant, Ulysses S. *Personal Memoirs of U. S. Grant*. 2 vols. New York, NY, 1885-1886.

Gregory, John B. *History of Milwaukee, Wisconsin*. 4 vols. Chicago, IL, 1931.

Hagood, Johnson. *Memoirs of the War of Secession from the Original Manuscripts of Johnson Hagood, Brigadier-General, C.S.A.* Privately printed, 1989.

Hassler, Warren W. *Crisis at the Crossroads: The First Day at Gettysburg.* Tuscaloosa, AL, 1970.

Hay, John, Dennett Tyler, ed. *Lincoln and the Civil War Letters and Diaries of John Hay.* New York, NY, 1939.

Helgerson, Ken and Marcia. *Men of Iron: Stories of the Civil War in Their Own Words.* College Station, TX, 2011.

Hennessy, John J. *Return to Bull Run: The Campaign and Battle of Second Manassas.* New York, NY, 1993.

Herdegen, Lance J., and William J. K. Beaudot. *In the Bloody Railroad Cut at Gettysburg.* Dayton, OH, 1990.

Herdegen, Lance J. *The Men Stood Like Iron: How the Iron Brigade Won its Name.* Bloomington, IN, 1997.

———. *Those Damn Black Hats! The Iron Brigade in the Gettysburg Campaign.* El Dorado Hills, CA, 2008.

Hinck, Elizabeth Eaton. *Undismayed: The Story of a Yankee Chaplain's Family in the Civil War.* Privately printed, 1952.

Hinkley, Juilian Wisner. *Service with the Third Wisconsin Infantry.* Madison, WI, 1912.

History of Crawford and Richland Counties, Wisconsin. Springfield, IL, 1884.

History of Vernon County, Wisconsin. Springfield, IL, 1883.

Hudson, Helen. *Civil War Hawks: Story and Letters of the Hawk Family in Civil War.* Hagerstown, IN, 1974.

Hurn, Ethel Alice. *Wisconsin Women in the War between the States.* Madison, WI, 1911.

Indiana at Antietam. Indianapolis, IN, 1911.

Indiana at Gettysburg. Indianapolis, IN, 1913.

Johnson, Robert U., and Buel, Clarence C., eds. *Battles and Leaders of the Civil War.* 4 vols. New York, NY, 1884-1887.

Jordan, Brian Matthew. *The Battle of South Mountain in History and Memory, September 14, 1862.* El Dorado Hills, CA, 2011.

Kellogg, John A. *Capture and Escape: A Narrative of Army and Prison Life.* Madison, WI, 1908.

Kessinger, Lawrence. *History of Buffalo County, Wisconsin.* Alma, WI, 1888.

Klement, Frank L. *Dark Lanterns: Secret Political Societies, Conspiracies, and Treason Trials in the Civil War.* Baton Rouge, LA, 1984.

———. *The Copperheads of the Middle West.* Chicago, IL, 1960.

———. *The Gettysburg Soldiers' Cemetery and Lincoln's Address.* Shippensburg, PA, 1993.

———. *Wisconsin and the Civil War.* Madison, WI, 1963.

Krumwiede, John F. *Old Waddy's Coming: The Military Career of Brigadier General James S. Wadsworth.* Baltimore, MD, 2002.

Ladd, David L., and Ladd, Audrey J., eds. *The Bachelder Papers: Gettysburg in their Own Words*. 3 vols. Dayton, OH, 1995.

Laven, Robert R. *The Last Troops of Autumn: A Military History of the Seventh Wisconsin Volunteer Regiment: 1861-1863*. Baltimore, MD, 2008.

Libby, Orin Grant. *Significance of the Lead and Shot Trade in Early Wisconsin History*. Madison, WI, 1895.

Linderman, Gerald F. *Embattled Courage: The Experience of Combat in the American Civil War*. New York, NY, 1987.

Long, E. B., and Barbara Long. *The Civil War Day by Day: An Almanac, 1861-1865*. Garden City, NY, 1971.

Love, William D. *Wisconsin in the War of the Rebellion*. Chicago, IL, 1866.

Madaus, Howard Michael, and Richard H. Zeitlin. *The Flags of the Iron Brigade*. Madison, WI, 1998.

Mahon, John K. *History of the Militia and the National Guard*. New York, NY, 1983.

Mahood, Wayne. *General Wadsworth: The Life and Times of Brevet Major General James. W. Wadsworth*. New York, NY, 2003.

Major General James S. Wadsworth at Gettysburg and Other Fields. State of New York Monuments Commission. Albany, NY, 1916.

Martin, David G. *Gettysburg, July 1*. Conshohocken, PA, 1996.

Matrau, Henry, *Letters Home: Henry Matrau of the Iron Brigade*. Reid-Green, Marcia, ed. Lincoln, NE, 1993.

McLean, James L. *Cutler's Brigade at Gettysburg*. Baltimore, MD, 1987.

McPherson, James M. *Battle Cry of Freedom*. New York, NY, 1989.

Meade, George Gordon, ed. *The Life and Letters of George Gordon Meade*. 2 vols. New York, NY, 1913.

Mitchell, Reid. *Civil War Soldiers*. New York, NY, 1988.

Morse, William Lowry. *Grandad and The Civil War*. Privately printed, 1994.

Murfin, James V. *The Gleam of Bayonets: The Battle of Antietam and the Maryland Campaign of 1862*. New York, NY, 1968.

Murray, R. L. *First on the Field: Cortland's 76th and Oswego's 147th New York State Volunteer Regiments at Gettysburg*. Wolcott, NY, 1998.

Nichols, Edward J. *Toward Gettysburg: A Biography of John F. Reynolds*. University Park, PA, 1958.

Nolan, Alan T., and Vipond, Sharon, eds. *Giants in Their Tall Black Hats: Essays on the Iron Brigade*. Bloomington, IN, 1998.

Nolan, Alan T. *The Iron Brigade: A Military History*. New York, NY, 1961.

Otis, George H., and Gaff, Alan D., ed. *The Second Wisconsin Infantry, with Letters and Recollections by Other Members of the Regiment*. Dayton, OH, 1984.

Partridge, Jr., George Washington, and Whitehouse, Hugh L., ed. *Letters from the Iron Brigade*. Indianapolis, IN, 1994.

Pfanz, Harry W. *Gettysburg: The First Day*. Chapel Hill, NC, 2001.

———. *Gettysburg: Culp's Hill and Cemetery Hill*. Chapel Hill, NC, 2001.

Pope, John. Cozzens, Peter, and Girardi, Robert I., eds. *The Military Memoirs of General John Pope*. Chapel Hill, NC, 1998.

Porter, Horace, Wayne C. Temple, ed. *Campaigning With Grant*. Bloomington, IN, 1961.

Quiner, Edwin B. *The Military History of Wisconsin*. Chicago, IL, 1866.

Ray, William, *Four Years with the Iron Brigade: The Civil War Journal of William Ray, Company F, Seventh Wisconsin Volunteers*. Lance J. Herdegen and Sharon Murphy, eds. New York, NY, 2002.

Reid, Whitelaw, *A Radical View: The 'Agate' Dispatches of Whitelaw Reid, 1861-1865*. 2 vols. James G. Smart ed. Memphis, TN, 1976).

Rhea, Gordon C. *Cold Harbor: Grant and Lee May 26-June 3, 1864*. Baton Rouge, LA, 2002.

————. *The Battle of the Wilderness, May 5-6, 1864*. Baton Rouge, LA, 1994.

————. *The Battles for Spotsylvania Court House and the Road to Yellow Tavern, May 7-12, 1864*. Baton Rouge, LA, 1997.

————. *To the North Anna River: Grant and Lee, May 13-25, 1864*. Baton Rouge, LA, 1997.

Robertson, Jr., James L. *Stonewall Jackson: The Man, the Soldier, the Legend*. New York, NY, 1997.

————. *The Stonewall Brigade*. Baton Rouge, LA, 1963.

Ross, Sam. *The Empty Sleeve: A Biography of Lucius Fairchild*. Madison, WI, 1964.

Sauers, Richard A., ed. *Fighting Them Over: How the Veterans Remembered Gettysburg in the Pages of the National Tribune*. Baltimore, MD, 1998.

Sears, Stephen W. *George B. McClellan: The Young Napoleon*. New York, NY, 1988.

————. *Chancellorsville*. Boston, MA, 1996.

————. *Gettysburg*. Boston, MA, 2003.

————. *Landscape Turned Red: The Battle of Antietam*. New Haven, CT, 1983.

Sheridan, Philip H. *Personal Memoirs of P. H. Sheridan*. 2 vols. New York, NY, 1888.

Sherman, William T. *Memoirs of General William T. Sherman by Himself*. 2 vols. New York, NY, 1875.

Shue, Richard S. *Morning at Willoughby Run: July 1, 1863, Gettysburg, Pennsylvania*. Gettysburg, PA, 1995.

Smith, Donald. *The Twenty-fourth Michigan of the Iron Brigade*. Harrisburg, PA, 1962.

Smith, Timothy H. *John Burns: The Hero of Gettysburg*. Gettysburg, PA, 2000.

Soldiers' and Citizens' Album of Biographical Record of Wisconsin Containing Personal Sketches of Army Men and Citizens Prominent in Loyalty to the Union. 2 vols. Chicago, IL, 1888.

Steensma, Robert C., ed. *The Civil War Letters of James E. Northup and Samuel W. Northup*. Sioux Falls, SD, 2000.

Stevens, Charles A. *Berdan's U.S. Sharpshooters in the Army of the Potomac, 1861-1865*. St. Paul, MN, 1892.

Stine, J. H. *History of the Army of the Potomac*. Philadelphia, PA, 1892.

Taylor, Emerson Gifford. *Gouverneur Kemble Warren: Life and Letters of an American Soldier.* Boston, MA, 1932.

Tevis, C. *The History of the Fighting 14th [Brooklyn].* New York, NY, 1911.

Trowbridge, L. S., and Farnsworth, Frederick E. *Michigan at Gettysburg.* Detroit, MI, 1889.

Trudeau, Noah Andre. *Bloody Roads South: The Wilderness to Cold Habor, May-June 1864.* Boston, MA, 1989.

Turner, Ann, ed. *A Chronology of Indiana in the Civil War.* Indianapolis, IN, 1965.

Underwood, George C. *History of the 26th Regiment of North Carolina Troops in the Great War, 1861-'65.* Goldsboro, NC, 1901.

Veil, Charles H. and Herman J. Viola, ed. *The Memoirs of Charles Henry Veil.* New York, NY, 1993.

Venner, William Thomas. *The 19th Indiana Infantry at Gettysburg: Hoosiers' Courage.* Shippensburg, PA, 1998.

Wainwright, Charles S., Allan Nevins, ed. *A Diary of battle: The Personal Journals of Colonel Charles S. Wainwright, 1861-1865.* New York, NY, 1962.

Walterman, Thomas. *There Stands "Old Rock;" Rock County, Wisconsin, and the War to Preserve the Union.* Friendship, WI, 2001.

Watrous, Jerome A. *Richard Epps and Other Stories.* Milwaukee, WI, 1906.

Wert, Jeffry D. *A Brotherhood of Valor: The Common Soldiers of the Stonewall Brigade, C.S.A., and the Iron Brigade, U.S.A.* New York, NY, 1999.

Williams, T. P. *The Mississippi Brigade of Brig. Gen. Joseph R. Davis: A Geographical Account of its Campaigns and a Biographical Account of its Personalities, 1861-1865.* Dayton, OH, 1999.

Index

Walther, Capt. George H., *photo*, 113, 136

Ward, Dr. Andrew J., 283, 416, 419, *photo*, 41, 81

Warham, Pvt. Richard, 177

Warner, Capt. Fred, 469-469n

Warren, E. T. H., 262

Warren, Gen. Gouverneur K., 470-472, 623; Wilderness, 479-480, 483, 498; Spotsylvania, 501, 504-505; North Anna, 509, 511-512; Petersburg, 514, 522, 527, 529, 536, 545, 555-556, 561-562, 572-572n, 573-574; Lincoln's visit, 567; removed from command, 575-576, 585-587; postwar, 602; *photo*, 551

Washington Chronicle, 105

Watrous, Henry, 68

Watrous, Sgt. Jerome, 66, 68, 104, 115, 159, 299-300, 307-308, 452, 459; off to war, 64; Second Bull Run, 212-212n; South Mountain, 238; Antietam, 243, 282, 283-283n; march to Gettysburg, 354; Gettysburg, first day, 403-406; Gettysburg, third day, 438; Wilderness, 488, 493-494; Petersburg, 515-518, 524, 526, 547-548, 570-572; Lincoln's visit, 565; Lincoln's assassination, 588-589; postwar, 601, 603-604, 609, 611n, 612, 614; *photo*, 566

Waukesha Freeman, 33-34

Weeks, Lt. Charles, *photo*, 534

Weidman, John, 233

Weirich, Joseph I., 125

Weldon Railroad, battles of the, 522, 527-528, 529-529n, 530, 535, 545-546, 554, 557, 565, 591, 616

Whaley, Sgt. Edward A., 230-230n

Whaley, Drum Maj. William, 86, 88

Wheeler, Corp. Cornelius, 368; *photo*, 97

White, George W., *photo*, 93

White, Lyman L., *photo*, 93

Whittemore, N. H., *photo*, 20

Whitty, Pvt. James, 233-233n, 483, 495-496

Wiard, Norman, 460

Wight, Sgt. Wallace, 320

Wight, Capt. William, 320

Wilcox, Franklin, 227, 230

Wilderness, battle of the, 476, 479, 484, 491, 493, 496-498, 519, 523n, 529, 538, 543-544, 553, 555, 563, 581, 591

Wilkinson, Senator Morton S., 331

Will, Paul, 67

Williams, Pvt. George, 141

Williams, Pvt. Jared, 535-535n

Williams, Col. Samuel J., 399, 446-447, 495; *photo*, 496

Winder, Charles, 255n

Winsor, Sgt. C. A., 532, 536

Wisconsin military units:

1st Cavalry, 545

1st Infantry, 7, 9, 11, 20-21, 25, 29, 42-43, 59, 61n, 112, 137, 144, 242, 278

2nd Cavalry, 468

2nd Infantry, Company A, Citizen Guard, 108, 196, 619; *Company B, La Crosse Light Guards*, 9, 284, 326, 619; *Company C, Grant County Grays*, 20, 121, 139n, 619; *Company D, Janesville Volunteers*, 14, 177, 228, 619; *Company E, Oshkosh Volunteers*, 189, 285, 477n, 619; *Company F, Belle City Rifles*, 9, 13, 28-29, 520, 619; *Company G, Portage City Guards*, 9, 619; *Company H, Randall Guards*, 10, 44, 261n, 619; *Company I, Miner's Guard*, 26, 43, 97, 619; *Company K, Wisconsin Rifles*, 188, 619; *La Crosse Light Guard*, 108, 190-191, 215, 224, 300-301, 303, 306, 308, 326, 442, 444-445, 449, 452, 465-466, 509, 623; organizing for war, 3, 7-9, 11n, 12, 15-17, 21-22, 35, 38-39, 41-45, 47, 64, 70, 72-73, 77-81, 85, 87, 89, 91-92, 95, 97, 103, 105-106, 112, 115, 128-129, 131, 134-135, 139, 141, 146-147, 152, 156; First Bull Run, 23, 25-26, 27-27n, 28-30, 32; Gainesville, 164-171, 175-176, 179, 181-182, 184, 186-187; Second Bull Run, 203; South Mountain, 221-222, 225, 227, 233, 237; Antietam, 240, 245, 247, 249-250, 254, 256, 259-260, 262-263, 266- 267, 269, 271, 273, 275, 278-279, 281, 283; Fredericksburg, 321, 323;

Lance Herdegen speaking at Camp Randall in Wisconsin in 2012.

About the Author

Award-winning journalist Lance J. Herdegen is the former director of the Institute of Civil War Studies at Carroll University. He previously worked as a reporter and editor for United Press International (UPI) news service covering national politics and civil rights. He currently serves as the historical consultant for the Civil War Museum of the Upper Middle West.

Lance is widely regarded as the world's leading authority on the Iron Brigade. He is the author of many articles, and his books include *Four Years with the Iron Brigade: The Civil War Journal of William R. Ray, Seventh Wisconsin Volunteers; The Men Stood Like Iron: How the Iron Brigade Won its Name*, and *In the Bloody Railroad Cut at Gettysburg*, and *Those Damned Blackhats! The Iron Brigade in the Gettysburg Campaign*.